THE !KUNG SAN

THE !KUNG SAN

Men, Women, and Work
in a Foraging Society

RICHARD BORSHAY LEE
University of Toronto

CAMBRIDGE UNIVERSITY PRESS

CAMBRIDGE

LONDON   NEW YORK   NEW ROCHELLE

MELBOURNE   SYDNEY

Published by the Press Syndicate of the University of Cambridge
The Pitt Building, Trumpington Street, Cambridge CB2 1RP
32 East 57th Street, New York, NY 10022, USA
296 Beaconsfield Parade, Middle Park, Melbourne 3206, Australia

First published 1979
Reprinted 1980

Printed in the United States of America
Typeset by Huron Valley Graphics, Ann Arbor, Michigan
Printed and bound by Vail-Ballou Press, Inc., Binghamton, New York

Library of Congress Cataloging in Publication Data
Lee, Richard B
The !Kung San: men, women, and work in
a foraging society.
Bibliography: p.
Includes index.
1. !Kung (African people)
2. San (African people)
I.   Title.
DT797.L43   968'.004'961   78-25904
ISBN 0 521 22578 7 hard covers
ISBN 0 521 29561 0 paperback

Why should we plant,
when there are so many mongongos in the world?
/Xashe, a !Kung man from Mahopa

Contents

Tables and figures

FIGURES

Preface

THE origin of this study of the !Kung San dates back to 1961, when I was a student at the University of California. With Desmond Clark, Sherwood Washburn, and Irven DeVore, my teachers at Berkeley, I began discussing the possibility of looking at a contemporary hunting and gathering society from an evolutionary perspective. We agreed that such a study could yield valuable insights, but that at the same time the undertaking faced some formidable difficulties of theory and methods. First, how were we to avoid the implicit racism and biological reductionism of earlier anthropological work on this subject? Many nineteenth-century writers had treated contemporary "savages" as "living fossils" or "missing links," an approach that had become thoroughly discredited. Second, how could the hunters of 10,000 years ago living in a world of their own making be compared with the hunters of today living in vastly altered circumstances?

To the first problem I argued that the ecological approach was essential, because through it we could explore comparatively the continuities and discontinuities in subsistence, energetics, spatial organization, group structure, and demography without doing violence to the absolutely crucial recognition of the uniqueness of human culture. By contrast, the more conventional social anthropological categories – kinship, marriage, ritual, descent, and ideology – would be much more difficult to deal with from a long-term evolutionary perspective.

To the second problem the answer seemed to be the making of a candid and detailed assessment of the historical circumstances of each case study. The effects of outside contact had to be fully accounted for before we attempted to draw the evolutionary implications of the data.

What finally tipped the balance in favor of undertaking the !Kung field-work was the conviction that detailed ecological and demographic data on a hunting gathering people would provide valuable records in their own right, useful for testing a variety of current hypotheses about

society and economy, whether or not the evolutionary record could be
enhanced. And there was the factor of urgency. The hunting and gathering way of life was disappearing rapidly, and many valuable research
opportunities had already been lost by failure to collect concrete data on
the material existence of these peoples.

Fieldwork was carried out in 1963–4, 1967–9, and 1973; the project
that started out with a two-person research team (DeVore and Lee) grew
to include over a dozen long- and short-term investigators. The larger
multidisciplinary project has been published in *Kalahari Hunter-Gatherers* (Lee and DeVore 1976), along with a number of articles, but the bulk
of my own research on !Kung ecology and society has yet to appear in a
unified account. The present volume provides such an account by drawing together material published elsewhere plus a substantial body of previously unpublished data; the latter forms by far the larger proportion of
the book.

Previously published have been Chapters 7 and 9, along with parts of
Chapters 3, 4, 11, 12, and 15. Chapters 1, 2, 5, 6, 8, 10, 13, and 14 consist
in the main of new material.

The main elements of theory and method are set out in the Introduction. Chapter 1 is an informal history of the project and of the impact of
anthropologists and !Kung on each others' lives.

Chapter 2 briefly introduces the major language and cultural divisions
of the contemporary San, reviews the names they are known by, and
attempts to plot their current numbers and economic statuses.

Chapter 3 introduces the Dobe area in the northwest corner of Botswana and presents a detailed analysis of the numbers and distribution
of the San and non-San population during the period 1963–73. The second part of the chapter describes the two kinds of San living groups in
the area–*camps* based mainly on hunting and gathering, and *client
groups* associated with the black cattle posts – and documents the size,
kinship structure, and age composition of these groups, and the dynamics of their variation through time. The third part of Chapter 3 is a history
of the San peoples of the Dobe area, covering their archeological origins
and, in particular, the period from their initial contacts with whites and
blacks in the 1870s and 1880s to the early post-Independence era of the
1960s. A preliminary assessment is made of the effects of black presence
and European contact on Dobe !Kung diet, seasonal movements, settlement history, political organization, and management of conflict. An account of more recent changes and a more detailed historical assessment
are reserved for Chapter 14.

Chapter 4 draws a picture of the natural world of the !Kung. We start
with geology and topography and their effect on the patterning of soils
and vegetation in the dune and molapo system. Certain aspects of Dobe
area relief may be accounted for by the recent discovery that the Oka-

Preface

vango swamps are undergoing a process of rifting related to the Rift Valley system of Eastern Africa. The major vegetation associations are described, and their main constituents are listed. Fauna – especially mammals, birds, and reptiles – are discussed next, with particular emphasis on the economically utilized species. The problem of game diminution produced by destruction of habitat and fencing by non-San is also considered. Because the shortage of rainfall and groundwater is one of the key limiting factors in the Dobe area, the discussion of climate receives detailed attention. Rainfall is examined from dual points of view: first, as it is perceived by the !Kung and used as a basis for decision making about their seasonal subsistence round; and second, as a climatologist would view it, with measurements of seasonal and annual fall and plots of long-term rainfall fluctuations. This latter topic is considered further in Chapter 12.

Chapters 5 through 8 are core descriptions of the hunting and gathering subsistence economy. Chapter 5 defines the main characteristics of the foraging mode of production in terms of division of labor, sharing, reciprocity, and work organization. It then goes on to take a detailed look at the technology of subsistence under four headings: tools used for getting water, tools used for gathering and carrying, tools used for hunting, and tools used for food processing. Particular attention is given to carrying devices, an important category of tool that deserves closer examination by evolutionists than it has so far received.

Chapter 6 presents an inventory of the 105 plant species used by the !Kung as food. Because these vegetable foods provide 60 to 70 percent of the !Kung diet, the dozens of fruits, nuts, berries, gums, roots, bulbs, and leafy greens lie at the very heart of the successful long-term adaptation the Dobe area !Kung have achieved. A concluding section documents the regional differences in the strengths of the major food species.

The mongongo fruit and nut (*Ricinodendron rautanenii* Schinz) stands in a class by itself. Alone it provides up to half the !Kung vegetable diet, and in its reliability, abundance, and caloric returns it rivals or exceeds the value of the cultivated staple crops of many agricultural peoples. Chapter 7 discusses the botany, ecology, and nutrition of the mongongo; plots its geographical distribution; and traces it through the !Kung system of production from collecting, transporting, processing, and cooking to its distribution and consumption within the camp. The documentation of the richness, abundance, and variety of the !Kung major plant foods serves to bring home to the reader that the foraging mode of production is no haphazard catch-as-catch-can existence, but rather a stable and successful adaptation built on a firmly based food supply.

Chapter 8, the longest in the book, is about hunting. Much attention pro and con has been given to the importance of hunting in human history: Some regard it as the master mechanism of human evolution

(Laughlin 1968); others, struck by the primacy of plants and other non-meat foods in the diets of recent hunter-gatherers, downplay its importance to a recreation for men while the women do the real work of subsistence (e.g., Morgan 1972; Tanner and Zihlman 1976). Here I try to place the role of hunting among the !Kung in proper perspective. Hunting activities though less productive than gathering, are the major preoccupation of the men and are a central ritual, social, and emotional focus for !Kung camp life. And the nutritional returns from hunting are by no means negligible: Game animals provide between 30 and 40 percent of the total calories of the !Kung. The first half of Chapter 8 details the hunting process–the way men actually hunt large and small game above and below the ground. Special attention is paid to the men's remarkable tracking abilities as they read out a whole range of crucial information about a prey animal by studying a few indistinct marks in the sand.

Another important aspect of hunting is the hunter's demeanor during and after the hunt. Arrogance and boasting are strongly disapproved of by the !Kung; humility is the proper stance, and the society has devised an array of humility-enforcing devices for bringing people into line. Despite a strong egalitarian ethic, some men are much more successful at hunting than others, and a minority of good hunters provides the bulk of the meat supply. How the !Kung manage success and failure in this key area offers a real clue to the underlying principles of their collective existence.

Chapters 9 through 11 take up a series of special problems by bringing to bear very fine-grained quantitative data on critical systems of hunter-gatherer life. Each studies an aspect of the cultural core's interface with biological systems, and each attempts to anchor social and economic processes in the energetic quanta of the natural sciences. Chapter 9 presents in considerably expanded form the results of a 28-day work diary of a Dobe camp originally published a decade ago (Lee 1968a, 1969a). Three kinds of !Kung work are identified: subsistence work, manufacture and maintenance of tools, and housework (in the original study only subsistence work was considered). An estimate is made of the per capita work effort for males and females in terms of hours per week and caloric units.

The results show that during the study period the !Kung had a more than adequate diet achieved by a subsistence work effort of only 2 or 3 days per week, a far lower level than that required of wage workers in our own industrial society. The distribution of work effort between males and females, as well as between aged and young and residents and visitors, reveals some interesting patterns. The impact of the recently introduced iron tools on work effort is also evaluated.

The data of Chapter 9 refer to the work of a single !Kung camp in a single month (July 1964). To determine whether these results were representative of the levels of work and consumption of the Dobe population as a whole, we took weight and fatness measurements on hundreds of !Kung throughout the Dobe area at different times of the year. Chapter 10 reports on the height, weight, and skinfold thickness measurements of 641 !Kung adults and children over a 19-month period in 1967–9. The main question asked is: Is there a hungry season among the !Kung, and if so when does it fall and who bears the brunt of it in terms of weight loss? By dividing the population by age and sex and by geographic region, it was possible to make a fine-grained analysis of the allocation of nutritional stress among the members of the population. The results show a basic maintenance of growth for children and of fitness for adults throughout the year, with some minor but significant weight loss for one period, followed by a rapid recovery. The utility of the method of internal analysis of variance is demonstrated here. The fact that the nutritional stress fell more heavily at one water hole than at the others enables us to pinpoint the probable explanation for this weight loss with some precision. Given the circumstances, it seems likely that the weight loss arose out of cash economy penetration and not as a result of some failure of the hunting and gathering adaptation.

The articulation between the systems of production (getting food) and reproduction (having babies) is explored in Chapter 11. Foraging requires mobility: Both men and women have to travel far afield to find food. Women carry their babies for the first few years of life wherever they go. A premium exists, therefore, for women to space their pregnancies well apart, because too frequent births will give a woman, in the !Kung phrase, "a permanent backache." For nomadic women, births are spaced almost 4 years apart, but this changes rapidly with sedentarization. When the people settle down to village life, the spacing of births falls rapidly, causing a boom in population and some surprising dislocations in the culture of children and in child rearing. The causes and consequences of birth spacing are examined using a combination of Marxist and systems theory analysis.

Ownership, leadership, and the use of space are covered in Chapter 12. The question of ownership of the means of production is a crucial one, and it is necessary to examine the !Kung case in detail because there is much confusion about the nature – collective or individual – of ownership of land among hunter-gatherers. Among the !Kung, land is a collective resource owned by both men and women and inherited by a complex number of pathways from generation to generation. Examples are given of the ways land resources are successfully managed without resort to territorial defense.

The subtleties of leadership in an egalitarian society without hereditary offices are also explored. We look at the principles of landownership in actual practice by studying the spatial organization of a block of land south of the Aha Hills involving 12 living groups during the period 1920–70. The use of long-term rainfall statistics for the Kalahari helps to reveal the underlying principles of !Kung adaptation, and we come to realize that the events a fieldworker observes in a year or two of fieldwork are but a small segment of social patterns and processes that take years and generations to unfold.

Chapter 13 examines conflict and violence among the !Kung. Living at low population densities, with adequate food supply and an absence of territorial defense, the !Kung would appear at first glance to be a people for whom the major sources of conflict are removed. Yet the !Kung do fight each other and sometimes with fatal results. Some 22 cases of homicide in the period 1920–55 came to light during my fieldwork, and I recorded as well dozens of nonfatal arguments in which people came to blows. The !Kung distinguish three levels of conflict: talking, fighting, and killing. The characteristics of each kind of conflict are described in detail and illustrated with case histories. Despite the absence of authority figures responsible for maintaining order, the !Kung are not without resources for avoiding, limiting, and resolving serious conflict. The resulting picture clearly contradicts the Hobbesian notion that life in the simpler societies is a state of "war of all against all"; yet at the same time neither do the !Kung conform to the romantic image of them as the "harmless people."

The bulk of the monograph is devoted to the !Kung as hunters and gatherers, the still-dominant mode of subsistence during the 1960s. Chapter 14 considers the other facets of !Kung economic life. Some !Kung play a role in the pastoral economy of their black neighbors; others are attempting agriculture and stock raising on their own; still others work for wages as migrant laborers. In addition, inputs from the blacks affect hunting and gathering itself. A few !Kung men hunt and kill game with borrowed guns; some women use donkeys to haul mongongo nuts from distant groves. A Marxist framework of analysis is used to make sense of the complex transformations !Kung society is currently undergoing. The contradictions experienced by the !Kung in trying to move from the foraging mode of production to a mode of production based on farming and herding help to bring out the underlying dynamic of each mode. The important implications for the future of the San of capitalist development in Botswana and of the armed liberation struggle in Namibia are assessed in the concluding section of the chapter.

In Chapter 15 the major results of the study are recapitulated in order to draw their implications for anthropological and evolutionary theory. Two kinds of methods – uniformitarian and Marxist – are proposed for reconstructing the foraging societies and evolutionary stages of the human past. The uniformitarian approach starts from the postulate that the same kinds of processes that mold the ecological adaptation of contemporary foraging societies were also at work in the foraging societies of the past. This method draws upon the tight articulation between the demographic, energetic, nutritional, and spatial subsystems of !Kung ecology to show how a change in one of the parameters triggers changes in the other parameters as well. These findings are applied to a consideration of the evolutionary significance of !Kung subsistence, technology, work effort, and nutritional status, and to an analysis of the dynamic of movement that underlies their social ecology.

For problems that involve the level of consciousness and ideology, a uniformitarian approach is not sufficient. To reach a deeper understanding of !Kung foragers and their role in theory, we have to account for a much wider range of cultural and social variables. The Marxist framework of historical materialism is used to throw light on the complex issues of the evolution of male-female relations and the social relations of foraging production. A final section touches on the universal themes and contradictions of human nature as they are reflected in the lives of the contemporary !Kung foragers of the Dobe area.

In a project that lasts as long as this one, it is inevitable that the list of those who contributed to its ultimate success will be substantial. Help came in three forms: concrete aid and friendship in the field; specific input in reading chapters and refining the data, theory, and methods of the book; and general intellectual stimulation and nourishment. Of those mentioned below, many gave two or all three kinds of help.

I want to thank Ken Allen, R. J. Andersson, Megan Biesele, Lew Binford, Nicholas Blurton Jones, Joan and Phil Brown, Sue Bucklin, Alec Campbell, Peter Carstens, Desmond and Betty Clark, Irven and Nancy DeVore, Mark and Judy Dornstreich, Pat Draper, Brian Fagan, Morton Fried, Maurice Godelier, Mathias Guenther, Graham Guy and Marvin Harris.

Thanks are also due John Hansen, Henry Harpending, H. J. Heinz, Nancy Howell, Marshall Hurlich, Susan Hurlich, Gabautwe, Gakekgoshe Isak, Francis Johnston, Kasupe, Katjambungu, Richard Katz, Carol Kerven, Marie Kingston, Melissa Knauer, Mel Konner, Kopela Maswe, Adam and Jessica Kuper, Eleanor Leacock, Meg Luxton, Ben Magubane, Gideon Mangwala, Lorna Marshall, John Marshall, and Onesimus Mbombo.

I want to thank as well N!eishi, N!uhka, Dorothy Obre, John Pfeiffer, Paul Puritt, Rakudu, Rayna Rapp, Ed Rogers, Harriet Rosenberg, Sai//gain!a, Bruce Schroeder, Ted Scudder, Wally Secombe, Marjorie Shostak, George Silberbauer, Reay Smithers, Jacqueline Solway, Enoch Tabiso, Jiro Tanaka, /Tasa, /Tashe, Phillip Tobias, ≠Toma!ko!ko, Mr. Tomas, ≠Tomazho, Stewart Truswell, /Twan!a, Twiathema, and /Twi!gum.

Thanks are also due Francis Van Noten, Helga Vierich-Esche, Sherry Washburn, Stan Washburn, A. Wehmeyer, Marjorie Whiting, Polly Wiessner, Ed Wilmsen, Elizabeth Wily, James Woodburn, Cyril Wyndham, and John Yellen. To unnamed others a collective vote of thanks.

For technical assistance thanks go to artists Patsy Cunningham for Figures 5.1 and 5.3 to 5.7; Lois Johnson for Figures 7.1, 7.2, and 12.1 to 12.4; and Deborah Shulman for Figure 5.2; and to cartographer Jennifer Wilcox for the other maps and diagrams. John Glover and Nancy DeVore helped with the photos (credit Richard Lee/Anthro-Photo; all photographs were taken by the author). Bill Postl provided computer assistance, and Margo Videki typed most of the manuscript.

The financial support of the following is gratefully acknowledged: the National Science Foundation (U.S.); the National Institute of Mental Health (U.S.); the Wenner Gren Foundation for Anthropological Research; and the Canada Council. Thanks go to the University of Toronto for granting a year's leave of absence, and to that worthy institution and the Canada Council for Leave Fellowship and other support that made possible the writing of this book in 1976–8.

The government and the people of the Republic of Botswana deserve a special vote of thanks for welcoming me and other members of the Kalahari Research Group in their midst. Without their patience, hospitality, and support this and the other studies could not have been completed.

Finally, the !Kung. This book is part of our bargain: to tell the world of your life, good and bad, with clarity and with honesty. You shared your life with me; you taught me much; may you live well, in peace and plenty, always.

Zhuo, i !ha weyshi //kau ge.

Batho bothe, tsamaya senthle.

R.B.L.

Note on orthography

THE San languages are characterized by click sounds produced with an ingressive air stream when the tongue is drawn sharply away from various points of articulation on the roof of the mouth. The four clicks used in !Kung appear as follows:

/   Dental click as in /Xai/xai, /Du/da (in spoken English this sound denotes a mild reproach, written *tsk, tsk*)

≠   Alveolar click as in ≠To//gana, ≠Toma

!   Alveopalatal click as in !Kung, /Ti!kai

//   Lateral click as in ≠To//gana, //wama (in spoken English this sound is used in some dialects to urge on a horse)

Other features of the San orthography that should be noted include:

‾   Nasalization as in /twā

_   Pressing as in ma͟a

'   Glottal stop as in ts'i

"   Glottal flap as in //"xa (mongongo)

Tone markers; low as in !gwe‿; high as in !gu‾

For the nonlinguist, San words may be pronounced by simply dropping the click. For example, for ≠To//gana read *Togana* and for /Ti!kai read *Tikai*.

Introduction
!Kung ecology and society

THIS book is an ecological and historical study of the !Kung San of Botswana, one of the very few remaining peoples of the world who live as hunters and gatherers. Based on 3 years of fieldwork among the !Kung, the study presents a description of the dynamics of their hunting and gathering way of life in what proved to be the last decades of its independent existence. The discussion draws heavily upon three theoretical traditions in social science: the anthropological school of cultural ecology founded by Julian Steward; the Marxist framework of historical materialism, particularly the French school of Maurice Godelier; and ecological systems theory.

Before the theoretical and methodological bases of the approach are discussed, it is necessary first to consider why the hunting and gathering societies are important for social science.

THE SIGNIFICANCE OF THE HUNTER-GATHERERS

Peoples who live by hunting and gathering – Inuit (Eskimo), Australian aborigines, the Kalahari San – are among the few remaining representatives of a way of life that was, until 10,000 years ago, a human universal. Basic human social forms, language, and human nature itself were forged during the 99 percent of human history when people lived in hunting and gathering camps. Our contemporary societies of cities, states, and empires, of literature, science, and technology are all developments of the last few thousand years of agriculture and settled village life. The contemporary hunter-gatherers, therefore, have much to teach us, but we must proceed with extreme caution to avoid misusing or misreading the lessons they offer. The hunters are not living fossils: They are humans like ourselves with a history as long as the history of any other human group. It is their very humanity that makes them so important for science. These peoples, despite cultural and geographical diversity, have

1

a core of features in common, and this core of features represents the basic human adaptation stripped of the accretions and complications brought about by agriculture, urbanization, advanced technology, and national and class conflict (Lee 1974: 167–8).

Although our ultimate goal is to use data on hunter-gatherers to illuminate human evolution, we must acknowledge that nowhere today do we find, in Sahlins's apt phrase, hunters living in a world of hunters. All contemporary hunters are in contact with agricultural, pastoral, or industrial societies and are affected by them. Therefore, the first order of business is carefully to account for the effects of contact on their way of life. Only after the most meticulous assessment of the impact of commercial, governmental, and other outside interests can we justify making statements about the hunter-gatherers' evolutionary significance.

CULTURAL ECOLOGY

The core of common features that unites these peoples centers on their distinctive way of making a living–the techniques, knowledge, and organizational features whose sum total we call the hunting and gathering, or foraging, way of life. Ever since the pioneering research of Julian Steward (1936) on the social and economic basis of primitive bands, modern anthropology has seen the hunter-gatherer adaptation as one of the primary socioeconomic forms of human society. It is treated as such in the great majority of anthropological textbooks, and various authors have emphasized the logical and evolutionary priority of its organizational forms (e.g., Lévi-Strauss 1949; Steward 1955a; Service 1962, 1966, 1971; Lee and DeVore 1968), its systems of exchange (Sahlins 1972), technology (Oswalt 1973), or demography (Cohen 1977).

Steward (1955b) developed an approach to these societies based on study of the core features that he christened the method of cultural ecology and that he extended to include the study of tribal, peasant, and industrial societies in addition to hunting and gathering bands (Steward 1949, 1956, 1967). Steward's cultural ecology provides a framework of analysis that has some claim to being at once materialist, historical, and evolutionary and that has been widely influential in contemporary anthropology (Leacock 1954; Sahlins 1958; Wolf 1959; Service 1962; Fried 1967; Harris 1968, 1975; Damas 1969a,b; Leacock and Lurie 1972). It focuses on the core features of subsistence, economics, and technology, and attempts to understand social and political organization and other aspects of culture in terms of this core. Cultural ecology is not a brand of environmental determinism. Steward and his successors have specifically pointed to an *interplay* of environmental, social, economic, and cultural factors in determining the form of a given society. Nor is cultural ecology a form of economic determinism; Steward also noted that

SYSTEMS

Ecological systems theory (Margalef 1964; Levins 1966, 1968; Clapham 1973) and its application to human societies (Rappaport 1968, 1971a) provides us with a powerful tool of analysis. The !Kung San, like any other functioning society, are not just a haphazard collection of personnel and social and cultural elements. !Kung society is a complex web of systems, including ecological, energetic, demographic, and information subsystems, that are interconnected in intricate, mutually interdependent feedback relations (Rappaport 1968). This is not a sterile, mechanical set of systems reflexively acted upon by the environment, but rather a dynamic set of systems including physical and biological components in dialectic relations with conscious human actors. These humans make choices where they can and keep making adjustments to bring their lives into line with constantly changing ecological and human realities. If we understand the shape and interconnections of some of these systems in sufficient depth, we can go a long way toward revealing the underlying principles of the society. Examples of this kind of analysis are found in Chapters 9, 10, and 11 of this book.

Far from being incompatible, Marxism and systems theory come together in a field we could call *systems history*, after a phrase suggested by Mervyn Meggitt. Maurice Godelier, for example, has drawn attention to the important correspondences between the Marxist concept of contradictions and systems theory's notion of feedback:

> In order to explicate the dynamic of systems and their history, it is necessary to develop the notion of contradiction and to distinguish several types . . . Cybernetics, in showing how systems can be regulated by feedback, has posed in new terms the problem of the existence of contradictions in physical and social systems. The mechanisms of feedback ensure a system's relative independence by relating the internal variation of its components to the external conditions of its functioning . . . The condition under which a system can reproduce itself is thus not an *absence* of contradictions, but rather one in which contradictions are *regulated* and this regulation maintains a *provisional* unity. [Godelier 1974b:55; emphasis in original]

One of the best ways to understand how a system works is to watch it undergoing transformation to another system. For example, my own understanding of the !Kung hunting and gathering system was deepened when I saw it being transformed into a farming and herding system (Chapter 14).

The goal of this research in theoretical terms is to understand what Godelier (1972:335–8) has called the inner dynamic or underlying logic of a society. This inner dynamic is a set of principles that exists both in the base and the superstructure and that comprises a more or less logically consistent blueprint for living. The degree to which we succeed in uncovering the inner logic depends on the depth and rigor of our analysis of the society in the full complexity of its historical setting.

METHOD AND STRUCTURE

The main elements of the method used in this study can now be specified. It is a multidisciplinary approach that starts with a detailed description of the core features of !Kung life–subsistence, technology, group structure, land use, and work effort–and moves on from these to draw cultural, ideological, and political aspects of !Kung life into the analysis. Starting from this core, or base, I gradually build up a picture of the society by articulating, feature by feature, those aspects of the superstructure that make sense and are rendered intelligible in terms of the core. Another main dimension of the study draws upon the biological underpinnings of !Kung existence. The health and nutritional status of the people, the chemistry of their food, their climatic adaptation, their energy budgets, and their reproductive physiology are aspects of biology that affect their culture core and are affected by it. The third dimension of the study is the historical one. By long-term fieldwork and by maximally extending the time dimension, we can begin to place this "ahistorical" society into history to get a sense of its trajectory in historical materialist terms as a foraging society on the threshold of a triple transformation to agriculture, to feudalism, and to capitalism (cf. LeRoy Ladurie 1960, 1976).

A critical focus concerns the roles men and women play in !Kung society. The study of the relative contributions of the sexes to the tasks of subsistence, tool making, housework, and child rearing allows us to inquire into the fundamentals of the human division of labor (and power) in a social setting remote from the hierarchically organized, industrialized, urban, class societies of the West.

This social and cultural study spills over into related fields; it draws heavily upon the natural sciences while at the same time seeking the historian's sense of time and movement. The method incorporates elements from social and physical anthropology, ecology, economics, demography, nutrition, and history. Here are some of the main features:

1. Long-term fieldwork by participant observation using the !Kung language, to collect a broad range of ethnographic data
2. Systematic quantitive collection of core data on population, botany, economics, nutrition, and demography
3. Delineation of critical systems and subsystems and the tracing

of their interrelations (the work of specialists in medicine, demography, and child-rearing studies is important here)

4. Analysis of internal variation by sex (as well as by age and geographic region) in key variables and the pinpointing of causes.

5. The plotting of year-to-year, and decade-to-decade, variations in ecology, resources, and group dynamics

6. The placing of the Dobe area !Kung into the broader historical and regional context of southern African history and development from 1870 to 1980

7. The detailed study of the conscious and unconscious beliefs, values, and attitudes by which the !Kung organize and make sense of the world and which in turn motivate their behavior; the pinpointing of key contradictions

These seven main elements of method combined with the ecological and evolutionary goals of the research dictate the topics to be covered and the structure of the book before you.

After an introduction to fieldwork among the San in Chapter 1, Chapter 2 reviews the terminology by which the San are known and their current status. Chapters 3 through 8 present core data on group structure, ecology, technology, and subsistence. Chapters 9 through 13 represent analyses of critical systems and subsystems: work effort, nutritional stress, reproduction and birth spacing, land use, and the management of conflict. Chapter 14, along with parts of Chapters 3 and 12 attempts to provide the historical context, and Chapter 15 summarizes the lessons of the !Kung for anthropology and social science.

1
Fieldwork with the !Kung

W HAT is it that separates the enterprise of the scientist from that of the poet or novelist? Both are seekers after knowledge, but unlike the poet, a scientist must subject his findings to the tests of the scientific method. If a set of observations can survive the scrutiny of the agreed-upon canons of the community of observers, the material passes from the realm of the inspired guess or poetic truth into the realm of what we like to think of as data about the world as it is.

But knowledge of the human world is mediated by two further intervening variables. First, the observing scientist does not stand in completely objective relation to the people studied. Modern anthropology no longer believes that the scientist of culture is neutral; today's epistemology includes the *observer along with the "natives" in the field of view.* When acknowledged and used creatively, the observer's likes and dislikes, his prejudices and enthusiasms, become an instrument of discovery, a part of the learning process itself and not external to it. Second, the "natives" themselves are far from neutral in this enterprise. What image *they* present to the observer may spring from their collective vision of who they are and who they take the observer to be.

The ethnography that results from this encounter of two realities is not a photograph mechanically reproducing a portrait of a people, but rather a dialectic of congruent and contradictory elements between observer and observed. It is only in recent years that the full complexity of this interplay has become apparent to practicing social scientists.

Much of this book is an account of the !Kung as they are (or were) and of the process of discovery by which a multitude of observations has been built up into a coherent picture of the external workings and underlying reality of this foraging society. But before beginning, the reader should have a brief accounting of the other side of the equation – of the observer himself and the history of his relations with the people. The account to follow details the !Kung fieldwork as it unfolded from 1963 to 1973 and

8

traces the mutual impact of the researchers on the lives of the !Kung and of the !Kung on the lives of the researchers. The goal is to convey the experience of fieldwork.

As an undergraduate majoring in anthropology and philosophy at the University of Toronto in the late 1950s, I became interested in Africa and in cultural evolution through contact with Ronald Cohen, and in biological evolution and the philosophy of science through work with Robert C. Dailey. A paper ("Primate Behavior and the Origin of Incest") I gave at the 1960 meeting of the American Anthropological Association led to a meeting with Sherwood Washburn and Irven DeVore and an invitation to study primate behavior with them at the University of California, Berkeley. Soon after settling in Berkeley, I realized that my long-term research interest lay in studying people, not primates. My hunch was that research on contemporary hunter-gatherer groups – subject to critical safeguards – could provide a basis for models of the evolution of human behavior.

Happily, Washburn and DeVore were enthusiastic about this approach, and they encouraged me to plan fieldwork with a contemporary hunter-gatherer group.

Also while at Berkeley, I was introduced to the work of Julian Steward and others on the Great Basin and Californian hunter-gatherers through courses with Robert Murphy and R. F. Heizer, as well as to the work of the zoologists H. G. Andrewartha on population ecology and Peter Marler on animal behavior. My theoretical interests at the time straddled the boundaries between cultural and physical anthropology. My strong commitment to evolutionism and scientism was tempered by an equally strong commitment to humanism. These two elements continued to define the two parameters of my fieldwork and my subsequent writings and are found in the present book.

J. Desmond Clark, who had just joined the Berkeley faculty after some 20 years of research at the Rhodes-Livingstone Museum in Zambia, was especially enthusiastic about this research. Clark was instrumental in focusing our attention on Southern Africa as a research locale and in particular on the !Kung San, a hunting and gathering people in the northern Kalahari Desert.

THE SEARCH FOR A FIELD SITE: 1963

Financed by a grant from the National Science Foundation, Irv DeVore and I embarked for the Bechuanaland Protectorate (later Botswana) in the summer of 1963. We entered the Kalahari Desert by Land Rover from the northeast in mid-August, teaming up with Adam Kuper, a South African anthropologist who was heading for fieldwork with the Bakalahari, a Bantu-speaking pastoral people in the western desert. Together we combed Northwestern Botswana in our initial survey, but we found few San except those closely tied in to European and Tswana cattle posts. We were intrigued by reports of a large cluster of semiindependent !Kung groups in the extreme west of the country on the South-West African border around a place marked Xangwa on the maps. But in our initial attempt to reach the area, we were turned back by an overzealous expatriate officer of the Bechuanaland colonial administration. (Botswana did not receive its independence from Britain until 1966.)

After DeVore returned to the United States in September, I made my way back to Maun with two Land Rovers, accompanied by Marie Kingston, a friend from Canada; Onesimus Mbombo, a Rhodesian schoolteacher, to act as interpreter; and Enoch Tabiso, a member of an acculturated San group near Livingstone. Tabiso had been Desmond Clark's gardener in the Zambian town of Livingstone. This time I picked my way more carefully through the network of colonial and tribal administration. Mrs. Elizabeth Pulane, the queen mother and regent of the Batawana tribe, interviewed me and gave me a letter in Setswana to her local representative, Mr. Isak Utugile, the headman of the !Kangwa (Xangwa) district. I met Isak in Nokaneng; he turned out to be a gruff, impressive white-haired man of about 60, who spoke no English (I later found that he spoke fluent !Kung, in addition to his native Setswana, and Seherero). He had been the headman since 1948, and because no European had ever lived in his district before, he interviewed me intensively through an interpreter for 7 hours before agreeing to accompany me to !Kangwa and introduce me to the !Kung.

On October 7, 1963, we set out from Nokaneng heading west through the acacia forest along a little-used track. The first !Kung village was 100 km ahead, with no people and no water in between. The trip took us 8 hours; we stopped frequently to cool the overboiling engine and clean the thick mat of grass seeds that continually formed on the radiator screen. I used the stops to learn a few words of greeting in !Kung and to marvel at the changing vegetation and rich bird life. It was almost dark when we chugged laboriously into !Goshe, the first water hole in the !Kangwa valley, with me in a state of nervous anticipation. Isak called the people out, and shyly in twos and threes they came forward – about 35 people in all. Reassured by Isak, the people became animated and milled around the trucks, chatting gaily. In those days the arrival of a vehicle was a rare event. Isak told them I was a white man who had come to live in the area and learn their language. They should be nice to me, and I would give them tobacco. This was my cue to pass out handfuls of tobacco to everyone and to repeat my newly learned greetings over and over again.

Then we moved on to !Kangwa itself, arriving in the pitch dark to stay for the night. The next morning Isak told me that 15 km to the west an independent group of !Kung was living at a small water hole called Dobe. We decided to move on there immediately, and Isak assigned his son

Plate 1.1. On the Maun–Dobe road.

Gakekgoshe, a man about my age, to show me the way. We arrived at Dobe in midmorning to find it temporarily deserted. Most of the people were out hunting and gathering. After 15 minutes, a small, wizened man emerged from the bush and came over to our Land Rovers. He told us his name was ≠Toma//gwe ("≠Toma sour plum") and that he lived here with his wife, two married sons, and his wife's brother and their families. He agreed provisionally to let us camp at Dobe for a few days and to help us learn the language. We offered to drive him across the pan to our camp-site, but he refused, saying the trip would kill him.

≠Toma//gwe and his group became the primary focus during the first weeks of my fieldwork and were to play host to a dozen anthropologists in later years. And though all the other Dobe residents and many other !Kung rode in our Land Rovers and Jeeps, ≠Toma//gwe has never set foot in one.

EARLY MONTHS AT DOBE

We pitched a tent on a pleasant open spot near the Dobe camp (it later flooded out when the rains came) and began to work. The first priorities were to find out who lived there, what they were eating, and how to speak the language. Notes were taken logbook style in stenographic notebooks. For a reason I cannot now fathom, I recorded the time of each observation plus the times I woke up, ate meals, and went to bed. Much of this information turned out to quite useless, and the logbooks were very difficult to retrieve even useful information from; later in fieldwork a much more efficient system was devised.

My early notebooks are filled with lists of people, of words, and especially of plants and animals. While learning to be a serious fieldworker, it seemed a safe bet that collecting as much information as possible on the flora and fauna would stand me in good stead. I quickly learned to ask for the names of things in !Kung (*a!ku re o a che?* = "what is the name of that?") and used the phrase constantly on daily nature hikes. The !Kung enjoyed this kind of work; they are superb botanists and know their environment intimately. Also this was an easy way to communicate directly with !Kung early on, without having to rely on interpreters. Finally, the plant and animal lists were a concrete indication of my progress. My field notes were interspersed with comments like "five new plants today!" and my totals grew month by month from 75 species by the first Christmas to 420 species at the end of 1964.

Learning to speak !Kung was a laborious task. No !Kung–English speaker was available, so one had to work with two interpreters. Onesimus Mbombo translated my questions from English to Setswana, and Gakekgoshe Isak (the son of Headman Isak and a fluent !Kung speaker) from Setswana to !Kung. The answer came back like a broken telephone from !Kung to Setswana and Setswana to English. This cumbersome system spurred me on to learn !Kung quickly, but in fact during the early months I learned more Setswana than !Kung. By March 1964 I could use Setswana in interviews and to elicit more !Kung vocabulary. The !Kung word can be described as an explosion of sound surrounded by a vowel. The bundle of clicks, fricatives, and glottal stops that begins most words makes !Kung a difficult language to record, let alone learn to speak; and the difficulty is compounded by the extremely rapid-fire delivery of !Kung speakers. Nevertheless, month by month my facility progressed until it was possible to dispense with the services of the English–Setswana interpreter a year into the fieldwork.

INTENSIVE FIELDWORK

The first few months at Dobe were productive, but I still wondered if a more isolated population of hunter-gatherers could be found. In early 1964 the camp was moved to the Tsodilo Hills, a treasure house of ancient San rock paintings about 200 km northeast of Dobe. While Sue Bucklin, a young American archeologist, studied the paintings, I walked over the hills collecting and pressing plants and learning the language from the small group (11 people) of !Kung camped in the hills. This handful of Tsodilo !Kung residents turned out to be an isolated group, and this fact strengthened my conviction that the Dobe area should, after all, be the main focus of study.

The serious, sustained part of the fieldwork got under way in mid-February. Returning to the Dobe camp, I found I had been named and adopted into a fictive kinship network. My name, /Tontah, was a pun on /ton meaning "white man," but was also one of the standard !Kung names. This put me into the widespread network of social relationships that flow out of the fact of shared personal names. Through this I was able to establish a kin tie with hundreds of !Kung throughout the Dobe area and beyond. I was also adopted as a "son" by a Dobe man named N!eishi, the wife's brother of ≠Toma//gwe, our original Dobe contact. From this adoption flowed a whole series of "genealogical" kin ties that provided alternative pathways for reckoning relationships. It also, I later learned, involved me in a host of economic obligations, which at times all seemed to be coming due at once.

Feeling secure in my new kin role and armed with a few hundred words of !Kung vocabulary, I resolved to try for a more total immersion in the culture. In March, without an interpreter, 3 weeks were spent living at the summer water holes north of Dobe, subsisting almost entirely on wild foods, supplemented with a bit of milk from the Herero cattle posts. The routine consisted of daily walks to the water hole, hunting with the men, accompanying the women on mongongo-gathering trips, and sleeping in a grass shelter in the camp. The people were kind and friendly, although conversation was limited by my poor command of !Kung. I tried to provide at least as many calories as I consumed so as not to be a burden on the people. If I succeeded in this effort, it was not by much margin. This immersion plunged me into the life of the !Kung in a way no amount of interviewing could. I came to have a healthy appreciation for the cheerfulness and effortlessness with which they faced a way of life that was for me quite uncomfortable.

One thing that struck me about the nutting camps was the amount of leisure time people appeared to have. Half or more of the adults seemed to be resting or sleeping in the camp on any given day. Some systematic observations on this problem were in order and on July 6, 1964, I started a daily work diary of the Dobe camp activities. The whole camp was checked at sunrise and sunset to determine what each individual was doing each day. The comings and goings of !Kung visitors were also recorded to count the number of mouths being fed each day; and the hunters were checked as they came home each day with or without meat. Women were monitored as well to see what species of plant foods they had gathered, and samples of their backloads were weighed on a simple scale. I tried to interfere as little as possible in the day-to-day flow of activities in the camp, although not entirely successfully. The resulting work diary covered a 4-week period and formed the basis later for an input-output analysis of !Kung subsistence (Lee 1969a).

SYSTEMATIC DATA

As the first anniversary of Dobe fieldwork approached, I began to round off my observations in preparation for returning home and to lay the groundwork for a possible longer-term study in the future. This involved (1) development of a standard format and numbered file for the 200 genealogies collected; (2) a rough attempt to estimate ages of the population by arranging people into age series ranked from youngest to oldest and pinpointing key birth dates through the use of event calendars (work carried forward later much more systematically by Nancy Howell); (3) setting up a comprehensive checklist of all the plants and animals and collection of specimens of all the plants for identification at the Salisbury Herbarium; and (4) setting up a card file of all the vocabulary collected – about 1100 items in all.

But the most significant work of systematization concerned the final census of the Dobe area in November 1964. I went through the entire population at the nine water holes, household by household, and assigned a unique master number to each individual, including those who had been born or had died during the period starting August 1963. The numbering started with my "father" N!eishi as 001 and included 433 people in all. This census provided the baseline for all the observations by a dozen investigators over the next 10 years and ensured that the unity and integrity of the study population would be maintained as it later grew to include some 980 people.

In October, Irven and Nancy DeVore returned to Africa to join me at Dobe, and the concluding months of the field study proved particularly fruitful. Irv and I worked closely together and made several trips to isolated bush camps to examine and plot recently abandoned campsites and to follow the men on hunts. Stan Washburn joined us from Berkeley, and he proved to be a brilliant photographer (see Howell et al. 1965:178–93).

By this time our base camp at Dobe had become quite substantial, consisting of a large grass hut for the DeVores, a smaller one for me, a kitchen tent, and several other tents and structures for Onesimus, Gakekgoshe, and the other workers. Like it or not, our Dobe camp had become quite an attraction to the local people. Every day brought a delegation of !Kung and Herero visitors seeking tobacco and medicine for sundry ailments. This magnet had its advantages: There was a constant flow of informants from distant camps willing to be interviewed, and we carried out many long discussions in the shade of the grove of peltophorum trees

Plate 1.2. Anthropologist's camp at Dobe.

in the center of our camp. For Christmas 1964, we slaughtered a Christmas ox and feasted the !Kung for 3 days and nights, the first in what was to become an annual ritual (Lee 1969b).

But the drawbacks of a popular base camp were also considerable. We felt that the presence of our camp disrupted the normal flow of activities through Dobe and put an undue strain on the hospitality of the Dobe !Kung residents. We tried to minimize this disruption, but we were not always successful. This tension in our work continued between the need for a base camp to store supplies and provide minimal comforts for the researchers, and the need for observation conditions that were minimally disruptive of the flow of !Kung life.

INTERLUDE: 1965-7

We left Dobe on New Year's Day 1965, and by March I was living in Cambridge, Massachusetts, and had started working on my thesis, "The Subsistence Ecology of !Kung Bushmen," completed in June of that year.

Attention now turned to the plans for the symposium on man the hunter, which DeVore and I were organizing with Sol Tax. The symposium took place in Chicago in April 1966 and convened a worldwide panel of scholars who had done fieldwork with contemporary hunter-gatherers. The book, mistitled *Man the Hunter,* brought together a mass of new data on hunting and gathering peoples and brought home to us the tremendous gaps in our own knowledge of the !Kung. It also underlined the urgency of further fieldwork with the few remaining viable groups. Further, we became aware that much more needed to be known about the contemporary adaptations, social organizations, histories, and acculturation status of surviving groups before the data on hunter-gatherers could be of much use to evolutionists. Because nowhere could we find, in Marshall Sahlins's apt phrase, "hunters living in a world of hunters," it was particularly important that we account for the impact of colonialism on even the most isolated groups. Finally, it was clear that the range of data required was far more than could be collected by one or two observers. These considerations led DeVore and me to embark on a more ambitious 3-year study involving collaboration with a number of specialists in anthropology and related fields.

Much of the rest of 1966 was spent writing the research proposal for the new field project and recruiting graduate students and other collaborators to take on specific aspects of the research. The National Institute of Mental Health funded our proposal, and the newly independent Government of Botswana granted a research permit early in 1967. In June we launched the second field study.

DOBE AND /XAI/XAI: 1967–9

After a brief visit to the Hadza, a foraging group in Tanzania, I returned to the Dobe area in August 1967, newly married to Nancy Howell. Howell, a sociologist, was planning a demographic survey of !Kung women; I planned to pursue an expanded range of topics to include social organization, kinship, and nutritional studies in addition to subsistence ecology. We set up a new camp at Dobe not far from the old one, and it eventually grew to include seven tents and other structures accommodating up to 10 researchers. Happily, my !Kung language facility had improved in the 2.5 years I had been away, and all my subsequent work was carried on in !Kung without an interpreter. The next 20 months of fieldwork resolved itself into a pattern in which long periods of isolation and sustained research were interspersed with short periods of intense activity facilitating the work of visiting researchers.

The first fieldwork had been about 30 percent interviews and 70 percent observation. This time the ratios were reversed, with much more of my time spent visiting people in their camps and sharing long mornings and afternoons of conversation. Information was recorded in NCR carbon notebooks with numbered pages. Filling about one 50-page notebook a week, I paused every few weeks to file the original page alphabetically by topic, retaining the second and third copies as a running record of the fieldwork. Gradually a file built up of about 4000 pages of notes under about 70 different headings, ranging from "Adolescence" and "Age Reckoning" at the beginning to "Water," "Weather," and "Work Effort" at the end.

In early 1968, Howell and I moved our camp from Dobe to /Xai/xai, 40 km to the south across the Aha Hills. /Xai/xai had a much bigger resident population than Dobe (140 in seven camps compared with 30 in one or two camps) and a larger hinterland to the east, south, and west with many seasonal water holes. The !Kung shared their water hole with about 70 Herero and their livestock, and this seemed a challenge for me to come to grips with the role of acculturation in the lives of the !Kung. We stayed at /Xai/xai for 14 months, and I consider this period by far the most productive of my 3 years of fieldwork.

Language fluency opened up whole new research areas for me and expanded others. Also the prospect of spending a full year based at one place encouraged me to set in motion longitudinal systematic observations on group movements, seasonal nutrition, and other topics.

First priority was understanding the dynamics of the /Xai/xai groups historically and spatially. This involved lengthy discussions with old people on the history of /Xai/xai and on the disposition of the various groups at the time of the coming of the blacks into the area (1880–1920). Extending genealogical knowledge back in time made possible the linking of several hundred living !Kung into a handful of sibling groups that flourished in the late nineteenth century. Going over much of the southern hinterland on foot, on donkey back, and by truck, accompanied by local informants, facilitated reconstruction of the mosaic of a dozen interlocking group territories that existed around the time of Bantu settlement of /Xai/xai about 50 years before (see Chapter 12).

The oral histories touched on a number of cases of conflict, including over 20 homicides, and it became clear that this subject should be pursued systematically. Eventually, over 100 case histories of lethal and nonlethal arguments and fights were collected.

The first months at /Xai/xai were culturally eventful ones, with two major dance movements in full swing. A young man named /Gaugo (/gau ="flower") had gone to work as a migrant laborer in the Witwatersrand gold mines, and there he had observed the organized "tribal" dances of migrant workers from various ethnic groups in the mine compound. Inspired by the precision drill of the troupes and by their subtle mockery of the white boss's authoritarianism, /Gaugo came back to /Xai/xai and organized a dance troupe of his own from among the /Xai/xai women. His dance featured rhythmic chants and shouted commands in Fanagalong, the lingua franca of the mines, and incorporated elements of African Zionist church and prophet movement rituals in a mixture that was uniquely !Kung. The entire population of /Xai/xai would turn out to watch and participate in his all-night, all-day dances.

As /Gaugo's movement slowed, there was an upsurge of the women's drum dance (*!gauts'i*), a dance that had been steadily expanding to the west and south from its original focus in the !Goshe area. In the well-known !Kung trance dance (Lee 1968b; Marshall 1969) the women provide the singing while the men dance and enter trance. In the women's dance, the roles are reversed. A man plays the drum while the women dance and go into trance. The women of /Xai/xai often danced four or five nights a week. Several nights were spent at the all-night dances, taking notes and enjoying the music. Later in the year Richard Katz, a Harvard-trained psychologist, made a detailed study of men's trance dancing (Katz 1976).

The systematic and longitudinal observations took several forms. We were concerned to see how the passage of the seasons affected !Kung nutritional status. Did people lose weight at one time of year and gain it back at the next? Was there a hungry season, as there is in many agriculture societies around the world? Nancy Howell and I devised a methodology for monitoring these cycles by periodically weighing everybody on a regular basis. Later on, we added skinfold and height measurements, and in order to get a regional picture, we traveled around the entire Dobe area to measure people at every water hole. Eventually we made over 3000 observations on some 641 individuals. These data were particularly useful in monitoring the nutrition of people in critical categories: newborns, growing children, adolescents, and pregnant and lactating women.

The population register begun in 1964 was continued and expanded, with new numbers being added as visitors arrived in the area and more babies were born (up to No. 846 in April 1969). Nancy Howell developed an expanded master file in which every individual had a biography that included age, birthplace, kinship, and a marital and reproductive history. Inspired by the example of F. G. G. Rose, who photographed over 200 Australian aborigines in his classic kinship study of Groote Eylandt (Rose 1960), I added photographic portraits of 700 people to accompany the biographies.

In 1968, I developed a seven-page written questionnaire and administered it to the adult men of the Dobe area; Howell worked out a somewhat different questionnaire for the adult women. The men's interviews covered about 20 major topics including birth, descent, naming, land-ownership, marital history, residence, travel, languages spoken, livestock owned, agricultural experience, wage work experience, hunting success by species, initiation, trance-dancing skills, visiting patterns, and traditional trading partnerships (*hxaro*). The interviews lasted from 30 minutes to 2 hours and often were accompanied by much side discussion that provided important, if tangential, insights. Over 150 of these interviews were collected, representing about 90 percent of the men of the Dobe area.

LIFE AT /XAI/XAI

The camp at /Xai/xai was at the end of a very long supply line. It was 40 km to the main camp at Dobe; over 350 km from Dobe to Maun, the nearest phone, the nearest doctor, and the nearest garage; and over 500 km from Maun to the railhead at Francistown. These were trips one did not undertake lightly. Driving around the Kalahari exacts a tremendous toll on motor vehicles. In the dry season the heavy sand grips the wheels, making four-wheel drive a necessity. For most of the year the daytime heat of 35 to 40 °C (95 to 105 °F) plus the heavy sand makes engine boiling inevitable.

The stretch from Nokaneng west to !Goshe was only 100 km, but it usually took 5 to 8 hours to cover in four-wheel drive through heavy sand. We nicknamed this stretch *the Middle Passage,* and crossing it marked a symbolic transition for us from the world outside to the insulated reality of the Dobe area. The worst time of year for driving, however, is the rainy season, when miles of road may be under water. It was often necessary to have someone walking ahead through the knee-deep water to warn the driver of hidden potholes. A breakdown in the dry season might mean a 40-km walk to the nearest water point. In the rainy season, it could take 2 days to dig out of the mud. If a vehicle could not be fixed on the spot, towing was usually out of the question. One abandoned the vehicle where it came to rest and hitchhiked to the only garage in Maun, then hitchhiked back to the vehicle with the spare parts in hand. The people of Ngamiland are resourceful when it comes to motor trouble, perhaps more so than anthropologists. In the event of a major breakdown, the passengers on the district transport, for example, would climb down and make camp by the side of the road, cooking and washing, hunting and gathering for a week or more until the truck was fixed. In 3 years of fieldwork I suffered through mechanical breakdowns without number and performed repairs I would never think of attempting anywhere else. I grew to thoroughly dislike the vehicles we drove and paradoxically to be moved to tears of thankfulness whenever one of them actually functioned for 100 km at a stretch.

The !Kung loved the vehicles! To go from one water hole to another by truck was like jet travel for the !Kung. They would climb onto the back, perch on top of the gear, and sing their *dots'i* ("truck song") lustily as we lurched along. There were many versions of the song, but my favorite lyrics were the ones that went as follows:

> While the truck does the work, we sit around and get fat
> Those who work for a living, that's their problem!

Whenever we announced we were going somewhere, a dozen people would show up ready to ship out on an hour's notice, and whenever we weren't going anywhere we were importuned and browbeaten to do so. As often as not, we would load up the truck, say our good-byes, and lumber off–only to break down a kilometer or two up the road and come straggling back on foot.

The rigors of desert travel by vehicle made us happy to settle into /Xai/xai for long periods of pedestrian life. Except for periodic trips to the water hole to fill our water drums and to the bush to collect firewood, there was no need even to start our truck. And for one memorable 6-week period, it was completely inoperative, its closed back area a storage shed and chicken coop, its cab a guest room.

At /Xai/xai we built a pleasant camp consisting of a large office tent, two smaller sleeping tents, and a mud-walled kitchen structure with a canvas roof. The camp was set up within a 20-minute walk of all the !Kung camps, but was directly associated with none to preserve our neutrality. Our household consisted of Nancy Howell, myself, and Gakekgoshe Isak. In those unliberated days, Nancy cooked for the three of us, Gakekgoshe did the dishes, and I, the *bwana*, kept the truck and the equipment running, read the rain gauge and thermohygrograph, and played the anthropologist. (Today I would do it differently.)

At a place like /Xai/xai, even if you have an office tent and other amenities you are subject to the forces of nature. In the spring and summer months of heat, the sand is so hot it burns the soles of your feet. Walking in the sun you can lose a half kilo of body weight per hour through sweating. In the winter nights the temperature inside the sleeping tent falls below freezing, and ice forms on the drinking water. The summer thunder showers can dump 2.5 cm of rain in a few hours and send gale-force winds racing through the camp. One December we returned to camp to find our sleeping tent destroyed by a windstorm–the canvas shredded and the aluminum poles twisted into fantastic shapes. In case of emergency the hospital was a minimum of 17 hours away *if* the truck was working. We took comfort in reminding ourselves that if the area was less difficult to live in and more accessible, it probably would not have remained a hunting and gathering stronghold and we would not be there.

The routines of camp life proceeded: up at dawn; a quick breakfast of mealie meal porridge, the local staple; down to the water hole to see the cattle being watered and to catch up on the day's events; hiking to one of the !Kung villages for a morning of talk; back to camp for lunch and a rest in the hottest part of the day; a second interviewing session in the late afternoon; and home at dusk. Bathing at the end of the day was a

Plate 1.3. Driving in the rainy season.

most pleasant ritual and we became adept at making the most of 2 liters
of water. Dinner was a time for pleasant conversation with Gakekgoshe
in !Kung over the day's events. At night the stars overhead had an almost
unbearable beauty, with the crystal clear high desert air and the central
spine of the Milky Way galaxy arching overhead. It is with good reason
that the !Kung named the Milky Way *!ku!ko!kumi* (the backbone of the
sky).

Life at /Xai/xai assumed a timeless quality untouched by world events.
The news of 1968 tragedies such as Martin Luther King's and Robert
Kennedy's assassinations reached us days and weeks after the events.
Gradually our existence merged into a different rhythm of water hole
trips, hunting, gossiping, gathering, and dancing.

THE /DU/DA POPULATION

One day in March, Irv DeVore drove into /Xai/xai from the border road,
having followed it up from Ghanzi in the South. He reported meeting a
large group of friendly !Kung camped along the border at !Kwidum, a
seasonal pan 25 km southwest of /Xai/xai. This was exciting news: None
of the /Xai/xai people were there, and we had assumed the area to be
unoccupied. Could this be a group that had never been contacted before?
At the first opportunity Howell and I dashed down to !Kwidum to find
out. There we found two camps totaling 37 people from groups we had
never seen before. They were full-time hunter-gatherers with no contact
with cattle people. They dressed traditionally, and several of the women
wore their hair long in elaborate ornamented coiffures, a style that had
largely died out in the Dobe area as a result of Bantu influence. Their kin
ties linked them more closely to the South and the Southwest than to
/Xai/xai and the Dobe area, and their speech patterns, though quite intelligible to us, showed distinct dialect differences that made them seem
exotic and foreign. Despite differences of detail, they were clearly !Kung,
however. On a later trip I was met by a man named /Tontah, a namesake; he greeted me warmly and showed me through the camp, introducing me to each of the residents in turn: "And this is our father . . . and
this is our mother . . . and this is our daughter . . . and this is our
wife . . . " demonstrating that the network of name relationships was
clearly in operation.

The first encounter at !Kwidum introduced us to a new subpopulation,
which we named the /Du/da population after the water hole 60 km south
of /Xai/xai where they were mainly concentrated in 1968–9. These were
the most traditional hunter-gatherers we encountered throughout the
fieldwork, and the information gathered on them, especially by Pat
Draper, forms a unique record. This is all the more important because
their life of isolation proved to be short-lived. Soon after we met them

they were contacted by the South African police with serious results (see below, "Return to Dobe: 1973").

EXPANSION OF THE RESEARCH GROUP

A number of long- and short-term researchers began studies of the !Kung in 1967–9. Irv DeVore was particularly conscientious in introducing new fieldworkers to the Dobe area. These included James Woodburn, the British social anthropologist, who had studied the Hadza in Tanzania; Marjorie Whiting, an American nutritionist, who made a very useful collection of food samples for laboratory analysis; and Drs. Stewart Truswell and John Hansen, then of the Cape Town University Medical School, who made examinations on over 80 !Kung in a 10-day trip (Truswell and Hansen 1976). In early 1968 three Harvard graduate students joined us in the Dobe area. Patricia Draper came to study child-rearing practices among both nomadic and settled !Kung (Draper 1975, 1976). Her husband, Henry Harpending, an anthropological geneticist, planned to collect blood samples and genealogical information from Dobe !Kung and later from !Kung throughout Northwestern Botswana. John Yellen, an archeologist, initiated a study of recently abandoned campsites at Dobe and its hinterland and excavated prehistoric sites in the Dobe vicinity. Draper, Harpending, and Yellen remained in the field for well over a year, and all went on to lead major research projects of their own in Botswana in the 1970s.

Later in 1968 Truswell and Hansen returned to continue their medical work, and Trefor Jenkins, a South Africa–based medical geneticist, also visited us. In September Richard Katz came out to do a study of !Kung healers and trance dancers from the point of view of humanistic psychology. In 1969 (after our departure) Mel Konner came to study infant behavior; his wife, Marjorie Shostak, collected life history materials from !Kung women. A year later Megan Biesele arrived to study myth and folklore. Nicholas Blurton Jones, the British ethologist, joined the Konners briefly to work on the !Kung's knowledge of animal behavior and other topics. (A collection of all these studies later appeared in Lee and DeVore 1976.)

By the end of 1968, Howell and I were beginning to think about winding up our work. That Christmas was to be our last at /Xai/xai, and I resolved to feast the !Kung in high style as a way of thanking them for all the cooperation of the past year. I made a point of seeking the largest, meatiest ox I could find so that the roast would be a memorable one for the !Kung. Imagine my surprise when the "roast" turned out to be of a different kind. The giant ox I had chosen became the subject of ridicule and derision, not happiness and gratitude. Soon after I bought the ox, and long before it was to be slaughtered, I was criticized by the !Kung for my poor judgment. According to which version you believed, the ox was too old or too tough or too thin. The Christmas "feast" was shaping up as a disaster.

When the day of the celebration arrived, I was surprised to find that the ox when slaughtered was meaty and tender after all, and the feast proved a big success. Why then had the !Kung been so critical of me and my ox beforehand? The search for the answer to that question proved a critical turning point in my understanding of the !Kung and of myself. What they were criticizing in me, I later learned, was not my judgment of beef, but the aloofness and arbitrariness of my behavior over the previous year. The !Kung are a fiercely egalitarian people and have a low tolerance for arrogance, stinginess, and aloofness among their own people. When they see signs of such behavior among their fellows, they have a range of humility-enforcing devices to bring people back into line.

Ridiculing a hunter's kill is one such leveling device, and it had been employed on me with great finesse and telling effect, even though I was the buyer of the meat, not the hunter. When the whole incident fell into perspective, I came to realize that there was affection as well as anger in their feelings toward me and that paradoxically the farce was a way, not of writing me off, but rather of bringing me into closer contact with them. This realization did not hit me until long after I left the field, and it convinced me that my next field trip had to be done on an entirely different basis. To make a significant person-to-person contact with the !Kung, it was essential to simplify my life style and to discard the massive material culture I had imported into their midst. The next trip, I resolved, would be done on foot with a knapsack and a sleeping bag. The opportunity for this, however, did not come until 4 years later.

INTERLUDE: 1969–73

We returned to North America in mid-1969 at the height of the anti-Vietnam War protest. The changing political climate could not fail to affect our work among the !Kung as well. As our fieldwork progressed, we began to see the !Kung and other San in a new light, as increasingly encroached upon by the mining, ranching, and military operations that were spreading throughout the more remote areas of Southern Africa. What about the future of the San? With changes in the land tenure system in Botswana, we could see a time when the !Kung would become landless squatters on the land they had traditionally occupied. This process had already occurred in other parts of Botswana. The military threat was even more disquieting. The !Kung, formerly so isolated, were being drawn into the political and class conflicts sweeping the Third World.

These considerations led us to reexamine the relation of our research group (now numbering 12 members) to the people we had studied. At a meeting in New Hampshire in 1973, the Harvard Kalahari Research Group decided that our responsibility to the San went beyond simply publishing the results of our studies in the appropriate journals and included a responsibility to work with them in their struggle for land and cultural survival. Out of these discussions came the founding of the Kalahari Peoples Fund, a nonprofit foundation that provides funding and personnel to the San to help them secure their land base and develop their communities (see Lee and DeVore 1976:22–32).

The KPF was a new departure for our research group, and to pave the way for our new kind of practice inside Botswana and to see how the Dobe !Kung were faring, I planned a third trip to the Kalahari in mid-1973 after a 4-year absence.

RETURN TO DOBE: 1973

This was the shortest of my three field trips; the returns in data were modest, but on a personal level the trip was important. Traveling to Botswana, I reflected on the changes in my life since last seeing the !Kung. I had become a father and had pictures in my knapsack of my 3-year-old twin boys to show everyone. Also I had moved from the United States back to Canada, but my marriage to Nancy Howell had foundered, and we had separated the year before. My heart was a mixture of painful and euphoric emotions as I was driven in a rented Land Rover across the 100 km of the Middle Passage. This time I had come back with a knapsack, a notebook, and a sleeping bag–determined to keep a low profile and live off the land.

The driver and I had set a date for him to come back and pick me up some weeks later. Until then I was to be on my own. I wondered how the !Kung would react to my newfound penury. Without the power implicit in the trucks and equipment, I was a curious creature indeed–a white man on foot. As we ground along the Middle Passage, I wondered what had become of my language facility. I hadn't spoken more than a few words of !Kung for over 4 years, and my mind seemed a blank. I laboriously practiced a few words of greetings just as I had on my first trip 10 years before.

We pulled into !Goshe in the early afternoon to see the people standing in front of their huts. After a few seconds' hesitation, I was greeted with a tumultuous welcome. As people pressed around hugging me and shaking my hand, the warmth of their greeting seemed to unlock the !Kung in me. The words poured forth, and I suddenly was able to greet everyone by name. Big changes had overtaken the area. On the way up the !Kangwa Valley we passed the new government schoolhouse, and as we rolled into Dobe I noticed that ≠Toma//gwe and his sons had a new kraal and 60 goats in the center of their camp.

Soon after I had settled into ≠Toma//gwe's camp, one of his sons said, "Our old friend /Tontah is back with us. We should slaughter a goat in his honor." His youngest brother replied, "Look, if we slaughter a goat every time we have a white man visit us, we will soon have no goats left. Why don't we go out hunting instead?" The next morning Gakekgoshe, the two brothers, and I set out hunting to the north, and within a few hours the younger man had shot and killed a young kudu, which we butchered and brought back to camp for a hearty feast. It was a perfect welcome for me at Dobe!

As I walked around the Dobe area, the people marveled at the pictures of the two boys, and the twins were duly named and adopted into the kinship network. David Lee, the older twin, was named N!eishi after my !Kung "father," and Alexander, younger by a few minutes, was named ≠Toma after my "older brother." My !Kung friends berated me for not bringing the boys with me and made me promise to do so on my next trip. Also there was intense speculation about my change in economic status. The people had literally never before seen a white man without a vehicle. Had I had a falling out with my older brother, Irv DeVore, they wondered, and had he taken my vehicle away? Later, when Gakekgoshe and I toured the camps on borrowed donkeys, the !Kung's spirits were considerably lifted. They joked that we had discovered a new and more reliable kind of vehicle, one that ate grass instead of petrol; they named our donkeys Land Rover and Jeepy.

One research goal was to bring the records of the population up to date by making a complete census of the Dobe and /Du/da populations. As the demographic data came in, they showed a marked excess of births over deaths, but overall the size of the resident population had remained the same as in 1968–9. The reason was the continual exodus of people to the South African government station across the border in Namibia, where free food and wage work were available. When we surveyed the border itself, the grim realities of the political situation became apparent. The border fence had been reinforced and was now almost 3 meters high with 17 strands of barbed and unbarbed wire. Furthermore, the South African–controlled side of the fence was bristling with military installations. There was a police camp every 40 km or so up and down the entire 800-km length of the border. Our sector of the fence was regularly patrolled by !Kung trackers employed by the South African police. Who were these !Kung? They turned out to be largely from the /Du/da groups we had first encountered in 1968. The !Kung trackers were being used by the South Africans to look for signs of freedom fighters from the South-West African People's Organization (SWAPO) crossing over into Namibia to liberate their country.

For me, the wheel had come full circle; I realized how closely in reality my scientific work and political work were linked. I had left the isolated

Plate 1.4. Lee on board Land Rover.

!Kung to get involved against the war in Vietnam. I returned to the Kalahari 4 years later to find the makings of the next Vietnam right in the Dobe area.

For this and other reasons, the 1973 field trip was painful for me. The personal difficulties I was going through at the time were much on my mind. This was brought home to me by the candid comments from several !Kung friends who said, "/Tontah has aged. /Tontah, you are an old man now. Your beard is full of gray." My first reaction was resentment. I wasn't old. I was young! Where did they get off saying I was an old man! But on thinking further about their comments, I admitted they had a point. I *had* aged. And it was a good thing I had too, because much of my adult life had been spent hiding my feelings from the world, trying to appear cheerful even if I felt depressed, burying anger inside me. In the past year I had tried to change this. I had learned to cry, and my face now showed some of the pain I had always felt, but not admitted. I had associated aging with degeneration, something to be feared and avoided. But becoming older was also growth, a positive thing, even a necessity if one was to live in the world.

It came as a shock that my perception of the !Kung and my misperception of myself were so closely bound up. Only as I became three-dimensional to myself could the !Kung become truly three-dimensional to me. When I was cheerful, the !Kung came out cheerful in my writing. But as I experienced sadness, some of their sadness came through. And as I experienced anger, some of their anger became visible and tangible to me. As I came to accept the fact of my aging, so could I accept their way of doing things.

Finally, on the day I was leaving Dobe, one of my "sisters," whom I hadn't seen before on this trip came in from one of the bush camps. We greeted each other warmly, and she looked at me carefully for several seconds. "You're not old," she finally said. "People told me you were old, but now that I can see you, I see you are not old. You are an adult!"

2

San, Bushman, Basarwa: a question of names

T HIS chapter introduces the San people of Southern Africa, their cultural groupings, their history, and the people who have studied them. The goal is to place the !Kung in a broader cultural-historical context. When the Dutch settled the Cape of Good Hope region in the 1650s, they found two cultural groupings among the native inhabitants. The cattle-herding nomads who occupied the Cape valleys became known to the Dutch as Hottentots, and the Dutch established a lively trade in cattle with them. Occupying the higher ground and in the mountains were a hunting and gathering people, apparently loosely organized, whom the Dutch originally labeled *San* or *Sonqua*, a Hottentot word meaning "aborigines" or "settlers proper" (Hahn 1881). The Dutch also applied the descriptive term *Bojesman* to these hunter-gatherers; this term took hold, and soon the Sonqua became known to the world as the Bushmen of South Africa. Both the Bushmen and the Hottentots spoke a click-filled language that was quite unrelated to the Bantu languages spoken by the other indigenous peoples of Southern Africa, such as the Xhosa, the Swazi, and the Sotho to the east. The names Hottentot and Bushmen gained wide currency in the scientific and popular literature and were enshrined in Isaac Schapera's classic ethnography, *The Khoisan Peoples of South Africa: Bushmen and Hottentots*, published in 1930. But as names for these two peoples they were far from satisfactory. Like so many of the band and tribal societies of the world, these Southern African peoples were tagged with names not of their own choosing that bore little or no relation to the names they used for themselves. Further, such names often had derogatory or racist connotations. To call someone a Hottentot in Cape Town is still considered an insult today.

In an effort to remove some of these connotations, scholars have recently reintroduced more linguistically accurate terms: Hottentot has been dropped in favor of *Khoi-Khoi*, a term of self-appellation for the descendants of the cattle people of the Western Cape (Carstens 1966).

Plate 2.1. Farm San at Ghanzi, Botswana.

The term *Bushmen* has both racist *and* sexist connotations, and it has
been dropped in favor of *San,* a comparatively neutral term originally
applied by the Khoi-Khoi to their hunting and gathering neighbors (Wilson and Thompson 1969:40–1). The Kalahari Research Group adopted
the term San in 1973, and it is used throughout this book and others by
our research group as the cover term for all the peoples formerly called
Bushmen (Lee and DeVore 1976). Acceptance of the term San is not
universal, however. Readers who want to pursue the continuing debates
over use of the terms San, Bushmen, Khoi-Khoi, and Hottentot should
consult Böeseken (1972, 1974, 1975), Elphick (1974, 1975, 1977), Barnard (1976a), Jenkins and Tobias (1977), and Guenther (1977).

However, even San is not an entirely satisfactory term. First, it too has
a derogatory connotation, meaning "a rascal" in Khoi-Khoi. Second, because of the tremendous linguistic diversity among the Kalahari San of
today, over a dozen self-applied terms are in use by various peoples, and
San is not one of them! The cover term for Bushmen in Botswana has
been *Masarwa,* a Setswana word whose root may have originally meant
"people of the west." But it too has uncomplimentary connotations, as
exemplified by the Setswana insult *Mosarwa ke wena!* ("Bushman you
are!"). The widespread use of this term generated an interesting corre-

spondence in the pages of *Kutlwano,* the Botswana news magazine. A bright high-school student pointed out that it was government policy to treat the Masarwa as full citizens with equal rights in the country. Yet this was inconsistent with the name Masarwa, which connoted inferiority and outcast status. Part of the problem, he argued, was in the prefix *Ma,* which in the Setswana system of noun classes refers to subordinate and enemy peoples. Why not change the prefix to *Ba,* he suggested, and place the *Ba*sarwa on an equal footing, at least linguistically, with the full Tswana tribes such as the *Ba*mangwato and *Ba*kwena? This suggestion met with approval, and the government took steps to implement it. The *Bushman* Development Officer in the Ministry of Local Government duly became the *Basarwa* Development Officer, and the term is now standard usage in the country. In this book the reader will find San as the general term for Bushmen, and Basarwa as the specific term when Botswana government usage is mentioned.

The !Kung are bemused by this terminological activity. Their name for themselves is not Bushman or San or Basarwa; neither, for that matter, is it !Kung! They call themselves *Zhũ/twasi* ("real people"), and they extend this to include all !Kung speakers as well as other San. A lively old blind man at !Goshe with a keen sense of humor put it all in perspective. When the !Goshe people first heard the term Bushmen applied to themselves, they were tickled by its strange sound. Old Dam decided that if they were Bushmen he was the biggest Bushman of them all, and he nicknamed himself *Bushimani n!an!a* ("big, big Bushman"), a handle he retains to the present day!

The origin of the term !Kung is obscure. German missionaries applied it to San speakers in South-West Africa in the last century (Vedder 1910–11). Bleek (1928b) traced it to Angola, arguing that it is the word "they" in Angola !Kung dialect. Contemporary studies have applied a variety of other terms to the !Kung and their languages: Zhu (Westphal 1971), JU and žu/'hoasi (Snyman 1975), !Xũ (Snyman 1970; Westphal 1971). For our purposes, the term !Kung is well established in the literature and refers to a clearly bounded ethnic and linguistic grouping in Southern Africa. Therefore, we have decided to continue to use !Kung in preference to these other terms to refer to people who are ethnically and linguistically !Kung. Finally, !Kung is easier to pronounce than žu/'hoasi.

THE CAPE SAN

Some 300 years ago San covered the whole of Southern Africa. It is impossible to estimate the number of San at the time of arrival of the Europeans. Modern archeology has shown that every region of Southern Africa – deserts, mountains, savannah, and coasts – was densely occupied by Later Stone Age peoples, who were almost certainly the ancestors of the historical San. Their beautiful rock paintings and engravings at hundreds of sites throughout the subcontinent attest to their cultural achievements.

Whatever their number (200,000 seems a reasonable figure), the San were subjected to genocidal warfare at the hands of the Dutch settlers, the ancestors of the present-day Afrikaaner rulers of South Africa. Decade after decade, from the 1690s to the 1830s, the San were hounded by the settlers and driven to take refuge deep in the desert or high in the mountains. In the eighteenth century the Dutch governor at the Cape regularly sent out vigilante units called commandos, whose task it was to hunt down the San, kill the men, and lead the women and children into slavery on the white farms. The commandos were required to file careful reports on the numbers killed and captured, and these reports, unearthed from the Cape archives in the 1830s by Donald Moodie, grimly document the campaigns of extermination (Moodie 1840–2).

Contrary to some popular notions, the San did not simply submit meekly to slaughter. At first they were easily overcome by the superior arms of the Dutch, but later they began to restructure their groups to make them more effective militarily. A system of war leaders called capitaans evolved to organize resistance, and in some mountainous areas the San were able to hold out for years against the commando attacks. This little known chapter in South African history has been ably documented by Shula Marks (1972).

Today the San of South Africa are virtually extinct, an eloquent testimony to the white man's "civilizing" mission in that part of Africa. The descendants of the San have been absorbed into the so-called cape coloured population, but all traces of their language have been lost (Marais 1939).

THE KALAHARI SAN

The tragic fate of the Cape San forms a necessary background to a discussion of the Kalahari San, because the latter experienced a very different history. The Cape San found themselves directly in the path of predatory white settlers. In the Kalahari, by contrast, the incoming groups were mostly Bantu-speaking cattle people, such as the Bakalahari and the Batswana from the Southeast, and the Herero from the Northwest. These encounters were not without violence, and there are many accounts of armed clashes in the oral histories of both sides. However, the element of genocide was absent, and in many parts of the Kalahari a coexistence developed with trade and intermarriage between San and non-San peoples. In the South, especially among the Tswana, the San became serfs of well-to-do Tswana families. In this semifeudal system, the San worked on the Tswana cattle posts and performed domestic

Plate 2.2. Cattle-post San in the Khwebe Hills.

chores, and the Tswana in turn housed and clothed the San and provided them with legal protection in the Tswana courts. There is no doubt that the San were subordinate to the Bantu, and remnants of discrimination continue to the present, but by comparison with their cousins under the Dutch, the Kalahari San have fared relatively well. Also because of the vast distances in the Kalahari and the scarcity of water, a substantial proportion of the San, such as the Dobe area !Kung, were only minimally affected by African or European contact until recent years. It is important to note that the Kalahari San are not refugees from other areas. All the archeological evidence indicates a long history of development in situ for the San peoples of the Kalahari (Fourie 1928; John Yellen, personal communication).

The Republic of Botswana, with an estimated San population of 24,400, is the home of over half of all the contemporary San; Namibia has about 11,500, and the People's Republic of Angola has 4000. A few hundred San live in Zambia and Zimbabwe, making a total of about 40,500 people in all the countries. Their distribution is shown in Figure 2.1.

Within this small population exists an astonishing linguistic and cul-

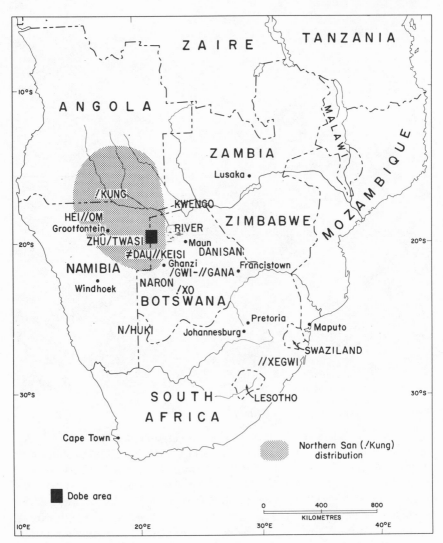

Figure 2.1. Distribution of the living San in Africa.

tural diversity, with the !Kung only one of three major language groupings. Thanks to the pioneering work of the late Dorthea Bleek (1929) and
the more recent work of linguists Ernst Westphal (1963, 1971) and Tony
Traill (1974, 1975, 1976), we are now beginning to make sense of the San
language divisions. Westphal established the distinction between the
Tshu-Khwe and the Bush divisions of languages. Although both groups
of languages were spoken by people who hunted and gathered for a living, the first group (Tshu-Khwe) was actually closely related to Khoi-Khoi
(Hottentot). The second division in Westphal's scheme consisted of

The Southern San peoples

This is a linguistically distinct cluster of scattered groups, located mainly in a broad belt across Southern Botswana with a few outliers. Most of these languages have the fifth bilabial click as well as the four other clicks found in !Kung and the Tshu-Khwe languages. Traill argues that all three languages can be related to the languages of the Cape San.

!Xo. The main group is the !Xo San of Namibia and Southern Botswana, numbering about 2000 people in 40 small communities. The !Xo include some recent hunter-gatherers as well as groups closely associated with Bakwena and Bakalahari cattle posts. The western !Xo have been studied by Heinz (1966, 1972, 1975), Traill (1974), Eibl-Eibesfeldt (1972), and Sbrzesny (1976). Helga Vierich of the University of Toronto has been making extensive studies of the eastern ≠Thua, an as yet unclassified sub-branch (Vierich 1977).

N/huki. This is the language of a small group of tourist-oriented San in the Kalahari Gemsbok Park of South Africa. In the early 1970s Traill reported that only one N/huki speaker remained (1974); the rest spoke Nama, the language of neighboring Khoi-Khoi groups. The N/huki have not been seriously studied (see Bjerre 1958), but striking photographs of them appeared in the well-known *Family of Man* photographic exhibition (1960).

//Xegwi. In the Lake Chrissie region of the Eastern Transvaal lives a small group of San speaking a language related to /Xam, the language of the Cape San. Studies of these people in the 1950s counted fewer than 80 speakers living on European farms (Potgieter and Ziervogel 1955; Lanham and Hallowes 1956). By 1976 only two speakers remained (Traill 1976:1). These plus the N/huki are the only surviving San in South Africa.

The Northern San peoples

In contrast to the linguistic diversity of the other San groups, the northern San all speak a single language (!Kung) with intergrading, mutually intelligible adjacent dialects. !Kung is linguistically distinct both from Tshu-Khwe and from the southern San languages. The !Kung number over 15,000, with the majority in Namibia and the remainder divided between Angola and Botswana. Some 25 years ago a large proportion of the !Kung were hunter-gatherers. By 1977 the situation had changed fundamentally, as the following survey makes clear. The three-part division of the !Kung was originally set out by Fourie (1928:84).

!Kung. In the extreme north of Namibia and across the Okavango River in
Angola live scattered groups of the !Kung proper. Only fragmentary reports exist about these northern people. They were the first of their ethnic
group to be contacted by nineteenth-century explorers and missionaries,
and their name for themselves (!Kung) has come to be applied as a cover
term for all !Kung (Bleek 1928b; Esterman 1946–9; Almeida 1965). Numbering about 3000 in Namibia and 3500 in Angola, the !Kung exist in close
association with neighboring Bantu groups. The Angola !Kung were seriously disrupted by the Portuguese during Angola's war of liberation. Not
only were the !Kung recruited as trackers, but the Portuguese were reported to have bombed villages believed sympathetic to the insurgent
Popular Movement for Liberation of Angola (MPLA) (Rotsart, personal
communication). In this book, the term !Kung applies generally to the
!Kung, not simply to this northern group.

≠Dau//keisi. On the Ghanzi and Gobabis farms live about 3000 !Kung
speakers. They are tied into the European farm labor system, but periodically move to the bush for hunting and gathering. Variants of their name
≠Dau//keisi, meaning "north side people," such as Makaukau, Kowkow,
and Auen, are widely cited in the literature going back to the nineteenth
century. Baines's (1864) and Chapman's (1868) descriptions of the
"Makowkow" provide the earliest English-language accounts of the
!Kung San. Curiously, there are no modern studies of these people.

Zhũ/twasi. The most traditional of the three regional divisions of the
!Kung includes the 6000 in Northwestern Botswana and Northeastern
Namibia. The term means "genuine people" in the !Kung language and is
a term of self-appellation. Along the Okavango River and around Grootfontein in Namibia these central !Kung are involved in farm labor and in
government settlement schemes. Elsewhere, the Zhũ/twasi are far more
traditional. An isolated population of Zhũ/twasi was contacted by the Marshall family of Cambridge, Massachusetts, in 1951 in a remote part of
Namibia that became known as Nyae Nyae (Marshall 1976). Since 1960,
close to 1000 Nyae Nyae !Kung have been settled by the South African
occupation authorities at a place called Chum!kwe. Across the border in
Botswana in 1963, Lee and DeVore contacted a population of !Kung in a
region that became known as the Dobe area. All the Zhũ/twasi on both
sides of the border continue to do some hunting and gathering, but only in
the Dobe area and perhaps around /Du/da are there groups for whom
hunting and gathering are the mainstay of subsistence. In addition to
extensive studies by the Marshall family (1957, 1959, 1960, 1961, 1965,
1968) and by the Kalahari Research Group (Lee and DeVore 1976), the
central !Kung have been studied by Wiessner (1977) and by Wilmsen
(1976, 1977).

3

The Dobe area: its peoples and their history

THIS chapter covers demography, group structure, and history. First, I introduce the Dobe area and look at its population in broad outline, examining size, sex and age composition, fertility, and mortality. Next, I focus in, with a water hole by water hole survey of the actual living groups of the Dobe people. The goal is to describe their living arrangements and to illustrate the dynamic processes at work in structuring their collective life. The last third of the chapter is a history of contact, tracing the history of the Dobe area from the 1870s to the time of my fieldwork in the 1960s. The purpose of this section is to place the Dobe people into the context of contemporary Africa to see how they have survived for so long as hunter-gatherers in a world of nonhunters.

Between the Okavango swamps on the east and the South-West African plateau on the west lies a vast, sparsely populated sandy plain about 400 km across. Called the Kaukauveld on some maps, the plain is bisected by the north-south line of the Namibia–Botswana border. Drainage is from west to east, and at various points dry river valleys and pans incise the landscape and expose the underlying rock formations. Surface water also appears here, and it is this water that has made possible the peopling of these valleys, first long ago by San hunter-gatherers and in the very recent past by Bantu-speaking pastoralists. In years of high rainfall water may flow in these riverbeds for a few days or weeks, but it never reaches the Okavango swamps. Instead, the water is dissipated and absorbed in the sandy flatlands west of the swamps we nicknamed the Middle Passage.

One of the largest and most isolated of these desert valleys is the !Kangwadum, which runs west to east through the center of the Kaukauveld north of the low ranges of the Aha Hills (Figure 3.1). Even more isolated is the /Xai/xai Valley just south of the Aha Hills. Protected by a waterless belt of country on the north, east, and south 50 to 150 km wide, these two valleys have remained hunting and gathering strongholds well

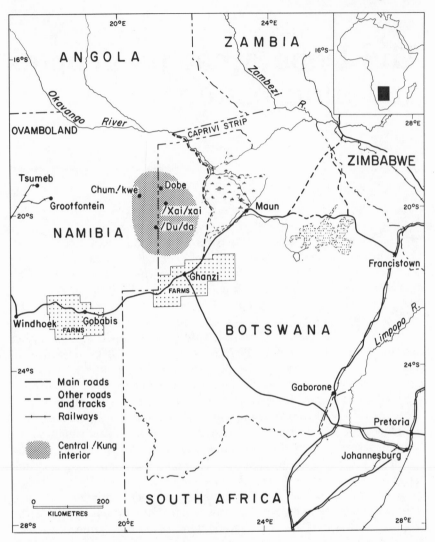

Figure 3.1. The Northwest Kalahari.

into the twentieth century. The isolation, lack of surface water, and low and erratic rainfall made penetration of this area difficult for blacks and whites alike. As a result, the impact of European colonialism, so brutal elsewhere in Africa, was greatly slowed in the Dobe area. The !Kung of these valleys have continued to hunt and gather into the 1960s and 1970s because that was the only economic alternative locally available to them.

The semipermanent water hole of Dobe is one of nine in the part of the !Kangwa Valley east of the Namibia border. The Dobe area includes

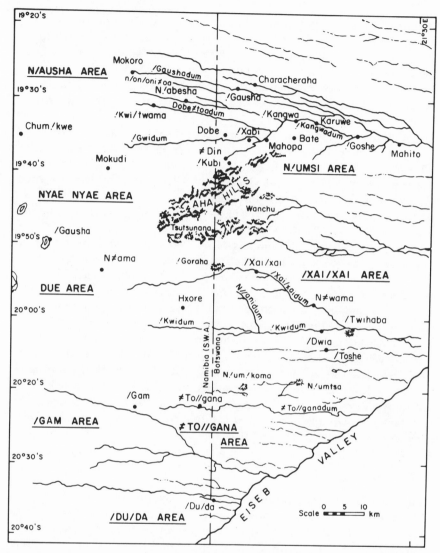

Figure 3.2. The Dobe area.

these nine water holes and their hinterlands as well as the water hole of /Xai/xai in the /Xai/xai Valley and its very extensive hinterlands (Figure 3.2). At its maximum, the Dobe area extends 140 km from north to south and 65 km from east to west, enclosing a space of roughly 9000 km², about three-quarters in Botswana and one-quarter in Namibia. On the east and north, the Dobe area is bounded by uninhabited waterless country; on the south, the area abuts the country of the /Du/da !Kung population; on the west it abuts the country of the Nyae Nyae !Kung

(Fig. 3.1). In former years there was a steady flow of visitors between the Dobe, the /Du/da, and the Nyae Nyae peoples, and these three groups together could be called the interior !Kung. Since 1965 this flow has been increasingly interrupted by the building of a fence along the Namibia–Botswana border by the South African authorities, and today the Dobe people are following a different historical course from that of their relations in Namibia.

Until the 1920s the Dobe area was occupied exclusively by hunting and gathering !Kung. Today, the 460 !Kung residents share their water holes with some 340 Bantu people and several thousand head of livestock. At the time of my main census (November 1968), another 125 marginal !Kung made periodic visits to the Dobe area from their bases elsewhere, and 145 !Kung lived isolated lives in the /Du/da area to the south, making a total of 730 !Kung in the study area.

These straightforward numbers – 460, 340, 125, 145 – are simple to state, but required considerable effort to develop (cf. Appendix A). An accurate count of the number of people in the Dobe area took many months to prepare, and the more complex data such as dates of births and deaths and determination of people's ages required even more work. The difficulty of this task helps me appreciate why there are so few reliable demographic data on hunting and gathering peoples. I started a registry of vital events in July 1963, a record that was maintained until July 1973. But the real demographic work with the Dobe !Kung was done by Nancy Howell, a professional demographer. Howell is responsible for the age analysis and for the retrospective fertility histories presented here and for very valuable advice. For a full account of !Kung demography, consult her mongraph (Howell 1979).

COUNTING THE !KUNG

Hunting and gathering peoples are notoriously difficult to keep track of. They move the location of their camps frequently, and even within a single camp the composition of the group changes from week to week or from day to day. The !Kung are no exception to this rule: They move from camp to camp with distressing frequency; some alternate among two or more water holes, dividing their time equally among the several locations; others move right out of the Dobe area several times a year or for years at a time. To complicate matters further, dozens of visitors move through the Dobe area each year. Like comets, some move on a regular and predictable path; others show up for a few days and may not be seen again for years.

Accurate census data are the foundations on which a sound demographic and ecological analysis must rest, and getting a firm fix on the numbers of !Kung was one of the highest priorities of the research. It is

Table 3.1. *Population of the Dobe area: 1964–73*

Year	Residents	Marginals	Total !Kung counted	Blacks
1964	379	87	466	340
1968	457	127	584	[b]
1973	457		457[a]	

[a]Residents only.
[b]In this and subsequent tables a blank means "no information" or "not applicable."

relatively easy to count the number of people in a camp on a given day, but it is more of a challenge to keep track of these people over a 12-month period as they move through the annual round. I began counting the !Kung in October 1963, but not until a year later did I feel familiar enough with the population to attempt an area-wide census. And it was only in 1968, well into the second field trip, that I was confident I was recording everyone in the population. These remarks are important to an understanding of the population data that follow. Because of the nature of hunter-gatherer nomadism, the longer an observer stays in an area, the larger the population will be – not because the population is growing through an excess of births over deaths, but because of the nature of hunter-gatherers' visiting and its cumulative effect on the observations. Take the Dobe area as an example. Some visitors visit every year; therefore, any 12-month fieldworker will enumerate them. But others come only once in 2, 3, or 4 years; therefore, only a 2-, 3-, or 4-year study will record them all. Our recording extends over 10 years, but even this long a study misses those who visit less frequently than once in 10 years. Given that the category *visitors* is an open-ended one, it becomes essential to define a *resident* population. We define as a resident anyone who spends 6 months or more a year living within the Dobe area. In fact, most of our residents spend 11 or 12 months of the year inside the area, so that the 6-month rule is a minimal definition. All others who spend less than 6 months in the area – even as little as 1 day – are classified as *marginals*. In November 1964, the Dobe area contained 379 residents and 87 marginals; 4 years later the numbers stood at 457 residents and 127 marginals; and in 1973 the figure for residents was again 457 – marginals were not counted in the latter census (Table 3.1).

To go beyond simple numbers, it is necessary to have a knowledge of the ages of people. Lack of age data was a main stumbling block in the demographic study of the !Kung. None of the !Kung knew their own ages or the ages of their children. None knew the year of his birth or, for that

matter, what the current year was. To estimate ages by looks alone was a
risky procedure because !Kung may look much younger (or older) than
they actually are. How were we to get a handle on this problem? The
!Kung turned out to have a social custom that proved useful in determining their ages. Most of their kinship terms have an older-younger specifi-
cation built in. Relative age is important in !Kung kinship because for
every pair of persons, or dyad, the older of the two determines what kin
term is to be used, and the younger defers to the older. Parent-child kin
terms, of course, have relative age built in (e.g., father-daughter), but the
!Kung extend this feature to cousin, sibling, and in-law terms as well.
There is even a special kin term (≠*dara* = "friend, agemate") for people
who are so close in age that older-younger specifications do not apply.
Because each !Kung can, in effect, state his or her age relative to dozens of others, it is possible for an observer to rank order an entire population from oldest to youngest. In 1968–9 Nancy Howell canvassed the
entire population of Dobe and /Du/da and developed four regional interconnected rank orders containing over 800 people. Next Howell assigned
absolute ages by a curve-fitting technique using model life tables from
Coale and Demeny's book (1966). She adapted and greatly refined a technique originally developed by F. G. G. Rose for a similar study of Australian aborigines on Groote Eylandt (Rose 1960). The Howell method
yielded results that were both internally consistent and jibed well with
age estimates based on the use of event calendars. The technique is
discussed in more detail in Howell (1973, 1976a,b; 1979). The age-sex
composition of the resident population based on these age estimates is
shown in Table 3.2. Several points should be noted about the figures.

Totals. The dramatic 20 percent rise in the resident population from 1964
to 1968 is more apparent than real. It is more a result of my improved
knowledge of the population than of a natural increase or immigration.
Between 1968 and 1973 the population remained stable. Although births
greatly exceeded deaths during the period, out-migration drained away
the additional population.

Age ranking. All three censuses show a substantial proportion of people
over the age of 60. This high proportion (8.7 to 10.7 percent) of elderly by
Third World standards contradicts the widely held notion that life in
hunting and gathering societies is "nasty, brutish, and short." The argument has been made that life in these societies is so hard that people die
at an early age. The Dobe area, by contrast, had dozens of active older
persons in the population. Quite a few made contributions to the food
supplies, and many others were respected healers and ritual specialists
who were cared for and fed by the younger people long after their productive years had passed. The dependency ratio measures the burden that

Table 3.2. *Age-sex composition of resident population*

	Males		Females		Total	
Age[a]	No.	%	No.	%	No.	%
1964						
Old	14	8.1	23	11.2	37	9.8
Adult	112	64.7	123	59.7	235	62.0
Young	47	27.2	60	29.1	107	28.2
Total	173	100.0	206	100.0	379	100.0
1968						
Old	17	7.8	23	9.5	40	8.7
Adult	141	65.3	145	60.2	286	62.6
Young	58	26.9	73	30.3	131	28.7
Total	216	100.0	241	100.0	457	100.0
1973						
Old	19	9.1	30	12.1	49	10.7
Adult	125	60.1	140	56.2	265	58.0
Young	64	30.8	79	31.7	143	31.3
Total	208	100.0	249	100.0	457	100.0

[a]Old = 60+, adult = 15–59, young = 0–14 years.

nonproductive young and old place on the adult producers in a population. Developing countries with growing population and a young age distribution show a high dependency ratio of 80 to 115 (i.e., 80 to 115 nonproductive people per 100 effectives); developed countries tend to have a lower dependency ratio (45 to 80) indicating a lighter burden of nonproducers per effective (United Nations 1970). The !Kung dependency ratios are shown in Table 3.3, along with comparative data for some developed and developing countries. By comparison with other Third World populations, the percentage of young people (and hence the dependency ratio) is relatively low: 30 percent of the !Kung are under age 15 compared with 43 percent in Lesotho and 48 percent in Iraq. As a result, the economically active section of the !Kung population is not burdened by the need to support a high proportion of dependents. Unlike the case in many Third World peasant societies, the !Kung young people are not pressed into the food quest at an early age.

Sex ratio. Women greatly outnumber men in the older age categories. This is an expected situation because the !Kung, like most of the world's populations, show higher mortality rates for men than for women. More surprising, however, is the surplus of females over males in the youngest age group (0–14 years). Table 3.4 sets out the sex ratio for each age

Table 3.3. *Dependency ratios*

	Age[a]				Child
	Young (%)	Adult (%)	Old (%)	Dependency ratio[b]	dependency ratio[c]
Dobe area					
1964	28	62	10	61	46
1968	29	63	9	60	46
1973	31	60	11	72	54
Mean	29	62	10	66	49
Comparative data					
Developed countries					
Japan	24	69	7	45	35
United Kingdom	24	63	13	59	38
Canada	30	62	8	61	48
United States	29	61	10	64	48
Developing countries					
Namibia	40	55	5	82	73
Lesotho	43	52	5	92	83
Guinea	44	49	7	104	90
Iraq	48	47	5	113	102

[a]For Dobe area: young = 0–14, adult = 15–59, old = 60+ years. For comparative data: young = 0–14, adult = 15–64, old = 65+ years.
[b]Number of young and old per 100 adults.
[c]Number of young per 100 adults.

Table 3.4. *Age-sex ratios: resident population, males per 100 females*

1964	
Old	60.9
Adult	91.1
Young	78.3
Overall	84.0
1968	
Old	73.9
Adult	97.2
Young	79.4
Overall	89.6
1973	
Old	63.3
Adult	89.3
Young	81.0
Overall	83.5

old = 60+, adult = 15–59, young = 0–14 years.

Table 3.5. *Birth and death rates: 1963–8*

Year	Crude birth rate[a]	General fertility ratio[b]	Crude death rate[c]
1963	55	169.4	4
1964	23	79.9	15
1965	39	114.5	26
1966	18	53.0	13
1967	70	212.1	20
1968	41	139.5	16

[a]Births per 1000 person-years lived.
[b]Births per 1000 women aged 15–49 years.
[c]Deaths per 1000 person-years lived.
Source: Howell (1976b:141–2).

group in the three censuses. In most of the world's populations the sex ratio at birth falls between 105 and 110 males per 100 females. Infant and child mortality is higher among males than among females, so that by the age of puberty there is parity between the sexes. In the !Kung case, the sex ratio among the young ranges from 78 to 81, an astonishing anomaly if it proves consistent. There is good reason to believe, however, that the skewed sex ratio is produced by an accident of small numbers. Of 101 babies born between 1969 and 1973, 55 were males and 46 females, for a ratio of 119.6. In a population of this size it is expected that sex ratios at birth may fluctuate from decade to decade. In contrast, the adult sex ratios represent the differential effects of mortality on men and women.

Fertility and mortality. So far, we have seen a population with a fairly high proportion of old people and a low proportion of people in the younger age categories. Superficially, the Dobe population pyramid looks like that of a developed country, for example, like that of the United States around 1900. A population in a developing country, by contrast, would have a lower proportion of old people (4 to 7 percent vs. 9 to 11 percent) and a much higher proportion of children (38 to 48 percent vs. 28 to 31 percent). To understand the shape of the population better, we have to know the birth and death rates that have produced it (Table 3.5). Howell has calculated the crude birth rate (CBR) as 41, which is about typical for Botswana as a whole (Howell 1976b:141). The crude death rate (CDR) for this period is 16, according to Howell (1976b:141)–higher than the United States figure of 9, but lower than the national Botswana rate of 23. This death rate of 16 is very low for a population without access to medical care, and an explanation is required. One is led to consider two possible explanations: (1) that the !Kung are a healthy and vigorous population with a low incidence of infections and degenerative diseases; and (2) that our expedition in some ways reduced the level of mortality temporarily through medical intervention. The true story probably combines both these factors. Medical examinations by a team of doctors showed that the Dobe area !Kung *were* a healthy population with few signs of such degenerative conditions as heart disease and high blood pressure (Truswell et al. 1972; Truswell and Hansen 1976; Truswell 1977). On the other hand, both the doctors and other members of the research group gave emergency medical care that probably saved lives during the period 1963–73.

Rate of natural increase. Whatever the explanation, the Dobe area !Kung are an expanding population. Over the long run we expect hunter-gatherer populations in general to have a positive, but very low, rate of natural increase. Any sustained marked excess of births over deaths would lead to a rapid population increase – even a population explosion – and the current Dobe population seems to be in just such a situation. With a CBR of 41 and a CDR of 16, the rate of natural increase is 25 persons per 1000 population, which translates to a growth rate of 2.5 percent each year, a rate that, if continued, would double the population in only 28 years (Howell 1976b:141). Migration has somewhat offset this rate of growth. The population grew through immigration *and* natural increase from 1963 to 1968, but out-migration during the period 1969–73 counteracted the growth, leaving the Dobe area in 1973 with the same number of residents it had had in 1968. There is good evidence that the current 2.5 percent growth rate is a recent phenomenon. Howell collected the retrospective reproductive histories of all the resident women of reproductive age and beyond during 1968–9 (Table 3.6). In all, 165 women between the ages of 15 and 80 were interviewed, and these women reported a total of 495 births – an average of 3.0 births per woman. For women past childbearing age, the completed family size (i.e., the total number of live births to a woman over her reproductive span) was 4.7. By world standards, this is a very low level of fertility for a noncontracepting population. When infant and child mortality was calculated for the 495 births, Howell found that about 40 percent of those born died before reaching maturity, a level of fertility and mortality that produces a population with a steady growth rate of less than 0.5 percent each year (Howell 1976b:150). The growth rate of the last 60 years shows an overall pattern, therefore, that is characteristic of what was probably the case in hunter-gatherer populations in general. How then are we to explain the higher birth and lower death rates of 1963–73? The answer lies in recent economic and demographic changes that are dealt with in Chapter 11.

Table 3.6. *Retrospective fertility: number of live births by current age of mother*

No. of births	Age of mother											Total
	15–19	20–24	25–29	30–34	35–39	40–44	45–49	50–54	55–59	60–64	65+	
0	13	4	3	2	3	2						27
1	3	7	3	4	5	3	3	2		1		31
2		5	1	3	3	2	2		2	2	1	21
3		4	6	1	3		2	2		1	2	21
4		1	2	5	2		2	3			1	16
5			1	4	1	3	2	2	4	3	2	22
6						3	1	2	1		4	11
7					1	0	1	0	1	2	4	9
8							1	1	1	2		6
9							1			3		1
Number of women	16	21	16	19	18	13	15	12	9	12	14	165
Number of children	3	33	36	53	40	40	61	50	45	60	74	495
Mean children per woman	0.2	1.6	2.2	2.8	2.2	3.1	4.1	4.2	5.0	5.0	5.3	
Total cohort fertility							4.1	4.2	5.0	5.0	5.3	

Source: Howell (1976b:146).

THE WATER HOLES

There are nine permanent water holes in the Dobe area, each varying widely in the size of its San and non-San populations and each with its distinctive cultural character, range of resources, and genealogical history. To introduce the water holes, let us take a brief walking tour of the area, starting in the east and moving to the west. As late as the 1960s most !Kung who traveled to the Dobe area from outside traveled by foot or on donkey. Only in the last decade has the truck traffic been regular enough to make it possible for !Kung to hitchhike across the Middle Passage; internal travel is still mainly on foot. The basic unit of measure of !Kung long-distance travel then and now is the !Kung walking rate of 4 to 5 km per hour.

To reach the Dobe area on foot from the east, you strike out from the main Maun–Shakawe road at the town of Nokaneng. In winter it is a hard 2-day march of over 100 km (67 miles) until you reach the first water hole at !Goshe, a large settlement of sedentary !Kung. This water hole, the easternmost settlement of the interior !Kung, is situated at the point where the !Kangwa River bed emerges from a deeply incised course through bedrock. !Goshe water is shared by the San with Bayei and Batswana herders. From !Goshe the path west is easier; a 3-hour (16-km) walk paralleling the river course passes the beautiful natural spring of !Kangawa Matse ("small !Kangwa") and brings you to !Kangwa, the administrative center of the district. The rock spring of !Kangwa has been on the maps since the nineteenth century (as Lewisfontein, Xangwa, or Khownwa). And since 1948, the Batswana headman has had his *kgotla* ("council") here. The !Kung are in a minority at !Kangwa. The largely Herero population of the village has doubled since the opening of the trading store in 1967 and a primary school in 1973.

About 8 km south of !Kangwa is the traditional cattle post of Bate, and south of it is the European-owned artificial well at /Ton!kan, where cattle bought by the store from the local pastoralists are grazed. !Kung live at both places, and at /Ton!kan young !Kung men work for wages caring for the European cattle.

From !Kangwa west the country becomes flatter, and the path crosses innumerable cattle trails leading from the many Herero hamlets of Mahopa to the two main water points at Mahopa. The !Kung here are outnumbered by the Herero, and some !Kung work for the Herero. At !Xabi, a small Tswana hamlet 10 km west of !Kangwa, the trail branches west and south. The western fork leads to Dobe, a small water hole with resident !Kung, no blacks, and since 1963 a semiresident population of anthropologists. Less than 1 km further west the trail abruptly stops at the Namibia border and its wire fence.

Plate 3.1. In the !Kangwa Valley at !Kangwa Matse spring.

Branching south from !Xabi, an hour's walk brings you to the giant baobab tree that marks the turnoff for the !Kubi water hole. The !Kubi Herero and !Kung settlements are situated in a sandy belt between the floodplain of the river course on the north and the gentle slopes of the Aha Hills on the south. The pans of !Kubi and nearby ≠Din have notable archeological sites first excavated by John Yellen in 1968–70.

From !Kubi south the trail begins to rise gradually to enter the heavily wooded Aha Hills. These low hills are not more than 100 meters above the plain, but the flatness of the surrounding terrain gives them a dramatic aspect. The hills give way on the south to a level sandy plain with dense mongongo groves, and finally the path leads down into the broad basin of /Xai/xai, home to 150 !Kung and 50 Herero and Tswana. The path through the hills is 27 km between water points, a difficult 6-hour hike through loose sand that serves to isolate /Xai/xai from the rest of the Dobe area.

If you continue on to the southeast following the /Xai/xai Valley, you reach, after 35 km, the rock massif of /Twihabe with its network of caves. /Twihabe marks the end of the Dobe area. From there it is an arduous 3-day hike 125 km across waterless country to the main road at the Tswana town of Tsau. During historical times there was a major trek route from /Twihabe to Tsau; it fell into disuse in the 1960s and 1970s, but today the trail has been reopened and widened for trucks. To reach the /Du/da area from /Xai/xai, you walk in a different direction, south through a rich and variegated country dotted with seasonal water holes. A leisurely 2-day walk through Hxore, !Kwidum, and ≠To//gana brings you, after 60 km, to the water hole of /Du/da itself just east of the Namibian border.

The population at the nine main Dobe area water holes is listed in Table 3.7 (Mahopa consists of two water holes 2 km apart, but they are counted as one). The tenth locality, !Gausha, is a larger summer pan 12 km northwest of !Kangwa, where residents and marginals regularly congregate each summer. In 1968, the San population per water hole ranged from 16 to 176, with a mean of 58, but the variability from water hole to water hole and at a single water hole from year to year was extremely high. This variability is illustrated in Table 3.8, which shows the percentage change in population at each water hole from 1964 to 1968 and from 1968 to 1973. When the nonpermanent water hole of !Gausha is excluded, the fluctuations at the permanent water holes show changes as great as +353 percent or −73 percent in the 5-year period 1968–73, although the overall total shifted not at all. Clearly, this is a population with considerable internal migration. To understand !Kung population and group dynamics, we should look more closely at the nature of !Kung group structure.

Table 3.7. *Population by water hole*

Water hole	San 1964			San 1968			San 1973 (resident only)	Blacks 1964
	Resident	Marginal	Total	Resident	Marginal	Total		
Dobe	35	0	35	48	0	48	45	0
!Xabi	10	0	10	10	10	20	19	12
Mahopa	33	10	43	67	20	87	18	65
!Kangwa	36	0	36	35	1	36	63	72
!Kangwa Matse	9	0	9	17	4	21	5	
Bate	41	3	44	15	1	16	68	29
!Kubi	23	25	48	34	38	72	24	65
!Goshe and Nokaneng	75	0	75	69	18	87	73	30
/Xai/xai	117	30	147	141	35	176	142	67
!Gausha	0	19	19	21	0	21	0	0
Total	379	87	466	457	127	584	457	340

Table 3.8. *Changes in resident population, by water hole*

Water hole	Population			Percent change		
	1964	1968	1973	1964–8	1968–73	1964–73
Dobe	35	48	45	+37	−6	+29
!Xabi	10	10	19	0	+90	+90
Mahopa	33	67	18	+103	−73	−45
!Kangwa and						
!Kangwa Matse	45	52	68	+16	+31	+51
Bate	41	15	68	−63	+353	+41
!Kubi	23	34	24	+48	−29	+4
!Goshe	75	69	73	−8	+6	+3
/Xai/xai	117	141	142	+20	+1	+21
!Gausha		21				
Total	379	457	457	+21	0	+21

LIVING GROUPS

The definition of !Kung living arrangements presents a most challenging problem to the observer. The !Kung commonly live in camps that number from 10 to 30 individuals, but the composition of these camps changes from month to month and from day to day. Intercamp visiting is the main source of this fluctuation, but each year about 13 percent of the population makes a permanent residential shift from one camp to another. Another 35 percent divides its periods of residence equally among two or three different camps both in and out of the Dobe area.

The nature of hunter-gatherer social units has long been the subject of controversy among anthropologists. Service (1962, 1966:34–8), for example, following Radcliffe-Brown (1930) and Lévi-Strauss (1949), has argued on formal grounds that the basic social unit of hunter-gatherers is the virilocal-patrilocal, territorial, exogamous band. A group of males related through the male line owns and exploits a common territory and exchanges women with other male-centered groups. Recent field studies, however, have shown quite a different picture. The living groups of Pygmies, Eskimo, Dogrib Indians, and Austrialian aborigines tend to be open, bilateral, nonterritorial, and flexible in composition (Hiatt 1962; Helm 1965; Turnbull 1965; Lee and DeVore 1968). Many ethnographers would agree that the earlier formulations are inadequate because they are overly rigid and fail to account for the observed facts. But the problem remains of what to do analytically about the apparent chaos of hunter-gatherer social arrangements.

The Dobe area !Kung are a case in point. Their camps are not "bands" in Service's sense, for they do not consist of a core of males related

Plate 3.2. Three old blind healers from !Goshe.

through the male line. But neither is the camp a random assortment of unrelated individuals whom adverse circumstances have thrown together. In essence, !Kung camp consists of kinspeople and affines who have found that they can live and work well together. Under this flexible principle of organization, brothers may be united or divided and fathers and sons may live together or apart. Furthermore, through the visiting network an individual may, during the course of his life, live for varying times at many water holes, as establishing residence at one camp does not require one to relinquish a claim to any other.

The constant circulation of population makes it appear at first that there is no stable basis of residential life and that the !Kung are a mobile people who can live anywhere and with anyone, but in no one place for very long. For example, at Dobe in October 1963 there were two camps, one with 28 members, the other with 10 members. In December, 18 members of the larger camp left on an extended visit to Chum!kwe, and the remaining 10 people made a joint camp with the smaller group to form a camp of 20 people. In January 1964, when 1 woman died, these two segments split up and abandoned Dobe altogether. The water hole remained unoccupied until May 1964, when the two segments recombined and were joined by 22 other people who came in from five other camps. This group of 41 people wintered at Dobe in one camp. Then, in August, the camp split up into a camp of 11 and a camp of 24. Of the 22 people who had wintered at Dobe, 6 returned to other camps and 16 remained at Dobe. The two Dobe camps of 11 and 24 remained approximately stable for the remainder of the first field trip (i.e., until January 1965). Thus at different times of the year the population of Dobe was counted as follows:

October 1963	38 people in two camps
December 1963	20 people in one camp
January–April 1964	nil
May 1964	41 people in one camp
August 1964 to January 1965	35 people in two camps

After the start of my second field trip, it became apparent that !Kung living arrangements *do* have a stable basis. I returned in 1967 to find many of the 1964 living groups more or less intact, and plotting the changes in group structure that did occur enabled me to begin to discern some of the forces at work in the life cycle of a !Kung camp.

In the discussion to follow a distinction is made between two kinds of living groups (LGs). One kind has a coherent internal structure. These groups are usually fairly large (10 to 30 members) and economically self-sufficient; they are usually, but not always, based on hunting and gathering. The other kind is attached to black cattle posts. These groups are usually units of one or two families whose menfolk work on the cattle; sometimes they are large groups (25 to 30 or more individuals) and sometimes small (as small as a single !Kung woman married to a Herero man). Marshall (1960:327, 1976:156–62) labeled these two types "bands" and "groups," respectively. Because of the misleading formal connotation of the term *band,* I have called the first kind of grouping a *camp* (Lee 1965:51–2, 1972a:345), a closer translation of the !Kung term *chu/to* (literally, "the face of the huts"). The term *n//abesi* that Marshall says translates as "bands" (1960, 1976:156) has never turned up in the Dobe area. It is possible that she means *n≠abesi* ("a cluster of camps at a single water hole"). For the second kind of living group, I have used the term *client group,* reflecting the dependent status in relation to the blacks.

The living groups of 1964, 1968, and 1973 are listed by water hole in Tables 3.9, 3.10, and 3.11, respectively, and are summarized in Table 3.12. Camps ranged in size from 4 to 34 members and mean camp size varied from 17.8 to 20.8, with a 10-year mean of 18.9. Client groups tended to be much smaller, with a mean size of 5.6 to 8.6. This size difference relates to the fact that a hunting and gathering camp has to

Table 3.9. *Living groups: 1964*

Water hole	Camp LG no.	Leader	Size	Client group LG no.	Leader/ Patron	Size	Water hole total Camp	Client group	Total
Dobe	1	N!eishi	11				35		35
	2	≠Toma//gwe	24						
!Xabi				3	Isak	10		10	10
Mahopa				4	Katjambungu	17		33	33
				5	Lotsa	8			
				6	Kathikona	1			
				7	Vethepa	1			
				8	Yona	6			
!Kangwa	10	Bo	22	9	N//u	13	22	14	36
				14	Vetetha	1			
!Kangwa Matse				11	Noiye	4		9	9
				12	Kangwadyata	4			
				13	Kamburungu	1			
Bate	15	!Xoma	19	17	Kakuna	6	29	12	41
	16	Kxaru	10	18	Kathedi	6			
!Kubi	19	N/ahka	23				23		23
!Goshe	20	/Tishe	23	23	Ibatha	5	66	9	75
	21	/Ti!kay	11	24	Tubego	4			
	22	Bo	19						
	25	Kau≠dwa	13						
/Xai/xai	27	//Kau	13	29	Halingisi	10	98	19	117
	28	//Kain!a	9	33	Dam	6			
	30	≠Toma!xwa	30	34	Kamakau	2			
	31	Sa//gai	18	35	Kakurumehe	1			
	32	≠Tomazho	28						
Total							273	106	379

have a minimum size of 10 to be viable, whereas client groups are never self-sufficient.

The economic basis of camps and client groups

In 1964 the camps were all based primarily on hunting and gathering subsistence; in later years this was usually but not invariably the case. Several camps (LGs 6, 7, 21, 22, and 23) owned cattle and/or goats and practiced agriculture in 1968. In 1973, two large camps (LGs 13 and 14) had been set up at the European well near Bate, where the cattle of the Botswana Trading Association store were grazed. While several of the young men worked for wages on the BTA cattle posts, the women and the rest of the men hunted and gathered.

Client groups, by contrast, are all associated with the cattle people and are usually dependent for their subsistence on the milk, meat, and grains of the blacks; but here too there are exceptions. Living groups 4 and 26 of 1968 were fairly large ad hoc gatherings of people related to a core !Kung family who worked on cattle. A group as large as LG 26/68 (44 people), of

Table 3.10. *Living groups: 1968*

Water hole	Camp LG no.	Leader	Size	Client group LG no.	Leader/ patron	Size	Water hole total Camp	Client group	Total
Dobe	1	N!eishi	15				48		48
	2	≠Thoma//gwe		33					
!Xabi				3	Isak	10		10	10
Mahopa	6	Rakudu	10	4	Katjambungu	19	31	36	67
	7	!Xoma	21	5	Lotsa	10			
				8	Kathikona	6			
				9	Kondomba	1			
!Kangwa	11	Bo	14	10	N//u	6	18	17	35
	12	/Twi!gum	4	13	≠Toma	4			
				14	/Ti!kaytsiu	2			
				15	/Twi	5			
!Kangwa Matse	16	Kau≠dwa	12	17	Kashe	5	12	5	17
Bate	18	Kxaru	15				15		15
!Kubi	19	Kumsa≠dwin	24				34		34
	20	≠Dau	10						
!Goshe	21	/Tishe	34				69		69
	22	/Ti!kay	17						
	23	Bo	18						
≠Dabashe	24	≠Dau	21				21		21
/Xai/xai	25	Tsan!kot≠din	21	26	Halingisi	44	72	69	141
	27	Kau	15	28	≠Toma!xwa	3			
	29	Sa//gai	16	31	Dam	15			
	30	≠Tomazho	20	32	/Gantsu	5			
				33	/Twi	1			
				34	//N	1			
Total							320	137	457

course, would not be supported on the cattle of even the wealthiest black family. Consequently, much of their food came from hunting and gathering trips to the hinterland. Although some groups may be associated with a single black patron family for years, most of these client groups are temporary aggregations. A young man may spend a few years in the employ of a cattleman and then move on, either to rejoin a camp or to form another group working on cattle.

Camp cores and the K"ausi

Apart from these black-associated groupings, the basic !Kung local group is the camp, a noncorporate, bilaterally organized group of people who live in a single settlement and who move together for at least part of the year. These camps tend to be much more stable than groups. What gives the camps their stability is the existence in each of a core of related older people – usually siblings and cousins – who are generally acknowledged to be the owners (*k"ausi*) of the water hole. Around each water hole is a bloc of land (*n!ore*), which contains food resources and other water points and which is the basic subsistence area for the resident group. The

Table 3.11. *Living groups: 1973*

Water hole	Camp LG no.	Camp Leader	Camp Size	Client group LG no.	Client Leader/patron	Client Size	Water hole total Camp	Water hole total Client group	Water hole total Total
Dobe	1	≠Toma//gwe	23				45		45
	2	Kam//a	4						
	3	!Xoma	18						
!Xabi Mahopa				4	Isak	19		19	19
				5	Katjambungu	18		18	18
!Kangwa	6	N//u	21	8	Goba	10	38	25	63
	7	Bo	17	9	Dama	3			
				10	Koruke	6			
				11	Kahopa	6			
!Kangwa Matse				12	Karambuka	5		5	5
Bate	13	Kxaru	25	15	Lotsa	8	55	13	68
	14	Kasupe	30	16	Licheku	4			
				17	Brown	1			
!Kubi	18	N/ahka	24				24		24
!Goshe	19	/Tishe	30	22	Moseley	6	67	6	73
	20	/Ti!kay	19						
	21	Bo	18						
/Xai/xai	24	Tsau	27	23	Halingisi	29	104	38	142
	25	/Ti!Kay	15	26	Dam	7			
	29	≠Toma!xwa	24	27	/Twi	1			
	30	Kau	22	28	//N	1			
	31	≠Tomazho	16						
Total							333	124	457

Table 3.12. *Summary of living groups*

	1964	1968	1973	10-year mean
Camps				
Number of camps	15	18	16	
People in camps	273	320	333	
Mean camp size	18.2	17.8	20.8	18.9
Range	9–30	4–34	4–30	
Proportion of residents in camps (%)	72	70	73	
Client groups				
Number of client groups	19	16	15	
People in client groups	106	137	124	
Mean group size	5.6	8.6	8.3	7.5
Range	1–17	1–44	1–29	
Proportion of residents of client groups (%)	28	30	27	
Total				
Number of resident living groups	34	34	31	
Resident population	379	457	457	
Mean living group size	11.1	13.4	14.7	

k"ausi are generally recognized as the "hosts" whom one approaches for permission when visiting at a water hole. The k"ausi are simply the people who have lived at the water hole longer than any others. They include both male and female kin and their spouses. The name of one member of the core group through time becomes associated with the camp as a whole, and the camp becomes known by that person's name: Examples are ≠Toma//gwe chu/to (LG 2/68) at Dobe and Kxarun!a chu/to (LG 18/68) at Bate. This leader is *not* in any sense a headman. Marshall (1960:344ff) originally argued that ownership of each water hole resided in the person of a band headman who was always male and who inherited his position patrilineally. My own research indicated that no headman existed among either the Dobe or the Nyae Nyae !Kung, and recently Marshall has revised her view accordingly and has retracted the headman concept (1976:191–5).

The k"ausi provide continuity with the past through an association with a water hole that may extend over 50 years or more. Rarely, however, does this association go back as far as the grandparent generation of the oldest k"ausi. To put it another way, the half life of a core group's tenure at a

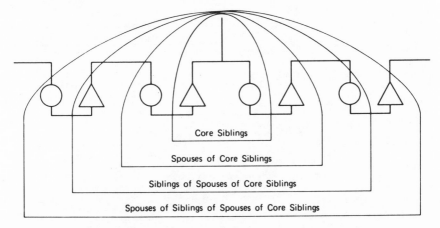

Figure 3.3. Group formation through a chain of siblings and spouses.

water hole can be estimated at 30 to 50 years (Lee 1972b:129). A second integrative role for the k"ausi is the genealogical focus they provide. A camp is built up gradually through time by the addition of in-marrying spouses of the core siblings. These spouses in turn may bring in *their* siblings and their spouses, so that the basic genealogical structure of the camp assumes the form of a chain of spouses and siblings radiating from the core, as shown in Figure 3.3. At a given time the camp is composed largely of persons related by primary ties: Almost every member has a parent, a child, a sibling, or a spouse to link him or her to the core.

Camp membership: Structure and dynamics

Let us look at the recent history of some of the camps to see how principles of continuity and affiliation operate. Table 3.13 lists the 16 Dobe area camps encountered in 1963–4. In subsequent years all camps went through changes: births, deaths, loss of members to other groups, gain of members from other groups. All the groups experienced the loss through death of key core members. But by 1973, 10 of the 16 groups were essentially intact: 9 of them living at the same water hole as in 1964 and 1 of them at a new water hole (Table 3.14). Of the 6 remaining camps, 4 disbanded and the members dispersed to other camps or to client groups (LGs 1, 25, 28, and 30/64). In 1 case (LG 26/64) the camp disbanded, but a large core segment moved intact to Bate to form a new camp; and in the last case the camp and the core split to form two camps (LG 32/64).

To illustrate the process of group structure, it can be examined from a developmental perspective. Figure 3.4 shows the genealogy of the main camp at !Kangwa (LG 10/64) as it was in November 1964. The evolution of the camp started around 1910, when //Gau (1) married /Xashe (2) and brought along her younger brother Dam (3), who in turn brought in his

Table 3.13. *Continuities 1964–73: selected camps*

1964 LG	Core leader	1968 LG	1973 LG
Dobe 1	N!eishi	Intact at Dobe LG 1	Disbanded members in LGs 2/73, 3/73, 5/73
Dobe 2	≠Toma//gwe	Intact at Dobe Lg 2	Intact at Dobe LG 1, loss of large segment to LG 14/73 at Bate
!Kangwa 10	Bo	Intact at !Kangwa LG 11, augmented by new members from LGs 3/64, 16/64, 25/64, 32/64	Intact at !Kangwa as LG 7
Bate 15	!Xoma	Moved en bloc to Mahopa as LG 7	Moved en bloc to Dobe as LG 3, with new members from LGs 1/68, 25/68
Bate 16	Kxaru	Intact at Bate as LG 18, augmented by new members from LG 31/64	Intact at /Ton!an as LG 13, augmented by new members from LGs 16/68, 30/68, 17/68, 11/68, 26/68
!Kubi 19	N/ahka	Altered by addition of new leader from LG 15/64 and loss of half of 1964 members to Chum!kwe, SWA; still discernible as LG 19/68	Intact at !Kubi as LG 18, with addition of 20/68, also from !Kubi
!Goshe 20	/Tishe	Intact as LG 21/68, augmented by LG 14/64 from !Kangwa	Intact as LG 19/73 with little change
!Goshe 21	/Ti!kay	Intact as LG 22/68, augmented by LG 23/64 from !Goshe	Intact as LG 20/73 with little change
!Goshe 22	Bo	Intact as LG 23/68, augmented by new members from LG 24/64 and several marginals	Core intact as LG 21/73; substantial changeover in other members, with new people drawn from LGs 16/68, 12/68
!Goshe 25 (A !Goshe resident group wintering at Nokaneng)	Kau≠dwa	Disbanded: members dispersed to LGs 16/68, 27/68	
!Gausha 26 A marginal group in 1964, but members became residents in subsequent years	N≠isa	Intact at ≠Dabashe (another summer water hole); loss of members to LG 3 at !Xabi and to Chum!kwe, SWA; gain of members from LG 19/64 (!Kubi)	Disbanded: core joined with segment from LG 2/68 to form new group at Bate: LG 14/73
/Xai/xai 27	//Kau	On death of leader, segment merged to form LG 25/68	Intact: the core of much expanded camp LG 24/73 with segments from LG 26/68
/Xai/xai 28	//Kaihan!a	Disbanded: members merged with LG 26/68, a large ad hoc group	
/Xai/xai 30	≠Toma!xwa	Disbanded: on death of three core members, others dispersed to LGs 25/68, 26/68, 27/68, 28/68	
/Xai/xai 31	Sa//gai	Intact: hardly changed as LG 29/68	Intact as LG 30 despite death of two core members
/Xai/xai 32	≠Tomazho	Intact with few changes as LG 30/68	Split into two groups: LGs 25/73, 31/73

Table 3.14. *Camp size fluctuations: 1964–73*

Location	1964 LG no.	Leader	Sex	1964	1968	1973
Dobe	1	N!eishi	M	11	15	Disbanded
	2	≠Toma//gwe	M	24	33	23
!Kangwa	10	Bon!a	M	22	14	17
Bate	15	!Xoma	M	19	21	18
	16	Kxaru	F	10	15	25
!Kubi	19	N/ahka	F	23	24	24
!Goshe	20	/Tishe	M	23	34	30
	21	/Ti!Kay	M	11	17	19
	22	Bo	M	19	18	18
	25	Kau≠dwa	M	13	Disbanded	
!Gausha	26	N≠isa	F	19	21	Disbanded
/Xai/xai	27	//Kau	M	13	21	27
	28	//Kaiha	M	9	Disbanded	
	30	≠Toma!xwa	M	30	Disbanded	
	31	Sa//gai	F	18	16	22
	32	≠Tomazho	M	28	20	Split

two wives, the sisters N!ai (4) and Sa//gai (5). The family of /Xashe (not shown) died or moved away, leaving 1 and 3 as the core sibling unit at !Kangwa. When the children of the cores (6, 7, 8, 9, 10) grew up, their spouses (11, 12, 13, 14) moved into !Kangwa. One of these spouses (12) brought in two of his siblings (15, 16), and these siblings were later joined by their spouses (17, 18).

By 1964, 2, 3, and 5 had died, leaving 15 adults in the !Kangwa camp. Of these, one (1) was the only survivor of the original core; five others were the offspring of the core members and constituted the 1964 core. Four others were the spouses of the core, two were siblings of the spouses, and two were the spouses of the siblings of the spouses of the core. The in-marrying sibling group (12, 15, 16) were in middle age, and because they had lived at !Kangwa for 25 years, they were also considered to be k"ausi of the water hole. In fact, the camp was named after 12, the eldest brother of the in-marrying sibling group.

Nine years later (1973) the core of the !Kangwa camp had shifted and expanded as a new generation grew to maturity (Figure 3.5). Numbers 21 and 22 were doubly legitimate, being the offspring of both the new and old core sibling group; 12 was still the central figure, but since the death of his wife (6) in 1971, he had remarried (20). Compare the genealogical positions of 1, 6, 7, 11, 12, 15, 16, 17, and 18 in 1973 with their positions in 1964. Most had moved from peripheral to central positions in relation to the core sibling group.

Marrying-in, it is by now clear, does not mean simply the addition of

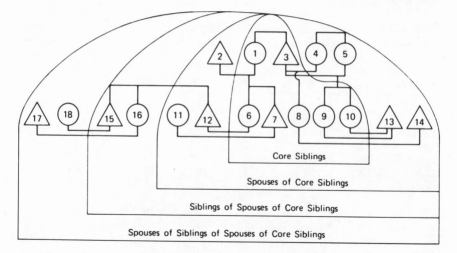

Figure 3.4. Genealogy of the !Kangwa main camp: 1964.

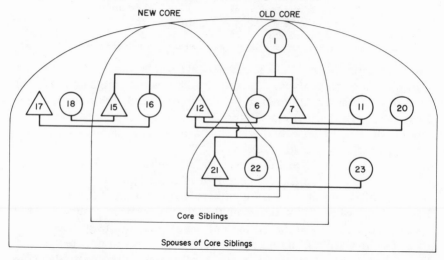

Figure 3.5. Genealogy of the !Kangwa main camp: 1973.

one person to the group. The in-marrying spouse may bring along a sibling or two or three or even a whole family! The joining of two families
through the marriage of their children is one of the important sources of
new alliances. But whereas in most societies this alliance is expressed
through gift exchange, reciprocal visiting, and mutual interest in the
offspring, among the !Kung the marriage may also be the occasion for
the entire families of bride and groom to combine in a single camp. The
in-marrying spouse may be accompanied not only by his or her siblings
but also by parents, grandparents, and parents' siblings. In the case of a
second marriage, a mature widow or widower may bring in his or her

married children and their spouses. These spouses, in turn, may bring in their married siblings.

Each of these processes of group formation is illustrated in the diagram of the Dobe camp in 1964 (Figure 3.6). The core siblings, //Koka (1) and her younger brother N!eisi (2), moved into Dobe around 1930. After the former owners died or moved away, 1 and 2 became the k"ausi. They brought in their spouses (3, 4, 5); the children of these marriages (6, 7, 8, 9) later brought in their spouses (10, 11) to live at Dobe (segments 1 and 2). After N/ahka (11) had been married to /Xashe (6) for several years, her entire family joined her at Dobe, including her six brothers and sisters (13, 14, 15, 16, 17, 18), her parents (19, 20), her maternal grandfather (21), and her mother's brother (22). Later, when two of her siblings (17, 18) married, their spouses also came to Dobe (23, 24) (segment 3).

On the other side, in 1955, ≠Toma (9) married a 45-year-old widow, Tin!kai (12), who brought her adolescent son (25) to Dobe. Around 1960, the son married a woman (26), who, in turn, brought her younger brother (27) along. Finally, in 1964, the last link was established when 27 married and brought his wife (28) to Dobe.

Of the 28 persons in the Dobe diagram, 6 are cores and another 6 are spouses of cores; 9 more members are the siblings, parents, and children of the in-marrying spouses, and 7 are more distantly related. All camp members, however, can trace their relation to the core through the primary ties of sibling, parent, offspring, or spouse.

The closeness to the core is reflected in the amount of time spent at Dobe. For example, six members (17, 18, 21, 22, 23, 24) spent only about 3 months at Dobe in 1964. By November of that year, segment 2 had split off to form another camp, and in the November census it was counted as LG 1/64, whereas segments 2 and 3 were counted as LG 2/64. The two LGs operated independently during 1965–7, but reunited for 6 months in 1967–8. Splitting again in May, they were again counted as separate living groups (LGs 1 and 2) in 1968. By 1973, the former segment 2 in Figure 3.6 had disbanded, and its members had joined various camps and client groups. The former segment 3, with several of the children grown and married, had become a major part of the core of LG 14/73 at the European well south of Bate. And the original segment 1 was still going strong at Dobe at LG 1/73 with 23 members.

In the two cases discussed, the core groups are composed of siblings of *both* sexes. This is typical of most of the core groups in the Dobe area. An analysis of 12 camps in 1964 showed that a brother and sister formed the core in 4 cases, two sisters and one brother in 2 cases, and two brothers and one sister in 1 case. In addition, 4 camps had cores composed of two sisters, and 1 had a core composed of two brothers. These combinations are to be expected in a strongly bilateral society such as the !Kung, and

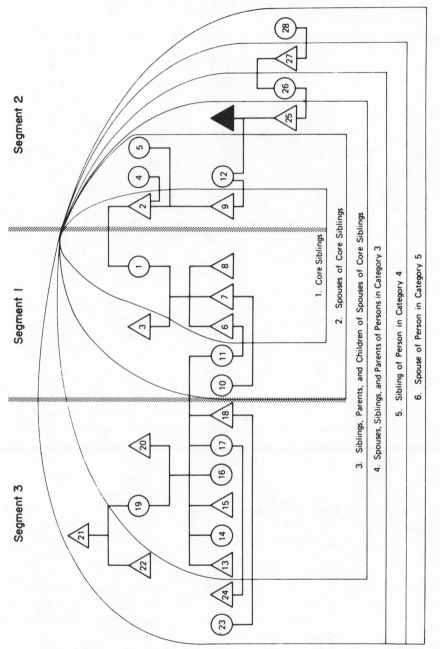

Segment 1   Segment 2   Segment 3

1. Core Siblings

2. Spouses of Core Siblings

3. Siblings, Parents, and Children of Spouses of Core Siblings

4. Spouses, Siblings, and Parents of Persons in Category 3

5. Sibling of Person in Category 4

6. Spouse of Person in Category 5

Figure 3.6. Genealogy of the Dobe camp: 1964.

the results serve to emphasize the futility of trying to establish whether the !Kung have matrilocal or patrilocal residence arrangements.

Dependency ratios

We have already noted that hunting and gathering camps require a minimum size of 10 in order to be viable. Another important constraint on camp structure is the proportion of effective food producers to dependents. People under the age of 15 or over 60 do not contribute much to the food supplies. They are supported in the main by the food-getting activities of the adult camp members between the ages of 15 and 59. The age breakdowns and dependency ratios of the independent camps of 1964, 1968, and 1973 are shown in Tables 3.15, 3.16, and 3.17. There is a remarkable range of variation in the dependency ratios, from zero, with no dependents at all (LG 2/73), to 200, with twice as many dependents as adults (LG 28/64). However, the values tend to cluster around 65 to 75: approximately 2 dependents for every 3 producers. There is good evidence that dependency ratios affect camp continuity and that camps with very high (125 or over) and very low (25 or under) ratios tend to take steps to bring in more producers or more dependents, as the case may be. Failing that, groups with too few or too many dependents disband or merge with other groups. For example, LG 16/64 had only 2 children in a camp of 10. By 1968 there were 4 children in a camp of 15. Similar shifts were noted in other low groups, such as LGs 19/64, 20/64, and 21/64. In 1968, LGs 1, 6, 12, 16, 20, and 30 all had child dependency ratios of 33 or less. All these camps had disbanded or merged by 1973.

Three other groups with low dependency ratios in 1968 (LGs 11, 25, and 29) raised their ratios and remained intact in 1973. Analogous processes were at work in groups with very high dependency ratios. In 1964 LGs 2, 27, and 31 had dependency ratios of 100, 160, and 125, respectively. By 1968 the ratios had fallen to 57, 62, and 78. The 1964 living group with the highest dependency ratio – LG with 3 adults and 6 dependents (ratio 200) – had disbanded by 1968. These upper and lower dependency limitations seem to operate more forcefully than upper and lower size limitations, although as in the case of size, the dependency ratio constraints still offer the camps a wide latitude of acceptable values from around 30 (1 dependent for every 3 producers) to around 90 (3 dependents for every 3 producers).

Also the dependency ratio constraints do not operate mechanically, but rather dialectically. A low or a high value does not lead automatically to the breakup of a camp, and two camps with the same value may respond in different ways. For example, LG 7/68 at Mahopa and LG 24/68 at ≠Dabashe had an identically high dependency ratio of 91 and a child dependency ratio of 73 (Table 3.16). But whereas LG 7 adjusted its membership and remained intact, with a lower dependency ratio, in 1973 (as

Table 3.15. *Age breakdown by camps: 1964*

Location	1964 LG no.	Leader	1968 LG no.	1963 LG no.	Age[a] Old	Adult	Young	Total	Child Dependency Ratio[b]	Ratio[c]
Dobe	1	N!eishi	1		3	8		11	38	
	2	≠Toma//gwe	2	1	2	12	10	24	100	83
!Kangwa	10	Bo	10	7	1	14	7	22	57	50
Bate	15	!Xoma	7	3	2	11	6	19	73	55
	16	Kxaru	18	13		8	2	10	25	25
!Kubi	19	N/ahka	19	18	1	17	5	23	35	29
!Goshe	20	/Tishe	21	19	3	15	5	23	53	33
	21	/Ti!kay	22	20	2	8	1	11	38	13
	22	Bo	23	21	1	10	8	19	90	80
	25	Kau≠dwa			1	10	2	13	30	20
/Xai/xai	27	//Kau	25	24	3	5	5	13	160	100
	28	//Kaihan!a			2	3	4	9	200	133
	30	≠Toma!xwa			5	17	8	30	76	47
	31	Sa//gai	29	30	4	8	6	18	125	75
	32	≠Tomazho	30	31	2	17	9	28	65	53
Total in camp					32	163	78	273	67	48

[a] Old = 60+, adult = 15–59, young = 0–14 years.
[b] Number of young and old per 100 adults.
[c] Number of young per 100 adults.

Table 3.16. Age breakdown by camps: 1968

Location	1968 LG no.	Leader	1964 LG no.	Age^a Old	Adult	Young	Total	Young	Total	Dependency Ratio^b	Child Dependency Ratio^c
Dobe	1	N!eishi	1	3	10	2			15	50	20
	2	≠Toma//gwe	2	2	21	10			33	57	48
Mahopa	6	Rakudu		0	8	2			10	25	25
	7	!Xoma	15	2	11	8			21	91	73
!Kangwa	11	Bo	10	1	10	3			14	40	30
	12	Twi!gum		1	3	0			4	33	0
!Kangwa Matse	16	K"au≠dwa	25	0	9	3			12	33	33
Bate	18	Kxaru	16	1	10	4			15	50	40
!Kubi	19	Kumsa≠dwin	19	0	17	7			24	41	41
	20	≠Dau		1	7	2			10	43	29
!Goshe	21	/Tishe	20	2	21	11			34	62	52
	22	/Tikay	21	2	11	4			17	55	36
	23	Bo	22	2	11	5			18	64	45
≠Dabashe	24	≠"Dau		2	11	8			21	91	73
/Xai/xai	25	Tsau!ko≠din		4	13	4			21	62	31
	27	Kau-chimburu		0	9	6			15	67	67
	29	Sa//gai	31	4	9	3			16	78	67
	30	≠Tomazho	32	2	16	2			20	25	13
Total in camp				29	207	84			320	54	40

^a Old =60+, adult = 15–59, young =0–14 years.
^b Number of young and old per 100 adults.
^c Number of young per 100 adults.

69

Table 3.17. *Age breakdown by camps: 1973*

Location	1973 LG no.	Leader	1968 LG no.	Age[a] Old	Adult	Young	Total	Dependency Ratio[b]	Child Dependency Ratio[c]
Dobe	1	≠Toma//gwe	2	4	12	7	23	92	58
	2	Kan//a		0	4	0	4	0	0
	3	!Xoma	7	3	10	5	18	80	50
!Kangwa	6	N//u		1	13	7	21	62	54
	7	Bo	11	2	10	5	17	70	50
Bate	13	Kxaru	18	3	17	5	25	47	29
	14	Kasupe		1	13	16	30	131	123
!Kubi	18	N/ahka	19	2	15	7	24	60	47
!Goshe	19	/Tishe	21	1	17	12	30	76	71
	20	/Ti!kay	22	3	13	3	19	46	23
	21	Bo	23	4	9	5	18	100	56
/Xai/xai	24	Tsau!Ko≠din	25	3	17	7	27	59	41
	25	/Ti!kay		1	10	4	15	50	40
	29	≠Toma!xwa	27	4	9	11	24	167	122
	30	Kau 385	29	3	13	6	22	69	46
	31	≠Tomazho		3	9	4	16	78	44
Total in camp				38	191	104	333	74	54

[a] Old = 60≠, adult = 15–59, young = 0–14 years.
[b] Number of young and old per 100 adults.
[c] Number of young per 100 adults.

Plate 3.3. Young boys collecting marula nuts at /Ton!kan.

LG 3/73), LG 24 disbanded. Ironically, some of its members merged with others to form LG 14/73, a camp that had an *even higher* dependency ratio (131) than LG 24/68! This last example pinpoints the dialectical nature of !Kung group processes. The necessity to work harder to provide for a large number of dependents is one of the limiting factors on the age composition of !Kung groups. But it is not an insurmountable obstacle. If enough good reasons counterbalance the disadvantages, even groups where dependents outnumber producers can be viable, *if the members are prepared to work harder*. Work effort is the sliding scale for adjustment between group composition and resources (see Lee 1972c:89–90).

Let us look more closely at LG 14/73. Here 13 adults lived with 16 children, but 5 of those children were strong lads aged 10 to 14, who made a real contribution to the food quest. Plate 3.3 shows the boys after a day's gathering in July 1973 bringing a load of marula nuts into camp. I suspect that had these boys been in a more typical living group, they would not have been working to provide food at such an early age. But the fact that they *were* working pinpoints the existence in the majority of !Kung camps of an unutilized reserve of labor power.

Finally, the 1973 dependency ratios show a definite tendency toward

Table 3.18. *Age-sex composition of marginal population: 1968*

Age[a]	Males		Females		Total		Sex ratio: Males/100 Females
	No.	%	No.	%	No.	%	
Old	0	0	6	9.0	6	4.7	0
Adult	42	70.0	36	53.7	78	61.4	117
Young	18	30.0	25	37.3	43	33.9	72
Total	60	100.0	67	100.0	127	100.0	90

[a]Old = 60+, adult = 15–59, young = 0–14 years.
Dependency ratio (old and young per 100 adults) = 65.
Child dependency ratio (young per 100 adults) = 57.

higher values. This is a reflection of the high number of births in the period 1968–73. If this trend continues, many of the Dobe area camps will soon look like LG 14/73 (two others already do), and the relatively leisured life of the hunting and gathering !Kung will be gone forever.

THE MARGINAL POPULATION

Who are the marginals and how do they differ in characteristics from the resident population? During the 12-month period preceding the November 1968 census, 127 nonresident !Kung visited the Dobe area for periods ranging from 1 day to 6 months. These people came from Chum!kwe to the west, N!aun!au to the north, the /Du/da area to the south, and the river villages to the east. The age and sex breakdown of the marginals is shown in Table 3.18. The marginals lack group structure when they appear in the Dobe area; they are mainly individuals, small families, and segments attached to camps. They are a younger and more mobile population; only 4.7 percent are over the age of 60, compared with 10 percent in the resident population; and the proportion of young is higher as well: 34 percent compared with 29 to 31 percent of the resident population. Men outnumber women in the adult age group (15 to 59 years). This is probably attributable to the presence of a number of young men who visit the Dobe area in search of women for casual liaisons or marriage or both. The single male travels much more widely and frequently than the single female. The fairly high proportion of young and the high child dependency ratio among marginals (57) compared with 40 for the 1968 resident population can be explained by the presence of young married couples living outside the Dobe area who come to visit parents or siblings in the area. For example, during the 5-month period *following* the 1968 census (December 1, 1968, to April 30, 1969), I recorded a further 45 marginals entering the Dobe area, for an average of 9 per month. This group included 3 old persons, 20 adults, and 22 children, for a dependency ratio of 125. When the 1968 marginals are combined with this group, the total comes to 172 marginals representing about 27 percent of all the !Kung seen in the Dobe area during 1967–9.

THE /DU/DA POPULATION

The most isolated hunter-gatherers encountered in 3 years of fieldwork were the population centered at the /Du/da water hole on the Botswana–Namibia border 70 km south of /Xai/xai. These !Kung had no goats or donkeys and few dogs, and they planted no crops. Between March 1968 and mid-1969, Pat Draper, Nancy Howell, Henry Harpending, and myself made five visits to their camps strung out along a 100-km stretch of the border fence. The observations on the /Du/da people constitute some of the best data we have on a full-time foraging ecology unaffected by the presence of cattle pastoralism. On the other hand, as our work progressed it became apparent that the movements of the /Du/da people were being controlled in crucial ways by their contacts with the South African Border Police Patrols, a point discussed in Chapters 12 and 14.

The /Du/da population was counted in four study periods. In March 1968, 37 people in two camps were enumerated at !Kwidum, a summer waterhole on the border southwest of /Xai/xai. The following month (April), 9 more were seen camped west of /Xai/xai at a summer water hole in the midst of the rich tsin fields of Hxore. In September of that year, a further 76 people were counted at the /Du/da water hole itself, part of a total aggregation of 120 people in three large camps. This was the largest residential concentration of hunting and gathering !Kung we ever saw (Chapter 15). Four months later we again returned to /Du/da to find 23 additional people as part of a group of 93 living in a single very large camp in January 1969. As of March 1969, the /Du/da population stood at 145, of whom 2 died in a bush fire, leaving a total of 143. In August–September 1969, Draper enumerated a further 10 /Du/da people on a visit to ≠To//gana, a border water hole midway between /Xai/xai and /Du/da.

The age-sex composition of the /Du/da population in early 1969 is shown in Table 3.19. The living group composition and dependency ratios of the September 1968 census are shown in Table 3.20. The /Du/da population differs from that of the Dobe area in several interesting respects. The proportion of elderly is lower at /Du/da than in the Dobe area (5 percent vs. 9 to 11 percent), and the ratio of children to adults is higher, making the /Du/da population a younger one than that of the Dobe area. These differences do not necessarily imply that the /Du/da population has a higher fertility and a higher mortality than does the Dobe population. A number of the /Du/da people reported histories of

Table 3.19. *Age-sex composition of /Du/da population: 1969*

Age[a]	Males No.	%	Females No.	%	Total No.	%	Sex ratio: Males/100 Females
Old	4	5.3	3	4.4	7	4.9	133
Adult	42	56.0	44	64.7	86	60.1	95
Young	29	38.7	21	30.9	50	35.0	138
Total	75	100.0	68	100.0	143	100.0	110

[a]Old = 60+, adult = 15–59, young = 0–14 years.

Table 3.20. */Du/da living group composition: September 1968*

LG no.	Leader	Age[a] Old	Adult	Young	Total	Dependency ratio[b]	Child Dependency ratio[c]
1	Kxau!xoma	2	27	13	42	56	48
2	Kum/to	1	21	16	38	81	76
3	/Tontah	4	21	12	37	76	57
Total		7	69	41	117	70	59

[a]Old = 60+, adult = 15–59, young = 0–14 years.
[b]Number of young and old per 100 adults.
[c]Number of young per 100 adults.

living on European farms in the Gobabis and Ghanzi districts to the south. Several reported parents and siblings still living there. Therefore, it is probable that the /Du/da people represent a younger and more mobile segment of a farm San population in which young adults and children are somewhat overrepresented and elderly somewhat underrepresented.

Also of interest is the sex ratio favoring males overall and in the younger age category (Table 3.19) compared with the sex ratio favoring females in the Dobe are (Table 3.4). These sorts of variations are to be expected in small populations. The variability, however, draws attention to the fact that /Du/da men will have a shortage of eligible spouses in coming years, a shortage that may lead to considerable out-marriage in the future, perhaps in the Dobe area direction, where a corresponding surplus of young women is growing up.

In some ways the "sudden" appearance of the /Du/da camps in the middle of the Northwest Kalahari and their histories of residence on European farms brings to mind the outstation or back to the bush movements among Australian aborigines, Canadian Inuit, and other foraging peoples. In the case of the /Du/da !Kung, however, their newfound or rediscovered

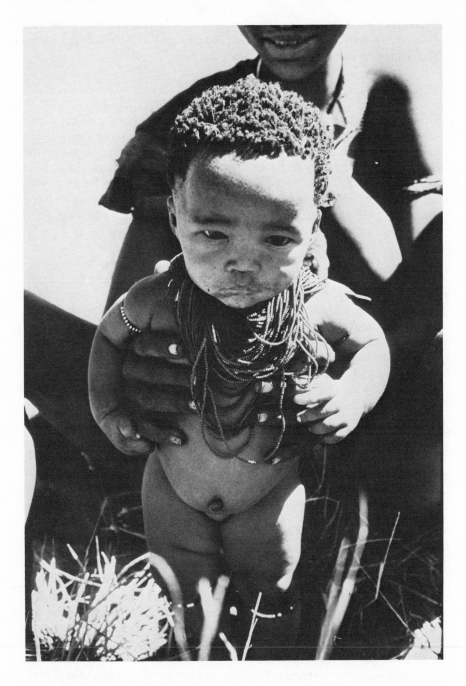

Plate 3.4. An infant girl of the /Du/da group.

freedom of movement was to be short-lived. Instead of becoming foragers anew, they soon found themselves caught up in the workings of the South African military machine (see Chapters 12 and 14).

A HISTORY OF CONTACT

This history of the Dobe area is based on oral histories gathered from many informants, San and non-San. Written records were virtually unknown for this area until the Marshalls arrived in 1951. None of the !Kung had any knowledge of the dates of historical events; these were filled in by discussions with literate Batswana who were familiar with the Dobe area and its people. The story that emerges is a fascinating one that may help explain how hunters and gatherers can continue to be viable in a rapidly changing world.

Pre-contact

There is no evidence in their oral tradition that the !Kung of the interior have migrated there from elsewhere. This corroborates the !Kung belief, quoted by Lorna Marshall, that "they have lived in the Nyae Nyae area since time began" (1960:325). Recent archeological work strongly supports this view. The discovery of Middle Stone Age materials at ≠Din near !Kubi, beneath a layer of water-borne silcrete and calcrete hardpan, indicates an antiquity of man in the Dobe area of at least 11,000 years (Yellen 1971).

At /Xai/xai, directly beneath recent !Kung campsites, Yellen, and more recently Wilmsen, have excavated deposits showing uninterrupted occupation, with contemporary San artifacts (tin cans, glass fragments, etc.) intergrading with Later Stone Age materials in a deposit 2 meters deep. By the data of archeology and by their own account, the Dobe !Kung cannot be considered refugees from more favorable habitats. The Dobe area has, if anything, been an area of out-migration during the historical period.

The interior !Kung have had trading relations with Bantu peoples on their periphery for over 100 years. The evidence for this is the presence of iron-tipped weapons, pottery, and smoking pipes in the upper levels of Later Stone Age deposits. In 1963 the !Kung had no knowledge of iron forging or pottery making, and they did not raise tobacco. Old people I interviewed stated that their grandfathers had these things before the first non-San came to the interior. Men in their sixties and seventies could remember their grandfathers' telling them that they began hunting with bone arrows and did not obtain iron for arrows until they were well into adult life. The technique for making bone arrowheads was still common knowledge, but as there was an abundant supply of iron fencing wire, none of the men hunted with bone. The art of chipping flint was not known in the Dobe area. It is probable that these black goods (and also some European goods such as beads and buttons) reached the interior through !Kung trading intermediaries some years before the arrival of the first blacks and Europeans. The depth of these black trade goods in the deposits suggests the possibility that the San–black contacts may extend back several hundred years (E. Wilmsen, 1979a).

Early contacts

The first known visits to the interior by non-!Kung took place in the 1870s. Tawana cattle people, who had recently set up their capital at Tsau, southeast of the Dobe area, began making hunting trips to the interior. The Tawana, one of the major Tswana tribes, were an expansionist people with a hierarchical organization and a flair for administration. They had already subjugated by peaceful means or otherwise a number of non-Tswana peoples in the Okavango delta, and bringing the !Kung under their sphere of influence seemed to present no great problems. One Tswana account of their initial contacts with Dobe area !Kung is worth quoting in detail:

> You see the zhu/twasi (!Kung) of today have both cheekiness and guile. Well, it wasn't at all like that in the beginning. When we Tswanas first came into this area, all we saw were strange footprints in the sand. We wondered what kind of people were these? They were very afraid of us and would hide whenever we came around. We found their villages, but they were always empty because as soon as they saw strangers coming they would scatter and hide in the bush. We said, "Oh, this is good; these people are afraid of us, they are weak and and we can easily rule over them." So we just ruled them. There was no killing or fighting. We would say, "Come here, give me water" or "Come here, and bring me my horse" and they would bring it . . . It was good that they were so afraid of us, because if they had tried to fight, we would have slaughtered them.

In the initial period and for many years after, the Tswana presence was modest and seasonal in the form of annual summer hunting trips to the Dobe area and to the Nyae Nyae pans. The !Kung acted as trackers and helped butcher the meat and carry it back to camp. In return, they received balls of compressed tobacco, a major trade item in the Kalahari and one that continues to be important today. The early hunting parties were described by a middle-aged !Kung man whose grandfather had worked for the Tswana during this period:

> The type of work that we !Kung entered then was called *n/i// wana!ha* ["shoulder the meat-carrying yoke"]. The country was teeming with game and the Tswanas came up on horseback with

guns. They put us under the carrying yoke. We had to carry the
meat that they shot from the kill sites back to the camps; and then
at the end of the summer hunting season, a line of porters would
carry bales of *biltong* ["dried meat strips"] back to Tsau. Then there
they would be paid off in balls of *shoro* ["tobacco"], which they
carried back to the West. The !Kung also did their own hunting and
brought the hides and biltong in for tobacco.

European penetration of the Dobe area also occurred in the 1870s, but
was much more sporadic. One Hendrik Van Zyl was hunting elephant
and rhinoceros in the Ghanzi region and in 1879 made a trip to /Gam. He
is known to have visited /Xai/xai and !Kubi. One of the white hunters
with Van Zyl had an affair with a !Kung woman at the latter place, and a
child was born. Living at !Kubi today are several !Kung with strongly
European features. They acknowledge white ancestry and trace their line
back to a white they call "Falsai." Quite probably they are referring to
the Van Zyl (pronounced "fansail" in Afrikaans) hunting party of 1879.
We know Van Zyl did not make any later trips because he was killed in a
skirmish with the Namas near Ghanzi the following year (Silberbauer
1965:114–15).

Although occasional hunting parties of whites came through the interior, the bulk of the nineteenth-century contacts were with the Tswana.
At first the Tswana came only to hunt and barter. Later they brought
cattle out to graze the rich grasslands for the summer months. At the end
of the hunting and grazing season, the Tswana would gather all the
hunting parties at a large water hole like /Xai/xai, and intense trading
would take place at the site of the ox wagons (koloi). The !Kung would
bring in their hides, furs, bales of biltong, and pots of wild honey; in
exchange they would receive such items as balls of tobacco, clay pots,
ironware and beads, and clothing of European manufacture. Large
groups of !Kung would congregate, and there were dancing, trading, and
marriage brokering among the !Kung themselves as well as trading with
the Tswana. At the end of the festivities, the oxen were inspanned and
driven back to Tsau, and the !Kung dispersed to their home areas.

The Mhapa and Kubu

It was the custom of the Tswana when a new tract of land was brought
under their control for the paramount chief to parcel out the land to
aristocratic Tswana lineages in a kind of feudal tenure. The lineages, in
turn, could hunt and graze their cattle there, allocate grazing to others,
and ensure that peace and order prevailed in the lands under their jurisdiction. Members of the Tawana clan Batau ("Lions"), under a man
named Mhapa, migrated from Ghanzi to Tsau in the late nineteenth
century. The paramount chief granted them rights over all the lands

west of Tsau, south of the Aha Hills. Later, another Tawana family of the Bakubu ("Hippo") clan, originally from Serowe, under the leadership of Murubela, were given rights to all the western lands north of the Ahas. In this way, the whole of the !Kangwa Valley fell under Kubu jurisdiction, and /Xai/xai and most of Nyae Nyae became Mhapa's fiefdom. Originally the areas claimed stretched far into what was then German South-West Africa. Tswana camps were set up throughout Nyae Nyae and as far west as Karakuwisa, 100 km inside German-held territory.

Tswana impact on the Dobe area at the turn of the century was modest. They continued to make annual visits to the interior, but it was another 25 years before any non-!Kung permanently settled in the area. Besides hunting and trading, the setting up of !Kung-operated cattle posts in the interior was the main business of the period 1890–1925. According to the !Kung version of events, it was they who played an active role in bringing cattle to the interior on a year-round basis. A 70-year-old /Xai/xai man, who had married the daughter of a leading *n!ore k"au* ("landowner") at /Xai/xai, gave the following account:

> When I was young the elephants, buffalo, and rhino were thick at /Xai/xai. Before I was born white hunters would visit /Xai/xai and shoot the elephants with guns. My ≠*tum* ("father-in-law"), ≠Toma!gai, worked for the whites. When they left, the zhu/twasi were all alone. My ≠tum said, "Let's go to the Tswana, bring their cattle here and drink their milk." So then my ≠tum organized the younger men and went east to collect the cattle. The Tswana who gave them the cattle were Mhapa and Hadi. Then they chopped a brush fence kraal under the camel thorn trees and kraaled them here. The Tswana came up to visit and hunt, then they went back, leaving the San drinking the milk. Then my ≠tum got shoro from the Tswana and smoked it. When the shoro was all finished the young men collected all the steenbok skins and I went east to bring back more shoro. The boys shouldered the tobacco and brought it back.
>
> Later they drove the cattle out to Hxore pan, where they built a kraal and ate the tsin beans of Hxore while the cattle drank the water. So they lived, eating tsin, hunting steenbok and duiker, and drinking milk. When Hxore water was dry, they loaded the pack oxen with sacks of tsin (for the !Kung to eat) and drove the cattle back to /Xai/xai.
>
> At the end of the season the cattle boys loaded the pack oxen with bales and bales of eland biltong and went east with it to collect the balls of shoro and sometimes bags of corn. These they would deliver to my ≠tum, ≠Toma!gai.

This account provides a good description of the Tswana mafisa system, in which rich Tswana families farm out cattle to other tribesmen on a sharecropping basis. The client tends the herds and drinks the milk, but the ownership of the herd and its offspring remains with the patron. It is difficult to estimate what proportion of the Dobe area !Kung were involved in mafisa in this early period; a rough estimate would be 10 to 20 percent of the men. It is worth noting that although the British declared a protectorate over Bechuanaland as early as 1895 (Sillery 1952), British presence was not felt in the Dobe area until many years later. The border between Bechuanaland and South-West Africa was surveyed in 1933 (Marshall 1976:59). Corporal Webb of the Protectorate police made the first official tour of the Dobe area from the British side in 1934.

Saukumbama

The great rinderpest epidemic of 1897 provides the earliest datable event that is also remembered by Dobe area !Kung. Called *saukumbama* in Setswana, the rinderpest wiped out entire cattle herds in many parts of Southern Africa, including the Tawana area around Tsau (Bley 1971:124–6). The Dobe area, protected by its waterless belt, was unaffected by the epidemic. In fact, cattle belonging to the Mhapa and Kubu were among the few herds to survive intact in Tawana country. Breeding stock brought from the Dobe area later provided the basis for rapidly rebuilding the tribal herds. Several of the !Kung in their seventies during the 1960s remembered the epidemic, and this fact can be used to determine their actual ages.

The German–Herero War

The next event peripherally to affect the lives of the Dobe !Kung was the German war against the Herero of South-West Africa. In January 1904 the Herero people rose in rebellion against an oppressive German regime. The locus of the revolt was 500 km west of the Dobe area. The resistance was met with unusual ferocity by the German army, which carried out mass exterminations of captured Herero men, women, and children. In all, it is estimated that 65,000 of the 80,000 Herero were killed by the Germans or died in the desert trying to escape to Bechuanaland (Gorges 1918; Bley 1971:150). The !Kung became aware of the fighting when parties of Herero refugees appeared in their area on the way to safety under British rule in Bechuanaland. Corporal Webb, a retired police officer, told me that the Germans pursued the Herero across the desert as far east as Gautsha and Gura in Nyae Nyae; there they found Tswana cattle posts and, thinking they had reached British territory, turned back. When my informant traveled through the Dobe area and points west in 1934, he found the initials of German units carved in the baobab trees at Gura and Gautsha. A photograph of these appears in Marshall (1976:55–7).

Several hundred Herero passed through the Dobe area in 1905–6, but they did not stop. They continued east and were given a place to settle among the Tawana and other tribes. Most had lost their cattle en route, so they went to work for the Tswana in the mafisa system and gradually rebuilt their herds. They soon became the most successful cattle raisers in Northwestern Botswana. But even today they harbor a strong desire to return to their former lands in Namibia.

The Dobe area !Kung were scarcely affected by the war. My /Xai/xai informant recounted:

> I heard that Herero were passing through, but I didn't actually see them. I was at /Gam and heard that they were mainly going north through ≠Din and !Kangwa. A man named /Ti!kai saw their camps in the !Kangwa Valley. He brought word that the Herero had come from the west and were continuing east, and that they were chased by war. Some people were afraid that the Germans would come and kill us too, but we didn't see any signs of the Germans, just the Herero fleeing. We decided that this was a fight between Germans and Hereros; they wouldn't kill us.

The Dobe people were lucky; many San were killed along with the Herero by the Germans in the Waterberg and other districts of South-West Africa during the war (Gorges 1918). The memory of the genocide of the Herero–German War continues to form a bitter legacy among blacks on both sides of the border, even though the South Africans have long ago replaced the Germans as the white oppressors of the people of South-West Africa (Namibia).

Internal shifts in population

Throughout the period leading up to the Bantu colonization and after, the !Kung of the Dobe area continued in the main to be full-time hunter-gatherers. The milk from even 200 head of cattle could not support more than about 40 people, and the standing population of the Dobe area is believed to have been 10 times that number. Also the presence of the cattle was intermittent. There were periods of each year when the herds were completely withdrawn, and the !Kung had only the long-distance trade with the East as a way of keeping contact with the blacks.

Nevertheless, the presence of the cattle affected the distribution of the groups in space. In particular, there was an eastward shift of population as some of the original residents of the !Kangwa Valley moved to the Nokaneng area to live with the Tswana at their main villages, and other groups moved in to run the cattle posts at !Kubi, Mahopa, and !Kangwa. A man named N//au!gusi came from the !Gwidum area immediately west of Dobe around 1920. He was given a herd of cattle by Murubela of the Kubu clan. After marrying a local girl and calling in his relatives from !Gwidum to help him, N//au!gusi became an important person in the valley. At various times he managed cattle posts at Mahopa and

!Kangwa before settling with a large group at !Goshe. His descendants still live at !Goshe today, along with the descendants of others who came from even further west to work on Murubela's cattle. The result is that the easternmost water holes in the !Kangwa Valley are inhabited by people whose roots are elsewhere.

At /Xai/xai, analogous processes were at work. The water hole had always been a central meeting place for !Kung from many areas long before the arrival of the blacks, and when the cattle posts came, they tended to attract groups from the hinterland to become semipermanent residents at /Xai/xai. Instead of an eastward displacement, as in the !Kangwa Valley, there was a drawing together of groups from several directions. In both cases, land rights had become affected by the presence of cattle, and this point has to be carefully weighed in any reconstruction of hunter-gatherer land use patterns (see Chapter 12).

/Xai/Xai on the eve of colonization

Today /Xai/xai pan is a 1000-meter-wide treeless, grassless basin pockmarked with pit wells (Plate 3.5). Some 50 years ago, before cattle had permanently been settled there, it presented a very different aspect. Ramadjagote Harry, a Motswana from Tsau born in 1903, remembers coming to /Xai/xai in the early 1920s to hunt elephants. The elephant grass that filled the basin was higher than a man's head, and hippopotamuses lived hidden in the extensive reedbeds of the pan. The pan lay in a lush valley flanked by dense stands of *Grewia* bushes, and the river course itself was dotted with ponds that held water throughout the year and attracted flocks of migrating waterfowl. It is hard to believe this description when faced with the dustbowl reality that is /Xai/xai today, but the picture is true and serves to underline how rapidly a semiarid environment can degrade when cattle are introduced.

Black Settlement

By the mid-1920s the Herero refugees from the German war were beginning to build up their herds of cattle in the east. Murubela, the Tswana overlord of the !Kangwa Valley, allocated to three Herero families grazing rights at !Kangwa, and they set up the first non-San permanent villages in the Dobe area. These families and those that followed were drawn largely from the Tsau–Nokaneng area, which was becoming increasingly overcrowded and overgrazed. In the early 1930s a few more families and their livestock moved into the Dobe area. When Corporal Webb of the Bechuanaland police visited the area in 1934, he reported that the Herero were occupying the water holes at /Xai/xai, !Kubi, !Kangwa, and Mahopa in Bechuanaland and that Tswana cattle posts were located at several points in South-West Africa (by this time under South African jurisdiction). Black families continued to move into the area during the 1940s, and

Plate 3.5. /Xai/xai pan today.

villages were set up at Bate, Karuwe, and !Goshe. By 1948 there were an estimated 150 blacks, with 2000 head of cattle, resident in the Dobe and Nyae Nyae areas.

The Tawana headman

For many years the relations between the colonists and the !Kung had gone unregulated. There were occasional reports of cattle theft by !Kung and retaliatory whippings by the Herero, but by and large, for a frontier situation, the Dobe area was peaceful. !Kung intergroup relations presented a somewhat different picture. Especially in the Nyae Nyae area, intergroup fights were not uncommon, and fatalities occurred at a rate of about one every 2 years. These acts of violence took place largely outside the legal jurisdiction of either Bechuanaland or South-West Africa, although the Tswana settlers did intervene informally in a double homicide at /Xai/xai in the early 1940s to prevent the conflict from spreading further (see Chapter 13).

The situation changed after 1946, when a !Kung man killed one of the Bantu colonists in an argument over the !Kung's wife. It was many months before the police patrol could reach the Dobe area to arrest the suspect and take him back to Maun to stand trial. The tribal government felt at the time that a more permanent representative of their authority was required, and in 1948, Isak Utugile was appointed headman of the Dobe area. His terms of reference were to maintain law and order especially in the areas of assault and stock theft. He administered customary law and judged disputes from his *kgotla* ("court") at !Kangwa until his retirement in 1973. Isak was an effective presence in the area. Only two !Kung homicides occurred during his tenure; in both cases the offenders were taken to Maun for trial, and there have been no homicides since 1955. After many years of service to the community, Isak died in 1976.

Border troubles

The black population of the Dobe area remained stable until 1954, when a major influx of Herero pastoralists occurred from Makakun in the East. In the late 1940s there had been an outbreak of tsetse fly into cattle-raising areas that had been formerly free of fly. This forced hundreds of pastoralists to evacuate the infested areas and put an even greater pressure on the grazing in the shrinking fly-free zones. The Dobe area 100 km west of the tsetse fly front appeared to offer an attractive living space to the displaced Herero. Accordingly, some 18 families totaling over 120 people with 4000 head of cattle, trekked west in 1954. But instead of settling at the Dobe area wells, the migrants leap-frogged these wells and moved directly into South-West Africa, where they occupied the water holes of the Nyae Nyae area. There was a long-standing precedent for such a move. Pastoralists from Bechuanaland had been summering cattle in South-West Africa since the 1890s, and some of the Dobe area blacks spent the entire year at their South-West Africa cattle posts.

The Marshalls made their first expeditions to the Nyae Nyae pans between 1951 and 1955. At that time they found a few of the water sources supporting black cattle posts. Laurence Marshall returned for a brief visit in 1956 to find what appeared to be a major black encroachment on the San in the Nyae Nyae region. His reports to the South-West Africa administration led to the expulsion of these Herero in 1957 and the closing of the border to all movements of cattle (Marshall 1976:60). The blacks were forced to withdraw to wells on the Bechuanaland side, and today the majority are bunched at two wells within 10 km of the border. Since 1957 the South African police have patrolled the border road and have shot on sight any cattle that stray across the line into South-West Africa. In 1965 the border was closed completely to cattle when a wire fence was built along its entire length. The !Kung residents on the Bechuanaland side, however, were not immediately affected by these restrictions. They continued to hunt and gather on the South-West Africa side and to visit their kinsmen in the Nyae Nyae area. Even after the fence was built, they continued to cross into South-West Africa (which they call *Sottibessi*), while the authorities evidently looked the other way.

Europeans at Chum!Kwe

In 1960, the South Africans put into operation their plan to settle and "civilize" the interior !Kung. A government station was set up around a newly dug bore hole at Chum!kwe, and the !Kung of Nyae Nyae were called into the settlement. The Marshall family cooperated closely with the authorities in setting up the scheme. Metal dog tags were issued to those !Kung whose names were listed in the Marshall genealogies as being bona fide residents of Nyae Nyae. Presentation of a dog tag entitled the bearer to a weekly ration of mealie meal (cornmeal) at Chum!kwe. When Dobe !Kung who were not in the Marshall genealogies presented themselves at the station, they were told to go back to Bechuanaland, where the British would take care of them. The !Kung's strong emphasis on sharing initially foiled this crude attempt to divide and rule. A lively trade in dog tags sprang up, and many tags reached the Dobe area through the hxaro trading networks. Later, when the South Africans required locally appointed headmen to give their occupation of Namibia some semblance of legitimacy, a man named ≠Toma–the Marshalls' key informant and the star of their movie, *The Hunters*–became the headman of Chum!kwe. His son, /Xashe, learned to speak fluent Afrikaans and became the official interpreter for the Bushman affairs commissioner.

The Dobe area in the 1960s

Initially cut off from the Chum!kwe settlement scheme, the Dobe !Kung continued their hunting and gathering existence into the 1960s, augmented by some work on the Herero cattle. Later, the restrictions on settling at Chum!kwe were eased, and about 25 Dobe people did emigrate between 1969 and 1973.

I arrived in 1963 and was present during the last year before the border fence was erected, an event that altered the movements of game through the area. In 1966, at the time Botswana achieved its independence from Britain, the Dobe area was still quite isolated from the rest of the country. Government presence was limited to about one vehicle per month, mainly veterinary teams inoculating the blacks' cattle. The opening of a branch store of the Botswana Trading Association (BTA), a private, white-owned firm at !Kangwa, in 1967 had the effect of opening the area up to the east even as it was being closed to the west. The BTA store sold food staples and dry goods at inflated prices, but its main purpose was to purchase Herero cattle on the hoof at prices much lower than those offered by the Maun livestock dealers. !Kung young men were hired to herd the BTA cattle and periodically to run drives of the purchased stock out to Maun. The availability of store-bought sugar, a principal ingredi-

ent in local beer, stimulated a thriving business in home brew. The
!Kung women of !Kangwa became successful penny capitalists, charging
five cents a cup for their product. The increased vehicle traffic encouraged !Kung men to seek work in the South African gold mines, and about
20 men went to the Witwatersrand as contract laborers during the 1960s.
Also the regular traffic of anthropologists after 1967 created a minor
industry in its own right and contributed to a general expansion of
knowledge of the ways of the outside world. The Botswana government
sent up bags of seed from the agricultural extension office to be distributed to the San for planting, and in the good rains of 1967–9, a number of
!Kung families planted and harvested crops of maize, sorghum, and melons. In later years, unaccountably, the seed program was discontinued,
and !Kung agriculture suffered a setback.

The end of my main period of fieldwork in 1969 found the !Kung still
primarily hunter-gatherers, but turning increasingly to small stock raising, horticulture, and wage labor as their opportunities expanded. The
dramatic changes of the 1970s occurred after my main field period and
are dealt with in Chapter 14.

4

The environment

T HE Dobe and /Du/da areas are part of a vast basin 1000 to 1200 meters above sea level bisected by the Botswana–Namibia border on the northern fringe of the Kalahari Desert. Their limits lie between 19°15' and 20°30' south latitude and 20°45' and 21°20' east longitude, encompassing an area of about 11,000 km², not all of which is utilized by the San. The Aha Hills in the northern third of the area are the most conspicuous feature shown on the standard maps of Southern Africa. Dobe and /Du/da are water holes in the northern and southern reaches of this area, respectively (Figure 4.1).

This chapter first looks at the topography, geology, soils, and vegetation associations of the region. It goes on to examine the fauna in detail and concludes with a discussion of climate. Of particular interest is the seasonal and year-to-year variability in climate and resources that is so important to an understanding of the hunting and gathering adaptation of the San inhabitants of the area.

TOPOGRAPHY

The first impression of a traveler to this region is an immense flatness, where the sky dominates the landscape. The Aha Hills rise only 100 meters above the surrounding plain, and from their top one sees what seem to be endles vistas of brush and savannah stretching to the horizon in every direction. Thus the observer is surprised to find in the !Kung language of travel a rich vocabulary of climbing and descending as they discuss trips from one water hole to another. For example, a trip to Nokaneng is always referred to as *kowa //hai* (literally "to descend to the east"). As one gains familiarity with the area, one realizes tht the !Kung are right: There are slight elevation differences from place to place, and I soon came to appreciate how important these differences are in the structuring of drainage, vegetation zones, and key plant resources.

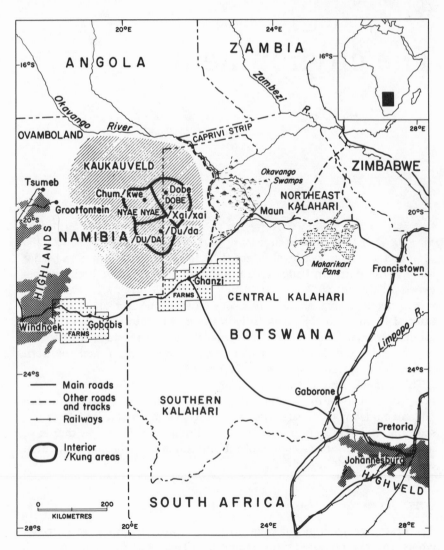

Figure 4.1. The Kaukauveld, showing the Dobe and /Du/da areas.

At several points in the landscape the sandy plain is broken by dry river courses: the !Kangwa, the /Xai/xai, and the Eiseb, each with its tributary streams. Some of these river courses can be traced for 100 km. They rarely hold flowing water, perhaps twice in a decade, but when they do the flow of water can be considerable. Some sections of their courses are broad and difficult to trace, but others are deeply cut and suggest periods in the past of wetter weather and more permanent flow. For example, although there are no topographic surveys to prove it, I estimate that the

Plate 4.1. The Botswana–Namibia border in 1964 (facing south, Botswana on the left; compare Plate 14.5).

bed of the !Kangwa River may fall as much as 50 meters in its course from the Namibian border to !Goshe, 37 km to the east.

The Kalahari Desert, a vast basin filled with sand, was formed during the Tertiary era when surrounding highland areas in Namibia and Zimbabwe were elevated by as much as 1000 meters with no corresponding rise in the center. In much of the Kalahari Desert the bedrock is overlain by a mantle of windblown sand many meters thick. In only a few localities are the underlying rock formations exposed; in the Dobe area the rock outcrops include the Aha Hills and /Twihaba, N!umtsaa ("Two Rocks"), and N!um!koma ("Small Rock") east and south of the Ahas (Figure 4.2). These rocks, formed of Otavi dolomite, underlie much of the Dobe area and form an important source of subsurface water. Dolomite is also often riddled with sinkholes and caves, and an extensive underground network of caves exists at /Twihaba (Cooke and Baillieul, 1974). A gigantic vertical sinkhole in the heart of the Ahas is called Wanchu ("Devil's House") by the !Kung.

Elsewhere in the Dobe area, especially directly north of the Aha Hills in the upper reaches of the !Kangwa Valley, extensive sheets of calcrete and silcrete hardpan are exposed. This is such an unusual feature of the landscape of the Northern Kalahari that the !Kung name for the !Kangwa Valley and all its water holes is simply *n!umsi* ("rocks or stones"). This

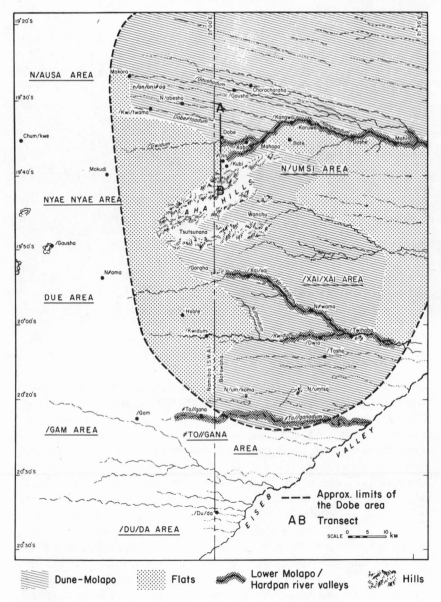

Figure 4.2. Physiography of the Dobe area.

hardpan, composed of calcium carbonate, is derived from underlying bedrock. Slightly soluble, it is drawn upward in aqueous solution by osmotic
pressure and deposited in sheets up to 50 cm thick. In some areas hardpan is still in the process of formation, and much of it is of very recent,
perhaps post-Pleistocene, age; Middle Stone Age artifacts have been
found by Yellen (1971) *beneath* layers of hardpan.

Most of the hardpan, like the surrounding sandscape, is extremely flat, and between Dobe and !Kubi the bed of the !Kangwa River winds through the hardpan incised a few centimeters below grade. When one reaches !Kangwa, however, the topographic relief becomes much sharper. The riverbed is about 2 meters below grade at !Kangwa, 4 meters at !Kangwa Matse, and 7 to 8 meters between vertical banks at a point midway between !Kangwa Matse and !Goshe. Here the down-cutting of the river has exposed the oldest rocks of the region, the coarse-grained granites of the basement complex. Deposits of high-quality chert are also exposed in this section and are a source of flints for the flint-and-steel fire-making kits used by the !Kung. I walked the length of the riverbed from the border to !Goshe in 1968, and I was impressed by the depth of the down-cutting in what had appeared to be such flat country. This impression was reinforced by what happens after a heavy rainfall: Then, for a few hours, the lower !Kangwa becomes a raging torrent with cascades to challenge a white-water canoeist. Another puzzling feature of the !Kangwa River is its extremely tortuous course of entrenched meanders and oxbows. In aerial photos the lower !Kangwa looks a bit like the lower Mississippi in miniature. East of !Goshe, the country becomes much flatter, and within a few kilometers the !Kangwa River course disappears in the extensive mud flats of Mahito in the Middle Passage.

For several years I was at a loss to explain the down-cutting, the vertical banks, and the entrenched meandering of this river in an otherwise flat stretch of semidesert. The explanation probably lies in the recent discovery that the Okavango delta is undergoing rifting and that Botswana contains an emerging southwestern branch of the great African Rift Valley.

According to Scholz (1976:35–42), the Okavango delta is sinking in relation to areas northwest and southeast of it. Eventually the delta will form the floor of an incipient Rift Valley. The faults that bound the delta on the northwest and southeast can be traced to geological formations in Zambia, which in turn are linked with the main western rift arm between Zaïre and Tanzania (Reeves 1972). To the south and west of the Okavango delta, the Dobe area appears to lie on the *high side* of the upstream Gomare fault and the Middle Passage on the *low side,* an orientation that, if confirmed by subsequent study, would account for the considerable down-cutting of the !Kangwa River in recent years (Grey and Cooke 1977, Fig. 1). Similar down-cutting can be observed in the /Twihaba Valley south of the Ahas and possibly in the Eiseb as well.

Despite their geological interest, the hills and riverbeds of the Dobe area are not the salient topographic features for the hunting and gathering !Kung. Most of the Dobe area is covered by a mantle of sand from 3 to 30 meters in depth. This sand varies in color from red to white to gray and in texture from coarse to fine-grained. Color and texture, in turn, correlate with each other and vary from place to place, with loose red and white sands on the tops of dunes and fine, compacted gray soil in the bottoms of the dry river courses between the dunes. These soil and elevation differences provide the key to an understanding of the vegetation and plant resources of the Dobe area.

The dune and molapo system

Apart from the hills and dry rivers, the main feature of the Dobe area is a system of fixed longitudinal dunes running parallel to each other 8 to 80 km in length and oriented 102° to 282° roughly east-west. These dunes, with crests 1.5 to 8 km apart, are designated *alab dunes* by Grove (1969), adopting a term first used by Monod (1958) to describe similar formations bordering the Southern Sahara Desert. *Molapo* is a Setswana word used to describe the longitudinal depressions or small valleys between the dunes. It corresponds to *omaramba*, a Herero word used by J. Marshall (1957), L. Marshall (1976), Story (1958), and others. Formed by prevailing easterly winds at a time when annual rainfall was less than 250 mm, the alab dunes are presently fixed by vegetation. Similar formations in Senegal are believed to be younger than 20,000 B.P. (Michel 1967).

The dune crests and flanks are characterized by deep, loose red and white sands. These support a distinctive association of broad-leaved trees and shrubs with many edible species. The molapos, both in the interstices of the dunes and in the more deeply incised river valleys, are characterized by compacted, fine-grained gray soils. They support an association of complex-leaved thorn trees and shrubs with a distinctive array of edible species. Soil texture and composition appear to be a function of elevation. The reddest, loosest sands are found on the crests of the dunes. The dune flanks and flats have buff to white compacted soils, and the molapos have gray, highly compacted soils.

Yellen provides the explanation for these soil differences:

> Drainage of rain water from the dune crests and flanks has largely removed the finer silty constitutents of the dune soils and concentrated them in adjacent molapo beds. On the lower flats and in the molapos, this water has reduced the ferric oxide component of the soil to soluble ferrous oxide which has been leached out. The result is a gradual and regular vertical shift in soil composition from loose, iron-rich sand on the dune crests down to a more compact soil, lacking in iron but richer in silt in the molapo bottoms. [Yellen and Lee 1976:34]

VEGETATION ASSOCIATIONS

The Kalahari is not the driest of the world's deserts. Compared with the Namib of Namibia, which receives less than 25 mm (1 in.) of rain a year,

Table 4.1. *!Kung habitat types*

≠To	A dune with *Ricinodendron rautanenii*
!Hu	A dune or flat with loose red or white sand
//Go	A plain with loose white sand
≠Da	An open flat with compacted white gray soil
N//o	A gray soil area with *Acacia* spp.
/Dwi	A thicket with close-spaced trees, usually *Terminalia prunioides*
Dum	A molapo, large or small
N!umsi	Hills or hardpan areas with rock exposed

the Kalahari is well-off; most of it receives 250 mm (10 in.) or more a year. Though highly variable, the rainfall does permit a substantial vegetation of trees, shrubs, and grasses that grows richer as you move from south to north. In the Dobe area we have recorded about 220 plant species (see Appendix B). Where the Dobe area most resembles a desert, however, is in the extreme scarcity of surface water.

The existence of hills, riverbeds, dunes, and molapos provides differences in relief of only a few meters – barely perceptible to the eye in the case of the dunes. Yet these small differences, along with the accompanying soil changes, produce a remarkably varied vegetation cover in the Dobe area. The !Kung themselves make fine distinctions in habitat types (Table 4.1). For our purposes four different associations can be distinguished: (1) dune, (2) flats, (3) molapo, and (4) hardpan (and river valleys). Surprisingly, the hills do not exhibit a vegetation association of their own. Where they are overlain by sand, their vegetation resembles that of the dune association; on rocky outcrops the hardpan association appears.

Plant geographers such as Keay (1959) and Cooke (1964) have not made such fine distinctions. They tend to divide the region in half, with the southern half classified as "Kalahari grassland on mixed open Acacia-wooded steppe" and the northern half as "bushveld and grassland." This follows the South African ecological practice of distinguishing between *thornveld,* where acacia species dominate, and *bushveld,* in which broad-leaved forms are dominant (Acocks 1953; Wellington 1955). In fact, both types of habitat occur throughout the area: the bushveld on the dunes and flats and the acacia thornveld in the molapos and river valleys. In the most recent vegetation map of Botswana, Weare and Yalala (1971) also distinguish two zones, but their's is an east-west, not a north-south, distinction. The Middle Passage area they classify as "northern Kalahari bush and tree savanna," and the Dobe area proper and points west as "northwestern tree savanna." They too fail to identify the dune–molapo distinction.

Of the earlier fieldworkers, only Maguire seems to have noted the ecological significance of the molapo–dune topography. Maguire (ca. 1954) divides the Nyae Nyae region into three vegetation types: the dune association, the omaramba (basin) association, and the intermediate association; the last is never precisely defined.

We now go on to consider each of the four vegetation associations in more detail.

1. The dune association

Unlike the moving dunes of the Namib and Southern Kalahari deserts, the dunes of the Northern Kalahari are fixed by vegetation. The dunes support relatively open forests of *Ricinodendron* (the famous nut tree) and open woodlands of *Burkea, Pterocarpus,* and *Terminalia.*

The major trees of the dune association are *Ricinodendron rautanenii, Burkea africana, Pterocarpus angolensis, Baikiaea plurijuga,* and *Terminalia sericea.*

Other important constituents include *Combretum collinum, Bauhinia petersiana, Ximenia caffra, Strychnos pungens, Strychnos cocculoides,* and *Guibourtia coleosperma.*

Ricinodendron rautanenii (the mongongo nut), the major plant food of the Dobe area !Kung, is found only on the crests of the fixed dunes. Because of the loose nature of the soils, there is no standing water on the dunes at any season of the year. The only source of water on the dunes is the rainwater that collects in the crotches of the mongongo trees from November to March. Although the volume of water stored is minute, the proximity of the supply to the nut groves makes this an important source of water for the San.

2. The flats association

Intermediate in elevation between the dunes and the molapos are plains of buff to white compacted sands. These plains, or flats, support a vegetation that has affinities to both the dune and molapo associations. It also contains species not found elsewhere.

The flats may be divided into two intergrading types on the basis of soil differences: (2a) looser buff sands supporting species that extend into the dune association and several other diagnostic species, and (2b) compacted white sands supporting species that extend into the molapo association and several other diagnostic species. In many areas these two types form a mosaic pattern, with patches a few centimeters lower in elevation supporting a 2b association and patches a few centimeters higher supporting a 2a association. We came to know such mosaics well because our Dobe base camp was located in the midst of one such area. Termite hills, some up to 4 meters in height, abound in these mosaics.

Upper flats with loose sand (2a) have the following diagnostic species: *Lonchocarpus nelsii, Acacia erioloba, Acacia* sp. cf. *hebeclada,* and *Aca-*

cia erubescens. They also contain *Terminalia sericea, Grewia retiner-uis,* and *Sclerocarya caffra.*

Lower flats of compacted sand (2b) have the following diagnostic species: *Acacia hebeclada, Acacia erubescens,* and *Ziziphus mucronata.* They also contain *Hyphaene benguellensis, Terminalia prunioides, Combretum imberbe,* and *Grewia flava.*

3. The molapo association

Two subtypes can be distinguished here, again on the basis of slight differences of elevation and soil composition: (3a) small molapos in the upper reaches of internal drainage systems and in the cols between dunes and molapos, and (3b) well-defined molapos in the interstices between the dunes, usually in the lower reaches of internal drainage systems.

Small molapos (3a) have compacted soils of light gray verging on buff. Here are found dense thickets of *Terminalia prunioides* interspersed with stands of *Sclerocarya caffra.*

Well-defined molapos, with gray, compacted silty soils and occasional beds of hardpan (3b), support *Acacia mellifera, Acacia tortilis, Dichrostachys cinerea* (L.) Wight & Arn, *Croton gratissimus, Boscia albitrunca,* and *Grewia flava.*

The molapo association, especially 3b, intergrades with the hardpan association.

4. The hardpan association

The soils here are very complex. In the upper !Kangwa Valley between Dobe and !Kubi there is a mosaic pattern of hardpan pavements interspersed with patches of gray black gumbolike soils that turn into thick mud in the rainy season. At Mahito, east of !Goshe, the gumbo soils extend for several square kilometers. Also included within this same association are the rocky terrains of the lower !Kangwa Valley and of the highest elevations of the Aha Hills. These diverse settings support a rather similar vegetation characterized by *Commiphora angolensis, Commiphora pyracanthoides, Combretum imberbe, Hyphaene benguellensis,* and *Adansonia digitata.*

Certain species are common to both the hardpan and the molapo associations. These include *Combretum imberbe, Hyphaene benguellensis, Dichrostachys cinerea* (L.) Wight & Arn, and *Grewia flava.*

The most important food plants of the two associations are *Adansonia digitata* L., *Hyphaene benguellensis, Grewia flava,* and *Citrullus lanatus.*

Vegetation and land use

The molapo zones, being the lowest parts of the landscape, contain all the sources of permanent and seasonal standing water. The permanent water holes are confined to main river bottoms where the bedrock is

exposed. Most of these water holes are natural fissures in the rock, but all
have been improved and maintained either by the San themselves or by
the Bantu herders.

The seasonal waters that exist for 1 to 6 months of each year are found
both in the main river bottoms and in the dune interstices, where local
drainage patterns produce a catchment. These latter vary in size from
small depressions 5 meters in diameter and a few centimeters deep,
which hold water for a few weeks after heavy rains, to great ponds up to
100 meters long, which may hold water several months after the rains
have ceased or year-round in years of high rainfall.

Precisely because of the abundant water supply, the molapo and hardpan areas have been the most heavily grazed by the Bantu cattle, and the
effects on vegetation have been more pronounced here than in the other
two associations. One result has been an encroachment of bush, particularly *Acacia mellifera* and *Dichrostachys cinerea*, in the immediate vicinity of !Kangwa and /Xai/xai valleys and in the major molapos feeding
them. Nevertheless, the main outlines of the four vegetation zones are
still identifiable.

A few of the major marker species distinguishing vegetation zones
should be mentioned. *Ricinodendron rautanenii* (the mongongo) is found
only on the dune crests in red or reddish white loose sand. It is diagnostic
of the dune association. *Commiphora angolensis*, with its characteristic
yellow green peeling bark, is found only on the hardpan or other rock.
Terminalia sericea and *Terminalia prunioides*, two very abundant
species, are sharply segregted ecologically. *T. sericea* is ubiquitous on
looser buff to white sand, but never on compacted sand. *T. prunioides* is
found only on compacted buff to gray sands, never on loose sand. Thus the
two species mark the dividing line between dunes and upper flats on the
one hand and the remaining associations on the other. Figure 4.2 shows
the patterning of dunes, molapos, rivers, and hills in the Dobe area. Figure
4.3 shows a north-south transect through part of the same area.

The discussion of soils and vegetation presented above provides a work-
able scheme that is adequate for the cultural ecological purposes of this
book, but it is not the last word on the subject. Although extensive collections of plant material for identification were made both by me and by
Dr. Marjorie Whiting, we did not collect soil samples or carry out statistically valid random sample plant surveys and transects. It is hoped that
future investigators will fill these gaps and present a more accurate and
possibly modified picture of the vegetation zones of the Dobe area.

FAUNA

Despite recent changes, the Dobe area presents an impressive array of
African plains game. With over 50 resident mammals, including 11 spe-

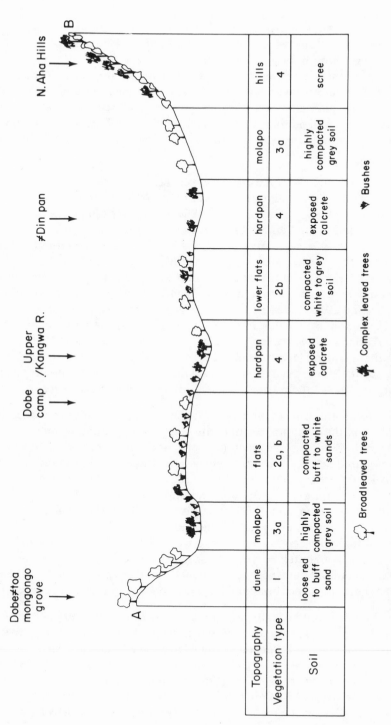

Figure 4.3. A north-south transect through the Dobe area (see text for explanation).

cies of ungulates and a dozen other edible game species, the area still provides the !Kung with a solid hunting subsistence base. At the same time, the !Kung hunters have to compete for their prey with representatives of all the major predator species, as lion, leopard, cheetah, wild dog, and hyena, to mention a few, are all resident in the Dobe area. In addition to the 58 mammals some 90 species of birds, 25 species of reptiles and amphibians, and perhaps 85 to 90 species of invertebrates are also known to the !Kung, making a total of about 260 species in their animal universe.

Mammals

Because of the broken nature of the vegetation, the area does not support the large herds of migratory plains game that are found on the open stretches of the Southern Kalahari. Wildebeest, for example, seen in herds of thousands in the Central Kalahari Game Reserve, occur in herds of 10 to 20 in the Dobe area. Game numbers and varieties have certainly diminished in the Northwestern Kalahari in the last century. The hunter Van Zyl killed elephant and rhinoceros at /Gam in the 1870s. Older Tswana informants reported seeing buffalo, rhinoceros, and hippopotamus at /Xai/ xai around 1915. Today elephant and buffalo are only occasional summer visitors, and rhinoceros have disappeared completely. John Marshall (1957) reported seeing springbok in Nyae Nyae as late as 1950, but none are there today. Happily, some of these disappearances are reversible, at least in the short run. Yellen reported that for 2 years after the very heavy rains in 1973–4 there was a resident hippopotamus near !Kubi.

Ungulates. In terms of biomass, ungulates are the most important mammals, and the most prominent of the ungulates are kudu, wildebeest, and gemsbok. Giraffe, eland, roan antelope, and hartebeest are also present. The nonmigratory warthog, steenbok and duiker are extremely plentiful and are the most frequently killed of the ungulates. Rarely seen and very rarely hunted are buffalo, zebra, and impala.

To give some idea of abundance, fresh warthog, steenbok, and duiker tracks can be seen every day of the year. Kudu, wildebeest, and gemsbok tracks might be seen several times a week. Tracks of giraffe, eland, hartebeest, and roan antelope would be seen perhaps once a month or once in 2 months; buffalo have been sighted only about a dozen times in 10 years, zebra perhaps three times and impala only once in the same period.

Carnivores. Paradoxically, all the major Southern African predators are found in the Dobe area, including lion, leopard, cheetah, hyena (two species), wild dog, and a dozen smaller forms. Their kills and spoor are frequently encountered on trips through the Dobe area; yet the !Kung do not seem to be afraid of them. The !Kung sleep in the open without fires when necessary and make no provision to protect or fortify their living sites. Ten of the smaller carnivores are occasionally hunted and eaten by the !Kung.

Table 4.2. *Mammals of the Dobe area*[a]

Animal	Occurrence[b]	Animal	Occurrence[b]
Ungulates		Leopard	U
Buffalo	R	Lion	C
Duiker	VC	Banded mongoose	C
Eland	U	Slender mongoose	C
Gemsbok	C	Yellow mongoose	C
Giraffe	U	Serval	VR
Hartebeest	U	Wild cat	C
Impala	VR	Wild dog	C
Kudu	C	Zorilla	C
Roan antelope	U		
Steenbok	VC	*Other*	
Warthog	VC	Ant bear	C
Wildebeest	C	Baboon	VR
Zebra	R	Bat (3 species)	C
		Elephant	R
Carnivores		Galago	C
Aardwolf	C	Scrub hare	VC
Bat-eared fox	C	Mouse (12 species)	VC
Caracal	U	Pangolin	C
Cheetah	C	Porcupine	C
Genet	C	Shrew	C
Honey badger	C	Springhare	VC
Brown hyena	VR	Bush squirrel	U
Spotted hyena	C	Ground squirrel	C
Black-backed jackal	C	Vervet	R

[a] A complete listing is presented in Appendix C.
[b] VC = very common, daily sightings of tracks; C = common, weekly sightings of tracks; U = uncommon, monthly sightings of tracks; R = rare, few sightings per year or less; VR = very rare, one or two sightings in a decade.

Other mammals. The elephant is the only large nonungulate mammal in the Dobe area. A few pass through the area each rainy season and return to the Okavango swamps usually with the onset of winter. In an exceptionally wet year, such as 1973–4, a dozen might be seen. Of the small- to medium-sized mammals, four are important in the diet: ant bear, porcupine, springhare, and scrub hare. The pangolin (scaly anteater) is less common, but is also eaten. Completing the list of mamals are 1 shrew, 2 species of squirrel, 3 species of bat, and 14 species of mouse and gerbil. None of these small mammals are eaten by the !Kung. Finally, there are 3 primate species: the tiny galago is a very common resident, the vervet monkey an uncommon resident, and the baboon an occasional visitor. None are eaten by the !Kung. A summary of the mammals is found in Table 4.2 and a complete listing is presented in Appendix C.

Table 4.3. *Birds of the Dobe area: most common species*

Gome birds	*Rapacious birds*
Black korhaan	Bateleur
Crested francolin	Gray kestrel
Crowned guinea fowl	Hooded vulture
Knob-billed goose	Lappet-faced vulture
Kori bustard	Martial eagle
Laughing dove	Secretary bird
Namaqua sandgrouse	Scops owl
Ostrich	Tawny eagle
Red-billed francolin	White-backed vulture
Red teal	Yellow-billed kite
Ring-necked dove	
Swainson's francolin	
Summer migrants	*Conspicuous residents*
Abdim's stork	Blacksmith plover
Cattle egret	Blue-eared glossy starling
Hamerkop	Cardinal woodpecker
Marabou stork	Crimson-breasted shrike
Saddlebill stork	European nightjar
Spurwing goose	Go-away bird
Wattled crane	Gray hornbill
	Hoopoe
	Meyer's parrot
	Mzilikazi's roller
	Scaly weaver

Birds

About 100 species of birds are resident in the Dobe area, and another 40 are summer migrants. Of these, the !Kung have identified at least 90 species. Considering the dryness of the area, birdlife is surprisingly abundant. Bird calls are a constant background sound throughout the daylight hours, and an hour's hike at any season will turn up a dozen species. The ostrich is still very common in the area, though rarely hunted for food. Its eggs, however, are frequently collected, their contents eaten, and the shells cleaned and used for water canteens and in bead making. Other important game birds include guinea fowl, francolin, duck and teal, korhaan, sandgrouse, quail, and dove. Nine species are systematically hunted for food. The most common species are listed in Table 4.3.

Reptiles, amphibians, and aquatic species

In all, 25 species of reptiles and amphibians have been recorded, including 10 snakes, 7 lizards, and a variety of tortoises, chameleons, and frogs. The 6 poisonous snakes loom large in the lives of the !Kung. Al-

Table 4.4. *Reptiles and amphibians of the Dobe area*

Poisonous snakes	*Chameleons*
Black mamba	*Rhampholeon* sp.
Boomslang	An unidentified species
Horned adder	
Puff adder	*Lizards*
Sand adder	Land leguaan
Spitting cobra	Marbled gecko
	Striped-plate lizard
Nonpoisonous snakes	Striped skink
Jalla's sand snake	*Zygodactylus* sp.
Rock python	Two unidentified species
Two unidentified species	
Turtles	*Frogs*
Large leopard tortoise	*Pyxiecephalus* sp. (a large bullfrog)
Small leopard tortoise	*Rana* sp.
A terrapin	
An unidentified species	

though snakebites are rare (only three cases occurred in 10 years, none fatal), the !Kung take precautions to clear their campsites of brush that would conceal a snake, and whenever they find a poisonous snake, they kill it with a club or digging stick. (Women appear to be as proficient as men at killing snakes.) Only 5 of the 25 species are regarded as edible by the !Kung, and of these only the large leopard tortoise and the rock python are regularly hunted for food. The small leopard tortoise is also hunted, and the other edibles include the leguaan and the bullfrog (Table 4.4).

Fish are not present in the Dobe area, but aquatic species such as terrapin, leeches, clams, and snails are found in isolated water holes, indicating a time in the past when the area was connected to a river system by flowing water.

Invertebrates

Of the countless invertebrates in the Dobe area, about 85 to 90 species are known to the San, including an abundance of scorpions, spiders, ticks, millipedes, and centipedes, and some 70 species of insects (Table 4.5).

Insects do not play an important role in the diet. One species of ant lion has an annual outbreak around the end of November. Tens of thousands swarm within a few days, and the !Kung women and children enjoy collecting them and eating them by the hundreds. In 1963, the swarming occurred on November 24, in 1964 on December 3, in 1967 on November 19, and in 1968 on November 22. Three different species of click beetle

Table 4.5. *Invertebrates of the Dobe area*

Animal	No. of species	Animal	No. of species
Class Arachnida		Order Odontata	
Scorpions	2	Dragonflies	2
Spiders	5	Order Isoptera	
Ticks	2	Termites	4
		Order Hemiptera-	
Class Myriapoda		Heteroptera	
Centipede	1	Aphid	1
Millipede	1	Shield bug	1
		Order Neuroptera	
Class Hirudinea		Ant lions	3
Leech	1	Order Lepidoptera	
		Butterflies	3
Class Unionidae		Moths	12
Freshwater clam	1	Order Diptera	
		Flies	6
Class Helicidae		Mosquito	1
Land snails	2	Order Hymenoptera	
		Ants	2
Class Insecta		Bees	2
Order Dictyoptera		Wasps	3
Cockroach	1	Order Coleoptera	
Mantises	3	Blister beetles	2
Order Phasmida		Click beetles	6
Walking sticks	2	Dung beetles	4
Order Saltatoria		Poisonous beetles	6
Cricket	1	Other beetles	2
Grasshoppers	7		

were eaten in March 1964. They were considered a delicacy rather than a staple. I did not see caterpillars eaten in 1964, but in 1968 six edible species showed up, all of them considered a rare treat. Wild honey was a superb delicacy, but highly subject to seasonal fluctuation. No honey was seen in 1963–4, but it was fairly common and highly prized in 1967–9.

The most important of the insects for subsistence are the species of chrysomelid beetles used by the !Kung for poisoning their hunting arrows. The entomologist Charles Koch has suggested that as many as eight species of poisonous grubs are used by the !Kung (Koch 1958; Shaw 1963; Marshall 1976:146–52). In the Dobe area three grubs, *Diamphidia nigro-ornata, Diamphidia vittatipennis,* and *Polyclada flexuosa,* were observed to be used by the !Kung, and each of these had its own parasite of the genus *Lebistina.* These grubs produce a slow-acting but highly effective poison, which when applied to arrows, can kill a wounded animal in 6 to 24 hours (see Chapter 5).

BARA	≠TOBE	/GUM	/GAA	/HUMA
Summer	Autumn	Winter	Early Spring	Spring Rains
HOT RAINY	COOLER DRYING	COOL VERY DRY	HOT DRY	HOT DRY/WET

| D | J | F | M | A | M | J | J | A | S | O | N |

Figure 4.4. Seasons of the !Kung.

CLIMATE

The Northern Kalahari Desert has a mean elevation of 1000 to 1200 meters above sea level; it lies within the summer rainfall area of Southern Africa. These factors combine to produce a climatic regimen of hot summers with a 4- to 6-month rainy season and moderate to cool winters without rainfall. At 20° south latitude, the sun is directly overhead from early December to early January, but the hottest mean temperatures may occur from October to February. In June and July, the coldest months of the year, night temperatures fall to freezing or near freezing, but they rise during the day to a comfortable 24 to 27°C. Temperatures are fairly consistent from year to year, but this is not the case with rainfall. The annual precipitation may vary from year to year by as much as 500 percent.

Seasons

The !Kung accurately divide the year into five seasons (Figure 4.4): spring rains, main summer rains, autumn, winter, and the spring dry season.

!Huma (spring rains). The !Kung year begins with the onset of the first rains in October and November. These are light convectional thunder showers that often fall on one area and miss other areas entirely. The combination of heat and atmospheric conditions makes this a spectacular season for lightning. According to the U.S. Weather Bureau, Botswana has one of the highest incidences of lightning in the world (Irv DeVore was struck by lightning in Dobe in 1964, but was uninjured). Electrical storms of an hour's duration are common at this time of year. These first rains also have the effect of triggering growth in plants and reproduction in animals, and overnight the parched landscape is transformed into one of lush greenery. The !Kung take advantage of the water that collects in the hollows of trees by leaving their permanent-water camps and moving out into temporary camps in the mongongo forests.

Bara (main summer rains). From December to March the heaviest rains fall, bringing with them a season of plenty. In most years migratory ducks, geese, and other waterfowl flock to the seasonal pans in great numbers; elephant and buffalo may migrate from the Okavango swamps into the Dobe area. The major summer plant foods – fruits, berries, melons, and leafy greens – also make their apperance, and the !Kung camps are widely distributed at seasonal water points in the hinterland. The onset and duration of the main rains are highly variable, and the timing of rain is almost as important to the ecology as is the total fall.

≠*Tobe (autumn).* A brief autumn occurs in April or May after the rains have ceased but before the onset of the really cold weather. The still warm weather and lowered humidity favors high rates of evaporation: The seasonal pans shrink and dry out at this time of year. The !Kung may converge on the larger summer pans that still hold water. Food is abundant, with plenty of the summer berries and melons still available. The April mongongo nut harvest puts a major new food into the diet.

!Gum (winter). The cool dry season extends from the end of May through August. It is heralded by a sharp drop in nightly temperatures, with the peak cold in late June. In 1964, Dobe experienced 6 weeks of freezing and near-freezing nights. The !Kung winter camps, usually around a permanent water hole, are well stocked with firewood to burn through the cold nights. Fortunately, the days are crisp and clear, warming up to 24 to 27 °C. The diet is varied during the winter months. Mongongo fruit and nut, baobab, and many species of roots and bulbs provide the staples. The clear, pleasant days are ideal for walking; winter is a time for visiting relatives at distant camps. The good tracking conditions encourage more hunting and the setting up of snarelines. Through time, plant foods become increasingly scarce as foods are eaten up in wider and wider radii around the permanent water holes.

!Gaa (spring dry season). The early spring begins in late August with a rapid increase in daily temperatures and ends in October or early November with the onset of the first rains. This is the least attractive time of year. Although humidity remains low, the days are exceedingly hot, with highs from 33 to 43 °C (92 to 110 °F) in the shade. Work is difficult, and the better foods may be available only at distances from camp. It is in this season that the !Kung make use of the widest variety of plant foods. Fibrous roots, ignored at other times of the year, may be dug and eaten without enthusiasm. Surprisingly, there is a great deal of hunting during !gaa. The men say the heat makes the animals less wary and their movements more predictable, so they are easier to stalk and kill. This fact is reflected in the

Plate 4.2. /Gausha pan in the dry season.

kill statistics: October was a consistently good hunting month in terms of the number of large animals killed (Marshall 1976:140). But by and large, spring is a time of waiting and eagerly scanning the horizon for the first sign of rain.

Temperature and climatic stress

Because of its tropical latitude and midcontinent location, the Dobe area experiences consistently hot days in spring and summer. Its relatively high elevation (1100 meters) accounts for its rapid diurnal cooling and for the cold winter nights. Figure 4.5 shows the curve of minimum and maximum temperatures for 1963–4. There are spring and summer highs of 35 to 38 °C and lows of 16 to 19 °C. Autumn is cooler, with highs of 28 to 34 °C and lows of 10 to 15 °C. The cold months of June and July show lows around −1 to +4 °C and highs around 25 °C. It is apparent that the !Kung, in common with most high desert dwellers, experience both heat and cold stress (Table 4.6). In terms of work ecology, the critical temperature datum is the daily maximum, which indicates the heat conditions under which the people must hunt and gather. From October to March the people of the Dobe area can expect daily highs of 35 to 45 °C (95 to 113 °F), meaning that subsistence work must be carried out under conditions of extreme sweat loss. For example, a person walking in the sun at

Table 4.6. *Heat and cold stress in the Dobe area: percent of days each month with extreme temperatures: 1967–9*

Conditions	1967 Oct	Nov	Dec	1968 Jan	Feb	Mar.[a]	Apr	May	June	July	Aug	Sept	Oct	Nov	Dec	1969 Jan	Feb.[a]	Mar	Apr
Heat stress																			
Percent of days 33 °C or over	56	38	42	40	5		7	4	0	0	39	100	100	50	76	70	0	0	58
Number of days of valid observations	9/31	24/30	31/31	30/31	22/29	0/31	15/30	27/31	30/30	28/31	28/31	20/30	31/31	26/30	29/31	27/31	11/28	11/31	26/30
Cold stress																			
Percent of nights under 10 °C	0	0	0	0	0		10	44	93	96	96	75	26	0	0	0	0	0	0
under 5 °C	0	0	0	0	0		0	0	77	71	60	0	0	0	0	0	0	0	0
under 0 °C	0	0	0	0	0		0	0	37	0	0	0	0	0	0	0	0	0	0
Number of nights of valid observation	3/31	28/30	30/31	30/31	21/29	0/31	16/30	27/31	30/30	28/31	25/31	20/30	31/31	26/30	30/31	29/31	0/28	11/31	26/30

[a] No record.
Source: Yellen and Lee (1976:31).

Plate 4.3. Mahito pan during the rains.

38 °C (100 °F) sweats at the rate of roughly 800 cc of water loss per hour, an equivalent of 3 liters (over 6 lb of water!) in a typical working day.

At the other extreme, during June, July, and August the !Kung can expect about 60 nights when the temperature falls below 5 °C. Here the problem is the opposite one: how to keep warm through the cold nights. Physiologists have tested the San's cold adaptation and have found them not particularly well adapted to cold (Wyndham et al. 1964). The Dobe !Kung's adaptation to cold winter weather is mainly cultural. They do not make any special warm winter clothing, no doubt because the cold hours fall late at night when they are sleeping, not moving around or working. They do employ three techniques against the cold: (1) they make use of the abundant supply of firewood to build extra large fires in front of their huts when they go to sleep; (2) they sleep three or four to a blanket, in families or in single-sex groups; and (3) if it is simply too cold to sleep, they get up and sit around the fire to keep warm and then go back to sleep after the sun comes up.

Another response to the stress of hot and cold temperature can be seen in the !Kung's seasonal activity rhythms. At latitude 20° south there is an annual variation in day length of just under 2 hours. In midwinter (July) the sun rises at about 7:00 A.M. and sets at 6:00 P.M. In midsummer (January), the sun rises at about 6:00 A.M. and sets at 7:00 P.M. During

the winter the !Kung get up late and stay around their campfires until
midmorning. They concentrate their subsistence activities in the warmer
middle hours of the day (10:00 A.M. to 5:00 P.M.). During the hot summer days they arise at dawn and work until 10:00 A.M. When possible
they spend the hottest midday hours resting in shade. Usually there is a
second period of activity in the cooler evening (5:00 to 7:30 P.M.).

Fortunately for the !Kung, the combination of wet *and* cold is rare. A
summer rainstorm or hailstorm can drop the temperature by as much as
15 °C (from 30 to 15). Their huts and clothing are far from waterproof
and a good shower leaves them soaking. But after a few hours the sun
usually comes out and rapidly dries everybody. By the time the cold
weather comes the rainy season is long gone. The spring and summer
rains are usually welcomed with rejoicing and prayers of thanks. But the
!Kung have a special fear and a special name (*tia!hau*) for a late May
rain that leaves them shivering with damp and cold. The absence of a
word for snow in the !Kung vocabulary indicates that winter precipitation is felicitously rare.

Rainfall

The rainfall is concentrated in the hot summer months (October to May),
and from June to September the Dobe area is completely dry. The relationships between two major air masses determine the weather patterns
in the Kalahari. A subtropical high-pressure area centered over South-
eastern Africa covers the Kalahari for most of the year; this is seasonally
affected by the movement of a low-pressure area over tropical Africa to
the north. The ways the interactions of these two air masses produce rain
over the Kalahari are discussed by the geographer R. C. Brown in his
recent study, "Climate and Climatic Trends in the Ghanzi District":

> Both the tropical low pressure and the sub-tropical high shift with
> the overhead position of the sun during the year resulting in a sea-
> sonal system of winds and precipitation in the Ghanzi district. In
> winter the tropical low pressure moves northwards and the sub-
> tropical high shifts in the same direction but less far. The district is
> at this time characterised by high pressure, outflowing winds and
> virtually no rainfall. The sub-tropical high dominates the weather
> in the whole of southern Africa in both winter and summer, but in
> summer it weakens and allows the inflow of maritime air between
> the low and high pressure areas, bringing moisture into the Ghanzi
> district from the east and north-east.
>   It was formerly believed that rainfall maxima over all of tropical
> Africa (including Ghanzi) was associated with instability at the inter-
> tropical convergence zone, a well defined discontinuity separating
> north-east from south-west trades. However, Thompson states that

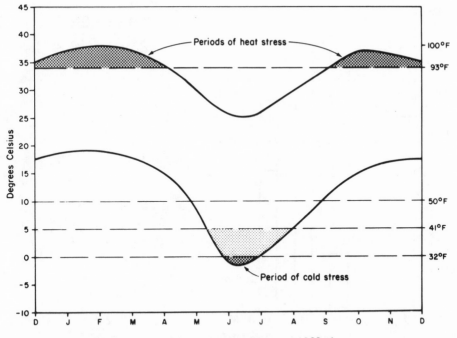

Figure 4.5. Minimum and maximum temperatures: 1963–4.

the zone does not at any time move south of the equator. Moist air is now believed to move into the Kalahari with synoptic disturbances associated with the deepening of the tropical low pressure and the weakening of the sub-tropical high as noted. This weakening is caused by strong surface heating in summer leading to increased instability. The heating has penetrated aloft and ousted the high pressure only after October in the Kalahari.

The moist air stream originates in the anti-cyclone lying to the south-east of the continent over the Indian Ocean, but usually enters the Kalahari from the northeast or north since its passage east is stopped by the Drakensberg. By the time this air reaches the Kalahari it has travelled such vast distances that it has lost most of its initial water content. This moist air stream is occasionally supplemented by a tongue of air from the north-west when the sub-tropical high pressure lies further north on the south-east African coast in December and January. However, the even longer track from the Indian Ocean means that this air stream only infrequently gives rise to rainfall. [Brown 1974:133–4]

Even slight changes in the year-to-year movement of these air masses can have a dramatic effect on the amount of rainfall the Dobe area receives. In such a climatic regimen averages say little. The most strik-

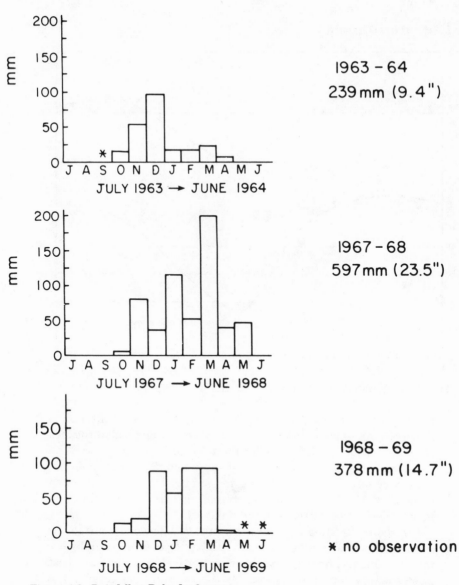

Figure 4.6. Rainfall at Dobe for 3 years.

ing fact is the enormous yearly variation in amount and distribution of rainfall. Figure 4.6 shows the rainfall at Dobe for two rainy seasons and most of a third. Rainfall varied from 239 mm in the drought of 1963–4 to 597 mm in the good year of 1967–8, a swing of 250 percent. Month-to-month and place-to-place variations further increase the uncertainty of precipitation.

In spite of this variability, the !Kung have come to recognize a pattern in the coming and going of the rains and have learned to read its signs. Several of their rainfall types are outlined below:

1. *//Gebi//gebi!go:* a strong, dry "male" east wind in September and October that brings clouds over the Dobe area, but no rain. *//Gebi// gebi* means "time of biting flies" (i.e., the wind that blows away the biting flies).

2. *//Gebi//gebidi:* the wind that brings the first sprinkles of rain that actually reach the ground, usually sometime in October. It is a "female" wind and has a cooling effect on the overheated land.

3. *!Xaima:* the first strong shower, usually in November. This might bring 8 to 12 mm of rain (0.3 to 0.5 in.) and is joyously welcomed. As soon as the rain stops, small groups move out to camp at the temporary water sources, grateful for the opportunity of a change of scenery and a change of company.

4. *Baran!nn!a* or *!gan!a:* a big summer shower. Anywhere from 3 to 10 of these occur from December to March, dropping from 12 to 40 mm of rain in a single storm. These are the main rains that fill the summer pans and facilitate the summer pattern of up-country land use. The start of such a shower is usually greeted with the prayer, *Na!gu ꞏn!e mi chi o!* ("Give me water to drink"), addressed to the sky and shouted into the teeth of the storm.

5. *N!aitebi:* a rare storm that goes on from morning till night or around the clock. These giant rainfalls of 40 to 60 mm (1.6 to 2.4 in.) soak through the fragile huts and clothing, leave standing pools of water in even the sandiest soil, and may make the rivers flow. The !Kung are ambivalent about such a storm. It leaves them personally damp and uncomfortable, and if it comes too late in the season it may rot and ruin the late summer bush foods.

6. *Tia!hau:* a very late shower after the cold has set in. It rots the food and generally leaves people cold and miserable.

The !Kung emphasis on the timing and duration of rainstorms underlines the point made by geographers (e.g., Wellington 1964:30–44) that timing and spacing of rain may be more important ecologically than the actual amount of the fall. Therefore, the rainfall totals, though useful, are not at all a perfect indicator of whether a year was hard or easy. A couple of centimeters of rain in March or April, for example, is not nearly as important to the growth of vegetation as the same amount falling in November when the plants need it most. But consider also the not unknown situation where a promising November or December rain is followed by drought in January. In that case, the vegetation triggered into growth cannot be sustained and withers. If the midsummer drought lasts as long as 5 weeks, not even the most abundant fall in February or March will regenerate the vegetations. As Wellington says: "From a [rancher's] point of view the spring rains, if sufficient to produce a good flush of grass and herbs, can be of great benefit to his stock, but if they

Table 4.7. *Drought frequencies at Maun, Botswana, over a
46-year period (lat. 20°00' S, long. 23°26' E)*

Condition	Number	Percent
Years of normal rainfall[a]	29	63
Years of drought[b]	17	37
1st degree (mild)	5	11
2nd degree (severe)	11	24
3rd degree (very severe)	1	2
Total	46	100

[a]Normal rainfall is annual rainfall more than 85% of mean.
[b]Definitions of drought severity adopted from Wellington (1964:40–
3): 1st degree, 70–84% of mean rainfall; 2nd degree, 55–69% of
mean rainfall; 3rd degree, less than 55% of mean rainfall.
Source: Lee and DeVore (1976:81).

are very light they do more harm than good, by stimulating vegetal
growth which cannot be maintained" (1964:32).

Drought probability

Having looked at the variations within years, let us examine area rainfall
in a longer-term perspective. As averages mean little, it is more useful to
discuss rainfall in terms of extremes: for example, by tabulating the number of years out of every 10 in which drought is experienced. The nearest
weather station for which long-term rainfall records are available is
Maun, 300 km east of Dobe. Figure 4.7 illustrates the fluctuations in rainfall at Maun over the last half-century. Table 4.7 summarizes these data.
Over 46 years, drought occurred in 17 years (37 percent), and in 12 of
these years (26 percent) drought was classified as severe (less than 70
percent of average rainfall occurred). In other words, the probability of
drought occurring at Maun is about 2 years in 5, and of severe drought 1
year in 4. I would argue that the situation at Dobe would be, if not more
acute, at least comparable to the situation at Maun (Lee 1972b) because
Dobe has had a lower average rainfall: 350 to 400 mm compared with 462
mm at Maun. Brown (1974:136) showed that drought occurred at Ghanzi
in 3.34 years out of every 10, and Wellington (1964:42–3), in a long-term
study of South-West African rainfall, found an incidence of drought in 30
out of 77 years (3.9 years in 10) in the northern part of the territory directly
adjacent to the Dobe area.

Local variability

Another source of variability is the difference in rainfall from place to
place in a single month or season. In a cluster of five stations within an
area 200 km across, annual totals may be comparable, but the fall in a

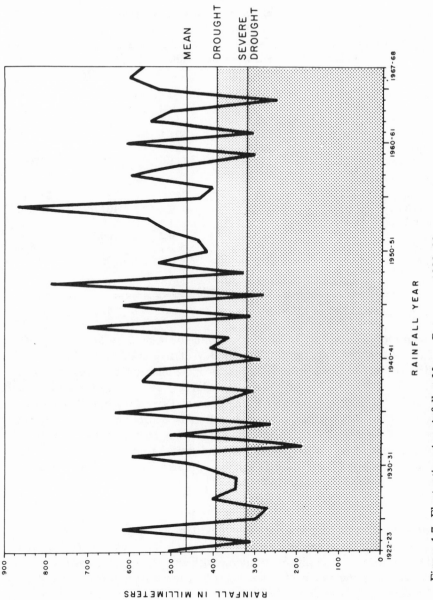

Figure 4.7. Fluctuations in rainfall at Maun, Botswana: 1922–68.

Table 4.8. *Local variations in rainfall (in millimeters) among five localities in the Ghanzi district: 1966–7*

Time	Kalkfontein	Scarborough	Ghanzi	Oakdene	Cume
1966					
July	0	0	0	0	0
August	0	0	6.3	0	0.5
September	0	12.0	41.2	14.5	25.7
October	16.0	10.5	24.1	0	24.5
November	3.5	34.0	35.2	43.2	29.0
December	73.5	116.0	111.6	90.5	75.4
1967					
January	127.0	167.6	242.0	183.0	223.2
February	81.0	136.0	139.2	161.5	131.3
March	38.0	35.5	14.5	6.3	50.0
April	25.0	89.5	6.2	55.4	86.3
May	18.5	13.5	9.1	21.0	6.5
June	0	0	0	0	0
Total	382.5	614.6	629.4	575.4	652.4

Source: Lee and DeVore (1976:82).

given month may vary from place to place by a factor of as much as 10.
Table 4.8 shows the rainfall for 1966–7 at five stations in the Ghanzi
district south of Dobe. In the early rains of October to December this local
variation is crucial because these rains largely determine the overall size
of the wild food harvest later in the season. For example, in November,
Kalkfontein received only 3.5 mm, whereas Scarborough 50 km away
received 34.0 mm. As a result, the desert may be blooming in one area
and a few hours' walk away, the land may be still parched. (Brown,
using the same Ghanzi data as are presented here, independently arrived
at the same conclusions; 1974:134.)

Too much rainfall?

After completing the analysis of drought probability and publishing it
(Lee 1972b), I was introduced to a climatic shift of a different order: too
much rainfall. I had assumed, along with the !Kung, that basically you
cannot have too much of a good thing. Then the anthropologist, Polly
Wiessner, reported from the Dobe area that the superrecord rains of
1973–4 were having some unusual effects. In particular she noted a
marked diminution of the mongongo nut crop owing to damage to the
trees at the flowering stage from mechanical action of the raindrops
(Wiessner 1977). The rains of 1973–4 were indeed phenomenal: 1183.9
mm (47 in.) were recorded at Maun, 258 percent of normal and about 37
percent higher than the previous record high of 870 mm set in 1954–5.

Closer examination of the effects on the Dobe area subsistence suggests that rain had knocked out the mongongo crop, though the fruit came back as usual the following year (1974–5) when 601.7 mm of rain fell at Maun (Wiessner 1977:27). However, although mongongo had been adversely affected by the heavy rains, other important species thrived on it. The tsin bean (*Bauhinia esculenta*) and the tsama melon (*Citrullus lanatus*), two major Dobe area species, yielded bumper harvests in 1974, more than offsetting the shortfall in the mongongo crop. Mathias Guenther, who visited Ghanzi in May 1974, reported seeing millions of tsama melons along the Lobatsi–Ghanzi road (personal communication).

Rainfall and long-term adaptation

The message of the foregoing discussion is clear. There is no such thing as a typical rainfall year for the !Kung. They must continuously adapt their subsistence strategy to high rainfall years, to low rainfall years, and to marked local variability. Theirs is a long-term adaptation to the problem of living; the ethnographer sees only a small segment of the overall pattern in a given year of fieldwork. There is a real danger of generalizing from too small a segment of the pattern. For example, I did not fully appreciate until years later the effects of the drought on what I had observed of !Kung subsistence strategy in 1963–4. And the effects of the very high rainfall of 1973–4 added yet another dimension to my understanding of !Kung adaptation. The corrective for the problem of generalizing from a short-term perspective is to assemble a longer run of data, by trying to observe behavior over a 5- or 10-year period. A further aid to understanding is the use of long-term climatic data such as the rainfall records over a 50- to 70-year period. In this way we can begin to close the gap between the time perspectives of the ethnographer on the one hand and the archeologist and historian on the other, as Emmanuel Le Roy Ladurie has done in his study of a millennium of climatic change in rural France based on long-term records of vineyard yields (Le Roy Ladurie 1960).

5

Technology and the organization of production

THIS chapter examines the general properties of the hunting and gathering, or *foraging*, mode of production and goes on to cover in detail the technology of production: the tools for gathering, hunting, obtaining water, and carrying with which the !Kung secure their livelihood. The purpose of analyzing the toolkit is to set out clearly the first of the three factors of production involved in the Marxist analysis of production. The second and third factors – labor and land – are described in Chapters 9 and 12, respectively.

How is it possible that the !Kung San of Dobe have remained to the present time as foragers in a world of nonforagers? Ecological factors such as lack of surface water, erratic rainfall, and soils too poor for agriculture are part of the explanation; economic and cultural factors also play a role. Whatever the cause, though many !Kung have tried experiments with agriculture and stock raising, few have amassed the necessary capital and experience to cross the threshold of farming and herding. In 1963–4 the proportion of subsistence derived from hunting and gathering at most camps varied between 80 and 95 percent, with only the !Goshe camps obtaining as much as 30 percent of their calories from domesticated sources. With the good rains of 1967–9, the proportion of domestic foods – milk and grain – rose somewhat, to 45 percent at !Goshe and 20 to 25 percent at the other camps, while at /Du/da, hunting and gathering provided 100 percent of the subsistence. As a result, the observer is able to see a spectrum of economic adaptations from full-time hunting and gathering to mixed foraging and herding, with the base of subsistence still firmly in the hunting and gathering sector. This preponderance enables us to study hunting and gathering, not simply as a technique of subsistence but as a full-fledged way of life, with its associated superstructure of kinship, ideology, and behavior.

THE FORAGING MODE OF PRODUCTION

The concept *mode of production* includes political as well as economic dimensions. The discussion to follow applies to hunting and gathering peoples organized as bands: the !Kung, Mbuti, and Hadza in Africa; the Indians of the Great Basin; the Dene and Cree of sub-Arctic Canada; the Inuit; the Australian aborigines; as well as other peoples of similar technology and organization. It does not apply to groups such as the Northwest Coast Indians, who, strictly speaking, lived by hunting and gathering (and fishing) but who were organized politically into chieftainships with highly developed systems of production and stratification. Meillassoux (1973) and Jordaan (1975) have adopted similar definitions in their useful attempts to define a foraging mode of production.

The foraging mode of production starts with a system of subsistence based on the hunting of wild game animals and the gathering of wild plant food as well as the procuring of fish and shellfish. But the mode of production (as distinguished from a mode of subsistence) includes not only the ways of making a living but also the ownership of the factors of production (land, labor, tools), the way people organize around production, and the way the products of labor are allocated. Technical aspects of foraging are considered later in this chapter. First, we look at the broader aspects of social and economic forms. Central to the foraging economy are a sexual division of labor; a simple technology; a collective, nonexclusive ownership of land and resources; and widespread food sharing within and among local groups according to the principle of *generalized reciprocity*. Each household can manufacture most of the tools and utensils needed for its survival.

What lends the foraging mode of production its distinctive character, compared with modes of production based on agriculture, is that in the former much of the reproduction of the means of subsistence is left to nature. Farmers and herders mold nature to make it reproduce the way they want it to; hunters live more or less with nature as a given. More than any other kind of society, foragers must fit their organization into the niches afforded by nature. This fact of the hunter-gatherers' life leads to several important features of their mode of production: (1) they must be mobile and cover a wide area in order to find sufficient food; (2) the environment sets upper limits on group size; (3) because of the annual and regional variability in resources, hunter-gatherer group structures must be flexible enough to adjust to the changing opportunities; (4) the need to move around sets limits on the amount of material wealth a family can possess; and (5) despite a variety of ideologies of landownership, all hunters have developed elaborate rules for reciprocal access to resources.

Unlike agricultural and pastoral economies, which depend on husbanding, or saving, resources produced in one season for consumption in another, the relation between production and consumption in the foraging economy is immediate. Among tropical foragers most food is distributed and consumed within the local group within 48 hours of its collection. Thus there is a rhythm of steady work and steady leisure throughout the year, with no single season of peak effort, such as the harvest season of farming peoples. Coupled with this rhythm of work is an *extensive* rather than *intensive* utilization of land: The food producers have to range widely in order to find food. Mobility is an important feature of this system of production; a hunter or gatherer has to cover about 2000 to 3500 km on foot each year in the food quest.

The division of labor by sex is virtually universal. Men hunt and gather; women primarily gather and very occasionally hunt; both sexes fish and gather shellfish. The actual productive process may be individual *or* cooperative. Men may hunt singly or in groups; women may gather alone or with others.

It is in the distribution and consumption of resources that the collectivist character of the foraging mode of production clearly emerges. Food is never consumed alone by a family; it is always (actually or potentially) shared out with members of a living group or band of up to 30 (or more) members. Even though only a fraction of the ablebodied foragers go out each day, the day's returns of meat and gathered foods are divided in such a way that every member of the camp receives an equitable share. The hunting band or camp is a unit of sharing, and if sharing breaks down it ceases to be a camp. This principle of generalized reciprocity within the camp has been reported for hunter-gatherers on every continent and in every kind of environment (Sahlins 1965).

The ownership of the means of production, land and tools, varies. The view of hunters as not owning land is inaccurate. In a few cases, such as the Hadza of Tanzania, any person may camp wherever he wants without restriction (Woodburn 1968a,b), but the more common situation is for the land to be divided into tracts or "countries" used primarily but not exclusively by a band or camp. At the core of each camp is an individual or group of individuals who is regarded as "owner." This core is usually a kin-based collective from whom one must seek permission to use the resources on a given tract. This kin group may be the members of a patrilineage, as in Australia (Peterson 1978), or a composite group of owners related through the male line, the female line, or a combination of both (Helm 1965; Damas 1969a–c). Both men and women may be members of the landowning collective.

Whether the "owners" are patrilineally related males or bilaterally related, their ownership is far from exclusive. Regardless of the ideology of land rights, all hunter-gatherer groups regularly permit visits from other groups and make reciprocal visits to other groups. My impression is that many hunter-gatherers spend the greater part of their lives outside their home "country" than within it.

A second inaccuracy is the view of hunters as having no private property. Land and its resources are collectively owned and utilized, but tools and other belongings are the property of the owner. Nonperishable goods are dealt with differently from foods. Meat may be distributed throughout the camp, but the bow and arrow that killed the animal belongs to the hunter. Material goods are important items of trade, and dyadic trade networks are a key means of cementing social relations; but the "worker" owns the means of production.

Two of the key diagnostic features of the Marxist analysis of modes of production based on the state and classes are the mode of appropriation of the surplus product and the degree of exploitation of labor (Hindess and Hirst 1975:27, 67). How do foraging societies compare in this regard? Despite the absence of classes, some foraging peoples, particularly in Australia, show some degree of male dominance and of control of younger men and women by elder males. How widespread these practices are and whether they constitute "exploitation" in the sense of appropriating a disproportionate share of the labor of others are questions for continuing investigation. For the moment we can say that the existence of privilege, status differences, and hierarchy appears to be far less developed in foraging societies as a group than in any other kind of human society. These general comments serve as a necessary background to the discussions in this and later chapters.

!KUNG TECHNOLOGY

Technology is a basic element of any mode of production. The !Kung foraging system has generated a simple but effective toolkit for carrying out the tasks of subsistence. The central features of the economy – sharing, self-sufficiency, and mobility – impose certain design criteria on the tools themselves. !Kung tools are few in number, lightweight, made from locally available materials, and multipurpose. Yet one should not exaggerate the element of simplicity in !Kung tools. Some, like the nut-cracking stones, are little more than unimproved calcrete cobbles picked up at random; others, such as the hunting bow, exhibit complexity of design and require considerable skill to manufacture.

The following sections describe the basic subsistence technology in four categories: (1) tools for obtaining water, (2) gathering and carrying tools, (3) hunting tools, and (4) food-processing tools. In each section, I discuss the tools themselves, the materials and techniques of manufacture, and the behavior that accompanies their use. Informative discussions along similar lines are found in Marshall (1976:98–103, 144–55) for the Nyae Nyae !Kung and in Steyn (1971:275–322) for the Nharo San of the Ghanzi district.

TOOLS FOR OBTAINING WATER

Scarcity of water is a primary ecological constraint on the life of the !Kung San. The people organize their lives around the permanent and temporary water sources of their n!ores, and the trip to the water source to fill the household's water containers is an event that takes place every day of the year. The !Kung have a hierarchy of water sources at their disposal (see also Chapter 12). First are the 10 permanent water holes that hold water throughout the year and that rarely, if ever, fail. Next are the semipermanent water holes that hold water through most years but may dry up in drought years. Third in importance are the large and small summer water holes or pans that can be expected to hold water for a few weeks to a few months during the rainy season (December to March). In years of high rainfall the larger pans may hold water through the winter and into the next rainy season. These three sources I have called *standing water*. Next in importance is tree water, which collects in the hollow holes of mongongo and other trees during the rainy season. The amounts provided are minuscule: A single tree may yield from 1 to 20 liters per season, compared with hundreds of liters for even a small summer pan such as !Kwidum. Yet these trees are strategically placed in food-rich sandy soils where standing water is unavailable, and therefore their small quantities are eagerly sought. At the bottom of the hierarchy of water sources are the water-bearing roots of such plants as *Fockea monroi, Raphionacme burkei, Raphionacme hirsuta,* and *Ipomoea verbascoidea.* These roots are dug during the dry season and enable groups to camp for short periods in areas that completely lack standing water. This is the least desirable of the water sources because of the added work involved in searching daily for the roots and in digging them out of the hard molapo soils. The Dobe and /Du/da !Kung try to arrange their annual subsistence rounds so that all but a few weeks of the year are spent camped in the vicinity of standing water.

Drawing water is mainly the work of women. Typically, the trip to the water hole takes place in late afternoon and is a pleasant occasion for washing up and conversation involving several women and their children. Permanent water holes are usually clefts in the rock with a small pool of water at the bottom. The women have to clamber down and often squeeze themselves into a tight spot to fill their containers. A younger woman or an adolescent girl places herself at the water's edge, the containers are handed down to her, filled, and then passed back up. Extra

Plate 5.1. Filling ostrich eggshells with water (!Kwidum pan, 1968).

amounts are drunk on the spot or used for washing up, and then everything is refilled for the trip back to camp.

Summer waters collect in flat depressions a few meters across in the molapos. A shallow pit in the center is often hollowed out to collect the remaining water and reduce evaporation as the pan dries out. The women squat in the tall grass at the edge of the water surface and fill their containers by pouring from a tortoise shell bowl or, in recent years, from tin-enameled cups obtained in trade. When water is plentiful in midsummer, both women and men troop down to the pan to bathe and frolic.

The *ostrich eggshell canteen* remains the most widely used water container among the nomadic !Kung. Each shell, when emptied, holds slightly over 1 liter of water (the average volume of six shells was 1.11 liters, or 37.4 oz). The eggshells are an attractive white color and are reasonably durable; if handled with care, an eggshell can be used for several years. The eggs are found in clutches of 10 to 15 in the shallow depression that the ostrich digs in the open sand to serve as a nest. When a clutch is found, each egg is pounded gently but firmly in the sand to jar the amnion and kill the embryo inside. Back in the camp a small hole is drilled at one end and the contents emptied, cooked, and eaten. Each ostrich egg contains the equivalent of two dozen hens' eggs. The taste is very different, however–much stronger and more gamey than a hen's egg. I did not like the taste of an ostrich egg omelette, though the !Kung consider it a delicacy. The empty shell is rinsed with water and deodorized with aromatic herbs; with the addition of a grass stopper, it is ready for use as a canteen. Although leak-proof, the shell of the ostrich egg "breathes" slightly, and through the evaporation of small quantities it keeps the water deliciously cool, a property not found in metal or glass containers. The eggshells are only occasionally decorated with incised designs; when done, this is for the purpose of beauty rather than identification. Each married woman owns a stock of 5 to 10 eggshell water containers, though not all these are filled on a given trip to the water hole.

The main disadvantages of the ostrich eggshell, apart from its fragility, are its weight and bulk. An empty eggshell weighs 225 to 275 g (8 to 10 oz) and occupies a space equivalent to a large cantaloupe. Carrying five or more eggshells in a kaross limits the amount of food or other goods that can be carried on a long trip. One solution to the problem is the use of *antelope stomach sacs* as water containers. Empty and shriveled, a stomach sac is almost weightless and occupies very little space, but each can be filled with up to 4 liters of water–the equivalent of four eggshells. The sacs are carried in pairs by a man on a carrying yoke. The sac too has a disadvantage: It is very fragile and easily ripped if it comes into contact with a stray branch on the trail. For this reason, it is not nearly as popular as the ostrich eggshell.

Large *pods of the baobab tree* are sometimes made into water containers. These are smaller in volume (700 to 950 ml) than the ostrich eggshell, more fragile, and tend to rot through in time. *Empty whisky bottles* obtained in trade are also in use.

Another special tool used in obtaining water is the *dipping sponge,* a bound bundle of grass that is lowered into the hollow of a tree to retrieve water. The bundle is lifted and the water squeezed into a cup or other container. Frequently, the !Kung use a handy *hollow grass stem* or reed to suck water out of a hollow tree. Unlike the southern San, they do not make sip wells in the sand.

Water storage for more than a day is not practiced in the Dobe area. This is in marked contrast to the southern /Gwi San, who have been known to bury several hundred ostrich eggshells of water at a single locality in the rainy season for later use in the dry season (Alec Campbell, personal communication).

GATHERING AND CARRYING TOOLS

There is a basic division of labor between the sexes: The men are hunters of game and the women gatherers of plant foods. The men, however, do combine gathering with hunting. For instance, if no game has been killed on a hunt, the men gather some vegetable food as they return at the end of the day so that they will not come home empty-handed. The organization of work is simple. The sexes are almost always segregated in food-getting activities. Typically, the women of a camp go out in groups of three to five, with a well-defined objective of collecting certain plant species. They spend the day or part of it working over an area and return to the camp each evening with their food. They never remain out overnight.

Only a single tool, the digging stick, is used in gathering. Carrying, on the other hand, involves the use of several ingenious multipurpose containers and an elaborate body of knowledge. The study of carrying technology and its evolutionary implications deserves more attention by scholars than it has received.

Gathering tools

The digging stick is 100 to 140 cm (3.5 to 4.5 ft) long and about 20 mm (0.75 in.) in diameter. It is cut from the smooth, straight stalk of *Grewia flava* or *Dichrostachys cinerea,* peeled, and smoothed; the end is sharpened to a wedge-shaped point. The shaft is not weighted with a bored stone (Figure 5.1a). When a root is dug out, the digging stick is used in one hand with a sharp downward motion to loosen the sand, which is scooped out of the hole with the other hand. Depending on the size and depth of the root and the hardness of the soil, up to 20 minutes can be required to dig out a root (see Chapter 6).

This versatile tool is also used in hunting to dig out burrowing mammals, in water getting to dig out water-containing roots, and as a carrying device to transport large roots impaled on it or suspended from it with twine.

For the remaining part of the vegetable diet (fruits, nuts, gums, melons, and leafy greens), and this includes about 75 percent of the vegetable calories, no special gathering tools are used.

Carrying devices

The kaross. Foremost among the carrying devices is the woman's kaross (*chi !kan*), a formidable one-piece combination garment-cum-carrying device that also does service as a sleeping blanket (Figure 5.1b). The men manufacture these for the women from the hide of female kudu, gemsbok, wildebeest, or eland. After an animal is killed, the fresh raw hide is pegged out and sun-dried. When dry, the edges are trimmed and the hide carefully scraped both inside and outside with a metal adze. (The inside shavings are edible.) Then the hide is thoroughly soaked and softened with a tanning agent from the plant, *Elephantorrhiza elephantina*. The dried and softened hide is vigorously rubbed between the hands to make the leather permanently supple. Then it is turned over to the women, who dye the hide to a rich red brown using the powdered bark of the tree, *Pterocarpus angolensis*. The resulting garment, which now has the color and texture of suede, is worn draped over the wearer's back. When tied at the waist with a leather thong, the lower half of the kaross conceals the wearer's backside, and the upper half forms a pouch for carrying vegetables, water containers, firewood, and babies. The kaross is ideal for carrying heavy loads; the center of gravity is close to the body and the weight can be distributed in an arc around the carrier's waist (see Chapter 7 for a description of the kaross as used in gathering mongongo nuts). In !Kung thought, the kaross is so characteristic of women and their work that the knot (*!kebi*) that ties the kaross at a woman's waist is also an affectionate colloquial term for "women" (*!kebisi*). For example, if you hear the sound of voices in the bush heading toward the camp and you ask, "Who's that?" the response will often be, "It's the !kebisi" (literally, the "knots").

A man does not wear a kaross; a few old men wear cloaks of leather, but they do not use these for carrying.

Leather bags. A variety of sturdy leather bags are used by both men and women. These bags are made by the men from the supple skins of the steenbok and duiker. Both men and women wear small "handbags" over the shoulder and under the armpit for keeping handy tobacco, fire-making kit, sewing materials, and other items. The women's bags are brightly decorated with beadwork (Figure 5.1c,d).

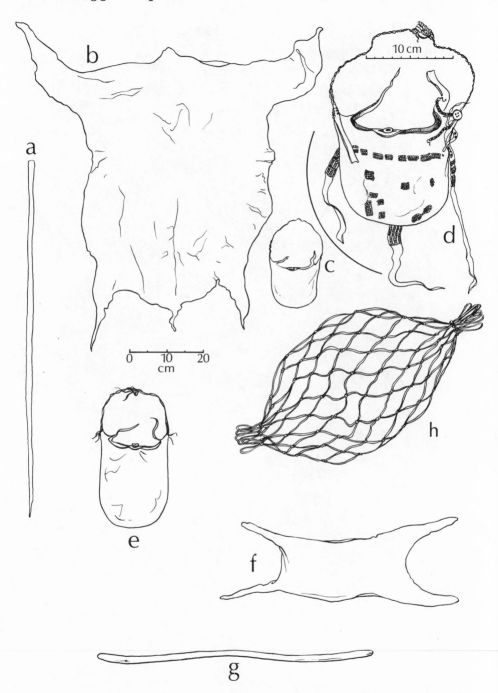

Figure 5.1. Gathering and carrying equipment: (a) digging stick; (b) kaross; (c) small bag; (d) same, detailed; (e) man's bag; (f) baby carrier; (g) carrying yoke; (h) man's net.

Plate 5.2. Women carrying loads.

For carrying foodstuffs and larger items, large bags called /tausi are used, ranging from 3 to 10 liters in capacity–up to the size of a grocery shopping bag (Figure 5.1e). The /tausi can be rolled up into a tight ball and stowed in the smaller bag until ready for use. It consists of two parts, right and left, cut from the same pattern and sewed together around the edges with sinew and a bone or metal needle. A strong shoulder strap of twisted sinew is attached at the top corners, and the bag is ready for use.

For carrying a young infant, a mother employs a special leather baby carrier tied around her waist and over her shoulders that fits inside the kaross on her hip and allows the baby access to the breast (Figure 5.1f). This special baby carrier is lined with soft grasses and other absorbent materials and is frequently cleaned and aired. When an older, toilet-trained child is carried, he sits directly in the main pouch of the kaross or is carried on the shoulder by a woman or man.

Carrying net. Men make an ingeniously intricate knotted net, called /wisi-, for use as a carrying device (Figure 5.1h). The sinews of gemsbok or kudu are made into twine by rolling on the thigh. These lengths of twine are then knotted together in a geometric hammock-shaped pattern that, when extended to its full size, forms a net 100 cm long and 40 cm across. This wide-meshed net can be lined with long grass and used to carry quantities of such small items as nuts and berries. The net is slung from the shoulders by means of looped straps attached to either end. Though of smaller capacity than the women's kaross and harder to pack, the men's net has two advantages: It is compact when empty, and when loaded it is carried in such a way that it can be easily slung off if game is sighted. (For a discussion of the nets and bags in use, see Chapter 7.)

Carrying yoke. The carrying yoke (!garo) is easily made from a rough wooden branch (Figure 5.1g). The branch is selected for balance, and then an area is smoothed on the underside for placing on the shoulder. Full bags, nets, bundles of meat, and haunches of freshly killed game are slung from either end, and the load is shouldered by a man for the long trips between camps. Sometimes a digging stick placed on the other shoulder is levered under the back part of the carrying yoke to relieve some of the strain on the main shoulder. In the old days, bagsful of balled tobacco were carried this way by parties of men from Tsau to /Xai/xai, a distance of 160 km (see Chapter 3).

Importance of carrying devices. Because the essence of the !Kung adaptation is mobility, and because their daily diet consists mostly of hundreds of small nuts, berries, and roots, San life would not be possible without some means of carrying quantities of these small foods back to the camp or home base. We have seen that !Kung carrying technology is

Table 5.1. *Carrying vocabulary* (see Figure 5.2 for illustrations)

To carry on the back		*To carry otherwise*	
1. A child	maa	11. On the head	ku≠tem
2. A load (males)	//xam	12. On the belt	!uu
3. A load (females)	//kei	13. To drag (not shown)	!gwe_
4. A kaross package	!guu	14. To carry firewood in a kaross	!gaba
To carry on the shoulders		*To carry with a carrying yoke*	
5. A child	chi	15. To stick a load through (not shown)	/di
6. An object	!kai	16. to hang a load from	//gau
7. A bag or quiver	!wana	17. To impale a root and carry	n!n//xam
8. A carrying yoke	//wana		
9. A kaross	//gama	18. To carry with two carrying yokes	du tsiu !garo
10. A spear	!kei//kun		

well developed and designed. A similar degree of development is noted in the vocabulary, which has a multitude of terms for different ways of carrying. A partial list is shown in Table 5.1 and illustrated in Figure 5.2. One cannot overstate the importance of carrying and carrying devices for San life and for the life of hunting and gathering peoples in general. The !Kung carry mainly with containers of leather and sinew. The foragers of North and South America and Southeast Asia developed basketry to a high degree, and the Australian aborigines had their ubiquitous bark or wooden tray, the *pithi*. The universality of the carrying device and its functional importance among all recent hunter-gatherers has implications for the evolution of human subsistence during the Pleistocene because a device for carrying vegetable foods would seem to be a prerequisite for human economic and social life. This point is developed further in Appendix E, an essay on the role of the carrying device in the origins of human economy.

HUNTING TOOLS

Hunting technology and organization represent a highly developed sector of the !Kung economy. The techniques of hunting and the inventory of prey species are discussed in Chapter 8. This section describes the hunter's toolkit. Six major weapons and several subsidiary hunting tools constitute the !Kung hunter's traditional arsenal. Eight different kinds of raw materials are used in the manufacture and repair of the hunter's kit. The six major weapons are (1) the bow and arrow complex consisting of the bow, iron-tipped arrows, arrow poison, the arrow poison kit, and a bark quiver; (2) the iron-tipped spear; (3) the springhare probe; (4) the club; (5) rope snares; and (6) hunting dogs. Subsidiary hunting tools include the adze/ax, the iron knife, fire and fire-making equipment, the digging stick, and oracle disks. Tools used for carrying meat back to camp include the carrying yoke and the knotted net.

The basic raw materials used in making the hunting tools and carried by the men in their repair kits include sinew for bowstrings and binding, twine of vegetable fibers (for snares), iron fencing wire (for arrowheads), poisonous grubs for arrow poison, bone chips for arrow link shafts, grass stems for arrows, whetstones of basalt, and wild cotton for polishing rope snares.

Guns and steel traps are not of great importance in the Dobe area. Only one !Kung man (the tribal constable) owns a rifle, which he fires only a few times a year. A few men own steel traps, but rarely use them. The traditional bow and spear hunting kit, albeit improved with the addition of iron tips, continued to provide almost all the hunted meat during the 1960s. Nontraditional hunting methods are discussed in Chapter 14.

The bow and arrow complex

The bow. The hunting bow is made from a carefully chosen flexible shaft of the bush *Grewia flava* or *Grewia bicolor*. The shaft is carved and smoothed with an iron knife and then repeatedly heated in hot sand and gently bent using the hands and knee to induce a gentle curvature. If the bow shows the slightest flaw or crack during the bending process, it is discarded. The bow is tightly bound with thongs at both ends to support the bowstring. The bowstring itself is twined from long strips of sinew from the back muscles of gemsbok or other antelope. Sitting on the ground, the hunter holds two or more of the 10- to 15-cm strands of wet sinew in his left hand and with the heel of his right hand rolls the strands skilfully into twine against the upper outer surface of his right thigh. (The same technique is used for making twine from vegetable fibers.) New strands are added to the string and intertwined with the old until a uniformly thick bowstring about 80 cm long is built up and finished with a loop at one end. While still wet, the bowstring is attached to the bow with a special knot at one end, and the preformed loop is pulled over and seated above the thong at the other end. As it dries, the bowstring shrinks under pressure to the point where the assembly becomes a working hunting bow with about a 9-kg pull. The completed bow is ritually strengthened by being rubbed with the blood of a freshly killed antelope. It is also usually decorated near the ends with brass bands cut from a casing of an empty rifle cartridge. With proper maintenance, the hunting bow has a useful lifetime of many years.

The arrow. The hunting arrow has a main shaft about 35 to 40 cm in length made from the stem of the perennial grass, *Phragmites australis*

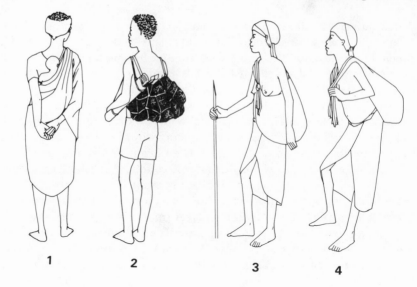

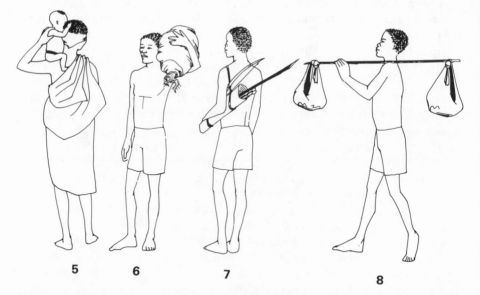

Figure 5.2. !Kung carrying positions (see Table 5.1 for explanation).

9

10

11

12

14

17

18

16

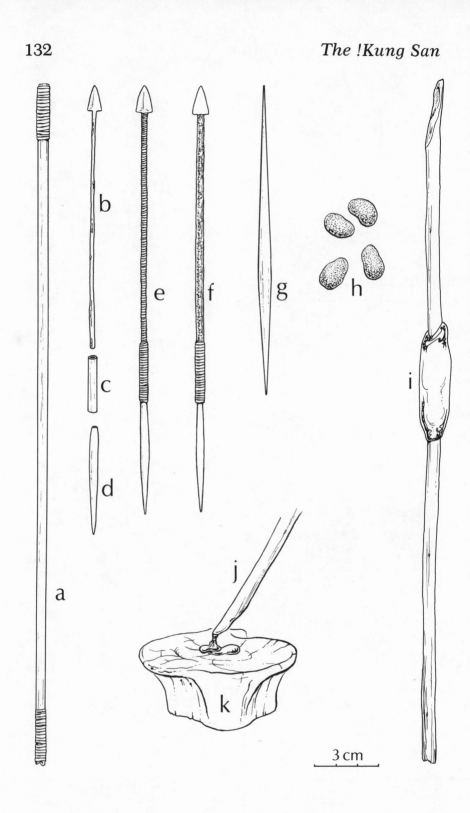

(Story 1964:94) (Figure 5.3a). Into the end is inserted a bone link shaft (d) about 5 cm long carved from the humerus or femur of giraffe, kudu, or gemsbok. The link shaft is joined to the metal arrowhead (b) by a joint (c), a hollow section of grass stem 2 cm long. Until 90 years ago, the arrowhead and link shaft were a single unit carved of bone. Several of these can still be seen in use, unpoisoned, for hunting birds (g). Today the link shaft is still made of bone, but the arrowhead is hammered from iron fencing wire.

When European ranchers in Ghanzi and Gobabis first began fencing their paddocks around the turn of the century, the !Kung and other San soon learned that a short length of fencing wire could be hammered into a very effective arrowhead with better penetrating power than the old bone points. Cut fences came to be a chronic problem for the ranchers, as the San would saw off sections of wire with stones in order to make arrowheads. A happy solution was achieved when the fence builders hit on the idea of leaving an extra length of wire on the ground at the beginning and end of every roll. For the cost of a few meters of wire, the fence builders saved their fences and provided the San with the makings of a several-lifetime supply of arrowheads! Today, the hunters of the Dobe area get all the wire they need from the cuttings around the cattle enclosures erected by the veterinary department for inoculating Herero cattle. Fencing wire has become almost a free natural resource of the Dobe area, and surplus wire is made into attractive anklets and bracelets for the women.

To make an arrowhead, 8 to 10 cm of stiff wire is heated and straightened, and the tip is beaten into a small, flat triangular blade 12 mm (0.5 in.) from base to apex and 7 mm (0.25 in.) at the base. The tangs of the arrowhead and the link shaft are coated with resin and inserted in the joint, which is then tightly bound with sinew to make a permanent assembly (Figure 5.3e,f). The whole composite arrowhead is then inserted in the top of the main shaft and the entire arrow checked and rechecked for balance, strength, and straightness. If the arrow is correctly assembled, the composite arrowhead will remain securely in a wounded animal, and only the main shaft will work itself out of the wound and fall to the ground. The link shaft principle is designed so that an animal cannot work an arrow out of a wound by rubbing it against a tree.

Arrow poison. Compared with the long bows and sturdy wooden arrows of other hunting peoples, the !Kung bow and arrow seem almost like toys. With a 9-kg pull and a tiny 15-g arrow made of a grass stem, the !Kung

Figure 5.3. Arrow points and poisoning: (a) arrow main shaft; (b) metal arrowhead; (c) joint; (d) bone link shaft; (e) complete arrowhead, unpoisoned; (f) same, poisoned; (g) bone arrowhead; (h) poison grubs; (i) gum; (j) poison applicator; (k) poison mixing cup.

bow has knockdown power for only the smallest antelope–steenbok and
duiker–and other like-sized game. What gives the !Kung bow and arrow
its formidable killing power is the arrow poison, a potent toxin obtained
from the pupal forms of three chrysomelid beetles, identified by the entomologist, the late Dr. Charles Koch, as (1) *Diamphidia nigro-ornata* Stal,
parasitized by *Lebistina subcruciata* Fairmarie; (2) *Diamphidia vittatipennis* Baly, parasitized by *Lebistina holubi* Peringuey; and (3) *Polyclada flexuosa* Baly, parasitized by *Lebistina peringueyi* Liebke (Koch
1958; Marshall 1976: 147–8).

The first two species are the most common, and the !Kung consider
their poison the most powerful. The !Kung call the beetles *!hwah,* which
is also the generic term for poison. The diamphids feed exclusively on the
leaves of *Commiphora pyracanthoides* and *Commiphora* sp.; the third
species, *gai,* feeds on the leaves of the marula nut tree, *Sclerocarya
caffra* (Story 1964:93). Each December, the larvae of the diamphids
emerge on the *Commiphora* bushes to feed. Soon they fall to the ground
and burrow into the earth, where they secrete a sticky substance that,
mixed with earth, becomes a hard protective coating for the pupal stage.
Later in the summer the !Kung men come to the base of these bushes
and excavate to a depth of 60 cm to retrieve 30 or more pupae from a
single bush. The living pupae are carried in the hunting kit, wrapped in a
piece of cloth or leather, and are used as needed. The poison remains
potent for many months after the pupa is dug up. To prepare the poison,
a few grubs (Figure 5.3h) are taken out and each one rolled between the
fingers to soften the insides. The viscous orange contents of several pupae are squeezed out of their casings into a special cup (k) made from the
proximal end of the humerus of a large antelope such as gemsbok or
kudu. The gum (i) of several species of *Acacia* may be mixed with saliva
and spat on the poison in the cup to improve its sticking properties.

The pupae are mixed with a slender wooden pestle (j) into a thin
orange paste, which is then applied directly to the iron arrow shaft. The
iron shaft is sometimes first tightly wrapped with sinew so that the poison will adhere more effectively. Occasionally an arrow is touched up by
applying dabs of poison directly from the grub to the arrow. Great care is
taken when handling the poison to see that there are no cuts or nicks on
the fingers; nor is the poison allowed to touch any part of the sharpened
blade. Even a small quantity of fresh poison in the bloodstream is enough
to kill or seriously injure a person. After the arrowhead is coated with
poison, the arrow is inserted butt end down in the sand to dry near the
fire. After a few minutes, it is ready for use. The potency of the poisoned
arrow, initially very high, declines rapidly, so that after a month it is said
to be at half-strength and after a year it is apparently completely harmless. As a consequence, men are in the habit of touching up a few arrows
with added fresh poison the day before a hunt, and periodically arrows

are completely scraped of old poison and a new dose applied. Tipped with full-strength poison, a well-placed arrow can kill a 200-kg antelope in 6 to 24 hours. (For a discussion of various aspects of San arrow poison, see Koch 1958; Shaw 1963; Story 1964:93; Marshall 1976:146–52.)

The quiver. The finished arrows, along with a supply of blanks and a pair of fire drills, are carried in the quiver (*!kuru*), an ingeniously manufactured sleeve of heavy bark capped by a cover of hide at either end. The quiver symbolizes the male role in economic life in the same way that the *!kebi* of the kaross symbolizes the female role.

The quiver is made from the smooth, thick bark of the stiff roots of *Acacia hebeclada* or *Acacia tortilis*. The hunter looks for a tree with a section of root that is perfectly smooth, straight, and at least 60 cm in length and 7 to 13 cm in diameter. With the metal ax, the root is chopped free from the tree at both the upper and lower ends and the section is brought back to camp. The bark is heated and pounded so it can slide off the wood as a hollow cylinder. The circumference is then reinforced with leather rings cut from the leg hide of a large antelope. These rings are slipped over the top of the sleeve and spaced along the length of the quiver to give added strength against splitting. The bottom end is finished with a cup of leather formed from the hide of the kneecap or the scrotal sac of an antelope. A removable cup of leather attached to the quiver with a thong forms the cap, and the quiver is completed with the addition of a leather shoulder strap.

The complete hunting kit consisting of bow, quiver, and spear, is carried over the left shoulder in a standardized bundle. The spear tip is wedged into the bottom cap of the quiver, and the bow is intertwined with the quiver's shoulder strap. The whole assembly weighs only a few kilograms and it accompanies a !Kung man wherever he goes. Not only on hunting trips but also on visits to other camps, gathering trips, and group moves, the !Kung hunter has to be prepared to hunt on a moment's notice if game is sighted. The contents of a man's quiver include 10 to 15 finished arrows, some made by himself and others traded with his hxaro partners, and a number of blank unfinished main shafts. Perhaps four or five of a man's arrows are fully poisoned and ready to shoot on a given day; an equal number of additional arrows could be made operational with another hour's work. Spare arrowheads and link shafts are often carried in a smaller container made from the tip of the horn of a gemsbok. So the quiver set is a portable workshop as well as a hunting weapon. Only a few of the older men, especially in the South, use a quiver bag, a popular item among the Nharo and the Nyae Nyae !Kung. This bag contains the quiver, bow, spear, arrowhead container, and poison kit. Most of the Dobe area hunters, however, carry the first three items in an open bundle as described above and the last two items in the small

Plate 5.3. Man carrying load.

shoulder bag along with the flint-and-steel fire-making kit and raw sinews for repair.

The iron-tipped spear

The !Kung spear blade and several other important weapons and tools such as the knife, adze/ax, springhare hook, and cooking pots are made from iron, a material not found in the San toolkit before their contact with agricultural societies. These items of ironware are now an integral part of the !Kung material culture and have been since the turn of the century, (Figure 5.4). In the Dobe and Nyae Nyae areas they have completely supplanted earlier piercing, cutting, and chopping tools of bone, stone, and wood. The interior !Kung were introduced to iron over a century ago when they established trading relations with Bayei and Mbukushu iron-working agriculturalists, who migrated south from the upper Zambezi and upper Okavango rivers to the west side of the Okavango swamps. Both the !Kung spear blade and !Kung iron knife show clear stylistic affinities to their Mbukushu counterparts. Originally, the !Kung must have imported the finished product, but they quickly learned to haft the Mbukushu blades to locally made wooden shafts and handles when the originals wore out. Nowadays the !Kung have developed their own iron-working skills to the point where they can fashion spear, knife, and ax blades from blanks, as well as making the wooden parts. Iron smelting, however, is still not in their repertoire. Iron for arrowheads was probably first obtained from the Bantu, but as noted above European fencing wire has long supplied the bulk of the !Kung's needs. In Chapter 9, I try to assess the impact of iron and other new tools on the efficiency of the hunting and gathering mode of subsistence.

Iron-working skill is generally distributed throughout the !Kung population, although a few men are acknowledged to be better at it than others. To make a spear or other blade, the !Kung artisan requires an iron blank and simple metal hammering and filing tools. All these are obtained in trade from the Bantu or scavenged from junkyards by !Kung trading partners living in European areas. The rest of the equipment is available locally.

The !Kung spear consists of a pointed wooden shaft about 2 cm in diameter and 90 cm long and an iron blade about 30 cm long fashioned from a solid rod of iron 10 to 15 mm in diameter (Figure 5.4a). For iron working, no bellows are used, so a windy day is preferred to provide maximum heat. A large fire of logs of a hard wood such as *Combretum imberbe* is allowed to burn down to a heap of glowing coals. One end of the iron rod is wrapped with grass or cloth to provide a handle; the other end is plunged deep into the coals and left there until it is red hot. The glowing rod is removed from the coals and pounded on an anvil stone with a heavy metal object, such as the blunt end of a European axhead

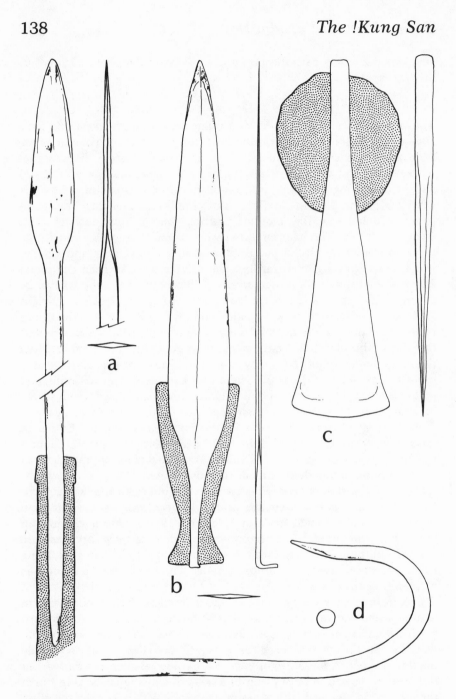

Figure 5.4. Iron working (one-third actual size): (a) spear point (front, side, and cross-sectional views); (b) knife blade (front, side, and cross-sectional views); (c) adze blade (front and side views); (d) springhare probe tip (side and cross-sectional views).

or a broken automotive spring blade, until the rod cools and has to be plunged back into the coals. Through repeated heating and pounding, the rod end is gradually flattened and shaped into a spear blade. Further shaping and refining is done with a European rasp or file, one of which is usually found in most camps. The cutting edge is honed to sharpness with a whetstone of local basalt. A similar process is used to manufacture adze/ax blades (Figure 5.4c), knife blades (b), and the springhare hook (d).

The spear shaft is made from the wood of *Acacia* spp. and is easily carved in a few hours using an adze for the rough work and a knife for the finishing touches. Making the spear blade, by contrast, may take 2 days of hard work. Properly maintained, a spear blade may last for 10 years and will outlive many shafts.

The spear is not used as a weapon of attack, but is employed to finish off an animal that has been weakened by poisoned arrows or wounded by the hunting dogs. If a wounded animal is active, the hunters hurl the spear aiming for its heart or throat. But if possible they try to minimize this, because many body wounds spoil the hide for use as a kaross. The throat is the preferred site for delivering the coup de grace. Apart from hunting, the spear blade is also used as a heavy-duty woodworking tool to smooth a wooden shaft after the adze/ax has done the rough work.

Other major hunting weapons

The springhare probe. The springhare probe (Figure 5.5a) is an unusual weapon for the !Kung in that it is a special-purpose tool for killing a single species: the springhare, *Pedetes capensis.* The probe consists of an iron hook attached to a 4-meter-long shaft made up of several lengths of light flexible wood lashed together with sinew and gum mastic. The wooden sections, cut from the stalks of *Grewia* spp., are carefully straightened and smoothed and tapered to fit together at the ends in tongue-and-groove fashion. The gum mastic is a sticky black pitch that exudes from the root of *Ammocharis tinneana* when sections of it are heated in the fire. The sinew lashing is applied while the gum mastic is still soft; it reinforces the pitch and causes it to harden under pressure. The resulting bond can withstand twisting and pulling up to the full strength of a man.

The springhare is a nocturnal animal that sleeps in a long narrow burrow during the daytime. The hunter probes a likely burrow to a depth of 3.5 meters; if he feels the animal within, he hooks it with a sharp upward motion. The top end of the probe is then secured at the mouth of the burrow and the hunter excavates to the section of the burrow where the animal is trapped; he retrieves the animal struggling on the hook and kills it with a blow from his digging stick.

The springhare probe, over twice the height of a man, is an unwieldy weapon to drag through the bush. But with it the hunter has a high

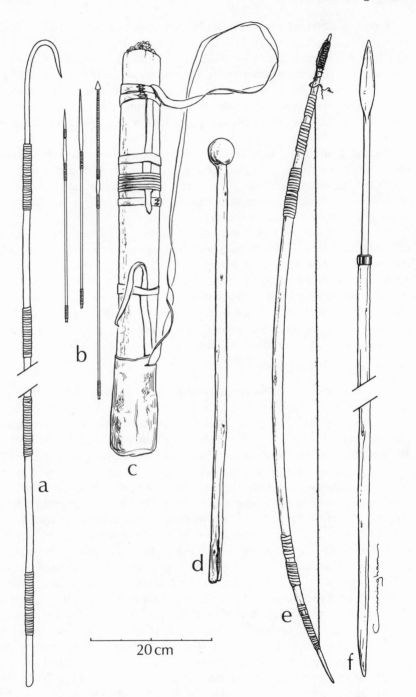

Figure 5.5. The main hunting weapons: (a) springhare probe; (b) arrows; (c) quiver; (d) club; (e) bow; (f) spear.

success rate, finding an animal and killing it on perhaps 50 percent of the days he goes hunting for one, compared with a success rate of 20 to 25 percent for other species. The returns, however, are modest. The springhare weighs 2.5 to 3.5 kg (5 to 8 lb) and yields only about 1.5 to 2.0 kg of meat per kill. Yet the appeal of a fairly reliable kill close to home is sufficient to make hunting with the springhare probe one of the most popular techniques.

The club. The wooden club or knobkerrie (Figure 5.5d) is carried like a swagger stick under the arm, or a longer one may be used as a walking stick. It is 50 to 100 cm long, carved from a single branch of hard wood such as *Peltophorum africanum* with a small bulb at one end. The wood is chosen so that the bulb is formed from a natural knot. Most men carry clubs wherever they go, even if their quiver sets are not with them. Although the clubs are not engraved, great care is lavished on sanding and polishing them to an ultrasmooth finish that is admired by other men. The club is used to finish off wounded or cornered animals. It is also used as a throwing weapon to knock down birds or such small mammals as mongoose, and it is the favored weapon for killing poisonous snakes found in the vicinity of the camp.

Snares. Rope snares are widely used to trap steenbok, duiker, hare, and such game birds as guinea fowl, francolin, and korhaan. The basic material for the snares is a twine (also widely used for many other tasks) made from the fibers of the leaves of *Sansevieria scabrifolia*. This common plant grows in dense localized groves in molapo soils. A bundle of 50 to 100 leaves can easily be collected in an hour. A single leaf is stripped of its outer covering by being drawn through the narrow aperture formed by pressing the edge of a digging stick against the sole of an upturned sandal. What remains is a handful of long, strong vegetable fibers that are ideal for making rope. While still moist, the fibers are rolled into twine using the same technique described for making a bowstring of animal sinews. The twine can be made up to any length by adding more bundles of fibers. It is common for the men to make lengths of twine 1 meter long and tapered at each end because this is the preferred length of a single snare. In snare making, a 5-cm length of smaller gauge tightly twisted twine looped at the end is intertwined with the main rope to accommodate the trigger. The rope is finished by tightly stretching and then vigorously polishing it with a bundle of matted wild cotton to smooth the rope and remove fiber ends. The result is a strong, professional looking rope that is indistinguishable from its machine-made hemp or sisal counterpart.

A working snare consists of six parts:

1. A 2-meter cut sapling to act as a spring
2. A rope snare 1 meter long
3. A tiny wooden trigger plug 1 cm long
4. A wooden trigger peg 20 cm long by 2 cm thick
5. Six to eight noose spreaders (short, straight twigs made from grass, reed, or wood)
6. Bait (for birds only; not for mammals)

The thicker end of the sapling is buried up to a third of its length to anchor it firmly against the lateral stresses the snare exerts, and the rope is securely knotted to the upper end. To prepare the snare site a ring of spreaders is stuck in the ground, and the trigger peg is buried for most of its length in the center. The business end of the rope containing the trigger is tied into a simple noose, and under great pressure the sapling is bent over and the noose arranged around the ring of spreaders while the rope is held down by hand. Now comes the most difficult part. The trigger is looped around the trigger peg so that it barely holds the noose in place despite the strong upward pressure exerted from the bent sapling. To set the trigger exactly right takes years of experience. If the trigger is secured too loosely, even a gust of wind will spring the trap; if the trigger is too tightly secured, the foot or head of the prey will fail to dislodge it. In a correctly set snare an animal stepping into the noose releases the trigger, which instantly tightens the rope around the paw and lifts the animal high in the air. The hunter checking his snares the following day finds the animal thrashing about and finishes it off with a club. In the case of birds, the creature's pecking at the bait releases the trigger, and the noose strangles the bird.

But the snare is a less than perfect mechanism. Even after an animal is caught, it may chew its way through the rope, or if it is big enough it may even work the sapling loose and drag it off to deeper cover. All too often the hunter arrives at the snare to find it sprung, but with no animal in it.

Dogs. Dogs are a valuable adjunct in the tracking of all game, large and small, and are especially useful in the killing of steenbok, duiker, warthog, and gemsbok. Their use was widespread in the Dobe area during the 1960s, but apparently much less so in the Nyae Nyae area in the previous decade. John Marshall (1957) noted that dogs were not a significant factor in hunting at /Gausha during his fieldwork in the 1950s. By contrast, at Dobe water hole perhaps a third of the meat taken in 1964 was killed with the aid of dogs, and during one period the proportion rose as high as 75 percent. In 1967–9 dogs appeared to be somewhat less important in hunting than in 1964, suggesting that the use of dogs is situationally variable and therefore not an integral part of the !Kung hunting complex. Nevertheless, when properly trained dogs are available, they can be highly productive.

The typical !Kung dog is a small animal (50 cm tall at the shoulder) of undistinguished appearance. It is a short-haired breed varying in color from all black to all buff with many piebald forms. The blood lines are difficult to trace. According to Brian Fagan (personal communication), there were no domesticated dogs in the Later Stone Age of South Africa until the arrival of the Bantu. It is possible that dogs are a recent import into !Kung culture.

Whatever their antiquity, !Kung dogs are widely used in hunting. In interviewing 151 adult men in the Dobe area, I learned that 119 of them (79 percent) had owned or hunted with dogs, and most (92 out of 119) had successfully killed game. The highest success rate was reported by the oldest men; 73 percent of dog-owning men 60 years old and over (11 out of 15) had killed game with the help of dogs. This proportion fell to 69 percent (16 out of 23) for men aged 50 to 59, and to 57 percent for the remaining men 49 years old and under. Usually a man owns one or two dogs. For hunting small game, two dogs may be enough, but for hunting gemsbok a minimum of four or five dogs is required. The dogs are used as an aid in tracking; their sense of smell supplements the !Kung hunters' superb visual acuity (see Chapter 8). When tracking an animal, the hunter crumbles the prey's dung under the dog's nose to help the dog identify its quarry; dogs can be trained to follow wounded prey even if its tracks are mingled in a herd of several animals. The dogs are also used to kill prey. If a steenbok or hare is sighted, the dogs are whistled ahead; they race off and can catch and kill the animal within a minute. They can help to keep larger game such as a wounded gemsbok or warthog at bay while the hunters fling their spears at it. The dogs are very courageous and casualty rates among dogs are fairly high; they are often gored or hooked and occasionally are killed scrapping with wounded animals. When meat is plentiful, a man's dogs are fairly well fed, but in slow periods of hunting the dogs often become thin and weak.

One of the main hunters of the Dobe camp (and my "older brother"), a man named ≠Toma, owned a wonderful pair of dogs in 1964. Anyone who met them remembers Swoïya and Foïya, two handsome, healthy, and alert animals whose condition contrasted sharply with that of the often miserable curs owned by other !Kung. Swoïya was the mother of Foïya and of several other good hunting dogs in the vicinity. I hunted with them and ≠Toma several times and was always impressed by the dogs' eagerness, stamina, and controlled ferocity when an animal was at bay. They always responded instantly to ≠Toma's whistled commands, and when they killed a small buck they would wait panting over the kill for ≠Toma to come and never tore impatiently at the viscera as other dogs did. During the 4 months of 1964 in which I kept close track of kills,

Swoïya and Foïya were involved in the killing of at least 20 steenbok and duiker and 12 warthogs. ≠Toma once told me, "If you don't have dogs you don't even bother to hunt warthog." On one memorable day in December, the two dogs along with several others brought an adult male cheetah to bay and killed it. For this and their other exploits, the two dogs were richly rewarded. ≠Toma set aside a portion of every kill for them—even kills they had not been involved in–and he set out dishes of shelled nuts and other foods for them on the days when there was no meat in the camp. The Herero knew about ≠Toma's wonderful dogs and wanted to buy them. One offered him a goat for each dog, but ≠Toma was holding out for an ox for each. Swoïya had several litters, and the pups were eagerly sought after.

When I came back to Dobe in 1967, I was shocked to learn that Swoïya and Foïya were dead. ≠Toma and his father, N!eishi, had been hunting with some Herero west of the border between Bechuanaland and South-West Africa in territory occupied by South Africa when their party was apprehended by a South African police patrol. The Herero were arrested and their mounts and dogs were confiscated and shot. ≠Toma and N!eishi were not arrested, but their dogs, including Swoïya and Foïya, were shot while they stood helplessly by. ≠Toma was terribly upset by the incident and the people of the Dobe area were filled with indignation. But by late 1967 ≠Toma, a perennial optimist, had obtained a small black pup, a grandson of Swoïya, and was busy teaching it to hunt.

Secondary weapons and tools

These tools are not used directly in killing animals, but they play important supporting roles in hunting. They are used to make and repair weapons, to butcher meat, to smoke out or dig out cornered prey, and, in the case of the oracle disks, to prepare for hunting by locating animals through divination. Their use is almost equally important in gathering and in processing plant foods.

The adze/ax. The adze/ax is a dual-purpose tool, with an iron blade that can be set in its wooden socket in two ways: at right angles to the plane of the handle as an adze for woodworking and hide scraping, and parallel to the plane of the handle as an ax for chopping wood. The position of the blade is easily changed, and this makes the adze/ax a most versatile tool. The wooden handle is carved from the bulbous root of an acacia tree; a natural knot is chosen as the site for drilling the socket to hold the blade (Figure 5.6a,b). The wedge-shaped blade is fashioned from an ingot obtained from the Bantu or from suitable European scrap metal; I have seen an excellent ax blade made from a railroad spike. (The nearest railroad is 500 km away.)

The tool is used more frequently in the adze than in the ax position; the

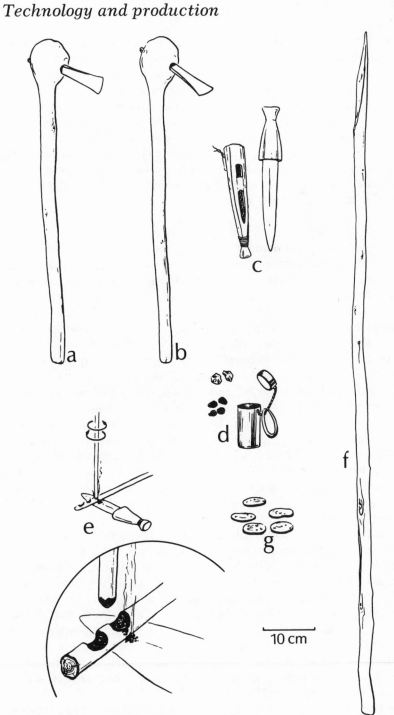

Figure 5.6. Secondary weapons and tools: (a) adze/ax in ax position; (b) same, in adze position; (c) knife; (d) flint-and-steel fire-making kit; (e) traditional fire drill; (f) digging stick; (g) oracle disks.

former offers much more delicate control in the fine woodworking required in making such things as the bow, digging stick, and mortar and pestle. The adze is the only tool used for scraping hides, a task where an especially sharp edge is required and where a slip of the hand could puncture the hide. The ax position is mainly used for chopping wood to make tools, utensils, and house posts. (Firewood is rarely chopped; instead, even the largest logs are fed into the fire bit by bit.) On the hunt, the ax is handy for chopping carrying yokes to bring home meat and for chopping holes in trees to gain access to honey. In butchery the ax is always used for the heavy work of chopping through bone; the knife is used for cutting through the softer parts.

The knife. The knife has an iron blade and a wooden handle and scabbard (Figure 5.6c). It is perhaps the single most essential household and manufacturing tool in the !Kung economy, owned by every adult man and by many of the women. A woman who does not own a knife regularly borrows her husband's or that of another woman, as the knife is in constant daily use. With it, the !Kung artisan can work with fiber, sinew, leather, bone, wood, bark, plant and animal foods, and even with fire. The rather intricate design of the !Kung knife, with the distinctive fluted ends on both handle and scabbard, shows a marked affinity to the design of the Mbukushu knife. Knives of similar pattern labeled "!Kung" are found in the collections of the State Museum in Windhoek, indicating that the adoption of this design is widespread in South-West Africa. Along with their clubs, the !Kung lavish much attention on the esthetics of their knives. The wooden handle and scabbard may have elaborate matching markings, and the scabbard usually has a portion of the side cut away for a see-through effect. The knife blade is the most challenging metal tool made by the !Kung "cold hammering" technique. It measures between 10 and 20 cm in length and 3 to 4 cm across at the base, tapering to a rounded tip. It is hammered to be only 2 mm thick at its thickest point (Figure 5.4b). The base of the finished blade has a 6- to 10-cm tang. The blade is wrapped in a rag, and the tang is beaten red hot and burned into the base of the handle. By repeated heating and burning, the tang is forced deep into the handle and forms a reasonably solid bond that withstands hard use. By a similar process, the tip of the blade is burned into the roughed-out scabbard. After each burning the charred wood is scraped out of the slot with a wire, and eventually a deep slot is excavated to accommodate the entire blade in a neat fit. It is probable that the attractive see-through design of the scabbard was dictated not by esthetics per se but rather by the need for access to scoop out debris from the inner slot during manufacture.

The knife is worn by a man over his shoulder or attached to the belt by a thong from the scabbard. The knife is used for a multitude of tasks. A comprehensive list of uses could run for pages; just a few can be mentioned here: cutting sinews for stringing beads, trimming leather and cutting out the shape of leather bags, whittling the bone link shafts for arrows, carving the trigger and spreader pegs for snares, cutting strips of inner bark for the lashing for house posts, cutting grass for thatching, scraping the ash off a root after it has been roasted, providing a platform for transferring a glowing tinder from a fire drill to a fire.

Meat is always butchered with a knife. When the blade becomes a little dull the butcher stops and casually hones it on whatever piece of bone happens to be protruding within reach. Full-scale honing is done on a basalt whetstone or against the shank of a spear or ax. The !Kung like to keep both edges of a knife blade as sharp as possible along its entire length. They were conspicuously lukewarm to offers of jackknives and hunting knives. Although a number of European steel knives have found their way into the Dobe area in recent years, the !Kung continued to prefer the traditional kind and were still actively making them in the 1960s.

Fire. Fire is one of the most important tools of a hunter-gatherer's life, and the original harnessing of fire represents one of human evolution's key advances. Fire has one direct and one indirect use in !Kung hunting. When a ground-dwelling animal such as warthog, ant bear, or porcupine takes refuge in an underground burrow, it may be smoked out by building a fire at the burrow's mouth. If the animal dies from asphyxiation in the burrow, it is dug out with digging sticks. Fire is also used indirectly in hunting in the late winter and spring to set bush fires. Vast areas measuring hundreds of hectares may be burnt off this way each year. Visitors to the Kalahari have noted the blood-red sunsets of August and September when dozens of local bush fires create a pall of haze on the horizon. These fires burn off old vegetation and encourage new growth, which attracts game animals to the burnt-out areas. Fire can be a dangerous tool. In August 1968 a party of /Du/da people set a bush fire. The wind suddenly shifted and the fire engulfed them killing two people and burning several others. Bush fires alter the landscape in significant ways that ecologists are only beginning to understand, and the effects of burning by humans may be traced far back into the Pleistocene. It is possible that humans have been cooking their environment for as long as they have been cooking their food (Komarek 1966, 1967; Jones 1969; Lewis 1971; Esche 1976).

The traditional method of making fire by a fire drill is a skill all !Kung men and women still possess. The most common method of fire making, however, is through the use of a flint-and-steel kit. These kits are sold in trading stores throughout Southern Africa; for the equivalent of about 50 cents in United States money, you get a small, cylindrical brass cup (2 by

5 cm) with a cap and a steel ring (Figure 5.6d). The buyer provides two additional items for local sources: chips of flint the size of gun flints and bits of a dry local fungus called *konu* to act as tinder. A supply of tinder is charred in advance and placed in the cup along with a chip of flint. The lid of the cup is tightly secured. When one wants to make fire–for example, to have a smoke while out hunting or gathering–he takes the kit out of his bag, removes the flint from the cup, and positions the cup and flint in his left hand in such a way that when the steel is struck against the flint a shower of sparks falls into the tinder in the cup. The tinder is set aglow by blowing on it, and the live coal is tapped out into the waiting pipe. If a cooking fire is to be built, the live coal is tapped out into a prepared wad of soft grass, which is blown into flame in a process the !Kung call *nchun !hara da* ("blow-shatter fire"). In the dry Kalahari firewood is rarely a problem. Dead wood is plentiful and even living wood is dry enough to burn instantly if put into a fire.

The traditional fire drill is a less efficient fire maker than the flint-and-steel kit, requiring about 90 seconds to nchun !hara da, versus about 20 seconds for flint and steel. Nevertheless, many men carry the fire sticks in their quivers and use them occasionally. The sticks are about 50 cm long and 1 cm in diameter. Two different kinds of wood are used: a hard wood such as *Catophractes alexandri* for the drill, and a softer wood such as *Ricinodendron rautanenii* (mongongo) for the base. The operator cuts a notch near the tip of the base stick held flat on the ground, with a knife blade to receive the coal, and places the tip of the drill stick in the notch (Figure 5.6e). He twirls the drill stick rapidly between his hands with a firm downward pressure, taking care to keep the drill tip from slipping out of the notch. After 10 seconds smoke begins to spiral up from the drill tip, and after 40 to 50 seconds a dribble of smoldering dust collects on the knife blade. After a minute or so, the glowing dust pile is carefully tapped into a wad of soft grass and blown into flames.

Drilling fire looks deceptively easy in the hands of a skilled operator; yet real muscular strength and control are required to get the fire started. Even experts in the task are sweating with exertion after a minute's drilling. It is not surprising that the flint-and-steel technique has become popular in recent years. It provides greater efficiency, and after the initial idea has taken hold all the components of the kit can be replenished locally if the originals wear out. Flint and tinder are plentiful, the brass cup can be replaced with a tortoise shell container, and when the steel ring wears out a knife or metal scrap can be substituted. Thus the !Kung have achieved a greater degree of efficiency in fire making without relinquishing self-sufficiency. Matches and lighters, of course, give instant fire, but bring with them dependency on the trading post and foreign technology.

The oracle disks. The last of the secondary hunting tools are the leather disks used for divination, which Marshall (1976:152–5) has aptly called the oracle disks. Hunting being an unpredictable business, the hunter needs all the help he can get. In addition to keeping their equipment in top trim and their knowledge of game movements up to date, the hunters make wide use of divination as well as of many other magical aids (Chapter 8). The oracle disks are a set of circular, stiff leather disks 5 to 7 cm in diameter, cut from the hide of buffalo, kudu, wildebeest, and other antelope (Figure 5.6g).

Any man may divine, and most older men make and own a set of five disks. The disks are used to seek information about hunting and to predict the behavior of humans at distant places. As an example of the latter, when our truck made a trip out of the Dobe area, the disks were consulted daily to predict the time of the truck's return (with its eagerly awaited cargo of tobacco).

The day before a hunt, the hunter or a friend holds a divining session. Spreading a kaross on the ground, he sits down and removes the disks from his kit bag. He stacks them in his hands in a prescribed order and then, shaking and blowing on the disks, as a crap shooter handles a pair of dice, the diviner asks his question of them in a loud ritualized voice and then throws them down on the kaross. The pattern of their distribution on the kaross, whether they overlap or not, and whether they are heads-up or tails-up are keys the diviner uses to make his interpretation. Each disk is named and is stacked in a definite order. The set makes up a complex and distinctive cast of characters, which varies widely, however, from diviner to diviner. N!eishin!a, from Dobe, named his disks (1) the camp owner; (2) his wife; (3) lion, death, or sickness; (4) the young in-law (male); (5) hyena, the one who asks for things.

Kasupe, a /Gausha man who came to live in the Dobe area, named his disks (1) me, (2) my son, (3) my wife, (4) my other son, (5) hyena, the outsider. Lorna Marshall reports on several other sets of disks in the Nyae Nyae area with quite different names (Table 5.2). Despite these variations, common elements appear. The first disk is always male and closely associated with Ego; the last disk is invariably the hyena, an outsider; and the ones in between are allies of varying loyalties to Ego, such as sons, wives, and sons-in-law. Lion, the most dangerous and negative disk, does not appear in every set; when it does, its position varies from third to fourth to fifth. The dramatis personae of the !Kung oracle disks shows some interesting correspondences to a suit of playing cards. In the oracle disks one can see the rudiments of Jack, Queen, King, Ace, and Joker. However, the characters of the disks bear little relation to the interpretation of a throw of disks. Both Marshall and I found that position and pattern of the throw are more important than the

Table 5.2. *Identity of oracle disks in sets from Dobe and Nyae Nyae areas*

	Dobe			Nyae Nyae[a]		
	1	2	3	4	5	6
Disk	Nleishi	Kasupe	Kasupe (obverse)			
1	Camp owner	Me	Me	Big male disk	Eland bull	Self
2	His wife	My son	Young in-law	Small male disk	Eland bull	His son
3	Lion, death, sickness	My wife	My people	Big female disk	Eland cow	His wife
4	Young in-law	My other son	Lion	Small female disk	Eland cow	His daughter
5	Hyena, the asker	Hyena, the outsider	Hyena	Brown hyena	Brown hyena	Outsiders, lions
6				Brown hyena		Brown hyena

[a]Data from Marshal (1976:152–5).

name of the disk, and that a single disk can assume a variety of identities on successive throws (Marshall 1976:153).

A single divining session may last an hour, during which 25 to 50 "questions" are asked. Each time the disks are thrown down, their patterns analyzed, and the disks gathered up for another throw. If others are present, they discuss and debate the interpretation in an intent but cheerful atmosphere. Looking over the shoulder of the thrower at several sessions, I got the impression of highly subjective and arbitrary elements in most of the readings; the oracle disks seemed more like a projective test than a method of divination. In one session where N!eishi threw the disks to find out when a truck driven by Irv DeVore was to arrive, a sequence of 10 throws was interpreted as showing the truck drawing nearer and nearer, an interpretation that bore little relation to the actual arrangement of disks on the kaross. In another sequence of five throws by Kasupe on the same question, the disk attribued to Irv DeVore was "Me" twice; "young-in-law" three times; "my people" four times; and "lion" twice. Only "hyena" never came out as Irv DeVore. In the same way that skiers are encouraged to "think snow," it may be that the !Kung hunters "think meat" and so psych themselves up for a day of hunting.

FOOD-PROCESSING TOOLS

Among the many kinds of plant and animal foods known to the !Kung, only berries and gums are eaten as collected. Most other vegetable foods and all meat have to be processed in some way to be edible. In addition, many foods are mixed together to increase palatability. Cracking, pounding, and cooking are the three most important kinds of food processing.

Cracking stones. Without the aid of nut-cracking stones (Figure 5.7a), it would be impossible for the !Kung to exploit the abundant but extremely hard-shelled mongongo nut. With the stones, the !Kung have made mongongo into a primary food staple. Any reasonably hard stone may be used, including plentiful calcrete cobbles from the widespread hardpan molapo deposits. The hammerstone is fist-sized, with no flakes struck off. The anvil stone may be any size and shape and may weigh 5 to 10 kg. Neither of these stones is improved in any way, and only the pecking marks show evidence of human use. The nut is held on the anvil stone between the fingertips of the left hand and is cracked with two to five sharp blows with the hammerstone in the right hand (see also Chapter 7). Cracking stones are also used for cracking long bones to extract the highly prized marrow.

The nut groves are located on sandy dune soils, which lack natural sources of calcrete for cracking stones. Through the generations, pairs of these stones have become distributed by the !Kung throughout the nut

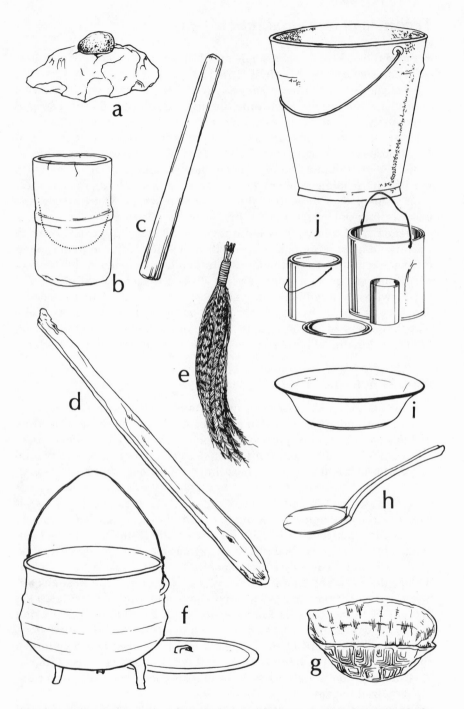

Figure 5.7. Food-processing tools: (a) nut-cracking stones; (b) mortar; (c) pestle; (d) ash paddle; (e) fan; (f) three-legged pot; (g) tortoise shell bowl; (h) serving spoon; (i) enamel basin; (j) pail and cans.

forests of the Dobe area. When making a new camp in the groves, one simply picks up the stones from nearby abandoned campsites. It is only occasionally necessary for a woman to carry her own cracking stones from one camp to another.

Mortar and pestle. Fire is usually thought of as one of the most important inventions in human history owing to its importance as a means of making indigestible foods edible. Among the !Kung its importance cannot be overestimated. But there is another tool, almost equal in significance to fire, which has received comparatively little attention. The !Kung mortar and pestle (Figure 5.7b,c) is an extremely useful tool for pounding foods to break down fiber and reduce particle size and for mixing different kinds of foods together. The mortar is a deep, round, straight-sided wooden container carved from a cross section of the trunk of a hard wood such as *Peltophorum africanum*. The mortar is about 40 cm high by 20 cm in diameter, with a bottom thickness about a third of the total height to withstand years of heavy pounding by the pestle. The latter is a solid wooden shaft 50 to 60 cm long and 5 cm thick. Unlike the larger mortars of the Bantu-speaking agriculturalists, which are pounded with giant pestles held in both hands from a standing position, the !Kung mortar is pounded from a seated position with the pestle held in one hand. It is portable and can be easily carried from camp to camp tucked in a woman's kaross. The great advantage of the mortar is its use as a pulverizer and a mixer. For example, the tasty and nutritious mongongo nut has an indigestible inner shell that clings to the nutmeat and is difficult to peel off. Many people eat the nutmeat inner shell and all, but this makes the nuts much harder to chew and digest, a particularly acute problem for older people. Pulverizing the nuts in the mortar reduces the fragments of inner shell to fine particles and makes chewing and digestion much easier. Furthermore, the nutmeats eaten alone are extremely constipating. To counteract this problem, the !Kung pound and mix the nutmeats with meat, roasted roots, and leafy greens. The addition of these more easily digested foods helps promote regular bowel action and incidentally provides some very interesting flavor combinations. A root such as sha (*Vigna dinteri*), pounded and mixed with nuts, makes a combination that looks and tastes like tangy creamed cottage cheese. Leafy greens such as //guea (*Talinum crispatulatum*) produce a delicious salad, and mongongo pounded with roasted hide and roots makes a crunchy mixture like bacon rind in strong cheese. As one would expect, these mortar recipes are most frequently prepared by older persons, whose teeth and digestion are weaker. I would speculate that the use of the mortar (in addition to cooking) may add significantly to the years of life of older !Kung people. Finally the mortar is culturally significant as a homing signal and as a means of locating other groups (Chapter 7).

Fire and fire tools. The cooking fire (*da*) is a central element in the domestic, subsistence, and symbolic life of the !Kung. Around it, the !Kung spend most of their nonworking hours. Every household has one; at it all the meals are cooked, and around it the evening conversations take place and the household members spread their sleeping mats when they turn in for the night. A new marriage is launched when the bride's relatives build a hut for her and help her kindle a fire in front of it. In day-to-day living, it is rarely necessary to start a cooking fire from scratch. When a new camp is established, a fresh fire is started with a fire drill or flint and steel, but thereafter household fires tend to smolder around the clock. When a woman comes back in the afternoon from a day of gathering, she builds a little wood pile on the old ashes and searches through the ash for a smoldering ember, which she places in a bed of soft grass tinder and skillfully blows into flames. When more grass is needed, she may casually reach back and grab a handful from her hut wall to feed the nascent flames. In the unlikely event that her fire has gone dead, she simply calls over to a neighbor, and a child saunters over with a live coal held in a supple stick bent over double.

Food is either roasted or boiled. In the first case, a root or piece of meat is carefully buried in a mixture of hot sand and glowing embers at the edge of the fireplace. The appearance of steam rising from the mound of sand indicates that cooking is proceeding. When the food is done after 5 to 30 minutes, depending on size, it is removed and knocked sharply against a rock or log to dislodge adhering sand and coals; then it is scraped to remove charred parts. Inevitably, some sand and ash are eaten with roasted food, a fact that probably has both positive and negative consequences for digestion and nutrition. The teeth of all older people, for example, are worn smooth on the occlusal surfaces.

In tending the fire a woman uses an ash paddle (Figure 5.7d) 50 cm long to shift coals, ash, and sand around and over roasting foods, and to pry the food out of the fire when it is cooked. A fan (Figure 5.7e) made of a bundle of kori bustard tailfeathers is used to fan the flames.

Boiling food is a relatively recent process, dating from the introduction of Bantu ceramic pots in the middle of the last century. A few of these are still in use, but pottery has been largely replaced by the three-legged iron pot of the European trade (see below).

The !Kung cooking fire is also a sleeping fire. Each evening just before sundown the men and women of the household go out to collect firewood. The women usually collect the smaller branches as fuel for cooking, while the men look for the heavy deadfalls, 2 to 4 meters long and weighing up to 30 kg for the sleeping fire. A large log is fed into the fire bit by bit through the night, and on very cold winter nights three or four such logs may be consumed.

The accumulation of ash from cooking and sleeping fires can be considerable; every week or so the woman of the household uses her ash paddle to scoop out the equivalent of a bushel basket or more of ash, which she carries to the back of her hut and dumps. The result of this periodic housecleaning in long-term camps – occupied for 3 to 5 months – is a characteristic village pattern of a mound of ash behind each hut and a cooking area that is scoured out to a depth of 10 to 20 centimeters below the land surface.

The pot. The three-legged pot (Figure 5.7f) is a ubiquitous trade item that has found its way into most !Kung households. It is supplied by the manufacturers in blackened cast iron; it has a lid and a wire handle, and comes in an almost infinite range of sizes from 1 to 80 liters. The !Kung favor smaller pots – 1 to 4 liters – which are lighter and more easily carried. They cook meat of every kind in these pots and they much prefer boiled meat to roasted meat. They cook the fruit of the mongongo nut in the iron pots, but they still prefer to roast roots rather than boil them.

The three-legged pot has become such a widely used item in !Kung kitchens that it is hard to visualize their domestic life without it. I once asked /Twi!gum of !Kangwa, "How did you !Kung live long ago before you got the iron cooking pots from the white man?"

/Twi!gum regarded me with a twinkle in his eye and replied, "It is well-known that people can't live without iron cooking pots, so we must have died!"

Serving utensils. Dishes and plates, or their equivalents, were unknown among the !Kung during the 1960s. In keeping with the collective nature of !Kung life, people at a single fire all eat from the same bowl. An exception is the mongongo fruit stew: The pot is first offered to one person, who eats his fill; it is then passed to the next and so on around the fire. The people usually eat with their hands, but many families own a store-bought metal fork or tablespoon for serving. A straight wooden pick, about 15 cm long and sharpened at one end, is often used to spear meat from a pot. This pick has ritual significance as well; it is used by young girls in seclusion during the first menses ceremony, when they are not allowed to touch food directly.

Two traditional serving utensils are still in use: the shell of the large leopard tortoise makes an attractive and durable bowl up to 1 liter in capacity (Figure 5.7g). Meat, mongongo stew, and many other foods may be passed around the fire in this colorful dish. A large, well-formed spoon (Figure 5.7h) carved from a hard wood is sometimes used by the !Kung as a ladle and serving spoon, but it is rapidly being replaced by store-bought metal spoons. Similarly, the !Kung have adopted another trade item, the enameled tin basin (Figure 5.7i); it is gradually replacing the tortoise shell bowl as the all-purpose dish of the household. The enameled basins are as lightweight as the tortoise shell bowls but are much larger and more durable. Women use these basins for preparing and serving food (not for cooking), for fetching water, and as a scoop for cleaning the ashes out of the fire. Galvanized water buckets, other enameled containers, and empty tin cans are found as well in !Kung households (Figure 5.7j).

FOOD STORAGE

Food storage facilities, so important for many hunter-gatherers (Steward 1968), are minimally developed among the !Kung. Most food is consumed within 48 hours of being brought into camp. Stores of mongongo nuts could easily be built up at the beginning of the harvest season (April and May), but this is not done. The day's collection of mongongo nuts is piled in plain view at the side of the gatherer's hut. Some households have a small storage area built at eye level in the crotch of a tree at the side or back of the hut. Branches are interwoven and the spaces packed with grass to make a relatively closed container. Here are kept the hunter's weapons and poisonous grubs, out of reach of dogs and children. A piece of dried hide and some strips of biltong may also be kept there; occasionally one can see a few kilograms of mongongo nuts stored there as well. Other personal possessions, such as beads, clothing, and blankets, are stowed inside the hut, hung from the branches that form its inner framework.

When a large kill is made, part of the meat may be cut into strips for drying into biltong. Racks are built for this purpose, consisting of a horizontal pole resting on two forked uprights. Meat is cut into strips up to 2 meters long and hung out to dry. After a few hours of intense sunshine, a film develops on the outside of the meat making it fairly impervious to flies. In 1 to 3 days, the meat is fully dry and can be kept in this state for 2 months or more. Drying meat attracts attention as well as flies, and most of the biltong is distributed to relatives and neighbors within a few days. What is left is eaten by the household, and all of that is usually gone within a month of the kill. The explanation for this prodigality is both ecological and sociological. Stored in a dry place, biltong will keep for many months without spoiling, but one good rainstorm will turn the dried sticks into a sodden mass that quickly becomes flyblown. It is better to distribute the meat widely than risk having it rot in your hands. Furthermore, if a hunter withholds a substantial portion of the meat from a kill, it draws the hostility of his neighbors. Conversely, total or near total distribution of meat, done with a modest demeanor, draws the good feelings of his neighbors, feelings that later make him a welcome guest at the neighbors' distributions. The prime reason, in short, for the lack of food storage facilities lies not simply in the ecological circumstances but in the practice of food sharing, one of the core values of the ideological system that surrounds the foraging mode of production.

TOOLS AND PRACTICES NOT FOUND AMONG THE !KUNG

To put the !Kung material culture into sharper perspective, it is useful to mention what kinds of tools, materials, and practices are *absent*. The !Kung have no basketry containers and they do not practice stone boiling. They make no pottery, and the few pots they have are obtained in trade with Bantu. They do not hunt with nets, nor do they practice the driving of game. They have no weapons of war, and none of their tools are modified for fighting. When they do fight each other, they do so strictly with the tools of hunting: bow and arrow, spear, and club (Chapter 13).

6

An inventory
of plant resources

THE security of !Kung life in the Dobe area is attributable in large
part to the fact that vegetable food and not meat is the primary
component of their diet. Plant foods are abundant, locally available,
and predictable; game animals, by contrast, are scarce and unpredictable, and though the !Kung hold meat in high esteem, they never depend
on it for their basic subsistence. This fundamental aspect of their subsistence the !Kung share with the vast majority of the world's tropical and
subtropical hunter-gatherers for whom plant foods are primary and meat
secondary (Lee 1968a:30–48).

This chapter describes the vegetable diet from four perspectives. First,
the various groups of plant foods (fruits, nuts, berries, roots, etc.) are set
out. Second, the differential use of these resources by the !Kung is discussed, documenting the !Kung hierarchy of major and minor foods.
Third, the food hierarchy is related to subsistence strategy, year-to-year
variations, and group movements. And fourth, differences in major food
hierarchies are examined at four localities within the !Kung range and
between the !Kung and other foraging populations in order to document
regional variations. In the last section, the !Kung's use of wild plants is
compared with the use of such plants by the agricultural Tonga of the
Gwembe Valley of Zambia (Scudder 1971). Major !Kung foods are also
considered in detail in Appendix D.

The !Kung are superb botanists and naturalists, with an intimate
knowledge of their natural environment. Over 200 species of plants are
known and named by them (see Appendix B), and of these a surprisingly
high proportion is considered by the !Kung to be edible. During my initial
fieldwork, I collected 85 of their edible species (Lee 1965, 1968a, 1969a).
This was in the drought years of 1963–4. Later, in the good rainfall years
of 1967–8, I found more plant types in use, and further research identified 20 more food species. The final list for the Dobe area stands at 105

edible species. If one were to include the Nyae Nyae (Story 1958, 1964) and Cigarette !Kung areas (Maguire ca. 1954), possibly another 10 minor species would be added. I am fairly confident that the Dobe list includes all the important food plants of the central !Kung interior, though the list of minor foods may be expanded.

It is evident that the !Kung have a remarkably broad subsistence base, including 29 species of fruits, nuts, and berries; 41 species of roots and bulbs; 18 species of edible gum; and a variety of beans, melons, leafy greens, and other plants. Close examination, however, shows that the Dobe !Kung are highly selective in their food habits. Only 14 of the 105 species constitute almost three-quarters of the calories in the vegetable diet, and one species alone, the mongongo, accounts for nearly half the total. These 14 major species are indicated by asterisks in Tables 6.1 through 6.5.

THE EDIBLE PLANTS

Let us look first at the inventory of the five major groups of edible plants – fruits and nuts, berries, gum, roots and bulbs, and others – to get a general sense of the role each plays in subsistence. For convenience of reference, each food plant has been assigned a code number: F1 through F14 for fruits and nuts, B1 through B15 for berries, G1 through G18 for gum, R1 through R41 for roots, and O1 through O17 for other plants.

Fruits and nuts

The 14 fruit-bearing trees listed in Table 6.1 provide a major proportion of the !Kung diet. They are also among the most conspicuous features of the landscape: The giant baobab trees, over 25 meters in height, are the largest living things in the Dobe area. Fruit trees are found in all habitats: !Hani (F5) and baobab (F1) are prominent in molapo soils; wild orange (F9, F10) and mongongo (F7) are abundant on the dune crests. The mongongo with its excellent nut is available year-round. Other fruits have a shorter season: baobab (F1) from May to October; !hani (F5) from June to October; and !gi (F6) from mid-November to mid-December. Nutritionally, this is the strongest of the five groups: Several species – baobab (F1), mongongo (F7), and marula (F8) – provide both a fruit that is rich in carbohydrates, vitamins, and minerals, and a nutmeat that is high in calories and proteins.

Berries

Large open stretches of flats and molapos support a vegetation of low shrubs and bushes (Table 6.2). Berry bushes of the genus *Grewia* are an important component of this shrubland and in many areas may be the

Table 6.1. _Edible fruits and nuts_

Code	!Kung name	Tswana and/or English name	Genus, species	Part eaten
*F1	≠M	Muana, baobab	_Adansonia digitata_	Fruit, nut
F2	Twih	Maroro, custard apple	_Annona stenophylla_	Fruit
F3	Zan	Motopi, coffee tree	_Boscia albitrunca_	Fruit
F4	/Twi	Motsaudi, chivi tree	_Guibourtia coleosperma_	Nut
*F5	!Hani	Mokulani, vegetable ivory palm	_Hyphaene benguellensis_	Fruit
F6	!Gi		_Ochna pulchra_	Fruit
*F7	//"Xa	Mongongo, mangetti	_Ricinodendron rautanenii_	Fruit, nut
*F8	Gai	Marula	_Sclerocarya caffra_	Fruit, nut
*F9	N!o	Mahorohwani, wild orange	_Strychnos cocculoides_	Fruit
F10	Tha	Wild orange	_Strychnos pungens_	Fruit
F11	/Duru	Wild medlar	_Vangueria_ sp.	Fruit
F12	!Xo!xoni	Sour plum	_Ximenia americana_	Fruit
*F13	//Gwe	Morutonoga, sour plum	_Ximenia caffra_	Fruit
F14	N≠a̱	Mokalu, buffalo thorn	_Ziziphus mucronata_	Fruit

*Major species.

dominant forms. At /Xai/xai vast groves of !gwa bushes (_Grewia retinervis_, B9) extend back from the pan for almost 1 km on the north side. North of Dobe mixed groves of kamako (B6), n/n (B8), and /tore (B10) are of comparable size. In the South around /Twihaba and /Du/da, extensive groves of !goroshe (B14) exist on sandy white soils. Berries lack the high protein content of some of the tree foods, because none of the berries' seeds are edible. The grewias have a dry, fibrous, pleasantly sweet flesh surrounding a very hard seed. The !goroshe has a superb mangolike orange flesh surrounding an equally hard seed. Each summer and fall many thousands of grewias and other berries are consumed by the people of the Dobe area. _Grewia_ stalks are also widely used in the making of digging sticks and fire drills.

Plate 6.1. Giant baobab trees with edible fruit at !Kubi.

Table 6.2. *Edible berries*

Code	!Kung name	Tswana or English name	Genus, species
B1	≠Tedikuzū		*Cephalocroton puschelii*
B2	Dare		*Clerodendrum* sp.
B3	Ma̱i	Mogau	*Dichapetalum cymosum*
B4	Chaha		*Diospyros chamaethamnus*
B5	Zoma		*Grewia avellana*
B6	Kamako	Mogwana	*Grewia bicolor*
B7	!Khwe (!o!kwe)		*Grewia falcistipula*
*B8	N/n	Morethlwa	*Grewia flava*
*B9	!Gwa	Mokomphata	*Grewia retinervis*
B10	/Tore	Maphate	*Grewia* sp. (possibly *flavescens*)
B11	Da/m		*Grewia* sp.
B12	!Kama!koro		*Grewia* sp.
B13	Kakatadebi		*Lannea edulis*
*B14	!Goroshe	Wild mango	*Salacia luebbertii*
B15	N!ana		Not identified

*Major species.

Table 6.3. *Edible gum*

Code	!Kung name	Tswana and/or English name	Genus, species
G1	N!ha	Moloto	*Acacia erubescens*
G2	N≠ṉ	Mhahu	*Acacia fleckii*
G3	/Tana	Mohoto, camel thorn	*Acacia erioloba*
G4	!Gun	Mokwelekwele	*Acacia* sp. cf. *hebeclada*
G5	//Koie	Mooka, sweet thorn	*Acacia karroo*
G6	!Gan	Mongana	*Acacia mellifera*
G7	/Tadi	Moshu	*Acacia tortilis*
G8	!Xu	Musheshe	*Burkea africana*
G9	≠Doni		*Combretum apiculatum*
G10	!Xabi	Mokabi	*Combretum hereroense*
G11	≠To	Moswire	*Combretum imberbe*
G12	/Dwa		*Combretum psidioides*
G13	N//abe		*Combretum zeyheri*
G14	≠Dwah	Mudubana	*Combretum* sp. cf. *collinum*
G15	//Gaiya		*Combretum* sp.
G16	/Twi, !xhai	Moselesele	*Dichrostachys cinerea*
G17	!Hu	Muchiara	*Terminalia prunioides*
G18	Ziow	Mogonono	*Terminalia sericea*

Edible gum

Several of the most conspicuous and abundant tree species (of the genera *Acacia, Combretum,* and *Terminalia*) exude a translucent resin that is nontoxic to humans (Table 6.3). Curiously called *gum* in the !Kung language, this edible resin is collected through most of the year by men, women, and children alike. Gum is not systematically collected: It is gathered from the trunks of trees as opportunity arises. Rarely does a collector bring in more than a few grams in one day. The !Kung do not rate this food highly, claiming it is hard on the digestion. No data are available on the chemical constituents of these gums.

The tree species in this group are widely used by the !Kung for many nonfood purposes: making houses, weapons, tools, and medicines. A large proportion of their firewood comes from species in this group, such as G3, G4, G8, G11, G17, and G18.

Roots and bulbs

The largest group of edible plants comprises the 41 species of roots and bulbs of the Dobe area (Table 6.4). This large variety of known edible forms is a tribute to the !Kung's powers of observation and classification. Root foods are difficult to find: In the dry season only the faintest wisp of a dried-up vine provides the clue that an edible root is below. And many of the dozens of roots and bulbs found in the area are quite toxic to man. Over the generations the !Kung have sorted through their land and learned which root plants are edible and how to find them.

A further difficulty is the problem of digging roots: Some are buried 50 cm or more below the ground, and in hard soil these can take a half an hour to dig out. The rewards, however, are not inconsiderable; several of the species are tasty treats raw or cooked (e.g., R9, R22, R25, and R33), and topping the list is the superb Kalahari truffle (*Terfezia* sp., R30), reported to be the peer in taste of the Perigordian truffles of France. Most of the root foods, however, are basically fibrous and tasteless and are a major source of carbohydrate in a diet consisting largely of fruits, nuts, and meat. Roots and bulbs are eaten year-round, but particularly in the winter and spring when other foods are scarce.

The family Asclepiadaceae is represented by 11 edible species including the genera *Fockea* and *Raphionacme*. These are water-bearing roots, extremely important items in the survival kit of the San. !Kung groups are able to live for days or weeks at a time completely independent of standing water by digging and chewing the roots of *Fockea monroi* and other species (Plate 6.3).

Roots and bulbs vary widely in the size of the underground part, in the depth below ground, and in the ease of digging out. We have recorded plants with edible storage organs weighing as much as 16.8 kg (37 lb)

Table 6.4. *Edible roots and bulbs*

Code	!Kung name	Genus, species	Comment
R1	/Gwitsau	*Brachystelma* sp.	Small bulb
R2	!Gama	*Ceropegia multiflora*	Root
*R3	/Tan	*Coccinia rehmannii*	Abundant large root
R4	N≠wara	*Coccinia* sp.	Abundant root
R5	Nh/wi	*Coccinia* sp.	Root
R6	!Gwara!kai	*Corallocarpus bainessi*	Root
R7	Uhru	*Cucumis* sp. cf. *C. kalahariensis*	Large root
R8	!Gau	*Cyperus fulgens*	Abundant small bulb
R9	!Hwi/wa	*Cyperus rotundus*	Small bulb
R10	!Goro!go	*Dipcadi longifolium*	Bulb
R11	N!əmshe	*Dipcadi marlothii*	Bulb
R12	!Goro, /gən	*Dipicadi rigidifolium*	Bulb
R13	N/ara	*Dipcadi viride*	Bulb
R14	≠Do	*Eulophia hereroensis*	Abundant bulb
R15	≠Dau	*Eulophia* sp.	Abundant bulb
*R16	!Xwa	*Fockea* sp. poss. *monroi*	Abundant water root
R17	N/omshan	*Hoffmannseggia burchellii*	Rare root
R18	//Hokxam	*Hydnora* sp.	Rare root
R19	Nh!oru	*Ipomoea verbascoïdea*	Water root
R20	//Haru	*Lapeyrousia coerulea*	Bulb
R21	≠Tədi	*Lapeyrousia* sp.	Bulb
R22	/Twe	*Nymphaea* sp.	Water lily root
R23	!Gi!gi, gwe	*Raphionacme burkei*	Water root
R24	N/won/washe	*Raphionacme hirsuta*	Water root
R25	/Tama	*Raphionacme* sp.	Small root
R26	!Gəmn!n!gow	*Rhyssolobium* (?) sp.	Rare root
R27	N//ama	*Sarcostemma* sp.	Root
R28	Tun	*Scilla* sp.	Uncommon bulb
R29	N!am	*Scilla* sp.	Uncommon bulb
R30	Chocho	*Terfezia* sp.	Truffles (a fungus)
R31	N≠wara!ko!ko	*Trochomeria macrocarpa*	Root
R32	Gani	*Vigna* (?) *decipiens*	Root
*R33	Sha	*Vigna dinteri* (cf. *Neorautanenia* sp.)	Abundant root
R34	Nchun	*Walleria muricata*	Bulb
R35	!Xo!kama	Asclepiadaceae	Root
R36	≠Dwa n/i!kosi	Asclepiadaceae	Root
R37	!Ganibe	Asclepiadaceae	Root
R38	//Kore	Not identified	Root
R39	Tedi	Not identified	Root
R40	!Gwi	Not identified	Root
R41	//"Aizheri	Not identified	Root

*Major species.

Plate 6.2. Children collecting truffles at /Xai/xai.

and located 60 cm below the surface (*Coccinia sessilifolia,* O7). At the other extreme is the sedge, *Cyperus rotundus* (R9), which weighs 4 g and exists in dense clusters 0.5 cm below the surface.

These characteristics are known for each of the 41 species, and in a day's gathering factors of size, depth, and hardness of soil are carefully weighed before choosing which roots to dig and which to pass by.

Other plants eaten

This group includes leafy greens (six species), melons (two species), beans (two species), cucumbers (two species), and other items such as heart of palm, grass seed, pods, and a mushroom (Table 6.5). Although it appears to be a residual category, it includes some important species. Foremost are the famous tsin bean (*Bauhinia esculenta*) and Tsama melon (*Citrullus lanatus*). Also important are the leafy greens, which are combined with other plants into tasty salads during the seasons they are available (November to March). It is interesting that five of the species in this group do double duty, providing an edible top *and* an edible root (O3, O7, O8, O14, O15). In all cases, the top is more important in subsistence than the underground part.

One kind of food – grass seed – should be more important than it is. Only two species are considered edible out of the dozen or more locally abundant edible grasses, and even these two are hardly ever used, even in years of drought when neighboring Bantu agriculturalists make exten-

Plate 6.3. A large water root, !xwa.

Table 6.5. *Other plants eaten*

Code	!Kung name	Tswana and/or English name	Genus, species	Part eaten
O1	!Kwe!kwe	Tepe, pig spinach	*Amaranthus* sp.	Leaves
O2	//Kai		*Aristida* sp.	Grass seed
*O3	Tsin	Morama, bean	*Bauhinia esculenta*	Beans, root
O4	≠N≠dwa	Mochope	*Bauhinia petersiana*	Beans
*O5	Dama	Mokate, tsama melon	*Citrullus lanatus*	Melon
O6	Dcha	Mokapana, bitter melon	*Citrullus naudinianus*	Melon
O7	Kitwan		*Coccinia sessilifolia*	Cucumber, root
O8	/Horu		*Corallocarpus bainessi*	Leaves, root
O9	!Gwaashe		*Dipcadi glaucum*	Leaves
O10	//Gən	Mokola	*Hyphaene* sp.	Heart of palm
O11	Karu		*Mukia maderaspatana*	Leaves
O12	//Kai		*Panicum* sp.	Grass seed
O13	//Gwa		*Pentarrhinum insipidum*	Cucumber
O14	Tataba		*Stapelia kwebensis*	Leaves, root
O15	//Guea		*Talinum crispatulatum*	Leaves, root
O16	N!washu		Not identified	Pod
O17	//Hai din !wobe	Mushroom	Not identified	Whole plant

sive use of them. Only one species of edible mushroom appears on the list; yet mushrooms, along with truffles, are one of the prime wild delicacies foraged by agricultural peoples in other parts of the world.

A HIERARCHY OF RESOURCES

Not all foods in the !Kung diet are of equal value. Some are prized and eaten daily; others are despised and rarely eaten; still others are eaten daily, but without much enthusiasm; and some are eagerly sought after, but rarely found. A complex set of criteria involving objective and subjective elements goes into structuring the food resources into a hierarchy of classes of desirability. A plant species may be regarded by the !Kung as a major food for one or more of several reasons. Certain foods are prized because of their abundance, because of the long season during which they are available, or because of their wide distribution. Other foods are prized because of the ease with which they are collected. Fruits are generally more popular than roots for this reason, as the latter have to be dug out of the ground. In the case of roots, the size of the root, its depth, and the hardness of the soil are taken into consideration. Then there are foods that are especially good tasting and/or are believed to be highly nutritious. On the negative side are plants that rate high on abundance and ease of collecting, but that have an unpleasant taste or toxic side effects. Plant foods are evaluated pragmatically and rationally; few species are restricted by magicoreligious taboos. In sharp contrast is the evaluation of animal foods, all of which are subject to complex, cross-cutting sets of taboos.

Using six criteria–abundance, duration of eating season, ease of collecting, tastiness, lack of side effects, and nutritional value–the !Kung consciously evaluate their plant foods and classify them as *strong* or *big* foods or as *weak* or *small* foods. These criteria and judgments plus my systematic observations of the frequency of use and amounts used make it possible to arrange the universe of edible plants hierarchically in terms of the overall importance of each species. This scheme divides the 105 edible species into six classes. These are listed in Table 6.6 and summarized in Table 6.7. There is 1 primary species (mongongo); in addition, there are 13 major, 19 minor, 30 supplementary, 19 rare, and 23 problematic species.

The mongongo (fruit and nut) is in a class by itself. All the Dobe !Kung agree it is their most important vegetable food. It is superabundant, found near all water holes, and available in all months of the year; it is easy to collect, tasty, and highly nutritious. Only meat rivals the mongongo as the most desirable food of the !Kung. I asked one informant to tell me what his idea of an ideal diet would consist of. Without hesitation, he listed four items: meat and mongongo for strength, honey for sweetness, and wild orange fruits for refreshment.

Thirteen additional species are major foods. These are foods that rate high on most, but not all, the criteria of desirability. Most are seasonal and therefore not available year-round, and most are not universally distributed at all the water holes. All are abundant, and each may exceed the mongongo in importance at certain water holes at certain times of the year. Baobab, for example, is tasty and abundant, but is mainly concentrated at a few water holes such as !Kubi and is rare or absent at others. Marula is found at most of the water holes, but its nutmeat is smaller than that of mongongo and its shell is harder to crack.

Nineteen of the species are listed as minor foods; these rate high on one or two of the criteria of desirability. Included are seven species of roots and bulbs that, taken individually, are not important, but that as a group become a major item of the diet during the winter dry season when the major summer foods are not available. All the species of class III are

Table 6.6. *Plant foods by classes*

Code[a]	!Kung name	Common name	Genus, species
I. Primary (n = 1)			
*F7	//"Xa	Mongongo	*Ricinodendron rautanenii*
II. Major (n = 13)			
*F1	≠M	Baobab	*Adansonia digitata*
F5	!Hani	Vegetable ivory	*Hyphaene benguellensis*
*F8	Gai	Marula	*Sclerocarya caffra*
F9	N!o	Wild orange	*Strychnos cocculoides*
F13	//Gwe	Sour plum	*Ximenia caffra*
B8	N/n	Morethlwa	*Grewia flava*
B9	!Gwa	Mokomphata	*Grewia retinervis*
B14	!Goroshe	Wild mango	*Salacia luebbertii*
R3	/Tan	Nakgwa	*Coccinia rehmannii*
R16	!Xwa	Water root	*Fockea* sp. poss. *monroi*
R33	Sha	Chada	*Vigna dinteri*
O3	Tsin	Tsin bean	*Bauhinia esculenta*
O5	Dama	Tsama melon	*Citrullus lanatus*
III. Minor (n = 19)			
F10	Tha	Wild orange	*Strychnos pungens*
F11	/Duru	Wild medlar	*Vangueria* sp.
B4	Chaha		*Diospyros chamaethamnus*
B6	Kamako	Mogwana	*Grewia bicolor*
B10	/Tore	Maphate	*Grewia* sp., possibly *flavescens*
G6	!Gan	Mongana	*Acacia mellifera*
G18	Ziow	Mogonono	*Terminalia sericea*
R4	N≠wara		*Coccinia* sp.
R8	!Gau		*Cyperus fulgens*
R14	≠Do		*Eulophia hereroensis*
R15	≠Dau		*Eulophia* sp.
R30	Chocho	Truffle	*Terfezia* sp.
R34	Nchun		*Walleria muricata*
R39	Tedi		Not identified
O6	Dcha	Bitter melon	*Citrullus naudinianus*
O7	Kitwan	Kitwan cucumber	*Coccinia sessilifolia*
O9	!Gwaashe		*Dipcadi glaucum*
O10	//Gən	Heart of palm	*Hyphaene* sp.
O15	//Guea		*Talinum crispatulatum*
IV. Supplementary (n = 30)			
F6	!Gi		*Ochna pulchra*
F12	!Xo!xoni	Sour plum	*Ximenia americana*
F14	N≠a	Mokalu	*Ziziphus mucronata*
B5	Zoma		*Grewia avellana*
B7	!Khwe		*Brewia falcistipula*
B11	Da/m		*Brewia* sp.
G1	N!ha	Moloto	*Acacia erubescens*

Table 6.6. (*cont.*)

Code[a]	!Kung name	Common name	Genus, species
G2	N≠<u>n</u>	Mhahu	*Acacia fleckii*
G3	/Tana	Camel thorn	*Acacia erioloba*
G4	!Gun	Mokwelekwele	*Acacia* sp. cf. *hebeclada*
G7	/Tadi	Moshu	*Acacia tortilis*
G8	!Xu	Musheshe	*Burkea africana*
G10	!Xabi	Mokabi	*Combretum hereroense*
G11	≠To	Moswire	*Combretum imberbe*
G16	/Twi	Moselesele	*Dichrostachys cinerea*
G17	!Hu	Muchiara	*Terminalia prunioides*
R1	/Gwitsau		*Brachystelma* sp.
R2	!Gama		*Ceropegia multiflora*
R5	Nh/wi		*Coccinia* sp.
R6	!Gwara!kai		*Corallocarpus bainessi*
R7	Uhru		*Cucumis* sp. cf. *C. kalahariensis*
R10	!Goro!go		*Dipcadi longifolium*
R12	!Goro		*Dipcadi rigidifolium*
R20	//Haru		*Lapeyrousia coerulea*
R25	/Tama		*Raphionacme* sp.
R31	N≠wara!ko!ko		*Trochomeria macrocarpa*
R32	Gani		*Vigna* (?) *decipiens*
R35	!Xo!kama		Asclepiadaceae
O4	≠N≠dwa	Mochope	*Bauhinia petersiana*
O11	Karu		*Mukia maderaspatana*

V. Rare (n = 19)

F2	Twih	Custard apple	*Annona stenophylla*
F4	/Twi	Chivi tree	*Guibourtia coleosperma*
B1	≠Tedikuzū		*Cephalocroton puschelii*
B2	Dare		*Clerodendrum* sp.
B3	Ma<u>i</u>	Mogau	*Dichapetalum cymosum*
B12	!Kama!koro		*Grewia* sp.
B13	Kakatadebi		*Lannea edulis*
G12	/Dwa		*Combretum psidioides*
G13	N//abe		*Combretum zeyheri*
G14	≠Dwah	Mudubana	*Combretum* sp. cf. *collinum*
R9	!Hwi/wa		*Cyperus rotundus*
R11	N!əmshe		*Dipcadi marlothii*
R19	Nh!oru		*Ipomoea verbascoïdea*
R21	≠ədi		*Lapeyrousia* sp.
R22	/Twe	Water lily	*Nymphaea* sp.
R23	!Gi!gi	Water root	*Raphionacme burkei*
R24	N/won/washe		*Raphionacme hirsuta*
R27	N//ama		*Sarcostemma* sp.
O8	/Horu		*Corallocarpus bainessi*

VI. Problematic (n = 23)

F3	Zan	Coffee tree	*Boscia albitrunca*
B15	N!ana		Not identified

170

Table 6.6. (*cont.*)

Code[a]	!Kung name	Common name	Genus, species
G5	//Koie	Mooka	*Acacia karroo*
G9	≠Doni		*Combretum apiculatum*
G15	//Gaiya		*Combretum* sp.
R13	N/ara		*Dipcadi viridae*
R17	N/omshan		*Hoffmannseggia burchellii*
R18	//Hokxam		*Hydnora* sp.
R26	!Gəmn!n!gow		*Rhyssolobium* (?) sp.
R28	Tun		*Scilla* sp.
R29	N!am		*Scilla* sp.
R36	≠Dwa n/i !kosi		Asclepiadaceae
R37	!Ganibe		Asclepiadaceae
R38	//Kore		Not identified
R40	!Gwi		Not identified
R41	//"aizheri		Not identified
O1	!Kwe!kwe	Pig spinach	*Amaranthus* sp.
O2	//Kai		*Aristida* sp.
O12	//Kai		*Panicum* sp.
O13	//Gwa		*Pentarrhinum insipidum*
O14	Tataba		*Stapelia kwebensis*
O16	N!washu		Not identified
O17	//Hai din!wobe		Not identified

[a]F=fruit (* and nut), B=berry, G=gum, R=root or bulb, O=other plant.

Table 6.7. *Summary of number of edible plants, by class*

Type of plant	Class						
	I	II	III	IV	V	VI	Total
Fruits	1	5	2	3	2	1	14
Berries	0	3	3	3	5	1	15
Gum	0	0	2	10	3	3	18
Roots, bulbs	0	3	7	12	8	11	41
Other	0	2	5	2	1	7	17
Total	1	13	19	30	19	23	105
Total, classes I, II, III		33					

seasonally limited. When available, each species is eaten several times a week. On this basis they can be distinguished from the major foods of classes I and II, which are eaten daily.

The largest class is supplementary foods, with 30 species. As the name implies, these foods supplement the foods in classes I, II, and III or are eaten when the more desirable foods become locally exhausted. The list includes 6 species of fruits and berries, 10 of edible gum, 12 roots and bulbs, a bean, and a leafy green. In general, the foods of class IV are both less abundant and less tasty than the corresponding foods of class III.

The rare foods (19 species) were observed to be eaten on only a few occasions each year. Many were quite scarce; others were plentiful but were downgraded because of poor taste or undesirable side effects. Mai (*Dichapetalum cymosum*, B3) is an abundant low shrub that grows on white sand, but its tasty fruits are believed to cause nausea and hallucinations if eaten in any quantity. The leaves of *Dichapetalum* are highly toxic to cattle, and a number of domestic stock die each year from ingesting the poison. The meat from the dead cattle is quite edible, however, and the !Kung get an unexpected windfall of cow's meat each year in handouts from their Bantu neighbors.

A food might be classified as rare if the Dobe area lies on the edge of its distribution. An example is the /twi bean tree (*Guibourtia coleosperma*, F4), which occurs only on the northern fringes of the Dobe area. In its own area northwest of Dobe, the /twi bean is a major food, equaling the mongongo in importance (Maguire ca. 1954).

Finally, there are the 23 species listed as problematic foods. The !Kung said these were edible, but I did not observe them to be eaten during the study period. For example, zan (*Boscia albitrunca*, F3) is a common tree and the fruits were highly regarded by the !Kung as food when they were available, but they were never available. Zan did not come into fruit in the drought year of 1963–4 *or* in the good rainfall years of 1967–9, and so it is relegated to the problematic category. Most of the other species were not eaten because of their unattractive taste or because more desirable foods were available.

Year-to-year variability

The hierarchy of food classes is based on observations made in 35 months of fieldwork between 1963 and 1969. In a previous study (Lee 1965), I presented an earlier version of the food classes based on only 15 months of fieldwork. Although essentially similar, the 1965 list and the 1969 (present) list differ in certain important details. A comparison of the two illustrates the differences in results from a single year of fieldwork and a multiyear study (Table 6.8). The most obvious difference is in

Plate 6.4. The wild orange fruit, n!o.

Table 6.8. *Comparison of food class assignment in single-year (1965) and multiyear (1969) studies*

Class	No. of species: 1965 study	No. of species: 1969 study
I. Primary	1	1
II. Major	8	13
III. Minor	14	19
IV. Supplementary	32	30
V. Rare	13	19
VI. Problematic	17	23
Total	85	105

Major species (class II): 1969	Class in 1965, if different
Baobab fruit	
Vegetable ivory fruit	
Marula nut	
Wild orange	IV. Supplementary
Sour plum	
N/n berry	
!Gwa berry	IV. Supplementary
!Goroshe berry	V. Rare
/Tan root	III. Minor
!Xwa (water) root	
Sha root	III. Minor
Tsin bean	
Tsama melon	

the totals, with an increase from 85 to 105 species. The mongongo remains alone in class I at the top of each list, but the additional species
are distributed through four of the other five classes. The most interesting changes are the increase in major species from 8 to 13. Five species
were moved up in importance, two from class III, two from class IV, and
one from class V.

The wild orange (*Strychnos cocculoides*) was listed as a supplementary species (Class IV) in 1965. In 1967–9 it was a major food at
!Kangwa, at /Xai/xai, and other places as well. Drought evidently adversely affected the wild orange, and although the !Kung rated it highly,
I rarely saw it eaten in 1964. Even more striking in this respect is !gor-
oshe, rated rare (Class V) in 1964, but a major food in 1967–9. Part of the
explanation is that my coverage of the food areas south of /Xai/xai was
fairly cursory in 1964, and it was precisely there that !goroshe proved to
be a major species in 1967–9. At /Du/da thousands of !goroshe rinds were
seen in 1968, when it outranked mongongo in importance as a food plant.

Other examples of more thorough observation include the *Grewia* berry, !gwa, which is by far the most important berry at /Xai/xai, a point I failed to realize in 1964. The two roots, /tan and sha, were first lumped with other roots and bulbs in class III. Further evidence of their abundance, year-round availability, distribution at all water holes, and widespread use made it clear that they too were major foods. A similar process of upgrading accounts for the increase in minor foods from 14 to 19 species. Of the new species not seen in 1963–4, most were added to classes V and VI (rare and problematic); an exception is *Terfezia* sp., the Kalahari truffle, which was absent in 1964 but common and easily obtained in the winter of 1968 at /Xai/xai and other southern water holes.

FOOD CLASSES AND SUBSISTENCE STRATEGY

The way the !Kung hierarchically evaluate their plant inventory in order of importance as food suggests a productive analogy to the way they utilize space in the short run in subsistence activities. The !Kung typically occupy a campsite for a period of weeks and eat their way out of it. For instance, at a camp in the mongongo forest the members exhaust the nuts within a 1.5-km radius the first week of occupation, within a 3-km radius the second week, and within a 4.5-km radius the third week. The longer a group lives at a camp, the farther it must travel each day to get food. This feature of daily subsistence characterizes both summer and winter camps. For example, at the Dobe winter camp in June 1964 the gatherers were making daily round trips of 9 to 14 km to reach the mongongo groves. By August the daily round trips had increased to 19 km.

This progressive increase in walking distance occurs because the !Kung are highly selective in their food habits. They do not eat *all* the food in a given area. They start by eating out the most desirable species, and when these are exhausted or depleted they turn to the less desirable species. Because plant food resources are both varied and abundant, in any situation where the desirable foods are scarce, the !Kung have two alternatives in food strategy: (1) they may walk further in order to eat the more desirable species or (2) they may remain closer to camp and exploit the less desirable species. In fact, both alternatives are practiced simultaneously: The younger, more active camp members go farther afield to bring back foods of classes I and II, and the older, more sedentary camp members collect class III and IV foods closer to home. Because the day's foods are pooled within families and shared out to other families at adjacent fires, the net effect is that every camp member has a variety of food available at the end of the day–a modest form of primitive communism.

There was a general, but not invariable, tendency at each camp for the class I and II foods to be exhausted first; then the class III foods were eaten out, followed by the class IV foods. I never observed the complete exhaustion of foods around a camp because the !Kung always moved camp well before the foods of class IV had become scarce. However, when there were compelling social or political reasons for keeping a group together in spite of an unfavorable food situation, it was sometimes necessary for gatherers to walk long distances even for class III and IV foods. (Such a situation was observed at /Du/da in 1968–9 and is discussed in Chapter 12.)

To sum up, !Kung short-run subsistence strategy has two fundamental dimensions: a spatial dimension in which the gatherer moves farther and farther from camp in order to eat the desirable foods, and a hierarchical dimension in which people remain in one area and eat their way through classes of foods of decreasing desirability.

A REGIONAL GEOGRAPHY OF MAJOR PLANT FOODS

No two water holes have the same constellation of major foods. Even within the Dobe area a food that is of great importance at one water hole may be of minor value or absent at another. For example, although most of the 14 major foods (including mongongo) are *present* at both Dobe and /Xai/xai, only 5 species are *major* at both water holes. As one goes farther afield, the list of common species grows smaller and new major foods appear. This section compares the lists of major plant foods, first within the Dobe area and then in a broader regional perspective at five different places in the Kalahari.

Table 6.9 compares the 14 major foods at the Dobe water hole and at /Xai/xai, 35 km to the south. Of the 14 major foods, 13 are present in the Dobe gathering area – only tsin beans (O3) are missing – but not all the foods are of major importance. N!o oranges (F9), !gwa *Grewia* (B9), !goroshe berries (B14), and the tsama melons (O5) are minor at Dobe. Similarly, at /Xai/xai water hole, baobab (F1), marula (F8), n/n *Grewia* (B8), and !goroshe berries are of minor importance, and the vegetable ivory (F5) is absent. Only five foods are major at both places: mongongo (F7), sour plum (F13), and the roots /tan (R3), !xwa (R16), and sha (R33).

Table 6.10 expands the focus to include three additional localities: /Du/da, south of /Xai/xai; /Gausha, in the Nyae Nyae area west of /Xai/xai (Maguire ca. 1954; Story 1958, 1964; Marshall 1976); and ≠Kade Pan, a /Gwi San area in the Central Kalahari Game Reserve 500 km southeast of Dobe (Tanaka 1976). Of the 14 major foods, 7 are major at /Du/da, 6 at /Gausha, and 5 in the Central Reserve. Only one food is major at all five localities, the ubiquitous /tan root (R3), and several other species are major in all four !Kung areas: mongongo (F7), !xwa (R16), and sha (R33).

In addition, the three non-Dobe localities have a total of 14 major species that are not on the Dobe area list of major foods. For example,

Table 6.9. *Comparison of major foods at two water holes*

Code	Major food	Water hole		Relative importance at each
		Dobe (1)	/Xai/xai (2)	
F7	Mongongo	****	****	Equal
F1	Baobab	***	**	1 > 2
F5	Vegetable ivory	***	A	1 > 2
F8	Marula	***	**	1 > 2
F9	N!o orange	**	***	2 > 1
F13	Sour plum	***	***	Equal
B8	N/n *Grewia*	***	**	1 > 2
B9	!Gwa *Grewia*	**	***	2 > 1
B14	!Goroshe	**	**	Equal
R3	/Tan root	***	***	Equal
R16	!Xwa root	***	***	Equal
R33	Sha root	***	***	Equal
O3	Tsin bean	A	***	2 > 1
O5	Tsama melon	**	***	2 > 1

****=primary, ***=major, **=minor or supplementary, *=present but rare, A=absent.

the mokalu berry *Ziziphus mucronata* (F14), which is a supplementary species in the Dobe area, is a major one at /Gausha, according to Marshall. The dcha melon (*Citrullus naudinianus*, O6) is a secondary food at Dobe and /Xai/xai, but a major one at /Du/da, observed eaten by the hundreds in January 1969. The most striking differences appear at ≠Kade Pan in the center of the Kalahari Desert. Tanaka lists eight major species that are not on the Dobe major food list. Every one is present in the Dobe area, but as a minor or lesser food. For example, *Ochna pulchra* (F6) is a minor food in the Dobe area, prized for its pleasant taste and good nutrition but downgraded because of its short season – about 5 weeks in November and December. At ≠Kade Pan the season is similarly short, but in the absence of mongongo, baobab, vegetable ivory, and marula, the *O. pulchra* assumes a much greater importance. *Raphionacme burkei* (R23) is only a supplementary species in the Dobe area because of its bitter taste, but at ≠Kade Pan in the absence of the !xwa water root (R16), *R. burkei* becomes a major source of water. *Aloe zebrina* is present in the Dobe area south of /Xai/xai, but is not considered by the San to be human food. At ≠Kade Pan, however, it is a major source of water in the dry season. These contrasts underline the point that the Central Kalahari is a poorer food region than the Dobe area, and in poor food areas less desirable foods may assume major importance.

Although 28 foods are listed in Table 6.10, no one water hole has them

Table 6.10. A regional geography of major foods

Code	Major foods	Water hole					No. of water holes where this food is present	No. of water holes where this food is major
		Dobe	/Xai/xai	/Du/da	/Gausha[a]	Central reserve[b]		
In Dobe area								
F7	Mongongo	***	***	***	***	A	4	4/4
F1	Baobab	***	*	A	***	A	3	2/3
F5	Vegetable ivory	***	A	A	*	A	2	1/2
F8	Marula	***	*	A	*	A	3	1/3
F9	N!o orange	*	***	*	*	*	All	1/5
F13	Sour plum	***	***	*	*	*	All	2/5
B8	N/n Grewia	***	*	*	*	***	All	2/5
B9	!Gwa Grewia	*	***	***	*	***	All	3/5
B14	!Goroshe	*	*	***	*	?	All?	1/4
R3	/Tan root	***	***	***	***	***	All	5/5
R16	!Xwa root	***	***	***	***	A	4	4/4
R33	Sha root	***	***	***	***	?	All?	4/4
O3	Tsin bean	A	***	***	***	***	4	4/4
O5	Tsama melon	*	***	*	*	***	All	2/5
Outside Dobe area								
F6	Ochna pulchra	*	*	*	*	***	All	1/5
F14	Ziziphus mucronata	*	*	*	***	*	All	1/5
B10	Grewia flavescens	*	*	*	***	*	All	1/5
R4	Coccinia sp. (n≠wara)	*	*	*	***	A	4	1/4
R5	Coccinia sp. (nh/wi)	*	*	***	*	?	All?	1/4
R7	Cucumis kalahariensis	*	?	*	*	***	All?	1/4
R23	Raphionacme burkei	*	*	*	*	***	All	1/4
R28	Scilla sp.	*	*	?	*	***	All?	1/4

R30	*Terfezia* sp. (truffles)	*	*	*	*	***	All	1/5
R?[c]	/Dobi	?	?	?	***	?	?	?
O4	*Bauhinia petersiana*	*	*	***	*	***	All	1/5
O6	*Citrullus naudinianus*	*	*	***	*	***	All	2/5
O15	*Talinum crispatulatum*	*	*	?	*	*	All	1/5
O?[d]	*Aloe zebrina*	A	Present, not eaten	?	?	***	All?	1/4
	No. of major foods	9	9	10	10	13		
	Major foods unique to each water hole (code numbers)	F5 F8	F9	B14 R5 O15	F14 B10 R4 R?	F6 R7 R23 R28 R30 O4 O?		

[a]Data from Marshall (1976).

[b]Data from Tanaka (1976).

[c]Root mentioned by Marshall; not coded for this study.

[d]Plant mentioned by Tanaka; not coded for this study.

***=major or primary, *=present,

A=absent, ?=uncertain if present.

all in significant amounts. The number of major foods *per water hole* is remarkably uniform: 9 or 10 in the !Kung areas; 13 in the South. Diet selectivity, therefore, appears to operate at all the water holes.

This regional comparison allows us to make a further evaluation of the strength of the major plant resources. Five species are of areawide importance, being major foods at four or all five of the water holes. These are: mongongo (F7), /tan root (R3), !xwa water root (R16), sha root (R33), and tsin bean (O3).

Six species are of regional importance; they appear as major foods at two or three of the water holes, but are of minor or lesser importance at others. These are baobab (F1), sour plum (F13), n/n *Grewia* (B8), !gwa *Grewia* (B9), tsama melon (O5), and *Citrullus naudinianus* (O6).

The remaining 17 species are of local importance; although most are present at all, or all but one, of the water holes, they assume a major role at only one of the five (see bottom of Table 6.10).

If a regional economic geography of a hunting and gathering society were to be written, it would include not only a discussion of the topography, climate, and plant resources, but also an evaluation of the more subtle differences in the importance of the major plant foods. It is these subtle differences that contribute to the strong regional cultural differences in the Kalahari, in much the same way that local foods specialties contribute to the varying regional flavors of rural France.

SAN–TONGA COMPARISONS

The use of edible wild plants by African agriculturalists is extensive, though this aspect of their subsistence is rarely studied by ecologists. An exception is the intensive study of plant gathering by the Gwembe Tonga of Zambia, carried out by Thayer Scudder (1971). Comparing the use of wild plants among the Tonga with that of the Dobe !Kung, Scudder makes some striking observations that illuminate the differences between foragers' and farmers' use of space.

The Tonga, situated in the Gwembe sector of the Zambezi Valley, 500 km east of Dobe, use at least 131 species of edible wild plants compared with 105 species for the !Kung. Of these, over 50 species of leafy greens are used by the Tonga as relishes to flavor their daily meals of cultivated cereals. By contrast, the !Kung use only 6 species of leafy greens in their diet. The Tonga area is better watered than the Dobe area, and this may account in part for the much larger number of leafy greens available to the Tonga, but there are other factors as well. The Tonga also use the wild plants as emergency food in times of crop failure, and here a striking fact emerges: The Tonga consume portions of 21 species that are also known to the !Kung and found in their area, but are not considered to be food by the !Kung (Scudder 1971:20). The Tonga live at a population density approximately 100 times that of the Dobe !Kung. When Tonga crops fail, enormous pressure is brought to bear on the Gwembe wild plant foods–far greater than that exerted by the !Kung on their plants even in time of drought.

For example, *Acacia albida* yields an abundant seedpod that is harmless to livestock, but toxic to humans. The !Kung ignore the seedpods of *Acacia* spp. even though thousands of kilograms of them could be harvested each year. Yet the Tonga during hunger periods collect quantities of these pods and eat them after an elaborate process of soaking, boiling, and leaching involving three changes of water over 24 hours.

The fact that the Tonga eat *A. albida* and many other species ignored by the !Kung is an index of the seeming paradox that an agricultural people may utilize wild plant and animal resources *more* intensively than a hunting and gathering people. Similarly, this comparison suggests that the !Kung environment may contain many more edible plants than are classified by the inhabitants as edible, a further indication of the security of the foraging way of life.

7

The mongongo

THE mongongo (*Ricinodendron rautanenii* Schinz) is the super-abundant, highly nutritious fruit and nut that is the major food resource of the hunting and gathering !Kung. This chapter deals with the botany and ecology of the mongongo and the role this important food plays in the life of the people. Why devote an entire chapter to the study of a single food species? Because the mongongo, though a wild food, functions in the !Kung subsistence as a staple, and with respect to its abundance, nutritional returns, and reliability, the mongongo equals or surpasses the cultivated staple crops of many agricultural peoples. Focusing on the mongongo serves to demonstrate the security and adaptiveness of hunter-gatherer life and helps correct the common misconception that the way of life of these people is precarious and unpredictable. Among even the most acculturated !Kung, the mongongo nut and fruit continue to constitute between one-third and one-half of the calories from the vegetable component of the diet. In the account to follow, we take up first the ecology, botany, and nutrient composition of the mongongo; then we go on to describe its local distribution, seasonality, methods of collection and preparation, as well as mongongo cuisine, sharing and reciprocity, and contribution to the diet. Finally we consider the question of whether the !Kung have ever tried to propagate this marvelous plant, and if not, why not.

MONGONGO ECOLOGY AND BOTANY

Ricinodendron rautanenii Schinz is a large fruit-bearing tree of the family Euphorbiaciae identified by H. Schinz (1898) in German South-West Africa. In the Dobe area the tree and fruit are known to the Herero as *mangetti* (Marshall 1960, 1965, 1976); to the Tswana as *mongongo* (Miller 1952); and to the !Kung as //"*xa*. Mongongo is used here in preference to //"xa because the latter is difficult to pronounce and because the

Plate 7.1. The mongongo.

former has gained some currency in the literature (Lee 1968a, 1969a; Pfeiffer 1969:338–46; Harris 1975:237–9).

The mongongo is found only in a relatively narrow belt across subtropical latitudes of Southern Africa. The northern border of its distribution runs through Southern Angola, Zambia, and Mozambique; its southern border runs through Ovamboland, Northern Botswana, and the Transvaal. The mongongo is particularly successful on a Kalahari sand base. It is found mostly at altitudes of 1000 to 1500 meters and its distribution falls very roughly within the zone defined by the 350- and 700-mm isohyets. The /Du/da area lies close to the southerly edge of its distribution. Traveling down the border road, one passes abruptly out of the mongongo zone about 20 km south of /Du/da. The southern limits in our area follow the Eiseb Valley (Figure 7.1).

The tree is of medium height, standing 8 to 12 meters when mature. It has a thick, stout trunk up to 1 meter in diameter, and it is not unusual for three or four trunks to grow in a cluster; though single trunks are also found (Plate 7.1). The crown is broad and spreading, casting a deep shade when the tree is in leaf during the summer and autumn rains (December to May). The larger branches grow at a very gentle angle to the ground; the trees can be easily climbed and are a favorite playground

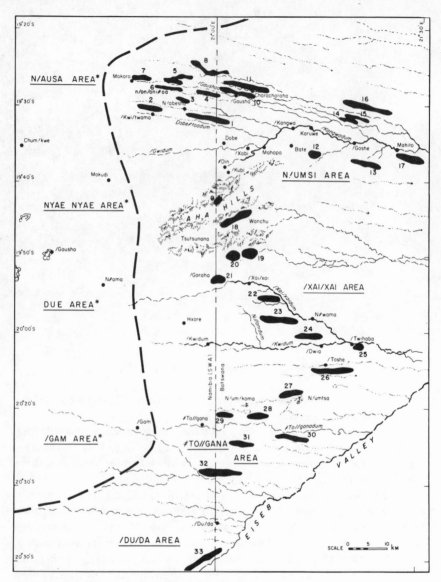

Figure 7.1. The distribution of 33 mongongo groves.

for children. The wood is very light in weight and useless for building or
manufacturing purposes. Brief descriptions of leaves, buds, flowers, and
fruits may be found in White (1962:203) and in Story (1958, 1964).

In our area the mongongo grows exclusively in two kinds of habitats.
By far the most common site is in linear groves a few hundred meters
across and several kilometers long along the crest of the fixed dunes. The
soil here is loose, fine-grained sand of reddish white hue. The mongongo

Plate 7.2. Collecting mongongo in the groves.

is one of the main constituents of the dune vegetation association (Chapter 4). It is also found in irregularly shaped groves in sandy soils on all the major rock outcrops that dot the Northwest Kalahari, including Tsodilo, Aha, /Twihaba, and N!um!koma (see Figure 7.1). The mongongo is never found in calcrete or compacted soils, on clay, or in areas subject to flooding. It appears that relatively high elevation and good drainage are prerequisites for the species.

The plant propagates from the edible kernel. Under each producing tree one finds up to a dozen mongongo saplings 1 to 2 meters high. According to the !Kung, a mongongo tree will start to bear fruit after 25 years of growth.

About half the trees in a grove bear fruit; the other half are sterile. The !Kung call the former trees "female" (//"xa di) and the latter "male" (//"xa!go), and their description agrees with that of the botanists (Story 1958:31).

The fruit of the mongongo is shown in Plate 7.2 and in cross section in Figure 7.2. It is composed of five layers, two of them edible. The skin (exocarp) is pale green when the fruit first falls and ripens to a rich red after several months on the ground. The skin is peeled off and discarded. The flesh (mesocarp) is green or red in color, dry and spongy in texture, and tastes like a date though less sweet; it may be eaten for 6 to 8 months after the fruit has fallen to the ground. The nut's outer shell (endocarp) is extremely tough and difficult to crack. This has proved a major barrier to commercial exploitation of the mongongo nut and has preserved this excellent food for exclusive use of the indigenous people of Africa. The nutshell makes up about half the total weight of the fruit. It is buff-colored and faintly pockmarked, with a dimple at the broad end that serves as a guide for the experienced cracker. The inner shell (testa) is only 1 mm thick and encloses the kernel like a glove. It can be peeled off only with difficulty, and many people chew and swallow the inner shell along with the kernel. The nutmeat or kernel itself is roughly the shape and size of a small hazel nut. It is skinless, creamy yellowish white in color, and breaks neatly into halves (the cotyledons) in the hand. Parts of the kernel tend to cling to the inner shell, especially early in the season. Longer roasting and careful cracking produce a cleaner looking nut for the more fastidious. The taste is not unlike that of dry roasted cashews or almonds. After prolonged roasting the kernel turns butterscotch brown or darker and takes on a unique flavor resembling fine old cheese.

Some mongongos, perhaps 1 in 20, are extra large. These are twins, containing two individual kernels of normal size and a correspondingly larger quantity of fruit. The nuts of these large fruits are cracked and eaten in the normal way. A second odd form of mongongo is the *tchoro* ("spoiled nut"). When opened, the tchoro has a vestigial, inedible kernel in an empty shell case. Tchoro nuts can be identified in the field by the experienced collector by sight and by the inexperienced collector by weight. When hefted, the tchoro nuts, lacking a kernel, are slightly lighter than normal nuts. They are discarded by the collector. According to the !Kung, a tchoro nut results when an immature fruit falls before the kernel has had a chance to develop. This may explain why the !Kung tend to avoid the first fall of fruits and instead wait for the bulk of the fruits to drop before making regular collecting trips. Some groves have a high proportion of tchoro nuts (up to 10 percent at ≠Ha≠hama grove 22, for example), and this high incidence the !Kung interpret as a sign that the mongongo forest is in decline.

Figure 7.2 also shows the constituents of the fruit and nut. The flesh makes up 26.7 percent and the kernel 9.0 percent of the fresh fruit, for an edible/waste ratio of 35:65. Later in the season when the flesh is eaten away, the kernel constitutes 14.8 percent of the whole nut for an edible/waste ratio of 15:85. Despite the high proportion of waste, the mongongo has remarkably high energy yields. The flesh has 312 Cal per 100 g and the kernel 640 to 655 Cal per 100 g, so every kilogram of whole fruits actual size 3cm X 2cm

	FRESH WHOLE FRUIT eaten Apr-Sept			NUT ONLY less flesh & skin eaten Oct-Mar	
	g/100g	x cal/g	cal/100g fruit	g/100g	cal/100g
A. skin	12.5			—	
B. flesh	26.7	x 3.12	83.3	—	
C. outer shell*	51.8			85.2	
D. inner shell					
E. nutmeat	9.0	x 6.41	57.7	14.8	94.9
	100.0		141.0	100.0	94.9
edible/waste ratio	35/65			15/85	
yield per 12 kg backload	16,920 cal			9,490 cal	

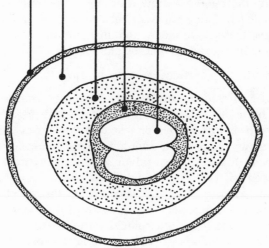

Figure 7.2. The mongongo fruit in cross section and its constituents (* indicates "inedible").

brought home yields over 1400 Cal. Each typical backload of 12 kg provides 11,000 to 17,000 Cal for the collector and family.

Table D.1 in Appendix D shows the nutrient composition of the mongongo in greater detail, along with the composition of a number of other important species. The nut has a high fat content (58.4 g per 100 g), is rich in protein (28.3 g per 100 g), and has a high energy value. Eating 200 mongongo nuts a day provides the consumer with 2500 Cal and 77 g of protein. Both in its energy value and in its vitamins and minerals, the mongongo compares favorably with the world's most nutritious foods, cultivated or otherwise. It is worth noting that the !Kung have at least three other wild foods that are as nutritious as mongongo: (1) the tsin bean (*Bauhinia esculenta*), which provides 544 Cal per 100 g and contains 31.6 g per 100 g protein; (2) the marula nut (*Sclerocarya caffra*), which provides 642 Cal per 100 g and contains 30.9 g per 100 g protein; (3) the baobab nut (*Adansonia digitata*), with an energy value of 506 Cal per 100 g and a protein content of 34.1 g per 100 g for the kernel alone (Wehmeyer, personal communication on CSIR.NNRI sample No. 667/67). This abundance serves to underline the point that foraging peoples are in many ways more richly endowed with food than agriculturalists or industrial peoples.

SEASONALITY

The mongongo year begins in April with the fresh fall of fruits. Because it may be early or late depending on the rains, the fall is an eagerly awaited event. In 1964, a drought year, the fall started on April 13; in 1968 on April 1. But in 1969, after the exceptionally good rains of 1967–8 and 1968–9, the fruits were on the ground by March 20. Occasionally the !Kung jump the gun and throw sticks up to the branches to knock down some of the early fruits, but most people wait for the fall. In a few weeks all the year's fruits have fallen, and they remain on the ground until they are gathered by people or eaten by animals.

Fall and winter gathering (dry season: April to September)

Starting in April and continuing until September, harvesting mongongos is one of the major subsistence activities of both men and women. Harvesting starts in the groves closest to home. Fruits are collected only when necessary, and no attempt is made to stockpile mongongos when they are easy of access. A freshly fallen fruit has a fuzzy green skin and spongy green flesh that is particularly pleasant eaten raw. After the flesh is eaten, the whole nuts are set aside for roasting and cracking. With the approach of the winter months of June and July, the fruits ripen and cure on the ground to a rich red color. By August the flesh has dried to a powdery texture, and insects are beginning to make inroads, eating away some of the flesh, but leaving the kernel intact inside the strong outer shell. The !Kung say that late rains, after the fruits have fallen, can hasten the spoilage of the flesh. Frost action combined with late rains may also shorten the period when the flesh is edible, though the kernel itself seems impervious to all these climatic factors.

Spring gathering (end of dry season: September to November)

From September to November the trees, which had lost their leaves in the fall, begin to come into leaf and start producing the next year's crop of fruit. By this time about half the fruits on the ground have lost their flesh to the insects. The fruits are collected and brought back to camp, where they are sorted into two piles. Those with usable flesh are soaked and cooked; the others are lightly roasted to char off remaining flesh and to prepare the nuts for cracking.

Summer gathering (rainy season: November to March)

The onset of the main rains and the work of the insects finish off what is left of the fruit, and for the next 4 months only the nuts remain, polished clean by the insects and weathered to a pale buff gray. Now more distant groves become accessible with the seasonal water points. Some of the mongongo trees themselves become water sources as rainwater collects in the hollow boles. Groups of gatherers are more widely dispersed, moving frequently from water point to water point to be as close as possible to the mongongo groves as well as to a variety of other summer foods. The deep shade and well-drained soils of the groves make them attractive summer camping places. In early summer the trees flower; then the female trees begin to bear the next year's crop of fruits.

Early fall gathering (end of rains: March and April)

As soon as the fruits of the current year fall, the previous year's crop is disregarded. During the summer, the mechanical action of raindrops buries last year's nuts in the soft sand. This makes the nuts difficult to see and troublesome to collect. Being buried also makes them more liable to attack by the soil microfauna. Nevertheless, at least a third of the uneaten nuts are still edible after having lain on the ground for a year.

Annual variations in yield

There is little firm evidence on the variation in the total crop of mongongos from year to year. In good rainfall years the fruits may ripen earlier, but the effect this has on overall output is unknown. For example, there appeared to be about the same amount of mongongos in Dobe ≠toa (grove 1) in the good year of 1967–8 as in the drought year of 1963–4, indicating that the mongongo is not adversely affected by drought.

A rare year of extremely high rainfall, on the other hand, *can* damage the crop. At Maun in 1973–4 1183 mm (47 in.) of rain fell, and similarly high rainfalls occurred at Dobe and elsewhere in Northern Botswana. Polly Wiessner (personal communication) reported that the mongongo crop of March and April 1974 was drastically reduced; the mechanical action of the raindrops during heavy January storms apparently destroyed the mongongo buds at the flowering stage. In the following year (1974–5), the mongongo crop appeared to be back to normal in some groves, though somewhat reduced in others; and by 1975–6 the crop appeared to have recovered to normal levels (Wiessner 1977:27; E. Wilmsen and J. Yellen, personal communications). Elephants browsing through the groves in rainy years can also damage the trees by breaking off branches to reach the fruits.

AN INVENTORY OF GROVES

The !Kung call a mongongo grove a //"*xa*/*to* (literally "the face of the mongongo") in the same sense that a camp or village (*chu*/*to*) literally means "the face of the huts" (/*to* = "face"). The dunes that support the groves are called /*to* or ≠*toa*. This term is almost synonymous with mongongo in everyday speech, so that when one asks, "Where is so-and-so?" and the answer is, "*A u a ≠to*" ("he went to the dune"), one knows he is collecting mongongos. Each water hole has its series of //"*xa*/*tosi* or ≠*tosi*, and much evening discussion around the campfire is devoted to daily situation reports on the status of each of the groves. On any day a camp member can give a rundown of the heaviness of the fall and the current availability of fruits in every grove.

Each of the 10 major water holes of the study area has at least one large grove within a 10-km radius, and several have as many as five groves (see Figure 7.1). Nevertheless, some of the water holes are considered to be much more well endowed with mongongos than others. For example, both Dobe and !Goshe have several groves lying within 25 km that remain untouched because peoples' needs are supplied closer to home. On the other hand, Bate and !Kubi are water holes where annually the residents exhaust their own grove early in the season and for the rest of the year draw upon the groves of other water hole groups.

Table 7.1 and Figure 7.1 show all the 35 mongongo groves used by the !Kung in 1963–9. There are certainly others, especially west of the border, that I do not know about. However, these latter groves are used mainly by people based in Chum!kwe. Lorna Marshall has discussed the mongongo-gathering activities of the Nyae Nyae !Kung (1960:335–6, 1965, 1976:114–16).

Not all the nut groves are equally exploited. Some are eaten out every year, others only some years; still others are barely utilized and most of the fruits remain untouched. These differences are expressed in the three-class ranking of the groves in Table 7.1. Only 17 of the 35 groves

Table 7.1. *An inventory of 35 mongongo groves*

Grove no.	Grove name	Location and comments	Class[a]
Location: Dobe, !Xabi, !Kubi, Mahopa			
1	Dobe–N//abesha	Starts 5 km N of Dobe, extends W of border; thoroughly utilized	A
2	!Kwi/twama	Starts 19 km WNW of Dobe; occasionally used	C
3	Shum!kau	Starts 14 km NW of Dobe; a small grove	A
4	//Gakwe≠dwa	Straddles border 16 km N of dobe	A
5	≠Tm≠toa	NW of Dobe; a secondary grove	B
6	N/on/oni≠toa	A major, well-utilized grove 19 km NW of Dobe	A
7	Mokoro	A large grove 26 km NW of Dobe	C
8	!Gaian!ko	A large, rarely used grove	B
9	Gai//garaha	A sparse stand in north central Aha Hills; !Kubi's only grove	A
10	!Gausha	A major grove 12 km NW of !Kangwa; heavily utilized	A
11	Characharaha	The main grove for !Kangwa; heavily utilized, 11 km NW of !Kangwa	A
12	Gani/ti	Bate's only grove; 5 km SE of Bate	A
13.	!Goshe	!Goshe's closest grove; starts 3 km from !Goshe	A
14	/Dutsusi	Rarely used grove N of !Goshe	C
15	Kam≠twa	Rarely used grove N of !Goshe	C
16	Che!gu	Rarely used grove N of !Goshe	C
17	Mahito	10 km ESE of !Goshe; a large well-utilized grove	A
Location: /Xai/xai			
18	Wanchu	A sparse but extensive stand 16 km N of /Xai/xai in heart of the Aha Hills	A
19	!Gihm	Very dense stand 7–10 km N of /Xai/xai	A
20	N/haihm	Very dense stand 7–10 km N of /Xai/xai	A
21	!Garaha	10 km W of /Xai/xai on a rock outcrop	A
22	≠Ha≠hama	5 km SE of /Xai/xai; the nearest nut grove	A
23	≠Ton!a	10 km SE of /Xai/xai	B
24	/Dwia≠toa	19 km SE of /Xai/xai near /Dwia summer water	B
25	/Twihaba	37 km SE of /Xai/xai in hills near Drodsky's caves	C
26	/Toshe	30 km SE of /Xai/xai; a large, dense grove	B
Location: ≠To//gana, /Du/da and south			
27	!Guro≠toa	A large grove on north flank of N!umtsa; 30 km S of /Xai/xai	C
28	N≠isa≠toa	A medium-sized grove 3 km SE of N!um!koma	C
29	//Gum//geni	A large grove E of the border, 36 km S of !Garaha	A

Table 7.1. (*cont.*)

Grove no.	Grove name	Location and comments	Class[a]
30	≠To!gum	13 km SE of N!um!koma; rarely used	C
31	Choga	10 km S of N!um!koma; rarely used	C
32	!Garo≠tem	A large grove 10 km north of /Du/da; main grove for /Du/da	A
33	≠Dwi!kun	7 km S of /Du/da; major source for /Du/da	B
34	≠To≠din	23 km SW of /Du/da; a major grove; may be continuous with 33	B
35	N//o!kau	A large grove S of Eiseb Valley, 38 km S of /Du/da; these form the southern limits of the distribution of mongongo	B

[a]A=eaten out every year, B=eaten out only some years, C=rarely eaten out.

are eaten out every year. The rest provide a cushion of subsistence margin in leaner years.

MONGONGO WORK

In the following sections the labor involved in collecting and processing mongongos is discussed in some detail. The reason for this emphasis is that in hunting and gathering, and other simpler societies, subsistence effort forms a very large proportion of the total energy expended by the population. Mongongo collecting, with its efficient techniques and high yields, thus makes a major contribution to the positive energy balance achieved by the !Kung in their annual round.

Collecting techniques

In all regions and throughout the year, mongongo collecting is a major activity of both women and men. The process is so simple that even a visiting anthropologist can learn the knack in an afternoon and make himself useful. Arriving at an unexploited grove, the collectors fan out, one tree to a person, and begin the process of bending over and picking up each fruit to put in the kaross, the versatile one-piece garment-cum-carrying device. Where the fall is thick, it is worthwhile sitting or kneeling to gather the 20 to 30 fruits within arm's reach. Otherwise, a woman bends gracefully from the waist, one leg forward and bent at the knee while she picks up a few fruits within reach. The digging stick is used as a staff to support the gatherer's weight. Some women like to pick up single fruits between their toes and thus reduce the amount of bending. A collector arranges her gathering in such a way that every 20 minutes or so, when she has collected a few kilograms of whole fruits, she returns to a central, well-shaded point to dump out what she has collected. Then she returns to the "front" to gather another small load. Three to five such round trips provide a full backload of 10 to 15 kg of whole fruits. Women collect about 20 to 30 fruits per minute of active collection, though this activity may occupy only a fraction of the time spent in the groves. When the women have collected what each considers a full load, they convene at the central place where they relax, smoke, and drink water from ostrich eggshell canteens. If the flesh of the mongongos has been eaten away, the collectors may crack and eat a portion of their nuts on the spot. If time is short, they may crack and eat a few nuts raw. With an hour or more to spare, the women build a small fire to roast the nuts, a process that makes them much easier to crack. And if the gatherers have an afternoon to spend, they crack up to half their nuts, eating all those that crack imperfectly and saving all the nuts that crack neatly with the inner shell intact. The inner shell keeps the kernels from becoming crushed or dirty in the backpack during the trip home. This preliminary cracking can reduce the weight of nuts to be carried home by 75 percent.

Although no large animal can shell the nuts, several species of mammals eat the flesh of the fresh fruit. The eating habits of two species are actually helpful. Elephants eat the whole fruit, digest the skin and flesh, and void the nuts. The !Kung may find two dozen or more nuts in a single large pellet of dry elephant dung. Even more accommodating is the greater kudu; after ingesting the fruits, this animal regurgitates quantities of the nuts. While gathering, !Kung find neat piles of 50 to 60 nuts deposited by kudus. The nuts are fleshless, finely polished, and ready for roasting and cracking.

Packing and carrying home

When ready to head for home, a woman spreads her kaross on the ground next to her pile of nuts. Then she piles all the nuts on the upper half of the kaross. She slips her leather !kebi belt thong under the kaross and sits on the lower half. Gradually, she ties herself into the kaross; first using the !kebi belt and then grasping the upper corners, she works the load closer to her body; then she lifts the whole load while at the same time tying the securing knot over her left shoulder and under her right arm. She adds other gathered foods, ostrich eggshells, and finally the baby, while continuing to distribute the weight of the nuts to the most comfortable position. Then, leaning into the load, she sets out walking steadily at 4 to 5 km per hour. The kaross is a superbly designed carrying device. The load is carried widely distributed and thus very close to the worker's center of gravity. No tump straps are used, and both hands are left free. There is little strain on the shoulder, although occasionally one sees red marks on the left shoulder where the strap has been rubbing. The only disadvantage of the kaross is the slight tendency for it to leak at the pouring spout fold when the woman is in motion. On the main paths leading into camps one often finds a trail of nuts that have fallen every 10 meters or so from the outlet of a kaross. Grass may be stuffed in the outlet to help hold the nuts inside. Losses from this source are negligible.

The men's carrying device, the net (*/twi si-*), is more complicated to use and has a much smaller capacity than the woman's kaross. After about 5 to 8 kg of nuts have been gathered the men proceed as follows:

1. Two digging sticks are staked out in the ground 1 meter apart.
2. The thong net is spread out between the poles.
3. Thatching grass is packed lengthwise inside the net to form a bottom and sides, taking the form of a reed canoe.
4. Inside this "boat" mongongo nuts are packed, taking care that the lining of grass remains solid.
5. As more nuts are added, the net fills out fully and more grass is added on the sides and top. The top of the net is tied shut with a spare piece of thong.
6. The full net looks like a very fat cigar about 60 cm long and 30 cm thick in the center.
7. The end pieces are then removed from the poles and used as shoulder straps.

The net takes a long time to pack, and its straps cut into a man's shoulder. But it is a carrying device that can be cast off in a split second enabling a man instantly to start hunting if the opportunity arises while he is on a gathering trip.

A third device, used by both sexes, is the carrying bag (*/tau˙*) employed when a small amount of mongongos (under 5 kg) is to be collected. It is worn over one shoulder. If it is very full, the top is sewn shut with a spare piece of thong.

The */tau˙* plays a special role in the sharing economy of the !Kung. A family member often asks another to collect nuts for him. If the other agrees, he hands him his own bag rolled up and tied so that it will fit easily into the other's pack. The collector simply fills the bag and delivers it back to its owner. The adaptive feature of this custom is that the person making the request specifies the amount of nuts he wants. This avoids the potential embarrassment that would ensue if the giver had to decide whether he was expected to donate 10 percent, 20 percent, or 50 percent of his load of nuts to the asker. Men carry the */tau˙* bags over the shoulder; women carry them inside the kaross or, more rarely, balanced on the head.

CAMPING IN THE GROVES

Elaborate carrying arrangements are not necessary when the group is camped in the mongongo groves. It is simpler to move the whole camp when the supply of nuts is exhausted within a 2- or 3-km radius. In the groves, the !Kung enjoy the deep, rich shade and cool, clean reddish white sand. Often the trees themselves provide water for the groups, which may return to sites near these water-bearing trees year after year. There are plenty of cracking stones nearby. Over the years hundreds have been transported to the groves, so that now all the gatherer has to do is seek out previous years' camps to find sufficient pairs of stones for the group's needs.

!GI SPEECH

Groves extend for miles along the well-wooded crests of dunes, and at any given time several groups may be using the same grove or two parallel groves. People are not always aware of the location of other groups in their vicinity, and in this vast and sparsely populated country the unexpected meeting of two groups is usually a cause for rejoicing. A stage in the processing of mongongo nuts plays an intriguing role in the communication between distant groups. After the nuts are cracked and shelled, they are often pounded in a mortar and mixed with other foods. The pounding is one of the most characteristic sounds of the !Kung camp. The !Kung call this sound *!gi kokxoie* ("mortar speech"), and they use it as a primary *audible* sign of human presence, associating it with the warmth and fellowship of the campsite. It also has remarkable carrying power, especially at night. Aided by atmosphere and wind conditions, the pounding of mortars can be heard in a camp 8 km away. The sound is at first so faint and intermittent that one is hard-pressed to distinguish it from such natural sounds as woodpeckers or the creaking of dead trees. But once the noise is identified, camp members perk up and try to identify the direction of the sound and which group is making it. Similarly, when one group is on the march to join another and is not sure of the other's location, the members may pick up the mortar speech and use it as a homing signal to lead them into camp. When two groups are camping close by, one can tell that the other group has turned in for the night when the mortars stop pounding. First three mortars are working, then two, then one, and then silence.

MONGONGO IN THE CAMP

For most of the year each household keeps a pile of mongongos at the side of the shelter. Rarely is there more than 2 or 3 days' supply on hand. When a woman returns from the groves, she stands over the pile, unties the securing knot of her kaross, and lets the day's collection of fruits pour out on the pile. Only after she has off-loaded does she drink, smoke, or wash. Eyes of the campmates casually look up to see how many mongongos have been brought home. Bags belonging to others are delivered, and usually without further ado, the woman prepares for processing the fruits. The first step is to sort out flesh-bearing nuts from those without flesh and to treat each lot differently. There are three basic and several secondary steps in the processing of mongongo including cooking the flesh, roasting the nuts, cracking and shelling the nuts, pounding the nuts in a mortar and mixing with other foods, and expressing the oil of the nut.

The processing of one mongongo may extend over several days. The flesh may be eaten on one day, the nut shelled on the next and set aside, and the nutmeat eaten the days after. Or the fruit may be processed and consumed in the space of an hour.

Cooking and eating the flesh

Even if the kernel were inedible, the flesh of the mongongo would alone make it a major food. The flesh is abundant and easily prepared. The taste is attractive and the yield of calories and minerals high.

In the past, the fruit was eaten whole and raw. Nowadays it is usually prepared in an iron cooking pot (Plate 7.3). A pot is filled with fruits and water and set on the fire to steam. Steaming softens the skins and makes them easy to peel off. After the fruits are peeled, a fresh change of water is used and the batch of peeled fruit is set on a high fire to cook. After 10 minutes of cooking, the pot is set on a lower flame and the fruits are stirred continuously with a special stick cut for the purpose. The stirring separates the flesh from the nut and at the same time the movement of the nuts produces a grinding action that turns the flesh into a rich maroon pulp, the consistency of applesauce. After 10 minutes, when most of the pulp has been freed from the nuts, the flesh of the fruit is ready for eating. The flesh is served in one of two ways. An enamel cup may be dipped into the gruel and passed to a recipient, who is expected to eat the whole cup. More commonly the whole potful is passed around the circle with each person present eating an appropriate amount. A hand-carved ladle is used to spoon out the cooked flesh.

In eating the flesh an etiquette is observed. Some of the pulp from the lip of the container is drunk, then a few of the nuts which are coated with cooked fruit are picked up, licked and sucked clean of fruit. The nuts are then spat out themselves on the ground. Those nuts revert to the giver, who collects them after the meal and sets them aside for later roasting. Sucking the nuts clean provides an enjoyable and pleasant meal and at the same time helps the giver by preparing the nuts for roasting.

Mongongo fruit is rarely mixed with other foods, but is eaten alone as a sweet dish. When I was first introduced to the dish, a woman named N≠isa, leader of LG 26/68, described it with the word *sukari*, a !Kung adaptation, via Setswana, of the English word "sugar." Next to honey it is one of the sweetest items in the San diet.

Plate 7.3. Cooking mongongo fruit.

Roasting, cracking, and shelling the nuts

This phase of mongongo processing is illustrated in Plate 7.4. In it, the subtleties and skills involved in cooking at an open fire become evident. A few branches are allowed to burn down to coals; then with a special spatula, the cook mixes the hot coals into a small pile of dry, loose sand. When the sand and coals are well mixed, she moves about 100 nuts to the base of the pile and then deftly buries them in the sand. She trims the smoking pile of hot sand to ensure that all the nuts are buried and none is in direct contact with live coals; then she lets them roast for 2 or 3 minutes. She kneads the pile of sand and nuts to turn all the nuts at least once and to shift their orientation slightly. This makes for more even roasting. If necessary, she adds more coals from the main fire, which is burning a few centimeters away from the roasting area. Then, after another 2 or 3 minutes, she quickly scoops the roasted nuts out with her spatula, checking to see that none is charred. A well-roasted nut looks blue gray owing to soot and ash from the fire.

The trick of the roasting fire is to provide a medium (sand) of uniform temperature and to distribute the nuts within the sand so that all are equally heated. By adding coals that are flaming or too hot, one risks ruining some of the nuts. On the other hand, if too few coals are added, no roasting will take place.

Roasting drives off some of the moisture in the outer shell and makes it easier to crack. After the nuts have cooled, the cracking begins. The cracker positions herself with the whole nuts on one side, an anvil stone in the center, and a dish to receive the nutmeats on the other. She picks up a nut with her left hand, positions it narrow end up on the anvil, and makes two deft, sharp blows with the hammerstone held in her right hand. Then she repositions the nut flat and makes one or two more blows; these are usually sufficient to open the nut. Sometimes the nut cracks with the first blow; occasionally five or six are necessary. When cracked perfectly the outer shell is split into neat halves leaving the inner shell intact. About half the nuts crack this way. The rest have to be picked apart by the cracker. A very few get smashed and are discarded. Nuts that are tchoro or burnt are also discarded.

I measured the rate of cracking for one woman, who cracked 558 nuts in 156 minutes for an average of 3.6 nuts per minute. On another occasion, I observed five women and three men cracking and eating. Their rates varied from 4 to 6 nuts per minute during active cracking. Given these rates, a reasonable estimate of cracking rates falls in the range of 200 to 300 nuts per hour. Estimating an allotment of 20 to 30 minutes to crack 100 nuts and 200 nuts per kilogram, each kilogram of nuts requires 40 to 60 minutes for cracking. An average backload of 10 to 15 kg can be cracked in 6 to 15 hours.

Plate 7.4. Roasting and cracking mongongo nuts.

Nuts that crack well are deposited in the dish for later eating. Nuts that break into several pieces are often eaten on the spot. Cracking rates per hour depend in part on how hungry the cracker is. If she is very hungry, she stops to peel many nuts and eat them; if she is not hungry she deposits most or all of the nuts in the dish. This steady eating underlines the difficulty of estimating quantities of food consumed: So much eating goes on *outside* of formal mealtimes.

Cooking and eating the kernel

Nutmeats are eaten whole, inner shell and all; whole, with inner shell removed; pounded in a mortar; or mixed with a variety of vegetable and animal foods. Although it is not ground into flour or meal, mongongo is nevertheless used as a base for a number of important dishes. In all these dishes, the mortar (*!gi*) plays a central role.

Hungry !Kung, especially men and younger people of both sexes, eat the nutmeat as well as the inner shell. Being chewable but indigestible, fragments of the inner shell pass through the system and are voided in the feces. I found chewing the shell rather unpleasant. Some people take an extra few seconds to peel the inner shell off before eating the nutmeat. The problem here is that the inner shell clings to particles of the nutmeat. A special effort can be made to tap the inner shell free beforehand, but this procedure is not always effective. So even the very fastidious have to tolerate some pieces of shell in their daily portion of nuts.

The mortar and pestle are also widely used to pound the nutmeats and mix them with meat and a variety of other foods.

Finally, when pounded to an oily pulp, the nutmeat may be used as a body rub. The oil is rubbed all over the body, especially in the winter dry season, to clean the skin and keep it supple. During this season washing tends to produce chapping and drying out. When one sees a !Kung adult or child with face and arms a glistening golden color, it is usually mongongo nut oil that has been used.

SHARING AND RECIPROCITY

Because it is regarded as a national resource, the mongongo is widely shared according to specified rules at every stage of its processing through the subsistence system. The trees or groves themselves are not individually owned. Most of the groves are associated with the family or sibling unit that has lived in its vicinity for a long time. Any one of several people may be asked to let a group eat in a grove, and permission is rarely refused (Chapter 12). Other groves that are closest to Bantu cattle posts, such as !Goshe or /Xai/xai, are used by everyone without asking permission. Marshall (1960:334) has described an example of territoriality in a grove, but the circumstances surrounding this incident are not clear.

Close kinsmen and affines frequently ask each other to fill bags with nuts. This service is symmetric with people of the same age, but is asymmetric between older and younger people. For example, at Dobe ≠Toma//gwe and his wife often sent a bag out to be filled by one of their three sons, but were never observed to fill bags in return. On the other hand, any of the three sons would fill a bag for either of his brothers when requested to do so. !Kung also may fill a bag for a nonkinsman campmate, and this appears to be reciprocal.

A household owns (k"ai) the nuts in the pile at its doorway. Any member of the household may crack and eat whatever he wants. In addition, siblings, parents, nieces, and nephews of the married couple may crack these nuts at any time. It is a common sight for a child from a neighboring household to sit down at a fire and roast and crack some nuts for herself or himself. Mongongo nut pulp is not a good substitute for milk, but it becomes increasingly attractive for toddlers and growing children.

Adults are somewhat more circumspect about eating nuts of another household. Typically a person comes over to a fire to talk while a householder is roasting nuts. When the nuts are done, the owner pushes a pile of nuts and pair of stones over to the visitor, who proceeds to crack while continuing the conversation. Sitting in on many such conversations, one rarely heard any specific references to the nuts, such as "let me crack some" or "these are good nuts." The nuts are simply shared without comment.

The flesh may be eaten by any number of people, but always at the fire of the owner because the nuts revert to the one who collected them. Shelled whole nuts may also be passed around the fire, but more often a cup is filled with them and sent over to a neighboring fire via one of the children. The mixed dishes of nuts and other foods are freely distributed around the fire, but rarely passed beyond it.

In sum, gathered nuts are shared at every stage, usually by receivers *coming* to the owner's fire. It is not customary for a receiver to *carry away* nuts from a fire, but shelled nuts may be *sent over* to another fire by the owner.

The distribution mechanisms of the Bushman camp are far from perfect. When conflict breaks out, sharing breaks down. Interruptions in the pattern of flow of nuts or of sitting patterns for the evening meal are indications of cleavages and disagreements within the camp. If the cleavage persists, the camp will split. Group or individual conflict is a common theme in !Kung song and conversation, as shown by this song composed in 1968 by a woman at /Xai/xai.

Zhu/wa na ka //"xa	People don't give me any mongongo
N/e mi /tu !gi !gi	To throw in the mortar (!gi !gi)
N/e mi /taa mi tsu.ee	So that I can give some to my uncle, ee
Kama zhu/wa na ka //"xa	Because people don't give me any mongongo
N/e mi /tu !gi !gi	To throw in the mortar
N/e mi /taa mi tsu.ee	So that I can give some to my uncle, ee
Zhu o chi dole, kama	People are bad because they don't
si /wa na ka //"xa	give me any mongongo
N/e mi /tu !gi !gi	To throw in the mortar
N/e mi /taa tsutsu ee	To give to old uncle, ee

THE NUTRITIONAL CONTRIBUTION OF MONGONGO TO THE DIET

Given the obvious importance of mongongo in the lives of the people, it is useful to know the actual productivity of the groves and thus determine quantitatively the contribution of mongongo to the diet.

Yield of fruits. The total yield of fruits from a grove is difficult to calculate. Although it would be feasible to count the total number of fruit-

Table 7.2. *Estimates of total annual yield of mongongo fruits and their energy values*

Yield	No. of edible fruits	Energy Value Cal	kJ
Per tree	950	12,046	2,600
Per linear kilometer	95,000	1,204,600	260,000

Table 7.3. *Estimate of size and output of 11 mongongo groves*

Grove no.	Grove name	Size (linear km)[a]	Annual production fruits × 10^6	Cal 10^6	kJ × 10^6
1	Dobe–N//abesha	11.5	1.1	13.9	3.2
2	!Kwi/twama	6.4	0.6	7.6	1.8
3	Shum!kau	3.2	0.3	3.8	0.9
4	//Gakwe≠dwa	6.4	0.6	7.6	1.8
5	≠Tm≠toa	9.6	0.9	11.6	2.7
6	N/on/oni≠toa	6.4	0.6	7.6	1.8
7	Mokoro	4.8	0.5	5.8	1.4
8	!Gaian!ko	9.6	0.9	11.6	2.7
9	Gai//garaha	4.8	0.5	5.8	1.4
10	!Gausha	9.6	0.9	11.6	2.7
11	Characharaha	12.8	1.2	15.2	3.6
	Mean	7.7	0.73	9.28	2.2

[a]Data from Yellen (1972).

bearing trees in a grove, I have not done so. Nevertheless, with several informal counts in hand, it is possible to estimate roughly the number of trees in a grove and the yield of fruits per tree (Table 7.2).

Yield per grove. The lengths of 11 of the groves mainly in the Dobe area have been very roughly estimated by Yellen (1972) based on his on-the-ground surveys of Dobe !Kung foraging patterns. The estimated production of these groves is shown in Table 7.3.

Total annual production. Based on informal discussion with !Kung informants and on field observations, the Dobe area groves appear to be representative, in length and in density of trees, of the mongongo groves in other areas. Bearing in mind the roughness of the estimate, we can use these figures for an approximation of the overall production from all the 35 groves. Given a mean length of 7.7 km per grove, the 269.5 km of groves in the area produce annually some 25.6 million fruits and 325 million Cal.

Production and carrying capacity. What do these estimates mean in human terms? How many people can be supported by these levels of production and for how long? Because not all groves are equally utilized, answering this question necessitates an estimation of the proportion of the annual fall actually eaten by San.

17 A groves (100% eaten) yield	157.76 × 10⁶ Cal	
8 B groves (50% eaten) yield	34.42 × 10⁶ Cal	
10 C groves (10% eaten) yield	9.28 × 10⁶ Cal	
Total	201.45 × 10⁶ Cal	

The mean standing population of the Dobe and /Du/da areas during 1967–9 was estimated at 550 persons; therefore, the number of person-days of consumption per year is 200,750. When the number of person-days of consumption is divided into the production figure for the *utilized* groves, an estimate can be made of the calories available from mongongo per person per day. This estimate falls remarkably close to 1000 Cal (240 kJ) per person per day. The daily energy requirement of !Kung is approximately 2000 Cal (Lee 1969a:89; Chapter 9). This means that mongongo flesh and kernel can provide up to half the total energy requirements for the entire population year-round, even when only 62 percent of the capacity of the groves is utilized.

This is not to imply that every !Kung eats sufficient mongongo every day to provide 1000 Cal. In fact, mongongo consumption is higher early in the season (April to July) when the fruits are easily available and falls to much lower levels as they become locally exhausted and people turn to other foods. Furthermore, most of the fruits collected after the rains have started (November to March) have lost their flesh to insects. This loss probably reduces the overall yield of mongongo calories by 20 percent. Therefore, a more reasonable estimate of production per capita is 800 Cal per day or 40 percent of daily requirements. The short-term consumption of mongongo in a given camp can vary widely, from as high as 90 percent for people who are camped right in the nut groves and are eating little else, to as low as 5 to 10 percent in camps during the late rainy season when local supplies are exhausted. It is instructive that the consumption of mongongo rarely falls to zero. There were always a few nuts in evidence in practically every camp observed.

HAVE THE SAN PROPAGATED THE MONGONGO?

Nutritious, tasty, abundant, the mongongo nut plays a central role in the daily life of the Dobe area !Kung. The people have made a study in depth of the botany, ecology, and growth habits of the tree and know the principles of its reproduction and dispersal (Story 1964). They have also played a role, partly unconscious, in the propagation of the plant. For example, growing on abandoned campsites on reddish white sand around Dobe are numerous mongongo saplings up to 2 meters high. These are several kilometers distant from the nearest producing grove and have obviously sprouted from fertile nuts carried there by San. Elsewhere, if one finds mongongo shrubs growing far from the groves and far from abandoned campsites, one can attribute their presence to transportation by elephants in dung.

The San acknowledge their role in dispersing the mongongo plant, but they add that plants do not grow to maturity except in the proximity of already established groves. Indeed, there are few examples of isolated trees. Virtually all mature trees are found within the maximum of a few hundred meters of other trees. For some reason, isolated clusters of saplings have not survived to maturity.

Nevertheless, considering the great importance of the mongongo and the long distances walked by the !Kung each year to reach the groves, one would imagine that some attempt would have been made to grow mongongo trees in the sandy soils near the permanent water holes, thereby making possible a more sedentary life. I asked /Xashe, "Why don't you try growing the mongongo tree at Mahopa?"

"You could do that if you wanted to," he replied, "but by the time the trees bore fruit you would be long dead."

"And besides," he continued, "why should we plant when there are so many mongongos in the world?"

8

Hunting

!K UNG men are excellent hunters, and they devote a great deal of time and effort to the pursuit of game. In energy returns hunting is a less rewarding activity than gathering, and vegetable foods provide the major part of the diet. On the other hand, the hunt and its products hold a central place in the life of the camp and in the community. The formalized distribution of meat is always an eagerly anticipated occasion. Graphic descriptions of hunts, both recent and distant, constitute an almost nightly activity of the men around the campfire. In storytelling, men can portray a hunt, step-by-step, in microscopic and baroque detail. And the food returns of hunting are far from negligible. Throughout the year the proportion of meat in the diet rarely falls below 20 percent, and during peak periods when the hunting is good may reach 90 percent, with a per capita consumption of meat of over 2 kg per day! Furthermore, animal products may provide essential nutrients that are lacking or scarce in the vegetable diet. Overall the hunt provides around 40 percent of the calories of the !Kung.

In this account we consider the basic techniques of hunting (tracking, stalking, shooting, killing, and butchery) as well as some specialized techniques (snaring, underground work, and capture of small game). Then we present an inventory of all the 55 species of mammals, birds, reptiles, and insects eaten by the !Kung, with more detailed discussion of species of big game hunted and not hunted by the !Kung. The chapter concludes with a discussion of hunting as a career and a life's work, including socialization as a hunter, hunting magic and ritual, initiation, and data on hunting success. The material covered here forms only a bare introduction to the subject. More extensive research on hunting has been conducted by Edwin Wilmsen, from whom a more substantial account can be expected in the future. The chapter also touches on the excellent work of S. A. Marks on hunting among the agricultural Valley Bisa (Marks 1976), though it should be noted that the Bisa hunt almost entirely with guns.

Plate 8.1. Butchering warthogs for cooking and distribution.

THE WORLD OF THE HUNTER

It is useful to introduce the subject with a glossary of some of the terms used in hunting. To hunt is *!gai,* and a hunter is called a *!gaik"au* ("hunt owner"). Game animals, large and small, are called generically *!ha* ("meat") and distinguished from the *zhum* or *!hohm* ("clawed or predatory animals"). All the species are individually named as well, and each has, in addition to its everyday name, a secret name that is used under special circumstances (as when an animal is wounded but not yet dead). The small antelopes, steenbok and duiker, are known collectively as *≠da≠hxaisi* ("daughters of the plains") because they prefer the open habitat of the plains; they are hunted interchangeably.

The basic toolkit consists of the bow (*n!au*), arrows (*chisi*), and a quiver (*!kuru*). The last epitomizes the hunter and hunting more than any of the weapons. When a man is actively hunting, he *//kama!uru* ("shoulders his quiver"); when he is not hunting, he is *kwara!uru* ("without a quiver"). The bow, on the other hand, is a bawdy metaphor for the penis. When a man jokingly says *mi kwara n!au* ("I have no bow"), he implies he is at a loss sexually.

A hunting trip of several days' duration is *guni*. Hunting without a strong lead is *!gai n//o* ("hunting around"). Stalking an animal is *lo* ("to follow"). A very close stalk is *sum*. Shooting an arrow is *chi//a;* to miss your shot is *chi//a da-ma* ("shoot failing"); and to strike home is *//'xopo* or *tah*.

A struck animal *!gaa u⁻* ("takes off like a shot") or *kxokxoni* ("staggers") or *!gow a /te* ("falls down"). To finish off a wounded animal with a club, you *n≠em!kū a* ("strike-kill it"); with a spear or knife, you *!n !kū a* ("stab-kill it"). Then the hunter *cho ka !ha* ("butchers the meat"), *//gau//hwanasi* ("loads it on carrying yokes"), and *//kama//hwanasi* ("shoulders the yokes") for the trip back to camp. There the meat is *n/wa* ("boiled") or *sau* ("roasted"); the members of the camp are *//kai/kiakwe* ("assembled"), and the *!ha* ("meat") is *≠twi n//o* or *hxaba* ("distributed"). Afterward, *n//ae* ("men") gather at a fire to *du n≠wao !gai ga* ("tell the story of the hunt") until *n!a //gai* ("dawn breaks," literally "sky rips open").

There are many dozens of synonyms, metaphors, and euphemisms for the words and phrases listed above; hunting vocabularly has undergone a fantastic elaboration in !Kung speech. These terms, nevertheless, give some sense of the hunter's world.

THE HUNTING PROCESS

The goal of hunting is to kill game to provide food. Killing for sport is unknown. All !Kung hunting techniques have three basic steps: the preparations for the hunt, the act of hunting itself, and the killing and butchering (see Marks 1976:114ff.). The first and third steps are common to all hunting. The act of hunting may take many forms. A distinction is made between snaring, which requires fixed facilities, and all other techniques, which depend on mobile searching for game. The latter method provides most of the meat. The search for game may focus on aboveground or below-ground animals. Underground work involves blocking an animal in the burrow and digging it out. Four important species are taken this way. Above-ground work includes knocking down and snaring very small game, chasing small- to medium-sized game with dogs, and the classic hunt for the large mammals in which poisoned arrows are used. This last technique is the one popularly associated with !Kung Bushmen hunting and made famous by the giraffe hunt in John Marshall's film, *The Hunters* (1956). The following discussion considers each of the steps and techniques in turn, starting with snaring and concluding with big game hunting.

SNARING

Snaring is a modest technique used largely by older men and young boys whose mobility is limited. It is time-consuming and provides little meat per man-hour, but it is a particularly good technique for the older hunter because it maximizes know-how and experience while making minimum demands on eyesight, endurance, speed, and energy reserves. Young boys set snares for rather different reasons: to gain experience in their craft through the study of animal behavior and through the feedback from successful and unsuccessful snaring.

Winter is the snareline season. Each hunter who is wintering at his home water hole starts to build his snareline in May and continues to refine and improve the lines until October, when they are abandoned. Impromptu snares may also be set up at temporary winter camps where the hunters are spending a few days. Snaring is rare during the rainy season because the rains ruin the delicate trigger mechanisms. The hunters of the camp agree before the snares are built where each man will set up his lines. A man surveys his snaring area for fresh tracks of steenbok, the major animal snared. The steenbok is a nonmigratory small antelope with a restricted home range – a characteristic that makes it eminently suitable for snaring. The hunter gradually lays down an unobtrusive line of brush, 200 to 300 meters long, that zigzags from bush to bush until by degrees he closes off a tract of ground with a brush barrier. The object of this operation is to habituate the animals to crossing his line at a limited number of gaps. Each day he inspects his line for fresh tracks. If the animals are breaching his line regularly at one gap, he then sets a rope snare in the gap.

The snare, described in detail in Chapter 5, consists of a length of rope with a noose and trigger on the ground at one end and a springy sapling bent over at the other. When the forefoot of the animal falls within the noose, the trigger is released and the animal is caught. Its struggles serve to tighten the noose more securely around its foot. Birds caught pecking at the baited noose are strangled, but the antelopes are not injured and must be dispatched with a club by the hunter making his daily rounds of the snarelines. On his round the hunter also repairs the brush fence and resets the snares. Often a man checks the lines of his brother, father, or son, as well as his own, so that it is not necessary for each man to go out every day.

At the height of the snaring season each hunter has one to three lines in operation, and each line has seven to nine gaps set with snares. At the Dobe camp in 1964 hunters who had set 20 to 25 separate snares averaged one small animal per hunter per week through the winter. A hunter's success in snaring seems to depend on his interpretation of game tracks and the patience with which he habituates the animals to crossing his lines where he wants them to. At the Dobe camp during the 4-week period from July 7 to August 2, 1964, 18 animals were killed, 11 of them in snares. The snared animals included five steenbok, two hare, one honey badger, and three game birds (two korhaan and one kori bustard). Although snared animals constituted 61 percent of the kills during the period, they accounted for only 20 percent of the meat; 40.8 kg out of a total of 205.9 kg.

The Bisa, by contrast, used a much wider variety of snares than the !Kung and these were of many different types. Trapping and snaring for the Bisa has fallen largely into disuse (Marks 1976:80–5).

MOBILE HUNTING

Preparations for the hunt

In the mobile hunt (!gai) the hunter carries with him the equipment necessary to kill over 40 different species of animals, from the smallest mongoose up to a giraffe. The hunter may have a single species as his objective, but he does not neglect the possibility that other game may come along. Therefore, the preparations for the hunt are standard and generalized, with attention to both technical and informational aspects. The first ensures that the toolkit is assembled and all the components are in working order; the second provides the best information available on where the best hunting is to be found.

The evening before the hunt, the hunter sits by his fire checking his kit. First he empties his quiver, lays the arrows carefully on the ground, and examines each arrow in turn, testing the link shaft and binding for a tight fit and sighting down the length of the arrow to check for straightness. If the arrow is out of true, he straightens it by twirling it lightly over a small fire and bending it gently in his hands. If he is not satisfied, he returns the arrow to his quiver making a mental note not to use it. After checking his arrows, he selects the three or four he will shoot and puts the rest back in the quiver. Then he may apply touch-up poison directly on the foreshaft to provide a little added killing power.

Next he examines his bow, pulling the bowstring a few times to check whether the tension is correct. He may oil the bow itself to condition the wood against cracking. Then he checks his spear and springhare hook to ensure that all the hafts are tight and that the wood is both straight and supple. In this extremely dry climate wood becomes brittle and often cracks or breaks in the hunt.

The technical preparations conclude with the assembly of the kit. The quiver is capped and its handle intertwined with the spear, bow, and digging stick to make a neat bundle. The springhare hook is carefully hung in the branches of a tree, out of reach of children. Into the shoulder bag go the following items:

1. Knife, for butchery and a variety of other tasks, such as cutting branches or twine and making quick repairs in the field
2. A whetstone (optional)

3. A flint-and-steel fire-making kit (if none is available, the traditional fire drill is stowed in the quiver)

4. Lengths of sinew, for making instant repairs on link-shaft bindings

5. Snares, to set for birds if a nest is encountered; also doubles as binding to tie up small game for carrying home

6. A net bag (optional) if gathering is planned as an alternative or for carrying filleted meat

7. Iron adze/ax, for butchery, opening beehives, or cutting carrying yokes

8. Smoking pipe and tobacco (if available)

The whole kit is hung from a customary branch near the man's hut or inside the hut if rain is threatening. In the morning there is little more for a man to do than shoulder his kit and move out.

In deciding *where* and *what* to hunt, the hunter seeks both empirical and magical forms of data. In the actual choice of routes and tactics, the empirical data play an important role. The magical data from divination and dreams are more important in telling a man whether to hunt and giving him a feeling of confidence, and are particularly sought after by hunters who feel they are down on their luck. Dreams and omens are widely used by the Bisa hunters as well (Marks 1976:102). First the hunter consults with the men and women of the camp to get reports on game sighting, game tracks, and weather conditions. Some of the questions he asks, depending on season, include these:

Spring: If rain clouds are sighted, on what localities did the rain actually fall?
Late summer: Which of the seasonal water points still hold water?
Late winter, early spring: What is the state of the grazing in different localities? Is there any new growth on burn patches?
Midsummer: If an animal has been killed in an area, how many others were there? Were any wounded but not pursued? Have the females dropped their young?
Anytime of year: Are there signs of occupied burrows?

Discussion of these questions may occupy several hundred hours a year of a man's time. Yet this is not considered by the !Kung as work (see Chapter 9). It is both part of a hunter's job and a pleasure to sit with a group of four or five men discussing the current situation, the habits of game, and the hunts of the recent and distant past. Even men who are not hunting contribute their experiences. Women participate in these discussions too. They cover much ground on their gathering trips and because they are as keen observers of the environment as are the men, their observations are sought and taken seriously.

Based on the information and opinions of others, on the oracle disks, and on his own observations of the environment, the hunter decides on a rough strategy for the day's hunt. This includes a direction to set out in, a set of working leads based on recent tracks, and perhaps backup alternatives like digging out a springhare or gathering nuts if nothing else turns up. With this plan in mind, the hunter turns in for the night.

The search for game

In the morning the hunters, singly or in twos or threes, shoulder their weapons and set out. They move in the direction determined the day before at a brisk pace, scanning the ground a meter or two ahead of them for signs of game. As fresh spoor is sighted there is a great deal of discussion about what the animal is doing, where it is going, and whether it is worth following. If the trail becomes very fresh, the men fall silent and communicate with each other by sign language as they move quickly but quietly through the bush (see Howell 1965:184–5; Marshall 1976:136). When hunters lose sight of one another, they signal each other by prearranged birdlike calls that act as homing signals but do not alarm the animals.

The man in the lead, if two or more are hunting, follows the spoor and stops only when the track divides or seems to disappear; then the hunters fan out to search for the correct spoor and resume tracking. This can be a laborious process, and if fresher spoor crosses the one they are following, the hunters may instantly switch to the more promising lead. So a day's hunting is made up of a series of spatially connected pathways; each point of intersection represents a decision by the hunters to follow the pathway that offers the better chance of success.

Hunting from a blind does not require initial tracking; the hunter waits for the prey to come to him. This method is infrequently used among the Dobe area !Kung. There are six stone blinds at ≠Gi water hole near !Kubi that have a considerable antiquity, according to John Yellen. They are very occasionally used for night hunting by !Kung men from !Kubi. I was also shown two small pit blinds dug at the edge of ≠Ta flats near N!um!koma, 35 km south of /Xai/xai. Fairly large herds of kudu, wildebeest, and gemsbok congregate on these flats, attracted by the salt licks (*hwanasi*). A hunter approaches the flats cautiously at dawn, and if he finds animals present crawls carefully out to his pit to wait there in absolute stillness for the animals to approach the ring of licking places that lie within a 20-meter radius of the blind. If he is lucky and the wind is right, he may get a chance at a shot. But it is not a particularly successful spot. ≠Toma !kom!gowsi, who dug the blinds and who is an excellent hunter, claims to have killed only a few kudu here over a period of years. ≠Toma, along with all the other !Kung hunters, has found the great majority of his kills through mobile hunting and tracking.

How to track

This section discusses some of the basics of tracking and how the variables in a situation are weighed in arriving at a decision about which lead to follow (see also Marks 1976:117ff).

The !Kung are such superb trackers and make such accurate deductions from the faintest marks in the sand that at first their skill seems uncanny. For example, both men and women are able to identify an individual person merely by the sight of his or her footprint in the sand. There is nothing mysterious about this. Their tracking is a skill, cultivated over a lifetime, that builds on literally tens of thousands of observations. The !Kung hunter can deduce the following kinds of information about the animal he is tracking: its species and sex, its age, how fast it is traveling, whether it is alone or with other animals, its physical condition (healthy or ill), whether and on what it is feeding, and the time of day the animal passed this way.

The species, of course, is identified by the shape of the hoofprint and by the dung or scat; this is the simplest information to be deduced, and any 12-year-old boy can accurately reproduce in the sand the prints of a dozen species. The sex of the animal is identified in some species by the print's shape, in others by the print's size and the length of the stride. A set of adult hoofprints and a set of immature prints moving together signify, of course, a mother and her young. Similarly, the !Kung use their knowledge of the seasonal social organization of different species to determine the age-sex composition of a group of animals. The size or age of an animal correlates directly with the size of its print. The depth of the print indicates the weight of the animal. An old or infirm animal may be distinguished by a halting gait or uneven stride length. Evidence of crippling is eagerly sought and is discerned when one hoofprint is deeper than the others.

The number of animals in a herd is difficult to determine, especially if they are many and their tracks crisscross, but given the relatively small herd size of the current ungulate populations, it is usually easy to distinguish three from four, or four from five, animals if the herd is followed for a kilometer or two. Feeding animals stop every 10 meters to browse or graze; animals that are not feeding move in a relatively straight course. Their speed is shown by the depth of the print, the amount of sand kicked up, and the distance between footfalls. A galloping animal leaves clusters of very deep prints spaced far apart, sharp at the leading edge and blurred at the following edge, with a considerable scatter of sand behind. What the animal is feeding on can be observed in several ways. Examining the dung is perhaps the least useful technique because it indicates the diet for hours or days previously. More helpful is observing the scatter of fresh forage that has fallen from the lips of the animal as it moves along feeding or examining which plants have their tips missing in the vicinity of the animal's milling prints.

Knowledge of the animal's habits aids in determining the time of day it passed by. Some of the signs are surprisingly simple. If the tracks zigzag from shade tree to tree, the animal went through in the heat of the day. If the tracks go under the west side of the trees, the animal was catching the morning shade; if under the east side, the afternoon shade; and if under either side, the animal passed at midday. Milling tracks within a small radius out in the open suggest the animal was there at night and was sleeping. Tracks leading into a dense thicket indicate the animal rested up during midday.

The number of minutes or hours elapsed since the animal went through can be determined from changes in the spoor. This is crucial information; to obtain it, the !Kung have developed their discriminating powers to the highest degree. After a print has been made, it provides a miniature physiographic feature that is acted upon by natural processes. Consider a simple example. When fresh, the print is clean-cut, but after an hour (or less if the day is windy) a fine covering of windblown sand collects in the depression. Later twigs and grass fall in, and then insect and other animal tracks are superimposed. The moisture content of the soil 1, 2, 3, or 4 cm below the surface and the rate at which soil dries out after being exposed by a footfall are two variables that are exceedingly well studied by the !Kung. When an animal is being closely followed, the present position of the shade in relation to the animal's footprint plus these other signs can indicate within 15 minutes the time the animal passed by.

All these kinds of information are interpreted and processed by the hunters and are weighed in deciding whether a spoor is worth following. Distance ahead is the most important variable. Fresh spoor of an animal only a few hundred meters ahead is a first-rate lead. If the animal is more than 2 km ahead, pursuit is not considered feasible. Next in importance come factors of wind direction and vegetation cover. If the wind is blowing the hunters' scent *toward* the animal, the chances of success are small, unless the men circle to downwind. Thick vegetation cover is preferred to open plains. In deep bush the hunter can creep forward well concealed. In the open it is harder to move in close without startling the prey. In a bare molapo it is almost impossible to get close. Next in importance come the factors of the animal's speed and behavior as it moves. A fast-moving animal, even if it is unaware of the hunter's presence, is poor quarry. It will quickly widen the distance between the hunters and itself. An animal that is feeding and resting, moving slowly from bush to bush, is a promising target. The hunter by a series of deft moves can take advantage of the cover to get close enough for a shot. Thus the ideal lead for a hunter is a slowly moving animal, upwind, 500 meters ahead or less, resting and feeding in deep bush, and with a marked limp for good measure.

Table 8.1. *Weights of some small and underground game species and their edible yield*

Animal	Male: gross weight (kg)	Male: edible yield kg	%	Female: gross weight (kg)	Female: edible yield kg	%	Immature: gross weight (kg)	Immature: edible yield kg	%
Small game									
Duiker	18.5	9.3	50	20.2	11.1	50	13.6	6.8	50
Steenbok	11.1	5.6	50	11.2	5.6	50	8.2	4.1	50
Hare	2.4	1.4	60	2.3	1.4	60	1.8	1.0	60
Honey badger	9.8	4.9	50						
Wild cat	5.5	2.8	50	4.6	2.3	50			
Underground game									
Springhare	3.5	2.5	70	3.2	2.2	70			
Ant bear	63.5	38.1	60	41.0	24.6	60			
Porcupine	17.2	8.6	50	19.1	9.6	50			

Source: Reay Smithers (personal communication).

If none of these conditions is present, any sign of small or underground game is sufficient to turn a hunter aside. We now consider small game and underground game before going on to discuss the killing of the major larger antelopes.

Small game killing'

The weights and edible yields of some small and underground game species are listed in Table 8.1. In mobile hunting, small game is knocked down with a throwing club, shot with an arrow, or chased with dogs. Club, dogs, and/or spear are used to finish off the animal at close quarters. The ≠da≠hxaisi (steenbok and duiker) are the most common small game animals killed. Rarely tracked for any distance, they are usually sighted frozen in the shadows or they may break cover immediately in front of the hunting party. Dogs are most effective in this situation: They chase the prey, wound or kill it, and wait over the kill for the hunter to arrive at the kill site. If there are no dogs, the hunter throws his club or walking stick at the prey; the men are surprisingly accurate with these unpromising instruments. If the animal is stunned and takes off, a merry chase follows: The hunter retrieves his club and goes crashing through the bush striking at the prey until it is beaten insensible. Usually the animal is clubbed rather than stabbed to death to ensure that the valuable hide is undamaged.

Poisoned arrows are also used for small game, though my impression is the the !Kung regard this as a form of overkill. A full dose of poison, well placed, can kill an animal as small as a steenbok or duiker in half an hour or less. Even the iron-tipped arrow itself has considerable knock-down power for these small animals. Yet we know of cases where a duiker has been tracked for 2 days in the same way as a large antelope.

The ≠da≠hxaisi are systematically hunted, but other small game are not neglected. Next in importance is the common hare, followed by the bat-eared fox, genet, and the several species of mongoose. The meat of this last group of animals may be fed to the dogs if other meat is available back at the camp, but people do eat this meat on occasion.

Game birds – mainly guinea fowl, francolin, and korhaan – are hunted with snares on an ad hoc basis. The snare is baited with a pea-sized edible bulb. During the breeding season, the hunter often finds a nest of eggs with the mother hen absent; he then sets a snare baited with one of the eggs to trap the hen on her return. Other game birds are knocked down with throwing clubs, then retrieved by dogs.

The young of all small game species are frequently run down on foot and captured in the hand. For the ≠da≠hxaisi, immatures may constitute a third to a half of the animals killed.

Underground game killing

Four important species are hunted below the ground: springhare, ant bear, porcupine, and warthog. The last two are hunted above ground as well. The aardwolf (*Proteles cristatus*) and the pangolin or scaly anteater (*Manis temmincki*) may also be taken underground.

Chapter 5 describes how the springhare is relatively easily captured by means of the 4-meter-long springhare probe. The other underground species are much more formidable: they live in large burrows; they readily attack a man, if cornered; and each is armed with a respectable means of defense – quills for the porcupine, claws for the ant bear, and tusks and hooves for the warthog. For all three, the basic hunting process is similar. The hunter examines a series of recent burrows to see if they are occupied. Most of the burrows are dug originally by ant bears, often but not always in the base of an anthill. The other two species occupy burrows abandoned by ant bears.

The porcupine and the ant bear are nocturnal animals. The hunter's task is to find one lying up in a burrow during the day. If he finds a porcupine-occupied burrow, he can go into the burrow himself with his spear and try to kill the animal underground, or he can block off the entrance and start digging down to the animal just as he would for a springhare. If the larger ant bear or a warthog is found, the hunter may build a fire at the mouth of the burrow, hoping to stupefy the prey with smoke and goad it to break out into the open. Then the hunter and, if available, his dogs, can wound and kill the prey at close quarters. If the animal fails to break out and dies of asphyxiation in the burrow, the hunter has to drag or dig it out. Which technique is used depends on the terrain. If the ground is hard, as it is around an anthill, and/or if the burrow is deep, digging out becomes unprofitable. Similarly, an ant bear that dies in its burrow may be wedged in so tightly that hauling it out is extremely difficult. Trying to goad the animal to the surface is the tactic of choice for these species.

This is dangerous work and demands personal bravery on the part of the hunters. A man enters a burrow only if he is hunting with a partner, who kneels poised at the mouth ready to haul out the hunter by the ankles. If the burrow is in soft sand, there is the danger of cave-in if the ant bear thrashes about. Several men bear the scars of ant bear claws on their faces and shoulders, and our records show that at least one man died from injuries and another from being smothered in a cave-in. The theme of a dangerous underworld inhabited by a society of ant bears exists in the mythology of the !Kung (Biesele, in press).

Porcupines are frequently killed above ground. If a sleeping porcupine is encountered on the trail, it is immediately set upon with whatever weapons are available – clubs, spears, digging sticks, or any piece of dead wood that is ready to hand. A merry chase follows, with shouting, crashing through the bush, and confusion, but the porcupine is usually killed. Such an episode is shown in Marshall's film, *The Hunters* (1956).

The ant bear (along with the pangolin) is the most subterranean of all the larger game species; it is rarely observed in daylight above ground. Only after heavy rains, when its burrow is temporarily flooded, is an ant bear found in the morning curled up at the mouth of its burrow. Then it may be shot with a poison arrow.

The warthog is basically an above-ground species that goes to ground in certain circumstances – the sow when she is dropping a litter and either sex when it is under attack. Many warthogs are killed on the surface, especially with the aid of dogs. When they do go to ground, they must be smoked out into the open. As the cornered warthog breaks out of its burrow, there are moments of high drama. The hog may be slashing out at the dogs, and the hunter must dodge around to spear the prey while avoiding hitting the dogs or being himself attacked by the hog. Warthog hunting often maims and occasionally kills dogs. When a sow and a litter of piglets break out, the confusion and excitement are compounded. In spite of these difficulties warthog is the most frequently killed of the larger game animals (Table 8.5).

Big game hunting

By *big game* is meant the six large antelope species whose adult forms weigh over 100 kg: kudu, gemsbok, wildebeest, eland, hartebeest, and roan. All these, plus the giraffe, are hunted in the classic manner with bow and arrows. The killing of the adults of any of these seven species is a major event, and though few hunters kill as many as five big game animals a year, the meat from these seven species probably provides over 50 percent of the annual wild game supply of a camp. Easier to kill are the young of these species, especially the first three. These can be run down and clubbed as are steenbok and duiker. The returns in meat from the young are much smaller. Several other species usually classified as big game by white hunters are not hunted systematically by the !Kung; these include zebra, elephant, ostrich, lion, leopard, and cheetah.

There are five elements in the successful killing of big game. We have already considered the preparation for the hunt and the tracking of game; here we discuss the stalking, wounding, and killing of the animal.

When a very fresh lead is being followed, the hunters move extremely carefully, without a sound, taking pains to see that the animal is always upwind, even if this means leaving the actual spoor of the animal. As the hunters close the distance to a few hundred meters, it is often possible to catch glimpses of the prey through the underbrush. Now comes the final stalk: One man moves forward, crouching at first, then crawling, then inching forward on his belly to get in as close as possible for a shot. The upper limit for reasonable accuracy seems to be 25 meters, and 10 meters is considered the optimum distance for a shot. It may take the hunter 20, 30 or even 40 minutes to cover the distance. Beforehand, the hunter has chosen two or three arrows to carry forward with his bow, leaving the rest of his kit behind. As he moves forward, he watches the animal closely, especially its ears, for any signs of alarm. When it raises its head or turns in his direction, the hunter freezes, holding still for several minutes at a time if necessary; then when the animal's head turns or drops, the stalker moves forward again. If the animal is skittish and keeps moving away, the hunter may have to risk a less than ideal shot before the prey moves out of range. Usually the hunter does not have a clear view of the prey; only the outline of the back or the legs may be visible through the bush. Before shooting, the hunter may have to figure out what trajectory his arrow should follow to avoid branches and trees in its path.

Reaching his optimum range, the hunter tries a shot: He draws the bow, takes careful aim, and silently lets fly. After this first shot, he holds stock-still; if he has missed completely, there is a chance the animal has noticed nothing and the hunter gets a second shot. If the animal bolts, the hunter may still hold his position because sometimes the prey moves only a few steps and stands still again, allowing the hunter a second shot from a standing position.

If the arrow strikes home, clearly wounding the animal, the next phase of the hunt begins. The hunter breaks cover and runs forward on a diagonal path trying to intercept and get another shot at the now-alarmed animal as it runs by. He may shoot all his arrows hoping to put more poison into the prey and thereby hasten its collapse. The hunter tries to hit a spot that will lame or hobble the animal.

In the meantime, the second hunter has moved in the direction of the animal's probable escape route, positioning himself for one or more shots as the animal runs by. The first hunter may help the second by chasing the prey in the latter's direction.

Ordinarily the hunters are fortunate to wound one animal a day. When two or more animals are being stalked, each hunter may choose an animal to creep up on. Hunters shoot as many animals as possible, even if not all can be followed. This increases chances of getting at least one and allows hunters to choose the most promising spoor. If their final approach is exceptionally good, it is not unknown for two hunters to shoot at and wound four or even five different animals in a single flurry. It is hunts like these, when five buck are killed in one day, that men discuss around the campfire for years and generations afterward.

In a few seconds the animal runs out of range. It is not pursued, for there is far more important work to be done. The first task is to retrieve and account for all the arrows shot. By this means the hunter can quickly confirm whether his animal is well wounded or even wounded at all. If he finds all his arrows, he is out of luck. If one is missing, this supports his visual impression that the animal is wounded. Next he begins to track the fleeing animal. If necessary, he must sort out its tracks from those of other animals in the herd. He looks for various signs. Blood on the ground indicates a good wound, but not an ideal one because the bleeding may flush much of the poison out of the animal's system. Finding a main shaft alone is an excellent sign, indicating a deeper wound with little bleeding and the detachable arrowhead inside the prey. Finding the whole arrow intact suggests it has been worked out of the wound by muscular contraction. In this event, the hunter examines the foreshaft carefully; if little poison remains, it indicates that most of the poison has already been absorbed and the animal may still die. I think another reason the hunters try to account for and retrieve all the arrows is to prevent someone's accidentally stepping on a stray arrow and poisoning himself at a later date.

Having made the initial diagnosis and retrieved their arrows, the hunters break off to get their full kits and to discuss the situation. They must consider many possibilities. How seriously is the animal wounded? Will it die or will it recover and keep going? Even if it is fatally wounded, how far can it travel before it collapses? Will that be too far away for the meat to be carried back? They also take into account the presence of large carnivores in the vicinity. Will the lions scavenge most of the kill before the hunters can reach it? To answer these questions, the hunters pick up the wounded animal's trail and follow it for several kilometers, observing carefully. They assess the animal's speed–how fast it is increasing the distance between them; its direction–whether it is moving away from or toward their base camp; and its strength–whether it shows signs of weakening.

The last is an indication of how rapidly the poison is taking effect, and this is the crucial factor. The hunters look for a number of signs. Zigzagging, milling, and stamping tracks indicate the prey is agitated, an early symptom of the poison. Bursts of running in panic tire the prey and hasten the working of the poison through the system. Signs of black blood or blood in the feces show the poisoning is well advanced. The dung of a fatally wounded animal has a peculiar smell, and this is a most hopeful sign. If the wound is well placed, an hour of tracking enables the hunters to estimate the probable time and location of the animal's death. More often only an approximate idea of the animal's condition and direction is gained because the poison works slowly at first. In either case, after an hour or two of tracking the men break off the trail and go home to the camp.

The poison takes an average of 6 to 24 hours or more to work, and once the nature of the wound is established there is no point in tracking the animal to its deathplace. If pursued too closely, the prey may be spurred to run much further before dying. The !Kung prefer to let the poison do the work for them. Only on rare occasions when hunters find themselves tracking as night falls do they stay out overnight, and as they never carry blankets, they have only their fire to keep them warm. Sometimes if the animal is lightly wounded, the hunters go home with the intention of resuming tracking the next day. However, the major reason the hunters leave the wounded animal before it is killed is to organize a party at camp to carry the meat back the following day.

FINISHING OFF, BUTCHERY, AND CARRYING HOME

All game must be killed and the meat brought back to camp from the kill site. For the small animals, the task is simple. From initial wounding to final killing can take an hour or less. The animals are light, weighing from 1 kg for a mongoose to a maximum of 20 kg for a female duiker, and can be easily carried home intact by a single hunter. For a secure load, the hindlegs are tightly bound together and attached to a club or digging stick as a makeshift carrying yoke. With the antelopes, the fore- and hindlegs may be forced together and bound to make a tighter bundle. An incision through the hamstring tendon forms an eye through which the binding is threaded. Then the load is shouldered and carried home to be butchered and cooked.

For the large animals that are left out overnight, the procedure is far more elaborate. First there is a culturally specified way of informing the camp about the kill; second, there are certain taboos to be observed by the hunter during the night; and third, a carrying party must be organized. In the morning this party must pick up the trail, find the animal if they can, dispatch it if necessary, and then butcher the meat and arrange it into parcels for carrying home.

Returning home on the day of the hunt, the hunter is naturally pleased with himself; but he must not show it. Announcing a kill is to the !Kung a sign of arrogance and is strongly discouraged. Humility and understatement constitute the appropriate behavior (Lee 1969b and below).

/Xashe, an excellent hunter from /Xai/xai and the southern districts, explained the correct behavior as follows:

> When you come home empty-handed, you sleep and you say to yourself, "Oh, what have I done? What's the matter that I haven't killed?" Then the next morning you get up and without a word you go out and hunt again. This time you *do* kill something and you come home. My *tsu* ("older kinsman") sees me and asks: "Well what did you see today?" "Tsutsu," I reply, "I didn't see anything."
>
> I am sitting there with my head in my hands, but my tsu comes back to me because he is a zhu/twã ("person"). "What do you mean you haven't killed anything! Can't you see that I'm dying of hunger!"
>
> "Well, there might be something out there. I just might have scratched its elbow."
>
> Then you say, as he smiles, "Why don't we go out in the morning and have a look." And so we two and others will bring home the meat together the next day.

After the word gets around that a kill has been made, a party of three to six people – depending on the size of the animal and its distance away – is organized. Usually the party is all male; however, there is no taboo on women's participation in a carrying party, and on a number of occasions the party is a mixed one. During the night the hunter is in a ritually heightened state; he may drink water but is expected not to eat anything lest the nourishment give added strength to the dying prey. I suspect that among the younger hunters this custom is not adhered to closely. In any case, there is no restriction on sex, and the men say that when one's heart is sweet with the thought of the kill, intercourse is particularly good.

If a very large animal has been killed and if there is water near the kill site, the whole camp may move to the kill and make a new camp. More frequently, the small party brings the meat back to the camp. Setting out in the morning in high spirits, the group moves directly to the point where the tracking was discontinued the previous evening. If the direction of the animal is toward the camp, the party will try to intersect the trail at the closest point. Picking up the trail may be difficult, especially if there are many animals of the species moving about or if rain or high wind has obscured the track during the night. Eventually the spoor is found, and the party moves toward the kill. With luck, the animal has died only 1 or 2 hours' walk from the starting point (i.e., 5 to 10 km distance), but sometimes it is necessary to track the animal right through the second day and not kill it until the third. In the longest chase we know of an animal was tracked over an 8-day period before being killed. It is more likely that if a day's tracking discovers no sign of the animal's imminent collapse, the party will decide to abandon the chase and start hunting fresh spoor or even return home.

John Yellen estimates that perhaps as high a proportion as 50 percent of all the animals wounded by the !Kung are allowed to escape and are never eaten. They either recover from their wounds and survive or run so far away that the hunters decide not to pursue them. In the latter case, the animals die eventually and are eaten by the lions, hyenas, and vultures. This rate of abandonment is high by the standards of the professional white hunters of Botswana, among whom it is a point of professional concern that all wounded animals be dispatched by the hunter. Nevertheless, one must remember that the overall predation rate for the !Kung is so low that even if half the animals wounded are allowed to escape, this would have little effect in reducing the game population levels in the area.

If the signs are good the pursuers continue the chase. As they approach the animal, they may find it still moving, standing or lying exhausted, or already dead. In the first instance, an additional chase and the shooting of more poisoned arrows may be necessary before the animal is brought down. In the second case, the hunters approach the quarry warily and may attack it with thrown spears before bringing it down. Often it is sufficient to approach the helpless animal and stab it to death directly with a spear. In all cases the spear is methodically worked in and out of the throat to ensure the animal is dead.

If the animal has died during the night, lions, leopards, or hyenas may have beaten the humans to the kill site. When the hunters find a pride of lions actually in the act of eating the carcass, they proceed in as follows. First, they take care to find out how hungry the lions are. If the animals are just starting their meal, they will be difficult to dislodge, and the !Kung retreat discreetly. However, if they show clear signs of satiety, the !Kung proceed in a surprisingly bold manner. The hunters run forward shouting and waving their arms; this commotion is usually sufficient to drive the lions off the kill. Then the people salvage what they can of the meat and return home.

In the ordinary event, if their timing is right, the party arrives to find a dead animal unmolested by predators. Everyone is in good spirits, most of all the hunters, and in keeping with the humility ethic members of the party begin to banter about the miserably small kill and the useless exertions required to bring it home. (This joking is discussed in detail later in this chapter, under "Hunting Success and Status Differences.") The joking continues as they set about butchering the meat. Fresh branches are piled to receive the cut meat, and a fire is built to cook the liver and other parts that are customarily eaten by the party on the site. The first cut is to remove the arrow or arrows if they are still embedded in the flesh. The meat around the wound is cut carefully away and discarded. The rest of the meat is quite edible. A cut is made at the breastbone or on the haunch to find out how much fat the animal has. Fat animals are keenly desired, and all !Kung express a constant craving for animal fat. The animal is then butchered in one of two ways.

If the hide is to be preserved intact, for making into a kaross, skinning is done carefully, removing the hide in a single piece with the main cuts made around the neck, down the belly line, along the inside of the legs and around the distal ends of the tibiae and radii. The wet hide is removed; after being brought back to camp, it will be stretched out, inside up, on the ground with pegs placed every few centimeters around the perimeter.

If the hide is too thick or too damaged to be useful, it is roughly cut up and left adhering to the extremities but skinned away from the torso. Later it will be dried and eaten. Then, with the animal on its side, the major butchery proceeds in the following stages:

1. The hindhooves, with metatarsals and tarsals, and the fore-hooves with metacarpals and carpals, are skinned and cut away. The long bones may be split with rocks on the spot and the marrow eaten or rubbed on the body.

2. The upper part of the rib cage and the breastbone are chopped with an ax and removed to expose the abdominal cavity.

3. The viscera (heart, liver, lungs, stomachs, and other organs) are removed. The stomach contents are emptied and usually discarded. The blood from the abdominal cavity is collected in a bowl and may be poured into an emptied stomach sac for carrying home.

4. The haunches, left and right, are removed. The scent glands on the haunches are carefully cut out and discarded. If left intact, they would spoil the meat.

5. The anus is cut away with the rectum and bowel. All three are removed as a unit. The contents of the bowel and rectum are squeezed out and discarded.

6. The rump, pelvis, and lumbar vertebrae with the choice back steaks are removed together.

7. The shoulders (chuck) are removed along with the forelegs.

8. The rest of the backbone with the ribs and short ribs is cut away from the head.

9. The head with horns becomes a unit.

10. In larger animals the forelegs are removed from the shoulders,

and the lower part from the upper part of the haunches, for easier carrying.

The result is 11 basic packages for carrying: (1) breast, (2) viscera, (3) left haunch, (4) right haunch, (5) rump and lower back, (6) bowel and rectum, (7) left shoulder, (8) right shoulder, (9) upper back and short ribs, (10) head, and (11) hide.

When the butchering is complete, the chunks of meat are divided up into parcels for carrying home. Each carrier is given two lots, one for the back of the carrying yoke and a lighter one for the front for balance. The yoke is cut on the site for each man. He uses his club, spear, or digging stick on his other shoulder to balance and distribute the weight. Women carry their share packed in the kaross in the same way they pack vegetable foods.

Two further stages in the butchering process may be noted. Kxau!koma of the /Du/da southern population butchered a large male gemsbok and filleted the entire carcass on the kill site, removing all the bones. The strips of fresh meat were then packed in the grass-lined men's carrying net (/twisi). After eating the head and the viscera at the kill site, Kxau and two other men carried all the rest home, having reduced a 200-kg animal to three convenient loads weighing 23 to 27 kg each.

If the hunters stay near the kill site for several days, there is time enough to cut most of the meat into strips and dry it into biltong or jerky. This reduces the weight of the meat by 60 percent and makes it possible for one or two men to carry the biltong of an entire animal. Bundles of sticks of biltong are one of the commonest ways meat is distributed both within a camp or from one camp to another.

The carrying party with loads of meat weighing between 20 and 30 kg moves in single file back to camp. The pace is slow – 3 to 4 km per hour – and there are frequent rests. Usually the party brings everything home in one trip. But if there is too much to be carried, the remainder is hung from the outer branches of trees or left on the ground covered with thorn branches until someone can come back for it the following day. At hunting camps where several animals have been butchered, the party may have to make several return trips before all the meat is finally brought into camp.

KOPELA MASWE'S WARTHOG AND OTHER HUNTS

The foregoing sections describe the hunting process from its initial preparations to the final carrying home of the meat. Now let us see how these general features are expressed in an actual series of hunts. Because every hunt is in some ways unique, it is helpful to offer some concrete examples of the mode and timing of killing, the distances traveled, and the recovery and distribution of the meat.

Table 8.2. *Allocation of carcass of Kopela Maswe's warthog*

| Portion | Carrier | Weight | |
		kg	lb, oz
Head Back and viscera	Kopela Maswe	19.8	43, 9
Forelegs and shoulders Hindlegs and rump	N!eishi	23.9	52, 11
Breast Stomach and bowels	≠Toma//gwe (the father)	6.4	14, 0
Total		50.1	110, 4

Kopela Maswe's warthog hunt: October 25–26, 1967

≠Dau, a Dobe man in his late thirties, is known by his Tswana nickname, Kopela Maswe, which means roughly "bad news." He and his younger brother, N!eishi, went out to hunt on the morning of October 25. They found nothing until midafternoon, when they saw a female warthog in the open. They shot and wounded the warthog; it ran to ground, where they cornered it; then when it came charging out of the burrow, they shot it again at point-blank range. This stopped the animal in its tracks long enough to be finished off by Kopela Maswe's spear. No fire was built at the mouth of the burrow and no dogs were used in the killing. By this time the day was late, so the two hunters covered over the carcass with thornbush branches and returned to camp.

Arriving home, they said they had seen nothing, and as their animal was already dead, they enjoyed a hearty meal of wildebeest meat from a kill of the previous day.

In the morning of October 26 the two brothers and their father (aged 65) made up a party of three to go out to the kill site. They found the carcass undisturbed and immediately set about butchering it. The liver and the long ribs were removed, cooked, and eaten on the spot, and the butchering was concluded by noon. The carcass was divided into six parcels and allocated as shown in Table 8.2. These loads were placed on carrying yokes, one fore and one aft, and the three carriers brought the meat back to Dobe, a distance of 6 km, arriving there at 1:30 P.M. Within the hour the meat was cooked to feed the members of the Dobe camp. Because the edible/waste ratio for a warthog is close to 55:45, one can calculate the yield as 27.5 kg (60.5 lb) of raw meat.

≠Dau's yearling wildebeest hunt: October 25–26, 1967

On the same days as the warthog hunt, a 40-year-old Dobe resident, also named ≠Dau, set out to the west to hunt alone. First he shot and killed a pregnant steenbok. As the day was young, he hung the carcass in a tree and continued to hunt. Then he spotted a yearling steenbok, chased it, and killed it with his club. This one he also left in a tree. Then he tracked a small herd of wildebeest and closed in carefully, concentrating on an adult female. He shot at the female, but missed, and she fled. His second shot hit a male about a year old. It had horns about 20 cm long and the thick, matted red brown fur of the immature wildebeest. The shot was well placed, and because the animal was small the poison worked quickly. After an hour of tracking ≠Dau had overtaken and killed the wildebeest. There was still time in the day to butcher the animal. About half the meat was hung in the trees, and the other half was cut into biltong strips, bundled into the /twisi (men's net), and carried home.

On the morning of October 26, ≠Dau, joined by his wife's brother ≠Toma, made up a party of two to retrieve the rest of the meat. They reached the adult steenbok first, and found the carcass had been attacked in the night by genets, which had eaten away the anus to a depth of 8 cm. They went on to collect the young steenbok, which was undisturbed. Finally they retrieved the rest of wildebeest meat, some of which they roasted on the spot. All the meat was brought into Dobe camp by 6:30 P.M.

The weights of the two steenbok were 11.7 kg (25.6 lb) and 2.8 kg (6.3 lb). The wildebeest was not weighed, but its size suggested a weight of about 48 kg. The weights of the animals totaled about 63 kg (138.6 lb), and given a 50:50 edible/waste ratio the animals yielded a total of 31.5 kg (69.3 lb) of meat.

/Xashe's wildebeest hunt: March, 12–14, 1969

This hunt is unusual in that the work stretched out over 3 days.

Day 1. /Xashe, the older brother of Kopela Maswe, went hunting alone in a southwesterly direction on Wednesday, March 12. At midafternoon he crept up on a herd of wildebeest. His first shot hit an adult female; his second, an adult male. Noting that both were well struck, /Xashe broke off the trail and came back to camp to sleep.

Day 2. Thursday morning a tracking and carrying party of five was formed: the hunter, his younger brother N!eishi, his sister's husband Kxau Mahono, his father ≠Toma//gwe, and his 11-year-old son Kxau. They picked up the trail 10 km west of Dobe and followed the herd with the two wounded animals all day to the west. The prey were proving

stronger than expected, but /Xashe was sure his poison was fresh and his
arrows well placed. The wounded animals were also moving apart; as
the male appeared too strong, they decided to leave him and concentrate
on killing the female. By midafternoon it was clear she was going to die,
but her tracks were still heading steadily west.

It was growing dark, so the party decided to spend the night out. They
bedded down at a place called !Kwi/wama after covering about 25 km
during the day. None had a blanket or even a shirt to cover himself, but
they built a large fire and ate some mongongos for dinner; there was
plenty of water to be had from the pans along the route.

Day 3. They were up and on their way by dawn (5:30 A.M.) Friday.
Following the trail, they found that the wildebeest had died in the night
about an hour's walk to the west. Immediately they set about butchering
it; after cooking and eating the liver, they cut up the entire animal into
biltong strips. This meant leaving the skin, intestines, and head behind
in order to reduce the take-home weight.

It was a larger than average wildebeest. I did not weigh the meat, but I
estimate that about 90 kg was brought back to camp. The kill site was
approximately 25 km west of Dobe, and the carrying party covered that
distance in 7 hours at an average speed of 4 km per hour. After being
wounded, this wildebeest lived approximately 30 hours before the poison
killed it. Because it was moving quickly, over 12 hours were spent in
tracking it, mostly on day 2, and the party had to sleep out one night.
This represents 3 days of hard work for the hunter and 2 man-days of
work for three other men – a total of 9 man-days of work for 90 kg of
meat.

AN INVENTORY OF PREY SPECIES

Some 262 species of animals are known to the !Kung. Of these about 80
species are eaten. However, there is no hard and fast line between the
edible and inedible sectors of the animal kingdom. It is more useful to
think of several grades of edibility: (1) the handful of species whose meat
is eagerly sought, such as the antelopes and game birds; (2) species that
are not regularly hunted but are taken if the opportunity presents itself;
(3) animals that are not hunted at all, although some few people will eat
the meat if it is offered them; and (4) species that for various reasons are
never eaten because they are too small (such as lizards and mice), too
difficult to capture (such as elephants), tabooed (monkeys and hyenas),
or a combination of these factors. Of course, there are dozens of species
of insects (e.g., ants, flies) that offer nothing to man as food and are not
eaten.

In Table 8.3, 259 of the 262 species are arranged into these four classes of edibility; excluded are 3 species of mammals that are so rare they cannot be classified. Only 34 species are systematically hunted or, in the case of insects, gathered. A further 25 species are hunted occasionally, and 19 more species are eaten by some people, but not regularly hunted. It is worth noting that the lizards, snakes, and rodents attributed to the !Kung dietary in the literature (e.g., Service 1966) are not eaten by the !Kung of the Dobe area. These people get plenty of meat from the more attractive large species and so have no need to bother with such unrewarding small creatures.

Small game and underground species have already been discussed. The following sections consider the main big game species, with data on weight, mode of hunting, and the frequency with which each is killed.

Eight big game species

Much of the mammal biomass of the Dobe and /Du/da areas is accounted for by eight large ungulates: giraffe, warthog, gemsbok, kudu, wildebeest, eland, roan antelope, and hartebeest. Accordingly, these eight species provide much of the meat eaten in the !Kung camps. By contrast, the most important large mammals for the Bisa are elephant, hippopotamus, buffalo, impala, waterbuck, warthog, and zebra (Marks 1976:170–95). Except for warthog, none of these is common in the Dobe area. Table 8.4 shows the weights of these eight !Kung species arranged in order of the frequency with which they are killed by the !Kung. The edible yield of these animals is about 50 percent of the dead weight. If the hide is eaten, the edible yield is about 10 percent higher. The edible yield of animals with large horns falls slightly below 50 percent, as the horns are discarded. The weights of immature members of these species vary widely, from 5 to 10 percent of adult weight for a newborn to 50 to 80 percent of adult weight for a yearling or 2-year-old.

The warthog, the smallest of the big eight, is the most frequently killed. Throughout 1964 warthog were being killed at the Dobe camp at the rate of three per month. Each adult killed yielded 39 kg of meat. At the other extreme is the giraffe, by far the largest of the eight, with an edible yield per adult of over 500 kg of meat, 13 times the yield of the warthog. Giraffe, however, are rarely killed; none was killed by !Kung in the Dobe area in 1964 or in 1968, and only two were killed in the /Du/da area in 1968 compared with dozens of the other species.

In the middle are the mainstays of !Kung hunting: gemsbok, kudu, and wildebeest. These large, handsome antelopes, weighing from 159 to 272 kg, are killed at a rate of one per month at each camp in the Dobe and /Du/da areas. The edible yield ranges between 79 and 136 kg, two to four times that of the wart hog, with an average of about 100 kg of meat per animal.

The eland is the largest of the African antelopes. Specimens in our area

Table 8.3. *The animal kingdom arranged in classes of edibility in !Kung subsistence*

Edibility class	Mammals[a]		Birds		Reptiles, amphibians		Insects, other invertebrates		Total no. of species
	Species	Total no.	Species	Total no.	Species	Total no.	Species	Total no.	
Class 1: systematically hunted	Warthog Gemsbok Kudu Wildebeest Porcupine Giraffe Hartebeest Roan antelope Steenbok Duiker Springhare Hare Eland Ant bear Pangolin		Guinea fowl Francolin (3 spp.) Duck, goose (3 spp.) Korhann Ostrich (eggs only)		Large tortoise Small tortoise Python		Honeybee Ant lion Click beetle (3 spp.) Catepillar (2 spp.)		
Total class 1		15		9		3		7	34
Class 2: occasionally hunted	Buffalo Bat-eared fox Aardwolf Honey badger Genet Mongoose (3 spp.)		Kori bustard Dove (4 spp.) Sandgrouse (2 spp.) Waxbill (3 spp.) Quail		Land leguaan Bullfrog		Caterpillar (4 spp.)		
Total class 2		8		11		2		4	25

	Mammals	Birds	Reptiles and amphibians	Insects and invertebrates	Total
Class 3: eaten by some persons	Jackall, Zorilla, Wild cat, Caracal, Lion, Leopard, Cheetah	Ostrich (meat), Stork, Other (6 spp.)	Adder (4 spp.)		
Total class 3	8	7	4		19
Class 4: not eaten	Bat (3 spp.), Elephant, Shrew, Rat, mouse (12 spp.), Hyena (2 spp.), Primate (3 spp.), Wild dog, Squirrel (2 spp.)	All others	Other snakes (5 spp.), Other lizards (6 spp.), Other frogs, Turtle (2 spp.), Chameleon (2 spp.)	Other insects and invertebrates	
Total class 4	24	63	16	78	181
Total	55	90	25	89	259

[a]Impala, zebra, and several cats complete the list of 58 mammals, but are so rare they cannot be rated.

Table 8.4. *Weights of eight big game species and their edible yield*

Animal	Male: gross weight kg	Male: gross weight lb	Male: edible yield (50%) kg	Male: edible yield (50%) lb	Female: gross weight kg	Female: gross weight lb	Female: edible yield (50%) kg	Female: edible yield (50%) lb
Warthog	77	170	39	85	77	170	39	85
Gemsbok	204	450	102	225	227	500	113	250
Kudu	272	600	136	300	159	350	79	175
Wildebeest	250	550	125	275	204	450	102	225
Eland	454	1000	227	500	340	750	170	375
Roan antelope	227	500	113	250	181	400	91	200
Hartebeest	136	300	68	150	125	275	62	138
Giraffe	1134	2500	567	1250	1043	2300	522	1150

Source: Data from Smithers (1968 and personal communication).

weight up to 500 kg. In edible yield eland falls midway between the gemsbok-kudu level and that of the giraffe. They are killed far more frequently than the giraffe; at the /Du/da camps they were killed at a rate of one per month in 1968–9. The roan antelope and the hartebeest are occasionally killed; their yield of meat falls in the range of the kudu-gemsbok group.

All these animals are hunted in the classic manner, with bow and poisoned arrow. I have no data on differential mortality rates after wounding. Generally, the larger the animal, the more likely it is to survive the action of the poison.

In addition, two species are taken with the aid of dogs. Warthog may be driven to ground and brought to bay by three or four well-trained hunting dogs. In the case of gemsbok dogs are used in conjunction with arrow poisons, because unlike most antelopes, which flee from dogs, the gemsbok will stand and fight. All these species may be hunted from blinds. None is ever trapped, and only one (warthog) is taken by underground techniques. The killing of an adult of any of these species (warthog excluded) by a beginning hunter qualifies him for the first buck initiation ceremony (see below, under "The Making of a Hunter").

I did not collect data on the total number of each species killed at a camp during the course of a year. Some idea of the relative frequency with which these and other game animals are killed is provided by Table 8.5. During the 1967–9 fieldwork, I asked 151 men how many of each of the major species they had killed during their lifetimes. Only those men who have hunted exclusively with bow and arrow are included here; 24 men who have hunted with guns are excluded. The art of counting is not well developed among the !Kung. The numbers from 1 to 10 are represented by the 10 fingers or by numbers derived from them (e.g., the

Table 8.5. *Relative hunting success of 127 !Kung men*

Animal	Men with no kills		Men with 1 kill		Men with 2–4 kills		Men with 5–9 kills		Men with 10 or more kills		Total	
	No.	%	No.	%	No.	%	No.	%	No.	%	No.	%
Big game												
Warthog	32	26	16	13	15	12	14	11	50	39	127	100
Gemsbok	34	27	18	14	15	12	14	11	46	36	127	100
Kudu	37	29	13	10	20	16	14	11	43	34	127	100
Wildebeest	44	35	25	20	21	16	10	8	27	21	127	100
Occasional big game												
Eland	71	56	23	18	9	7	6	5	18	14	127	100
Roan antelope	90	71	6	5	11	9	5	4	15	12	127	101
Hartebeest	88	69	16	13	5	4	4	3	14	11	127	100
Rare game												
Giraffe	91	72	15	12	7	5	7	5	7	5	127	99
Ostrich	110	87	10	8	3	2	1	1	3	2	127	100
Zebra	119	94	5	4	3	2	0		0		127	100
Buffalo	120	95	3	2	4	3	0		0		127	100
Carnivores												
Cheetah	109	86	13	10	2	2	2	2	1	1	127	101
Leopard	109	86	9	7	5	4	3	2	1	1	127	100
Lion	118	93	5	4	3	2	1	1	0		127	100

number six is "hand plus one"). Numbers over 10 are usually covered by the word "many" and were recorded as such with no attempt to sort out 10 or more kills. The data in Table 8.5 are of little use in estimating the actual number of animals killed, but are helpful in suggesting a rank ordering of species from the most frequently to the least frequently killed.

Warthog tops the list of most frequently killed: 75 percent of the men have killed at least 1 and 39 percent have killed 10 or more warthogs. Closely following are gemsbok and kudu: 36 and 34 percent of the men, respectively, have killed more than 10 of these species. Wildebeest is next in importance: 65 percent of the men have killed at least 1, but only 21 percent have killed more than 10. Eland, roan antelope, and hartebeest form a group: 11 to 14 percent of the men have killed more than 10 of these species. The low kill rates for these species are attributable in part to their scarcity and localized distribution. Roan antelope are found only in the North, especially north of the Ahas. Eland are rare in the Dobe area, present 50 km north of Dobe, but more common in the /Du/da area and points south. Hartebeest are scarce in all areas.

The giraffe is grouped with the rare game. Because of its size and endurance, it is a difficult animal to kill. None was killed in the Dobe area during my 3 years of fieldwork. Nevertheless, some 27 percent of the men stated that they had killed at least one giraffe during their life-times and seven men (5.5 percent) claimed to have killed "many" gi-raffes. I suspect that with an animal as large as a giraffe, if three or four men are involved in a successful hunt they may all take credit for killing it. Multiple credits for a single kill may also be allowed for other large rare species such as buffalo and zebra, though apparently the credit for a kill of the other species is strictly limited to a single hunter even if several men were involved. Because a giraffe hunt usually involves a number of men (Marshall 1956), it may be necessary to divide the number of claimed kills by a factor of three or four to obtain a realistic estimate of the number of giraffe actually killed.

Rarely hunted species

Ostrich, zebra, buffalo, and elephant are residents of, or seasonal visitors to, the Dobe area; yet they are hardly ever hunted by the !Kung. By not hunting these animals, the hunters are overlooking a substantial source of meat. It is necessary to investigate the reasons why.

The ostrich, the world's largest living bird, is a common year-round resident. It lays its clutches of 8 to 15 eggs in shallow, unconcealed depressions in the sand. The eggs are easily collected by both men and women, and after the contents have been shaken out and eaten, the intact shells are used as canteens. As each ostrich egg contains the equivalent of two dozen hen's eggs, the eggs alone make a significant contribution to the animal diet of the !Kung. The adult birds would seem to be an equally attractive source of food. A male weighs 100 kg and a female 90 kg, and judging by the frequency of sighting they are at least as abundant in the environment as are kudu or gemsbok.

The reports of kills, however, are extremely low, much lower than for the giraffe. Men's reported hunting success of ostrich is set out in Table 8.5. Only 17 men have ever killed an ostrich, and of these, only 3 men claim to have killed 10 or more. Hunters offer two reasons for not hunt-ing the ostrich. The first is that it runs very fast. This makes it hard to hit and also enables it to cover great distances before dropping even if it is wounded. ≠Toma, the Dobe hunter, said: "I wouldn't hunt ostrich be-cause they run so fast. You need horseback for that." Ostrich are indeed fast. Driving in our Land Rover, we have clocked ostrich of both sexes running in the track ahead of us at a speed of more than 50 km per hour over distances of 8 km (Plate 1.1). The second reason given is that the meat tastes bad and few people eat it because of this. This latter reason must surely be a post hoc rationalization. It is intriguing to speculate that not hunting ostrich is a form of conservation of the population to ensure a plentiful supply of eggs for canteens.

The absence of the zebra from the hunting repertory is an even more puzzling omission. Zebra are common all over Africa and are hunted by many peoples. For the Hadza hunter-gatherers of Tanzania, the zebra is the most important large animal killed (Woodburn 1968a). The Burchell's zebra found in the Dobe area is a very large form weighing 350 to 400 kg. One would expect the zebra to be at least as attractive a prey species as a giraffe. Yet, the hunting success data (Table 8.5) show that only 8 out of 127 men have ever killed a zebra; 5 men claim one kill, and 3 men claim from 2 to 4 kills. No one has killed as many as 10 or even 5 zebra.

The reason given for not hunting zebra is a curious one. The !Kung say its meat smells bad (//o/xau, "bad smell") and therefore is not eaten. Again this may be a post hoc rationalization. This taboo extends to horse and donkey meat, neither of which is eaten. The zebra, though large, is not a particularly difficult animal to kill with poisoned arrows; the only reason I can offer for its not being hunted is its scarcity. Zebra are rarely seen in the Dobe area, and several of the men who have killed zebra did so 160 km southeast of the Dobe area in the !Gon!a area, which is known to be in a zone where large herds of zebra persist.

The African buffalo is a frequent visitor to the Dobe area, migrating by the hundreds in December and January west out of the Okavango swamps and into the desert (Tinley 1966). Buffalo also appear in winter and in rainy years may reside year-round in the Dobe area. Most of the buffalo stop short of the Dobe area and feed around the seasonal pans 10 to 50 km west of the Tsau–Shakawe Road. Every year a few dozen buffalo are sighted in the area. The Botswana buffalo is a very large animal (700 to 900 kg) and is reputed by the professional hunters to be one of the toughest large game species to hunt. Only seven of the men of the Dobe area have ever killed one (Table 8.5), and no one has ever killed more than three or four. Several hunters related that they had shot a buffalo just to see what would happen, and then not tracked the animal.

The reasons for not hunting buffalo are fairly straightforward. By general agreement it is a mean, cunning animal with tremendous endurance and fight. The men express fear that if they stalk a buffalo into a thicket (the kind of habitat the buffalo favor) the animal will end up stalking them! They also say that the buffalo is one of the few animals that will attack a man rather than flee and that it is even meaner if wounded. Given these liabilities, the buffalo is rarely hunted by !Kung, despite its magnificent size and high meat yield. Fewer men have killed buffalo than have killed lion and leopard.

The fourth animal in the rarely hunted group is the elephant, a frequent summer visitor to the Dobe area from the northern upper Okavango River direction as well as from the eastern swamps. If anything, the elephant comes in greater numbers than the buffalo. During the rains its presence is evidenced by the broken branches and shivered trunks of the mongongo and other trees and by the gigantic footprints and balls of dung along the game trails. Elephant are not prevalent enough to endanger the camps and villages, though occasionally they come within a few dozen meters of a camp in the nut forests at night and wake everyone into a state of alertness that lasts until dawn. Elephant were not included in the formal interviews on hunting success, but we were told by everyone that no living !Kung has ever killed an elephant or even participated in hunting one, except for a few men who have hunted them in the East with mounted Tswanas armed with guns. The reasons given for not hunting elephant are interesting. First, there is a belief that the elephant is a person in that it possesses intelligence as a human does. N!eishi n!a said: "We call it a *zhu/twā* ("person") because it cries like a person and when it drinks it uses its trunk like a person uses its hands."

In the recent past, however, the !Kung did hunt and kill elephant. N!eishi described how they did it:

> They set grass fires on one side and the people come in on the other side. The dogs worry it, then when it raises its ears the people throw in their spears one after another. I have never eaten elephant meat, but my father did. They didn't put poison on their spears. They just gathered many men together to throw their spears.

The essential factor in hunting elephant appears to be the ability to coordinate many hunters in a single game drive. Such drives appear to be beyond the organizational capabilities of the !Kung of the 1960s. As N!eishi put it: "There were many men of all ages in those days and they could kill elephant." Only one datum came to light on the possibility of elephant hunting by contemporary San. A !Goshe man with kin ties to the North told me that northern !Kung kill elephant today by shooting a poison arrow into the foot, the only point where an arrow will penetrate the tough hide. This story was not corroborated.

Carnivores

The big cats, the hyenas, and the wild dogs were almost never hunted by the !Kung under traditional circumstances. However, a man occasionally had to defend himself against attack by a predator if he surprised it on a kill or while it was hunting. There are several cases in our genealogies of people being killed by carnivores, but the risks were not high; perhaps 5 out of over 1000 deaths were caused by carnivores–a much lower figure than for deaths by homicide (Chapter 13).

Since the arrival of the Bantu, however, the !Kung hunters have participated in hunting carnivores, a practice almost exclusively confined to pastoralists protecting their stock against losses. (In designing a cover for our book *Man the Hunter* [Lee and DeVore 1968] a well-intentioned Chicago artist commissioned by the publisher produced a design that showed

Masai warriors raising their spears and shields over the carcass of a lion. Several urgent telegrams were required before we persuaded the publisher to replace this with a design appropriate for hunters rather than herders.) In the Dobe area when a cow is killed the Herero mount a game drive to track the culprit (usually a lion or leopard) and try to kill it. As many as 20 men may participate in such a hunt, with the Herero mounted on horses and donkeys and the !Kung more vulnerable on foot. The herero also set steel traps and poisoned meat to catch a marauding predator. At least two /Xai/xai !Kung men during 1964–7 were attacked and mauled in hunts of this type–one by a lion, the other by a leopard. Both survived, and in the second case the hunter actually killed the leopard with his knife. Table 8.5 shows the number of men who claim to have killed cheetah, leopard, and lion: 18 men have killed one or both of the first two species; only 9 men have killed lion. I believe multiple credits are a factor here, as they are in the credits for kills of rare game. In any event, hunting the big cats must be almost entirely a product of Bantu contact. It is, nevertheless, interesting to note that both buffalo and zebra are less often killed than any of the three carnivores.

THE MAKING OF A HUNTER

Hunting is the main occupation of !Kung men. All men are supposed to hunt and kill game. Traditionally there was no culturally approved way for a man to be a nonhunter. Today, some men work on the Bantu cattle posts and may hunt little or not at all during their period of work. However, except for a few of the most acculturated, all !Kung men over the age of 30 own or have owned a quiver set and have killed game with it. During the 1960s it was still important for a man to prove himself as a hunter in order to obtain a wife.

Women do not hunt. Meagan Biesele (personal communication) knew of one young woman in the !Gon!a area who used to hunt small game, and Marjorie Shostak (personal communication) reported that a few women described experiences of play hunting when they were children, but I know of no other instances of !Kung women hunting anything as large as a springhare. They do collect tortoises, lizards, and snakes (the last as large as a 3-meter-long python), and they accurately and energetically kill poisonous snakes, spiders, and scorpions if they find them in the camp or on the path, but basically they leave hunting to the men. I did not get the feeling that women's nonparticipation in hunting was a sore issue between the sexes (i.e., that the women wanted to hunt but the men would not let them, or that the men wanted women to share in the work of hunting but the latter did not want to). It was not an area of conflict. Much more in evidence was the women's complaints that the men did not bring in enough meat. Good-natured (and not so good-natured) accusations of men's laziness at hunting were a common re-frain in many camps.

!Kung children, male or female, are not pressed into service in the food quest at an early age. They are not expected to provide food in significant quantities until they are well into their teens. Learning to hunt, there-fore, is largely a play activity for the boys, and they receive little formal instruction from older men until they are about 12 years old. Play hunt-ing can begin as early as age 3. Older children make a little bow of wood and twine, with arrows of grass stems, and teach the toddler to shoot it, aiming first at still targets a few inches away and graduating to moving targets such as the ubiquitous dung beetle. Little girls participate in these games too, and frequently a play group of four to six kids pretends to cut up, cook, and serve an imaginary animal in the same way that North American children have an imaginary tea party. As the boys grow older, they graduate from shooting dung beetles and grasshoppers to shooting small birds such as waxbills. These tiny birds, related to the sparrows and finches and weighing a few grams, are plucked and may be cooked and eaten by little boys and girls. In the age range 9 to 12 other games are played, now exclusively by boys, that teach hunting skills and that may include adolescent males as well. N/ebi is a kind of javelin toss played by a number of boys: Each throws a light wand and bounces it off the ground to see who can throw it the farthest. /N!au ("spear") is a target-practice game in which a rough wooden spear with a ball of pad-ding at the end is hurled back and forth between two teams of boys to see whose aim is the most accurate. The main tracking skills, however, are acquired through the on-going study of nature as the young boys and girls learn to identify the hundreds of plants and animals in their environ-ment. Studying animal tracks is a major pastime of the older boys.

Before they actually go on a hunt, !Kung boys have listened to dozens of hunts described in the minutest detail in the storytelling around the campfire. This is a major component of their socialization as hunters. This vast body of knowledge is a treasure house of lore and information about animals and how to kill them. And the boys listen intently.

Around age 12 a boy starts accompanying his father, uncles, or older brothers on hunts. Within a couple of years his father makes him his first quiver set, with unpoisoned bone and metal arrows and a scaled-down quiver and bow. The boy becomes more active in shooting, with mon-geese, genets, hares, and game birds as the main targets; during the winter months the young adolescent boy also builds snarelines, often under the guidance of his father or grandfather. The assumption of adult status as a hunter comes with the first successful killing of an antelope, such as kudu or gemsbok, from the list of big game species (excluding

Plate 8.2. A young hunter takes the forehead cuts at the first buck ceremony.

warthog). The animal can be male or female and must be mature or nearly so and killed with a poisoned arrow. If these conditions are met, the first buck ceremony is held, an extremely important milestone in the life of a hunter. In the Dobe area of today the first buck ceremony is often delayed for years. To achieve the killing of the first antelope requires diligence and concentration on hunting. These are hard to combine with the demands of working on the Bantu cattle posts, and as a result a man may be 25 or 30 before he kills his first buck. In /Du/da, where no cattle posts are present, we found a situation that probably resembled the more traditional picture: adolescent boys 15 to 22 working hard at hunting and bringing in their first bucks by age 15 to 18.

Separate ceremonies are held for the first male and for the first female animal killed. For the male cuts and tattoos are applied on the right side of the chest and back and the right arm; for the female, cuts are made on the left side of the chest and back and the left arm. Separate cuts are applied to symbolically strengthen visual acuity, stamina, cunning, and the strength of the bow; the resulting tattoos, which are permanent, announce to the world the young hunter's new status.

Debe's first buck ceremony

Debe was a 30-year-old Dobe man, married with two children. On January 14, 1969, he shot and killed a juvenile male kudu. The following day he shot and killed an adult female kudu and he asked his relative, ≠Dau, to perform the first buck ceremony for the female. He had previously received the cuts for killing a male, so this, the second of the two ceremonies, was supposed to "finish" him. On the morning of January 16, while most of the women were out of camp, about 15 men and boys gathered in the center of the Dobe camp to perform the ceremony and to cook some of the kudu meat, including the special portions reserved exclusively for the older men.

The narrative continues from my field notes:

> On the shade side of the cooking fire sit the older men who can eat the special male portions, and on the sun side sit Debe and his agemates and the cutter. Among the older men the atmosphere is casual, with many side conversations going on. Among the novices there is a more serious air, with Debe looking the gravest. ≠Dau takes a razor blade (a trade item) and, lifting up a pinch of skin at the top of Debe's breastbone, makes a series of 10 short, vertical, parallel cuts through the pinch. The blood wells out of the cuts and combines to flow down Debe's chest.

> 1. Now the medicine, a mixture of *!gwa* ("a charred medicinal herb") and fat from Debe's kill is rubbed into the cuts. It makes a

bold, rough black smudge 4 cm by 2 cm on his chest. When the cuts heal a neat row of blue tattoos will remain.

2. The next cuts, made in the same manner, are on the left side of the chest over the heart. The !gwa ash and kudu fat mixture is again rubbed into the wounds, as it is in all subsequent cuttings.

3. Two more series of cuts are made on the left side of the stomach, 5 cm above the hip bone.

4. Two series of cuts are made on the back under the left scapula.

5. Cuts are made at five locations on the left arm: upper biceps, lower biceps, upper forearm, lower forearm, wrist.

6. The final cuts are made above the bridge of the nose on the brow in the midline.

≠Dau explains the cuts: "I cut his chest and put in medicine to lift up his heart and make him *want* to seek meat; I put [it] in his arm and wrist to make his arm soft [*swa*] and his aim correct; in his back to make sure that the game won't run away; in his brow so that he may see things quickly."

After the cuts, five more rituals are performed. ≠Dau rubs Debe's bow with blood from the kill. He loudly cracks Debe's knuckles on both hands: "We say if there is no thumb crack, then you don't have an animal coming up. But if it cracks it means you are going out tomorrow and kill something."

He rubs melted fat on the forearm and biceps and massages (*n//abu*) it firmly "to make the arm soft to make hunting better."

He pinches up a vein on the lower part of Debe's bicep with a thumb and forefinger and then pushes the vein down with his elbow "so that when you shoot, you shoot one arrow and the animal drops."

He rubs the severed ears of the kudu on Debe's head: "This is to make the animals come closer to us so we don't have far to shoot. We want the game to flap-flap its ears so we can walk right up to it and kill it. We don't want ears raised and alert!" And ≠Dau pantomimes the kudu's behavior using the ears as props.

After Debe is done other young men ask to have some cuts done as well. Bo, a younger initiated man, takes over from ≠Dau and under his guidance administers two small series of cuts (chest and brow) to Tsaa and one to /Gau (chest only). After these two are done, ≠Toma, a younger brother of Debe, in his midteens who hasn't killed anything big yet, steps into the circle almost in fun and the senior cutter, ≠Dau, massages his arms.

Now the men eat the meat; those over 35 years old eat the "men's portions" cooked in a separate pot, and the younger men including the initiate Debe, eat other portions. The right to eat the men's portions is according to age, not hunting accomplishment, and even though Debe has killed both a male and a female animal he will have to wait 5 years more before he can partake of it. The men's portion consists of the shoulders (≠*tore*), the belly, and several parts of the intestines. These parts are reserved for older men in all animals killed, not just those used in a first buck ceremony.

In the aftermath of the cutting and other rituals, ≠Dau tells a long and detailed hunting story for the benefit of the younger men, though all the men listen intently. He is a master of the art, and his deep resonant voice is accompanied by dramatic gestures imitating the desperate behavior of the wounded animal. Following this, ≠Toma //gwe launches into a loud and vituperative tirade against a man named /Xashe from !Kubi. "I am the owner of the meat, you are nothing! You never give me anything!" /Xashe responds in kind: "Shut up! Be quiet! It is *you* who is the nothing cheapskate!" This exchange is delivered in extremely good spirits, with the participants and listeners alike enjoying it immensely – a good example of an argument for the fun of it. After another hour, the meat is finished and the men begin to drift away. Debe turns the rest of the kudu meat over to his father for distribution and the camp atmosphere returns to normal as the women return to their fires.

HUNTING AND ADULTHOOD

With the killing of his first buck, the young man is considered much more favorably as a potential son-in-law. Marriage negotiation is a long, drawn-out process that may involve the prospective parents-in-law in discussions and gift exchanges for years before the children have grown to marriageable age, about 16 or 17 for girls and 23 to 30 for boys. Traditionally, the prime characteristics parents of a girl sought in a son-in-law were proved hunting ability and a willingness to live with his in-laws and provide meat for them for a period of years. This period of "bride service" is common among the Dobe !Kung and was even more frequent in occurrence among the Nyae Nyae !Kung during the 1950s (Marshall 1976:169). The period of probation began with the marriage ceremony itself. It was customary for a bridegroom to go out and hunt and kill an animal immediately after the marriage day. !Xam !koma, a young /Xai/xai man, married a girl named Chwa in 1965; the day after the ceremony he went out, killed a kudu, and presented the carcass to his father-in-law. This was considered a very good omen for the marriage.

The Bantu presence has changed the criteria for marriage ability. Previously, a young man who had not proved himself as a hunter was not

Plate 8.3. The cutter tells the hunt after performing the first buck ceremony.

considered ready for marriage. Today, a nonhunter such as Debe may still marry if he can convince his in-laws that he is able to provide for them through a Bantu work connection instead of by hunting. For example, a man working at a Herero cattle post can invite his in-laws for an extended stay to drink the milk and eat the meat from the master's herds. The in-laws expect the man eventually to become a good hunter and provide for them and their daughter after he leaves his employer's service.

A young man with no quiver *and* no job is considered a risky prospect as a son-in-law. But even here exceptions are now made. A 30-year-old /Xai/xai man named /Twi came back from his fourth contract as a mine laborer to find his father had arranged a marriage for him with an attractive 16-year-old named /Xoishe. In the weeks before the marriage was to be consummated the people of /Xai/xai noted with some amusement that the sophisticated traveler /Twi was shouldering a quiver even though he had spent most of the last 5 years in the mines and knew little about the bush. By the day of the ceremony /Twi had killed nothing by hunting, so in lieu of an antelope he presented his father-in-law, ≠Tomazho, with a goat he had purchased with mine wages. His father-in-law expressed himself satisfied with the substitution and slaughtered the goat on the spot for a wedding feast.

A newly married couple is expected to spend the first years of their married life with the wife's parents. Because there is usually a big age difference between spouses, with husband 7 to 10 or more years older than wife, a common reason given for bride service is that the girl is too young to leave her mother. During this initial period, which varies from 3 to 10 years, the husband is expected to hunt meat for the camp regularly. This period can be one of great productivity for a young hunter. In a sense he is on trial; yet the in-laws praise success (in the characteristically backhanded !Kung way) and tend to go easy in the event of failure. Because of the fluid nature of !Kung camp structure, the camp core group of older people wants to encourage the sons-in-law to stay with the group permanently, as more hunters mean more meat; they do not want to drive young men away by being hypercritical (Lee 1974).

After several years the couple may elect to return to the husband's camp or to go elsewhere. Or they may decide to stay on with the wife's group. Much discussion surrounds the making of this decision. In 1964 ≠Dau who had been living with his wife Sa//gai's relatives at Dobe for some 5 years wanted to return to his aged mother //Kokamahura at Bate 16 km away. ≠Dau's mother-in-law //Gumin!a was against the plan, complaining that though ≠Dau had produced very little meat for Dobe so far, they still had hopes of more from him. (In the !Kung scheme of things this was a compliment!) ≠Dau's mother came over from Bate, and several all-day discussions ensued (see Plate 13.1). Finally a compromise was reached whereby ≠Dau and Sa//gai and their two small children agreed to spend half the year at Dobe with her folks and half the year at Bate with his.

Hunting as a life's work

From the age of 25, a man's career as a hunter goes on for the next 40 years or until he dies, reaching a peak between the ages of 30 and 45. During this period most men have the optimum combination of physical strength and skill plus the wisdom of experience. Even after his prime, a man's skill and experience continue to grow with age. A man in his fifties or sixties may work with a younger man, often his son; the two hunters interpret the tracks together but the younger man does most of the shooting. Still older men remain active too, and some of them tend snarelines into their late sixties.

Although hunting is the steady, life-long occupation of all men, the number of animals they kill is not large. I estimate that over the long run a hunter averages only two or three large antelope a year and accounts for only 80 to 120 large kills over a lifetime of hunting – as well as, of course, a much larger number of smaller game. However, a large antelope yields a tremendous return in meat and calories. A single kudu or gemsbok weighing 200 kg provides some 300,000 Cal *or 1.37 percent of the total annual requirements* of a camp of 30 adults and children. Only

20 such kills a year would provide some 27.4 percent of the camp's *total* requirements. Given the composition of !Kung camps (see Chapter 3), a camp of 30 would contain 8 to 10 hunters, and to make up the total of 20 kills, each hunter would have to account for only 2 or 2.5 kills per year. The proportion of annual returns from *all* game sources, large and small, is about 40 percent; those from vegetable foods are 60 percent. If anything, my estimate of two to three kills per hunter per year may err on the high side. In a very careful study of /Xai/xai hunting during 1973 and 1975–6, Edwin Wilmsen recorded 44 large animals killed over a 19-month period, for a rate of 28 per year. As /Xai/xai had a standing population of about 45 men of hunting age or older, the killing rate works out to only 0.6 large animal per man per year (Wilmsen 1976; quoted with permission).

Taking two animals a year as an average, it is likely that rates of killing vary with the age of the hunter, being lower than average for the first 5 years of hunting, perhaps double the average or higher in the peak years from age 30 to age 45, and falling off in the later years. Even within these broad parameters hunting success can be erratic. A man may kill three large bucks in a month and none for 6 months. This irregularity of hunting activity has made it difficult to calculate hunting success rates by extrapolating from short runs of data.

Hunting success and status differences

The data from the retrospective histories of hunting success provide a way of measuring long-term hunting success and for determining whether there are any marked differences among men in hunting achievements. Looking again at Table 8.5, we can see marked differences. For example, 37 of the 127 men have never killed a kudu, one of the commonest game species, whereas 43 men have killed 10 or more. Similar differences can be seen for other species.

To illustrate the impact of individual differences in hunting skill, let us assume that the average number of kudu killed by those who have killed 10 or more is 15. Table 8.6 shows that these 43 hunters alone have accounted for 15 × 43 = 645 kudu, whereas the other 84 men in the study have accounted for only about 171. Table 8.6 makes the point that 34 percent of the hunters account for 79 percent of the kudu killed. Among the Valley Bisa the picture is even more dramatic. Over half of all the meat in one Bisa village cluster in the course of a year was produced by two of the nine resident hunters (Marks 1976:204).

Age is an important factor in hunting success. Is it possible that those who have never killed kudu are the youngest ones and the top kudu hunters are all older men? Table 8.7 shows that success in killing kudu does markedly increase with age, with 9 to 11 kills per man in the over 39 age groups compared with 3 to 5 kills per man in the younger age groups. However, age alone does not account for hunting success. Even

Table 8.6. *Differential success at killing kudu*

No. of men	No. of kills by each man	No. of kudu killed
37	0	0
13	1	13
20	2–4 (av. 3)	60
14	5–9 (av. 7)	98
84 (66%)		171 (21%)
43 (34%)	10+ (av. 15)	645 (79%)
127		816

in the oldest age group a significant number of men (11 of 33) claim 4 or fewer kudu kills. Even allowing for a certain amount of underestimation on the part of some of the older men, out of modesty, there is a fairly wide range of hunting achievements from modest to excellent within each age group. In the younger age groups, the better *half* of the hunters accounted for 95 to 100 percent of all the kills. In the older age groups the better half of the hunters accounted for about 70 percent of the kills. I estimate that the better than average half of the hunters over a span of years provides upward of two-thirds of the meat, and the below average half of the hunters provides one-third.

How do the !Kung men respond to the existence of these differences among them? Do hierarchies form? Do the best hunters dominate the politics of the camp and monopolize the women? Far from it. The !Kung are a fiercely egalitarian people, and they have evolved a series of important cultural practices to maintain this equality, first by cutting down to size the arrogant and boastful, and second by helping those down on their luck to get back in the game.

Men are encouraged to hunt as well as they can, and the people rejoice when meat is brought in, but the correct demeanor for the successful hunter is modesty and understatement. A /Xai/xai man named /Gaugo described it this way:

> Say that a man has been hunting. He must not come home and announce like a braggart, "I have killed a big one in the bush!" He must first sit down in silence until I or someone else comes up to his fire and asks, "What did you see today?" He replies quietly, "Ah, I'm no good for hunting. I saw nothing at all . . . maybe just a tiny one." Then I smile to myself because I now know he has killed something big.

The theme of modesty is continued when the butchering and carrying party goes to fetch the kill the following day. Arriving at the site, the

Table 8.7. Success in killing kudu, according to age of hunter

No. of kills per hunter		Age 15–28 yr		Age 29–38 yr		Age 39–48 yr		Age 49+ yr		All ages	
Range	Average	No. of men	Av. no. of kills	No. of men	Av. no. of kills	No. of men	Av. no. of kills	No. of men	Av. no. of kills	No. of men	Av. no. of kills
0	0	22	0	13	0	0	0	2	0	37	0
1	1	6	6	1	1	1	1	5	5	13	13
2–4	3	4	12	7	21	5	15	4	12	20	60
5–9	7	1	7	4	28	3	21	6	42	14	98
10+	15	5	75	7	105	15	225	16	240	43	645
Total		38	100	32	155	24	262	33	299	127	816
Kills per man			2.6		4.8		10.9		9.1		6.4
Kills by better half of hunters		100 (100%)		147 (95%)		180 (69%)		210 (70%)			
Kills by worse half of hunters		0 (0%)		7 (5%)		82 (31%)		89 (30%)			

members of the carrying party loudly express their disappointment to the
hunter:

> "You mean to say you have dragged us all the way out here to make
> us cart home your pile of bones? Oh, if I had known it was this thin
> I wouldn't have come."
>
> "People, to think I gave up a nice day in the shade for this. At
> home we may be hungry but at least we have nice cool water to
> drink."

To these insults the hunter must not act offended; he should respond in
kind, with self-demeaning words:

> "You're right, this one is not worth the effort; let's just cook the liver
> for strength and leave the rest for the hyenas. It is not too late to
> hunt today and even a duiker or a steenbok would be better than
> this mess."

The party, of course, has no intention of abandoning the kill. The heavy
joking and derision are directed toward one goal: the leveling of potentially arrogant behavior in a successful hunter. The !Kung recognize the
tendency toward arrogance (≠*twi*) in young men and take definite steps
to combat it. As ≠Tomazho, the famous healer from /Xai/xai, put it:

> When a young man kills much meat, he comes to think of himself
> as a chief or a big man, and he thinks of the rest of us as his
> servants or inferiors. We can't accept this. We refuse one who
> boasts, for someday his pride will make him kill somebody. So we
> always speak of his meat as worthless. In this way we cool his heart
> and make him gentle.

Even though some men are much better hunters than others, their
behavior is molded by the group to minimize the tendency toward self-
aggrandizement and to channel their energies into socially beneficial
activities. As a result, the existence of differences in hunting prowess
does not lead to a system of Big Men in which a few talented individuals
tower over others in terms of prestige.

Two further aspects of egalitarianism among !Kung hunters should be
mentioned: the use of hunting magic to improve poor hunting results in
the widespread practice of sharing arrows and ownership for kills. If a
hunter is down on his luck, he may request another man to touch up his
first buck tattoos. The older man spends up to an hour opening the old
cuts and rubbing fresh medicine into the tattoos. The knuckle cracking
and other rituals are also performed. If a hunter has made a small kill
and wants to make a big one, the blood from the small kill is rubbed on
his bow to strengthen it. If a man is very dissatisfied with his hunting
results, he may discard his present bow and quiver and build new ones

from scratch. Other forms of hunting magic revolve around the correct butchering and distribution of meat from previous kills. The !Kung believe that the women must never eat the men's part of the animals or hunting success will drop to zero. In one case of hunting failure the explanation offered was that an inexperienced young man had cooked meat for the women in a pot that had not been thoroughly cleaned with water, sand, and ash after the men's portions had been cooked in it. In days before the advent of the iron kettle, this kind of contamination must have been rarer because most of the meat was roasted in the fire. Only since the cooking pot has come into use has the danger of mixing tabooed parts arisen (Marks 1976:125).

Divination with the oracle disks is an important part of hunting magic. A man who is just getting back into hunting after a period of inactivity may consult the disks on several days in a row until he gets a favorable omen; only then does he go out. In a period of active hunting the hunter may use the disks to help him decide which of two directions would be the most promising. In a modest way the use of hunting magic helps to restore or maintain the confidence of the hunter and to give him the feeling that unseen forces are favorable to his quest.

The !Kung rule for allocating ownership of the meat from a kill is "the owner of the arrow is the owner of the meat." This holds true even if the owner of the arrow is not the man who shot it. (If two or more arrows hit an animal, the owner of the first arrow shot gets credit for the kill.) Ownership in the !Kung context consists primarily of the right to distribute the meat formally. Disputes over ownership are rare; in fact, the man take steps to blur the credits for a kill by circulating their arrows in the traditional hxaro trading system. A man will say to another, "Give me an arrow and if I kill something with it I will give the meat to you." Weeks or months later when he kills an antelope, he shares the carcass with his trading partner if the latter happens to be in his camp. If the arrow giver is elsewhere, the hunter saves a portion of the biltong for him. This trading of arrows strengthens the bonds between men and is especially used between such kin categories as brothers-in-law. In 1964 I asked four Dobe men to show me all the arrows in their quivers and to sort out the "owners" of each. The results are shown in Table 8.8. Alone of the four, Kopela Maswe had no arrows from other men. Each of the others had arrows that came from four to six different men, indicating how widely arrows are circulated. Two of the four men had no arrows *of their own* in their quivers. Women may own arrows too, trade them with men, and become owners of meat.

The reason for this high incidence of arrow sharing is not hard to find. A meat distribution brings prestige to the hunter, but it can also be an onerous task, bringing with it the risk of accusations of stinginess or improper behavior if the distribution is not to everybody's liking. A prac-

Table 8.8. *Arrow sharing: owners of contents of quivers of four Dobe men: 1964*

Hunter[a]	Name of donor	Relation to ego	No. of arrows given	Total arrows/ hunter
≠Dau (Kopela Maswe)	Self		14	14
/Gashe	Kumsa	MFBSS	3	
	/Ti!kay	?	8	
	Debe	WB	2	
	≠Dau	"Z"H	1	
	Kxau	WF	2	
	Kxau	?	2	
	Self		0	18
/N!au	/Twi	?	2	
	≠Dau	"OB"	5	
	Bo	WMB	1	
	Kxau	WF	3	
	Self		2	13
N!eishi	≠Dau	MBDH	2	
	≠Toma//gwe	F	4	
	Kumsa	MFBSS	9	
	≠Toma	?	1	
	/Gau	?	2	
	≠Dau	OB	1	
	Self		0	19

[a] ≠Dau, /Gashe, and N!eishi are brothers, the three sons of ≠Toma//gwe.

tice that tends to diffuse the responsibility for meat distribution and spread the glory (and the hostility) around is therefore a blessing in such tense situations. Lorna Marshall makes this apt comment on the practice: "There is much giving and lending of arrows. The society seems to want to extinguish in every way possible the concept of the meat belonging to the hunter" (1976:297).

The on-again off-again !Kung hunter

With the practice of meat sharing so firmly entrenched, with arrows shared to further defuse bitterness over meat distribution, and with the pervasive humility-enforcing devices to counteract the tendency toward competitiveness and self-aggrandizement, one would expect the !Kung hunter to be a well-socialized, cooperative member of the team who acts consistently for the good of the group by hunting a regular nine-to-five shift 4 days a week. In fact, though the men *were* in the main cooperative, their work rhythm at hunting was, to say the least, erratic. Many good hunters did no hunting at all for weeks or months at a time, while their wives and children waited patiently and ate the meat distributed by other hunters. The !Kung say that hunting is an unpredictable business and if your luck runs out you may have to stop hunting for a time. ≠Toma, the best hunter of the 1963–4 Dobe camp (see Chapter 9), stopped hunting for 3 months in 1963. He explained that his hunting power was "cold" and that the animals "refused" him. He stayed in camp awaiting inspiration, while his wife and kinspeople provided food for him. In 1964 his luck returned and he started killing warthogs at the rate of one to three per month with the aid of his famous dogs, Swoïya and Foïya.

Paradoxically, part of the explanation for this stop-and-go rhythm may have to do with !Kung's strongly held ideals of equality. After a run of successful hunts during which he has been the host at several meat distributions the hunter may stop hunting in order to give other men the chance to take the limelight. Marshall (1968:94) makes the point, and I am inclined to concur, that a *too* energetic hunter or gatherer might be appreciated up to a point, but then would begin to draw the envy and resentment of others. Also a period of hunting inactivity allows the hunter to enjoy the benefits of some of the reciprocal obligations he has built up. In a market-based society one would say the successful hunter has "earned" the right to accept the hospitality of others; among the !Kung there is no concept equivalent to "earned." Kumsa, a superb hunter from LG 26/68, stopped hunting for several months in early 1968. He visited relatives at !Goshe, who fed him and his family of five generously and gave him bags of their freshly harvested sorghum to take back to Dobe. Later in the year he was back at N!abesha hunting again.

The alternating rhythm of energy and inactivity illustrates beautifully one of the key contradictions in the communal life of !Kung hunter-gatherers: the pressure on the one hand to prove oneself by hunting and to be generous, and the counterpressure on the other against being too successful or too far ahead of one's fellows. The !Kung men arrive at a two-phase solution by alternating bursts of hunting to build up their "credits" with periods of inactivity "to cool their hearts and make them gentle," a good illustration of an economic system based on use value instead of exchange value.

9

Men, women, and work

How hard or easy is it for the !Kung to make a living? How is the work load allocated among males and females, young and old, residents and visitors? What are the relative proportions of subsistence work, tool making, housework, and leisure in the daily lives of the !Kung? This chapter examines work in its ecological setting by means of an input-output analysis of !Kung subsistence.

After defining !Kung work and the units of measurement, the chapter goes on to present the results of a work diary collected at Dobe in July and August 1964, including data on work effort in relation to group size, to sex and age, and to other variables. Questions of male and female efficiency and male hunting success are considered next, followed by a study of per capita caloric returns. Housework and tool making are then estimated in order to arrive at a final estimate of overall work levels in relation to the sexual division of labor. Although men work harder than women in subsistence and manufacture, women do more of the housework. There is no evidence for exploitation on the basis of sex or age.

The necessity of work is a basic law of human existence. All human societies in history and prehistory have had to work to survive. In state societies the nature of work has become incredibly complex, with mental work and machine operation becoming as important as the once universal manual work. And with the advent of capitalism some of the owners of capital apparently do not work at all. For most of the long history of human society, however, there were no leisure class, few machines, and no distinction between the mental and the manual laborer. Everyone worked and everyone used both hands and mind.

The beauty of the study of work is that work can be precisely quantified and can be tied into a whole gamut of social and economic variables. Underlying the network of social relations anthropologists are so fond of studying is a network of energy relations to which we pay little or no attention. Yet the basic units of social behavior and interaction have

Plate 9.1. Woman working: *Grewia* berry collecting.

never been satisfactorily defined and isolated, although the basic units of energy relations are relatively easy to define and measure. The advantage of the study of work for anthropology is that it anchors the ephemera of social life on the foundations of the natural sciences.

Energy studies cannot provide a complete accounting of social life; for that, a much wider range of variables must be brought into the analysis. But these studies can provide a baseline for internal analysis of structure and a common data language for comparison between cultures.

I was led to the study of energy relations almost in desperation more than 15 years ago, after my initial survey of the literature on the subsistence ecology of hunter-gatherers. How easy or difficult was it for them to make a living, I wondered? Opinions varied, with the majority of observers tending to support Alan Holmberg's view with reference to the Siriono, a group of hunter-gatherers in Eastern Bolivia; for them life was precarious, work was constant, and people expressed anxiety about food (Holmberg 1950).

The opposite view was admirably put forward by Rodney Needham (1954) in an intriguing paper, "Siriono and Penan: A Test of Some Hypoth-

eses." Needham disagreed with Holmberg. The Penan, a hunter-gatherer
group in Borneo that he studied in the early 1950s, had a very relaxed
attitude toward food and did not express anxiety about where their next
meal was coming from. My common sense tended to favor Needham's
view: If hunters and gatherers had been in business for so many thousands of years, surely they had worked out some sort of stable adaptation.
Yet I realized that neither Holmberg nor Needham had really answered
the question. Surely we could find a better way of determining whether
the Siriono and Penan are well off than by the presence or absence of
"anxiety." Anxiety, after all, is an infinitely divisible and expandable
phenomenon, and many people in North America feel plenty of anxiety
about food while living on salaries of $25,000 a year.

The methods of energetics, nutrition, demography, and ecology seemed
to offer a way out of this impasse. Armed with these tools of analysis, we
could ask and answer such questions as: How many days do people work
per week? How many dependents does each active worker support? How
adequate is the diet in terms of calories, proteins, and other nutrients?
We could examine socially significant categories of people – women, men,
the young, and the elderly – in energy terms. This line of research seemed
to offer a definite advance in rigor over the older, qualitative impressions
of ethnographers, and I embarked on my first fieldwork with the !Kung
San enthusiastically determined to build a better mousetrap to answer
the question: "How hard or easy is it to make a living?" This chapter
presents the results of my inquiry. Parts of this material were originally
presented elsewhere (Lee 1968a, 1969a), but all the data have been recal-
culated in the light of new information that has become available since
the original publication.

!KUNG WORK DEFINED

The main kind of work the !Kung do is subsistence work: hunting and
gathering. A proportion of their total time is also spent in manufacturing
and maintenance of their tools, clothing, and housing. Most observers
would have little difficulty considering these activities as work, and these
are the two main categories of work discussed in this chapter. Regarding
other categories of behavior, the definition of work becomes much more
difficult. When a hunter consults the oracle disks, is that work? When he
spends the evening in camp listening to reports of game sighting on the
eve of a hunt, is he working? Because these activities are carried out in a
socially pleasurable context, I have not considered them as work. More
ambiguous is the question of housework or domestic work. Cooking, nut
cracking, and cleaning are obviously work, but of what kind? Ironically,
this same issue has sprung up recently in our society. The Wages for
Housework movement argues that housework is exactly the same order

of work as clerical or industrial tasks and should be paid for as such (Edmond and Fleming 1975). This view of housework correctly highlights the existence of a vast pool of unpaid labor on which capitalism depends; but to accept the proposition that housework is work and the men and women within a household should share it equally does not mean that housework should necessarily be brought into the sphere of capitalist wage labor (see Redstockings Collective 1971). In the !Kung context I have considered housework as work of a separate category in order to make these data comparable with data on industrial and other societies. Although not presented in a specifically Marxist framework, the results of this study can be adapted to Marxist analyses of the labor process under capitalism (e.g., Meek 1973; Secombe 1973; Braverman 1974).

For the purposes of this study, *work* is defined as those activities that contribute to the direct appropriation of food, water, or materials from the environment. These include three main categories of activities:

1. Subsistence (gathering, hunting, drawing water), travel to or from subsistence sites, carrying subsistence loads back to camp
2. Manufacture and maintenance of the tools of subsistence and of other necessities such as housing and clothing
3. Housework

Activities in category 1 take place entirely outside the camp. Activities in category 2 take place both inside and outside the camp. Housework, by definition, takes place almost entirely within the camp. It includes such activities as food processing (e.g., nut cracking and cooking) as well as cleaning the living space, tending the fire, and collecting firewood. Butchery, when it takes place at the kill site, is classed with subsistence work; when it is carried out within the camp, it is included with domestic work.

Units of measurement

Units of time and energy are the ones most commonly used in the measurement of work (Durnin and Passmore 1967; Edholm 1967). Precise measurement of energy expenditure expressed in calories requires the use of a physiological monitoring apparatus, and the minute-by-minute sampling frame of a time and motion study. In neither area did my own methodology approach this standard. My much cruder approach was to count the number of people who did any work on a given day and in a limited number of cases clock them out of the camp in the morning and back in during the afternoon. This gave me a good count of the number of workdays in a week and an approximate idea of the length of a working day. This approach is not nearly as precise as studies using apparatus such as the Max Planck respirometer or the Douglas bag (Weiner and

Lourie 1969), but it does possess two distinct advantages over the latter type. First it interferes minimally with the flow of activities in the camp, and second it allows the observer to follow a number of people (up to 40 or more) through the day. The apparatus interferes considerably with normal activity, and only one or two individuals can be followed at a time. In addition, even the most careful monitoring depends ultimately on extrapolation (i.e., multiplying calories expended per person per minute in a particular activity by the number of minutes spent performing that activity), and extrapolation to weekly, monthly, or annual figures for whole populations can introduce very large errors, far outweighing the precision of the original observations.

The use of a random sampling framework can considerably reduce errors of extrapolation; and Johnson (1975) has correctly pointed out the shortcomings of studies such as the present one, which fail to randomly sample different groups at different times of the year (see also Minge-Kalman 1977). I fully agree with Johnson's cogent criticisms. However, the present study of work does retain some value, as a block of continuous observations in real time on a single group, with the proviso that these results alone cannot be considered representative of !Kung groups in general or even of the Dobe group at other times of the year. One reason for placing some confidence in the data presented here is that my colleague Pat Draper used a very sophisticated random sampling research design in her study of child rearing, a study that yielded as a by-product highly useful and representative data on the activities of adults in the several camps she studied. Her observations in the main corroborate the results presented here. She has pointed out that "although Lee's data refer to another population, the !Kung of the /Du/da area follow weekly work routines essentially similar to those in the north" (Draper 1976:210). Her discussion of regional differences in diet are mentioned below.

THE 1964 WORK DIARY

For a 4-week period during the winter of 1964 (July 6 to August 2) I observed the work and leisure activities of the residents and visitors at the main camp at Dobe water hole. Each morning I recorded the activities of every member of the camp, and each evening I recorded the total number of adults and children who ate the evening meal and slept in the camp. I did not break down the day's activities into hours or minutes, but rather set down each person's major activity under one of four basic headings: gathering, hunting, in camp, or visiting. Some further subdivisions were made: for gathering, the main crop (usually but not always mongongo nuts) was specified; for hunting, a distinction was made between mobile hunting and snaring; for those who stayed in camp, note was taken of the kind of activity (cooking, eating, hut building, etc.) if

one activity predominated; and for visiting, I recorded which water hole
away from Dobe was visited.

My main goal was to find out how hard people were working by getting
a broad picture of the ratio of subsistence work days to days not spent in
subsistence. Therefore, a day during which hunting or gathering was
carried out was counted as a workday even if the day was short. A day
spent in camp or visiting was not counted as a workday even if subsis-
tence-related work such as food processing or tool making was carried
on. First, let us look at subsistence effort (category 1); later we will discuss maintenance work (category 2) and housework (category 3) and add
them in to get a total picture.

The Dobe camp was studied during the midwinter dry season when all
the !Kung were clustered around the nine permanent water holes of the
Dobe area. The days were sunny and warm with high temperatures of 20
to 25°C; the nights were cool with near-freezing temperatures. Mongongo
nuts were the main food crop, with smaller quantities of roots and bulbs.
Berries, leafy greens, and other rainy season foods were scarce or absent.

At the time of the work study, both major segments of the Dobe population were living together in a single circular camp that varied during the
4 weeks from 23 to 40 people in 9 to 15 huts. The genealogy of the camp
is illustrated in Figure 3.6. The main adult residents numbered about 25
people. The camp core owners (*k"ausi*) included N!eishin!a and his son
and daughter, and N!eishi's older sister //Kokan!a and her husband and
their three sons. The residents spent most or all of the 28 days at Dobe. In
addition, a small number of visitors came for stays of 7 to 15 days, and a
rather larger group of visitors stayed for 1 to 6 days. In all, some 76
!Kung passed through the camp during the study. The period 1960–4 had
been one of exceptionally low rainfall and the 1963–4 rainy season had
been disappointingly short. There had been little rain in January and
February and only a few showers in March. Summer water holes had
dried up by April, necessitating a move back to the permanent water
holes earlier than the !Kung prefer. The crops of their black neighbors
had failed 2 years in succession, and the local Herero and Tswana
herders were experiencing real difficulties. Later in the year the Herero
women began joining their !Kung neighbors in gathering wild foods. It is
against this background that the data from the work diary should be
viewed.

WORK EFFORT AND DIVISION OF THE WORK LOAD

Group size and work effort

The number of people in Dobe camp each day varied widely from 23 to
40, with an average camp size of 30.9 (20.1 adults and 10.8 children).

The variations from day to day are shown in Table 9.1. Adding the group sizes for each day gives the total person-days of consumption: 179 the first week, 198 the second, 240 the third, and 249 the fourth – a total of 866 person-days of consumption.

How much work was carried out to support the camp for the 4-week period? If the 20 adults were working a 5-day week – the norm in industrial society – to support themselves and their dependents, the average number of workdays per week would be $20 \times 5 = 100$; a 4-day week for the adults would show 80 workdays, and so on. The actual number of days worked is much lower: Table 9.1 shows the number of people who worked on each day of the study, and Table 9.2 is a week-by-week summary of the work diary. On a given day from 0 to 16 people were out doing subsistence work. The person-days of work were 37 the first week, 22 the second, 42 the third, and 77 the fourth. The number of days of work per adult per week varied from a low of 1.2 to a high of 3.2, a range of figures that represents only 24 to 64 percent of the 5-day weekly work load of an industrial worker.

However, these figures cannot be accepted without a further adjustment. Week II (July 13 to 19) shows an unusually low work input of only 22 days. I contributed food on July 12 and 17, and this resulted in a decreased subsistence effort for the week. In my original study, week II was not included in the final results, which were based on weeks I, III, and IV (Lee 1969a:83–7). However, there are advantages to be gained from using all 4 weeks in the presentation of results; therefore, in the present study it seems perferable to retain week II and add the number of workdays that would compensate for the workdays saved by my provision of food.

The method of adjustment is briefly as follows: On July 12 and 17, I took five and nine people, respectively, by truck to collect mongongo nuts at groves not accessible on foot. These 14 person-days were counted as workdays in the original study; but judging from the weight of the nuts brought in by truck, each "truck-day" of work provided nuts equivalent to what could be brought in by 2.5 days of work on foot. Therefore, to the original 14 days of these trips was added another $14 + 7 = 21$ workdays in order to compensate for the truck input. This raised the work effort in week II from 22 to 43 days. The adjusted results are shown in the last two columns of Table 9.2. The work week for week II doubles from 1.2 days of work per adult to 2.4 days. Over the 4-week period, the change is small, with the total number of workdays increasing from 178 to 199 and the overall work week rising from 2.2 to 2.4 days of work per adult.

This low input of work required to feed a camp of hunting and gathering people challenges the notion that the life of hunter-gatherers is a constant struggle for existence, with subsistence work dominating their lives. The !Kung San, at least during the month of this study, appeared to

Table 9.1. *Dobe work diary: record of activities at Dobe camp for 28-day period July 6 to August 2, 1964*

Date	Adults[a]	Children[b]	Person-days of consumption[c]	Person-days of work[d]	Meat output (kg)[e]
Week I					
July 6	18	9	27	9	0
7	14	9	23	6	42
8	15	9	24	2	0
9	15	9	24	3	5
10	16	9	25	7	0
11	18	11	29	3	0
12	18	9	27	7	0
Week II					
July 13	20	11	31	5	0
14	16	9	25	0	0
15	16	9	25	1	0
16	14	9	23	0	0
17	19	12	31	11	36
18	17	9	26	3	0
19	23	14	37	2	0
Week III					
July 20	26	14	40	9	50
21	24	11	35	3	11
22	19	13	32	3	0
23	18	11	29	4	12
24	23	13	36	10	7
25	22	10	32	6	0
26	24	12	36	7	0
Week IV					
July 27	22	13	35	12	3
28	27	13	40	12	36
29	26	13	39	9	4.5
30	24	11	35	16	5
31	22	10	32	4	9
Aug. 1	24	11	35	8	0
2	22	11	33	16	0

Workday = a day in which one person collected food for the camp or a day in which one man went hunting.

[a] Daily count of adults in the camp.

[b] Daily count of children in the camp.

[c] Daily total of adults and children in camp. This count documents the variation in camp populations from day to day and week to week.

[d] Daily count of residents engaged in subsistence activities.

[e] Daily meat output in kilograms of edible meat.

Table 9.2. *Summary of Dobe work diary*

Week	Groups size Mean	Range	Adult-days	Child-days	Total person-days of Consumption	Work	Work week	Person-days of work (adjusted)	Work week (adjusted)
I (July 6–12)	25.6	23–29	114	65	179	37	2.3	37	2.3
II (July 13–19)	28.3	23–37	125	73	198	22	1.2	43	2.4
III (July 20–26)	34.3	29–40	156	84	240	42	1.9	42	1.9
IV (July 27–Aug. 2)	35.6	32–40	167	82	249	77	3.2	77	3.2
Total	30.9		562	304	866	178	2.2	199[a]	2.4[a]

[a]Seven workdays were performed by nonadults (see Table 9.3), hence the *adult* work week equals (192 × 100/562) × 0.07 = 2.391459).

spend less than half their days in subsistence and appeared to enjoy more leisure time than the members of many agricultural and industrial societies. This point gains added significance when we note that these observations were made during the dry season of a year of serious drought, a year when the !Kung's farming and herding neighbors experienced crop failure and livestock losses of a magnitude similar to that experienced in the Sahel of West Africa a decade later.

However interesting these overall figures on work effort may be, they tell us little about how work effort is allocated within the group. Of particular interest is the division of work between residents and visitors, between women and men, and between young and old.

Residents and visitors

On the days when Dobe people were not hunting or gathering they were either in camp, often entertaining visitors, or themselves visiting other camps. A total of 49 visitors joined the 27 residents at Dobe for stays that totaled 204 person-days, a block of time that constitutes almost a quarter (23.6 percent) of all the person-days spent at Dobe. The residents, for their part, spent 58 person-days visiting other camps (Table 9.3).

Time allocation differs markedly between residents and visitors, with the residents spending a much higher proportion of their time in subsistence than do the visitors. Table 9.3 shows that residents worked a 2.6-day week compared with a 1.7-day week for the visitors. Visits vary in length from 1 to 15 days, and most of the work visitors did do was done by those who stayed a week or more at Dobe. In !Kung etiquette, anyone is welcome to visit for a day or two and be fed. If you are staying much longer than that, you are expected to work and contribute to the food supplies of the camp by hunting and gathering in the host's area. Visiting men spend a higher proportion of their time gathering than do resident men. Gathering accounted for 40 percent of all the visiting men's work, but only 17 percent of the resident men's work. One reason for this difference is that only resident men tend snarelines and this accounted for about a third of all hunting days. The difference between resident and visiting women's work week is smaller: 1.8 days for the residents and 1.4 days for the visitors. When the women's work is adjusted to reflect the additional workdays required to provide the food equivalent to the truck trips, both resident and visiting women's work rises slightly to 2.2 and 1.7 days, respectively. Overall we see the residents working a 2.6-day week compared with a 1.7-day week for the visitors.

When a person visits Dobe and is fed by the Dobe people, he or she incurs an implicit obligation to reciprocate hospitality at a later date. Table 9.3 shows that visitors from other water holes spent far more time at Dobe than Dobe people spent elsewhere: 204 person-days of *in-visiting* versus only 58 days of *out-visiting*. This disparity implies that during

Table 9.3. *Activities at Dobe camp: men and women, residents and visitors*

| Population | Person-days (unadjusted) of | | | | | | Work week (unadjusted) | Adjusted work days | | Adjusted work week |
	Hunting	Gathering	Out visiting	In camp	Other	Total		Hunting	Gathering	
Residents										
Men	74	14	12	78	28	206	3.0	74.0	15.5	3.0
Women	0	54	35	122	1	212	1.8	0	67.5	2.2
Adults	74	68	47	200	29	418	2.4	74.0	83.0	2.6
Children	0	4	11	219	10	244	0.1	0	7.0	0.2
All residents	74	72	58	419	39	662	N/A	74.0	90.0	N/A
Visitors										
Men	9	6	1	45	0	61	1.7	9	6	1.7
Women	0	17	2	64	0	83	1.4	0	20	1.7
Adults	9	23	3	109	0	144	1.6	9	26	1.7
Children	0	0	2	58	0	60	0	0	0	0
All visitors	9	23	5	167	0	204	N/A	9	26	N/A
Residents and visitors										
Men	83	20	13	123	28	267	2.7	83	21.5	2.7
Women	0	71	37	186	1	295	1.7	0	87.5	2.1
All adults	83	91	50	309	29	562	2.2	83	109.0	2.4

N/A = not applicable.

Table 9.4. *Balance sheet of Dobe visiting: July 1964*

| Water hole | Person-days: | | Dobe net |
	Made visits to Dobe	Received visits from Dobe	
Mahopa	80	20	+60
!Xabe	13	7	+6
!Kangwa	9	6	+3
Bate	46	14	+32
!Goshe	9	0	+9
!Kubi	1	2	−1
/Xai/xai	46	9	+35
Total	204	58	+146

the month Dobe residents built up a considerable stock of credits with reference to visiting at other camps. It must be clearly emphasized that no !Kung would keep an exact count of days owed or days owing; nevertheless, it is instructive to examine the patterns of visiting in quantitative terms. Table 9.4 shows the person-days of visiting between Dobe and the seven other main water holes of the area. Note that Dobe people received at least one visitor from every other water hole and themselves made visits to all but one of the others. This table documents the constant flow of personnel throughout the Dobe area.

The net balance of +146 days in Dobe's favor is not surprising. Given seasonal availability of food, it is common for visitors to converge on a water hole if a particular resource is in abundance. Bate receives many visitors from February to April when morula nuts are falling; !Kubi gets many visitors from August to October during the height of the baobab season. News of a large kill at any nearby waterhole is sufficient to bring up to 50 people in for an overnight stay. I suspect that the presence of our expedition was itself a sufficient inducement to attract visitors during the month of the study. At other times of the year we observed Dobe people making more visits elsewhere. I believe that over the long run visiting reciprocity balances out.

Women and men

One of the most interesting findings of the work diary was the higher work effort of men compared with women. The work effort for visiting men and women was similar, but resident men were observed to work an average of 12 out of 28 days, whereas resident women worked about 9 out of 28 days. This finding contradicts the view that women are the workhorses of a foraging society: Men appear to work a third harder than do women. Gathered food, mainly provided by women, makes up the larger part of the food eaten by the !Kung. A total of 116 person-days was spent in gathering: 87.5 days by the women, 21.5 days by the men, and 7 days by two resident adolescent girls. Because gathered foods provided about 70 percent of all the calories consumed (see below), each person-day of gathering provided about 0.6 percent of the period's total food in calories.

A total of 83 man-days was spent in hunting, and this activity produced the other 30 percent of all the calories consumed. Thus each day of hunting provided 0.36 percent of the total food. Put another way, the total production of food over the 28 days came to about 2 million Cal. Each man-day of hunting provided about 7230 Cal and each person-day of gathering provided about 12,000 Cal. The men in 104.5 days of work (83 days of hunting and 21.5 days of gathering) produced 600,000 + 260,000 = 860,000 Cal. The women (and teenage girls) in 94.5 days of gathering produced 1,140,000 Cal. In short, women worked fewer days than men but produced more calories.

In an earlier presentation of these results (Lee 1968a:40) I made the difference in efficiency between women's and men's work appear even more striking than it should have been. I stated that a woman's work was 2.5 times as productive as a man's per person-hour. These adjusted figures show a smaller difference in efficiency ratio, with a day of gathering producing about 67 percent more calories on the average than a day of hunting.

Draper (personal communication) has also provided important unpublished data on men's and women's work effort in the /Du/da area. Between February and October 1969, Draper observed seven camps for periods of 4 to 11 days, for a total of 44 days. She recorded a total of 1268 adult-days of consumption and 408 adult-days of work. The overall work week was 2.3 days per adult, a figure not far from the 2.4-day work week at Dobe. Draper's observations span several seasons. She found work effort highest at the two summer camps observed in February and March (3.5-day work week), lowest at the two winter camps in June and July (1.2-day work week), and intermediate in April (2.2-day work week) and in August and October (2.3-day work week). Draper found a striking difference between men's and women's work effort at the /Du/da camps, with men working over twice as hard as women: 3.3 workdays per week for men, but only 1.3 workdays for women. Although this sex difference remains to be accounted for, it is clear that both the range and the mean of the /Du/da camp's overall work effort compare closely with the Dobe results.

Young and old

How is the work allocated among the age-sex classes? At what age do people enter the productive labor force? At what age do they leave it?

Thanks to the use of Howell's method for estimating ages, we are in a position to give some preliminary answers to these questions. Table 9.5 presents data on 28 Dobe adults (18 residents and 10 visitors) arranged into three age categories: old (60+), middle-aged (40 to 59), and young (20 to 39). Work effort for adults declines with age from 38 percent workdays in the 20 to 39 age group to 29 percent in the over 60 group. Differences according to sex should be noted: Overall the men work harder than the women in all age groups, but the hardest workers for the men are in the 40 to 59 group; for the women the 20 to 39 age group works the hardest. The declining work effort with age is more pronounced for women than for men; women's percentage of workdays drops from 36 to 22 with age; in the case of the men the old group and the young group appear to be exactly the same. The reason for this, I suspect, arises from specific circumstances: Dobe had one exceptionally active old man (≠Toma//gwe). Also three Dobe men (two young and one middle-aged) spent about 26 days – listed under "Other" in Table 9.3 – doing work at !Kangwa for the Tswana headman. Had they been present in camp for those days, their subsistence effort would have been higher, raising the levels of work for the younger men (20 to 39) probably to 45 or 50 percent.

Perhaps as interesting as the overall figures is the wide range of variation within age groups: Every age-sex category has at least one person who did little or no work during the time period, and most categories have one or more hard workers with over half of their days as workdays. Among the older men, ≠Toma//gwe, an energetic 60-year-old, went out to check his snarelines on 14 days, went hunting on 2 days, and gathering on 1 day, for a total of 17 workdays out of 28. At the other extreme was ≠Toma/twe from /Xai/xai, who came to visit his daughter Bau and did no work during his 6-day stay.

Illness may prevent a man from working and may increase the workload for others. Kasupe, a popular man in his fifties with seven children (see Chapter 12), was disabled with a badly infected leg and could do no work during his 16 days at Dobe; his wife /Tasa, with four of their children under the age of 15 to take care of, worked 10 of the 16 days she was at Dobe. Similarly, their eldest daughter N/ahka was the hardest worker among the younger women as she gathered food for her own three children and to help provide for her younger siblings. Even with Kasupe temporarily disabled, however, the burden did not fall too heavily on his immediate kin. I noted contributions to the family's food supply from all the other households of the Dobe camp. In addition, daytime curing ceremonies were held frequently for Kasupe by men and women healers from Dobe and elsewhere. That the burden of care for Kasupe was spread around the camp is demonstrated by the fact that Debe, Kasupe's eldest son, did no hunting or gathering in his 7 days at Dobe.

The age breakdown of the work diary showed some interesting anoma-

Table 9.5. *Age, sex, and work effort at Dobe camp*

Age group[a]	Men						Women						Both sexes	
	No. of men	Days of work	Days of consumption	High individual[b]	Low individual[c]	Percent work days	No. of women	Days of work	Days of consumption	High individual	Low individual	Percent work days	No. of persons	Percent work days
Old	3	19	49	17/28[d]	0/6	39	4	17	77	6/15	0/6	22	7	29
Middle-aged	4	34.5	80	18/28	0/16	43	5	25	86	10/16	3/28	29	9	36
Young	7	48	123	16/28	0/7	39	5	38.5	107	14/28	0/11	36	12	38
Total	14	101.5	252	18/28	0/16	40	14	80.5	270	14/28	0/11	30	28	35

Raw data[e]

	Men	Women
Old	17/28, 2/15, 0/6	6/15, 6/28, 5/28, 0/6
Middle-aged	18.5/28, 13/28, 3/8, 0/16	10/16, 3/28, 3/8, 8/28, 1/6
Young	16/28, 3/6, 9/21, 10/28, 4/11, 6/22, 0/7	14/28, 13.5/28, 8/28, 3/12, 0/11

[a] old = 60+, middle-aged = 40–59, young = 20–39 years.

[b] Highest proportion workdays.

[c] Lowest proportion workdays.

[d] 17/28 = present on 28 days; worked 17.

[e] Work behavior (number of days worked/number of days present) of each person studied.

lies. /Twi!kumsi, one of the oldest men in the population – estimated age 75 – and partially blind, spent 15 days at Dobe and actually put in 2 workdays of gathering. One of the youngest and healthiest members of the group, Sa//gai, a 23-year-old woman with two children, did no subsistence work at all during her 11-day visit.

To judge from the Dobe work diary, elderly !Kung are only moderately less active in subsistence than are people in their middle years. Not so the members of the youngest age categories. Only two people under 15 years of age did any significant subsistence work. Two 14-year-old girls each did a day of gathering and a day on the truck for mongongos for a total of 7 (adjusted) workdays during their 47 person-days of residence. The rest of the children were footloose and fancy-free. These data are strongly supported by Draper's (1976:209–11) systematic observations that children under 14 do almost no subsistence work. Because of the small sample size, the analysis of work effort by itself cannot be very informative; individual differences and situation-specific differences tend to blur general trends. Nevertheless, these data act as a check on qualitative ethnographic observations. My overall sense, after viewing men and women at work in many !Kung camps, is that the Dobe data are on the high side for old men, too low for young men, and fairly representative for women. My impression is that the male-female differences in work effort observed here hold true at other camps.

On the question of age at entry into the work force it is also necessary to refer to other data, as there were no people in the Dobe sample between the ages of 15 and 19 and only three between the ages of 10 and 14. Adolescent girls do not start regular subsistence work until marriage; therefore, variability in the age at marriage produces wide variations in the amount of work done by teenagers. For example, at /Xai/xai one married girl of 15 was observed regularly to accompany the women on gathering trips, whereas an older playmate, still unmarried, stayed in the camp. We have noted how work on black cattle posts delays boys' assumption of adult status as hunters. At /Du/da, however, where there are no cattle, Draper (1976 and personal communication) has observed boys of 15 to 18 actively hunting each week.

MEAT AND HUNTING RETURNS

During the 28-day study 18 animals yielding 206 kg of meat were killed by the hunters of the camp, and an additional 16 kg of meat were received as gifts from outside, for a total meat intake of 222 kg (490 lb) (Table 9.6). When this intake is divided by the 866 person-days of consumption, we see that meat consumption averaged 256 g (9.1 oz) per person per day. None of the kills was made with bow and poisoned arrows. Hunting with his excellent dogs, ≠Toma killed four warthogs, and

The !Kung San

Table 9.6. *Meat intake at Dobe camp: July 6 to August 2, 1964*

Date	Hunter	Technique of kill	Animal	Weight of meat Kg	lb
Meat from kills at camp					
July 7	≠Toma	Dogs	Warthog	36.3	80
	≠Toma//gwe	Snare	Steenbok	5.4	12
9	/Xashe	Snare	Steenbok	5.4	12
17	≠Toma	Dogs	Warthog	36.3	80
20	≠Toma	Dogs	Warthog	36.3	80
	≠Toma//gwe	Club	Honey badger	5.0	11
	≠Toma//gwe	Club	Python	8.6	19
21	/Xashe	Snare	Steenbok	5.4	12
23	N!eishin!a	Snare	Steenbok	5.4	12
	≠Toma//gwe	Dog	Hare	1.4	3
24	≠Toma	Dog	Bat-eared fox	4.5	10
27	≠Toma/gwe	Snare	Hare	1.4	3
	Kopela Maswe	Snare	Korhaan	0.5	1
	N!eishima	Snare	Korhaan	0.5	1
28	≠Toma	Dogs	Warthog	36.3	80
29	≠Toma//gwe	Snare	Kori bustard	2.7	6
30	N!eishin!a	Snare	Steenbok	5.4	12
31	/Xashe	Club	Porcupine	9.1	20
Total				205.9	454
Meat from other sources					
July 21	From Mahopa	Rifle	Kudu	5.4	12
23	From Bate	Bow	Kudu	5.4	12
24	From district officer	Rifle	Warthog	2.7	6
27	From /Xai/xai	Club	Korhaan	0.5	1
27	From /Xai/xai	Club	Korhaan	0.5	1
29	From Herero	Domestic	Beef	1.8	4
Total				16.3	36

these alone, weighing 145 kg (320 lb), provided 65 percent of all the meat in the camp. Snaring was actively pursued by several of the resident men, and it produced nine kills with a total weight of 32 kg (Table 9.7). Three more kills, totaling 22.7 kg, were made with clubs. In all, nine different species were brought into camp, but apart from warthog, only the five steenbok (27 kg) provided as much as 10 percent of the weight of all kills.

A small quantity of meat from outside Dobe flowed into camp from five sources (Table 9.6). !Kung visitors from Mahopa and Bate brought meat from kudu kills, and a visitor from /Xai/xai brought two small game birds killed on the way. A Herero man from !Xabi gave a small gift of cow's

Table 9.7. *Kills at Dobe camp, by technique and species*

	No. of kills	Meat yield	
		kg	%
Technique			
Dogs	6	151.1	73
Snares	9	32.1	15
Club	3	22.7	11
Total	18	205.9	99
Species			
Warthog	4	145.2	71
Steenbok	5	27.0	13
Porcupine	1	9.1	4
Python	1	8.6	4
Honey badger	1	5.0	2
Bat-eared fox	1	4.5	2
Hare	2	2.8	1
Kori bustard	1	2.7	1
Korhaan	2	1.0	1
Total	18	205.9	99

meat, and the district officer gave a few pounds of warthog meat from a kill he had made while on a tour of the Dobe area. Meat from outside sources made up only about 7 percent of the total weight.

In all, seven men (six residents and one visitor) did 78 man-days of hunting and four men did no hunting at all (Table 9.8). (Several other visitors did 5 man-days of hunting, not used in this tabulation.) Hunting success rates – percent of hunting days on which kills were made – varied from 0 to 38 percent. The average success rate of 23 percent means that one kill was made for every 4 man-days of hunting. Returns in kilograms of raw meat and in calories per day of hunting also varied widely. ≠Toma had an excellent record for the month; every day he hunted, he produced 9.4 kg of meat, a portion sufficient to meet the day's caloric requirements for 13 people and protein requirements of 20 people! Others did not fare so well. The hunting of two men, ≠Toma//gwe and his son /Xashe, provided meat in excess of their own caloric needs; the other men's hunting actually produced fewer calories than they consumed in the process of hunting! Overall, the men's hunting made a positive contribution to the energy balance, but not a particularly efficient one. In each day of hunting the hunter consumed about 2800 Cal and 90 g of protein; his work yielded 7900 Cal (raw basis) and 343 g of protein, for a net contribution to the group of 5100 Cal and 253 g of protein.

The Valley Bisa hunters studied by Marks (1976) offer an instructive

Table 9.8. *Hunting returns at Dobe camp*

	No. of kills	Yield of meat (kg)	Days of hunting	Hunting success (% days with kill)	Meat/ day of hunting (kg)	Calories day of hunting (3000 Cal/kg)	Protein/ day of hunting (130 g/kg)
Hunters							
≠Toma	5	149.7	16	31	9.4	28,200	1,220
≠Toma//gwe	6	24.5	16	38	1.5	4,500	195
/Xashe	3	19.9	9	33	2.2	6,600	286
N!eishin!a[a]	2	10.8	16	13	0.7	2,100	91
Kopela Maswe[a]	1	0.5	9	11	0.1	300	13
N!eishima[a]	1	0.5	8	13	0.1	300	13
≠Gau	0	0	4	0	0	0	0
Total/Average	18	205.9	78	23	2.6	7,900	343
Men not hunting							
/Twi!kumsi	0	0	0				
/N!au	0	0	0				
Debe	0	0	0				
Kasupe	0	0	0				

[a] Shared in one of ≠Toma's warthog kills.

comparison with the !Kung on the questions of success rates and meat yields per unit of work effort. The 12 resident and visiting hunters at one large village cluster had success rates varying from 0 to 50 percent, with most of the values falling in the range 9 to 33 percent, a level very similar to the !Kung's. On the other hand, the Bisa hunters used firearms exclusively, and the mammals they hunted tended to be larger than those hunted by the !Kung. As a result, the Bisa hunters provided excellent yields by !Kung standards. Even an average hunter brought in 25 kg per day of hunting compared with 9.4 kg per day for the best !Kung hunter. However, among the Bisa, hunting is a specialized profession, and the 12 hunters worked to feed villages with over 300 people. Year-round a Bisa adult could count on only about 55 kg of meat from local sources compared with 80 to 90 kg of meat per year for the !Kung (Marks 1976:202–4).

INPUT-OUTPUT CALORIC LEVELS

So far we have considered the level of work effort for the group and have seen how the work load is divided between males and females and between young and old. The task now is to estimate the quantity of energy yielded by this work effort. Because the actual time devoted to subsistence is modest, the question arises whether this low work effort produces a substandard diet.

During fieldwork no direct caloric observations were made. It was difficult to measure a single individual's daily food intake because this was eaten over a period of several hours in the late afternoon and evening and was made up of small portions from the supplies of different families. However, because foodstuffs are shared equitably throughout the camp, it was possible to measure gross per capita intake by estimating the total weight of food brought in and dividing it by the number of people on hand. A net per capita intake figure was calculated by deducting values for waste (inedible portions, bones, nutshells, etc.) and allowing for loss through cooking. An account of the methods and results follows.

The staple mongongo is particularly suitable for this kind of analysis; it is easy to count and weigh, and the percentage of edible constituents is precisely known. The fruit consists of edible flesh, a hard outer nutshell and a soft inner shell (both inedible), and a core of edible nutmeat. The whole fruit weighs 5.0 g, and the nutmeat makes up about 15 percent of the total weight of 0.75 g (Chapter 7).

During the study period most of the mongongos had already lost their flesh, and for this calculation only the nutmeat is taken into account. Small quantities of the flesh have been included with "other" vegetable foods.

There are approximately 200 whole nuts per kilogram and each kilogram of whole nuts yields 150 g of nutmeats. I weighed the total backload of nuts brought in by a sample of women. A woman's daily collection of whole nuts weighed between 10 kg (22 lb) and 15 kg (33 lb), although backloads of as much as 20 kg (44 lb) of whole nuts were recorded. Each backload contained, on the average, 2,500 whole nuts as well as smaller quantities of other foodstuffs. As the edible portion of whole nuts is 15 percent, each 12-kg backload of nuts contained 1800 g of edible nutmeats.

Records were also maintained for the number of nuts cracked and eaten by individuals and families on a single day. The cracking and shelling rate averages three to six nuts per person per minute. In 1 hour a person cracks and shells 200 to 300 nuts, and an hour's cracking yields 150 to 225 g of edible nutmeats. On the bases of cracking rates, time devoted to cracking, and total weight of whole nuts brought into camp, the Dobe !Kung were observed to eat about 300 nuts per person per day, a portion that yielded about 210 g of nutmeats when allowance is made for spoiled and crushed nuts. Each 100 g of nutmeats contains about 650 Cal (Appendix D, Table D.1; Figure 7.2) and 28 g of protein. These figures are more accurate than, and supersede, those presented in my earlier paper (Lee 1969a:88) in which calorie and protein yields were calculated at 600 Cal and 27 g, respectively, per 100 g. The result is a per capita intake figure for mongongo about 8 percent higher for calories and 4 percent higher for protein than that presented in 1969.

The per capita daily allotment of meat from hunting and from gift sources works out to 256 g (9.1 oz) of raw meat. Allowing for a 10 percent shrinkage in cooking, the caloric yield of this allotment is estimated at 690 Cal (based on a rate of 300 Cal per 100 g cooked). The protein content of the allotment– 15 percent of the weight– is estimated to be 34.5 g per cooked portion.

The remaining vegetable portion of the diet consisted of small quantities of some 20 species of roots, melons, gums, bulbs, and dried fruits, including some mongongo fruit. In reexamining the figures I published in 1969, I concluded that the amounts derived from this source were underestimated, particularly by not allowing for mongongo fruits. Accordingly, the figure for this category has been raised from 190 to 300 Cal.

In Table 9.9 the three main food sources (meat, nuts, other vegetable foods) are considered together in order to show the contribution each makes to the diet and to derive an estimate of daily per capita intake of calories and proteins. The results show a daily allotment of 2355 Cal and 96.3 g of protein per person. Because of the high protein value of the mongongo, the protein intake is unusually high, even by North American standards. It is also unexpected that a hunting people should get such a

Table 9.9. *Caloric and protein levels in !Kung diet: July–August 1964*

Class of food	Percent Contribution to diet by weight	Per capita consumption		Calories/ person/ day
		Weight (g)	Protein (g)	
Meat	31	230	34.5	690
Mongongo nuts	28	210	58.8	1365
Other vegetables	41	300	3.0	300
Total	100	740	96.3	2355[a]

[a]In the original study the overall per capita consumption figures were: weight, 630 g; protein, 93.1 g; and calories, 2140 (Lee 1969a:88).

high proportion of their protein from vegetable rather than from meat sources.

Does a per capita intake of 2355 Cal meet the energy requirements of the group? The !Kung are small in stature and weight. The average height and weight for adult males are 157 cm and 46 kg and for adult females 147 cm and 41 kg (Bronte-Stewart et al. 1960). The overall weights for the whole population of the Dobe area are somewhat heavier (Chapter 10.) However, the Dobe camp people themselves are smaller than the area-wide average, and their weights are very close to the Bronte-Stewart figures.) Basal metabolic requirements for individuals of such heights and weights are calculated at 1400 Cal per day for males and 1100 Cal per day for females (Taylor and Pye 1966:45–8). Given an activity regimen that varies from light moderate to severe exercise (including an hour of nut cracking per day and 32 km of subsistence travel per week), the requirements can be estimated at 2250 Cal for males and 1750 Cal for females, each day of an average work week. These figures apply to adults 30 years of age; caloric requirements are less for middle-aged and elderly persons. For children I have taken a median age of 8 years for all individuals under 15 years and estimated the daily requirements to be 2000 Cal (Taylor and Pye 1966:463).

To calculate the daily caloric requirement for the study group as a whole, it is necessary to take an average, weighted according to the precentage of each age-sex class in the population. Because the population consists of 30 percent adult males, 35 percent adult females, and 35 percent children under 15 years, the mean daily energy requirement for a group of 31 persons is 61,300 Cal, and for each group member, about 1975 Cal.

The per capita yield of foodstuffs during the study period was estimated to be 2355 Cal (Table 9.9); clearly the food output exceeds energy require-

ments by about 380 Cal per person per day. These data confirm that even
the modest subsistence effort of 2.4 workdays per week was more than
enough to provide an adequate diet for the !Kung during the study period.

Draper has documented the regional variations in the composition of
the diet. At /Du/da camps in 1969 she noted a lower level of mongongo
nut consumption and a higher level of meat consumption. As noted, work
effort was also higher at some camps, a difference discussed later in this
book (Chapters 12 and 15; see also Lee 1972c; Draper 1976).

These estimates imply a positive energy balance for the July 1964 Dobe
camp of 380 Cal per person per day. How is this modest surplus allocated? Three areas of allocation should be mentioned. Part of the surplus
goes to maintain the camp's hunting dogs, which varied in number from
five to eight during the study. The dogs eat what is left over when people
have eaten their fill, and it is worth noting that the physical condition of
the animals seemed to show more seasonal variation than the condition
of humans. In input-output terms, the dogs absorb the effects of marginal
variations in abundance of foodstuffs brought into camp, a role similar to
that played by pigs in the economy of New Guinea highlanders (Vayda et
al. 1961; Rappaport 1967, 1968). (However, unlike the highlanders, who
eat their pigs, the San have never been known to eat their dogs.) The
surplus is also used to meet the caloric demands of the !Kung trance-
healing dance. The dances involve the whole camp and go on from dusk
till dawn. With the men dancing and going into trance and the women
sitting up all night singing and clapping, a dance requires a substantial
amount of energy; the participants in a single full-night trance dance
may consume calories equivalent to those used in a full waking day,
which would amount to 61,000 Cal in the case of the Dobe camp. Dances
are often held in celebration of a large kill, and the day following is spent
cooking the meat and resting. There was no dance held at Dobe during
the study period, although a major one occurred the night of July 4,
immediately before the study commenced. At the various Dobe area
camps trance dances of both the men's and women's types tended to
occur at a frequency of one to four times a month.

The caloric surplus not given to the dogs or utilized in special events
such as dances may go into physiological accumulation of fat – an accumulation that is later metabolized during the lean season of the year. Exploration of this possibility forms the main subject matter of Chapter 10.

OTHER FORMS OF WORK:
MANUFACTURE, MAINTENANCE, AND REPAIR

Subsistence labor looms large in !Kung work, but it is by no means the
only kind of work necessary to their way of life. Manufacture and maintenance of the tools of subsistence and of other essentials, such as clothing

Plate 9.2. Other work: building a hut.

and housing, must also be considered in any comprehensive view of their
work lives. As a shorthand we will call this kind of work *tool making* and
tool fixing, even though under this heading are included such diverse
"tools" as karosses, dogs, sandals, storage structures, and huts, as well
as more conventional tools like digging sticks, spears, axes, and fire
sticks. Getting an accurate picture of the time spent in tool making and
fixing would be a laborious task if one had to rely on direct observation.
Intensively observing a group for a month, one would see only a fraction
of the toolkit actually being manufactured or repaired. The method I
have chosen instead is a rough and ready one, but it may offer a preliminary idea of the magnitude and complexity of this kind of work. Table
9.10 is a catalog of every subsistence tool discussed in Chapter 5 as well
as every item of clothing and housing that a !Kung family of four would
possess. Column 1 shows the time in minutes required to make the item
and indicates whether the maker is the man or the woman of the household or (in a few cases) both. Column 2 lists the useful lifetime of the
article in days, with a range of from 60 days for a biltong rack to 5475
days (15 years) for a set of oracle disks. Column 3 lists the cost of manufacture in minutes per person per day spread out over the lifetime of the

Table 9.10. *In-camp manufacture amd maintenance times for subsistence tools, clothing, and housing for household of four*

Tool	(1) Time for manufacture (min) Men	Women	(2) Useful lifetime (days)	(3) Cost of manufacture per day of useful life (min) Men	Women	(4) Time for maintenance (min) Men	Women	(5) Frequency maintenance needed (days)	(6) Cost of maintenance (min) Men	Women	(7) Total cost (min/day) Men	Women
Subsistence												
Eggshell canteens		360	730		0.50							0.5
Stomach canteen	60		180	0.3							0.3	0.3
Digging stick	60		180	0.3			15	30		0.5	0.3	0.5
Kaross	900		1825	0.5			120	60		2.0	0.5	2.0
Bags (4)	240	240	1825	0.13	0.13	20	20	30	0.67	0.67	0.8	0.8
Net	900		3650	0.25		60		180	0.33		0.33	
Yoke	15		5	3.0							3.0	
Bow	900		1825	0.5		10		5	2.0		2.5	
Arrows (15)	900		365	2.5		30		5	6.0		8.5	
Poison & kit	300		180	1.7		30		4	7.5		9.2	
Quiver	600		1825	0.36		30		180	0.17		0.5	
Spear	600		3650	0.16		30		30	1.0		1.16	
Probe	600		1825	0.32		60		30	2.0		2.32	
Club	300		1095	0.27		60		180	0.33		0.6	
Rope snares	600		365	1.6		60		30	2.0		3.6	
Dogs (2)		60	730		0.08	10	10	31	3.3	3.3	3.3	3.3
Adze/ax	600		1825	0.33		10		5	2.0		2.33	
Knives (2)	1200		1825	0.66		10	10	5	2.0	2.0	2.66	2.0
Flint-and-steel fire kit[a]	300		1825	0.16		10	10	1	10.0	10.0	10.16	10.0
Oracle disks	300		5475	0.05							0.5	
Nut-cracking stones (6 sets)												

Mortar & pestle	600		1095	0.55			30	30		1.0	0.55	1.0
Fire tools	180		365	0.5			30	30		1.0	0.5	1.0
Iron cooking pot (store-bought)[a]		900	1825		0.5		30	30		1.0		1.5
Basins/spoons (store-bought)[a]		600	1095	0.55	0.55		15	30		0.5		1.05
Tortoise shell & other things	300		730	0.41			15	30		0.5	0.41	0.5
Storage	300	150	180	1.6	0.83	0.5	15	30	0.5	0.5	2.1	1.35
Biltong rack	180		60	3.0		15	15				3.0	
Total				19.15	2.59				39.8	20.97		
Clothing: women												
Skirts (2)	120	160	1825	0.07	0.07		15	30		0.5	0.07	0.57
Baby carrier	60	60	365	0.16	0.16		30	30		1.0	0.16	1.16
Sandals	360		1825	0.2			15	75		0.2	0.2	0.2
Cloth		180	365		0.5		15	75		0.2		0.7
Total				1.94	1.06					2.3		
Clothing: Men												
Chuana	240	240	730	0.33	0.33		15	30	0.2	0.2	0.53	0.2
Shirt	180		365	0.49			30	60		0.2	0.49	0.2
Shorts	180		365	0.49			30	60		0.2	0.49	0.2
Sandals	360		1825	0.2		15	15	75	0.2		0.4	
Total					1.06				0.4	2.3		
Housing												
Hut	180	900	90	2.0	10.0	1	5	1	1.0	5.0		15.0
Clearing and bedding	180	180	90	2.0	2.0	1	1	1	1.0	1.0	3.0	3.0
Total				2.0	12.0				1.0	6.0	3.0	18.0

[a]Cost of manufacture based on cost of making ostrich eggshell beads that are traded for these items.

article. Columns 4, 5, and 6 repeat this sequence, but for the cost of maintenance of an article. Column 7 lists the total cost in minutes of work per day for a man and a woman to make and keep in repair each article.

For example, most households have a stock of six ostrich eggshell canteens for water. It takes a woman about 1 hour to prepare each one: drilling a hole, shaking out the contents, rinsing and deodorizing the interior, and making a small grass stopper (total 6 hours = 360 minutes). A canteen has a useful lifetime which averages 2 years (730 days). Therefore, the cost of the "tool" (six canteens) is about 0.5 minute per day (360 ÷ 730). Because the canteens are virtually maintenance-free, the total cost per day is still 0.5 minute. A kaross is made by the men and used and maintained by the women. At least 15 hours (900 minutes) of in-camp work are required to make one: stretching, drying, and scraping the hide; then trimming, tanning, and softening it. But the kaross has a useful life of 5 years or more, so the initial cost spread out over the lifetime of the article is only 0.5 minute per day. Maintenance of the kaross involves frequent processing of the leather with the red bark of *Pterocarpus angolensis* to keep it soft and suedelike, a task that takes a woman about 2 hours every 2 months, for a cost of 2 minutes per day. One important tool costs nothing: the nut-cracking stones. But the four main components of hunting–bow, arrows, poison, quiver–may together cost as much as 20.7 minutes a day. The cost of dogs was difficult to calculate. Building a shelter for a whelping bitch might take an hour's work. Maintaining a dog would require about 10 minutes' work a day, but not every household has a dog, and on days when there is little food left over, dogs have to fend for themselves. Three items of European manufacture presented an interesting problem of calculating costs of manufacturing. The flint-and-steel kit, the three-legged iron pot, and the enamel basins and metal spoons must be bought in a store or obtained in trade from other !Kung. I assigned to each of these the time required to make enough ostrich eggshell beads to purchase the item from a store: 300 minutes for the flint-and-steel kit, 900 minutes for the pot, and 600 minutes for the basin and spoons. Maintenance costs for these items are calculated in the same way as for locally produced tools.

The summary of results (Table 9.11) offers some surprising insights into tool making and fixing. First, we see the interdependence of men and women. Many of the tools used by women are made for them by men. Housing used by both men and women is made by the latter. Second, we see that in both making and fixing subsistence tools men carry a heavier share of the work than women: 19.15 minutes versus 2.59 minutes a day for manufacture, and 39.8 minutes versus 20.97 minutes for fixing. Work on clothing is comparable for men and women (2.34 versus 3.36 minutes), but in the area of housing women do much more of the work, with

Table 9.11. *Summary of household work time results*

Category	Manufacturing (min/day)		Repair and maintenance (min/day)		Total manufacturing and maintenance (min/day)	
	Men	Women	Men	Women	Men	Women
Subsistence	19.15	2.59	39.8	20.97	58.95	23.56
Clothing	1.94	1.06	0.40	2.30	2.34	3.36
Housing	2.00	12.00	1.00	6.00	3.00	18.00
Total	23.09	15.65	41.2	29.27	64.29	44.92

only 3 minutes a day for men and 18 for women. Overall the man's daily work load is estimated at 64 minutes compared with 45 for the woman, and these times should be added to the weekly subsistence work loads.

Before leaving the subject of tool making and fixing, we should consider the question originally raised in Chapter 5: What effect has the adoption of iron technology had on the subsistence system of the !Kung? In particular, how much has the introduction of iron shortened the time spent per day in tool making and fixing and other activities, compared with the period when the toolkit was mainly of stone and bone? Obviously nut cracking would have been the same for "stone-age" !Kung, but what about butchery, hide scraping, and woodworking with stone tools? And how much additional subsistence time would be necessary to collect stone suitable for working? It should be noted that abundant sources of chert and fine-grained silcrete exist in the Dobe area. Nodules are common in the exposed beds of the !Kangwa Valley and elsewhere. The massive accumulations of Stone Age artifacts in archeological deposits both north and south of the Ahas attest to this abundance. On the question of additional time required in tool making and repair and in butchery, I consulted Ed Wilmsen, an expert in lithic technology (Wilmsen 1974). Based on his own observations and experiments with flint knapping, Wilmsen suggests that the overall work effort *would not have been significantly greater* for pre-iron age !Kung, since stone tools can be made with extreme rapidity and are almost as efficient as iron in such areas as butchery and skin scraping (Wilmsen, personal communication). In light of these comments it may be that the work data presented here are not entirely without relevance to prehistoric hunter-gatherers.

HOUSEWORK AND OVERALL WORK EFFORT

The basis of housework is the hour or more of nut cracking required to provide a day's ration of mongongo nuts. Children over the age of 8 and *all adults of both sexes* do most of their own cracking. Children 4 to 7 eat

Table 9.12. *Work hours per week: men and women*

	Subsistence work	Tool making and fixing	Subtotal	Housework	Total work week
Men	21.6	7.5	29.1	15.4	44.5
Women	12.6	5.1	17.7	22.4	40.1
Average, both sexes	17.1	6.3	23.4	18.9	42.3

smaller quantities of nuts, and these are cracked for them by their parents or older siblings. Nursing infants and toddlers do not eat many of the hard-to-digest mongongo nuts, except when premasticated or pounded and mixed with other foods. Most of those nuts provided for children are cracked by the women. Both men and women prepare and cook food. Vegetable foods and very small game are prepared mostly by women; larger game (weighing 5 kg and up) are butchered and cooked mainly by men. Other kinds of housework, including tending the fire, serving food, cleaning the fireplace, washing utensils, and preparing the bedding, fall more heavily on women; collecting firewood is a job that falls more heavily on men. Overall, women do more housework than men, although because of the division of the nut-cracking work and because of the men's predominance in butchery, meat cooking, and firewood collecting, the difference between the sexes is not as great as one might expect: about 2.2 hours of housework per day for men and 3.2 hours per day for women. The difference appears more striking in the rhythm of the work. The woman's 3 hours is a steady daily input, compared with a man's daily input of only about 1.8 hours. However, when game is brought in, the men's butchery and cooking time can vary from 1 hour for a game bird to 4 hours for a warthog to 15 hours for a large antelope, a work effort that brings the men's daily time devoted to housework up to 2.2 hours.

What then are the final tallies in terms of hours per person per week for !Kung work effort of the three kinds: subsistence work, tool making and fixing, and housework? To arrive at the hours of subsistence work, we take the number of days in the work week from Table 9.3 and multiply it by the number of hours in a workday: 8 hours for men and 6 for women. To obtain the hours of work for tool making and fixing we multiply the minutes per day totals (Table 9.11) by 7 and divide by 60. And to arrive at the hours per week of housework, we simply multiply the daily figures by 7. Table 9.12 summarizes the figures: Men clearly have the heavier share of work in subsistence and tool making and repair. Women do more housework than men, but overall the men appear to have a longer work

Plate 9.3. Housework: cooking a meal with a grandchild's help.

week. The shorter subsistence workday of the women does not result in a lower return in foodstuffs; we have already noted that women provide more food per day of gathering than men provide per day of hunting. Women return to the camp earlier in the day than men. They use the time to ensure that the ostrich eggshell canteens are filled and that some food is prepared to await their husbands' arrival later in the afternoon if both happen to be out that day.

Do these figures suggest that men, by working the longer week, are exploited members of !Kung society? I think not. A major category of work still to be mentioned is child care, and to the child's own mother falls 60 to 80 percent of the work with young children, a proportion that more than redresses the apparent disparity between men's and women's work shown in Table 9.12. Neither do these figures support the notion that women are the exploited members of !Kung society. Their weekly work effort, *including housework*, is less than that of the men, and even adding the work of child rearing does not raise the women's total work load significantly above the range of the men's. It should be remembered that low fertility helps to space the periods of intensive infant and child care more widely, and after the age of 40 or 45 child care does not figure in the work lives of most women. These points are explored in greater detail in Chapter 11.

Apart from a few notes of comparison between Dobe and /Du/da, very little has been said about seasonal and regional variations in work effort and food intake. Yet this type of information is crucial if we are to place the Dobe camp data in a broader context to see whether the relative ease of subsistence and high quality of diet observed here can be considered representative of the !Kung as a whole. Chapter 10 discusses the search for a methodology to answer this question.

10

The allocation
of nutritional stress

THE !Kung San of the Dobe camp in a single month appeared to meet their nutritional needs with a modest amount of work effort. But how representative is this one case study of the !Kung population as a whole or even of the Dobe camp population at other times of the year? Answering this kind of question demands a new methodology, one that enables the observer to monitor the nutritional status of large numbers of people at widely separated camps over long periods. The method I have chosen, adapted from the standard medical-nutritional survey, is the systematic recording of weight, height, and skinfold thickness (i.e., fat accumulation) for a large number of people at different times of the year. Even without the seasonal dimension, a survey of this kind can make a useful contribution to nutritional anthropometry. We can study the body size and stature of the !Kung, in terms of both internal variability and comparative perspective, and attempt to find out why the !Kung, in common with other tropical hunter-gatherers, are so light and small (de Almeida 1965; Tobias 1975; Truswell and Hansen 1976). Observations on children and adolescents, coupled with reliable estimates of age, can yield useful cross-sectional growth data. But such data become really valuable when we make repeated observations on the same individuals; we can explore the degree of individual and seasonal fluctuation in weight and fat accumulation and attempt to relate these to seasonal changes in food availability. For example, there may be a period of the year when food and other resources reach an annual low point and when life becomes significantly more difficult. This model is exemplified by the ecological principle known as Liebig's law of the minimum (Dice 1952).

I was led to undertake such a study after a conversation in 1966 with the late Albert Damon, a Harvard physiological anthropologist. I had been discussing my 1964 work diary results and had just finished relating how interesting it was that food input exceeded work output by 145 Cal per person per day. Damon replied that it was not really so surprising; it was common sense to expect that input and output would match closely. After all, if food intake exceeded energy expenditure by a wide margin, the population would gain weight rapidly and visibly; on the other hand, if there was a significant shortfall, the population would equally rapidly decline into hardship and starvation.

Damon's point was well taken: For every 5000 Cal of excess consumption, a person gains about 0.5 kg of body weight, and for every 5000 Cal of excess energy expenditure a person loses 0.5 kg of body weight. In light of this fundamental fact of nutrition, it seemed simply logical, efficient, and even elegant to weigh the people periodically rather than to struggle laboriously to monitor their food intake and energy outflow.

This chapter reports the results of a 20-month nutritional monitoring study of 641 !Kung adults and children carried out in 1967–9. After a brief description of the techniques and conditions of the study and the sample size, I discuss the weight, height, and skinfold thickness of the Dobe area adult population in terms of sex and age categories. (Howell [1979] discusses the data on adolescent growth in more detail from a demographic perspective.) Then the determinants of the !Kung's short stature and small body size are considered. The major proportion of the chapter, however, concerns the seasonal and annual fluctuations in !Kung weights and tries to assess the degree of nutritional stress the !Kung may undergo.

TECHNIQUES AND SAMPLE SIZE

Starting in mid-September 1967 and continuing until April 1969, Nancy Howell and I periodically asked the people at whatever camp we were at to congregate in the morning and undergo a 1-minute routine of weighing and other measurements, in return for which each received a small quantity of leaf tobacco. Weight was recorded on a specially designed data sheet and note was taken of the clothes worn and any other special feature, whether the person was ill or pregnant or lactating. In a small camp such as Dobe, the whole group could be weighed and on the way to the day's activity in less than an hour. The observations were made on an Avery butcher's steelyard in pounds and ounces. Every morning the scale was balanced and checked accurate to ± 0.5 oz, an error factor of less than 0.10 percent. Subjects were weighed with shoes off in their minimal regular clothing, every item of which was recorded. Later we weighed dozens of samples of clothing in order to get an average figure for each item. We tried to take all our observations in the morning hours before the hottest part of the day, but we did not have any check on the subjects' urination or defecation.

Heights were measured on a special free-standing apparatus built to

Plate 10.1. Weighing a !Kung woman to determine seasonal weight changes.

our specifications in the shop of the University of Cape Town Medical School and provided by Drs. Stewart Truswell and John Hansen. It consisted of a wooden upright marked with 0.25-in. divisions and firmly attached at right angles to a plywood and metal base. This base enabled us to set up anywhere, even in soft sand. The heights of most of the adults were measured only once; in the case of children and adolescents, we took several readings over the study period to give some idea of longitudinal changes in stature.

Skinfold thickness was measured with a pair of Harpenden skinfold calipers provided by Dr. C. H. Wyndham of the Environmental Physiology Laboratory of the South African Chamber of Mines. For readers who are not familiar with the technique, a few words are in order about the use of the calipers. The observer locates the specific site on the body and takes a fold of skin between the tips of the calipers; the gauge gives a reading that is half the actual distance between the tips. Because the fold of skin represents twice the total thickness of the subject's skin and fat at that site, the gauge gives a reading that is supposed to represent the depth in millimeters of the accumulated fat plus skin at a given site. Observations were taken at three standard body sites: the midtriceps, the subscapular, and the abdominal (Weiner and Lourie 1969:12). In addition, a reading was taken at the lower triceps site. The Harpenden instrument measures to a maximum of about 50 mm in 0.1-mm divisions. Three readings were taken at each site at each observation, and an average was taken of the three. For example, a typical midtriceps series of readings would be 5.3, 5.1, and 5.2 mm, for an average of 5.2 mm. The standard error within an observation was about 2 percent. Additionally, measurements were taken with a tape measure of upper arm circumference for most adults and children, and of chest and head circumferences for a few of the children.

These weight-height-skinfold data were backed up by several related sets of information, including genealogies and marital and reproductive histories for most of the adults, age estimates for the entire population, and a clinical examination of 154 members of the sample by Drs. Truswell and Hansen (1976).

At first, our monitoring observations tended to be concentrated at the water hole where we happened to be residing. Later, Howell and I began to make systematic surveys at all water holes, attempting to record data on as many people as possible. These weight campaigns took place in July 1968, October 1968, December 1968 to January 1969, and April 1969; each included between 300 and 450 subjects. Because of the extreme mobility of the !Kung population, there were fairly few repeat observations from one campaign to another on the same individuals. The sequence of surveys did ensure, however, an even area-wide coverage of data distributed through several time points in the annual cycle.

Table 10.1. *Number of subjects of various ages observed for weight, height, and skinfold thickness*

	Age (yr)										Total no. of subjects	No. of subjects observed twice or more
	0–4	5–9	10–19	20–29	30–39	40–49	50–59	60–69	70–79	80+		
Weight												
Male	36	32	42	44	51	49	31	13	6	5	309	238
Female	42	37	56	48	54	40	24	22	7	2	332	269
Total	78	69	98	92	105	89	55	35	13	7	641	507
Height												
Male	31	30	38	37	40	41	28	13	6	5	269	
Female	34	34	53	46	47	37	24	20	7	2	304	
Total	65	64	91	83	87	78	52	33	13	7	573	
Midtriceps skinfold												
Male	21	24	36	39	47	44	26	10	6	4	257	122
Female	17	29	50	42	47	34	22	21	6	2	270	153
Total	38	53	86	81	94	78	48	31	12	6	527	275

After fieldwork was completed, all the data were punched on cards, converted to metric measure, and analyzed by computer at Rutgers, Princeton, and Toronto universities. In the case of the weights, each of the 3139 observations were individually corrected by deducting for the weight of the clothing worn; all weights, therefore, are presented as nude equivalents.

In all, 641 persons were weighed, 507 of them twice or more. Height was recorded for 573 of the weighed individuals, and skinfold thickness readings were made on 527 people, 275 of whom had two or more readings (Table 10.1). Of particular interest are the 308 subjects weighed on five or more occasions (Table 10.2).

BODY SIZE, STATURE, AND FAT ACCUMULATION

To the casual observer the !Kung appear a small, wiry, and fine-boned people. They are attractive and well proportioned, with rather thin legs and arms, deep chests, and finely formed heads. Closer study confirms this impression. Adult men are small, averaging 160 cm in height (5 ft 3 in.) and weighing 49 kg (108 lb). Women average 150 cm (4 ft 11 in.) and 41 kg (90 lb). The tallest man in our sample was only 180 cm in height (71 in.); the shortest was 144 cm (56.5 in.). The tallest woman was 165 cm (65 in.) and the shortest 137 cm (53.75 in.). !Kung weights and heights are presented in relation to age in Tables 10.3 and 10.4.

Several interesting points should be noted. Weight for males and females does not increase with age past 40 years. This nonincrease of weight with age is in marked contrast to the situation in Western coun-

Table 10.2. *Number of subjects of various ages weighed five or more times*

Sex	Age (yr)										Total
	0–4	5–9	10–19	20–29	30–39	40–49	50–59	60–69	70–79	80+	
Male	12	11	26	18	19	18	17	7	5	1	134
Female	13	20	33	26	19	24	17	16	5	1	174
Total	25	31	59	44	38	42	34	23	10	2	308

Table 10.3. *!Kung weights (in kilograms), by sex and age*

Sex	Age (yr)										Mean all ages
	0–4	5–9	10–19	20–29	30–39	40–49	50–59	60–69	70–79	80+	
Male (n = 309)	9.65	16.26	28.12	48.71	50.86	50.80	47.83	46.91	42.74	41.28	38.20
Female (n = 332)	7.65	15.05	28.27	42.81	42.30	41.11	41.15	37.73	35.52	36.11	31.88

tries, where weight continues to increase with age until age 55 to 65. Lacking longitudinal data on weight and aging, we do not know in the !Kung case to what extent the decline in mean weight in the older age groups is attributable to weight loss and to what extent to differential mortality of heavier people. Probably both factors are involved. Height also declines with age in males from about 160 cm in the 20 to 59 age group to about 157 cm in the over 70 age group; a somewhat similar decline occurs in the females, from 150 to 147 cm. Several factors may be involved in the decline of height with age: (1) most human individuals lose a few centimeters of their height in their later years through vertebral compression and postural changes; (2) there may be slightly higher mortality rates for taller people; and (3) there is the possibility of secular trend, the increase in adult stature in successive generations, a phenomenon that has been observed in many parts of the world and appears to be present among the Kalahari San as well (Tobias 1975:147-9; Truswell and Hansen 1976:172).

Midtriceps skinfold thickness, by age, is shown in Table 10.5. In common with other human populations, !Kung skinfolds are thicker in females than in males, although the degree of dimorphism is greater among the !Kung than it is for the Western standards. !Kung women's skinfold thickness is about 80 percent higher than that of !Kung men, compared with a 32 percent difference between males and females for Western standards (Jelliffe 1966:242). Unlike the situation in the developed countries, !Kung fat accumulation rises only very slightly with age, reaching a modest peak in the age group 40 to 49 (with a secondary peak for males in the 60 to 69 bracket). Obesity is not a problem for the !Kung, and their lean and wiry body form seems to favor longevity.

How do the !Kung compare in stature, weight, and fat accumulation with other populations? By the standards of the West, the !Kung are not only short but tend to be very lightweight and thin for their height. For example, the average !Kung male at 160 cm and 50.8 kg weighs only 83 percent of the Western standard weight of 60.5 kg for that height. The average !Kung woman at 150 cm and 42.3 kg is also only 83 percent of the 50.4 kg standard weight for that height (Jelliffe 1966:238-40). Similarly, the adult men's midtriceps skinfold thickness of 5.4 mm represents only 43 percent of the Western male standard of 12.5 mm. The !Kung women's 10.1-mm midtriceps skinfold thickness is 61 percent of the Western standard of 16.5 mm (Jelliffe 1966:242).

WHY ARE THE !KUNG SO SMALL?

Various explanations have been put forward to account for the small stature and thin physique of the !Kung and other San people. De Almeida (1965:5), after observing the !Kung in Angola, argued that the San stat-

Table 10.4. *Kung heights (in centimeters), by sex and age*

Sex	Age (yr)									
	0–4	5–9	10–19	20–29	30–39	40–49	50–59	60–69	70–79	80+
Male (n = 269)	80.8	106.7	134.9	160.6	160.3	160.9	160.8	160.0	157.4	153.6
Female (n = 304)	73.8	103.5	135.6	151.0	150.4	149.6	149.0	146.4	149.5	138.7

Table 10.5. !Kung midtriceps skinfold thickness (in millimeters), by sex and age

Sex	Age (yr)										Mean all ages
	0–4	5–9	10–19	20–29	30–39	40–49	50–59	60–69	70–79	80+	
Male (n =257)	8.3	6.8	5.8	5.5	4.8	5.7	5.5	6.3	5.7	5.0	5.8
Female (n = 270)	9.2	7.4	8.2	9.8	9.6	10.6	10.2	9.5	6.4	10.3	9.2

ure is a product of chronic semistarvation – a view that contrasts sharply with the evidence for their adequate diet and abundant leisure time (Chapters 6 through 9). Truswell and Hansen, who examined 154 !Kung in the Dobe area in 1967–9, also consider the San's small stature, low weight, and lack of fat to be products of undernutrition. Though they do not go nearly as far in this direction as de Almeida, their observations led them to conclude that "chronic or seasonal calorie insufficiency may be a major reason why San do not reach the same adult stature as most other people" (Truswell and Hansen 1968).

Taking the opposite side of the argument has been the South African physical anthropologist Phillip Tobias, who has argued that genes, not environment, have shaped the physique of the Kalahari San (Tobias 1961). In a later paper, Tobias presented evidence that the small stature and thinness of the San represent an efficient adaptation to the demands of a hunting and gathering way of life in a hot climate:

> The Bushman's body build, as reflected in his height-weight ratio seemingly differs but little from that of other African peoples living in hot though not desertic conditions. People in hot climates tend to have a lower body weight than those in temperate and colder climates. Coupled with a relative increase of body surface area, lower weight makes for a much greater cooling surface relative to body weight. This feature the Bushman shares with other Africans. The fact that the present day desert-dwelling Bushmen do not show it in more marked degree than other Africans who do not live under desert conditions confirms again the absence of anatomical features specifically related to life in the desert [Tobias 1964:76].

Tobias also attributes the light, linear, stringy build of the San to a long-term adaptation to a method of hunting with poisoned arrows that places a premium on fleet-footedness and the ability to creep up on an animal to shoot it at close quarters rather than on the heavier musculature of the prehistoric Eurasian bowman (Brues 1959).

My own views tend to agree with those of Tobias. Clearly, the !Kung fall far below the Western standards for height, weight, and fatness; but the existence of this shortfall in spite of an adequate diet leads me to question, not their way of life but the validity and applicability of the Western standards! It has become increasingly clear over the last 10 years that the body size we have come to accept as normal in the West is a product of overfeeding, underexercising, and declining standards of nutrition and health. Far from being a model for emulation by the rest of the world, the dietary level that has produced the Western standards of weight, height, and weight/height ratios appears to be implicated in a growing list of health problems including obesity, diabetes, cancer of the colon, and cardiovascular disease (Schaefer 1970, 1971; Gordon and

Kannel 1973; Jelliffe and Jelliffe 1974; Esche and Lee 1975). At the same time data from the developing world suggest that small body size and stature may be positively selected for in marginal environments. Given conditions of scarcity, it may be that smaller people are better able to survive to maturity and reproduce than are larger people with greater calorie and protein requirements. For example, Frisancho, in a demographic study of short and tall mothers in a squatters' settlement near Cuzco in the Peruvian Andes, found that the infant mortality rate was significantly higher among the children of the taller mothers than among the children of the shorter mothers (Frisancho et al. 1972, 1973). The advantages of smallness have been noted in industrial societies as well. Albert Damon and his co-workers, in a study conducted for the U.S. Armed Forces of the human body in relation to equipment design, found that after a certain age, smaller men showed significantly more resistance to fatigue, more endurance, and less energy expenditure per unit of work output than did larger men (Damon et al. 1966).

Smallness, therefore, may make sense for the !Kung's long-term survival. In spite of the apparent evidence for their slow growth and late maturation as children, and their smallness and thinness as adults, the !Kung are a hardy and vigorous people. Truswell and Hansen found almost no clinical signs of malnutrition among the !Kung. They also noted that the !Kung had an adequate intake of proteins, vitamins, and minerals and appeared to be remarkably free of some of the commoner Western diseases of aging such as coronary and hypertensive heart disease (Truswell et al. 1972; Truswell and Hansen 1976:181–94).

It may well be true, as Truswell and Hansen suggest, that under traditional hunting and gathering conditions !Kung do not reach their maximum genetic potential (1976:191), but implicit in this statement is the assumption that *bigger* is somehow *better*. For hunting, precisely the opposite may be the case. Tobias (1964:77) has reported the impression of George Silberbauer that among the central San groups "the taller members are almost invariably poor hunters, are clumsy and enjoy little prestige." This intriguing observation led me to examine systematically the relation between height and hunting success among the Dobe area !Kung. I interviewed 112 men about the number of animals of various species they had ever killed by traditional means (Chapter 8). (Men who had hunted with guns were not included in the tabulation.) Their heights were recorded in the course of the weight-height measuring campaigns, and the men were grouped in 10-year cohorts to ensure comparability within each cohort. Note that the cohorts in Figure 10.1 are divided differently from those presented in Table 10.4. The hunting success score used is a composite based on a scale of 1 to 4 for each of 14 larger species (1 kill = 1, 2 to 4 kills = 2, 5 to 9 kills = 3, 10+ kills = 4), with a theoretical maximum of 56. In the two youngest age categories (15 to 24

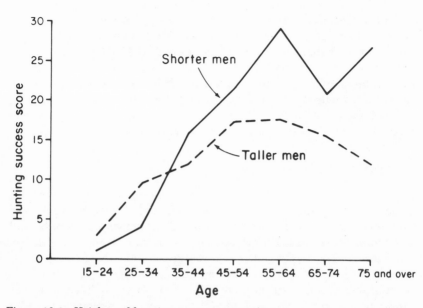

Figure 10.1. Height and hunting success among !Kung men.

and 25 to 34 years) taller men show significantly better scores than shorter men. After age 35, however, the shorter men's scores are better, and the gap increases with age, reaching a peak in the age group 55 to 64. Overall, the shorter men's score is 15.65 compared with 11.20 for the taller men, a difference that is significant to the 0.05 level. In the younger age groups, the higher scores for the taller men are probably attributable to factors of early maturation, with those who reach adult stature first having somewhat greater cumulative hunting success than the late maturers. But after age 35 the success rates first cross, then diverge sharply in favor of the shorter men. The scores indicate that over a lifetime of hunting the shorter men in the population may contribute as much as 35 percent more meat to the community than the taller men. Given this evidence, it is hard to accept the view that shorter stature constitutes a disability or that a short person has somehow failed to realize his "genetic potential."

At the same time, it must be acknowledged that the !Kung are small by world standards and that this smallness probably indicates some degree of undernutrition during childhood and adolescence, as Truswell, Hansen, and others have suggested. Also, as Tobias (1975:148–9) has recently pointed out, whatever advantages smallness confers on a traditional hunter is quickly lost when people move into a sedentary agricultural-pastoral way of life. !Kung who have been raised on cattle posts on an essentially Bantu diet of milk and grains grow significantly taller (and, in the case of women, heavier and fatter) than do !Kung raised on a diet of bush foods (Lee 1969c:48). But even though cattle post !Kung may consume more calories, there is no evidence that their diet is as well rounded or that their health is any better than the health of their bush-living relatives. As Truswell himself has recently stated, "Except for being a little short in stature – which causes no obvious inconvenience – there was no evidence that these [!Kung] Bushmen were unhealthy because of their diet. What is more, in several ways we found they were more healthy than people in western countries" (1977:216).

IS THERE A HUNGRY SEASON?

Throughout rural Africa the agricultural cycle produces a marked seasonality of food supply, with a period of plenty in the months following the harvest and a period of scarcity during the growing season that culminates in the so-called hungry season immediately preceding the annual harvest. There is evidence that marked fluctuations in body weight accompany this cycle, with a substantial annual weight loss during the growing season and a substantial weight gain after the harvest. For example, in a 6-month study of subsistence farmers in Northern Ghana, Hunter (1967:177–8) found an average weight loss of 6.2 percent for males and 6.5 percent for females between the harvest of December 1963 and the hungry season of June 1964. Fox has recorded losses and gains of a similar magnitude over three successive seasons among farming groups in the Gambia (Fox 1953; Harrison et al. 1964).

Hunting and gathering people are also subject to seasonal variations. Although their way of life is not based on agriculture, it is often assumed that the seasonal stress of food scarcity of hunters actually exceeds that of farmers. Harrison et al., for example, in their textbook, *Human Biology*, have stated:

> The vulnerability of the hunting diet lies not in its composition so much as simply in quantity resulting from its precariousness of supply. A severe failure may mean an all-round failure in both calories and aliments. By contrast the cultivators' diet is more secure as regards overall energy supply. [Harrison et al. 1964:433]

The possibility of seasonal nutritional stress appears to be an ideal topic for study by the periodic weighing method. If one period of the year is much more difficult than the others, this fact should be reflected in an overall loss of weight (biomass) caused by a reduction of body fat among members of the community. Also, according to Liebig's law of the minimum, it is not the average amount of food available that limits the well-being of a population; rather, the amount of food available at the time of year when food is least plentiful is the limiting factor. The nature of the problem seems to dictate study by a method that merely locates the most stressful period of the year, weighs and measures a number of people at that time, and compares their weights and skinfold thicknesses with the same measures taken on the same individuals at other times of the year.

Closer examination of the problem, however, shows that the solution is not nearly as simple as it first appears. First, before the possibility of seasonal variation can be tackled, the problem of individual fluctuations – not necessarily of a seasonal nature – must be considered. It is well established that a person's weight varies considerably from day to day and throughout the year (Durnin and Passmore 1967). Individual factors of health, disease, appetite, work effort, consumption, and fluid retention are the sources of this fluctuation, not to mention the special factors of pregnancy and lactation in women. At any given moment in even a quite stable population, some persons' weights are rising, others falling, and still others showing no change. For example, in Hunter's previously cited study in Ghana, even though the adult population as a whole lost over 6 percent of body weight from December to June, some people (16 out of 265) actually gained weight during the study (Hunter 1967:170). These fluctuations form a background against which the search for seasonal trends must be viewed. Variations of less than ± 1 percent in weight and ± 2 percent in skinfold thickness are probably nonsignificant for this reason.

Second, even the pinpointing of the season when weight and skinfold thickness should be lowest is difficult. At least two factors besides the availability of food can contribute to the annual low point: the incidence of communicable disease and the climatic adaptation. Although it is assumed that infection and malnutrition are closely related, it is by no means clear that the season of maximum ill health coincides with the season of food scarcity. In the case of the !Kung, malaria is most prevalent in the rainy season (December to March) and respiratory infections are most common in the winter (June to August), both times when food is considered to be relatively plentiful. Climatic factors can also complicate the picture; weight and fat loss may be an adaptation to the hottest time of the year, when sweating and evaporation rates reach their annual maximum and when fat deposits are metabolized to meet the added demands of cooling. Each of these factors, as well as possible shifts in the timing and intensity of the hungry period itself, can affect the seasonal distribution of body weight.

In the case of the Dobe area !Kung a number of leads point to the spring dry season (October and November) as the most likely stress period, if there is one at all (Chapter 4). The summer rainy season (December to March) is a time when both plants and animals are abundant. Seasonal foods, especially fruits and leafy greens, are abundant, and the existence of temporary water sources increases mobility and makes it possible for groups to reach otherwise inaccessible food sources. It is the birth season for animals, and the newborn of small and large game are easily killed. The fall (April and May) also appears to be a season of plenty, with the annual ripening of mongongo nuts, tsin beans, and several major *Grewia* berries. Winter (June to August) is a time when food continues to be plentiful; hunting is good, and numerous root foods are added to the diet of mongongos and meat. The extremely cold weather with freezing or near-freezing nights could increase caloric costs owing to the added metabolic demands of keeping warm. In September the warming weather heralds a season of declining food supply. Vegetable foods become eaten out in the vicinity of water points, and mongongo nuts may be available only at large distances. At this time of year the distance between food and water appears to reach an annual maximum and the weather is extremely hot and dry. Even after the rains come in November, the difficult period may continue, because new food sources lag several weeks behind the first rains. Given this sketch of the !Kung annual round, it seemed reasonable to look first at October and November as a possible hungry season. This decision was reinforced by the findings of Truswell and Hansen, who, after showing that Dobe San nutrition is *qualitatively* adequate, conclude with the observation that "the only nutritional weakness of the San's diet is a shortage of energy [calories] usually in the spring dry season" (Truswell and Hansen 1976:194).

July–October comparisons

In July 1968, Howell and I traveled through the Dobe area and weighed and measured some 294 !Kung. Three months later we again canvassed the whole area, and this time contacted some 353 !Kung, 215 of whom had also participated in our July study. Of these, 14 were pregnant or lactating women who were excluded from the sample. Data on the matched sample of 201 provide the basis for analysis of the changes in body weight and fat accumulation between July in the midwinter season of relative plenty (and the same month during which I had made the work study 4 years before) and late October in the spring dry season of possible scarcity.

The overall results are shown in Table 10.6. Weight showed a very slight gain of 96 g, which amounted to 0.3 percent over the July body weight. Skinfold thickness also showed minor variations, with two indexes falling slightly and one rising. The only measure that can be considered significant is a 3.7 percent increase in the thickness of the abdominal skinfold. Thus far there is no evidence for a hungry season among the !Kung; they seem to be maintaining their overall weight levels well. However, we should consider the possibility that there may be a hungry season for some but not for others. Perhaps males are gaining

Table 10.6. *Mean weight and skinfold thickness in July and October 1968*

	July	October	Change	
Weight (g)[a]	34,744	34,840	+96	(+0.3%)
Skinfold (mm)[b]				
Midtriceps	8.122	7.973	−0.149	(−1.8%)
Subscapular	6.855	6.819	−0.045	(−0.7%)
Abdominal	5.252	5.446	+0.194	(+3.7%)

[a]n = 201.
[b]n = 200.

Table 10.7. *Weight change from July to October 1968, by age and sex*
($n = 201$)

		Weight (kg) in:		Weight change (g)	
Sex, age (yr)	No.	July	October	Gain	Loss
Male					
60+	13	45.236	45.769	+533	
40–59	24	50.277	49.704		−573
20–39	23	50.087	50.357	+270	
10–19	13	26.824	27.041	+217	
0–9	17	11.369	11.689	+320	
Female					
60+	18	37.788	37.590		−198
40–59	26	40.255	40.402	+147	
20–39	18	43.215	42.595		−620
10–19	24	28.465	29.088	+593	
0–9	25	12.281	12.580	+299	
Total number	201				
Average, *both sexes*		34.744	34.840	+96	

while females are losing to yield the net observed result of stasis, or the elderly may be bearing the brunt of the losses. Also there is the problem of the children and adolescents: 79 of the 201 subjects were under the age of 20; their growth should be reflected in a higher overall weight in October compared with July.

Table 10.7 shows the weight changes by age and sex; there is a rather complex pattern of small weight losses and gains among the various age-sex categories. These are summarized, along with the changes of the midtriceps skinfold thickness, in Table 10.8. A weight gain of 1.2 percent was registered by older men (over 60), while losses of 1.1 to 1.4 percent

Table 10.8. *Age and sex differences in weight and midtriceps skinfold thickness (as percent change) from July to October 1968*

Age(yr)	Male		Female	
	Weight[a]	Midtriceps skinfold[b]	Weight[a]	Midtriceps skinfold[b]
60–85	+1.2	+17	−0.5	−4
40–59	−1.1	−2	+0.4	−7
20–39	+0.5	−1	−1.4	−3
10–19	+0.8	−8	+2.1	+5
0–9	+2.8	−4	+2.4	−1

[a]n = 201.
[b]n = 200.

were registered by men aged 40 to 59 and women aged 20 to 39. Children showed good weight gains for both sexes, as did adolescents. Women's skinfold thickness losses were slightly greater than those of men.

There is still no evidence for a weight loss in *any* category even remotely approaching the magnitude of loss observed among agriculturalists. The largest losses (1.1 to 1.4 percent) occurred among the active, healthy adults – a category of persons with maximal demands of providing for growing families. Among the elderly the picture is equivocal, with the old men gaining and the old women losing, the change being modest in both directions. The picture for children and adolescents shows some interesting anomalies: The weight gains and fat losses for the boys indicate the conversion of fat to muscle mass with overall growth. Adolescent girls show gains in weight *and* fat, a finding consistent with the adolescent growth spurt and the development of secondary sexual characteristics.

Three conclusions can be drawn from this July–October comparison: (1) the period of supposed annual maximal nutritional stress did not in the year selected produce any hardship or reduction of fitness for the !Kung population as a whole; (2) the minor variations observed, with a mixture of losses and gains, suggest that individual variations may be as important as seasonal variation in the timing of a person's ups and downs; (3) the patterns of weight and fat losses show that adults are bearing the brunt of what nutritional stress there is, while children continue their growth or remain stable through the period of difficulty. Put another way, the more active people are "financing" the growth of the children by absorbing the greater portion of the nutritional stress of the October dry season.

Twelve-month comparisons

The next step in the analysis is to place these July–October comparisons into a broader context. A subgroup of the population (111 people) was weighed in four time periods: January 1968, July 1968, October 1968, and January 1969. The mean weights of males, females, adults, and children for each time period are set out in Table 10.9, and the percent changes between periods are shown in Table 10.10. Several points emerge from the tables. January 1969 adult weights are actually lower than those of October 1968, suggesting that January may be closer to the annual low point than October. This possibility is strengthened by examination of the values for children, which show a substantial weight gain for the first 6 months of the year (January to July), a much smaller gain for the next 3 months (July to October), and virtual stasis for the last 3 months (October to January). In fact, the boys in the sample experienced a slight loss of weight between October and January (− 130 g). The overall loss of weight is small, and the maximum drop (that of adult males between October and January) amounts to only 1.2 percent. The overall difference between the adults' highest weights for the year (in July 1968) and their lowest (in January 1969) is 483 g, just over 1 percent.

Year-to-year variations can also be examined with these data. The children show a healthy growth in the 12-month period, with a 7.3 percent weight increase for boys and a 10.8 percent increase for girls. The higher growth rate for girls is probably a product of the differing age composition of the boys' and girls' sample, with boys having a larger proportion in the slow-growing 5 to 14 age group and the girls – with heavier mean weights – having a larger proportion in the faster-growing adolescent age category. The adults show no particular trend through the year; although the adult males show a 1.3 percent drop in weight between January 1968 and January 1969, the females' weight varies by less than 0.2 percent between the two periods. (Pregnant and lactating women were excluded from the sample.) During the first 6 months of the year, the men lost weight and the women gained; between July and October the signs were reversed, with men gaining and women losing. Only in the period October to January did both men and women lose weight. This last point, when combined with data for the decelerated growth of the children, reinforces the conclusion that December and January rather than October may be the annual low point.

A January minimum?

We return now to the 201 persons weighed in July and October and examine their weights in January 1969. This allows us to explore in greater detail the impact of the January low point on the age-sex categories of the population using exactly the same sample as was employed in the July–October comparison. Again pregnant and lactating women, whose weights follow cycles independent of season, are excluded.

Table 10.11 shows a consistent pattern of weight loss from October to January, with all adults losing except the older women, who gain. The

Table 10.9. *Weights over 12-month period* ($n = 111$)

	No.	January 1968		July 1968		October 1968		January 1969	
		kg	SD	kg	SD	kg	SD	kg	SD
Adults									
Men	36	49.468	5.85	49.276	6.09	49.427	6.30	48.841	6.20
Women	29	38.815	5.59	39.279	5.21	38.990	4.67	38.738	4.90
Total	65	44.715	7.80	44.816	7.57	44.771	7.65	44.333	7.56
Children									
Boys	20	19.348	8.59	20.783	9.21	20.888	9.33	20.758	9.38
Girls	26	20.113	9.28	21.732	10.12	22.080	10.40	22.276	10.29
Total	46	19.780	8.89	21.320	9.64	21.562	9.86	21.616	9.83
Whole population	111	34.382	14.83	35.079	14.37	35.153	14.34	34.919	14.11

Table 10.10. *Change in weight over 12-month period* $(n = 111)$

| | Jan.–July 1968 | | July–Oct. 1968 | | Oct. 1968–Jan. 1969 | | Jan. 1968–Jan. 1969 | |
	g	%	g	%	g	%	g	%
Adults								
Men	−192	−0.4	+151	+0.3	−586	−1.2	−645	−1.3
Women	+464	+1.2	−289	−0.7	−252	−0.6	−77	−0.2
Total	+101	+0.2	−45	−0.1	−438	−1.0	−382	−0.9
Children								
Boys	+1435	+7.4	+105	+0.5	−130	−0.6	+1410	+7.3
Girls	+1619	+8.0	+358	+1.6	+196	+0.9	+2163	+10.8
Total	+1540	+7.8	+242	+1.1	+54	+0.3	+1836	+9.3
Whole population	+697	+2.0	+74	+0.2	−234	+0.7	+537	+1.6

Table 10.11. *Weight change from October 1968 to January 1969, by age and sex (n = 201)*

Sex, age (yr)	No.	Weight (kg) in:		Weight change (g)	
		Oct. 1968	Jan. 1969	Gain	Loss
Male					
60+	13	45.769	44.556		−1213
40–59	24	49.704	49.020		−684
20–39	23	50.357	50.196		−161
10–19	13	27.041	27.134	+93	
0–9	17	11.689	12.037	+348	
Female					
60+	18	37.590	37.959	+369	
40–59	26	40.402	39.830		−572
20–39	18	42.595	41.582		−1013
10–19	24	29.088	29.144	+56	
0–9	25	12.580	12.799	+219	
Total number	201				
Average, both sexes		34.840	34.599		−241

magnitude of the losses is also greater, with men over 60 and women 20 to 39 losing 2.4 to 2.7 percent, and men and women 40 to 59 losing 1.4 percent (Table 10.12). Growth for adolescent children 10 to 19 is slowed almost to a standstill, but younger children up to 9 years still show overall gains: 3.0 percent for boys and 1.7 percent for girls. Clearly, in spite of the adults' weight losses, the growth of the young children is still being maintained through December and January.

Comparing January weights with those of the previous July provides a time frame more or less comparable to the 6-month span between the harvest season and the hungry season defined for the West African agriculturalists (Hunter 1967). How do the !Kung compare with the agriculturalists in the magnitude and severity of their weight loss? From Table 10.12, last column, we see that old men lost 1.5 percent from July to January, while the old women gained slightly. In the 40 to 59 group, it is again the men who sustain the greater losses, with a 2.5 percent drop compared with a 1.0 percent loss for the women. In the young adult category (20 to 39), however, the situation is reversed, with the men maintaining stasis and the women sustaining a 3.8 percent loss. Overall, adult men lost 1.25 percent of their weight from July to January and adult women 1.49 percent, with an average loss of 1.36 percent for both sexes.

We can reasonably draw three conclusions from the evidence pre-

Table 10.12. *Percent change in weights from July 1968 to January 1969, by age and sex (n =201)*

Sex, age (yr)	July–Oct. 1968 Gain	July–Oct. 1968 Loss	Oct. 1968–Jan. 1969 Gain	Oct. 1968–Jan. 1969 Loss	July 1968–Jan. 1969 Gain	July 1968–Jan. 1969 Loss
Male						
60+	+1.2			−2.7		−1.5
40–59		−1.1		−1.4		−2.5
20–39	+0.5			−0.4	+0.1	
10–19	+0.8		+0.3		+1.1	
0–9	+2.8		+3.0		+5.8	
Female						
60+		−0.5	+1.0		+0.5	
40–59	+0.4			−1.4		−1.0
20–39		−1.4		−2.4		−3.8
10–19	+2.1		+0.2		+2.3	
0–9	+2.4		+1.7		+4.1	
Both sexes	+0.3			−0.7		−0.4

sented. First, during the period 1968–9, the low point for body weight appeared to fall in January 1969 in the middle of the rainy season, and not, as had been predicted, in October and November at the end of the dry season. Second, the magnitude of the loss–between 1 and 2 percent of adult body weight–is a significant degree of loss but one that falls far short of 4 to 6.5 percent average loss observed among agriculturalists. Third, the loss does not fall significantly harder on males than on females or on the elderly than on those in the productive years. The nutritional stress experienced by the population is absorbed broadly among the various age-sex categories. The largest single loss–3.8 percent among women 20 to 39 years old–deserves some comment. About 29 percent of that loss was represented by 2 of the 18 women in the age category, who lost 4.5 and 3.9 kg, respectively, owing to illness. With the relatively small sample size of the present study, one or two extreme individual shifts can loom large in the overall weight standing of an age category. In view of this fact, we cannot assume that women aged 20 to 39 are necessarily the most vulnerable to nutritional stress; nor, for that matter, can we assume that women over 60 are the least vulnerable to stress simply because their weights rose from July to January. Instead, the picture that emerges is one of a slight degree of stress widely distributed among the age-sex categories of adults, accompanied by a sustained growth for children and adolescents. Measured objectively, the season of minimal weight among the !Kung is certainly not a hungry season by the standards of African agriculturalists.

The unexpected discovery of a January weight minimum leads us to ask why this should be the case. January is a period of increasing food supply, with seasonal fruits and leafy greens becoming available for gathering, while the newborn of many game species become prey for the hunters. But it is also a time of maximum dispersal, with groups moving out to the temporary water holes to enjoy these seasonal foods. Because our surveys reached only the main water holes, and not the temporary ones, it is possible that more sedentary people are overrepresented in our study and more mobile people are underrepresented. Therefore, the people who show the January weight loss are those who are not taking advantage of widely dispersed summer food supplies. For instance, at /Xai/xai 22 percent of the people in the weight study (17 of 78) were over age 60, a proportion of elderly that is twice as high as their proportion in the population at large. The age breakdown of the 78 /Xai/xai people in the July–January study was: 60+, 22 percent; 20 to 59, 50 percent; and 0 to 19, 28 percent. By contrast, the age breakdown for 47 /Xai/xai people not in the July–January study because they were dispersed at summer water points was: 60+, 4 percent; 20 to 59, 56 percent, and 0 to 19, 40 percent.

In Chapter 6 it was pointed out that at any given season the !Kung have two subsistence strategies available to them: to walk farther to reach the more desirable foods or to remain closer to home and accept foods of lower quality. It is likely that the low January weights are one of the consequences of choosing the latter subsistence strategy in preference to the former.

REGIONAL COMPARISONS

The Dobe area can be broadly divided into three subregions of roughly equivalent population size: Western N!umsi, centered around Dobe water hole; Eastern N!umsi, including the sedentary village of !Goshe; and /Xai/xai, south of the Aha Hills (Table 10.13; see also Figure 3.2). The people of the eastern region (!Kangwa, !Kangwa Matse, Bate, and !Goshe) are more acculturated than the people of the other two regions. At !Goshe water hole !Kung farm and raise cattle; at !Kangwa, with its European trading store, !Kung and other women entrepreneurs purchase the raw material for making and selling home brew. The western region, also with four water holes, has a strong black presence, with cattle posts at !Xabi, Mahopa, and !Kubi, but the !Kung are not as deeply involved in the farming-herding economy as are the !Kung of !Goshe. A number of young men work on the cattle posts and receive rations of milk and grain, and several families have attempted to raise crops in small fields, but the great bulk of their subsistence during 1967–9 came from hunting and gathering. That situation describes /Xai/xai as well, with numbers of

Table 10.13. *Regional comparisons*

Region	No. of water holes	Population 1968 Total no.	Population 1968 No. per water hole	Area accessible in 1 day's walk (km²)	Minimal economic density (persons/100 km²)	No. of Bantu cattle present: June 1968	Degree of !Kung participation in farming/herding	Adults' weight change, Oct.–Jan. (%)	Children's weight change, Oct.–Jan. (%)
Eastern	4	157	39	ca. 800	19	1544	Moderate-high	+0.4	+1.5
Western	4	159	40	589	27	2387	Low-moderate	−0.7	+1.3
/Xai/xai	1	141	141	293	48	542	Low-moderate	−2.3	−0.4

young men working on the cattle posts and several families planting crops. The western section has considerably more cattle than the other two regions (see Table 14.2), though some of these cattle are at cattle posts that do not share milk with !Kung visitors. The key difference between the western region and /Xai/xai, besides the former's greater number of cattle, is that in the western region the population is dispersed at four permanent water holes, whereas at /Xai/xai all the people are concentrated at one. In other respects – rainfall, presence of mongongo groves, other food resources – the three regions are equivalent; no one region has a significantly richer ecology than the others. The division of the Dobe area into these three regions allows us to examine the effect of farming and herding and the effect of the degree of population concentration on the July to January weight cycle.

Table 10.14 shows the weight changes for the adults and children of the three regions for the period July 1968 to January 1969. Before looking at the changes, we can note that eastern adults have the heaviest mean weights and /Xai/xai adults the lightest, with western adults in between. These differences are attributable in part to the differing age composition of the three subpopulations, with older, lighter people overrepresented in the /Xai/xai sample; but, in addition, eastern weights are higher cohort by cohort, probably as a result of dietary changes brought about by Bantu contact. The higher weights of western children compared with eastern and /Xai/xai children may also be attributed to the differing age composition of the samples, with more older children in the western subgroup.

However, it is the shape of the curves that interests us most. Both eastern and western adults lose weight from July to October, but whereas westerners continue to lose weight to January, easterners recover slightly. /Xai/xai adults present yet a third pattern, with a rise from July to October and a steep drop to January. From October to January, the changes are: eastern region, +0.4 percent; western region, −0.7 percent; and /Xai/xai, −2.3 percent. The curves for the children are also revealing: children in the eastern and western sectors show steady, positive growth for the 6-month period, but the /Xai/xai children actually lose ground slightly from October to January. /Xai/xai is clearly experiencing nutritional stress to a somewhat greater degree than are the other two regions.

The explanation of this pattern is twofold. The eastern region, with its partially agricultural economy, does not experience a January minimum. The availability of milk throughout the period and the upswing in the milk supply around the new year calving season may account for the weight gain from October to January in the eastern sector. The western people do not have the same access to milk. Therefore, their weights fall from October to January, reflecting a situation of slightly lower quality of food for the less mobile foragers. /Xai/xai shows the biggest decline from October to January, a drop of 2.3 percent for adults and even a slight

Table 10.14. *Weight change from July 1968 to January 1969, by region*

	No.	(1) Weight July 1968 (kg)	(1 – 2) Change July–Oct. 1968 (g)	(2) Weight Oct. 1968 (kg)	(2 – 3) Change Oct. 1968–Jan. 1969 (g)	(3) Weight Jan. 1969 (kg)	(1 – 3) Change July 1968–Jan. 1969 (g)	Percent change 1 – 2	Percent change 2 – 3	Percent change 1 – 3
Adults										
Eastern	24	46.819	−466	46.353	+179	46.532	−287	−1.0	+0.4	−0.6
Western	42	45.339	−412	44.927	−314	44.613	−726	−0.9	−0.7	−1.6
/Xai/xai	54	43.401	+343	43.744	−1002	42.742	−659	−0.8	−2.3	−1.5
Children										
Eastern	34	19.443	+192	19.635	+299	19.934	+491	+1.0	+1.5	+2.5
Western	23	21.605	+160	21.765	+285	22.050	+445	+0.7	+1.3	+2.1
/Xai/xai	24	18.920	+787	19.707	−87	19.620	+700	+4.2	−0.4	+3.7

falling off for children. The difference between the western region and /Xai/xai is probably attributable to the greater degree of population concentration at the latter site. At /Xai/xai all 141 residents were concentrated at a single water hole; in the western region the numbers were divided among four water holes spaced 2 to 7 km apart. The foraging area accessible within a day's walk to the 141 residents of /Xai/xai is approximately 293 km^2, for an economic density of 48 people per 100 km^2. By contrast, the area accessible to the 159 residents of the four western water holes totals 589 km^2 that *do not overlap*, for a much lower economic density: 27 people per 100 km^2. This fact alone would put greater pressure on the resources in the immediate vicinity of /Xai/xai and could account for /Xai/xai's lower January weights. Mobility, of course, would counteract the disadvantages of the too-dense /Xai/xai settlement, as within a few days' walk of /Xai/xai there exist abundant wild resources more than sufficient to meet the needs of the /Xai/xai population. In fact, after the January study /Xai/xai became 50 to 70 percent deserted for late January through April as the residents sought the plentiful resources of the seasonal water points. However, for those members of the community who seek the social rewards of year-round residence at /Xai/xai (see Chapter 12), a poorer quality food supply and declining weight for part of the year may be the price they have to pay. Given the long-term trend toward sedentarization throughout the Dobe area and the absence of any immediate prospects for secure transition to farming and herding, we may expect this seasonal cycle to increase in intensity. Edwin Wilmsen, who made similar observations at /Xai/xai in 1975–6, found a 6 percent adult weight loss from July to January (Wilmsen 1976, 1977) compared with 1.5 percent in 1968–9. Although Wilmsen attributes this loss to a deficiency in the hunting and gathering economy caused by periodic failure of wild resources, I believe the explanation lies elsewhere; in the problem of rapid sedentarization of groups and the sudden introduction of the cash economy. This possibility is discussed in Chapter 15.

POST-JANUARY RECOVERY PHASE

Our next weight campaign in April 1969 showed a marked rebound from the January low points. So few of the July–January study population were also in the April study that a new subpopulation of 88 had to be drawn, composed of subjects who were weighed in October 1968, January 1969, and in April 1969 (Table 10.15). The 59 adults dropped 1.2 percent in body weight from October to January, but gained 2.0 percent from January to April, for a net weight gain of 0.7 percent from October to April. The 29 children were stable from October to January, but gained 5.3 percent from January to April, for a net weight gain of 5.2 percent for

Table 10.15. *Weight change from October 1968 to April 1969 (n = 88)*

	No.	Weight Oct. 1968 (kg)	Change Oct. 1968– Jan. 1969 (%)	Weight Jan. 1969 (kg)	Change Jan.– Apr. 1969 (%)	Weight Apr. 1969 (kg)	Change Oct. 1968– Apr. 1969 (%)
Adults	59	44.457	−1.2	43.922	+2.0	44.782	+0.7
Children	29	20.115	+0.1	20.143	+5.3	21.213	+5.2
Total	88	36.435	−1.0	36.085	+2.6	37.015	+1.6

the 6-month period. April found the adult members of the study group fully recovered to the levels of the previous October or better, and the children showed very good overall growth.

The data from the October–April study confirm the existence of the January minimum, show the rapid recovery from the January low, and pinpoint January to April as a period of rapid growth for children and weight gains for adults. These findings are consistent with what we know of the seasonal availability of food. Truswell and Hansen examined 33 !Kung adults and 30 children in October 1967 and again in April and May 1968. They found good gains in weight and height for the children and a slight weight gain for adults, indicating a pattern similar to what we found a year later.

11

Production and reproduction

THIS chapter explores the dual role women play in !Kung society as producers, of food and the necessities of life, and as reproducers, to whom fall the major tasks of bearing and raising the next generation of gatherers and hunters. This dual role, which the !Kung women share with women in all preindustrial societies, places them in a strategically central position because for the !Kung the work of subsistence and of child rearing forms a large proportion of the total work carried out by the society. This is in marked contrast to the situation in industrial societies, where women are often marginalized by being excluded from the labor force and confined to the home or relegated to menial jobs of low productivity.

The work of the !Kung women in subsistence is of relatively high productivity – higher than that of the men, a point established in Chapter 9. And like the men, the !Kung women range widely through the countryside to find food. This need for mobility is a key factor in the foraging mode of production. Against this are the demands placed upon women in their other role: reproduction. Pregnancy, childbirth, lactation, and the need to care for and carry the young infant tend to draw a woman toward the home and to reduce her mobility. Women are thus at the intersection of two critical systems within the foraging economy: the productive system and the reproductive system, each with its conflicting demands. The one necessitates mobility and the other penalizes it. In hunting and gathering societies there is a tight articulation between these two systems so that a change of the variables in one system leads to adjustment of the variables in the other.

Three questions are to be considered. First, what are the factors that regulate !Kung fertility under traditional hunting and gathering conditions? Second, how might these factors be altered in a shift from a nomadic to a sedentary life? And third, what are the actual trends in fertility among the !Kung of the Dobe area in recent years. The predictive model of changing !Kung fertility was originally presented at a conference on population growth in 1970 and published 2 years later in a paper entitled "Population Growth and the Beginnings of Sedentary Life Among the !Kung Bushmen (Lee 1972d). Data to test the predictions of the model were collected in a restudy of the Dobe !Kung in 1973.

THE ROLE OF WOMEN IN THE !KUNG ECONOMY

Women's work – gathering wild vegetable foods – provides about two-thirds of all the food consumed by a !Kung camp. Men's hunting activities and gifts of food from other camps make up the remainder. Subsistence work occupies 2 or 3 days of work per week for each adult woman. On each workday a woman walks from 3 to 20 km (2 to 12 miles) round trip, and on the return leg she carries a load of 7 to 15 kg (15 to 33 lb) of vegetable foods – a combination of nuts, berries, fruits, leafy greens, and roots that varies according to season. Another 1 or 2 days a week are occupied in visiting other San camps situated 2 to 16 km distant from the home camp. Small quantities of food (1 to 3 kg) may be carried on both legs of the journey. When the entire group moves camp or when a family decides to visit a distant camp, the woman has to carry all her possessions – ostrich eggshell canteens, mortar, pestle, and cooking utensils – for distances up to 100 km. Her possessions, plus the water carried on long trips, weigh from 5 to 10 kg. Subsistence work, visits, and group moves require an adult woman to walk about 2400 km (1500 miles) during the course of an annual round. For at least half this distance she carries substantial burdens of food, water, or material goods.

But the major burden carried by women has yet to be mentioned. On most gathering trips and on every visit and group move, a women has to carry with her each of her children under the age of 4 years. Infants and young children have an extremely close relationship with their mothers (Draper 1976; Konner 1976). For the first few years of an infant's life mother and child are rarely separated by more than a few paces. Although solid foods are introduced at the age of 6 months or earlier, breast-feeding continues into the third or fourth year of life. For the first year or two an infant is carried on its mother's back in the special baby carrier (Chapter 5). A child aged 2 to 4 years is carried in the kaross or straddling its mother's shoulder. For the first 2 years of life, a child is carried everywhere. In the third year some baby-sitting occurs, and this increases in the fourth year. At age 4 years, well after the child has been weaned from the breast, it is weaned from the back. For gathering trips the 4-year-old may remain in camp while its mother goes out alone or

Plate 11.1. A /Du/da woman in late pregnancy carries her 4-year-old home from a gathering trip.

with a younger sibling. On visits and group moves the child walks part of the way and for part of the way is carried on its father's shoulder. By the age of 6 or 7 years, carrying ceases entirely, and the child walks wherever the group goes. For each of the first 2 years of life a child is carried by the mother for a distance of 2400 km; in the third year this decreases to about 1800 km; and in the fourth year to about 1200 km. Over the 4-year period of dependency, a !Kung mother carries her child a total distance of around 7800 km (4900 miles).

The reproductive system

The onset of puberty in girls is late, usually occurring between the ages of 15 and 17. First pregnancies are further delayed by several years by postmenarcheal adolescent sterility (Howell 1976b). Thus a woman does not bear her first child until she is between 18 and 22 years of age. The first pregnancy is followed by four to eight others spaced 3 to 5 years apart until menopause occurs after age 40. Howell has noted that !Kung fertility appears to be lower than among other populations, a point discussed in Chapter 3.

What is critical to the present analysis is not the overall fertility picture as expressed in birthrate, but the frequency with which successive births occur to individual women: the interval between births, or birth spacing, expressed in months or years.

The economic consequences of birth spacing

Because every child has to be carried, it is fortunate that generally the birth interval among the !Kung is as long as it is. The advantage of long birth spacing to hunter-gatherers is obvious. A mother can devote her full attention to caring for a child for a longer period, and the older the offspring is when its mother turns to the care of the subsequent young, the better are its chances for survival.

There is also the matter of the sheer weight to be carried by the mother. A women whose children are spaced 4 years apart has only one child to carry at any one time. By the time the next infant is born, the older child is mature enough to walk on his own. But, a woman whose babies are spaced only 2 years apart has to carry two children at once: a newborn to 2-year-old on her back and a 3- or 4-year-old on her shoulders. No sooner is the older child weaned from the shoulder than yet another newborn arrives. The !Kung of the Dobe area recognize the plight of the woman with high fertility and express it in the saying: "A woman who gives birth like an animal to one offspring after another has a permanent backache."

The actual work involved in raising young children in a hunting and gathering society is in large part a function of three variables: weight of children, the distance to be traveled, and the frequency with which children are born to a given woman. Each of these variables can be precisely

Table 11.1. *Average weight for 40 San children from birth to 8 years, by age*

Age	Weight (kg)	Range (kg)	Weight (lb)	Range (lb)	No. of observations	No. of individuals
0–1	6.0	3.1–8.7	13.2	7–19	32	12
1–2	8.8	7.3–11.8	19.4	16–26	21	12
2–3	11.6	8.2–14.1	25.6	18–31	15	9
3–4	12.4	10.9–15.0	27.4	24–33	15	7
4–5	13.4	9.5–15.9	29.6	21–35	31	11
5–6	14.7	12.3–16.8	32.3	27–37	20	10
6–7	15.3	11.8–17.7	33.8	26–39	13	7
7–8	17.6	12.7–19.5	38.7	28–43	17	5

quantified, and from their interaction a simple calculus can be developed to show more precisely the relation between birth spacing and women's work–between the reproductive system and the productive system.

WOMEN'S WORK

The weights of infants and children

!Kung adults are small in stature and light in weight by Western standards (Chapter 10). Birth weights and rates of infant growth for the first 6 months of life are comparable to Western standards. Thereafter, !Kung children grow more slowly than Western children. The weights of the former at each age run about 75 to 80 percent of the latter. For example, a 3.5-year-old American child weighs about 16.0 kg; a !Kung child of about the same age weighs 12.5 kg (Truswell and Hansen 1976:176).

The average weights of !Kung infants and children from birth to 8 years are shown in Table 11.1. The figures are based on 164 observations on 40 children weighed during fieldwork in 1967–9. The values vary from 6.0 kg in the first year of life to 17.6 kg in the eighth year. Note that these figures represent average weight during the year, not the weight attained at the end of the year. Presenting the data in this form enables us to calculate the average burden carried by the mother during each year of the child's life.

In the first year children weigh from 3.1 kg at birth to a high of 8.7 kg for an exceptionally fat older infant, with the average weight of infants being 6.0 kg. In the second year of life the mother's burden in 8.8 kg, with a range of 7.3 to 11.8 kg. By the fourth year this average has increased to 12.4 kg, with a range of 10.9 to as high as 15.0 kg.

Table 11.2. *Work load of women with children of various ages*

Child's Age (yr)	Average weight of child		Average annual distance to be carried		Work load for mother (kg-km)
	kg	lb	km	mi	
0–1	6.0	13.2	2,400	1,500	14,400
1–2	8.8	19.4	2,400	1,500	21,120
2–3	11.6	25.6	1,800	1,125	20,880
3–4	12.4	27.4	1,200	750	14,880
4–5	13.4	29.5			
5–6	14.7	32.3			
6–7	15.3	33.8			
7–8	17.6	38.7			

The distance to be traveled

I have estimated that a woman walks about 2400 km during a year's activity. Apart from food, water, and personal belongings, a woman carries each of her children under the age of 4 years for all or much of this distance. The weight she actually carries is determined by the age of the child and its rate of growth. Table 11.2 shows the different burdens of women with children of various ages. As a measure of work load, I introduce the useful, though somewhat cumbersome, unit *kilogram-kilometer,* which is simply a product of weight times distance (e.g., a load of 1 kg carried a distance of 1 km).

The interval between births

Given a mean birth interval among nomadic San of 4 years (for women of normal fertility), the work load of an average woman's reproductive career can be estimated. Her first baby is born in year 1, her second baby in year 5, her third in year 9, and so on. Each year she has a variable weight of child to carry, depending on the age of the child. For a 10-year period her work effort is as shown in Table 11.3.

During the 10-year period the average woman raises three children and carries an average burden of 9.2 kg per day. Her burden is least during the years she is carrying a newborn (6.0 kg per day) and greatest when she is carrying a 3-year-old (12.4 kg per day plus the burden of her pregnancy at the same time).

With shorter birth spacing, both the number of children and the weight of children to be carried increase. Table 11.4 shows the work effort required of mothers with four different birth intervals: 2, 3, 4, and 5 years. The table shows the number of babies and the weight in babies for each year of a 10-year period of the reproductive career.

Table 11.3. *Average daily burden over 10-year period for a woman of normal fertility*

	Year	Daily burden (kg)
First baby	1	6.0
	2	8.8
	3	11.6
	4	12.7
Second baby	5	6.0
	6	8.8
	7	11.6
	8	12.7
Third baby	9	6.0
	10	8.8

The work required of the mother progressively increases as the interval between births decreases. At one extreme, a mother with 5-year spacing has, at the end of 10 years, raised two children and carried an average daily burden of only 7.8 kg (17.2 lb). At the other extreme, a woman with 2-year spacing has, after the same period, had five children and carried an average daily burden of 17.0 kg (37.4 lb); and for 4 of the 10 years her daily burden was as high as 21.2 kg (46.6 lb). The 2-year interval represents a theoretical upper limit of birth frequency for San women living under hunting and gathering conditions.

For the majority of fertile women living as foragers the interval between live births varies between 5 and 3 years (see below). Shortening the birth interval from 5 to 4 years adds a daily burden of 1.4 kg to a woman's work load. Shortening the interval further, from 4 to 3 years, more than doubles the increase in burden to 3.0 kg for a total weight of 12.2 kg.

We have noted that actual work for the mother is the product of weight carried times distance traveled. To carry a child for 1 year requires between 14,000 and 21,000 kg-km of effort by the mother. To carry one child for the full 4 years requires a total of 72,280 kg-km and an average each year of 17,820 kg-km.

Table 11.5 shows how the amount of work is affected by different lengths of birth spacing. The required work effort increases slowly as the birth interval shortens from 5 to 4 years; it rises more rapidly as the birth interval is reduced to 3 years and extremely sharply as the interval is further reduced to 2 years. This table indicates some of the "costs" in work effort of raising children under nomadic, hunting and gathering conditions, and it also shows the added costs of an increase in the birthrate.

A mother with 5-year birth spacing has two children at the end of 10

Table 11.4. *Effect of different birth intervals on work effort of mother over 10-year period*

Year	2-yr interval		3-yr interval		4-yr interval		5-yr interval	
	Weight (kg)	Baby no.	Weight (kg)	Baby no.	Weight (kg)	Baby no.	Weight (kg)	Baby no.
1	6.0	1	6.0	1	6.0	1	6.0	1
2	8.8	1	8.8	1	8.8	1	8.8	1
3	17.6	1 + 2	11.6	1	11.6	1	11.6	1
4	21.2	1 + 2	18.4	1 + 2	12.4	1	12.4	1
5	17.6	2 + 3	8.8	2	6.0	2	[a]	[a]
6	21.2	2 + 3	11.6	2	8.8	2	6.0	2
7	17.6	3 + 4	18.4	2 + 3	11.6	2	8.8	2
8	21.2	3 + 4	8.8	3	12.4	2	11.6	2
9	17.6	4 + 5	11.6	3	6.0	3	12.4	2
10	21.2	4 + 5	18.4	3 + 4	8.8	3	[a]	[a]
Number of children at end of 10 yr	5		4		3		2	
Average weight (kg) of baby per year	17.0 (6–21.2)		12.2 (6–18.4)		9.2 (6–12)		7.8 (0–12)	
Number of years carrying 2 children	8		3		0		0	
Number of years carrying 1 or 0 children	2		7		10		10	

[a] No baby to be carried.

Table 11.5. *Work per mother per year according to birth spacing*

	Birth interval			
	2 yr	3 yr	4 yr	5 yr
Average work per year (kg-km)	32,064	22,824	17,808	14,256

years. Adding a third child during the same period (by lowering the birth interval to 4 years) adds only 3500 kg-km to a mother's work load. Adding a fourth child (by further lowering the birth interval to 3 years) costs 40 percent more than the cost of adding a third child: 5016 kg-km as opposed to 3552 kg-km. And adding a fifth child (by lowering the birth interval even further to 2 years) costs over 2.5 times as much per child as adding a third.

Given these high costs of short birth spacing, it is not surprising that under nomadic conditions the birth interval averages close to 4 years, even in the absence of contraceptive measures; the !Kung practice postpartum sex taboos, but only during the first year of the baby's life. This long birth spacing is adaptive both at the individual level and at the level of population. The individual woman is better equipped to care for each of her children if births do not follow too closely one after another, and this long birth spacing lowers overall fertility so that the population does not grow so rapidly that it threatens the food supply. Long birth spacing alone is not sufficient to keep the population in long-term balance with resources, but the !Kung's modest amount of excess fertility is readily absorbed by infant mortality, occasional infanticide, and out-migration.

In this context it is worth noting that the slow rates of growth of !Kung children noted in Chapter 10 are also adaptive. For people who have to walk a lot, small babies are easier to carry than large babies. This is another way that smallness makes sense in terms of the nomadic foraging way of life. If the !Kung children grew as fast as they should according to Western standards (Truswell and Hansen 1976), an intolerable burden would be imposed on the parents who would have to do the carrying, thereby reducing the survival chances of both generations.

MOBILITY, BIRTH SPACING, AND POPULATION GROWTH

I have examined the implications of higher and lower fertility levels for the economic adaptation of the hunting and gathering San. More babies and/or greater distances to travel mean more work for San mothers. Similarly, work effort declines with fewer babies and/or less walking. The

Table 11.6. *Effect of reduced mobility on fertility: work (kilogram-kilometers) per year for women with various birth intervals*

Mobility	Birth interval			
	2 yr	3 yr	4 yr	5 yr
Nomadic conditions:				
1200–2400 km/yr	32,064	22,824	17,808	14,256
More sedentary conditions:				
800–1600 km/yr	21,376	15,216	11,872	9,504

latter possibility–less walking or reduction of mobility–is of interest here. It is precisely what happens when hunters and gatherers shift to agriculture. Even partial agriculture allows more food to be grown closer to home and enables the population to maintain the same level of nutrition with much less walking.

What are the consequences for a !Kung mother's work load of a partial shift to food sources closer to home? To raise one child to the point where it can walk alone requires 4 years of carrying, for an average annual work load of 17,820 kg-km. This average is based on 1200 to 2400 km per year of walking. If walking is reduced by a third–to 800 to 1600 km per year–then the annual work load falls to 11,880 kg-km.

Table 11.6 sketches the implications of reduced work effort for birth spacing. Under nomadic conditions the mother with 5-year birth spacing has an annual work load of 14,256 kg-km. Under the more sedentary conditions, this falls to 9504 kg-km. A nomadic mother with 4-year birth spacing has a yearly work load of 17,808 kg-km. In a sedentary situation this declines to only 11,872 kg-km, which is less than that of a mother with 5-year birth spacing under the nomadic conditions.

In practical terms this means that with reduced mobility a woman may shorten the interval between successive births and continue to give each child adequate care while keeping her work effort constant. Put another way, a mother can have more children with no increase in work effort. Table 11.6 shows how, under more sedentary conditions, a mother may have a baby every 3 years with slightly *less* work effort than having a baby every 4 years requires under nomadic conditions (15,216 kg-km compared with 17,800 kg-km). Shortening the mean birth interval results in a general rise in the level of fertility, which, in turn, leads to an upswing in the rate of population growth.

I do not intend to imply that sedentarization alone causes population growth. In the first instance, reduction of mobility may produce a situation where the number of children remains the same but the amount of leisure time increases. I am suggesting that settling down removes the adverse effects of high fertility on individual women. Among hunters and gatherers high natural fertility is maladaptive, and even with 3-year birth spacing the mother's work load may be great enough to endanger her own fitness and affect the survival chances of her offspring. With sedentary life these restraints are removed, and 3-year birth spacing becomes no more strenuous for the mother than is 4-year birth spacing under nomadic conditions.

Thus, for the population as a whole sedentarization may lead to the upsetting of the low-fertility adaptation of the hunting and gathering life and trigger population growth, even in the absence of any expansion in the food supply. The cause of the sedentarization need not be the shift to agriculture, though such a shift is occurring among the !Kung San. Any change in the subsistence economy that allows reduced mobility may be sufficient to increase fertility. Such preagricultural examples of sedentarization as the exploitation of wild grains with a milling technology or the exploitation of coastal and riverine resources may have had a similar effect of increasing fertility by reducing mobility.

The relation between nomadism and long birth spacing has been known at least since 1922, when Sir Alexander Carr-Saunders referred to "the problem of transportation in nomadic societies." He pointed out that the necessity of carrying children for the first few years of life sharply limited the number of children a woman could successfully rear during her reproductive span (Carr-Saunders 1922). Birdsell (1968:236) spoke of at least a 3-year birth interval among Australian aboriginal women. To my knowledge the first person to pinpoint birth spacing as a key variable in the shift from hunting and gathering to sedentary life was Lewis R. Binford, as quoted by John Pfeiffer:

> Binford suggests that one result [of a more reliable food supply at the end of the Pleistocene] may have been an increased trend toward year round settlements reducing the need to pack up and move on to new hunting grounds, and permitting an adjustment of primitive birth control measures. As long as mothers had to keep on the move, they were limited to one child every three or four years because that was all they could carry but infanticide could be relaxed in more settled times with fish and fowl to supplement basic supplies of reindeer meat [Pfeiffer 1969:218].

Note that, contrary to the present theory, Binford pointed to infanticide as the key mechanism of hunter-gatherer population control. In his view, sedentarization triggers population growth through a reduction of infanticide and not through a shortening of the interval between live births. Birdsell also saw infanticide as the key mechanism, arguing that "difficulties of nursing and mobility in the Pleistocene may have made necessary the killing of 15–50 per cent of children born, since lactation alone would not have provided sufficient spacing of births to provide equilibrium" (Birdsell 1968:243).

My own view is that a high level of infanticide is *not* a necessary component of hunter-gatherer population control: The !Kung, under foraging conditions, are able to maintain very low fertility through long birth spacing with a rate of infanticide of less than 2 percent (Howell 1976b:147). In fact, we are now in a position to specify precisely how long the birth intervals are under hunting and gathering conditions and how these birth intervals change when the !Kung settle down to village life.

!KUNG BIRTH SPACING: A TEST OF THE HYPOTHESIS

Starting with July 1963, our research project maintained a registry of births (and deaths) in the Dobe population. During fieldwork, birth dates were recorded by direct observation. These dates are usually accurate to ± 5 days. When there was no observer in the field, birth dates were reconstructed through interviews. These dates are usually accurate to ± 30 days. In all, we followed the reproductive lives of 256 adult women over the 10-year period 1963–73.

A process of sedentarization was going on in the Dobe area, but this had a markedly differential effect on groups at different water holes. At one eastern water hole (!Goshe), the San had built a village of mud huts in the early 1960s and essentially occupied this same site throughout the study period. They continued to hunt and gather on short trips, but an increasing proportion of their subsistence came from cows' milk and cultivated grains. At the other extreme of mobility were the /Du/da subpopulation 60 km south of the Dobe area, who moved camp five or six times a year in a classic foraging pattern. The remainder of the population exhibited patterns intermediate between these two poles. This varied situation offered the investigator a natural laboratory for testing hypotheses about the social, economic, and demographic effects of sedentarization.

The year after the original study appeared in print (Lee 1972d), I returned to the Dobe area to complete the 10-year record of births and deaths and to acquire data for testing the hypothesis about the relation between birth spacing and sedentarization. The 256 adult women included virtually all the resident women of reproductive age (15 to 59 years) in the population. There were two sets of crosscutting variables characterizing the women in the sample (1) the stage of the reproductive career and (2) the number of children born. These variables yielded the nine categories of women listed in Table 11.7. Of the total, 119 women were not pregnant during the period from July 1, 1963, to June 30, 1973; 43 others had only one pregnancy; and for 2 women the data was insufficient. This left 92 women with two or more births and, hence, with at least one measurable birth interval.

Table 11.7. *Number of women of reproductive age in the Dobe area: 1963–73*

Stage of reproductive career	No. of pregnancies: 1963–73			
	0	1	2+	Total
Early[a]	24	22	16	62
Middle[b]	63	19	73	155
Late[c]	32	2	3	37
Total	119	43	92	254[d]

[a]Women for whom menarche occurred during 1963–73.
[b]Postmenarcheal women between the ages of 15 and 59.
[c]Women who underwent menopause during 1963–73.
[d]For 2 women of total 256, data were insufficient.

The first step was to consider all the birth intervals, acknowledging that infant mortality could shorten the interval considerably. The average interval between successive births was 37.23 months for all 92 women (165 intervals). That means that over 3 years elapsed between births whether or not the first baby died. Individual intervals ranged from a low of 11 months for a woman whose infant died in the first week of life and who conceived again soon after, to a high of over 8 years for a woman of very low fertility. This 37-month figure is very high for a population in which no form of contraception is practiced.

To eliminate the effects of infant mortality, I abstracted from the data those birth intervals in which the first child survived to the birth of the second. I further divided the population into two groups: more nomadic women and more sedentary women. Finally, I divided the 10-year run of data into two 5-year periods. This last division yielded three temporally related sets of data: (1) intervals falling within the period July 1, 1963, to June 30, 1968; (2) intervals falling within the period July 1, 1968, to June 30, 1973; and (3) intervals straddling the mid-1968 boundary. By comparing period 1 with period 2, we could discern possible secular trends through the 10-year period.

The results are set out in Table 11.8. The mean birth interval for nomadic women was 44.11 months and for sedentary women 36.17 months, indicating that throughout the period sedentary women tended to reconceive about 8 months earlier than nomadic women. This 8-month difference would significantly increase both the birth rate and completed family size for the sedentary women.

The difference between more nomadic and more sedentary women is even sharper when we examine the time dimension. The entire population was undergoing sedentarization during 1963–73, and this is reflected in the fact that the birth interval dropped from 39.89 months in

Table 11.8. *Mean length of intervals (in months) between successive live births to !Kung women: 1963–73*

	1963–8	1968–73	1963–73	Mean of all three periods
More nomadic women	42.27 (11)[a]	36.42 (12)	47.63 (32)	44.11 (55)
More sedentary women	38.35 (17)	29.82 (22)	40.12 (26)	36.17 (65)
All women	39.89 (28)	32.15 (34)	44.26 (58)	39.81 (120)

[a] Numbers in parentheses indicate number of intervals.

period 1 to 32.15 months in period 2. This shortening of the birth interval was particularly marked for more sedentary women, with a drop of 8.53 months, but the process is apparent also in the more nomadic women, who exhibited a decrease of 5.85 months. The increase in fertility was most marked at the most settled village of !Goshe, where there were four young women, each of whom in the period 1968–73 had had two successive live births spaced 22, 23, 21, and 20 months apart, respectively.

To illustrate the effects of birth spacing on actual people, here are case histories of several women representing the more nomadic and the more sedentary categories.

/Tam (born in 1933) is a married woman who alternates between !Kubi and /Xai/xai water holes, spending a large proportion of her time with her group (LG 20/68 and LG 18/73) foraging in her husband's n!ore in the southwestern Aha Hills. When photographed in 1968 (Plate 11.2) /Tam had three well-spaced children: //Koka born (born in 1960), !Xam (born in February 1963), and N!ai (born in March 1968). She had another child in September 1971, and when interviewed in August 1973, she was about 3 months pregnant. Three of her birth intervals fall roughly within the study period:

> February 1963 to March 1968   61 months
> March 1968 to September 1971   42 months
> September 1971 to January 1974   28 months

The average birth interval was 43.67 months with clear evidence of a shortening of the interval through the 10-year period.

N≠isa (born about 1941) has lived with her husband at cattle posts at Mahopa and Bate. In addition to an older son by a previous husband,

Plate 11.2. Long birth spacing: /Tam with her three children aged 8 years, 5 years, and 6 months.

N≠isa has had five pregnancies since the early 1960s: a girl, //Kushe (born 1962); a boy, /Tishe (born in February 1965); a boy, Bo (born in October 1968, deceased); and another boy, /Twi (born in March 1971). She was in the middle stages of pregnancy when contacted in July 1973. Her three birth intervals within the study period are:

February 1965 to October 1968   44 months
October 1968 to March 1971   29 months
March 1971 to October 1973   31 months

The average birth interval was 34.67 months and there was some evidence of shortening through the period, though N≠isa does not approach the very short intervals (20 to 24 months) of some of the !Goshe girls.

An example of the last is N!uhka (born in 1947), who has spent most of her life at cattle posts north of the Dobe area and who married a !Goshe man in the mid-1960s. She had one stillbirth prior to 1968 (undated) and a pregnancy that spontaneously aborted in September 1968. She had a baby girl in April 1970 and 23 months later a boy in March 1972, for a birth interval of only 23 months and a period between birth and reconception of only 14 months (Plate 11.3).

The data presented in Table 11.8 are specific to the period 1963–73, a time of increasingly rapid change for the !Kung. We have no way of knowing what the birth intervals may have been 10, 25, or 100 years ago when the !Kung were leading more nomadic lives. However, the data presented here convincingly demonstrate that the actual interval between live births continues to be well over 3 years for nomadic !Kung, even under present circumstances, and that this long birth spacing is achieved without recourse to infanticide or to any form of contraception. In fact, methodologically the technique tends to *underestimate* the mean of the birth intervals. Because only a 10-year time period is considered, the cutoff at July 1973 gives a truncated distribution of the full range of birth intervals and tends to overrepresent shorter intervals and underrepresent longer ones. For example, we do not know how many of the 43 women with only one birth in the 10-year period have ceased to be fertile and how many will give birth again after intervals of 60, 70, or 80 months (Sheps and Menken 1973; Howell, personal communication). If these longer intervals were added into the sample, I believe the mean birth interval for nomadic women would fall between 4 and 5 years, as postulated by the model. Unfortunately, the termination of fertility by gonorrhea was a factor in the lives of many of the 63 women of mid-reproductive age who had no pregnancies during 1963–73 (Howell 1979).

A second point brought home by the data in Table 11.8 is the rapidity of change during the decade. There is no statistical reason why the birth intervals in 1968–73 should be 7.75 months shorter than the intervals in

Plate 11.3. Short birth spacing: N!uhka with her two children age 3 years and 1 year.

1963–8. The difference, significant to the 0.05 level on the t-test, suggests that a change in the means of production toward reduced mobility can rapidly alter the balance in the system of reproduction and release, in effect, a flood of suppressed fertility. Schaefer (1971) and Freeman (1971) have observed similar bursts of fertility among the recently settled Inuit and other Canadian native peoples.

PRODUCTION AND REPRODUCTION: THE CAUSAL LINKS

Two further questions can now be asked: By what mechanism is long birth spacing maintained under foraging conditions? And what factors in the productive system underlie the shortening of birth spacing when the shift to sedentary life is made? To the first question the answer is that a long period of lactation appears to suppress ovulation in !Kung women. Mothers nurse their children for the first 2 to 3 years of the child's life. Nursing is vigorous, frequent, given on demand, and spaced throughout the day and night. During the latter half of the nursing period, the mother's sexual life is active, but conception does not occur. Although the exact mechanism is still in dispute, it seems clear that the long period of vigorous, continuous nursing suppresses ovulation in enough women enough of the time to produce an average birth interval in nomadic !Kung women of about 3.7 years (44.11 months).

Data on the relation between lactation and ovulation in other populations were at first difficult to interpret, but recently the relation has become clearer. Careful studies have shown a marked suppressant effect in Third World populations: Nursing mothers show much longer birth intervals than nonnursing mothers. These studies include populations in Rwanda (Bonte and van Balen 1969), India (Peters et al. 1958; Tietze 1961; Potter et al. 1965), Egypt (El-Minawi and Foda 1971), and Taiwan (Jain et al. 1970) as well as native North Americans such as Indians in New Mexico (Gioiosa 1955) and Alaskan Eskimos (Berman et al. 1972). The data have led demographer John Knodel to conclude: "There is ample evidence that lactation inhibits conception through prolonged postpartum amenorrhea" (Knodel 1977a:1; see also Van Ginneken 1974; Knodel 1977b).

The fact that studies from urban Western populations have shown the suppressant effect to be present, but in a weaker form, has led some Western authorities to express doubts that lactation has any contraceptive value beyond the first few months of the child's life (e.g., Guttmacher 1952). In a recent study of American nursing mothers, Kippley and Kippley (1975:163) have argued that cultural factors such as nursing schedules, the early use of pacifiers, midnight bottles, and supplementary feedings have tended greatly to reduce the effectiveness of lactation as a suppressor of ovulation in Western societies. For Western mothers who are committed to a program of what the Kippleys call "natural mothering"–no pacifiers, bottles, or solid foods used for first 5 months, plus 24-hour feeding on demand–much longer periods of lactational amenorrhea have been achieved. In a survey of 22 American La Leche League mothers who breast-fed their children from 12 to 37 months, the Kippleys found the mean length of breast-feeding to be 22.8 months and the mean period of amenorrhea to be 14.6 months (Kippley and Kippley 1975:163–78). These values are, of course, short by !Kung standards, but they are very long by Western standards, where most women who bottle-feed their babies resume menstrual cycles within 90 days of giving birth.

Although data on the incidence of postpartum amenorrhea are not available for the !Kung, we can infer from the length of the birth intervals and from the absence of evidence for the use of contraceptive devices or for postpartum sex taboos after 12 months that the !Kung women experience much longer periods of infertility following parturition and that their strong continuing lactation is probably involved in the persistence of the infertile period.

How does lactation suppress ovulation? Two kinds of related explanations have been offered. The first, called the critical fatness hypothesis, was originally developed by the Harvard biostatistician Rose Frisch to account for the timing of menarche in adolescent girls. Frisch found that the onset of menses was correlated with the attainment of a critical level of fatness, a level that was in fact a better predictor of the timing of menarche than was a girl's chronological age (Frisch and Revelle 1970; Frisch 1974; Frisch and McArthur 1974). She has also suggested that a critical threshold of fatness may control the cessation and resumption of menstrual cycles in adult women (Frisch 1975). Citing evidence for amenorrhea in poorly nourished wartime populations, Frisch has directed attention to fat loss as a possible way of controlling menses and ovulation. Howell has applied this hypothesis to the !Kung data seeking to determine whether the caloric demands of lactation are so great that fat stores in nursing mothers are reduced below a critical threshold to the point where menses and ovulation cannot resume. She is also considering the possibility that the gradual shift of the older nursing child to solid foods may permit the mother's fat levels to rise sufficiently to the point where menstrual cycles and ovulation are triggered (Howell 1976a, 1979; see also Kolata 1974).

There are a number of problems with the critical fatness hypothesis as an explanation of the !Kung women's long postpartum infertility. First, nutritional amenorrhea is usually a serious condition of ill health and reduced fitness; it seems unlikely that !Kung fertility is regulated by a mechanism that routinely reproduces wartime conditions of semistarvation. Second, the clinical evidence for the nutritional status of lactating !Kung mothers indicates adequate levels of overall nutrition and better than average levels of such key nutrients as vitamin B_{12}, folates, and iron (Metz et al. 1971, Truswell and Hansen 1976). Third, Howell, in a study (1979) of the weights of pregnant !Kung women, found that about half the women weighed showed levels of fatness below the critical threshold around the time of conception and about half above, a finding that does not support the hypothesis that a critical fatness threshold is linked with the ability to conceive among the !Kung.

Other studies have also failed to show a correlation between weight gain and the timing of conception. For example, nursing mothers in a Guatemalan rural study population were actually found to be *losing* weight at reconception, not gaining it (Bongaarts and Delgado 1977). Finally, a number of studies have criticized the general hypothesis of critical fatness or critical weight on methodological and empirical grounds (Johnston et al. 1971, 1975; Billewicz et al. 1976).

Given these problems, attention has turned to alternate explanations. The second possible mechanism relating lactation to suppression of ovulation concerns the strength and persistence of the sucking stimulus itself. Minaguchi and Meites (1967) reported that follicular growth and ovulation were inhibited by the suckling act itself, a finding that confirmed earlier observations by other researchers (e.g., Udesky 1950; McKeown and Gibson 1954; Topkins 1959; Keettel and Bradbury 1961). Topkins has stated:

> Recent evidence indicates that it is the stimulus of sucking of the infant rather than lactation which acts on the pituitary gland probably by way of the mid-brain. The decrease in the frequency of feedings and the cessation of nursing result in the re-establishment of ovarian function, the reappearance of menstruation and ultimately ovulation. Complete breast-feeding in the early months of life is a fairly effective method of suppressing ovarian function and conception. [Topkins 1958; quoted in Kippley 1975:149–50]

Subsequent research has confirmed this. Mosley, drawing on studies later reported by Tyson and Perez (1978) and others, could state:

> It is now well-established that lactation and post-partum amenorrhea rely heavily upon the effectiveness of the nursing stimulus which in turn causes secretion of the pituitary hormone prolactin. This hormonal reflex system has even been demonstrated in normally menstruating women who induce lactation simply by nipple stimulation. [Mosley 1977:8–9]

In other words, vigorous sucking–of a kind that is regular, frequent, and occurs round the clock–seems more likely to be responsible for the persistence of amenorrhea during lactation than does the falling of a woman's fat levels below a critical threshold.

Whatever the mechanism (and the interactions between the two are complex), the !Kung appear to be able to achieve periods of lactational amenorrhea that are two to three times longer than those of other populations of breast-feeding, noncontracepting mothers. The mean birth interval of 39.8 months (Table 11.8) for !Kung mothers implies a mean period from birth to conception of 30.8 months. If we assume that a woman's menstrual cycles resume on the average 3 to 6 months before she becomes pregnant again, that places the mean length of the period of amenorrhea in the range of 24.8 to 27.8 months, compared with 10 to 12 months for native populations in India, Alaska, and Rwanda (Berman et al. 1972:532).

How are we to account for this persistence? If vigorous, persistent sucking stimulus is the causal mechanism, then the !Kung present a good case. Observers of !Kung nursing mothers have been struck by the high frequency with which the children take the breast and the vigor with which the older children especially stimulate the nipples. In fact, the !Kung are quite striking in the degree to which they accept as the cultural norm the continued nursing of an older child with a full set of teeth and fully developed sucking muscles. It is common to see a 2- or 3-year-old standing to nurse at a seated mother's breast. In fact, the primary reason for weaning appears to be a following pregnancy; when a woman becomes sure she is pregnant she quickly withdraws the breast, saying to the child: "Look this milk is no longer for you, it is for your younger sibling" (Shostak 1976:251–3). But in the absence of a pregnancy a child may continue to nurse to age 5 years or more. Only when the child is as old as 6 years and the mother is still not pregnant are steps taken to wean the child with social pressure and mild ridicule ("You are too old for baby stuff like that"). This kind of late weaning is almost always confined to the last child of a mother in her forties and illustrates the interesting (but not uncommon for the !Kung) situation of a woman undergoing menopause while still lactating. We do not know how much nourishment the 3-year-old or 5-year-old child is getting from the breast (probably not very much), but if the sucking stimulus itself proves instrumental in inhibiting ovulation, then the !Kung child-rearing practices offer an ideal milieu to maximize its effectiveness.

Of course, the 3-year-old child running with his or her play group does not nurse as frequently as the 1-year-old who is carried on the mother's hip, but the vigorousness of the stimulus may compensate for the decline of nursing frequency.

The emphasis the !Kung place on carrying the younger child may now be more clearly understood: The constant stimulation of the breast by the carried child may contribute significantly to the birth control effect, rather like carrying your contraceptive on your hip. If the infant were left at home with baby-sitters for a 6-hour working day, the contraceptive effect might be reduced.

Australian aboriginal women in Arnhem Land organize their work groups differently from the !Kung. They leave their children in camp in the charge of older co-wives or other baby-sitters while they go out to gather. It is worth considering whether this fact alone may not account for the much shorter birth intervals and higher rates of infanticide that have been observed among aboriginal women compared with !Kung women (McCarthy and McArthur 1960; Rose 1960; Lancaster-Jones 1963; Birdsell 1968:243).

Finally, why does this system of long lactational amenorrhea break down when the shift to sedentary life is made? The rapidity of the change makes it unlikely that "removing the adverse effects of high fertility" accounts for the change, for we see birth intervals shortening from one pregnancy to the next in the same women. It is more likely that some more proximate or immediate cause is at work. The probable mechanism is not too hard to discern. The nomadic !Kung diet, though rich in nutrients, is deficient in suitable weaning foods – soft foods like milk and porridge that are easily digested by infants and toddlers. As a result, though infants are introduced to solid foods by 6 months, mother's milk continues to be an important part of the child's diet into the third year of life. At !Goshe and the other more settled !Kung villages there is a more plentiful supply of cows' milk and cultivated grains. The availability of alternative foods lessens the child's need for breast milk, and this may lower the level of lactation and the frequency of nipple stimulation. The result of the infant's reduced demands is that the woman's lactational amenorrhea may cease and ovulation may resume as early as 11 to 14 months after she has given birth, a situation that would lead to the 20- to 23-month birth intervals actually observed at !Goshe.

It must be emphasized that these are not either-or propositions. A variable such as diet affects different women differently. In some women it may lead to earlier conception; in others it may not. The net statistical effect, however, is a shorter birth interval and a rise in the birthrate.

THE EMOTIONAL ECONOMY OF REPRODUCTION

The more rapid succession of births is not an unmixed blessing, quite apart from the long-term consequences of population growth and shrinking food supply. This sudden embarrassment of riches in terms of births is already imposing hardships on !Kung mothers and children alike, a degree of stress that reveals the existence of a third system interlocked with production and reproduction – a system I will call the emotional economy of the San. Long birth spacing for the !Kung has meant that a great deal of energy, both physical and emotional, has gone into the raising of each child. Among the nomadic !Kung each child got its mother's exclusive attention for 44 months, a period that included 36 months of breast-feeding. By the time the child was weaned it had the teeth, motor development, language, and social awareness of a 3-year-old. The weaning transition was not without difficulties. The child would cry for the breast and to be carried in the back pouch and would throw tantrums if it did not gets its way. But after a few months the child usually adjusted to its new status of older sibling as the mother turned her attention to the new arrival. For the child who is weaned at 12 months instead of 36 months the trauma of separation becomes much more severe. Remember, the year-old child in traditional !Kung circumstances was carried full time by the mother, was nursed on demand, and probably obtained a large proportion of its calories from breast milk. From the point of view of the culture, the year-old child was just a third of the way toward the point at which it would have to give up breast and back.

When the mother of such a young child becomes pregnant, the effects are striking. The most miserable kids I have seen among the !Kung are

Plate 11.4. A young /Xai/xai mother with two babies under 3 years of age.

some of the 1.5- to 2-year old youngsters with younger siblings on the way. Their misery begins at weaning and continues to the birth of the sibling 6 to 8 months later and beyond. The mother, for her part, has not only a demanding newborn to care for but the constant intrusions of an angry, sullen 2-year-old. A grandmother or aunt may do her best to feed and cheer up the older child and to give the overworked mother some relief, but it is clear to the observer that something is out of kilter. The scene is in marked contrast to the relatively placid infant care in the nomadic camps documented by Draper (1976) and Konner (1976). In light of the emotional stress brought on by short birth spacing, it is not surprising that several of these women have asked for birth control assistance. The Dobe area has never had a regular medical presence until the last few years, but the !Kung women had heard rumors of a European pill that would make them stop having babies, and they sought this as a way out of their difficulties.

The unhappiness of the prematurely weaned !Kung babies and their mothers brought home to me how closely the emotional and psychological dynamics of life are tied into the productive and reproductive systems. The long birth spacing that makes such good sense for hunter-gatherers in economic and health terms also provides the opportunity for a high parental investment in each child, making possible the raising of what Becker and Becker, in another context, have called fewer children of higher quality. The children's personalities were molded by this system of exclusive attention for the first few years. The emotional security !Kung adults display may be related to the security they experienced in early childhood. Short birth spacing breaks the circle, and the emotional economy is put under stress, even though the nutritional and health needs of mother and child may be adequately met. Clearly, marked changes in the patterns of child care and maternal behavior will be required before the !Kung can adjust emotionally to their new economic and demographic realities. In the interim, a generation of !Kung children may be growing up bearing the psychological scars of the too-rapid transition.

12

Ownership, leadership, and the use of space

MARXIST and non-Marxist economists alike recognize three main factors of production: land, labor, and capital. We have already considered two of the factors in detail: labor or work in Chapters 6 through 9 and 11, and capital in the form of capital goods or technology in Chapter 5. Land and resources and the way they are controlled in the hunting and gathering economy remain to be considered. This is a crucial factor because the nature of the ownership of land by hunting peoples has been a matter of dispute among scientists for over a century. Learned discourses on the subject have shown an astonishing variety of opinion. Regarding the San of Southern Africa, some authorities have expressed the view that San local groups maintain strict territorial rights to their land, defending it rigorously against trespass. For example, Fourie reported that among the San "territorial boundaries are observed in the most scrupulous manner . . . Each family is inseparably united to its habitat and has a superstitious dread of any locality but its own" (Fourie 1928:85); other authorities have taken the opposite view, that San maintain no territorial rights at all, being a people, in Frere's words, "without . . . even a shadow of land tenures" (Frere 1882–3:259).

Even among modern researchers a range of opinion exists. In her early writings Marshall (1960:344ff.) spoke of a relatively clear-cut concept of landownership among the Nyae Nyae !Kung, with the responsibility for each water hole clearly residing in the person of a band headman, who was always male and who inherited his position patrilineally (a view she no longer holds; see also Heinz 1972). Yellen and Harpending (1972), by contrast, preferred an open model of land use in which groups more or less freely circulate throughout a region, using the resources of a given area one year and of a different area in another year. Recently, Barnard (1978) has documented variations in land use for four distinct San populations: !Kung, /Gwi, !Ko, and Nharo.

Related to the nature of landownership is the question of leadership:

How are decisions made in an egalitarian society and who makes them? Here too a variety of opinion exists; various authorities have attributed to the San strong chiefs (Schapera 1930), weak chiefs (Fourie 1928), headmen (Marshall 1960), or no chiefs or headmen at all (Frere 1882–3).

In the case of the !Kung San, our understanding of ownership and leadership is complicated by the fact that non-San people have been living among them for two generations. Grazing rights and rights of access to water holes for the blacks' cattle have made it more difficult in some cases to discern the preexisting patterns of ownership and use of land for the hunter-gatherers.

The purpose of this chapter is threefold: first, to examine concepts of landownership as they existed among the !Kung during the 1960s and to show how these principles are worked out in practice; second, to look at patterns of leadership and how these are being transformed in the face of outside pressures; and third, to present, in a detailed reconstruction, the spatial organization of a dozen living groups around /Xai/xai as they were in the 1920s *before* the arrival of the black settlers. In the concluding section I seek an underlying structural dynamic to account for the flexibility of !Kung land use.

N!ORES

The !Kung word for locality, land, or territory, *n!ore,* is applied to the block of land that surrounds each water hole and provides the resources on which the people of the water hole depend. Each n!ore is associated with a core group of owners (*k"ausi*), a point discussed in detail in Chapter 3. The sizes of these n!ores cannot be usefully measured because the size and shape vary from year to year depending on who is using the foods and on what neighboring living groups are doing. Roughly n!ores measure in the range of 300 to 600 km².

Within a n!ore, the water hole itself and the area immediately around it is clearly owned by the k"ausi group, and this ownership is passed from one generation to another as long as the descendants continue to live there. But this core area is surrounded by a broad belt of land that is shared with adjacent groups. In walking from one n!ore to another, I would often ask my companions, "Are we still in n!ore X or have we crossed over into n!ore Y?" They usually had a good deal of difficulty specifying which n!ore they were in, and two informants would often disagree, one saying, "We are already in Y"; the other saying, "No, we are still in X." Such observations convinced me that the !Kung do not define sharp boundaries between n!ores. Plant food resources are more clearly defined, but even here some ambiguity persists. In a grove of mongongos at //Gakwe≠dwa, north of Dobe, the eastern end belonged to !Kangwa people and the western end to Dobe people, but as one walked

Plate 12.1. The private life phase of the !Kung annual cycle: a small temporary camp at Tsutsunana.

east the Dobe nut trees graded gradually into the !Kangwa trees, and no one could specify where the dividing line was.

Such vague boundaries are disconcerting only to people from societies such as our own in which productive land is clearly divided by fences, hedges, and other markers. To the !Kung these ambiguities do not represent lapses or omissions. They are clearly functional and adaptive. Though I cannot prove it, I believe the !Kung *consciously* strive to maintain a boundaryless universe because this is the best way to operate as hunter-gatherers in a world where group size and resources vary from year to year. At the //Gakwe≠dwa grove, if one year the Dobe people eat their way further east, then the !Kangwas will eat their way further west the next. The important point is that the !Kung do not live in a universe where every calorie counts and must be carefully guarded. *Among the !Kung and other hunter-gatherers, good fences do not make good neighbors.*

Principles of n!ore use

Given the lack of boundaries, how do people plan their food-gathering activities over the course of a year? The answer to this question must be sought at three levels: within the living group, among neighboring groups, and between local groups and visiting groups.

Within the camp everyone has free access. The !Kung camp is a unit within which sharing takes place, and when sharing breaks down it ceases to be a camp. Who will gather on a given day and where are informally worked out. The food is in or on the ground or in the trees, and any member of the camp may gather where she or he pleases. Visitors join residents in the exploitation of resources, and the day's take is unobtrusively distributed within the camp at the day's end. Later in the year residents will pay reciprocal visits to the visitors' n!ore. No matter where they are from, as long as people are living together in a single camp the n!ore's food is theirs to share. This is one of the clearest principles of resource use stated by the !Kung.

A different kind of situation arises when a neighboring group wants to make a camp within a n!ore separate from the owner group's camp. In this case, the neighboring people must ask permission of the owner group. Where relations are good, the asking often takes the form of an invitation: "Come, let's go together and eat the dcha melons of X [referring to an area used by both groups]." If the owner group has other plans, it may respond: "No, you go and eat our dcha melons, we are staying by our water." (!Kung grammatical categories, unlike English, make a distinction between the inclusive and the exclusive first person plural, so that in the sentence above when the owners say "our melons" they clearly specify that the melons belong to the neighbors *and* themselves, but when they say "our water" they indicate that the water belongs to the owners alone.) The members of the neighboring group should also specify whether they will be eating the dcha melons by themselves or with visitors. The owner group might accept the neighbors but might not be agreeable to the visitors that accompany them.

A /Xai/xai man expressed the principle of inclusion and exclusion in the following terms:

> Within the camp people don't fight over food, but between camps people could disagree. For example, if people from /Gam came up to eat the tsin beans of Hxore and one of us /Xai/xai people happened to find them there, he might report back to us and we would start an argument with them . . . We would go there and seek out our in-laws in the /Gam group and say: "Look we have given each other children and today we are *n!umbaakwe* ['affines'] and the n!ore is ours [inclusive], but why when we weren't here did you come and bring with you 'strangers to boot?" My in-law might reply: "Oh, when I came here with them, I expected to find you here. How was I to know that you would be over there? But I understand your point and so I'll go home."
>
> In other words, as long as you eat together it is all right. Or if they come to you first, it is all right too. It's when they eat alone and you come along later to find them there, that's when fights start.

A third type of situation occurs when a more distant group wants to camp in part of a n!ore. Such a group must be especially careful to ask permission because it does not have a joint claim to the resources. By asking to camp, it incurs a reciprocal obligation to play host to the owner group at a later date. Usually if the visiting group is small and its stay is short, permission is freely given; but if the group is large and stays for months, the owner group may take steps to reassert its claim to the food resource. A case in point was the quiet drama played out in 1968–9 over the extensive tsin bean fields of Hxore, straddling the border 25 km southwest of /Xai/xai. ≠Toma/twe [363], a /Xai/xai man, is generally recognized as the senior owner of these fields. (The number in brackets immediately following a person's name refers to the code for the informant listed in Table 12.5.)

In April 1968, over 40 /Du/da southern people moved into Hxore as the tsin season began. They were joined by a few /Xai/xai people related by marriage, and together they ate out the year's tsin beans. By winter (June and July), they had moved back south to /Du/da.

The following year, in January 1969, an entirely different group moved into Hxore; led by ≠Toma/twe himself and composed only of /Xai/xai people, this group of 25 to 29 persons had no members in common with the group of the previous year. They started collecting and roasting the tsin beans almost 2 months before the tsin season started. I was puzzled by the 100 percent turnover of the personnel and by the fact that they had jumped the gun on the tsin season. The explanation was given me by Sa//gain!a [396], an old woman who is acknowledged to be one of the main owners of /Xai/xai (see below under "N!ore ownership"):

> Hxore has always been part of the /Xai/xai n!ores. We get our tsin there. Last year the /Du/da people just came up to eat it as visitors. When we saw them all at Hxore we told them: "Look we really count on that tsin there. Go back to your other n!ores." You see those people always lived south. Hxore was further north than they had come. Maybe they were looking for tobacco. Years ago the Boers carried them all off to work on the farms, but today they are coming back again.

To make sure the /Du/da people understood, the /Xai/xai party arrived in the tsin fields early, and by eating the beans reasserted their traditional rights in the area. After 1969 the southerners did not return in strength to Hxore, though small groups of them continued to make friendly visits to /Xai/xai.

In short, the !Kung do own the land they occupy. Although ownership is collective, not individual, and the boundaries are not well marked, the concept of ownership is there nonetheless. To summarize, members of the core group and their visitors may exploit the resources of the n!ore

Table 12.1. *Patrilineal versus matrilineal inheritance of locality (men)*

Inherited n!ore from:	Number	Percent
Father	60	39.7
Mother	40	26.5
Both father *and* mother	16	10.6
Neither parent	21	13.9
Does not know, or no n!ore	14	9.3
Total	151	100.0

Source: Lee (1972b:129).

without restriction. Neighboring groups may use the resources as well, but they must keep the owners informed of their movements and who they are camping with. More distant groups must ask permission more explicitly and should be modest in their behavior, in terms of length of stay and the number of people brought in. If these rules are followed, the use of resources operates smoothly. Disputes between groups over food are not unknown among the !Kung, but they are rare, far less common and less serious than are, for example, fights over sex, adultery, and betrothal.

N!ore transmission

An individual may inherit a n!ore from his father's family or from his mother's family or from both parents or from neither. There is a discernible patrilineal tendency, at least among males. Table 12.1 shows the inheritance of n!ores by 151 men of the Dobe area (representing over 90 percent of the adult male population). Although the majority take n!ores *not* in a strict patrilineal way, inheritance from father is the most common single alternative. (Unfortunately, comparable data were not gathered for females.) Polly Wiessner (in press) argues that all !Kung inherit *both* their father's *and* their mother's n!ore, and each individual gravitates to one or the other in adult life.

The interviews on n!ores also showed a considerable amount of internal migration among Dobe area men. Only 32 of 151 men (21 percent) were actually living in their natal n!ores at the time of the study. Of the 97 men living in the !Kangwa Valley, only 30 claimed n!ores there, and of the 43 /Xai/xai residents, 23 stated that location as their n!ore. The reasons given for leaving the natal n!ore by the 117 men who had done so were numerous, ranging from "I married out of my n!ore" to "I came to work for the Tswana." The responses are summarized in Table 12.2.

It is clear that black and European contact has been partly responsible for this internal migration. Historically, many people from !Gwidum,

Table 12.2. *Reasons given for leaving n!ore*

Reason	No. of men	Percent
I followed my parents	23	15
To work for the blacks	21	14
To marry in	16	11
Just visiting; I plan to return	14	9
Chased by Boers from South-West Africa; fence cut us off	14	9
No one to live with; old people died off	12	8
Other reasons (seeking water, food, tobacco)	14	9
Inappropriate (still living in n!ore)	32	21
Not ascertained	5	3
Total	151	99

Nyae Nyae, and /Gam migrated into the Dobe area from the west and south to herd the blacks' cattle (Chapter 3). However, factors internal to !Kung society, such as marriage and visiting patterns, have also played an important role. Wiessner (1977) has made a careful study of migration to and from /Xai/xai for the period 1964–74 (Table 12.3). Using a slightly different base population from my own, Wiessner found that during the 10-year period 15 percent of the population immigrated and 22 percent emigrated, but that only a third of the emigration and none of the immigration involved a Bantu or European work-related decision. (Wiessner excluded from her analysis temporary 1- to 3-year absences from /Xai/xai for work purposes.) From the available data, it is difficult to factor out what proportion of residential shifts over the last 50 years is strictly attributable to outside pressure and what proportion represents the normal group processes of foragers. My guess is that about half of the internal migration in recent years is accounted for by outside factors. Thus we can assume a considerably lower, but still significant, rate of migration for the pre-contact period.

Although the majority of people live in n!ores other than their natal ones, this is not to imply that ownership of n!ores is absent. Each n!ore contains a core of people with the longest time association. These people are generally accepted as owners, and it is they who are asked for permission to camp in an area. And the core group is by no means static. The ownership of the land passes from parent to child, but immigrants who come and stay for good are also gradually absorbed into the core. For example, at !Kangwa in LG 11/64 the members of the in-marrying sibling group of 40 years ago have become the n!ore k"ausi of today (see Chapter 3).

Table 12.3. *Migration to and from /Xai/xai*
(residents only): 1964–74

Base population: 1964		130
Additions: 1964–74		
Births	37	
Immigration		
For marriage	12	
For other reasons	7	
For Bantu work	0	
Total additions		56
Subtractions: 1964–74		
Deaths	21	
Emigration		
For marriage	9	
For other reasons	9	
For Bantu work	10	
Total subtractions		49
Net population: 1974		137

Source: Data from Wiessner (1977).

NAMED GROUPS

Although the n!ore-owning groups are a prime focus of social identity today, there is evidence that a rather different system of local organization may have prevailed in the last century. The remnants of a system of named, semilocalized groups among modern !Kung offer some intriguing clues to how space may have been organized in the past. These named groups were neither strictly tied to locality nor strictly based on kinship, but combined elements of both principles in determining group membership. Little is known about the functioning of these groups or how they articulated with groupings based on n!ore ownership because none is functioning today. Their existence, however, is well established.

Except for some references to them in the early German reports on the !Kung (e.g., Passarge 1907), these groups are rarely mentioned in the ethnographic literature. The cover term applied to them by the !Kung is *!ku·si* (literally "names"). It is not clear what connection they had with !Kung personal names or with the important name relationship discussed by Lorna Marshall (1957, 1976). For want of a better term, I have called them the *named groups*.

Forty named groups have come to light, most of which are associated with particular localities in the Dobe, Nyae Nyae, /Gam, and /Du/da areas (Table 12.4).

Many groups are named after animals and plants: the Giraffes, the Elands, the N≠wara Roots, and the Ants. The names of others refer to outstanding cultural or physical attributes: the Big Talkers, the Fighters, the Short Feet, the Carrying Yokes.

In the old days named groups were exogamous (a Giraffe could not marry a Giraffe), but informants were very clear that members of a named group *could* marry into any group other than their own. Today, the exogamy provision has broken down; Giraffes marry Giraffes without restriction. I asked one middle-aged woman who had married a man of her own named group what the old people had said about the union. She replied that by the time she married, the old people who cared had already died off.

Of 151 !Kung men interviewed in 1967–9, 62 (41 percent) did not know what named groups they belonged to. Of the 89 men who did know their named groups, 49 percent inherited membership from their fathers, 37 percent from their mothers, and 14 percent from other kin such as an older namesake.

Named groups were semilocalized, but marriage out and the option of inheriting membership from father *or* mother tended to disperse the members of the group. For example, the members of the Carrying Yokes, originally from ≠To//gama, were found to be living at !Kubi, Dobe, /Xai/xai, Mahopa, and Chum!kwe during the 1960s. There is no indication that the named groups were originally based on a unilineal principle of inheritance.

Today the named groups are a fading memory. Of the 40 groups known, only 3 continue to have large memberships: The Giraffes from Nyae Nyae, the Carrying Yokes from ≠To//gana, and the Duikers from /Xai/xai each has over 30 male and female members. About 30 other groups claim from 1 to 10 members among the men and women of the Dobe area, and the remaining groups with no living representatives are known by name only. Locality designations have replaced named groups as the main means of fixing peoples' social identity in space. When I asked informants what their named groups were, many replied, "I am a ≠Gi k"xau" ("an owner of ≠Gi") or "I am a Gam k"xau" ("an owner of Gam") or some other locality, and they insisted that that was the only "name" they were known by. In the past, named groups probably operated in much the same way that n!ore ownership groups operate today, with one significant difference: The named groups were exogamous, whereas n!ore groups are not strictly so. In other respects–inheritance of land, lack of territoriality, reciprocal access to resources, and visiting patterns–the named groups of the past seem very similar to the n!ore groups of today. Their existence, however, points to a time in !Kung history when the living groups were of a more corporate nature than are the living groups observed by ethnographers in the 1950s and 1960s.

Table 12.4. *!Kung named groups*

Region, group	No. of male members[a]
!Kangwa Valley	
1. The Owners (n//ok"xausi)	0
|Xai|Xai	
2. The Duikers (/tausi)	13
3. (≠daba≠hxasi)[b]	1
|Gam–≠To||gana (south of |Xai|xai)	
4. The Bitter Melons (dchasi)	0
5. The Rhinos (/tisi)	3
6. The Carrying Yokes (//wanasi)	15
!Gwidum–!Xwa area (west of !Kangwa)	
7. The Big Talkers (n/omsi)	4
8. The Pebbly Roots (/tansi)	2
9. The Long Roots (n≠warasi)	1
10. The Baobabs (≠msi)	1
Nyae Nyae (Marshall area)	
11. The Edible Gums (gumsi)	2
12. The Fighters (n!aiesi)	4
13. The Cold Ones (tsisi)	0
14. The Giraffes (≠dwasi)	16
15. The Ant bears (!xunsi)	1
|Du|da area (south of |Xai|Xai)	
16. The Short Feet (/xai!koasi)	3
Peripheral west	
17. The Scorpions (≠xaisi)	2
18. (tsanosi)[b]	1
19. (n!abak"xausi)[b]	1
Peripheral north	
20. The Elephants (!xosi)	2
21. The Dirty Fighters (!gasi)	0
Peripheral east	
None	
Peripheral south	
22. The Ants (n/on/onisi)	0
23. The Wild Cats (n/wasi)	2
24. The Elands (n!nsi)	1
25. The Lice (/desi)	0
26. (nauk"xausi)[b]	1
27. (≠takabesi)[b]	2

Table 12.4. (*cont.*)

Region, group	No. of male members[a]
Other groups not centered in one region	
28. The Medicine Roots (!gwasi)	2
29. The Steenboks (/tonsi)	5
30. The Gemsboks (!gwesi)	0
31. The Jackals (/tedisi)	1
32. The Springhares (n/umsi)	3
Other named groups mentioned	
33. The Impalas (kxarasi)	0
34. The Cutters (/tumsi)	0
35. The Kori Bustards (!gwisi)	0
36. The Diarrheas (//gomsi)	0
37. The Kaross Knots (!gosi)	0
38. The Penises (tahsi)	0
39. The Tortoises (zimsi)	0
(n≠tobosi)[b]	0
40. The Owners of Due (Due k"xausi)	0

[a]Of the 151 Dobe area men interviewed, 89 knew to which named group they belonged. The right-hand column shows the membership of each. Women shared equally in membership with men, but data on women were not statistically compiled.
[b]Meaning unknown.

LEADERSHIP

How group and individual decisions are made in a society without formal political or judicial institutions is difficult to discern. In egalitarian societies such as the !Kung's, group activities unfold, plans are made, and decisions are arrived at – all apparently without a clear focus of authority or influence. Closer examination, however, reveals that patterns of leadership do exist. When a water hole is mentioned, a group living there is often referred to by the !Kung by a single man's or woman's name: for example, Bon!a's camp at !Kangwa or Kxarun!a's camp at Bate. These individuals are often older people who have lived there the longest or who have married into the owner group, and who have some personal qualities worthy of note as a speaker, an arguer, a ritual specialist, or a hunter. In group discussions these people may speak out more than others, may be deferred to by others, and one gets the feeling that their opinions hold a bit more weight than the opinions of other discussants. Whatever their skills, !Kung leaders have no formal authority. They can only persuade, but never enforce their will on others. Even the !Kung vocabulary of leadership is limited. Their word for "chief," *//kaiha,* derived from the word *//kai* ("wealth"), is applied to Bantu headmen and chiefs, and even to English kings and queens; but only rarely do the !Kung use it of other !Kung and then usually in a derisory manner. One /Xai/xai man [336] nicknamed //Kaihan!a ("Big Chief") told us it was a joking name because when he was young he tended to put on airs; people called him Big Chief to take him down a peg.

The suffix *-n!a* ("old" or "big") is added to any person's name after age 40. When one person of a camp is singled out as *n!a* from other agemates, it usually means that he or she is the leader of the camp. Marshall (1976:191) called the camp leader the *k"xaun!a* ("big owner").

Paths to leadership

Analyzing the attributes of the acknowledged leaders of the living groups of the Dobe area, one finds a wide variety of skills, backgrounds, and genealogical positions. Some people are powerful speakers; others say very little. Some leaders are genealogically central; others are outsiders who married core women. Some have many children and grandchildren in the living group; others have few or no offspring. The majority of leaders are men, but women as well take leadership roles. At least four attributes can lead to leadership: (1) seniority in a large family, (2) n!ore ownership, (3) marriage to a n!ore owner, and (4) personal qualities. Most leaders have several of these in varying degrees.

Seniority. Being the oldest member or surviving member of a sibling group puts a person in a position of respect within the family; and if the family is large enough, the entire camp may be made up of that person's descendants, his siblings' descendants, and their spouses. Seniority alone, however, does not make a leader; many of the oldest people do not take leadership roles.

N!ore ownership. This is an important criterion; if a person is the senior descendant of a long line of n!ore owners, his claim to leadership is very strong. For example, Sa//gain!a [396] of /Xai/xai (d. 1971), quoted above, was a descendant of several generations of /Xai/xai owners, and though she was a soft-spoken person she was the acknowledged leader of her camp, a position shared with her husband. Her niece Baun!a (d. 1966) had equal claim to n!ore ownership, but as she was a strong, forceful woman as well she was doubly a leader of her /Xai/xai group. Her son Tsau later became the chief spokesperson for the /Xai/xai San in their relations with the Blacks (see below, under "!Kung leadership in the Contact Setting").

Marriage to a n!ore owner. This is the most common route to leadership positions among the !Kung. It always involves the marriage of an energetic, capable man from another water hole to a woman of the n!ore-owning group. The best example of this kind of leader is ≠Toman!wa, one of Lorna Marshall's main informants at /Gausha (Marshall 1960, 1976). He married !U, a woman of the n!ore-owning sibling group, and became the leader of the /Gausha camp, while !U's older brother Gao went to live in the Dobe area. ≠Toma is known to students of anthropology as the senior of the four giraffe hunters in John Marshall's classic film *The Hunters* (1956). Another example of a leader who married in is ≠Toma//gwe at Dobe. He married //Koka of the n!ore-owning group and settled at Dobe to raise a family that by the 1970s had grown to consist of a group of four married children and their spouses and eight grandchildren. ≠Toma//gwe is considered gruff and unreasonable by other !Kung, but his large family plus his connection to the owner group validates his leadership role. It is significant that though ≠Toma//gwe regards himself as an owner of /Gam, 70 km to the south, his children and grandchildren are now generally recognized as owners of Dobe, having inherited that n!ore from their mother //Koka. (Parenthetically, //Koka herself was an immigrant, having come to Dobe with her parents and siblings when she was a young child.)

Personal qualities. Some leaders, like ≠Toman!wa of /Gausha, have obvious leadership qualities, being excellent speakers and diplomatic mediators. Others, like ≠Toma//gwe, are gruff and unreasonable but have strong personalities. ≠Toma Leopard, the young leader of LG 24/68 at /Xai/xai, is charming, but also short-tempered, feisty, and fiercely independent; Kxarun!a of Bate and Sa//gain!a of /Xai/xai are mellow, grandmotherly, and soft-spoken. No single personality type or personality trait dominates the ranks of leaders. If anything, the leaders share *an absence of traits in common.* None is arrogant, overbearing, boastful, or aloof. In !Kung terms these traits absolutely disqualify a person as a leader and may engender even stronger forms of ostracism (see Chapter 13).

Another trait emphatically not found among traditional camp leaders is a desire for wealth or acquisitiveness. The leaders of the 15 or so living groups not closely tied to black cattle posts live in huts no larger and dress in clothing and ornaments no more lavish than those of the other camp members. Whatever their extravagances in speech, their personal style of living is modest and their accumulation of material goods is minimal. Whatever their personal influence over group decisions, they never translate this into more wealth or more leisure time than other group members have. !Kung leaders therefore adhere closely to the image of the "egalitarian redistributor" noted by Harris (1975:289) or the

modest band leader noted by Fried (1967:82ff.) as characteristic of egalitarian societies. A similar profile for leadership among the Australian
aborigines has been presented by Dawson (1973).

San headmen?

The existence of hereditary headmen or chiefs among the San has been a
matter of dispute. Long ago, Fourie wrote:

> At the head of each group is a big man or chief. Though usually
> considered to be a chief in name only and without any authority
> over the members of the group, he in fact does exercise consider-
> able influence in the life of the community because in him are
> vested certain functions, the performance of which are of vital im-
> portance to the welfare of his people. The family area with its food
> and water supply as well as the fire are all looked upon as belonging
> to him. Among the tribes of the Kalahari he is succeeded by a son or
> failing such, by the nearest male relative. [Fourie 1928:86]

Lorna Marshall in her early writings (1960:344–52) also spoke of a
hereditary headman in whom resided the ownership of the group's resources and who inherited his position patrilineally, a view Fried has
questioned (1967:87–9). Marshall has subsequently altered her views
and has recently (1976:191) stated that " 'headman' was a misleading
and unfortunate paraphrase" for *k"xaun!a,* meaning "big owner." Her
revised thinking on the subject of headman brings the data on the Nyae
Nyae !Kung into line with the data from the Dobe area; in the latter case
it is clear that the institution of the headman was absent among the
pre-contact !Kung. Further, there is good evidence that the concept of
headman came into currency only *after* the arrival of the blacks.

After reading Marshall's 1960 article and the earlier writings of others,
I made widespread inquiries in the Dobe area in 1964 to find out who
was the headman or chief (*//kaiha*) at each water hole. The answers
people gave were almost entirely negative. The younger people did not
know who, if anyone, was the headman, and the older people were obviously puzzled by the question. Some people offered a variety of names,
but most answered that the only headman they knew of was Isak, the
Motswana headman. Finally I discussed the question with K"au [336], a
senior /Xai/xai man originally from /Gam. "Before the Tswana came
here," I asked, "did the San have chiefs?"

"No," he replied. "We had no one we set apart like a chief; we all lived
on the land."

"What about /Gaun!a? Was he a chief of /Xai/xai?" I asked, citing the
name of a man the Herero had mentioned as a former San headman.

"That is not true," K"au responded. "They are mistaken. Because
among the blacks the chief's village is fixed; you come to him, speak, and

Plate 12.2. The public life phase of the annual cycle: 150 !Kung may meet daily at the /Xai/xai water hole.

go away. Others come, speak, and go. But with us San, we are here today, tomorrow over there, and the next day still elsewhere. How can we have a chief leading a life like that?"

"If San have no chiefs," I asked, "then how did /Gaun!a come to be labeled as the chief here?"

"I can tell you that. /Gaun!a was living at /Twihaba east of /Xai/xai when the Bantu came. They saw evidence of his many old campsites and so they called him '//kaiha.' But they named him something that no !Kung person recognizes."

"But even that is lies," the old man continued, "because /Gaun!a was not even the real owner of /Twihaba! His proper n!ore is N!umtsa, east of /Gam. /Twihaba properly belongs to the people of a ≠Toma whose descendants now live mostly in the east."

Other !Kung informants corroborated K"au's statements about the absence of headmen among themselves, but the most striking confirmation of the point came from a conversation with another K"au, a short, lively Dobe resident nicknamed Kasupe by the Herero, who had originally come

from the Nyae Nyae area. In her detailed discussion of the headman
Marshall (1960:344–52) had used the /Gausha water hole as a prime
example. The leader of her /Gausha band 1 was ≠Toman!wa, discussed
above, who had married into the core group. But the "headman" at /Gau-
sha was not ≠Toma, but his wife's younger brother, a crippled man
named Lame ≠Gao. The real headman, however, should have been one
Gao who, according to Marshall, "chose to renounce his headmanship
and to live with his wife's people in Band 21 . . . However, should Gao
change his plan and return to Band 1, the headmanship would automatically fall on him again, as he is the eldest son" (1960:350).

Marshall's Gao turned out to be none other than K"au-Kasupe living at
Dobe. When I asked him how it felt to be the absent headman of /Gausha,
he expressed surprise, shock, disbelief, and then laughter. With a keen
sense of the irony of the situation, Kasupe insisted that he was in no way
the headman of /Gausha; that his shrimp of a kid brother, Lame ≠Gao,
certainly was not the headman; that the !Kung did not even have headmen. If they did, he, Kasupe, would be the headman of //Karu, not /Gau-
sha, because the latter was his father's true n!ore. Finally, asked Kasupe,
if he was such a headman how did it happen that he, the boss, was living
in rags at Dobe, while underlings like his brother and sisters were living
in luxury at the South African settlement at Chum!kwe?

Kasupe's genuine surprise at being named the headman of /Gausha,
along with the abundant corroborating evidence from other informants,
convinced me that indeed the !Kung have no headmen. Years later,
speaking with /Twi!gum, one of the owners of !Kangwa, I casually asked
him whether the !Kung have headmen.

"Of course we have headmen!" he replied, to my surprise. "In fact, we
are all headmen," he continued slyly, "each one of us is headman over
himself!"

!KUNG LEADERSHIP IN A CONTACT SETTING

Given the conflicting nature of the evidence on the headman question,
we may legitimately ask how the idea of !Kung headmanship came into
being. The answer must be sought in the contacts of the !Kung with
blacks and Europeans over the last 80 years. The Tswana were a hierarchically organized, expanding people who brought under their rule a
number of tribally based societies in Western and Northern Botswana.
By the time they reached the Dobe area in the 1890s, the Tswana had
already become part of the British colonial protectorate of Bechuanaland
(Sillery 1952, 1965). Like the British, the Tswana employed a system that
combined elements of direct and indirect rule. Around the turn of the
century the Tswana Kubu and Mhapa clans were given stewardship of
the Dobe area by the Tawana paramount chief (Chapter 3), but because

the area was vast and their numbers were few they tried to recruit local !Kung to be spokespersons for the San camps at the various water holes. Later when they moved their cattle to /Xai/xai, /Gam, and !Kangwa, they put local !Kung men in charge of the livestock. Gradually a system of leaders came into being who were recognized as //kaihas by the Tswana but who had no equivalent standing among the !Kung themselves.

This contradiction between what we might call "inside" leaders and "outside" leaders continues to the present day. Inside leaders achieve their status by being n!ore owners or spouses of n!ore owners in combination with personal qualities of leadership. The outside leaders excel in their ability to deal with blacks and Europeans and in their entrepreneurial skills. Rarely are the two kinds of attributes combined in a single person. For example, at Dobe in 1973 there were two camps: the ≠Toma//gwe group (LG 1/73) which had lived there for many years, and a group led by !Xoma (LG 2/73), a vigorous and able man who had worked for blacks and Europeans for many years but who had little claim to the ownership of Dobe. !Xoma, because of his knowledge of and sensitivity to the outside world, was highly regarded by government people, anthropologists, and missionaries (see Chapter 14), but Polly Wiessner reported that whenever the outsiders were absent, !Xoma's !Kung neighbors would express a great deal of resentment toward him.

This hostility came to a head in the mid-1970s over a government-sponsored project to dig a well at Dobe to improve and stabilize the water supply and make stock raising possible for the Dobe residents. When it came time to register the well in a leader's name, the outside agents favored !Xoma, who was fluent in Tswana and who could make a highly articulate case for the !Kung before the District Council's Land Board in Maun. To the dismay of the outsiders, the Dobe !Kung chose as their leader a quiet and unaggressive man named ≠Dau, whose main claim to the role was the fact that he was the descendant of ≠Dauhwanadum ("≠Dau licks the molapo"), the senior owner of Dobe before //Kokan!a and ≠Toma//gwe moved in. At the long and contentious meetings held to discuss the issue of the well, ≠Dau sat quietly to one side listening and only rarely interjected a comment. Marjorie Shostak, who attended these meetings, felt that !Xoma would have been the ideal representative for the !Kung at the land board hearings, whereas ≠Dau seemed totally out of his element in such a setting. The fact that the Dobe people chose the latter man in preference to the former indicates that they were not yet fully aware of the threats to the security of their land and thus were not able to mobilize fully against it. Polly Wiessner pointed out that at the Chum!kwe settlement across the border ≠Toman!wa (the /Gausha leader) was initially elected as the "foreman" to represent the !Kung in their dealings with the South African authorities, but he was defeated at the next election, a fate that has befallen many of his successors as well.

In only a few cases have the traits of the outside leader and the traditional inside leader been combined in a single person. One example is Tsau at /Xai/xai. A tall and forceful man in his late thirties, Tsau was the son of the late Baun!a, a member of the n!ore-owning group, and therefore regarded as an owner himself. In addition, Tsau spoke Tswana and Herero fluently and displayed considerable skill as a negotiator and mediator. During the late 1960s Tsau became the spokesman for the /Xai/ xai San. Whenever a dispute broke out between the San and the Herero (as frequently happened), Tsau was called in to act as the defender of San interests in the matter. He assembled around him several other men, leaders of different groups, and they constituted an informal bargaining committee with the Herero, the Tswana, and the resident anthropologists. Because his kin ties to past n!ore owners gave Tsau a strong claim to legitimacy, he did not elicit from his own people the same degree of hostility and criticism that other !Kung leaders suffered when they tried to deal with outsiders. But the task he had undertaken was not without stress. When Tsau appeared to concede a point to the Herero in some delicate negotiation, some !Kung would grumble that he was selling them out and that he was becoming more of a black man than a bushman. After a few years in the role of informal headman, Tsau became discouraged by the pressure and took his family away to Chum!kwe, where he put his son in primary school, one of the first /Xai/xai children to attend.

The changing patterns of leadership reveal the existence of two contradictory systems of politics among the San. The old system based on genealogy and n!ore ownership favored a leader who was modest in demeanor, generous to a fault, and egalitarian, and whose legitimacy arose from long-standing n!ore ownership. The new system required a man who had to deny most of the old virtues. The political arena of district councils, land boards, and nationalist politics required someone who was male, aggressive, articulate, and wise in the ways of the wider world. As antithetical as these characteristics are to !Kung traditional values, the dynamics of the San's rapid incorporation into the national capitalist system of Botswana make it inevitable that these new leaders will have to come to the fore (see Chapter 14).

FLEXIBILITY IN SPATIAL ORGANIZATION

In moving through the annual round, the !Kung local groups satisfy their subsistence requirements with surprisingly little friction with neighboring groups. We have seen that subsistence space is bounded, but these boundaries are vague and not defended. N!ore-owning groups make ample provision for visitors to exploit the resources of their land, and they expect the same courtesies when they pay reciprocal visits to their neighbors. A common pattern is for groups from two or more water holes to join forces for the joint exploitation of a major resource such as tsin beans or mongongo nuts. During the winter dry season it is common to find from two to six different groups camping together at a permanent water hole.

How do we account for the flexibility of !Kung group structure and the fluidity of land use? Starting from the patrilocal band model of hunter-gatherer social organization (see Chapter 3), some anthropologists have viewed the flexible arrangements of contemporary hunters as a product of the breakdown of preexisting groups after contact with outsiders. El-man Service, for example, has postulated a patrilocal band organization of territorial, male-centered local groups as the major organization for all hunting peoples, an organization that gives way to more flexible groupings when the hunters suffer depopulation and political takeovers in the colonial period (see Service 1962, 1966, 1971; Williams 1968; Birdsell 1970; and the counter views in Lee and DeVore 1968; Damas 1969a; Guemple 1972). The !Kung at first glance seem to be a good example of Service's hypothesis: Their land use is flexible and they have been in close contact with black and European outsiders for over 50 years (Chapter 3). But, as we shall see, the patrilocal model leaves a great deal unexplained.

An alternative view of hunter-gatherer organization questions the universality of the patrilocal band model. This view considers that flexibility itself is a primary organizational principle and that the flexible arrangements of today would have been no less adaptive for the pre-contact hunter-gatherers. For example, it can be argued that the !Kung's flexibility is in large part a response to long-term environmental conditions in the Kalahari and not simply a response to recent acculturation.

Pursuing this line of inquiry may enable us to see !Kung organization in a new light. Instead of evaluating hunters by the degree to which they do or do not conform to an ideal model of patrilocal bands, we should consider the possibility that they are organized on an entirely different dynamic based on a different set of structural principles.

Two important features of the Kalahari environment stand out in any consideration of the effect of environment on the structuring of space by the !Kung. The first is the high variability in rainfall: within the year, from year to year, and from place to place within the same rainy season. The second feature is the sparse distribution of standing water in the central !Kung interior, with only a few dozen permanent water points in an area some 27,000 km², the size of Southern New England (Massachusetts, Connecticut, and Rhode Island). Let us consider each of these features in turn.

Rainfall variability

The Northern Kalahari, in common with all the drier areas of Africa, experiences a sharp alternation between the wet and the dry seasons of the year. Between 90 and 100 percent of all the rainfall occurs in the 6-month period from November to April; the other 6 months of the year are almost totally dry. This fundamental fact of existence alone strongly influences !Kung subsistence strategy. But there are other kinds of rainfall variability as well, such as year-to-year variations.

As discussed in Chapter 4, average annual rainfall has little meaning in an environment in which rainfall may vary from year to year by as much as 500 percent. During the 1963–4 rainy season, we recorded 239 mm (9.4 in.) at Dobe and in 1967–8, 597 mm (23.5 in.) were recorded; almost twice that amount fell in 1973–4. Given this variability, it makes sense to consider the extremes of rainfall rather than the averages – for example, to tabulate the number of years out of 10 in which drought is experienced. Figure 4.7 and Table 4.7 in Chapter 4 present these data; drought appears to occur in 2 years of every 5 and severe drought in about 1 year of every 4. The work of Brown (1974:136) and Wellington (1964:42–3) on drought probability shows that in the Northern Kalahari drought conditions can be expected to occur in 3 or 4 years in each decade.

A third source of variability mentioned in Chapter 4 is the difference in rainfall from place to place in a single month or season. In the critical early months of the rainy season (October to December) the rainfall can vary from place to place by as much as a factor of 10 (Table 4.8), causing the desert to bloom in one area while only a few hours' walk away the land is still dry and parched.

To such variable conditions the spatial organization of the !Kung must adapt, and the existence of this variability is a powerful argument against territoriality. For example, it would be sheer folly for the members of one group to stake out an exclusive claim to an area, for if the rain during critical periods was likely to miss it completely every few years, their carefully guarded ground would be quite useless to them. (However, see Heinz 1972 and Barnard 1978 for an opposing view.) Instead, the !Kung have devised a *long-term solution* to the problem of variability, though the ethnographer will observe only a small segment of the pattern in any given year of fieldwork. As we shall see, the !Kung are by no means unique among foragers in hitting upon this solution.

Water source scarcity

Consider now the second salient environmental feature: the distribution of water points in space. The sparse distribution of water on the ground is the spatial correlate of the temporal variability just discussed. Because of

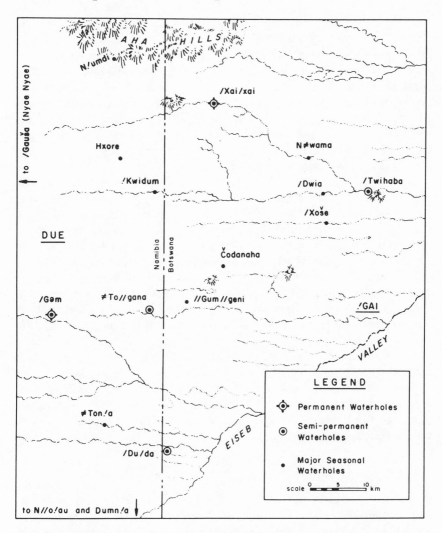

Figure 12.1. Distribution of water sources in the /Xai/xai–/Gam area.

the porosity of the sandy soils, the high rate of evaporation, and the infrequency of exposures of water-bearing rock, standing water points are few and far between. Figure 12.1 shows an area of the central !Kung interior south of the Aha Hills and north of Eiseb Valley. This includes the southern half of the Dobe area and parts of the Nyae Nyae and /Du/da areas on the west and south, respectively. The area straddles the international border and measures about 80 by 80 km for a total area of 6400 km^2 (2500 square miles). This entire area contains only five permanent water points (i.e., water holes that hold water throughout the year), and of these three have been known to fail within living memory.

In fact, the area contains a hierarchy of water sources arranged in order of their duration and reliability: (1) two have never given out in living memory (/Xai/xai and /Gam); (2) three have not failed in the last 5 years (/Twihaba, ≠To//gana, and /Du/da); (3) five (at least) are strong summer waters that may last through the winter of good years (/Dwia, N≠wama, Hxore, !Kwidum, and //Gum//geni); (4) about 50 are seasonal water points holding water from a few days to several months; (5) about 100 are mongongo, baobab, and *Terminalia* trees with small reservoirs in their hollow boles; (6) about 150 are sites in which the water-bearing root !xwa (*Fockea monroi*) is found.

In general, the lower a water source is in the hierarchy, the less efficient it is in satisfying the !Kung's moisture requirements. Tree water (class 5) is usually difficult of access and often must be soaked up in a makeshift sponge or sucked out in a reed straw. (Sip wells are known to the !Kung but rarely utilized.) Water roots (class 6) are even more difficult to get at, as the root itself must be dug from depths of up to 40 cm (15 in.) and the contents of as many as 20 roots must be consumed per day to satisfy the needs of one person (Lee 1965:172ff.). On the other hand, root and tree waters are widely distributed in close proximity to valuable food sources and therefore are often utilized despite their difficulty of access.

The !Kung's ability to operate successfully in this environment involves them in sorting out a complex set of variables about the current locations of food and water, the ease or difficulty of getting them, and the whereabouts and current activities of adjacent groups. And their subsistence plans must be continually revised in light of the rainfall situation through the growing season and beyond.

!KUNG SPATIAL ORGANIZATION

Given the ecological conditions, what land use pattern has emerged? Today (1963–79), international politics and pastoral occupation have restructured land use in non-hunter-gatherer ways. The current situation and how it evolved are interesting subjects in their own right and are discussed below. In order to understand the hunting and gathering pattern, we have to reconstruct a picture of the distribution of landholding groups as they were during the 1920s, before the black settlement.

In Figure 12.2 are plotted the landholding groups of the /Gam–/Xai/xai area 50 to 60 years ago. Each group's number is located on the map in the vicinity of the largest water hole each group's area contains. Clearly, there were many more groups holding land than there were permanent water holes to support them: 11 groups regularly wintered in the area, with occasional visits from at least 5 other groups; yet there were only five permanent water holes and of these only two were really reliable.

Plate 12.3. A late summer camp of 25 south of /Xai/xai.

And 11 is the minimum number that operated in this area. There may have been more groups, especially in /Gam. The members of these groups have moved entirely out of the area to the Ghanzi and Gobabis white farms or to the Tswana and Herero cattle posts around Lake Ngami. Further, this presentation does not take into account groups that have moved into the study area since 1930, such as the group from /Gausha that moved to /Xai/xai in the 1940s and groups from the Ghanzi farms who were moving into the /Du/da area in the late 1960s.

Such a large number of groups could be supported only if there were widespread agreement to maintain regular and free access to permanent water. The orderly, rather evenly spaced arrangement of groups in Figure 12.2 is characteristic only of the height of the rainy season when water and food are available throughout the area. As the summer waters evaporate with the coming of the winter, the 11 groups would converge to the pattern plotted in Figure 12.3 and summarized in Table 12.5 (column headed "winter").

Unless water was exceptionally strong, groups 2 and 4 would join group 3 at /Twihaba, and later in the season most or all of the people would pay a visit to group 1 at /Xai/xai. At the same time, groups 5, 6, and 7 would converge on ≠To//gana, while groups 8, 9, and 10 would converge on /Gam. Group 11 stayed around /Du/da, where it was joined by one or two groups from N//o!au and Dumn!a (see Table 12.5, foot-

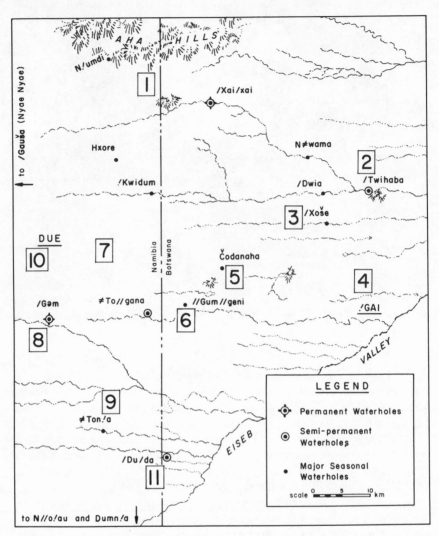

Figure 12.2. A reconstruction of the distribution of landholding groups in the /Xai/xai–/Gam area: 1920–30.

note). Later in the season, it was customary for groups at /Du/da and ≠To//gana to pay visits to relatives at /Gam.

In good years, groups had the option of wintering in any of several places: in the home area, at a permanent water hole, or visiting relatives at water holes outside the area. Also, the members of the groups that were primarily associated with one of the two very reliable water holes (group 1 at /Xai/xai and group 8 at /Gam) could spend most of their year enjoying the seasonal food resources of their neighbors. Reciprocal ac-

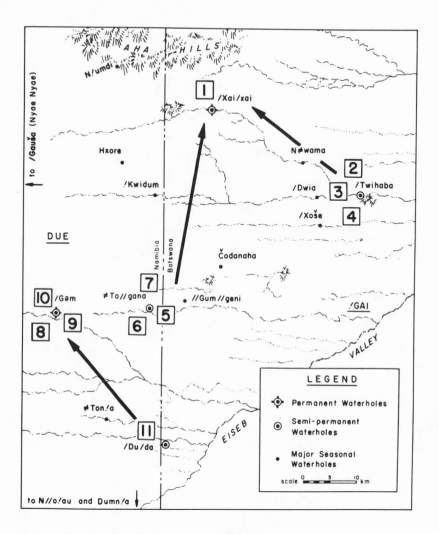

Figure 12.3. Patterns of convergence of landholding groups during the dry season and in drought years: 1920–30.

cess to resources at all times ensured that key resources would be available at critical periods.

In moderate winter dry season conditions, the 11 groups distributed themselves at five water points. Under very severe conditions, the groups underwent another phase of convergence (see Table 12.5, column headed "extreme dry recourse"). Four groups fell back on /Xai/xai, four others on /Gam, and three others alternated between /Gam and /Xai/xai. Thus in the most difficult drought years there might be as many as seven

Table 12.5. *Reconstructed living groups of the /Xai/xai and /Gam areas: ca. 1920–30"*

Group no.	Informant no.	Location during year — Summer	Location during year — Winter	Location during year — Extreme dry recourse	Current status	Living group no. — 1964	Living group no. — 1968
1	396	N!umdi	/Xai/xai	/Xai/xai	Sa//gain!a's group at /Xai/xai	31	29
2	346	Twihaba	Twihaba and /Xai/xai	/Xai/xai	No longer functioning; descendants at /Xai/xai	29	26
3	414	/Dwia	Twihaba and /Xai/xai	/Xai/xai	Ti!kai's group at /Xai/xai	32	30
4	429	!Kai	Twihaba and /Xai/xai	/Xai/xai	No longer functioning; descendants at /Xai/xai	33	31
5	335	Chodanaha	≠To//gana	/Gam or /Xai/xai	Still utilize n!ore part of the year; winter at /Xai/xai	27	25
6	543	//Gum//gemi	≠To//gana	/Gam or /Xai/xai	A few families still utilize n!ore; winter at /Xai/xai or /Du/da	[b]	26
7	363	North of ≠To//gana	≠To//gana	/Gam or /Xai/xai	No longer functioning; descendants at /Xai/xai	30	26
8	336	Around /Gam	/Gam	/Gam	No longer functioning; descendants at /Xai/xai	28	26
9	580	Due or ≠Ton!a	/Gam	/Gam	A functioning group now based at /Du/da	[c]	[c]
10	636?	Due	/Gam	/Gam	Moved to South African government settlement at Chum!kwe	[b]	[b]
11	684	/Du/da	/Du/da	/Gam	A functioning group based at /Du/da	[c]	[c]

[a] Several additional groups moved into this area from the west and south during the summer and may have opted to winter at /Gam and/or /Xai/xai during extremely dry years (e.g., Marshall's bands 1 and 2 from /Gausha, band 15 from Dum!a, and band 17 from N//o!kau) (Marshall 1960, 1976:156–9). Wilmsen (1976) has pointed out that another /Xai/xai-based group, alternating between /Xai/xai and !Kubi in recent years, was using the southern Aha Hills in earlier generations.

[b] Not in area in 1964.

[c] Southern marginal from /Du/da population.

groups at a single water hole. Such a situation was observed by the Marshalls when seven groups converged on /Gam in the severe drought winter of 1952 (J. Marshall 1957:36).

Traditionally, water holes such as /Xai/xai and /Gam have played important roles as entrepôts in the economic and social lives of the !Kung. Even before the Bantu built their cattle posts there, /Xai/xai was a trading center where people from all points of the compass came to visit, dance, and do hxaro trading (and sometimes fight; see Chapter 13).

/Ti!kai [414] described the traditional role of /Xai/xai as follows:

> /Xai/xai has always been a meeting place for people even before the blacks came. People came from the North, from !Kangwa and !Goshe, and from the South from /Gam (and from the West from /Gausha), stayed here, did hxaro, drank n!o [a choice wild fruit], ate //"xa [mongongo nuts], and then went back.
>
> They asked Kan!o [one of the owners] for permission. They also asked ≠Toma!gain [father of 396].
>
> /Xai/xai was favored because the water was so big. Choma [men's initiation ceremony] was danced here, but the main reason to meet was hxaro trade.
>
> People came in all seasons of the year–summer, winter, and spring. But they particularly came in spring [!gaa, September–October] when the trees were in flower [before the onset of the rains]. When the summer pans dried out, they ate !xwa [the water-bearing root]. When the !xwa got thin they came into /Xai/xai. This was because some of the n!ores did not have year-round water.

A closely comparable land use pattern has been observed in the Nyae Nyae area as recently as 1952–3 by the Marshall expedition. In his little-read but extremely informative thesis, John Marshall (1957) discussed how the Nyae Nyae groups arranged themselves with reference to water first under "normal" and then under drought conditions. Of the latter, he wrote:

> In very dry years, more of the bands would be concentrated around /Gautscha, Deboragu, and perhaps Khumsa. I do not know for sure whether Khumsa is a permanent waterhole. I am sure that there is a permanent waterhole northeast of /Gautscha to which bands 8, 9, and 10 would shrink if a winter of desiccation was complete. The distribution of the interior bands in such a winter season that so utterly rejects all juicy things would probably be:
>
> Bands 1, 2, 3 at /Gautscha, the highest yielding waterhole in the area, therefore able to support the 85 people of these bands.
>
> Bands 4 and 5 might hold out at Deboragu and would be joined by band 6. Deboragu is a weak water. The 29 people of bands 4, 5, and

6 would probably be able to survive, however. One man told us, speaking with affection for Deboragu, that, though it may look dry, scratch and you will find water.

Band 11 might flee to S'amangaigai and so the people would endure. [J. Marshall 1957:32–3]

HUNTER-GATHERER COMPARISONS

The spatial organization of many hunting and gathering peoples is similar to that of the two !Kung cases cited. For example, a division of the Eskimo year into a large-group phase and a small-group phase was first formally described by Mauss (1904–5) and documented by many observers (Boas 1888; Rasmussen 1931; Spencer 1959; Balikci 1964; Damas 1969c; the last source is particularly useful). In the case of the central Eskimo, the time of maximum concentration was also in the winter, but the environmental determinant was the accessibility of good seal hunting rather than the availability of water. For other Eskimo groups, the maximal aggregation was associated with a variety of ecological strategies, as summarized by Damas (1969c:135–8).

Among the Australian aborigines, the flexible land use pattern was for a long time obscured in anthropological studies by a confusion of the patrilineal totemic group with the on-the-ground living group. The totemic group indeed controlled real estate exclusively, but only for occasional ritual purposes and not for day-to-day living (Hiatt 1962, 1965; Berndt 1970). For the latter, the group that hunted, gathered, and lived together was made up of members of a number of patriclans and exhibited a genealogical composition and an annual concentration-dispersion pattern similar to that of the !Kung. In Arnhem Land and Cape York, the significant ecological determinant appeared to be the annual flooding of the plain, which caused the people to congregate in larger groups on the seacoast (Thomson 1939:209) or on higher interior ground (White and Peterson 1969; Schrire 1972; see also Hiatt 1965:24–9). In desert Australia, the concentration-dispersion pattern has been known for many years. Particular attention has been paid to the maximal grouping in the form of the corroboree or ceremonial gathering (Spencer and Gillen 1899:271ff.). The ecological significance of this gathering has been pointed out by Meggitt (1962:54–5) and Strehlow (1947:65). Here, as among the San, the environmental determinant was seasonal differences in water availability.

Examples could be multiplied: concentration-dispersion patterns and reciprocal access to resources have been documented for sub-Arctic Indians (Leacock 1955, 1969; Helm 1965), Great Basin Indians (Steward 1938, 1955a), Pygmies (Turnbull 1965, 1968), and Northwest Coast Indians (Drucker 1955). What are central to all these cases are a pattern of concentration and dispersion, usually seasonal, and a set of rules and practices for allowing reciprocal access to or joint exploitation of key resources. The worldwide occurrence of this pattern of spatial organization in vastly different kinds of environments indicates the degree to which it is basic to the hunting and gathering adaptation.

The concentration-dispersion pattern with its flexibility of group structure and rules of reciprocal access reveals the underlying spatial dynamic of the foraging mode of production. Such a dynamic makes much more sense of the foragers' adaptation than does the patrilocal band model.

Several of the adaptive advantages of the flexible model can now be spelled out. In the case of the !Kung, we have seen, first, that reciprocal access to resources allowed a much higher population density than could be supported if every n!ore had to contain a permanent water source (Figure 12.3). Thus, in the /Xai/xai–/Gam area, we find 11 groups in occupation instead of 2. Second, the pattern contained a mechanism for responding to local imbalances in food resources. It had the capacity to adjust to conditions of scarcity and to conditions of exceptional abundance. Third, the pattern offered many social advantages, not the least of which was the separating of individuals and groups in conflict, thus keeping the threat of violence to a minimum (see Chapter 13). Leacock (1969:14) cited a similar set of advantages for the flexibility of Montagnais groupings.

By contrast, the patrilocal pattern of spatial organization that encapsulates a group of males with their spouses and offspring within a territory is far less adaptive. Indeed, it would be difficult to visualize how a patrilocal territorial organization could function in the San case. I would predict that such a society could survive only to the extent to which its members could slough off their patrilocality and territoriality and approximate the flexible model outlined above.

In view of these adaptive advantages, it hardly seems likely – as Service has argued – that this flexible land use pattern is strictly a product of acculturation brought about by the breakdown of aboriginal bands. Flexibility appears to be adaptive in both the pre-contact and the post-contact situation. In fact, we are now in a position to trace what actually has happened to change !Kung land use patterns over the last 80 years.

CONTACT AND SPATIAL ORGANIZATION: 1890 TO 1969

Chapter 3 discusses the history of !Kung–black contacts in detail. Briefly, Tswana penetration of the interior began in the 1880s and 1890s when pastoralists began coming out to the /Xai/xai–/Gam area from their towns in the East for annual hunting and grazing expeditions. At the end of each rainy season, the various hunting parties, along with several groups of San, would rendezvous for some weeks of hunting, dancing, and trading. In the trade, the !Kung gave furs, hides, honey, and ostrich eggshell beadwork; in return, they received tobacco, clay pots, iron implements, and European goods. When the trading was done, the oxen were inspanned and the Tswana drove their wagons back to the East for the winter. During this period of initial contact, an annual concentration point occurred at the encampment known as *koloi* ("ox wagon" or "oxwagon camp" in Setswana).

During the 1920s, permanent Bantu-speaking settlers began to move into the area, bringing herds of livestock and enlarging and deepening the water holes at /Gam and /Xai/xai. A nucleus of semisedentary !Kung began to develop at these two points, in a process that has been observed worldwide among hunter-gatherers, around what L.R. Hiatt has aptly called "the magnets" of attractiveness. Missions and government stations constituted the magnets in Australia; in the Northern Kalahari, black cattle posts were the magnets.

Prior to black settlement, the !Kung had spent most of the year moving around the n!ores and a few months camped at the permanent water. Since the arrival of the blacks, a reverse pattern has evolved. Today, many !Kung remain most of the year camped at /Xai/xai and spend only a few months moving around the n!ores. In fact, the point of major population concentration in recent years has usually coincided with the Christmas feast offered the !Kung by their black neighbors (Lee 1969b).

The effects of contact on spatial organization are shown in Figure 12.4 (and Table 12.5, last column). Acculturation has produced fragmentation and discontinuous utilization of n!ores. Four groups (2, 4, 7, and 8) have ceased to function as subsistence units, having become wholly attached to black cattle posts. Group 10–along with many others from the Nyae Nyae, outside our study area–has joined the South African government settlement in Chum!kwe. Four other groups (1, 3, 5, and 6) move in and out of /Xai/xai on hunting and gathering trips of varying length.

Even though these semisettled groups spend most of the year at /Xai/xai (or Chum!kwe), each tries to spend at least a month or two in the home n!ore. Unlike the Australians, the !Kung San do not maintain totemic sites within their home localities. Nevertheless, the ties to the n!ore are certainly based on sentiment as well as economic expediency; this emotional content is expressed in the following quotation from a young woman member of group 3 now living at /Xai/xai:

> [You see us here today but] you know we are not /Xai/xai people. Our true n!ore is at /Dwia and every day at this time of year [November] we all scan the eastern horizon for any sign of cloud or rain. We say to each other, "Has it hit the n!ore?" "Look, did that miss the n!ore?" And we think of the rich fields of berries spreading as far as the eye can see and the mongongo nuts densely littered on

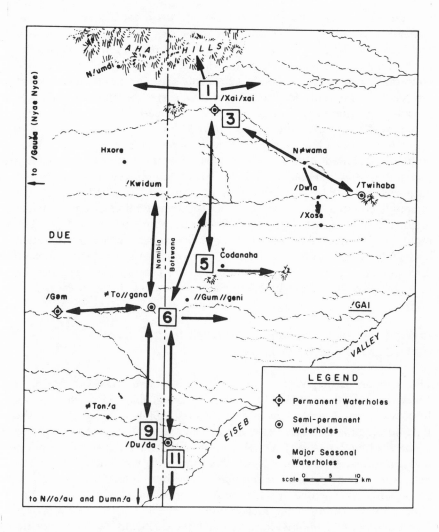

Figure 12.4. Land use patterns of active landholding groups: 1963–9.

the ground. We think of the meat that will soon be hanging thick from every branch. No, we are not of /Xai/xai. /Dwia is our earth. We just came here to drink the milk.

Only groups 9 and 11, from /Du/da, are using their n!ores in anything like the traditional manner. And in recent years, even these two groups have been affected. South African police patrols have ordered these groups to confine their camps and activities to within a close radius of the border so that they can be easily checked. (It was group 9 that moved up the border to eat the tsin beans of Hxore, as described earlier in this chapter, under "Principles of N!ore Use.") This order has produced two rather bizarre effects on spatial and social organization: (1) there is a highly unusual linear pattern of land use as the groups move up the border road from camp to camp and then down again, and (2) there are abnormally large groups of 90 to 120 people camping together at times of the year when one would expect them to be dispersed into much smaller groups. The !Kung say they are afraid to disperse for fear that the police patrols will go out after them (see Figure 12.4).

In short, contact has produced in !Kung land use a spectrum of effects including fragmentation and sedentarism in some groups and consolidation and increased mobility in others. The actual changes in land use can be accounted for by a combination of economic and political factors, although common to all situations is the introduction of an economic magnet and, along with it, an outside jural authority (Lee 1972c, e). The highly flexible spatial arrangements of today appear to be a continuation of flexible spatial arrangements of the pre-contact era. And these flexible arrangements, in turn, are adaptations to the perennial problems of the arid environment: recurrent drought and scarcity of surface water.

CONCENTRATION AND DISPERSION: A DIALECTIC OF
ORGANIZATION AND ECOLOGY

The division of the hunter-gatherer year into two phases – a period of concentration (the public life) and a period of dispersion (the private life) – was first described by Marcel Mauss (1904–5) in relation to the Eskimo. Such a division of the year appears to be characteristic not only of the Eskimo, but also of the !Kung San and most of the world's hunters and gatherers. I want to explore this pattern in more detail because I believe it will help us to understand better how ecological factors and social factors articulate in the foraging mode of production. For the !Kung, I will examine what factors brought people together, what factors kept them apart, and how these factors have shifted in response to recurrent ecological cycles and recent political developments.

As was true for the Eskimo described by Mauss, the nature of the ecology demanded flexibility in !Kung living arrangements. In drought years the large group (public life) phase had to be extended in time because water was available at only the few most reliable water holes. During years of higher rainfall the !Kung had a greater range of options: The minor water points might hold water through the winter and into the next rainy season. Thus people could live there throughout the year and remain more widely dispersed than in years of drought, thereby extending the private life phase.

What brought people together

Although the winter camp (public life) phase was dictated partly by the ecology, living together in large groups had many social benefits for the !Kung. This was the period of the year when social life was more intense, a period of large-scale trance dancing and curing, initiations, trading, storytelling, and marriage brokering.

The !Kung men's initiation camps (chomas) were held in winter every few years. The choma brought together the largest aggregations of !Kung. The reason for this is that at least seven boys of the correct age were needed to make the elaborate 6-week-long initiation program worthwhile, and a large number of local groups had to assemble to get together enough boys between the ages of 15 and 20. The families of the boys camped together and provided food for the initiation camp throughout the 6-week period. When very large groups of 20 or more boys were initiated together, the numbers in the adjacent camps must have been well over 200. In the five decades between 1910 and 1960, choma gatherings occurred somewhere in the central !Kung interior in 24 out of 50 years. For example, in the /Xai/xai-/Gam-≠To//gana areas, I recorded chomas as occurring in 1910, 1917, 1922, 1930, 1940, 1944, and 1950. In the !Kangwa Valley chomas were held in 1920, 1921, 1928, 1934, 1942, 1943, and 1960 (all dates approximate). In years when no choma was held in a local area, the initiates and their families would often travel 70 to 100 km to join chomas at distant points.

Even in the years when chomas were not formed, winter camps of 100 to 200 were common. The trance dancing and curing ceremonies brought together medicine men from far and wide. The curing medicine was thought to be especially effective when many performers entered trance at the same dance. As the big trance dances went on around the clock for 12 to 36 hours, subsistence had to be organized to provide support for the singers, dancers, and trance performers. This was difficult to do unless there were 50 or more adults in a camp, as to be effective the trance dance had to have 15 to 20 adults participating at any one time.

A third activity of the public life phase was hxaro trading. Hxaro is the term applied by the !Kung to their peculiar institution of long-distance exchange networks. Goods traveled for hundreds of kilometers across the Kalahari from one hxaro partner to another. Any individual had dozens of partners, many of whom he or she saw less than once a year. Fulfilling trading commitments and putting new goods into circulation were major activities at all !Kung camps, but especially at the large ones that brought together people who saw each other infrequently. The peculiarity of !Kung hxaro trading was the inordinate length of time separating the two parts of a transaction. Individual A gave B a trade item – such as a spear, arrow, or an eggshell-bead necklace – and A and B parted. Months or years later they came together again, and B gave A an item in return.

Hxaro trading is a traditional form of exchange among the San, but it has become particularly important as an avenue through which novel items of black and European manufacture have been disseminated into the interior of the Kalahari. Hxaro is the subject of a detailed study by Polly Wiessner (1977).

Marriage brokering was another of the activities bringing together large groups of San. Because of the small size of local groups and the frequent disparities in sex ratios, parents had to look far afield in arranging a marriage for their son or daughter. Rarely could an individual find a spouse from within the home group or adjacent groups. More frequently marriages brought together people from 40 to 80 km apart (Harpending 1976). The large winter camps gave families the opportunity of casting a wider net in seeking a spouse.

All these activities – religious, medical, economic, and marital – brought !Kung together and contributed to the intensity of social life. In general, the winter dry season was a period of higher social velocity, during which more time was spent interacting with large numbers of people. But life in large groups was not an unmixed blessing, and there were many occasions when water and food resources were abundant, but large groupings failed to materialize. The question can now be raised: Given the obvious advantages of larger grouping, why did the !Kung not spend more of their time together in one place?

What kept people apart

The major disadvantage of intense social life in larger groups is the increased frequency of conflict. Arguments and fights take place in !Kung camps of all sizes and at all seasons, but the larger camps seem particularly plagued with disputes (Chapter 13). For example, at /Xai/xai, a water hole with a large resident population (100 to 150), serious disputes broke out about once every 2 weeks during 1968–9. The comparable rate for water holes like Dobe and Mahopa, with resident populations averaging between 40 and 60, was three or four times a year. In the past, the choma initiation camps sometimes failed because of disputes on procedural matters. The big camps would split up, and the participants would disperse into smaller groupings in local areas.

Keeping very large groups together requires special efforts from individuals. They must maintain higher levels of cooperation and coordination of hunting and gathering activities than are necessary in smaller domestic groupings. For this reason, the largest aggregations of !Kung and of other hunters such as the Pygmies (Turnbull 1965, 1968) were inherently unstable; fights were likely to break out and lead to the breakup of the group.

The largest groupings the !Kung could muster thus had an inherent contradiction. People sought the stimulation of a more intense social life, but there was always the danger of serious conflict. The !Kung annual round was structured to allow both kinds of social life – the intensity of the public life, with its inherent dangers, and the domestic tranquility of smaller groupings in the private life.

The coalescing and splitting of hunter-gatherer local groups have often been considered as an adjustment to changing ecological conditions, and there is a great deal of validity to this view (Steward 1936, 1955a). Given the annual and regional variability in water and food supply, it is highly adaptive for !Kung to move frequently and to maintain flexibility in order to make the most effective use of their resources. But within the framework imposed by the ecology, conflict also plays a role in the rearrangement of groups. If people have a good enough reason for staying together – such as the performance of a ritual – they can do so, but only if they are prepared to work harder at it. Groups of over 100 people can be sustained for months, but only at the cost of an increasingly high input of subsistence effort per capita.

The problem of large groups and the added work involved in keeping them supplied with food offers an interesting tie-in between the objective material conditions of life and culture bearers' perceptions of those conditions (i.e., between the *etic* and the *emic* perspective). How are group size and work effort perceived and reacted to by individual members of the group? In a large gathering, an increasingly wide radius of food resources is eaten out with each succeeding week. Accordingly, the work effort required of individuals rises with each week. As work effort increases, the individual perceives his "costs" of staying together as increasing. He has to work harder than he did last week or accept a substandard diet or, if he slacks off, sustain the criticism of his fellows.

People get on each other's nerves, and as the situation tightens this leads to heightened irritability and a lowered threshold of conflict. As food becomes harder to provide, it becomes more important that everyone do his fair share of the work. In this atmosphere even small disagreements may erupt into conflict, and this conflict usually results in one or both parties splitting off to seek greener pastures. Hunters say "to hell with it." This is not to say that San argue only when food is scarce or when the group is large. They argue all the time about lots of things. What I am suggesting is that arguments in large, harder working groups are more likely to lead to a split than are arguments in smaller groups.

Unlike farming and city peoples, foragers have a great deal of latitude to vote with their feet, to walk out of an unpleasant situation. And they do so, not when their food supply is exhausted, but well before that point, when only their patience is exhausted.

Thus we see the dialectic between social and ecological factors, and between subjective and objective perceptions, that goes into the structuring of San collective life. The combination of seasonal ecology and the disruptive effects of conflict worked out so that in the traditional hunting and gathering society an average of approximately 3 months out of the year was spent in the larger groups of the public life and the other 9 months were spent in the smaller groups of the private life.

Contemporary society: Stabilizing the public life

Now let us consider how this state of affairs has been affected by recent contact of the !Kung with the outside world. When the Herero pastoralists set up their cattle posts at the large permanent water holes, the San built camps near the Herero and asked them for milk, tobacco, and trade goods. Gradually a pattern was established in which the Bushmen visited the cattle posts on a regular basis while continuing to depend on wild vegetable foods and game for the major part of their subsistence. As the herds of the Herero prospered, some !Kung families settled with the Herero to provide extra labor as cowboys and milkmaids. Their families acted as a conduit for funneling surplus milk to more isolated groups, so that all !Kung participated at least indirectly in the contact economy for periods varying from a few weeks each year to most of the year.

By the late 1960s, for example, at /Xai/xai there were 150 !Kung residents in seven camps, along with 70 Herero and over 500 head of cattle. This large semipermanent aggregation of San puzzled me. How could so many !Kung stay together in one place for so long? Then I realized that the San of /Xai/xai had achieved what amounted to a permanent public life situation. Instead of spending 9 months of the year dispersed and 3 months of the year together, they had reversed the ratio. Many !Kung lived at /Xai/xai for 9 months in the winter and spring and dispersed only for a short period at the height of the fresh food season in late summer and early fall.

How were they able to enjoy the public life situation without experiencing its disadvantages? Two reasons are involved. First, their overall subsistence was assisted by an input of Herero milk, meat, and agricultural produce, and this reduced the level of work effort by comparison with what would be required if the same size group were strictly dependent on wild foods. (Nevertheless, as noted in Chapter 10, the /Xai/xai !Kung, because of their higher degree of concentration, underwent a greater degree of nutritional stress during the January minimum than did the !Kung at other water holes.)

Without the Herero food, the /Xai/xai aggregation would not be possible (or possible only at the expense of unprecedented subsistence effort by the !Kung). But an additional element is also necessary: the legal umbrella provided by the Herero to maintain order among such a large number of feisty !Kung.

Arguments were common at /Xai/xai, but whenever a dispute came to blows or showed other signs of becoming nasty someone ran for the Herero. At this point one or more Herero intervened to separate the combatants and mediate the dispute. Formerly, the !Kung did their serious fighting with spears and poisoned arrows (Chapter 13). Now they can maintain an intensity of social life over long periods that would not have been possible under the traditional hunting and gathering conditions. Under the old order real conflict and the threat of conflict tended to work against the !Kung's desire for a more intense social life. It is the presence of the Herero as mediators, backed up by the legal sanctions of the Batawana Tribal Authority and, until 1966, by the British colonial administration, that provides the umbrella that enables 150 San to live together in relative harmony for the greater part of the year (see also Netting 1972). There is also evidence for the emergence of more formal leaders from among the !Kung themselves as a response to the contact situation (see earlier in this chapter, under "!Kung Leadership in the Contact Setting").

This example illustrates nicely how economic and demographic factors on the one hand and sociological factors on the other dovetail in the analysis. If the !Kung were more tightly organized, they could have maintained larger aggregations for longer periods. Instead, their relatively brief periods of intense social life were surrounded by much longer periods of relative isolation in small domestic groupings. The evidence of large gatherings being sustained in the face of quite unfavorable food situations demonstrated to me that the !Kung could live in larger groups if they wanted to. Put another way, their mean group size and intensity of land utilization were measurably lower than the levels that could be supported by the resources. The gap between what could be supported and what was observed as being supported can be explained by the avoidance of conflict situations.

The informal leadership, vague boundaries, and reciprocal access to resources worked well for the !Kung when the land was vast and the people were few. But with the transition to village life the old mechanisms have proved quite inadequate. The process of moving to a new mode of production involved the !Kung not only in changes in the economic base but also has necessitated the emergence of new kinds of political relations, new forms of leadership, and new methods of resolving disputes.

13

Conflict and violence

CHAPTER 12 documents the !Kung patterns of nonterritorial, collective use and ownership of land. Disputes involving land and resources are uncommon and rarely rise to violence. Therefore, one of the major causes to which human intergroup conflict is attributed is not present to any significant degree among the !Kung. Does this imply that the overall level of conflict among the !Kung is low and all forms of violence rare? Such a view of the !Kung has been presented by Elizabeth Marshall Thomas, (1959), whose popular book about them was entitled *The Harmless People*. A similar view was presented by Lorna Marshall, whose careful ethnographic studies have made such an important contribution to knowledge of the !Kung. She has argued that the !Kung are a people who fear fighting and therefore do everything possible to avoid it:

> Occasions when tempers have got out of control are remembered with awe. The deadly poisoned arrows are always at hand. Men have killed each other with them in quarrels–though rarely–and the !Kung fear fighting with a conscious and active fear. They speak about it often . . . Their desire to avoid both hostility and rejection leads them to conform in high degree to the unspoken social laws. I think that most !Kung cannot bear the sense of rejection that even mild disapproval makes them feel. If they do deviate, they usually yield readily to expressed group opinion and reform their ways. They also conform strictly to certain specific useful customs which are like instruments for avoiding discord. [Marshall 1976:288]

Basically the !Kung *are* a peace-loving people, but this by itself tells us little, as all peoples are more or less "peace loving." It is equally part of the story that the !Kung *do* fight and not infrequently with fatal results. During 3 years of fieldwork, I recorded 58 case histories of arguments and fights–34 of which led to blows. And homicide is not rare: from interviews with informants I tabulated 22 cases of homicide and at least 15 woundings occurring in the central !Kung interior between 1920 and 1969, the last fatality occurring in 1955 after the arrival of the Marshall expeditions.

Judging from the number of serious fights in the recent past, it is clear that the current fear of fighting referred to by Marshall is entirely justified. The data reveal that there had been some nasty punch-ups in the past and that not all the old feuds were dead. At least nine of the killings, for example, had occurred in the Nyae Nyae area among groups closely studied by the Marshall expeditions. Attractive as they are as people, the !Kung have occasionally killed each other, and these killings deserve to be explained, especially as they occurred in a context in which the circumstances appeared to favor an avoidance of conflict.

The purpose of this chapter is two-fold: (1) to document the extent, frequency, and seriousness of fighting among the !Kung and (2) to attempt to place !Kung hunter-gatherer violence into an ecological and evolutionary perspective. Draper (1978) has insightfully covered the same topic from the perspective of socialization and values.

LEVELS OF VIOLENCE

It is useful to distinguish, as the !Kung do, three levels of conflict: talking, fighting, and deadly fighting. A *talk* is an argument that may involve threats and verbal abuse, but no blows. A *fight* is a dispute that includes an exchange of blows but without the use of weapons. A *deadly fight* is one in which the deadly weapons – poisoned arrows, spears, and clubs – are used whether or not someone is killed. The 81 cases of violence I collected are divided among these three levels of violence as follows: verbal disputes, 10; fights without weapons, 34; fights with weapons, 37 (15 nonfatal, 22 fatal). In addition to the 22 confirmed fatal fights presented here, Marjorie Shostak (personal communication) has an account of 2 other uncorroborated homicides. (My notes also contain 14 cases of arguments and fights involving San and black or San and European.)

Of the 34 fights *without* weapons, 17 were eyewitnessed (8 by me and 9 by other research group members) and 17 were described in interviews after the event.

Eyewitness data on conflict are the most valuable, but are difficult to get. Seeing a fight start, one must resist the temptation to break it up. Even if one does not intervene, the presence of an outsider may have a restraining effect. In both kinds of cases, I tried to interview the principals soon after the fight occurred while the events were still fresh in their minds. In the case of the 22 homicides, all accounts were retrospective. The best data were obtained when several independent accounts corroborated one another. It should also be emphasized that the 34 fights with-out weapons all occurred in 1963–4 and 1967–9 within the Dobe area, whereas the 22 killings and 15 woundings were spread out over a period of 35 years and occurred in the Dobe, Nyae Nyae, and /Du/da regions.

In approaching this material it is useful to note how disputes escalate from one level to another and to attempt at each stage to determine what factors operate to limit conflict and what factors lead to its heightening.

TALKING: ARGUMENTS AND VERBAL ABUSE

The San do not fight much, but they do talk a great deal. In fact, they may be among the most talkative people in the world. Much of this talk verges on argument, often for its own sake and usually ad hominem, as ably documented by Lorna Marshall (1961, 1976). Accusations of im-proper meat distribution, improper gift exchange (*hxaro*), laziness, and stinginess are the most common topics of these disputes. Often they are followed by a group split, as one or both of the principals leaves the camp for a cooling-off period. N!eishin!a and his brother-in-law ≠Toma//gwe at Dobe, for example, have been coalescing and splitting for years. Every year or so one or the other packs up after an argument and takes off with his group, only to recombine the following season.

The most common kind of argument heard is called *hore hore* or *oba oba*, !Kung words that mean "yakity-yak." It is often punctuated by a joke that breaks the tension and leaves the participants rolling on the ground helpless with laughter. Simply because these arguments happen to be funny does not mean that they lack seriousness. They *are* serious, and they proceed along the knife edge between laughter and anger. In-deed, one of the purposes of this kind of argument is to provoke one's opponent to anger so that one can retort with injured innocence: "What's the matter, we were only kidding" (see Lee 1969b).

When disputants get really angry (i.e., when both parties drop the pre-tense of good humor), a talk ensues. The "talk" (*n≠wa*), first described by Marshall (1961:232), is an outpouring of verbal anger with extrava-gant statements delivered in a stylized staccato form. A good example of the n≠wa is John Marshall's film, *An Argument About a Marriage* (1973). Of this level of verbal conflict, the !Kung say that *si !x"asi dui* ("their hearts rise up"). The point of potential danger has been passed, and the combatants are no longer completely in control of the situation. Fighting may break out directly, or the talk may move on to another level: verbal abuse involving sex.

The third and final phase of conflict on the verbal level is *za* ("sexual insulting"). The za mode occupies the ambiguous position of being both the highest form of affectionate joking between appropriate kin in the

Plate 13.1. An argument involving women.

"joking relationship" and the deadliest affront leading directly to fighting. The primary za form addressed to males is *!ki nuwa n!u* ("may death pull back your foreskin"), a grave insult among a people who do not practice circumcision and among whom the glans penis is exposed only during sexual arousal. For females the most common za forms are *!ki du a !gum* ("death on your vagina") and *!gum/twisi≠dinyazho* ("long black labia"), the latter a reference to the elongated labia minora characteristic of San and Khoi-Khoi female genitalia. According to the !Kung, to be the recipient of za in anger arouses intense feelings of *dokum* ("shame"), leading to suicide or assault.

The complete sequence of levels may not be observed on a single day. Instead, the argument may last for weeks at the talk level. Za (verbal sexual abuse), however, is so climactic that its use leads directly to fighting or to a group split or to both. The escalation of conflict at the verbal level is illustrated in the following case history. (In this and the other cases, individuals' names have been changed.)

Case 1. /Wa divorces Gau

Gau was about 27 and /Wa 14 years old when they married in mid-1967. She came from a bush-oriented family with a reputation for fierceness; his family preferred to live near the Herero cattle posts at /Xai/Xai to drink surplus milk. The age difference between bride and groom is not atypical for !Kung marriages. In late 1967 the families of bride and groom were on such good terms that they made a common camp together, a kind of residence arrangement that occurs frequently between in-laws (Chapter 3). The camp consisted of 5 adults and 1 child from the groom's family, 8 adults and 1 child from the bride's family; with the young couple, a total of 17 people (from LG 25/68).

After 6 months of marriage, Gau started an affair with an older !Kung woman named Be, whose husband was away on a long trip; he began sleeping with her to the exclusion of his young bride. The latter's family complained, but Gau did not stop seeing the older woman. In an effort to patch things up in October 1968, Gau bought his wife a new dress, and the two of them began to build a hut of mud in the new Bantu style, an act that signified a stabilization of the marriage. He did not stop seeing the older woman, however.

/Wa's people were far from satisfied with this arrangement; especially annoyed was her classificatory uncle Debe, aged 35, a man with a fiery temper. On the evening of November 6, 1968, a big argument erupted, involving verbal sexual abuse that almost led to blows. The following day /Wa and her eight relatives moved out of Gau's camp and went off to live in the bush 50 km south of /Xai/xai.

I did not witness the actual argument, but I interviewed three of the principal participants the following day. The several versions show interesting divergences, but taken together they offer, in Rashomon fashion, a truthful composite of what happened. First is the account of /Tishe, the 65-year-old father of the husband Gau:

> When the mudding of the hut started three women [including the rival] came to help my son and his wife. After they did some work on the hut, food was cooked and served to the helpers, but not to the in-laws. Then /Wa [the wife] brought over some cow dung and ant-hill earth [for the hut], but her father pulled her away angrily saying that she wasn't to do any more work on the hut. Then the argument started, and today my in-laws have refused me and have gone to live elsewhere. The one who caused my in-laws to reject me was Debe; it was he who told my *n!umba* [kin terms for child's spouse's father] to pull his daughter out of my camp.

Gau, the husband, gave a rather different and more elaborate account of the affair:

> The argument was over meat. I got some cow's meat from one of the Herero. I cooked it and gave some to my father-in-law *and* to Debe. Then my wife gave some of the meat to Be. [Note: the 14-year-old wife and the 45-year-old rival, possibly because of the big age difference, were on rather good terms.]

Then Debe said, "Give some meat to N//au" [a blind kinsman of his who lived in a nearby camp], but by then it was all gone. So Debe got angry and said, "Why is it that there is none for blind N//au but there is plenty for that woman there [Be]?"

Then Debe got out his arrows and spear and wanted to shoot me. I started to run away, and he started to follow me with his weapons out, but my father-in-law pulled him back.

When I returned they asked me, "Why does Gau care for Be but doesn't care for his own wife?" They they looked daggers at me and were silent. They went to bed, but the next morning they moved away to build a new village.

Now you should write in your book that today Gau is dead, and it isn't sickness that killed him, it is people; today the arrows have come out and I am [as good as] dead.

Finally, here is the account of Debe himself, which adds material not provided by the other accounts:

When Gau cooked a pot of meat, he filled a tin can of it for his wife like she was a bird, but the full pot he set in front of Be. We said, "That's not the way to do it. You must give the pot to your wife and give the girlfriend the tin." But Gau replied, "This girl-wife hasn't entered my heart. She can't do anything right. It is you who have forced her on me."

When we heard that, we said, "Enough!" The marriage is finished and we took our child back. But then they started to za me. And the mother of Gau za-ed me and za-ed me, and za-ed me, and za-ed me. I wanted to kill myself. Can I ever live again with people who talk like that? I am just going away for good and never coming back.

As you see, I am a zhū/twa [person] under the view of god, I say that I, as of today, have no n!ore [locality] here, this very earth here, I have no n!ore, and I am just going to kill myself.

Commentary. Debe did not kill himself. (Suicide is very rare among the !Kung. I have recorded cases of five attempts at suicide, none of them successful.) Nor did Debe attempt to kill the husband. Instead, he gathered together a new group consisting of the original in-law segment and 10 other people, and they moved out to the bush to summer in their home locality. After a separation of a few months, Gau and his young wife got back together, and they were still together 4 years later.

Case 1 illustrates some general points about !Kung arguments. First, the deeper cause is a marital problem but the precipitating cause is improper food distribution. Second, the arguments tend to be mercurial and unpredictable in their courses. There is an absence of long slanging matches or ritualization at the verbal level. When the language gets abusive, an attempt at physical violence is likely to follow rapidly. Third, the effect of the resort to verbal sexual abuse is striking. On the one hand, it caused the protagonist to reach for his weapons, but on the other, it actually diverted Debe's wrath from Gau to /Tasa, Gau's 60-year-old mother. Although the data are somewhat ambiguous on this point, it is possible that /Tasa used the sexual insults to *intervene* and avert a direct confrontation between two men with poisoned arrows. Finally, the case illustrates how the conflict was resolved by the splitting up of the group. This important mode of !Kung conflict resolving was first described by Colin Turnbull (1965) for the Mbuti Pygmies; later it was found to be present in many other hunting and gathering societies (Lee and DeVore 1968:9).

FIGHTING: HAND TO HAND

Not all fights are resolved at the verbal level. On at least 34 occasions during 1963–9 peace making failed and people came to blows. There were probably other cases I did not hear about. Based on accounts of 17 incidents actually witnessed by the research group, !Kung fights tend to have the following characteristics. They are of short duration; the actual time during which blows are exchanged varies between 30 seconds and 5 minutes. Assaults are sudden and in earnest; once begun, there are no ritualized phrases or slanging matches interspersed with the fighting. An exception to this rule is the play fighting occasionally observed among young males aged 18 to 35. Here there can be lengthy sequences of posturing and sparring interspersed with bouts of wrestling. Of five such cases observed during fieldwork, two turned serious, three did not. Four of the five cases involved only males; one involved a husband and wife. There are no instances of play fights among women.

In the case of serious fights, the atmosphere among the bystanders tends to be hysterical, although the combatants themselves often fight in dead silence, grim-faced and tight-lipped. Wrestling and punching at close quarters rather than fisticuffs seems to be the major technique for both sexes. The object of the fighter is to get a headlock on his opponent and force him to the ground. We saw no evidence of kicking or intent to harm the genitals. After the first exchange of blows, attempts are made by third parties to restrain the combatants. The fighters are forcibly separated and held back facing each other. After the fighting ceases, there is an eruption of talking and shouting by everyone–again except for the combatants, who remain silent. The discussion of the fight may continue for several hours after the event, and punching may flare again. On the other hand, we have seen people burst into laughter only a few minutes after a fight. After the tension is broken, partisans of the opposing sides

Table 13.1. *Number of initiators and victims of fights, by sex*

Attacker	Victim		
	Male	Female	Total
Male	11	14[a]	25
Female	1[b]	8	9
Total	12	22	34

[a]In 10 of these 14 cases, a husband attacked his wife.
[b]A wife attacked her husband.

may be seen joking with one another whereas only minutes before they were grappling. We did not see formal attempts at reconciliation – such as handshaking – following a fight. However, the trance dance that sometimes follows a fight may serve as a peace-making mechanism where trance performers give ritual healing to persons on both sides of the argument.

The breakdown by sex of participants in fights is shown in Table 13.1. Women are involved in fights almost as frequently as men (23 vs. 26 times), but men are the *initiators* of the attack almost three times as frequently as women (25 vs. 9 times). In only 1 instance did a woman attack a man, although women attacked other women on 8 occasions. The severity of the attacks were mild. In most cases the only injuries sustained were a few cuts and scratches. In six instances, however, a riding crop or a stick was used and in two of these the victim suffered concussion and scalp wounds. In the most serious case, a brawl at !Kangwa in January 1969 in which a man received a deep gash on the skull, drunkenness was a precipitating factor. The misuse of alcohol, a substance unknown until the 1960s, appears to be an increasingly serious social problem in the 1970s (see Chapter 14).

The causes of these fights are not always easy to discern, because the precipitating event may give few clues to the underlying cause. Adultery was the most common single factor: Accusations of adultery cropped up in 2 (of 11) male-male fights and 2 (of 14) male-female fights, but was a factor in 5 (of 8) female-female fights. The incidence of fights within a family was high: In 10 of the 14 male-female fights a husband attacked his wife, and in the 1 female-male encounter a woman attacked her husband. Despite the higher frequency of male-initiated attacks, women fought fiercely and often gave as good or better than they got.

In total, 48 people appeared as principals in these 34 fights, 37 people appeared only once, but 11 others took part in two or more fights. One nasty man with a reputation for unruliness was responsible for 4 of the

34 fights; 3 others (2 men and 1 woman) each cropped up in three different fights.

Because of the small number of cases and the diversity of causes, the following case histories are in no sense typical or representative. However, they convey the style of !Kung combat.

Case 2. Kxau whips his wife //Kushe in dispute over blanket

I witnessed this scene at the /Xai/xai water hole in November 1968. Kxau, a 40-year-old man with a long history of adultery, was departing by donkey for a visit to Mahopa to see a lover, leaving his pregnant wife and their two children behind. His neglected wife //Kushe followed him down to the well where he was watering his donkey. She argued with him, asking him not to go, or if he did at least to leave their one store-bought blanket with her. Kxau flatly refused. Wordlessly she went to the donkey and pulled out the blanket from Kxau's kit. Wordlessly Kxau firmly took the blanket away from her and tucked it back on the donkey's back and tied it down. Again, she came forward and without a word tugged it away. Again he pursued her and pulled it back.

This entire pantomime was carried out by //Kushe with a 10-liter bucket full of water balanced on her head and with her 3-year-old son riding in her kaross! On her third attempt, still without a word, she pulled a piece of plastic from the donkey's back and staggered away with pail teetering and baby bouncing.

Kxau, his face grim, without a word chased her and in quick succession:

Tied his donkey to a fence
Grabbed the plastic from his wife and tucked it on the donkey's back
Took the full pail of water off her head and set it on the ground without spilling a drop
Went around behind her and roughly pulled their now screaming child out of the backpouch and set him on the ground
Started thrashing his wife on the shoulders and back with a donkey whip

Two women immediately rushed forward and dragged him off, his arm still upraised, shouting: "Are you crazy, hitting a woman like that?"

Kxau stopped struggling and breathing heavily returned to his donkey while the women continued to berate him. //Kushe darted in to grab the blanket, and stuffing it into her pouch she made off with her bucket and her child in tow. Still grim, Kxau then mounted his donkey and cantered off for Mahopa.

Commentary. The wife was unable to stop her husband from leaving, but she did get the blanket and she won the moral victory by provoking him to lose his temper and beat her in public, thereby invoking strong public criticism of his behavior. It was interesting that she chose to fight him while "wearing" both the bucket of water and the child, making her morally a doubly redoubtable target; to spill water and strike a child in anger are both strongly frowned upon by the !Kung. The husband had to set both bucket and child on the ground before taking a swing at his wife. The couple had a long history of strife. This same husband had provoked two other fights involving adultery during my 3 years of fieldwork. One was a battle royal at /Xai/xai in 1964 in which four people were injured, including Kxau's wife *and* his lover, while Kxau himself was untouched.

Case 3. Two young men play fight and it turns serious

I witnessed this fight at Dobe in December 1964. Kashe and Bo were ummarried young men in their late twenties who had just returned from a period of working on the Tswana cattle posts in the East. Both men had a reputation for fighting. Kashe had been involved in at least three other scraps and Bo in two others in recent years. The causes of the fight are obscure. Kashe accused Bo of za-ing his brother-in-law and he wanted to kill him because of the insult. Others of their agemates thought he was joking until he attacked one of them, a man named /Tishe, and landed several blows.

Kashe called out a challenge to Bo: "You and /Tishe together can't lay a hand on me."

"You shouldn't talk like that," Bo repied, "we are all men here and we are all strong."

Kashe said, "If you don't like my words then let's get into it."

The two men started grappling and fought their way out of the camp to a clearing 100 meters to the east. (I was told later that they moved out of the camp to fight because they didn't want the women to see their genitals exposed through their ragged shorts.) At first there was a playful element to the fighting, but it soon became serious. They punched and grappled and each got a hammerlock on the other. Kashe got Bo down on the ground and gouged his eyes with his nails so that Bo's face was covered with blood. Many people gathered round the fighters, and the tension became very high. Some tried to break it up, but others started side fights. Bo's mother, aged 60, attacked Kashe's mother's sister, aged 55. An aunt of Bo's wanted to pile in, but her husband prevented her and *they* started fighting. One man exploded with irritation at the fighting women: "Why should you fight? The boys are not using arrows or spears. Why should you start a big one?" Kashe's father yelled back, "If this is a big fight, let's get started. We are all men here. Get me my arrows!"

Plate 13.2. A 1964 fight at Dobe (case 3).

Soon after, two men plunged into the fray and pulled the grappling men apart. They made several more attempts to lunge at each other, but more people held them back. As they were held panting, Kashe yelled that he wanted to continue the fight, and Bo's mother continued to try to whip up a big fight, but then Kan//a, the strongest man in the population, interposed himself between the straining men and shouted at everybody to calm down and keep quiet. Kan//a had a reputation for being very strong and competent and very mild-mannered. His display of anger had a calming effect. (Later when I asked him which side he favored in the fight, he replied, "Oh, how can a man like me get in a fight. I wanted to thrash both sides!")

At this point, Kashe's father and Bo's uncle, who had been restraining the boys, exchanged looks and broke into laughter as if to say, "What a mess! The boys were trying to kill each other!" This released the tension, and the danger of more outbreaks subsided.

In the aftermath everyone returned to the camp, where knots of people discussed the day's events with animation. There was much laughter and little rancor. Even Bo's mother and Kashe's mother's sister, who had been fighting a few minutes before, were seen sitting side by side, while the two fighters reported to my hut for first-aid treatment of their cuts. A few days later the group dispersed to several different summer water points.

Commentary. It is not clear whether play fighting of this kind is traditional to the !Kung or a recent introduction from the blacks, among whom adolescent male play fighting and tests of strength are common. All the cases involved young men recently returned from work on the cattle posts.

Gakekgoshe, the son of Tswana headman Isak, told me that he rarely saw a play fight among traditional !Kung groups. Then he continued:

I think it is learned from Damas and Gobas (Bayei). Their boys are always trying each other's strength. It is not a Tswana custom. We always do each other with words, not fists. The !Kung don't use words because the only words they have are fighting ones. For instance, a fight like we saw today couldn't have happened among the San in the old days, because the grown men seeing the fight, their hearts would rise and the arrows would start flying. But today the boys can do it because it is play, they are copying the Gobas.

The events of case 3 support Gakekgoshe's comments. The tension between the two young men rapidly spread to other members of the group, and in the passion of the moment side fights broke out. For a few moments the situation was touch and go before order was restored. With no superordinate authority to turn to, the fight had to be broken up by the relatives and affines of the fighters themselves.

An element common to all !Kung fights (and for that matter to fights in most egalitarian societies) is the absence of any immediate authority figure to settle disputes (see Colson 1973:35–51). The people on the spot, often close kin or supporters of the protagonists, must do the settling by force of will. By and large, the !Kung are very successful in keeping quarrels below the deadly threshold, but their mechanisms for conflict management are far from perfect, and in the past flare-ups have led to violence with lethal results. In all the fights we observed steps were taken to keep the men in their prime from going out of control. Women and old men interposed themselves and often got hit in the bargain. Fighting between men aged 20 to 50 is considered the most dangerous, because these men hold a near monopoly on the poisoned arrows. The phrase, "We are all men here. Get me my arrows," from case 3, is a danger signal. The same phrase crops up in several of the case histories of fatal fights. When the poisoned arrows come out, the chance of a killing increases greatly, as the following discussion shows.

FIGHTING WITH WEAPONS

I have never witnessed a fight with arrows. The last fatal one occurred in 1955. The two offenders were taken to Maun for trial, and since then no further fights with spear or arrow wounding have taken place. Interviews with !Kung eyewitnesses and participants were the source of my information on 22 killings and 15 woundings that occurred beween 1920 and 1955. The uncorroborated killings reported by Shostak are not included in the tabulations. Homicide was an extremely sensitive topic to discuss. I had been in the field for 14 months before recording my first well-documented case. However, once informants became aware that I already knew of several killings, they became more open and provided extensive details of time, place, participants, and who shot whom, even in cases where the killer was still alive and active in the population. Unfortunately, less material is available on the exact events leading up to the actual fighting with arrows. These are cases of homicide or attempted homicide, acts of violence in which adults kill adults. Infanticide and senilicide, both of which are rare in any case, are not included in this discussion. Similarly, the !Kung do not practice any form of ritual murder or sacrifice; nor do they induce death by magical means.

My methodology follows a scheme set out by criminologist Marvin E. Wolfgang (1958) in his study, *Patterns in Criminal Homicide*, and used also by Bohannan (1960) in his excellent work on African homicide. For each of the 22 documented cases I attempted to establish data for 15 variables: sex and age of killer(s), number of killers, sex and age of victim, whether on the day of the killing there was a single or multiple victims, whether the victim was a principal in a prior argument, whether the killing was premeditated or spontaneous, and whether part of a feud. I also tried to establish the kin relation of killer and victim, the weapon used, the season and time of day of the killing, and finally what happened to the killer or killers. The 22 cases are listed in Table 13.2 and the variables are tabulated in Table 13.3. In the text, numbers preceded by *K* refer to the coding of the cases in these tables.

Arrow fights have several general features. They occurred most commonly *within* living groups or between neighboring groups. Only a few of the killings occurred as a result of special expeditions for the purpose of fighting. However, two informants said that raiding expeditions had occurred in the very distant past, during the youth of the grandparent generation of the oldest living people. In the 22 cases, the outbreak of fighting was usually spontaneous; only 5 killings were the result of premeditated sneak attacks. The !Kung fight in public, usually in full view of everyone,

Table 13.2. *!Kung homicides: 1920–69*

Code no.	Situation
K1	In a general brawl over a marital dispute, three men wound and kill another east of /Xai/Xai (1930s). See case 4.
K2	By general agreement, the senior of the three killers in K1 is himself killed in retaliation (1930s). See case 6.
K3	The notorious /Twi kills a man in a spear fight (/Du/da area, 1940s). See case 7.
K4	The notorious /Twi kills a second man, an event that later leads to the killing of /Twi himself (/Du/da area, 1940s). See case 7.
K5	In the course of being fatally attacked, /Twi manages to kill a third man and wound a woman (/Du/da area, 1940s). See case 7.
K6	The killer /Twi is ambushed and wounded and then killed by the collective action of a large number of people (/Du/da area, 1940s). See case 7.
K7	In a sneak attack one man kills another over the latter's wife. Wife first runs away with the killer, but becomes frightened and returns alone (≠To//gana, 1940s).
K8	A young man kills his father's brother in a spear fight, the closest killer-victim kin connection in the sample (/Du/da area, 1930s).
K9	A man accuses another of adultery. In the ensuing fight, the accused adulterer is wounded, but succeeds in killing the husband (Bate, 1930s).
K10	In anger over her adultery, a man stabs and kills his wife with a poisoned arrow and flees the area (/Xai/Xai, 1920s).
K11	≠Gau from Chum!kwe kills a /Gausha man with a spear to initiate a long sequence of feuding (Nyae Nyae area, 1930s). See case 5.
K12	≠Gau's enemies attack him in retaliation, but ≠Gau kills a second man in the attempt (Nyae Nyae area, 1930s). See case 5.
K13	A relative of ≠Gau's is killed in an earlier fight that is related to K11 and K12 (Nyae Nyae area, 1920s). See case 5.
K14	≠Gau's enemies attack him a second time at a place called Zou/toma, and ≠Gau kills a third man; two others are killed the same day: K15, K16. (Nyae Nyae area, 1930s). See case 5.
K15	The attackers kill a woman bystander of ≠Gau's group in the arrow fight at Zou/toma (1930s). See case 5.
K16	The attackers fail to kill ≠Gau himself at Zou/toma, but they do kill another man of his group (1930s). See case 5.
K17	A young man not of the /Gausha groups kills ≠Gau in a sneak attack, finally eliminating an unpopular man (1940s). See case 5.
K18	The younger brother of ≠Gau is attacked by another man in an argument, but in the ensuing fight, the man's wife is killed. ≠Gau's brother goes to jail in South-West Africa for this crime (1950s). See case 5.
K19	Returning home from jail, ≠Gau's younger brother is met on the road and killed by relatives of the victim in K18 (near South-West African farms, 1950s). See case 5.
K20	A black settler was having an affair with a !Kung man's wife. Catching them in flagrante, the husband shoots and kills the adulterer. The killer is later jailed in Maun, Botswana (!Kubi, 1946).
K21	A young man kills an older man with a club in a general brawl. The killer is later jailed in Maun (1952).
K22	In a general brawl a young man and his father kill a /Xai/xai man. Later both are taken to jail in Maun (1955); the last case of !Kung homicide in the Dobe area.

Table 13.3. *Some characteristics of !Kung homicides*

Code no.	Estimated year	Region	Sex, age, and no. of killers	Sex and age of victim	Weapon used	Single or multiple victims[a]	Part of a feud	Relation of victim to prior argument
K1	1935–8	/Xai/xai	3 M 50/20/?	M 50	Spear, arrow[b]	Multiple	Yes	Participant
K2	1935–8	/Xai/xai	M 40	M 50	Arrow	Single	Yes	Principal
K3	1946–8	/Du/da	M 25	M 25	Spear	Multiple	Yes	Principal
K4	1946–8	/Du/da	M 25	M		Single	Yes	
K5	1948	/Du/da	M 25	M	Arrow	Multiple	Yes	Bystander
K6	1948	/Du/da	M 25	M 25	Spear, arrow	Multiple	Yes	Principal
K7	1945	/Xai/xai	M	M	Arrow	Single	No	Principal
K8	1939	/Du/da	M 20	M 45	Spear	Single	No	
K9	1930–3	Dobe	M 30	M 30	Arrow	Multiple	No	Principal
K10	1920–4	/Xai/xai	M 25	F 20	Arrow	Single	No	Principal
K11	1930–4	Nyae Nyae	M 45	M	Spear	Multiple	Yes	
K12	1930–4	Nyae Nyae	M 45	M	Arrow	Multiple	Yes	Participant
K13	1920–4	Nyae Nyae	M	M 25			Yes	
K14	1936	Nyae Nyae	M 45	M	Arrow	Multiple	Yes	Participant
K15	1936	Nyae Nyae	M	F	Arrow	Multiple	Yes	Bystander
K16	1936	Nyae Nyae	M	M	Arrow	Multiple	Yes	Participant
K17	1940	Nyae Nyae	M 25	M 55	Spear	Single	Yes	Principal
K18	1952	West	M 50	F 40	Arrow	Multiple	Yes	Bystander
K19	1953–4	West	M	M 55		Single	Yes	Principal
K20	1946	Dobe	M 30	M 40	Arrow	Single	No	Principal
K21	1952	Dobe	M 25	M 45	Club	Single	No	
K22	1955	/Xai/xai	2 M 20/25	M 30	Spears	Multiple	No	Participant

[a]Killed *or* wounded. Blank = not ascertained.
[b]Arrow = poisoned arrow.

Kin relation of victim to killer	Season and time of day of killing	What happened to killer	Remarks
Kin	Summer	Later killed	
Kin	Summer evening	Lived	"Execution" of one of the killers in K1
Kin		Later killed ⎫ Later killed ⎬ Later killed ⎭	Three killings by a notorious killer (see K6)
Kin	Winter	Lived	"Execution" of killer in K3, K4, K5
	Night	Escaped	
Brother's son		Lived	Only close kin killing
Kin		Nothing	
Wife	Evening	Escaped	Only wife killing
		Later killed	First killing in a sequence of 9 (K11–K19)
		Later killed	
			Earlier killing related to K11 and K12
	Summer morning	Later killed	
	Summer morning		
	Summer morning	Lived	
Kin	Night	Lived	"Execution" of killer in K11, K12, K14
		Jailed, killed	South-West African police intervened; killer killed after release
		Lived	Killing of killer in K18
Unrelated	Spring evening	Jailed, lived	San killed a black, date exact
	Winter	Jailed, lived	Date exact
	Spring	Jailed, lived	Date exact

385

and many people get involved. The fight takes place in or near the camp–
the site of domestic activities. There are no special fighting grounds or
prearranged times for fighting. Nor are there any special weapons. To
illustrate some of these points, here is the case history of an arrow fight
that took place in the late 1930s and involved a number of men still active
in the community. The names of the principals have been concealed.

Case 4 (K1). A father is killed in a fight over his son's right to marry a
woman

The principals were, on one side, the victim (H) and his son (D), the first
narrator; on the other side, the senior killer (G), his son (S) another killer,
the man who started the fight (B), the woman over whom they fought
(T), and her brother (K), the second narrator. This is a composite account
of two participants, D and K, men now in their fifties. D reported:

> We were all living together at N≠wama [30 km southeast of /Xai/
> xai]. B started it by refusing me a wife. I wanted to marry T, and
> her mother and father gave me permission, but B had already mar-
> ried T's older sister and he wanted to take her as a second wife, so
> he refused me.
>
> There was a big argument and fighting broke out. B yelled at my
> younger sister, "What is your brother doing marrying my wife? I'm
> going to kill you!" He shot an arrow at her and missed. Then B
> came up to me to kill me, but my father came to my aid. Then S
> came to B's aid. S shot at me but missed; my father speared S in the
> chest under the armpit. S's father (G), seeing his own son speared,
> came to his aid and fired a poisoned arrow into my father's thigh. I
> was shooting at B but missed him.

The narrative continues with the account of K, the brother of T:

> Then H stabbed at G with his spear. G put up his hand to protect
> himself and the spear went right through it. S rushed at H with his
> spear and tried to spear him in the ribs. At first the spear jammed,
> but then it went through.
>
> In the meantime side fights were going on. My older brother
> dodged several shots and then shot D's sister in the shoulder blade
> (she lived). I dodged arrows by two men and then hit one of them in
> the foot with a poisoned arrow.
>
> After being hit with a poisoned arrow in the thigh and speared in
> the ribs, H fell down mortally wounded. Half-sitting, half-lying
> down he called for allies. "I'm finished, my arms are stilled. At least
> shoot one of them for me."
>
> But no more shooting happened that day. We went away and
> came back the next morning to see H writhing in his death throes.

He had been given cuts to draw off the poison, but the poison was in too deep and he died. We left N≠wama and all came back to /Xai/ xai.

Commentary. This case illustrates some general features of !Kung arrow fights. First, the protagonists are members of closely related living groups. A second point concerns the rapid escalation and drawing in of more participants and the unpredictable outcome: None of the four wounded were even principals in the original argument between B and D over the woman T. The aftermath of the incident involving further bloodshed is discussed below (case 6).

ANALYSIS OF HOMICIDES

Now let us look at the case histories from several points of view: geography and dating, sex of killers and victims, weapons and casualties, social settings, victimology, and conflict resolution.

Geography and dating

The killings occurred in all four subregions of the central !Kung interior: 3 in the !Kangwa Valley (north of the Ahas), 5 at /Xai/xai, 5 in the /Du/da southern regions, and 9 in the Nyae Nyae area and points west. Dating of all but 3 killings is only approximate, estimated from the ages of living people who were born shortly before or after the time of the incident. Cases K20, K21, and K22 are precisely dated because the offenders were arrested and taken for trial to Maun, where their names appear in the court records. Other homicides that had occurred prior to the 1920s came to light, but are not included. The analysis is limited to a period during which I am reasonably sure I have recorded all the cases: this makes it possible to calculate rates (see below). By decades, there were 2 homicides in the 1920s, 9 in the 1930s, 7 in the 1940s, and 4 in the 1950s. Though the data show that no one region or decade had a monopoly on the violence, there were two concentrations of incidents: K3 through K6 in /Du/da during the 1940s, and K11, K12, and K14 through K17 in Nyae Nyae during the 1930s and early 1940s. Each was attributed to a single killer, who precipitated a blood feud and who was himself later killed in retaliation.

Sex and number of killers

All the killers were males between the ages of 20 and 50. In 17 cases, there was a single killer; in 1 case (K22), two killers; and in 1 case (K1), three killers. In 3 additional cases between one and three men were involved. Two of the men were multiple killers. /Twi and ≠Gau each killed three victims (K3, K4, K5 and K11, K12, and K14) before being killed themselves in retaliation. There were no female killers and only 3

Table 13.4. *Incidence of females as killers and victims among the !Kung and other societies*

Society	No. of cases	Percent female killers	Percent female victims
!Kung	22	0.0	13.6
Tiv (Nigeria)[a]	122	4.0	18.0
Soga (Uganda)[a]	100	2.0	45.0
Luo (Uganda)[a]	47	9.0	25.0
Philadelphia[b]	(1948–52)	18.0	24.0
Britain[b]	(1900–48)	32.0	57.0

[a]Data from Bohannan (1960:240).
[b]Data from Wolfgang (1958:46ff.).

of the 22 victims were female. The low incidence of women in deadly fights contrasts sharply with the picture for less serious fights among the !Kung, in which over two-thirds of the cases involved females. The low incidence of females in deadly fights also contrasts sharply with the proportions of females reported as killers and as victims in other African societies and in Western industrial nations. Table 13.4 compares !Kung homicide rates, by sex, with rates in three other African societies and in Philadelphia and Britain. Female offenders, absent among the !Kung, make up 2 to 9 percent of the killers in the three African societies, and 18 and 32 percent of the killers in the two Western studies. Similarly, females as victims tend to be much more common in other African societies and in the West: 24 percent in Philadelphia, 45 percent among the Soga of Uganda, and a remarkable 57 percent in Britain. Among the !Kung, the male monopoly of the lethal hunting weapons may partly account for the absence of woman killers, but still leaves unexplained the low incidence of woman victims compared with other societies. The answer may lie in the relatively high status !Kung women have relative to men, a point discussed in detail in Chapter 15.

Weapons and casualties

A poisoned arrow inflicted the fatal blow in 13 of the 19 homicides in which the weapon is known. A spear was used in 7 cases (sometimes in addition to arrows), and a club in 1 case. The poison, from the larvae of *Diamphidia* beetles, is the same as that used on hunting arrows (Chapters 5 and 8). From a wound it is carried in the bloodstream and acts on the central nervous system. The only known remedy is to make cuts around the area of the wound and to suck some of the poisoned blood and lymphatic fluid from the victim's body. The poison will kill an untreated man in a few hours. With treatment, there is a 50:50 chance of survival. (In a general survey of the population, we counted 10 men with the characteristic oval scars on their body indicating treatment for arrow poisoning; some of these may be the result of hunting accidents, not fights.) The fatal weapons are exactly the same as those used in hunting. The !Kung possess no special technology for fighting, such as swords, battle axes, or shields.

In addition to the 22 killings, I recorded 15 cases of nonfatal woundings: 6 with poisoned arrows, 4 with spears, and 1 with a club. In the 4 other cases the weapon used is not clear. Although the list of woundings is not as complete as the list of killings, the figures offer some indication of the relatively high fatality rate (60 percent) as a proportion of total injuries in arrow and spear fights (22 out of 37).

The popularity of the poisoned arrow puzzled me. Why, I wondered, didn't the men fight with unpoisoned arrows and thus reduce the risk of death? To this question, one informant offered an instructive response: "We shoot poisoned arrows," he said, "because our hearts are hot and we really want to kill somebody with them."

Social settings and context

Data are incomplete on the size of the camp in which each killing took place. The question was not included on my original checklist and the size of the group had to be inferred from the season, locale of the incident, and whether the participants were drawn from one or several localities. For example, the fighters described in case 4 were drawn from living groups from //Karu, ≠To//gana, and /Dwia, indicating a large gathering of over 40 people (see Chapter 12, Table 12.5). By similar inferences it is possible to say that 15 killings took place in large camps of 40 or more people gathered for trading, initiation, or exploiting a food resource; 3 homicides took place in small living groups; and for 4 others the camp size could not be estimated.

Better established is the fact that the killings tended to be a part of a more general melee. In 12 of 21 killings at least one other person was killed or wounded on the same day. The most serious fight took place at Zou/toma, west of Chum!kwe, around 1936 when three people were killed and several wounded on a single day (K14, K15, and K16).

A feud killing is one in which a homicide is followed by one or more retaliatory homicides. By this definition, 15 of the killings occurred as parts of feuds; only 7 were single killings without retaliation. Probably four feud clusters are involved: two of 2 killings (K1 and K2; K18 and K19), one of 4 killings (K3 through K6), and one of 7 killings (K11 through K17). Put another way: 1 killing led to 6 others, 1 killing led to 3 others, 2 killings led to 1 other, and 7 killings did not lead to retaliation.

Case 5 (K11 through K19). A history of feuding

This sequence of killings took place in the Nyae Nyae area between the
1920s and the 1950s. It involves families who were closely associated
with the Marshall expeditions of 1952–9. The informant is one of the key
members of Marshall's band 1 at /Gausha; he married into the Dobe area
and has spent much of his life there. The account revolves around a man
named ≠Gau, who had a fierce reputation and was responsible for several killings.

≠Gau was a lion. He ate people. First there was a man named
Debe; they had a quarrel that arose over the foods of the bush, and
≠Gau killed him with a spear (K11). Later, the family of Debe attacked ≠Gau to avenge the killing, but in the attack ≠Gau killed
another man, ≠Toma. He hit him in the spine with a poisoned
arrow shot at long range (K12). Then ≠Gau grabbed his people and
left the area.

It had all started from a fight some years before, when my
father's generation had killed a man who was ≠Gau's brother-in-
law (K13).

My people and the men of nearby groups agreed to organize an
expedition to go and kill ≠Gau. So I joined a party that went after
him. We had a battle at Zou/toma near Chum!kwe where the poisoned arrows were flying. ≠Gau killed another man named /Twi
with a poisoned arrow in the side (K14), but we killed two of his
people, a woman named //Koka (K15) and a man named /Kashe
(K16). Others were wounded.

After this battle ≠Gau and his group ran away. We took all their
meat and their possessions and carried them home.

We said to ourselves, "Now we have done this fight. We should
stop it and go back and let him live. We will watch ≠Gau to see if he
does anything else."

Later, however, he started another fight, this time with a group of
young men in the bachelors' hut. He took their bows and arrows
and spears and broke them and threw them away. Soon after, a
young in-law of his named /Toshe sneaked up on ≠Gau in the dead
of night while he was sleeping and stabbed him in the heart with a
spear. ≠Gau leapt up and chased /Toshe a few steps, then dropped
dead (K17). The young man escaped and died many years later of
natural causes.

For years ≠Gau's younger brother wanted to seek revenge. Then
he started another fight in which a woman was killed (K18), but
this time the people sought the police patrol. The man was arrested
and sent to jail in Grootfontein (South-West Africa). Later, ≠Gau's

younger brother escaped from jail, but on his way back to Nyae Nyae people met him on the way and killed him (K19). That's when the good people came together and saw and understood each other. Now the good people are at Chum!kwe eating properly and living properly.

Commentary. Time has compressed the events of this long tale of killings. It is not entirely clear whether one, two, or three feuds are encompassed by the account. Clearly cases K11, K12, and K14 through K16 are part of a single feud; K18 and K19 are obviously connected; but K17 is both the concluding episode of the first feud and the triggering episode of the second. And it is not clear how K13, the earliest, fits in. This account also speaks of an expedition for the purpose of killing, an unusual feature in a society where most homicides tend to occur within coresident groups.

After K11, K12, and K13, but before K14, K15, and K16, the narrator was actually married to a daughter of the notorious ≠Gau! I asked him how he could marry the daughter of his enemy. He replied, "I divorced ≠Gau's daughter. He was a great killer, and I said to myself, 'I want to hunt eland, kudu, and gemsbok, but hunting men is what gets you killed.' I refused fighting, and so we split."

This is by far the most serious feud recorded in the data on !Kung homicide: 40 percent of all the killings are included in this one account.

Victimology

Wolfgang (1958) following Hentig (1948) has employed the term *victimology* to refer to the study of who gets killed and the relationship of victim to killer. This perspective is useful for analyzing !Kung homicides. The data show that unlike the situation in Western societies, where up to a quarter of homicides occur within the family, among the !Kung close kin do not kill one another. No case concerns killing a parent, a child, or a sibling, and only one describes a husband killing a wife. This case, concerned with the wife's infidelity, was the only instance of intentional homicide of a woman (K10). In K8, a young man killed his father's younger brother in an arrow fight. In the other cases the kin tie was more distant. In all cases the victim was personally known to the killer and probably related by some kinship connection. In no case was the victim a stranger.

There are several indications that among the !Kung, groups who kill one another also marry one another. One instance has already been noted above. In case 4, S killed H; years later the daughter of S married the son of H and they lived together at /Xai/xai. In four other cases, a widow or divorced sister of a dead man remarried a man from the opposing side. These marriages seemed more in the nature of peacemaking alliances than examples of the victor taking a prize, as in two cases of marriage both sides had lost a man, in one case the woman went to the victim's side, and in only one case did the woman marry into the killer's side.

Also worth noting is the point that homicides tend to recur in some families. One /Xai/xai man lost a father and a brother in two different fights (K8 and K3); another lost a father and a mother's sister in two different fights (K1 and K10); one unfortunate woman lost two husbands in two different fights (K3 and K22).

The most striking aspect of the killer-victim relation, however, is that in the majority of cases *the victim was not a principal in the verbal conflict that led up to the actual killing with arrow or spear.* In only 8 of the 18 cases on which I have data was the victim a principal in the previous argument. In 10 other killings, the victim was struck more or less at random: in 3 cases a man came to the aid of another and was killed; in 4 cases a peacemaker was fatally wounded; and 3 victims (2 of them women) were bystanders. The !Kung men are excellent shots when hunting game, but are poor shots when aiming at each other.

Of the 8 homicides involving a principal in a prior dispute, the circumstances include the following: a man attacked and killed a non-San who had been sleeping with his wife (K20); a man killed another and ran away with the victim's wife (K7); a man who had slept with another's wife was attacked by the husband but killed the husband (K9); and a man killed his wife in an argument over her adultery (K10).

Finally, 4 intentional killings were conflict-resolving homicides in which the community sanctioned and participated in the elimination of a man who had previously killed others. These killings can best be described as *executions:* All were premeditated and 3 involved sneak attacks.

Executions among the !Kung?

Political philosophers have argued that the state is necessary to provide an authority to control peoples' disruptive impulses. Following Hobbes, this school of thought contends that without a state, the natural aggressiveness of man would create a situation in which every man is pitted against every other–"the war of all against all" (Hobbes 1651).

The !Kung, though not particularly warlike or aggressive, seem at first glance to be a case in point. Their strong ethos of egalitarianism and their quick tempers have led to a number of fatal fights in the past. Furthermore, if a killing occurred it was more likely than not to be followed by a retaliatory killing: 15 of the 22 homicides were parts of blood feuds. However, there is some evidence that even among these egalitarian people there was a capacity for bringing conflict to an end through the agreed-upon execution of a known killer. In our accounts of four such killings the collective nature of the act is clearly stated, suggesting the jural concept of a state in embryonic form.

Case 6 (K2). Retaliatory killing

In case 4, we saw how G and two others killed H in a fight at N≠wama around 1935–8. Soon after the event, it was avenged by the retaliatory killing of G and the matter brought to a close. The informant is D, the first narrator in case 4. Because the killer here had the same name as the narrator, we shall call him D2.

> After my father's murder, D2, a man who was my *!Kun!a* ["older namesake"] complained, "Now my younger namesake D has no father, but S still has a father. Why is this?"
>
> I said, "You are right. I am going to kill B, who started it all."
>
> "No!" D2 said. "B is just a youngster, but G is a senior man, a n!ore owner, and he is the one who has killed another n!ore owner, H. I am going to kill *him* so that n!ore owners will be dead on both sides."
>
> One evening D2 walked right into G's camp and without saying a word shot three arrows into G, one in the left shoulder, one in the forehead, and the third in the chest. G's people made no move to protect him. After the three arrows were shot, G still sat facing his attacker. Then D2 raised his spear as if to stab him. But G said, "You have hit me three times. Isn't that enough to kill me, that you want to stab me too?"
>
> When G tried to dodge away from the spear, G's people came forward to disarm D2 of his spear. Having been so badly wounded, G died quickly, but no further move was made to harm D2. However, fearing more trouble, some of our people brought in the Tswana man Isak to mediate the dispute.

Commentary. This account is corroborated by informant K, a partisan of the other side. Although not explicitly stated, there must have been some prior agreement that this killing should go forward. How else can we account for the fact that G's people made no move to help him until after he had been hit with three poisoned arrows? Only then did they disarm the attacker. The later intervention of Isak introduces a complicating factor in the discussion. Two accounts specifically say that the killer's group sought Isak, and this suggests that the truce following the retaliatory killing was not an entirely secure one and that the Tswana, representing outside authority, would ensure no further violence. This account, dating from the 1930s, is one of the earliest to include an intervention by non-San in a San internal matter.

Case 7 (K6). A collective killing

The most dramatic account of a collective killing concerns the death of
/Twi, a notorious killer who had been responsible for the deaths of two
men (K3, K4) in the 1940s. A number of people decided that he must be
killed. The informant is ≠Toma, the younger brother of /Twi.

> My brother was killed southwest of N//o!kau (in the /Du/da area). At
> the time I was in the East working for the Herero. People said that
> /Twi was one who had killed too many people so they killed him
> with spears and arrows. He had killed two people already, and on
> the day he died he stabbed a woman and killed a man.

> It was /Xashe who attacked /Twi first. He ambushed him near the
> camp and shot a poisoned arrow into his hip. They grappled hand to
> hand, and /Twi had him down and was reaching for his knife when
> /Xashe's wife's mother grabbed /Twi from behind and yelled to
> /Xashe, "Run away! This man will kill everyone!" And /Xashe ran
> away.

> /Twi pulled the arrow out of his hip and went back to his hut, where
> he sat down. Then some people gathered and tried to help him by cut-
> ting and sucking out poison. /Twi said, "This poison is killing me. I
> want to piss." But instead of pissing, he deceived the people, grabbed
> a spear, and flailed out with it, stabbing a woman named //Kushe in
> the mouth, ripping open her cheek. When //Kushe's husband N!eishi
> came to her aid, /Twi deceived him too and shot him with a poisoned
> arrow in the back as he dodged. And N!eishi fell down.

> Now everyone took cover, and others shot at /Twi, and no one came
> to his aid because all those people had decided he had to die. But he
> still chased after some, firing arrows, but he didn't hit any more.

> Then he returned to the village and sat in the middle. The others
> crept back to the edge of the village and kept under cover. /Twi
> called out, "Hey are you all still afraid of me? Well I am finished, I
> have no more breath. Come here and kill me . . . Do you fear my
> weapons? Here I am putting them out of reach. I won't touch them.
> Come kill me."

> Then they all fired on him with poisoned arrows till he looked like a
> porcupine. Then he lay flat. All approached him, men and women,
> and stabbed his body with spears even after he was dead.

> Then he was buried, and everyone split up and went their separate
> ways because they feared more fights breaking out.

> There was talk among /Twi's people of a blood feud, but since
> blacks were living within a few days' travel, they gave up the idea,
> fearing retribution from the outsiders.

Commentary. This exceptionally graphic account brings out some of the drama of the action. The killer shot so full of arrows that he looked like a porcupine is a remarkable image of the capacity for collective action and collective responsibility in a noncorporate and nonhierarchical society. There is an air of unanimity of purpose here that is lacking in the previous account. Here the mere possibility of Bantu intervention was sufficient to deter further bloodshed while in case 6 the Tswana actually intervened. I interviewed the mother, father, and sister of the dead /Twi and the relatives of his victims. All agreed he was a dangerous man. Possibly he was psychotic.

The end of the fighting

Community-sanctioned or partially sanctioned killings of killers closed the books on four feuds totaling 15 fatalities. An additional 7 homicides were single occurrences without retaliation. In 2 of the latter cases (K7, K10), the killer escaped from the area and did not return. In 1 case (K8), where a man killed his father's brother, the group split and the two subgroups remained on cool terms for years. They minimized contact by not visiting each other's n!ores, though they did meet periodically at large winter water holes such as /Gam.

In 1 case (K9), in which one Dobe area man killed another, the killer not only remained in the area but married and had five children. The informants say that the victim's people did not retaliate because they feared Tswana intervention. Finally, in 3 cases of single killings (K20, K21, and K22) the law intervened and took the culprits to Maun for trial. None of the four defendants returned to the Dobe area, and no killings have occurred since 1955.

Clearly, the Tswana contact has played an increasingly important role in !Kung conflict resolution. Yet even before the arrival of the Tswana with their courts and customary law, the !Kung were not without resources for keeping violence in check. After the fighting, the parties would *//gau!kurusi* ("hang up quivers") to announce symbolically that the fighting was over for good. One informant had this to say about peacemaking in pre-contact times.

> In the old days the people would bury the dead and over the grave would look at each other with suspicion; there might be whispering of killing another. Then the one who wants to kill would cry out and writhe and tear his hair: "Oh why can't I kill one of them, since my man is dead?" But the elders would take hold of him and forbid further fighting.

> Then the elders would say: "We see that these people cannot live together properly. You people must separate and each group must go into its own n!ore and eat only in its own n!ore."

This is group fission on a grander scale, creating splits (as in K8) that might last for 20 years. But because of flexible group structure such a separation is not hard to maintain. And I suspect that the rather high incidence of marriages between former enemies signifies a way of reestablishing group alliances after the bitterness fades. Although these mechanisms continue to be much in evidence in recent years, the Tswana court has become the major means of conflict resolution among the !Kung. Early in the century the Motswana Murubela, leader of the Kubu clan, practiced a rough form of frontier justice in the Dobe area that is still remembered with awe. In a fight over adultery at !Kangwa, one !Kung man had killed another. Murubela was summoned, heard the evidence, and shot the offender on the spot! No further incidents of Tswana meting out summary justice have occurred in the Dobe area, but the one incident made a deep impression on the !Kung and may help to account for the fact that only one !Kung homicide occurred in the !Kangwa Valley between 1920 and 1946!

The latter date marked a second pivotal incident in !Kung conflict. A young man named Kxau shot and killed a Muyei settler who had been messing with Kxau's wife. In the ensuing outcry the Bantu colonists demanded that the Batswana tribal administration give them some protection against the "dangerous" !Kung.

As a result, Isak Utugile was appointed headman of the !Kangwa district, and he administered customary law there for the next 25 years. Since Isak became headman, !Kung have preferred to bring serious conflicts to him for adjudication rather than allow them to cross the threshold of violence. The *kgotla* ("court") has proved extremely popular with the !Kung. Many speak of the bringing of the *molao* ("law") to the district as a positive contribution of the Batswana. A number of the !Kung men have become knowledgeable in some of the finer points of Tswana customary law. The reason for the court's popularity is not hard to find: It offers the !Kung a legal umbrella and relieves them of the heavy responsibility of resolving serious internal conflict under the threat of retaliation. The court has also provided the !Kung some protection against unfair treatment and land grabs at the hands of the Bantu settlers (see Chapter 14). On the other hand, the impact of outside law should not be overestimated. Two homicides occurred in the Dobe area after the headman's appointment, and in Nyae Nyae one offender was killed after he had been jailed by the South African authorities.

DISCUSSION

In drawing together the strands of the analysis of !Kung homicide, one point stands out. The data fail to show a good fit between social conflicts and the person actually killed. A bystander or a third party is as likely to be killed as a principal in a fight. This unpredictability, coupled with the hysteria and absence of ritualizations that surround serious fighting, highlight the spontaneity of most !Kung fights. This is a society in which a high proportion of "crimes" are "crimes of passion." It may be useful to consider !Kung fighting as a kind of temporary insanity or running amok rather than as an instrumental act in a means–ends framework. Suggestive parallels to amok behavior exist in other areas of !Kung life, such as the violent displays of the inexperienced trance performers (Lee 1968b:41–2) and similar displays among grief-stricken adults and among young children during weaning.

Although the violent behavior itself may best be regarded as noninstrumental, this is not to say that adaptive consequences are lacking. The fear of violence, as Lorna Marshall has pointed out, is a prominent feature of !Kung life. It has been shown that this fear has a firm basis in experience; the effects of it upon their group structure should be spelled out. One of the principal means of resolving conflicts within groups is for the local group to split up and thus separate the parties to the conflict. Resolution or avoidance of conflict by group splitting is one of the major reasons why San groups appear to change in size and composition more frequently than the subsistence circumstances require. Because serious fights seem to be associated with larger groups, I suggest that fear of fighting tends to keep the living groups smaller in mean size than the numbers that the food resources of the local area could support. Actual fights, as far as I can determine, do not lead to redistribution of land (see Rappaport 1968). However, fear of fighting contributes to keeping groups small and frequently shifting in space (Chapter 12).

Some anthropologists have tended to treat conflict as a determinant of group structure that is somehow opposed to an ecological explanation. Thus, Turnbull (1965, 1968), in explaining the importance of group fission among the Mbuti Pygmies, has argued that it is conflict, not the search for food, that causes people to shift in space. Therefore, in his view, groups are structured more by social and political factors than by ecological ones. But the present analysis shows that conflict can usefully be considered in an ecological framework. Although conflict over resources is rare, the threat of conflict in general serves as an adaptive spacing mechanism that keeps groups well distributed on the land without recourse to any kind of territorial exclusivity.

Hunter-gatherer violence: An evolutionary perspective

We have examined !Kung conflict in detail, with special attention to homicide. That the !Kung do fight and sometimes kill has been thoroughly documented. It remains to be determined whether the !Kung violence rate is high or low by the standards of other societies. A total of 22 killings over 50 years in a base population of approximately 1500 gives a homicide rate of 29.3 per 100,000 person-years. This rate is high by African standards. Southall (1960:228) has calculated the homicide rates from court records for 23 Ugandan tribes during the late colonial period 1945–54. The figures range from 1.1 to 11.6 homicides per 100,000 population with a mode of 4.0 to 6.0.

The rates for urban industrial societies are also lower than the !Kung figure. In the United States in 1972, there were some 18,880 homicide victims for a rate of 9.2 per 100,000 population, one-third that estimated for the !Kung. Only in a few American cities did the homicide rate exceed that of the !Kung: Washington, D.C., 32.8; Baltimore, 36.8; Detroit, 40.1; and Cleveland, 41.3 (U.S. Bureau of the Census 1974).

At first glance, the !Kung homicide rate seems to rank very high, making the !Kung level of conflict comparable to the level in America's most troubled urban centers. However, these statistics unduly favor the United States. One reason the American homicide rate is as low as it is, is the availability of excellent hospital emergency room care for victims of knife attacks and gunshot wounds. Were it not for these medical facilities many more cases entered on the police books as aggravated assaults would be entered instead as homicides. Another hidden source of homicides is contained in automobile accidents, a significant proportion of which have a homicidal intent but are not reported as such in the crime statistics. But the most important difference between homicide rates among the !Kung and the modern nation-state has still to be mentioned. The figure of 22 dead plus a few other possible cases represents all the killing the !Kung did for 50 years; they do not engage in warfare. The American state, on the other hand, was waging a war in Vietnam characterized by massive bombing of the rural population. While 18,880 Americans were murdered at home, at least 10 times that number of Vietnamese and Americans died violently in 1972 as a result of the war. In calculating the rate, one should add the Vietnamese base population (30 million) to that of the United States (210 million). Adding Vietnamese, as well as American, casualties in Vietnam, and allowing for underreporting of domestic violence in the United States, brings the comparable American homicide rate to over 100 per 100,000 population. Even in times of peace, domestic underreporting alone would probably account for triple the current homicide rate of 9.2.

Other Western nations have recent homicide rates that are much lower than that of the United States. Canada, England, France, and Germany had homicide rates in the 1950s and 1960s that ranged between 1.0 and 2.5 per 100,000 population. Yet the same comments about emergency medical care and underreporting apply to the underestimation of homicide in these countries; and, of course, the tremendous slaughter of the populations of Europe during the two world wars is not represented in the annual reporting of domestic violence. If the millions of English, French, and Germans killed in 1914–18, and 1939–45 were prorated in the homicide statistics for these countries for the interwar and postwar periods, the rates for other industrial nations would equal or surpass the revised American figures of 100 per 100,000 population.

The balance sheet in this perspective clearly favors the hunter-gatherers, who manage to keep their killing rates low even in the absence of our elaborate system of police, courts, and prisons.

This revised view of the level of violence in one of the "simplest" societies on earth compared with the most "advanced" should lead us to reconsider the role so often ascribed to the state in the evolution of social control. It has been argued that the great advantage of the state in societal evolution is that it creates an overriding mechanism for containing and resolving social conflict. Sahlins (1968) has called the state a society especially constituted to maintain law and order. The vast administrative hierarchies of the state are, of course, absent in band and tribal societies. An alternative but complementary view is to regard the process of social evolution leading to the state as one of *externalizing* violence rather than *controlling* or *eliminating* it. Such a view enables us to see the evolution of social control in a different light. As human societies have evolved from bands (like the !Kung) to tribes and chiefdoms, each step up in the level of sociocultural integration has reduced the problems of violence at the previous level of integration, *but has opened up new forms of violence at the new level.* So, for example, in the nineteenth century the Batswana chiefdom imposed its order on the band-level San hunters in Eastern Botswana, only to wage intertribal warfare on a much larger scale against neighboring chiefdoms such as the Matebele and the Kalanga-Shona. Then at the end of the nineteenth century, the British industrial state brought the Pax Britannica to the warring chiefdoms of Southern Africa. But a generation later, the British mobilized thousands of Tswana warriors' sons to fight in the Mediterranean theater against the German and Italian national states. At each new level of integration, the scale on which violence is practiced becomes greater in terms of the numbers involved, the degree of organization, the length and intensity of the conflict, and the technological sophistication. Warfare, in Paul Goodman's phrase, has become less passionate precisely as it has become more violent. In this perspective the lowly !Kung, for all the fierceness of their poisoned arrows, may well be the harmless people after all.

The !Kung themselves should have the final word on the subject of violence. One afternoon I was interviewing about hunting success four men who had also been participants in several cases of homicide. As I asked them about how many kudu, gemsbok, and giraffe they had killed, it suddenly occurred to me to pose the question: "And how many men have you killed?"

Without batting an eye, ≠Toma, the first man, held up three fingers;

ticking off the names on his fingers, he responded: "I have killed Debe from N≠amchoha, and N//u, and N!eisi from /Gam."

I duly recorded the names and turned to Bo, the next man. "And how many have you killed?"

Bo replied, "I shot //Kushe in the back, but she lived."

Next was Bo's younger brother, Samk"xau: "I shot old Kan//a in the foot, but he lived."

I turned to the fourth man, Old Kashe, a kindly grandfather in his late sixties, and asked: "And how many men have *you* killed?"

"I have never killed anyone," he replied.

Pressing him, I asked: "Well then how many men have you shot?"

"I never shot anyone," he wistfully replied. "I always missed."

14

Economic
and social change
in the 1960s and 1970s

MOST of the world's recent hunter-gatherers experienced their major contact with *European* outsiders representing the commercial or bureaucratic advance guard of Western capitalism. Fur traders in Eastern North America and in Siberia, whalers in the Arctic, ranchers in Australia and Patagonia brought foraging people into sudden and often deadly contact (through disease and/or warfare) with the expanding frontiers of the European world system (Moorehead 1966; Wallerstein 1974). The Dobe area !Kung, by contrast, had a gentler introduction to non-San people. Except for a few white hunters, the main contacts the San had with outsiders before 1930 were with Tswana and Herero pastoralists and Bayei and Mbukushu agriculturalists. These were tribally based peoples whose lives were not so very different from those of the !Kung. Although the blacks grew food, raised animals, and made iron tools, their social systems, like the !Kung's, were based on kinship, and none had developed systems of exchange based on market principles or craft specialization. The Tswana were a chiefdom with the beginnings of internal ranking, and the !Kung were immediately accorded a position at the bottom of the Tswana social scale. But it should be emphasized that in the Dobe area the San were not enslaved or enserfed; nor were they propelled into the cash economy. The nature of the contact, in socioevolutionary terms, occurred between more or less adjacent stages within the sequence of precapitalist social formations. In the early days Tswana and !Kung men hunted side by side, each with bow and arrows, and even in recent years Tswana and Herero women have been observed gathering wild plants alongside !Kung women in times of drought.

Therefore, in tracing the roots of the changes in the Dobe area we must first consider San–black relations. It was not until the 1930s that European colonial presence was even felt in the !Kung interior, and it was 1960 before actual direct administration was established – with the founding of the South African settlement at Chum!kwe. Since that time

Plate 14.1.   !Kung women help a Herero neighbor (*right*) to stamp her meal.

the pace of change has increased, and by the 1970s a complex situation had developed with the San experiencing simultaneously the transition to farming and herding, the appearance of wage labor and schooling, and the potential loss of their land base. The San started the twentieth century on the farthest perimeter of the developing world system; by the late 1970s they were on the verge of being swept up in the national and class conflicts of the modern world. The purpose of this chapter is to describe each of these new challenges and to try to unravel the transformations that are taking place.

The analysis is considered in two parts. The first part concerns the changes that were occurring before 1970 when the locus of decision making still resided within the Dobe area community. These include:

1. Improvements in hunting and gathering
2. Mafisa work on blacks' cattle posts
3. Transition to farming and herding
4. Migrant labor, wage work, and penny capitalism

The second part deals with changes since 1970 and involves the shift of political power to agencies *external* to the Dobe area. These include:

5. The introduction of schools
6. Changes in land tenure
7. Opening of missionary activity
8. The Office of Basarwa (Remote Area Dwellers) Development in Botswana
9. Armed liberation struggle in Namibia and South African counter moves

Table 14.1 summarizes the main historical events of the last 110 years.

IMPROVEMENTS IN HUNTING AND GATHERING

Not all technological changes have led to a change in the mode of production. In the initial stages such changes can lead to a refinement of the existing mode. A case in point is the introduction of donkeys to the Dobe area. The donkey is not milked nor is the meat eaten, and it is too small an animal to be hitched to a plow, but the donkey is a handy means of transportation, and by 1968 out of 151 !Kung men some 58 claimed to own one or more donkeys. The animals were obtained in a variety of ways: bought with wages from work for Europeans, as a payment for work for blacks, and as hxaro exchanges from other !Kung. Donkeys were widely used for travel within the Dobe area and to the east across the Middle Passage, but not for travel to the west because after 1957 San livestock found in South-West Africa was confiscated and shot by the South African police. Donkeys were also used as beasts of burden to carry

Table 14.1. *Chronology of events in the Dobe–Nyae Nyae areas*

11,000 B.P.	Hunting and gathering population established in area by this time
1870s	First visits of Tswana hunters to area
1879	Visit of hunter Hendrik Van Zyl to /Xai/xai
1896–7	Rinderpest epidemic
	Division of area between Batau (Mhapa) and Bakubu clans of the Batawana
1904–5	Herero–German War: Herero refugees flee east through area
1910–25	Mafisa cattle enter Dobe area
ca. 1925	Arrival of first year-round black settlers
1934	First survey of border area by Bechuanaland Protectorate police
1948	Appointment of Isak Utugile as !Kangwa district (= Dobe area) headman
1951	Marshall expedition reaches Nyae Nyae
1954	Border road surveyed
1957	Expulsion of Herero and their cattle by South African police from areas west of border
1960	Start of South African settlement at Chum!kwe, South-West Africa
1963–4	First Lee–DeVore field trip to Dobe area
1965	Border fence built
1966	Botswana independence
	South African mandate terminated by UN. South-West Africa becomes Namibia; South African occupation continues
1967	Opening of BTA store at !Kangwa
	Second Lee–DeVore Field trip
1969–73	Reinforcement of border fence
	Start of South African military border patrol using !Kung trackers
1972	Tribal grazing lands policy (amended) legislation passed in Botswana
1973	Opening of !Kangwa school
	Third Lee field trip
1974	Establishment of Office of Basarwa Development in Botswana
	First !Kung children in !Kangwa school
	First government-assisted well digging
	Botswanacraft buying trips to Dobe area
1975	South African invasion of Angola
	Arrival of first missionary in Dobe area
1976	Dobe area closed to anthropological researchers
1977	Opening of second area school at /Xai/xai

bags of mongongo nuts and meat from kill sites back to camp. About 120 of the donkeys in the Dobe area in 1968 belonged to San, though not all of these were in regular use (Table 14.6). Though the price of a donkey in those days was $7 to $15, only a third of the men owned one, and many donkeys each year strayed or were lost to lions or sickness or were given away as hxaro. At Dobe, for example, there were no donkeys until 1969, and until then all the subsistence work was carried out on foot.

Surprisingly, donkeys were not used in hunting except to carry meat home. The men said that tracking was better on foot; the sound of the donkeys would frighten the quarry away. Occasionally !Kung men would join the Herero to hunt gemsbok from horseback, borrowing both weapons and mounts from the Herero.

The horse is the aristocrat of the domestic livestock of Botswana. In the 1960s the price of a horse varied between 3 and 6 cows, equivalent to 15 to 30 donkeys. Only two !Kung owned horses in 1968, although three others had owned one in the past, and five more men claimed to have owned a horse each when they were working in the East or on European farms.

The use of firearms in hunting had made only modest inroads into the Dobe area in the 1960s. In 1968 one man (the tribal police constable) owned a gun, and 26 others had hunted with borrowed guns and killed game with them. A further 28 men had had the experience of firing a gun, but 94 others had neither owned nor fired a gun. When the !Kung men hunted with borrowed guns, the kill belonged to the gun's Herero or Tswana owner, not to the hunter. Therefore, even though hunting with guns was more efficient than hunting with bow and arrow, only a small proportion of the meat so killed found its way into the !Kung subsistence economy.

Curiously, the introduction of more stringent game laws in post-Independence Botswana has strengthened rather than weakened the !Kung's reliance on bow-and-arrow hunting. In the colonial period, under Tswana tribal law, it was considered the right of every indigenous man to own a gun and to hunt game without restriction. In 1968, new legislation empowered the Botswana Game Department to put a number of species on the restricted list and to charge a tax for killing most other game animals. A "ticket" for killing one kudu, for example, cost R4 ($5.60) under the new plan. (In the 1960s 1 South African rand equaled $1.40 [U.S.]. Its value rose to $1.50 [U.S.] in the early 1970s, and then fell to $1.15 [U.S.] in the mid- and late-1970s.) The San were exempt from the fee system as long as they continued to use their traditional bows, arrows, and spears. The ruling cut two ways: On the one hand it was a humane recognition of the San's continued dependence on game for their survival; on the other hand, some observers felt it thwarted their transition to the cash economy and thus contributed to their underdevelopment. Whatever the effect, the Dobe San persisted as traditional subsistence hunters into the 1970s at least in part because of government fiat.

Commercial hunting hardly existed in the Dobe area during my fieldwork. A few men owned steel traps for capturing fur-bearing animals such as genet, wild cat, and bat-eared fox, but sales of these furs to traders during the 1960s contributed at best only R20 to R40 per year of cash income in the Dobe area. At the Chum!kwe settlement commercial hunting was better developed. One /Xai/xai man described how he would

Table 14.2. *Dobe area livestock census: June 1968*

Area	Cattle	Sheep	Goats
Eastern N!umsi			
!Goshe	568	5	96
!Kangwa, /Bate	976	0	197
Western N!umsi			
Mahopa, !Xabe,			
!Kubi	2387	120	1256
/Xai/xai	542	2	241
Total	4473	127	1790

Source: Veterinary Department, Government of Botswana, Maun.

Table 14.3. *Number of !Kung men working for Bantu*

Type of work	Men working in 1968	Worked previously	Lived with but never worked	Never lived with Bantu	Total
Cattle	39	83	11	11	122
Other	2	5			7
All	41	88	11	11	151
Percent	27	58	7	7	99

go out hunting large antelope with a government rifle to provide meat for
sale to road gangs and construction crews. And this practice was beginning to penetrate the Dobe area as well. By the mid-1970s Wiessner
reported (personal communication) that /Xai/xai San hunters were actually *selling* game meat to other San for cash, an unheard-of practice in
the 1960s.

MAFISA WORK ON BLACKS' CATTLE

A Veterinary Department livestock census in June 1968 showed a total of
almost 4500 cattle and 1800 goats in the Dobe area (Table 14.2). Of the
black population of 350, only 80–90 were men of working age. The demand for additional labor was therefore considerable, and a number of
!Kung men found work tending the livestock of their neighbors. In 1968,
41 !Kung men were actually working for the blacks, an additional 88 had
worked for them in the past, and only 11 of the 151 had never lived with
the blacks (Table 14.3).

!Kung worked cattle under three rather different sets of conditions. At !Goshe one living group (LG 20/64) operated under a classic mafisa system, a cattle share cropping arrangement found all over Botswana. They cared for the cattle of a Tswana master who lived in Maun and who visited infrequently. The decisions on the day-to-day management of the herd resided with the !Kung alone. All the milk was theirs to dispose of, and when an animal died they ate the meat, though they had to give an accounting of gains and losses to the master when he visited. If their work was satisfactory, he gave a calf or two in payment, and as a result several members of this group owned cattle of their own, which they herded along with the master's.

A second and more common kind of arrangement existed at !Goshe and most other water holes. A middle-aged !Kung man established a long-term relationship with a resident Herero or Tswana cattle-owning family. While he tended the cattle, his wife and sisters, and often other relatives, helped the women of the cattle post with chores. These open-ended arrangements have lasted for two generations in some cases and have involved the workers' children as well. An entire *camp* can be linked with a black patron, as were LGs 19/64, 22/64, 31/64, and 32/64; the younger men of these groups worked the cattle while other group members hunted and gathered. Client groups can also be involved, as in the case of LGs 3/64, 4/64, and 29/64.

In a third variant, which included all the other client groups, a single family or even a single individual worked on cattle. This arrangement was more often a short-term one, lasting 1 to 3 years, and ceased when the employee decided to move back to his parents' or his wife's camp. However, long-term relations lasting 10 to 20 years were not uncommon. For example, old Dam and between five and a dozen of his relatives spent the entire period 1963–73 living at Yehaveha's cattle post at /Xai/xai (LGs 33/64, 31/68, and 26/73).

In arrangements of the second and third types, the economic decisions were in the hands of the black owners, while the !Kung clients shared in the daily food of the cattle post and received other perquisites such as clothing, donkeys, and occasionally a calf of their own. The main advantage of this kind of arrangement from the workers' point of view was the steady diet of milk and grain and the possibility of offering hospitality to their camp-living relatives out of the master's and mistress' food supplies! The blacks, being themselves tribally based people with strong rules of hospitality, were relatively free with their surplus milk, and as a result many cattle posts received a few !Kung visitors every day throughout the year. The people of Dobe water hole, for example, made frequent trips to Mahopa to pass the day and drink the milk of Katjambungu's cattle. In July 1964 they spent 20 person-days there, a third of their total out-visiting time (Table 9.4).

Milk was and is the major product of the Bantu cattle posts, and life revolves around the morning and evening milkings. Milk is never consumed fresh, but is always poured directly into large gourds to be cultured into a tangy and refreshing sour-milk drink the Tswana call *maswi*, the Herero *omaihi*, and the !Kung *ku n!um* (meaning "ripe milk"). The Herero drink the whole soured milk as their staple diet; the !Kung get it in two forms: whole and skimmed (the latter is called *matuka* in Herero). In the summer months when milk was most plentiful, a number of !Kung women and men found work around the cattle post churning matuka in gourds. The gourd was hung from a tree by leather cords and rocked back and forth for 30 minutes or so to separate out the butter, which was skimmed off and given to the master, leaving the skimmed (cholesterol-free) soured milk to be consumed by the worker and her family (and if there was extra, by her dogs). As often as not, the whole milk was given to the visiting San with no work expected in return, and so over the years all the !Kung, even from the most traditional camps, have come to visit the cattle posts for at least a few days or weeks each year.

I was initially puzzled by this arrangment. It was not clear why the blacks gave the San so generously of their milk. Was it because they felt an indebtedness for the use of !Kung land? Or did they fear that the !Kung would steal their cattle if milk products were not freely given? Probably elements of both motives are involved, but there is a third and possibly more relevant explanation that has to do with the factors of production in pastoralism. Until the 1970s the blacks of the Dobe area were not plugged into the market system for their cattle. They sold off only a few head each year in order to buy consumer goods or to pay their taxes. As a result very large herds of cattle have built up in the area (4500 cattle and only 350 black people in 1968). With a 12:1 cow/person ratio, the blacks needed not only labor for herding but also help in handling the young and milking the cows. In subsistence cattle production the herders always must decide how much of the herd's milk output should be drawn off for human consumption and how much left to foster the growth of the year's crop of calves. With their own subsistence needs taken care of, the blacks could have let the calves take the rest, but Herero and Tswana herdsmen pointed out to me that calves not regularly taken away from their mothers so that the latter can be milked may grow up into unruly and semiwild adults. Therefore, it was to the herders' advantage to have their animals milked on a daily basis, even if the milk was not required by their own households. The San who milked the cows and consumed the milk were therefore providing a useful service to the blacks in managing the herds. Also advantageous to the herders was the fact that the San could be seasonally laid off when the milk supply declined.

Table 14.4. *!Kung planting experience*

Growing season	Men who planted		Men who did not plant		Total	
	Percent	No.	Percent	No.	Percent	No.
1968–9	51	62	49	60	100	122
1967–8	38	56	62	92	100	148
1966–7	15	16	85	90	100	106
Prior to 1966	55	82	45	66	100	148

TRANSITION TO FARMING AND HERDING

At the time of my first field trip in 1963, the Dobe area !Kung appeared to be full-time hunter-gatherers, with no agriculture or livestock (except at !Goshe). As the fieldwork proceeded, however, a more realistic picture emerged of the "pristine" nature of the Dobe area. I learned that most of the men had had experience herding cattle at some point in their lives and that many men had owned cattle and goats in the past. Further, the !Kung were no strangers to agriculture. Many had learned the techniques by assisting black neighbors and in years of good rainfall had planted crops themselves. For example, in the good rainfall years of 1967–9 about half the !Kung men made at least one attempt at farming, with varying degrees of success (Table 14.4). However, because of the extreme unreliability of the rainfall, none of the San had succeeded in establishing themselves on an agricultural basis. The same pattern occurred with livestock raising. Men often obtained cattle or goats in payment for working for the blacks, but only a few families had set themselves up as herders independent of a black patron. Here is a description of !Kung farming practices in the 1960s.

A typical field was oval, 0.25 to 1 ha in size, and had an outer perimeter that was heavily brush-fenced against the incursions of local livestock. The main technique was dry cultivation. There was no irrigation and very little slashing and burning. The farmer often chose as a site an abandoned cattle kraal because the animal droppings provided fertilization. Several households in a single camp would combine their efforts in putting in a field. The men did the heavier work of brush fencing, and men and women were observed to share equally in the clearing, hoeing, and planting. The hoe was used for most of the fields, though a few !Kung farmers at !Goshe, /Xai/xai, and Mahopa borrowed steel plows and oxen to plow their fields. After the field was sown, there was little attempt at weeding; no modern agricultural inputs such as herbicides or pesticides were available. Many fields were attacked by birds, locusts,

Table 14.5. *!Kung planting and success rates with four major crops*

| | Men who never planted | | Men who planted | | Of those who planted | | | |
| | | | | | Percent success-ful | No. suc-cessful | Percent with mixed results | Percent unsuc-cessful |
Crop	%	No.	%	No.				
Tobacco	36	54	64	97	68	66	14	18
Melons	47	71	53	80	61	49	20	19
Maize	48	74	52	77	35	27	30	35
Sorghum	66	101	34	50	48	34	26	26

and boring insects, and these agents coupled with the unreliability of rainfall destroyed much of the standing crop before it could be harvested. Although no yield figures are available, my impression is that even in 1967–8, a good year for rainfall, only about 10 to 40 percent of the total area planted in each field actually produced crops.

In all, the !Kung planted 10 different crops, including gourds, marijuana, sugarcane, and beans, but by far the most important crops – those planted by 50 or more families – were maize, melons, sorghum, and tobacco (Table 14.5). Surprisingly, tobacco was the most frequently planted crop: 97 of 151 men had tried to grow it, and 66 had succeeded. Tobacco is also the most difficult crop of the four to grow, requiring deep shade and daily watering. The fact that the !Kung devoted so much of their farming effort to a nonfood crop suggests that the motive of increasing the food supply was not uppermost in their minds.

Melons, of the highly diverse *Citrullus* or *Cocylanthus* genus, were the most successful food crop for the !Kung. These melons, cross-pollinated with wild and feral forms (see Appendix D), were grown in several varieties and were usually cooked before eating. The taste resembled that of summer squash. Maize is the prestige crop of Botswana, and the !Kung were eager to cultivate it. Ground maize, called "mealie meal," is the staple food of workers and peasants all over Southern Africa and was sold at trading posts in Botswana during the 1960s at 10 to 14 cents (U.S.) per kilogram. Seed, in the form of whole maize kernels, is also readily available. Probably two-thirds of all the acreage planted by the !Kung and their neighbors was devoted to maize, but the results were poor. Maize, an imported crop, requires a certain minimum rainfall and does poorly in the sandy soils of the Dobe area. When a !Kung farmer gets 50 or 100 ears of corn from a 0.5-ha field, he is considered to have had a good year.

Sorghum, the fourth major crop, is much more drought-resistant than maize, and those who planted it enjoyed a better rate of success (48 percent of the men who planted sorghum harvested it, compared with 35

Table 14.6. *Livestock holdings by !Kung men: 1967–9*

No. of animals	No. of men with		
	Cattle	Goats	Donkeys
0	110	99	93
1	22	21	31
2	9	7	10
3	2	7	8
4	2	4	4
5	2	9	4
6–10	2	2	1
11+	2	2	0
Total men	151	151	151
Total animals	ca. 102	ca. 155	ca. 120

percent for maize). And the yields per hectare appear to be much higher for sorghum as well. At !Goshe the !Kung harvested their sorghum in June 1968, and it was still being eaten by them and their guests in October of that year. The government's Agricultural Extension Department even distributed bags of drought-resistant sorghum seed to !Kung and other marginal farmers during the 1967 and 1968 growing seasons.

Despite these efforts, agriculture continues to be a very risky proposition for the Dobe area !Kung. Only at !Goshe, where the !Kung enjoy the patronage of an influential Tswana-Yei cattleman, has agriculture begun to provide a significant proportion of the subsistence. Under Mr. M. Morapedi's guidance, the !Goshe people had begun to cultivate what are, by !Kung standards, giant fields of 5 to 10 ha. The strategy for the !Kung at the other water holes seemed to be to put in the seed and hope for the best. At /Xai/xai, for example, some maize, melons, and sorghum appeared in the diet in April, May, and June 1968, but by July all these foods had been consumed and the people were back to bush edibles.

Unlike farming, livestock production *is* an economically viable adaptation in the Kalahari, and it continues to be the economic mainstay of Botswana. Some form of herding represents the main hope for the future development of San communities, and if established on a small scale could avoid the dangers of overgrazing and environmental degradation. During 1967–9 only about 100 head of cattle and 155 goats were owned by !Kung in the Dobe area, representing about 2 percent of the cows and 8 percent of the goats in the district (Table 14.6). To operate a pastoral household requires at least 5 or 10 head of cattle with at least 2 or 3 reproductive cows to provide milk. Only six !Kung families owned the minimum number and of these only one man had set up with his family as independent farmer-herders (LG 6/68). Most of the other people let their animals run with the herds of their black neighbors. A goat herd is easier to manage, and several families at Mahopa, Bate, and !Goshe have built kraals and assembled small herds consisting of their own goats and those of their relatives. These families put the children of the camp to work herding and watering the goats while the adult members combined farming with gathering and hunting. These are the modest beginnings of animal husbandry among the !Kung on their own, not as employees or clients of black masters. The advantage of goat herding is that the !Kung can get into it without a great capital investment; for the price of a cow one can buy 6 to 10 goats. The disadvantage is that goat herding ties the family members down and hampers them from going to the bush to find food, but does not provide any caloric input because, unlike cows, the goats are not milked. The main advantage of goats is their convertibility to other valuables: Several people obtained their first cow by selling a herd of goats. Apart from its exchange value, a goat's only other use is as meat.

The possession of a herd of goats or cattle, or of a field of maize and melons, puts !Kung farmer-herders in an anomalous position. The demands of the work routine require some obvious changes in their life style. First, their mobility is restricted by the need for daily supervision of the animals. It is not as easy for family members to go on an extended foraging trip or to pay visits to relatives at distant camps. Second, there are daily tasks to be performed and the children are pressed into service. Draper (1976) has described how the children of the sedentary villages are put to work tending the animals or helping with chores, a contrast with their carefree life in the bush camps (see also Kolata 1974). A more subtle change noted by Draper (1975) concerns the separation of men and women in daily work and the confining of the latter much closer to home. In bush camps both women and men go far afield in the food quest. In village life, the men maintain their mobility, following the herds, but the women become housebound with more of their time spent alone with their children and less with peers on common productive tasks. Perhaps the beginnings of the subordination of women can be glimpsed here in the reorganization of household work loads around the demands of farming and herding (see Lee 1975).

CONTRADICTIONS BETWEEN FORAGING AND FARMING

The most striking anomalies are observed in the tense relations between those families of !Kung who have begun to farm and herd and their relatives who continue the foraging life. There are real contradictions between the organization and ideology of farming and the organization and ideology of foraging. The most important of these is the contradiction between *sharing,* or generalized reciprocity, which is central to the hunting and gathering way of life, and the *saving,* or husbandry of resources, which is equally central to the farming and herding way of life. The food of the !Kung camp is shared out immediately with residents and visitors alike (Chapters 5 and 12); for herders to do the same with their livestock, or farmers with their harvested grain, would quickly put them out of business.

When a !Kung family harvests a crop or comes into possession of livestock, it comes under intense pressure to share the good fortune with kinfolk and affines. If the family gives in to these demands, its stocks are quickly depleted; but if it refuses, it is accused of being stingy and "farhearted." In grappling with these contradictions people at times make what appear to us to be strange choices. One enterprising Mahopa man named Debe assembled a small herd of goats and cattle and appeared to be on his way to becoming a successful herder. But when meat was scarce his relatives would visit from /Xai/xai, and under heavy social pressure Debe would slaughter one goat after another, until after several years he sold or gave away his remaining herd saying that the responsibilities were too heavy. Debe was also successful as a farmer, and his relatives were equally glad to consume his harvested crops. Later he tried to enlist the help of his /Xai/xai relatives in building a larger field for planting crops they could all enjoy. But they were so reluctant that Debe in disgust *hired* an itinerant black for wages to help him clear the land and build the brush fence – the first case we know of in which a San paid wages to a Tswana. Oscillating between exhorting his kinfolk to help him farm and hiring an outsider, Debe seemed to be caught in the contradictions between a communalistic and an individualistic style of work relations.

Another instructive case involved a man named Bo of LG 6/68, the leader of the only group whose members established themselves as independent farmer-herders. Bo took great pride in his herd of six cows and his fields of maize and melons, and he emphasized to all who would listen that he was on his own and not under Bantu patronage. Bo was also a rational man, and when his many kinsmen and affines came to his hamlet to share in his good fortune, he fed them a fine meal, offered his fire for overnight, and sent them on their way the next morning with a handful of his home-grown tobacco. Bo knew that nothing could dissipate his surplus more quickly or more surely than the arrival of kin on extended visits, so he sent them on their way. The effects of this were striking: People spoke of Bo as stingy and far-hearted; he became feared, and there were mutterings that he had learned techniques of witchcraft from black medicine men. Then his son's wife left her husband and other kin shunned Bo's camp, leaving Bo a successful but isolated farmer-herder. Finally, in 1970, Bo had had enough. He sold all his cattle and other stock for cash, packed his things, and walked across the border to settle at Chum!kwe in Namibia.

In making the transition from foraging to farming, ecological factors are clearly only part of the problem. Factors internal to !Kung society also provide obstacles, and the transition is not smooth and continuous but rather sharp, discontinuous, and conflict-ridden as the contradictory ideologies of sharing and husbandry are juxtaposed. With sufficient time, the !Kung could probably make the transformation to small-scale farming and herding successfully and could restore reciprocity and equality on a new and higher level of surplus accumulation, in which due recognition is taken of the farmer's right to his corn crop and the herder's right to his own flocks. But time is one thing the San have in short supply: Even as these new economic arrangements were being worked out, changes of an even greater magnitude were on the horizon. Capitalism was coming to the Dobe area.

MIGRANT LABOR, WAGE WORK, AND PENNY CAPITALISM

Cash and the cash economy were virtually unknown to the Dobe San in 1963. Several dozen men had worked for the blacks in the East or on European farms in the South, but they were usually paid in kind, not in cash. Only the handful of men who had gone to the mines or men and women who had worked for the government on tsetse fly control projects had had the experience of being paid in cash. The !Kung's innocence of the world of money was brought home to me by an incident that occurred in December 1964. I was on the point of leaving the field and was paying off one of the two local !Kung men I had hired. The man, ≠Dau, was one of the most experienced and worldly-wise of all the !Kung; he had traveled to Maun many times as valet to Headman Isak, and he used to regale the other !Kung with tales of the wonders of the outside world. ≠Dau had worked 2 months for me at a salary of £5 per month, so I handed him two crisp £5 notes and warmly shook his hand. His face fell and he moved away, obviously disappointed. Seeing this, I followed him and asked what was the matter. At first he was reluctant to speak, but at my urging he finally blurted out: "/Tontah, when you hired me you promised me ten monies, but now you have given me only two!"

It took several minutes of explaining with the help of Tswana friends to convince the incredulous ≠Dau that each of the monies in his hand was worth five and that indeed he had received his £10 in full. Other !Kung crowded around and marveled that by simply altering a mark shaped like a *1* to a mark shaped like a 5 you change a value of £1 to a value of £5.

Over the next few years the pace of labor migration increased, and when I returned in 1967 I found the !Kung men talking with more sophistication and assurance about the wider world. In 1963 none of the !Kung had been aware of the existence of the Atlantic Ocean, only 800 km west of them. (When I asked about the biggest water they knew of, they all

Table 14.7. *Wage work by !Kung men*

Type of work	South-West Africa	Botswana	South Africa
No wage work		91	
Tsetse fly control		19	
Chum!kwe settlement	15		
Witwatersrand mines			15
Farm laborers	8	1	
Anthropological expedition	2	5	
Cattle guard BTA		5	
Veterinary department		3	
Road gang	2		
Jail	2		
Well digging		2	
Safari company		1	
Brick making		1	
Nokaneng store		1	
Sehitwa store		1	
Total jobs[a]	29	39	15

[a]The 60 men who had worked for wages held a total of 83 jobs.

pointed north to the Okavango River, not west to the Atlantic.) By 1967 young men were bantering about the relative merits of Fanisisi (Francistown), Johanni (Johannesburg), and Binduka (Windhoek) as places to work.

A 1968 survey of work experience showed that although 91 men had done no wage work, 60 others had some experience of working for wages (Table 14.7). During the 1950s and early 1960s the Tsetse Fly Control program of Bechuanaland hired gangs of several hundred men and women for a month each year, at about 50 cents per day plus rations, to clear forest habitats near Tsau and Nokaneng that were favorable to fly transmission; 19 !Kung men had participated in the tsetse fly program. Similar short-term jobs at the Chum!kwe settlement in South-West Africa had involved 15 men, and 9 others had done European farm work in the Gobabis district of South-West Africa. Farm wages, if paid at all, varied between £1 and £2 ($2.80 to $5.60 U.S.) per month. Other men had found local work on road gangs, well-digging, and veterinary fencing projects; and 2 men even listed jail terms in South-West Africa as wage work, which indeed they were as convicts placed on work gangs were paid 20 cents a day!

During the period 1900–70 migrant labor to work in the gold fields of South Africa was a main source of income for hundreds of thousands of African men drawn from Lesotho, Swaziland, Mozambique, Botswana, and as far away as Angola and Malawi. This demand for labor was and is

Plate 14.2. The recruiting depot at Shakawe for migrant laborers to South Africa.

a major cause of rural underdevelopment in Southern Africa. In many
districts of Lesotho and Mozambique, for example, between a third and a
half of the able-bodied men are absent on mine work at any given time.
During the 1960s remittance payments from mine workers constituted
the bulk of the cash income in many rural districts of the countries on
South Africa's periphery (Wilson 1972:21–34).

By 1968, 15 Dobe area men, about 10 percent of the adult male population, had made the trip to Johannesburg; 8 of them had made two or
more trips, and 1 man had signed on for five of the 9 month tours of duty.
Men reported wages of between R12 and R18 per month ($18 to $25
U.S.), but from this total were deducted the worker's off-hours canteen
and bar bills, so that when the Dobe area workers were paid off at the
end of their contracts, most brought home only between R25 and R40 in
total.

In order to go to Johanni, Dobe area men had to walk out 100 km to the
main road at Nokaneng and hitch a ride north to the Witwatersrand
Native Labour (Wenela) recruiting depot at Shakawe. After receiving a
cursory medical examination, they would wait along with 150 other men
for the weekly flight to the mines. At Johannesburg they were sent to one
of the 40 or so giant gold mines on the Rand in the Transvaal or in the
northern part of the Orange Free State. The shorter men were classified
for surface work at lower pay; the taller and huskier ones were chosen for

the more dangerous and better paid underground work. Returning home after 9 months' work, the men were paid off in cash at the Wenela airstrip in Shakawe, where a variety of home-brew joints and prostitutes were waiting to relieve them of part of their pay. Many returning workers have brought gonorrhea back to the Dobe area as a result. With the rest of their money the men purchased clothes, shoes, saddles, blankets and yard goods, and sometimes donkeys to make their way back to the home area. The system of remitting mine wages back to families in the rural areas was unknown among the Dobe San. There was no post office, and neither the workers nor their wives could read or write. Instead, the !Kung had developed a standard method for translating the values gained through wage work back into significant values in the local exchange system. On returning home, the mine workers' behavior followed a consistent pattern.

For example, when young Bo returned to !Kangwa in September 1968, he was dressed to kill in fedora, plaid shirt, undershirt, sport jacket, long pants with cowboy belt, underpants, new shoes, and socks. Over the next few days his wardrobe dwindled as each item of clothing appeared in turn in the costume of a friend or relative. By the third day Bo himself was strolling around dressed only in his undershirt and his leather *chuana,* the standard breechclout of !Kung men. Bo had given away his entire wardrobe in the hxaro network, and we enjoyed seeing one of his kinsmen appear in fedora and chuana, another in sport jacket and chuana, and so on. At /Xai/xai, a 30-year-old man who had made four trips to the mines came back after a 5-year absence laden with goods. He turned the whole lot over to his father for distribution, saying that having been away for so long he was afraid of offending someone if he did the distribution himself. For the Dobe area !Kung the trip to the mines was still an adventure and a windfall. This indicates that they had yet to be incorporated into the South African sphere of rural underdevelopment in which such trips have become a matter of economic survival for thousands of African families.

Before 1967 the only opportunities for wage work were *outside* the Dobe area. In that year the mercantile system came to the area in the form of a retail store operated by the Botswana Trading Association (BTA) owned by Greek immigrants in Maun. The store, housed in the first modern building ever constructed in the !Kangwa Valley, sold mealie meal, soap, kerosene, clothing, saddles, and dry goods at inflated prices and purchased cattle from the Herero at reduced prices. In 1968 the !Kangwa store paid between R3 and R5 per hundredweight, about R1 to R2 per hundredweight less than the going rate for cattle in Maun. The San had few, if any, cattle to sell, but the store did have two effects on them. Five young men were hired for wages to tend and water the purchased BTA cattle. The pay was only R6 to R8 per month ($8.40 to 11.20

U.S.), but even this small amount has had a major impact in a world without cash. By 1973 a large camp of 25 people (LG 13/73) had built up around the workers at the BTA cattle post and well southeast of Bate. The cattle boys disposed of their wages in much the same way as did the returning mine workers. Every penny was rapidly disseminated within the population in the hxaro networks. Livestock was purchased as well. By 1973 virtually every member of LG 13/73 had a donkey to ride on, the first mounted "band" of !Kung.

But the major social impact of the store on both the San and their black neighbors came not from the wages but from a single store-bought commodity–sugar. Sugar is the prime ingredient in the potent home-brewed beer (actually a form of mead) that is the centerpiece of a new culture that has sprung up around the !Kangwa store. The beer, called *khadi*, is a clear amber beverage that looks and tastes like a sparkling hard cider. It is made from brown sugar and *Grewia* berries, with fermentation induced by a mixture of bee earth, honeycomb, and honey called *seretse*. Combined with 7.5 liters of spring water in an enamel bucket, these ingredients are allowed to churn and bubble for 24 hours. When the churning stops, the residue is strained out to be saved for further use, and the khadi is ready for drinking. A number of !Kung women have set themselves up as penny capitalists, buying the sugar at the store and selling the product at 5 cents ($.07 U.S.) a cup. A single batch of beer requires 20 cents' worth of sugar and yields 16 cups, for a gross income of 80 cents and a net income of 60 cents (equivalent to $.84 U.S.). The !Kung are scrupulous businesswomen. They do not give drinks on credit, and even close kin are charged the full price for each drink. However, after the day's business is done the same women are seen sharing their wild plant foods in the traditional !Kung way with their erstwhile customers at the evening meal.

Where does the money come from? A mine returnee with even R5 ($7 U.S.) in his pocket can provide 100 people with the price of a drink, and much of the cash is circulated from the workers to their friends, to the beer makers, and back into the community. Since 1967 !Kangwa has become the center of a new !Kung culture based on selling and drinking beer and listening (and dancing!) to hit tunes from Radio Botswana on transistor radios. !Kung drinking behavior resembles that of their Herero and Tswana neighbors, whose women also brew and sell beer. Drinking is confined to the hottest hours of the day, beginning at 10 in the morning and continuing to late afternoon. The hot sun overhead must speed the alcohol's effect because most people are thoroughly drunk by 2 in the afternoon. !Kung drinking parties are loud and rowdy, with shouting and laughter that can be heard a good distance away. Sometimes they take a nasty turn and fights break out, like the brawl at !Kangwa in which a mine returnee gave another man a blow with a club that fractured his

Plate 14.3. The arrival of the BTA truck bringing brown sugar for beer making.

skull. By nightfall the partygoers have finished for the day and disperse to eat the evening meal or to sleep off a drunk.

By 1973 the level of drunkenness had increased to alarming levels. As more money flowed into the !Kung economy from wage work and craft sales (see below) much of the proceeds went into drinking bouts that went on 7 days a week near the !Kangwa store. The magnitude of the problem was brought home to me late one night in July 1973 when I witnessed the arrival of the supply lorry at the BTA store. No supplies had come in from Maun for 3 months, and the truck's arrival was greeted with jubilation. When the goods were unloaded I saw why: Of a total cargo of 4 tons, almost 3 tons consisted solely of bags of sugar for making beer–enough sugar to make almost 3000 buckets of home brew! When the store opened its doors the next morning, Herero, Tswana, and !Kung women were lined up three deep at the counter to buy bags of brown sugar, and by the following afternoon it seemed as if everyone at !Kangwa over the age of 16 was happily drunk.

Not all the Dobe area !Kung were pleased with the new cultural life. Many expressed fear at the effects of drinking on people's behavior; the loss of control, the fighting, and the neglect of daily tasks were seen as signs of the breakdown of the fabric of society. Stories were told and retold, with a mixture of glee and apprehension, of the bizarre behavior

of people under the influence. A man named ≠Toma had stepped out of a
drinking hut to urinate and had blithely pissed into a Herero woman's
cooking pot filled with meat. In the uproar that followed he narrowly
escaped a thrashing by the woman's husband. A case was brought in the
headman's court, but ≠Toma disclaimed all responsibility saying that *he*
would never do such a thing; it was entirely the fault of the beer. The
headman was not persuaded by this argument and fined him a goat for
the outrage. On another occasion, the leader of LG 7/73, a respected
medicine man, got drunk and fell down a well. Having received cuts and
scratches, he was helped back to his camp, where he proceeded to vomit
into the central fire, spewing sparks and steam in every direction. This
helped him to sober up, and immediately he went into a self-induced
trance to speed his recovery; then he entered a deeper trance and effectively started healing a sick relative who had come to him for treatment.

Incidents like these juxtaposing adaptive behavior with out-of-control
behavior were widely discussed and helped convince many !Kung at other
water holes that !Kangwa was an evil place to be avoided. Travelers from
the South African settlement station at Chum!kwe described the same
kinds of behavior there, with frequent fighting, accidents, and loss of
workdays to drunkenness and illness related to drinking.

The !Kung San of the interior had entered the 1960s in their isolated
areas with their group structure and productive systems intact. Through
the decade, the Dobe area became open to outside penetration, starting
with the building of the Chum!kwe settlement in 1960 and continuing
with the opening of the !Kangwa store and its home brew supplies in
1967. The arrival of the anthropologists in 1963 and their continuous
residence from 1967 to 1971 also had its effect. But a 1960 visitor returning in 1970 would have had no great difficulty in recognizing the !Kung
he knew before. More store-bought clothes, more babies, and more
donkeys and goats were in evidence, but the basic pattern remained the
same. The decade of the 1970s, however, brought new challenges that
threatened to change fundamentally the basic pattern of !Kung existence. In the early part of the decade the Dobe !Kung passed from a
situation of local autonomy to one in which the direction of their lives
came increasingly under outside control. The remainder of this chapter
examines the emerging dominance of outside agencies in the areas of
education, land tenure, administration, and military matters.

SCHOOLING AND LAND TENURE

Plans were announced in 1968 to build a primary school at !Kangwa, but
almost 5 years passed before the school actually opened its doors in January 1973. The school, a two-room single-story structure, had two teachers
and offered Standards I to IV. The first class consisted of 55 Herero and

Tswana students aged 5 to 10, all enrolled in Standard I. The school day started at 7:30 A.M., ended at noon, and was followed by a lunch feeding program prepared by parent volunteers. In the afternoon the teachers offered literacy classes for children too old to register in Standard I and for adults. The medium of instruction was Setswana, and the curriculum both mornings and afternoons was the standard one for Botswana schools, consisting of learning to read and write Setswana, with English and arithmetic as secondary subjects interspersed with singing, art, and bible stories.

Of the 60 or so !Kung children of school age, *not a single one enrolled in January 1973.* When I spoke to them in July of that year, !Kung parents gave several reasons for their children's nonparticipation. Many said that the R3 ($4.50) annual school fee was too high for them. When I observed that R3 per year was not an outrageous amount for people who brew beer and work on the BTA cattle, they pointed out that in addition to the fees, each child had to purchase an obligatory school outfit consisting of shoes, underpants, sweater, shirt, and short pants for the boys, shoes, underpants, sweater, and dress for the girls. Such an outfit cost between R15 and R17 at the local store, plus the weekly cost of the laundry soap to keep the clothes clean. This sum put the cost of schooling out of the reach of all but a few !Kung families. For those who *could* pay for the fees and the outfits, there remained yet another problem of equal magnitude: how to feed and care for the children in !Kangwa 5 days a week for 8 months of the year. At !Goshe, for example, several families had the means to put their children in school but were reluctant to move to !Kangwa away from their flocks and fields. For the foraging !Kung the problem was even more acute. Even though the children would receive a nutritious school lunch, how was the rest of the family to forage for sufficient food in the immediate vicinity of !Kangwa, which already had a resident population of 63 !Kung? !Kung life depended on mobility, a demand that stood in direct conflict with the school's requirement of regular attendance.

But the high costs and problems of feeding did not exhaust the list of reasons the !Kung did not put their children into school in January 1973. Especially at water holes west and south of !Kangwa, parents expressed concern that the school was located at the village where the heaviest drinking took place. They feared their children might be beaten or neglected if they were left in the care of !Kangwa relatives. A fourth issue raised by a number of parents was the corporal punishment meted out by the schoolmaster. Some Tswana parents echoed this concern, and several who had enrolled their children withdrew them after they were caned by the teacher. A fifth reason given by some parents concerned reports from relatives who had children in the school at Chum!kwe, South-West Africa. According to these reports schoolchildren there were growing up to be disrespectful and contemptuous of their parents and even za-ed them, a form of verbal sexual insulting expressly forbidden between parents and children (Chapter 13).

In short, the !Kung were faced with a real dilemma. They had many good reasons for being suspicious of the school and its impact on their lives, yet if the children did not gain some literacy skills, they would find themselves severely disadvantaged in the rapidly evolving world of land claims, jobs, and international conflict that surrounded them. The central government was creating laws that would increasingly have a direct impact on !Kung lives, and unless the San could read and interpret these laws and make the appropriate responses their way of life would be in danger. The ability to read and write, therefore, was becoming an even more important skill than hunting in the struggle for survival.

A critical example of how the !Kung's lives were being affected by government edicts was the Tribal Grazing Lands Policy (TGLP) Act and its various amendments passed between 1968 and 1975 (Republic of Botswana 1975). These laws provided a mechanism for taking land out of communal tenure and putting it into what amounted to freehold tenure to encourage more businesslike farming and ranching practices. Until Independence, the great bulk of Botswana's land had been held under a tribal form of tenure. In this system the paramount chief of each of the eight Tswana tribes doled out parcels of land to senior Tswana lineage heads to allocate grazing and agricultural rights. The Kubu and Mhapa families controlled the !Kangwa and /Xai/xai valleys, respectively, under this system. Effectively, it was a form of communal tenure; no land taxes or grazing fees were paid, and no one could appropriate a piece of land for his own exclusive use. In the Dobe area, this tribal tenure coexisted with the !Kung n!ore system: Foragers and herders shared the water holes and the space around them. As one Herero man pointed out to me: "People don't eat grass, and cattle don't eat mongongo nuts."

With Independence came a plan to rationalize the country's cattle industry and take land out of tribal tenure and allocate it to individuals and syndicates on 50-year renewable leases. The lessees would survey and fence the land and would limit their herd sizes to the number of animals that could be supported in line with modern range management techniques. The proclaimed advantages of the new system of land tenure were the prevention of overgrazing, the control of diseases, and the introduction of better breeding lines. The modern rancher would be required annually to sell off surplus animals and thus ensure a steady supply of beef for the Botswana Meat Corporation, the giant state-owned abattoir in Lobatsi. The plan's proponents hailed it as the start of a new era in scientific and profitable animal production. But for students of economic history the TGLP appeared to be nothing short of the capitalist transformation of agricultural land. Like the Enclosure movement in seventeenth-century Britain and similar movements in many other Western countries, the Tribal Grazing Land Policy was a means of transforming inalienable communal land into valuable real estate the leases for which could be bought and sold. And like the Enclosure movement it threatened to transform the people who lived on that land from independent hunters and herders into tenants and landless squatters.

To the government's credit, safeguards were installed to prevent the too rapid takeover of tribal land by unscrupulous speculators. The National Policy on Tribal Grazing Land of 1975 specified that no leasehold application could be made for land that was within 5 miles of an existing communally used well. Outside this limit the new land tenure rules could apply, but it was usually necessary to dig a new well before securing the land. Also, land boards were set up in each district to screen every application before deed and title were granted. The process was a laborious one, requiring the submission of written documents and frequent appearances before the local land board to give testimony in Setswana (Republic of Botswana 1975:10–15).

In spite of the safeguards, the !Kung of the Dobe area and other Basarwa were at a great disadvantage under the new legislation. Lacking schooling, they were quite out of their depth in the legal complexities of land board negotiations. Also it was impossible for them to make the frequent trips to Maun to attend the land board hearings. And in addition few, if any, Basarwa had the financial or technical means of digging a well with a reasonable chance of striking water, a process that required special equipment and months of work at a well site often far from existing water. Therefore, without some additional safeguards or an agency acting on their behalf, it appeared as if the Basarwa would be quickly dispossessed of their land. Such a process had already occurred in the Ghanzi District, where several thousand San were squatters on European-controlled land (Guenther 1976). And several instances on a smaller scale had already occurred in the Dobe area between 1968 and 1973. For example, soon after the land board was set up, a Herero man named Kamundundu started digging a wildcat well at Characharaha Pan, a traditional mongongo area and summer water for !Kung people from !Kangwa (grove number 11, Table 7.1). Had he succeeded in striking water, he could have restricted the San's access to the area. After the !Kangwa San made several angry representations to Headman Isak, Kamundundu was ordered to stop digging his well, which was already 12 meters deep, and he was forced to return to his home area near Maun. Similar attempts at unauthorized well digging occurred at /Xai/xai and Mahopa, resulting in further San deputations to Isak. The old headman, then almost on the verge of retirement, advised the San that the best way to protect their land was to start digging wells themselves. Their traditional claims to the land were well established, and if they could find water the land board would grant them title and thus secure their land base. His advice struck a responsive chord in the San and starts were made on several wells.

BASARWA DEVELOPMENT INITIATIVES

The year 1973–4 marked a turning point for the Basarwa of the Dobe area. To understand why, we have to look at developments at the national level in Botswana, because the threats to the land base of the Dobe San were also being experienced by other San groups throughout the country. For the first time the issue of the future of the Basarwa in Botswana society became a nationally discussed question. Editorials, letters, and articles appeared in Botswana newspapers and magazines as the people of Botswana tried to come to grips with the question of whether the Basarwa were second-class citizens in a land committed to racial and ethnic equality. The choice of the name *Basarwa* was itself indicative of the changing climate of opinion (Chapter 2). The new awareness was the result of a three-pronged initiative. First, Basarwa people themselves were becoming more vocal in expressing their feelings of deprivation and of being excluded from the mainstream of society. Second, international attention was being focused on the racial struggles in the neighboring white-dominated states of South Africa, Rhodesia, and Namibia. The existence of an oppressed minority – the Basarwa – in the context of an African people who were themselves oppressed by the white supremacists created an uncomfortable anomaly in Botswana's political posture. A third theme emerged from within the young Botswana elite. Liberal, Western-trained Batswana and expatriate civil servants and legislators saw the Basarwa as in some ways analogous to the aboriginal minorities in Canada, Australia, Malaysia, and other Commonwealth countries, minorities with whom they shared some of the same social stigmas and disadvantages. It thus became a sign of modernity to acknowledge the existence of this minority and to make some provision for its special status and needs.

The result was the establishment in 1974 of the Office for Basarwa Development within the Ministry of Local Government and Lands. Armed with a budget of about $35,000, the Basarwa Development Office (BDO) was given the job of enumerating the Basarwa, finding out what their special needs were, and giving grants to local district councils specifically earmarked for Basarwa citizens. Education, bore holes and water rights, craft marketing, and agricultural extension work were the major kinds of projects funded by the BDO, which worked closely with international funding groups. In 1975 Basarwa development work was incorporated into the National Development Plan with a greatly expanded budget of between $180,000 and $375,000 per year.

The impact on the Dobe area was striking. Within 2 years of the establishment of the BDO six major developments occurred within the area.

First, a scholarship and feeding program was set up in 1974 to enable 22 !Kung children to attend the !Kangwa school; this was similar to a smaller-scale program for !Kung children at Kauri east of the Dobe area. The local district council agreed to match a $700 grant provided by the Kalahari Peoples Fund, an organization founded in 1973 by anthropologists who had done fieldwork with the San and who were concerned about their future (Lee and DeVore 1976:21–4). The program provided school fees and school outfits for each pupil and weekly rations sufficient for the pupils and their families. The program involved 22 children in 1974, 32 in 1975, and 42 in 1976. In 1977 a second Dobe area school opened at /Xai/xai with 30 !Kung and 4 Herero children as pupils. Similar scholarship programs were set up in several other Botswana districts. In this way the San were beginning to become equipped with the skills necessary for survival in the modern world.

Second, in looking for alternative sources of income to livestock production and wage labor, the BDO encouraged the San to market their traditional crafts for sale to tourists and for export. Some craft marketing had gone on for many years previously, with tremendous profit taking by the European middlemen and very poor returns for the San producers. In Ghanzi in the mid-1960s, one of the trading stores paid the San a standard rate of fifteen cents for a string of ostrich eggshell beads and sold the same string to a tourist for 10 times that amount. The same beads sold in Johannesburg curio shops for $7 to $15, up to 100 times what the San producer had received. In 1969 the government-owned Botswana Development Corporation founded Botswanacraft, a craft-purchasing and marketing agency. The agency's buyers traveled throughout the country purchasing both traditional and modern crafts of every ethnic group and paying the makers a standard two-thirds of the retail price. The people of the Dobe area went to work with a vengeance producing crafts, and from 1974 on, the area experienced a veritable cash explosion, selling between $300 and $500 worth of crafts *per month* to Botswanacraft. At /Xai/xai alone, for example, the income from sale of crafts between April 1975 and March 1976 came to $2235, for an average of $186 per month. Overall cash income at /Xai/xai for the period totaled $3450 (Wilmsen 1976) a point discussed further in Chapter 15.

Initially the influx of money caused a boom in beer making at !Kangwa, and the brewing of beer, drunkenness, and squabbling spread to the other water holes as well. The increase in drinking caused a crisis in the school program; several parents, fearing for their children's safety, withdrew them from school. Gradually the crisis was brought under control as anthropologists working with the BDO persuaded the San to drink less and to place part of their craft income into a trust fund for use in community

Plate 14.4. !Kung men earn cash by selling bow and arrow sets to the craft marketing board.

development projects before the monies were entirely consumed in buying sugar for beer.

As the pace of development increased at the national level, a third change occurred in the Dobe area. The !Kung of Dobe had never been missionized, though a Dutch Reformed missionary had been working at neighboring Chum!kwe since the mid-1960s. In 1975 Brother Charles Rotsart, a Belgian priest of the Catholic order of the Little Brothers of Jesus, was given permission to set up a mission in the Dobe area. Brother Charles had worked with !Kung communities in Angola before being driven out by Portuguese bombings of his mission. He was more interested in saving the !Kung's land base than in saving their souls, so his major efforts were directed to helping the !Kung organize their well-digging activities (the fourth major development). With funds from overseas sources such as Oxfam-U.K. and Oxfam-Canada, the Kalahari Peoples Fund, and church philanthropies, Brother Charles purchased dynamite and a jackhammer and compressor to aid the San in drilling through rock strata that lay between the surface and the water-bearing levels.

By 1977, the San of the Dobe area and points north had applied to register 20 well sites. But even with the encouragement of BDO personnel, the San had received land board approval for only 5 of these well sites. And progress at these was encountering many obstacles. As of mid-1978, only 1 approved well, at Dobe itself, had actually struck water; 4 others (at /Twihaba, Characharaha, /Dwi!ā, and N//ani) were in abeyance because the work groups could not be organized. Applications for 4 other sites were pending before the land board, and at the remaining 11 sites work had ceased with no immediate prospect of resumption (Basarwa Development Office Report 1977). Problems in well digging appeared to be both of a technical and an organizational nature. With the increase in international tension in Botswana as a result of the military conflicts in neighboring Namibia and Rhodesia (Zimbabwe), blasting materials (dynamite, fuses, detonators) have proved difficult to obtain. Without dynamite, progress is very slow and because of this slow progress at the existing well-sites, community motivation has been low for mobilizing the considerable labor required to dig at the other well sites. Although the San, with BDO assistance, have been more successful in handling the red tape of land board applications, the process is still slow, with the hearings spread out over a year or more.

Progress has been more substantial in agricultural development, the fifth area of change. The process for registering agricultural fields a few hectares in size is much simpler than the process for registering grazing land, which may involve over 100 km² of territory. Aided by a local BDO agricultural officer funded by the Kalahari Peoples Fund (Mr. Leonard Mathlare), the San have succeeded in registering and planting 11 fields at /Xai/xai, 15 at Dobe, and a number of others at !Goshe and at other water holes outside the Dobe area. The fields at !Goshe now range in size up to 15 ha; at Dobe and /Xai/xai the fields are between 1 and 2 ha. The BDO has also helped the San to purchase steel plows and borrow Herero draft animals to plow their fields. Mathlare also reports increased livestock holdings among the !Kung, with 20 head of cattle at Dobe water hole alone in 1977.

Ironically, the sixth consequence for the !Kung of the establishment of the BDO concerns their relations with the team of anthropologists who had been living with them on and off since 1963. Over the years the San and the anthropologists had developed bonds of friendship and sentiment that went beyond the researcher-researched relationship. !Kung sentiment expressed itself in the form of incorporating each of us into their kinship system, thereby giving us each a distinct social identity within the community. We reciprocated by founding the Kalahari Peoples Fund, a vehicle for discharging our responsibilities to the community by working with it in development projects. The wheel came full circle when the officers of the BDO, while applauding our efforts for San welfare, took a dim view of our research work and closed the Dobe area to researchers for an indefinite period starting in 1976.

Anthropologists continued to work with San in other parts of the country. In 1977 the BDO became the Extra-Rural Development Office (ERDO) which later was renamed the Remote Area Dwellers Office (RADO). In 1978, the office underwent other changes of structure and personnel, indicating a further downgrading of Basarwa development as a priority for governmental planning.

THE MILITARIZATION OF THE SAN

The shift in government priorities regarding the San becomes understandable in light of the rapidly changing political situation in Southern Africa. Since the early 1970s Botswana has found itself in the center of three rapidly escalating liberation struggles in bordering countries: in Rhodesia (Zimbabwe) to the east, in South Africa to the south, and in Namibia to the west. Much of the debate between scientists and administrators over the best development strategy for the Botswana Basarwa is rendered academic by this far more serious threat to the people of Botswana. The Dobe area !Kung, in particular, have been steadily drawn into the military events in neighboring Namibia. The roots of the Namibian conflict can be briefly traced.

From 1915 on, South Africa administered the former German colony of South-West Africa under a League of Nations mandate. Following World War II, when all the other mandate powers turned their mandates over to the jurisdiction of the United Nations Trusteeship Council, South Africa alone refused to relinquish its control over South-West Africa. After two decades of diplomatic struggle, the United States declared South Africa's mandate null and void in 1966 and turned nominal jurisdiction of the territory, named Namibia, over to the Council for Namibia, a United Nations body with headquarters in Lusaka, Zambia. In the same year, the people of Namibia, under the leadership of the South-West African Peoples Organization (SWAPO), launched an armed struggle to liberate their land from South African domination, a process discussed in detail elsewhere (Hurlich and Lee 1978). Since that time the struggle has intensified, particularly along the 800-km-long northern border between Namibia and Angola. In the period 1973–7 South Africa moved an estimated 50,000 troops into Northern Namibia and built a massive military base and air field at Grootfontein, a town only 260 km west of the San settlement at Chum!kwe. It was from this base that the South Africans launched their ill-fated invasion of Angola in October 1975.

Such a massive buildup could not fail to affect the San of the central !Kung interior. Their once-isolated border area had become part of the frontier between the white-ruled South and the front line states of independent Black Africa (Figure 14.1). Yet because of the area's isolation, the military impact came late and in a less drastic form than in other areas of Namibia. But it came nonetheless. As recently as 1964 the

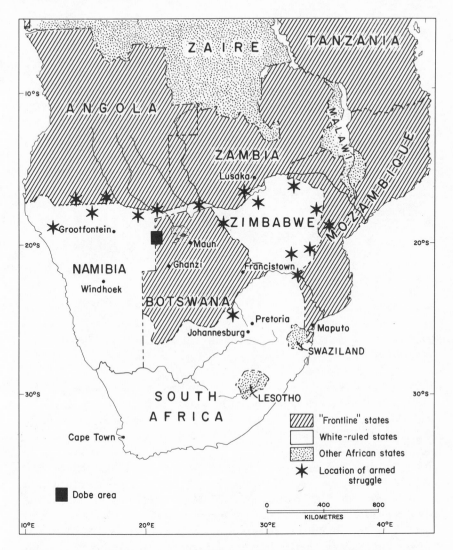

Figure 14.1. The Dobe area in relation to the liberation struggle in Africa.

border was marked only by a dirt track patrolled every few weeks by South African police. The !Kung moved freely back and forth, hunting and gathering on both sides of the line. In 1965 a fence was built the entire length of the border; it was periodically reinforced and increased in height, until by 1973 the fence, called *chipi* ("iron"), by the !Kung, stood 3 meters high and consisted of 17 strands of barbed and unbarbed wire. The !Kung were not specifically prohibited from moving across the line, but the existence of the fence had an inhibiting effect and cut off the !Kung increasingly from their foraging areas in Namibia. The fact that

Plate 14.5. The Namibian border fence in 1973 (a stile allows the !Kung to move back and forth).

the Nyae Nyae !Kung were settled at Chum!kwe on the other side of the fence did not make available any additional foraging space for the Dobe area !Kung; in fact, the gathering range for the latter was significantly reduced between 1960 and 1970, not increased as Williams (1977:761–3) erroneously suggested.

The South Africans also increased the frequency of their patrols through the period, from biweekly or weekly between 1965 and 1968, to daily *ground* and/or *air* patrols by 1977. More important, after 1970 the police recruited Namibian !Kung trackers to patrol the border on foot. They set up and supplied base camps every 50 km or so along the border and trained scouts to make daily trips up and down the line looking for fresh tracks of possible guerrilla incursions. In the Dobe–/Xai/xai sector there were several camps, including one at !Kwidum south of /Xai/xai and another at /Dwi!kā north of Dobe. Each morning a scout would set out from each camp; they would meet in the middle, spend the night at Dobe, and the next morning set off back along the border. Any tracks seen were reported to the police vans on their daily rounds. Although the San scouts carried only bows and arrows on their patrols, more recent reports state that they were receiving weapons training from the South African police (Basarwa Development Office 1977; *Windhoek Advertiser* 1977). The trackers and their families have been largely drawn from the

/Du/da southern population first contacted by us in March 1968. From being the most isolated !Kung foragers we ever saw (Chapter 3), they have been transformed in less than 5 years into the most acculturated of all the San in the study area. They are now fully incorporated into a force of wage laborers whose activities and movements are directly controlled by the South African police.

Accompanying this militarization of the /Du/da people has been a belated South African attempt to win over the "hearts and minds" of the Dobe area population. When the fence was built to its present height, the police saw to it that stiles were placed at 30-km intervals enabling people (but not their animals) to cross over into Namibia and back. Every week the police send word across of when a truck will be going into Chum!kwe. On the appointed day Basarwa and Herero line up at the stile. They are given a lift to the Chum!kwe store to buy what they need and are driven back to the border the same day. Since prices tend to be lower at Chum!kwe than at the !Kangwa store, these shopping junkets have proved popular with the Basarwa and their neighbors, and this has helped to soften the image of the Boers as ruthless and cruel toward nonwhites. Obviously this has been a calculated move on the part of the South Africans to secure the loyalty of politically unsophisticated minorities, while practicing severe repression against more politically conscious groups elsewhere in Namibia. Thousands of Namibians have been jailed or shot by South Africa in recent years. As SWAPO organizers are also active throughout the border areas of Namibia, it is almost inevitable that there will be an armed clash involving San on one or both sides in the near future, though such a clash has not occurred as yet. One cannot help but note the parallels between the South Africans' manipulation of the San for their own purposes, and the history of the American Special Forces attempts to train the Montagnard minorities of Vietnam to fight against the peasant armies of the National Liberation Front in Southeast Asia.

15

The lessons of the !Kung

W HEN I began my work with the Dobe !Kung in 1963, the hunting and gathering peoples occupied a curious role in anthropological theory and popular imagination. In scholarly circles there was by the 1960s no question of the hunters' evolutionary status: They were not missing links; they were as human as we. Recognizing our common humanity with the hunters, however, did not prevent many anthropologists from setting them apart in yet another way – as illustrations of humans at the limits of technological simplicity and of environmental harshness. Living at the edge, so to speak, they nevertheless faced what was to us their miserable fate with courage and dignity in adversity. Robert Flaherty's epic film, *Nanook of the North*, widely shown to generations of North American children and adults, was the paradigm of this view. Thornton Wilder's play, *The Skin of Our Teeth*, presented the same line in comic form with Mr. Antrobus, the earlyman-everyman, watching his pet dinosaur (and just about everything else) succumb to the onrushing ice age. Echoes of this theme are found in many introductory textbooks in anthropology, and such views of the foragers are even more common in related disciplines of sociology, history, and economics, where Marxist and non-Marxist scholars alike seem to agree on one thing: that life in the state of nature was, in a word, tough.

I was skeptical. This view of our hunting and gathering ancestors' initial adaptation made it appear as if survival had been touch and go all the way. How were we to square this image of precariousness and struggle with the indisputable fact that we humans have been a fabulously successful species? Our forefathers and foremothers expanded numerically to settle a multitude of environments on six continents long before the invention of agriculture and the Neolithic Great Leap Forward.

I began to suspect that hunting and gathering could not have been as precarious an existence as it was made out to be. For reasons that were not clear at the time, it seemed that researchers had unconsciously been skewing our sample of foraging peoples to emphasize the harsh, the stark, and the dramatic at the expense of the routine, the mundane, and the uneventful.

This line of thinking led to several further questions. How hard or easy *was* it to make a living as a hunter-gatherer? What actual measurements could be made? Was it even possible to observe hunters and gatherers today, or had the surviving groups been irrevocably changed by contact? The attempt to answer these questions led in turn to fieldwork with the !Kung San and eventually to the book you have before you. In this final chapter I want to review the major findings of this "revisionist" account of a foraging people and use this summary, in turn, to pose two further questions: Can the data from living hunters and gatherers be used to reconstruct a picture of hunters and gatherers in the Pleistocene? And can such data shed any light on the social conditions in contemporary societies?

In the study of contemporary foraging societies there are skeptics and believers. Some scholars have argued that the study of modern foragers yields little information of general value to anthropological science, and they take a dim view of attempts to apply ethnographic data in reconstructing the past. Others have approached the foragers with enthusiasm, finding in them a rich mine of data and insights for constructing models of the behavior of prehistoric people.

My own view is that the data from hunting and gathering studies *have* an important role to play in social science. Foraging was the way of life that prevailed during an important period of human history. The modern foragers do offer clues to the nature of this way of life, and by understanding the adaptations of the past we can better understand the present and the basic human material that produced them both. However, we must also acknowledge that the method has limitations. Much of the debate between the skeptics and the believers has suffered from a lack of clarity about the methodology of ethnographic inference. On one side, the skeptics have argued that we have no way of knowing what the behavior of early hunters may have been like. In their view the hunters of the Middle Pleistocene, for example, may have behaved entirely differently from any of the known modern hunters, and therefore ethnographic analogies may be entirely inappropriate (Freeman 1968; F. Clark Howell 1968:287–8). On the other side is a group of scholars who, far from denying the relevance of ethnographic data, have applied specific data from the !Kung directly and uncritically to the interpretation of archeological materials thousands of years in the past (e.g., Speth and Davis 1976).

In one important respect, the skeptics make a valid point. Modern foragers *are* different from each other and from ancient foragers. We will make no progress in this area by simply applying specific ethnographic data to specific archeological sites. But it seems equally implausible that the behavior of ancient foragers would fall entirely outside the range of behaviors of the modern ones. Though specific ethnographic data may be of little use in reconstruction, if we can discern the *principles underlying foraging behavior* in all its variability, we can apply these principles to more dynamic models of foraging societies past and present.

I believe that two lines of investigation, each with a distinctive kind of inference, can lead to insights on hunter-gatherers and human evolution. The first, called the *uniformitarian* approach, is a method for treating the quantitative ecological data in a more rigorous way in order to sort out which aspects of foragers' behavior are central and closely linked to structure and which aspects of their behavior are situational, variable, and not closely linked to structure. The second line of investigation yielding insights of a broader nature arises from an examination of the foraging mode of production and its associated superstructure. Whereas the uniformitarian approach deals primarily with *etic* categories, behavior that can be measured by a community of observers, the *Marxist* approach from mode of production deals with both *etic* and *emic* categories, the latter being the culture bearers' own categories for organizing experience and giving meaning to their lives. The Marxist approach recognizes above all that the populations we are dealing with are human, composed of actors who make conscious and unconscious choices based on their perceptions of external realities and on the set of rules or ideologies provided by their culture. Mechanical models drawn from animal behavior and animal ecology, however sophisticated, cannot do justice to any but the simplest of cultural ecological phenomena.

UNIFORMITARIANISM AND MARXISM

The first of the two methods for evolutionary analysis was set out informally in 1968 (Lee 1968c:353–4) and developed further in later papers (1972c:177–85, 1973a:85–94). It is called the uniformitarian approach to evolutionary reconstruction following the term widely used in nineteenth-century geology (Lyell 1830). Uniformitarianism holds that the same geological processes that can be observed in the present were operating in the past and that these processes, not sudden catastrophes, are largely responsible for producing the world's known geological formations. The philosophy underlying uniformitarianism makes the theory applicable to other fields as well. Nancy Howell (1976a) has applied the concept in a stimulating way to the study of human paleodemography, and following the lead of Bruce Trigger (1973:109), I want to use it for the analysis of human paleoecology.

We start with the assumption that some of the same processes we see at work in contemporary foragers were also at work in prehistoric foragers. What are these processes? We may have no way of knowing whether an ancient people had a Crow kinship terminology or cross-cousin marriage or whether they worshipped one god or several, but we can be quite sure that they ate, slept, moved around their range, reproduced and died, and that they lived in groups of some sort. Thus four fundamental variables provide our starting point: energy, space, resources, and vital statistics. Foragers have to expend energy in work in order to absorb energy in consumption. They have to move around their range in order to find the resources necessary to life. Their caloric intake has to provide for their own needs; for the needs of nonproductive young, sick, and old; and for the extra demands of reproducing the next generation. And they have to live in social groups as do all terrestrial primates, for their health, safety, and social needs. In other words, whatever the specifics of their ecology and culture, all foragers have to have some level of work and caloric intake, some sort of group size and group structure, some sort of access to local resources, and some sort of seasonal and annual round. These define the parameters of their existence, and the range of variability within the parameters is far from infinite. Caloric requirements, for example, are closely tied to body size, temperature, and level of work effort (Chapter 9); reproductive rates, as Howell has shown, vary within a surprisingly narrow range in human populations.

In showing the relationships between elements of the reproductive system, Howell (1976a:27ff) has made the important point that there is a tight articulation between the various components. A certain birthrate combined with a certain deathrate generates a given life expectancy and age pyramid. Too often an investigator reports a birthrate and a life expectancy that bear little or no relation to one another. Such anomalies demand explanation; yet, as Howell points out, many investigators have been unaware even of the existence of these anomalies!

Components of ecological systems behave in a similarly tightly articulated way. For example, a 400-kg antelope yields 600,000 Cal in meat, and at 2000 Cal per person per day, the antelope is large enough to provide food for 300 person-days. This could consist of 1 day's food for 300 people, 10 days' food for 30 people, or 30 days' food for 10 people. If an investigator postulated that 50 such animals were required to provide for the annual needs of a group of 30, we would have reason to be skeptical because such an input alone would exceed their *total annual requirements* by 40 percent without taking other food sources into consideration. In light of the articulation between group size, caloric requirements, and caloric yields, we can legitimately assume that in the example given, either group size should be much larger or number of animals killed much smaller. If both are accurate and all the meat was consumed, we must reluctantly conclude that each member of the group gained 30.6 kg (67.5 lb) during the year in question! The same kinds of articulation can be extended to include range size and work effort along with group size and caloric quanta. A further application of this method is explained below under "The Dynamic of Movement" as well as in Chapters 9 through 11. For our present purposes it is sufficient to say that a uniformitarian approach provides parameters within which key variables fluctuate, and the knowledge of their articulations allows us to test models of group structure and behavior of prehistoric foragers against the behavior of contemporary foragers by a best-fit method. Although this model does not answer all the criticisms of the misuse of hunter-gatherer data in reconstructing the human past, it does, I believe, lay to rest the objection that the behavior of prehistoric foragers may have fallen completely outside the range of behavior of contemporary peoples.

When we come to the cultural practices of foragers as distinguished from their ecological behavior, the problem of analogy to the past is greatly complicated. The uniformitarian approach is not adequate to deal with problems of consciousness. For this research area we need an explanatory framework that can account for the facts of material existence, the ideological superstructure, and the complex relations between the two. As suggested in Chapter 1, the Marxist framework of historical materialism can provide the key. In this final chapter I return to Marx for a deeper understanding of the nature of the foraging way of life. Marx saw the relation between the material conditions of life and the cultural and social level as a relation between base and superstructure. In a famous and much-quoted passage from the "Preface to 'A Contribution to the Critique of Political Economy' " (1859) he used this pivotal relation to propose a promising research strategy for understanding particular societies and societies in general:

> In the social production which men carry on they enter into definite relations that are indispensable and independent of their will; these relations of production correspond to a definite stage of development of their material powers of production. The sum total of these relations of production constitutes the economic structure of society–the real foundation, on which rise legal and political superstructures and to which correspond definite forms of social consciousness. The mode of production in material life determines the general character of the social, political, and spiritual processes of life. It is not the consciousness of men that determines their existence, but, on the contrary, their social existence that determines their consciousness. [Marx 1859:137]

In his later work, *Kapital* (1867), Marx proposed a more subtle kind of feedback relation between the foundation, or base, and the superstructure, with the causal flow in both directions and with base determining superstructure "in the final analysis" (Marx 1867). This should be kept in mind when interpreting the passage above. Marx never postulated hunting and gathering (foraging) as a distinct mode of production. It was always included together with other pre-class societies based on fishing, horticulture, and pastoralism in a category labeled "primitive communism," "primitive communalism," or "tribal ownership" (Hobsbawm 1965:122). The evidence from a century of anthropological research, however, strongly supports the view that it should be considered separately. Foraging was not only the original mode of production, but it was a way of life that characterized the first 80 to 95 percent of the total history of the human species. All the rest of Marx's historical epochs and modes of production – the Oriental (Asiatic), Ancient, Germanic, Feudal, and Capitalist – are products of the last 10,000 years (Hobsbawm 1965).

Marx made the important point that the distinct social and political forms and ideology of each society within a mode of production were closely related to the ways people organized their work and to the ways the ownership of the means of production was allocated. In applying this theory to the foraging mode of production, it is best to see which aspects of the cultural and social superstructure correspond most closely to the base, because these are likely to give a clue to underlying principles. Sharing is an example of such a cultural practice. Sharing deeply pervades the behavior and values of !Kung foragers within the family and between families, and it is extended to the boundaries of the social universe. Just as the principle of profit and rationality (the French call it *rentabilité*) is central to the capitalist ethic, so is sharing central to the conduct of social life in foraging societies. Sahlins (1965, 1972:185–277) found the principle of generalized reciprocity to be a universal among hunting and gathering peoples. Therefore, when we discuss sharing and other central features of !Kung foraging, we are not simply looking at a cultural practice unique to them, but rather at an expression of a universal theme in the foraging mode of production.

These two tools of analysis – the uniformitarian and the Marxist – yield different kinds of insights; yet both have a role in the understanding of human history. In the discussion to follow, we begin with the conclusions that rest on more precisely quantified data on food, tools, work, fitness, reproduction, and mobility. When we move on to consider the foraging mode of production, it is to draw the links between these basic facts and the superstructural categories of sharing, male-female relations, values, and what can be called the quality of life.

ABUNDANT FOOD AND SIMPLE TOOLS

What conclusions can justifiably be drawn from this study of !Kung ecology and how can these be applied to the past history of humanity? One conclusion is that among the !Kung, food supply is sufficient to their needs, and they achieve this state of affairs with only the simplest of tools. This finding challenges the widespread popular and scientific notion that the way of life of hunter-gatherers is precarious and full of hardship and that the life of man in the "state of nature" was "nasty, brutish, and short."

The foundation of !Kung subsistence rests on the 105 species of edible wild plants found in their area, crowned by the remarkable mongongo fruit and nut, which may alone provide up to half of their vegetable diet. But even when the mongongo harvest is poor, as it was in the unusually heavy rains of 1973–4, the !Kung are buffered from hardship by dozens of other major and minor foods. This variety of food sources provides a cushion against a wide range of ecological variability: some foods are adversely affected by drought, but others are drought-resistant; some foods are damaged by heavy rainfall; but other foods (like tsama melon) actually thrive on it.

The traditional !Kung are not experimenters introducing exotic cultigens into new environments. Theirs is a conservative adaptation based on locally occurring food plants that have become genetically adapted over many generations to the full range of conditions the environment has to offer. If anything, the flow of botanical knowledge may go in the other direction. The National Academy of Sciences (U.S.), for example, has singled out the San food plant, the tsin bean (*Bauhinia esculenta*), as one of a worldwide sample of 36 of the most promising plants for increased propagation to help alleviate world food shortages (National Academy of Sciences 1977).

Perhaps the most telling evidence of the security of life as hunter-gatherers is its extraordinary persistence. Foraging people have been operating in the Dobe area for thousands of years without any evidence for major discontinuities. Personnel have changed, but the way of life has remained the same. During this long period there has been little evidence for technological change: Only in the last 100 years have iron tools replaced those of stone and bone. These have conferred some gains in efficiency for the contemporary !Kung compared with their ancestors, though the gain was probably on the order of only a 10 to 20 percent saving in work time (Chapter 9). A more detailed analysis of the relative efficiency of stone and bone compared with iron tools would be well worth further investigation.

If asked to specify the most functionally critical areas of hunter-gatherer technology, I would emphasize plant gathering and processing utensils before those used for cutting, stabbing, and piercing. Northern and Arctic hunting peoples have much more complicated needs in terms of housing, clothing, and transportation than do foragers of the tropical or temperate zones; in the case of the latter the two most central tools are containers for gathering and tools for pulverizing and breaking down

Plate 15.1. Abundant meat drying at a seasonal camp at summer water.

rough and fibrous foods into more digestible forms. Containers for gathering are universal among lower latitude foragers. Skin karosses and bags are found among the !Kung, the bark tray or *pithi* is ubiquitous among the Australian aborigines, and baskets in great variety were the preferred containers in North and South America and Southeast Asia (Forde 1934, 1954). The carrying device may well be the earliest and most universal human invention (see Appendix E).

In regard to milling and grinding tools, the San are somewhat anomalous. Most foraging peoples have stone grinders of the mano and metate type for milling seeds and other fibrous materials. Such tools are found among the Hadza, the Australians, and throughout North America. By contrast, the !Kung have only the wooden hand mortar and pestle for crushing and stamping foods (Chapter 5). However, with this tool the !Kung can mix and render more palatable and digestible a remarkable variety of foods, including nuts, berries, greens, roots and bulbs, as well as meat, gristle, and dried hides. The use of the mortar is especially important for processing foods for children and for old people; its existence probably adds significantly to the lifespan of the elderly whose teeth and digestions are failing. The absence of grinding technology from most pre-Mesolithic archeological sites may indicate that ancient foragers had a lifespan that was somewhat shorter than that of contemporary foragers, a problem that could benefit from further research.

WORK LOAD AND WEIGHT LOSS

By itself, the evidence for the abundant food supply among the !Kung is not sufficient to document the security of their way of life. We have to know how much work they actually perform to satisfy their needs. The limited direct evidence for the !Kung (July 1964) suggests that they meet their needs with only 12 to 21 hours of subsistence work per person per week, a total that rises to 40 to 44 hours per week when times for tool manufacturing and maintenance and for housework are added into the total (Chapter 9). Studies of other hunter-gatherers (McCarthy and McArthur 1960; Woodburn 1968a; Sahlins 1972) show a similarly low level of work effort–a level that has led one observer to suggest that the foragers probably enjoy more leisure time than does any other level of society (Service 1966:100).

All these studies of work and leisure are short-term; the workers at one or two camps are monitored over a period of days or weeks. We do not know how representative these studies are of the level of work effort required over the long run. And the longer time span is of crucial importance for the study of the foraging adaptation because, to paraphrase Liebig's law of the minimum, it is not the average level of work effort that is crucial but rather the level of work effort required at the most difficult time of the year that sets the limiting conditions on a population.

The study of seasonal fluctuations in weights and skinfold thickness provides this broader perspective (Chapter 10). In a study of 200 adults and children, !Kung adult weights showed slight but significant annual fluctuations, with the peak weights in April to June and the minimum in December and January. The overall weight loss for adults varied between 1 and 2.5 percent. The children and adolescents showed more or less steady growth, accelerating in the period January to June and decelerating in the period July to December. These adult weight losses are small by the standards of African agricultural societies, for whom weights may vary by as much as 6 percent between the harvest season and the hungry season (Fox 1953; Hunter 1967), and the overall picture tends to strengthen the argument for the relative ease of subsistence and for the security of foraging life.

Recently this finding has been called into question by Wilmsen (1977, 1979b). In a study of seasonal weights at /Xai/xai, he found a *6 percent* adult weight loss from July 1975 to January 1976, a loss which he argues contradicts my earlier finding of no marked seasonal swings. However, there is a major obstacle in the interpretation of Wilmsen's finding. He also notes that during the time of his study the !Kung were heavily involved in the cash economy and in fact sold almost R2000 ($2300) worth of crafts to Botswanacraft as well as earning another R800 connected with his research project and R200 from other sources. Their degree of involvement in the cash economy complicates the interpretation of the findings about their weight loss. For example, by expending only R144 on store-bought food (less than 5 percent of their total income), the /Xai/xai !Kung could have compensated entirely for their lost weight and could have reduced their seasonal fluctuation to zero, still saving the great bulk of their cash income for other purposes. What were the !Kung doing when they should have been out hunting and gathering? We have to consider the possibility that they stayed at home precisely to manufacture the $2300 worth of crafts sold to Botswanacraft, a process that would take many hundreds of working hours away from subsistence. For example, a set of hunting bow, quiver, and arrows sold for $20 would require 30 to 40 working hours to manufacture; a spear or knife sold for $10 would require about 10 hours each of work time (Chapter 9, Table 9.10).

The fact that they lost so much weight in spite of having money in their pockets strongly suggests that what Wilmsen observed was a failure of the cash economy, not a failure of the hunting and gathering economy. Instead of showing the range of variability in nutritional stress among foragers, the Wilmsen study shows how fragile these economies are in the face of mercantile penetration. Only among foraging peoples in the Arctic and sub-Arctic latitudes is there clear evidence for starvation (Balikci 1968), and some of these may be attributable to overhunting and exhaustion of game brought about by commercial exploitation of fur-bearing animals (Bishop 1974; Rogers and Black 1976). Among the !Kung and other hunter-gatherers in the tropics and temperate zones – the original cradle of human evolution – there is little evidence for starvation owing to the overall failure of wild foods. Among prehistoric foragers, with an even richer range of food supply and habitats to choose from, one can postulate a security of life that was at least no worse and possibly much better than that observed among contemporary foragers.

DEMOGRAPHY AND MOBILITY

Perhaps one of the most useful applications of the uniformitarian approach lies at the interface between ecology and demography – in the problem of the determinants of human reproductive rates. In foraging societies there is a tight articulation between women's role in the reproductive system and women's role in the economic system. The demands of gathering take a woman out of the camp to forage in distant places; the demands of pregnancy, childbirth, and infant care reduce her mobility and add to her work load. In addition to the conflicting demands of production and reproduction on a woman's daily time budget, there are the long-term problems of population regulation that all hunting and gathering societies must face. Their reproductive rates must be sufficiently high to ensure the replacement of the current generation by members of the next, but a reproductive rate that is too high can rapidly lead to doubling and redoubling of the population and consequent exhaustion of local food resources.⁾

Ever since the time of Malthus (1798) scientists have postulated famine and other catastrophes as the ultimate check on the uncontrolled expansion of the human population. Recently anthropologists have called into question this dire formula for human survival. Stott (1969) and Birdsell (1968) have noted that among the hunting and gathering societies mechanisms have evolved to maintain populations in equilibrium at a level well below the carrying capacity of their land.

Binford (cited in Pfeiffer 1969), Birdsell (1968), and others have invoked systematic infanticide as the mechanism for keeping foraging populations in check; Sussman (1972) and Lee (1972d), following the lead of Carr-Saunders (1922), have argued that long birth spacing – up to 4 or 5 years – is sufficient to maintain population increase within low and manageable limits, a suggestion recently taken up in more detail by Cohen (1977).

Most observers agree that the need for mobility in the food quest provides the proximate cause of long birth spacing. In the !Kung case, an infant or young child has to be carried by its mother on all or most of her gathering trips, and the dangers of short birth spacing are aptly summed in the !Kung proverb: "Women who have one birth after another like an animal have a permanent backache!" Alternately, women who enjoy a long interval between births are said by the !Kung to have a "good back." Among the !Kung infanticide is rare; instead, long-term lactation and the consequent suppression of ovulation serves to delay reconception in nomadic !Kung females for 24 to 36 months after the birth of a previous child. The result is an average interval of 3 to 4 years between successive live births.

Striking confirmation of the hypothesized relation between long birth spacing and mobility has come from the evidence for dramatic changes in fertility when nomadic hunter-gatherers make the shift to sedentary village life. Among the Dobe area !Kung, where such a shift is taking place, there is an 8-month difference in mean birth interval between more nomadic and more sedentary mothers (44 vs. 36 months). At one water hole, birth intervals have dropped to as short a period as 20 months, causing the beginnings of a veritable baby boom and creating unexpected emotional hardships among mothers and babies alike (Chapter 11).

Although the physiological mechanisms underlying !Kung birth spacing are still not well understood, the fact of the association of shorter intervals with sedentarization is now well established. The close articulation between economic and demographic change observed among the

!Kung may offer important clues to demographic and social changes that accompanied the origin of agriculture 10,000 years ago.

THE DYNAMIC OF MOVEMENT

The fundamental building blocks of the uniformitarian approach – population, space, resources, and energy – have been applied to the problems of food supply, technology, work, and fitness and reproduction. In this section I want to put the variables together in an integrated way to explain foraging as a system and to draw out and amplify its underlying structural dynamic. In this way I hope to show how these principles can be applied to foraging societies generally in contemporary and archeological contexts.

Two comments are in order at the outset. First, though the approach used here is derived from systems theory, the operation of the model proposed is dialectical rather than mechanical. By this I mean that the flow between the variables is two-way rather than one-way. The system does not tend toward a static equilibrium; rather, within its parameters, the system's steady state is always one of movement. Second, the analysis itself is dialectical, exploring the complex interplay between material and ideological factors. It starts with a direction of movement: from observable *etic* categories to *emic* categories. Both kinds of data have roles in the analysis, but it is important to follow the sequence from etic to emic, explaining what can be explained by material factors first before moving on to a consideration of ideological factors. Although the starting point must be the material realm, that area cannot be relied on entirely for our explanations. We have to know when to move on to include social, political, and ideological factors because only these can provide a full explanation of the human complexities of !Kung foraging society.

The model of foraging adaptation starts with three of the variables discussed earlier in this chapter: numbers, resources, and work; additional variables, such as group size, seasonal variation, conflict, and cognitive variables, are incorporated later. The purpose is to show how size of groups, use of space, and work effort are systematically interconnected.

Let us consider each of the primary variables and how each may vary:

1. The *population* occupies the space, and its size is subject to increase through births and immigration and to decrease by deaths and emigration. By weighing the people, one can add the concept of biomass (see Chapter 10).

2. The *space* contains a patterned distribution of resources of a given density, including vegetable and animal foods perceived by the people to be edible. The amount and types of food may vary seasonally and on a longer-term basis (e.g., with a cycle of drought

years and years of high rainfall). The intersection of population and
space gives population density.

3. *Work* is the energy, expressed in calories, that the population
performs in order to maintain itself within its space.

These are the variables. The constant, or given, in this simple model is
the productive system: the tools, knowledge, and organization necessary
to make a living in that environment (see Chapters 4 through 8).

When a research worker enters into a field situation, he finds an on-
going system, and his task is to unravel all the relationships among the
components of that system.

Every population has to behave in a sufficiently businesslike manner to
ensure its own survival. Because the group we are studying is surviving,
the work level at which it is performing must be sufficient for maintaining the population at its current numbers. We can confirm this point
empirically by several simple measures, such as the population's weights
and skinfold thicknesses. If the subjects are maintaining weight, fitness,
and fat and muscle mass, we are reasonably sure that intake is adequate—a point discussed in detail in Chapter 10.

Holding body mass as a constant, however, enables us to specify more
clearly the relations between work effort and resources. We have to observe what happens when a change occurs in population and resources. If
numbers of people increase owing to a rise in births, and food resources
remain the same, work effort has to increase to feed the greater population—not only total work, but work per capita. Or if food resources decrease, as in a drought year, but the numbers to be fed remain the same,
then work effort per capita has to increase in order to maintain adequate
caloric levels. The reason for this per capita increase is that work effort is
partly a function of distance traveled between the home base and the food
supply. As discussed in Chapter 6, the longer a group stays in one place the
farther the workers have to walk each week to reach the food supply.
These relationships among numbers, work, and resources can be precisely
plotted and reduced to mathematical terms (e.g., Thomas 1971).

The key point is the central position of *work* in the model. Work effort is
the intervening variable between population and food supply. And work
is the major way individuals and groups of people respond to changes in
the parameters. If food supply decreases, humans do not respond by dying off like fruit flies; they respond by working harder.

Nothing has been said so far about the organization of this population
into groups. A great deal of scholarly effort has been directed to the study
of ideal group size for hunters, and a figure of 25 has been called the
magic number. However, given the tremendous seasonal variations
documented in Chapter 12 in the size and composition of groups, I feel
this approach is not as fruitful as the approach that starts from work.

Plate 15.2. The dynamic of movement: /Du/da groups preparing to move camp.

Let us assign a strictly arbitrary mean group size of 30. With a given age-sex composition, there is a level of work effort appropriate to that particular group size, with work effort measured in kilometers walked in order to find food. This distance increases through time as foods are eaten out over an increasingly wide radius. For example, let us say that the mean work effort in the 30-person group is 2 hours per adult per day. If the group size is doubled to 60, while resources remain constant, the mean work effort has to rise accordingly, let us say to 3 hours each day. If the group size is doubled again, to 120, the mean work effort must again rise, this time to 4.5 hours per adult per day. The point is that up to certain limits each of these group sizes is quite feasible, given the food resources; the difference is simply that the larger the group, the more work the individuals in it have to do.

There is a corollary to this relation between work and group size. Resources may be denser in one season than in another so that it may be possible to move from a scarce season group of 30 to an abundant season group of 120 with no increase in the mean daily work effort, at least in the short run. These relationships – work effort against group size and work effort against density of resources – can also be expressed mathematically.

Now we can ask: What determines whether populations of hunters arrange themselves into groups of 30, 60, or 120, or 25, 50, or 100, and for how long do such groups remain together? The principle of least effort specifies that people always arrange themselves into the smallest viable groups because doing so would always keep work effort at a minimum. Field observations, however, indicate radical departures from this picture. Among the !Kung large aggregations of 100 persons and over were observed, such as the /Du/da camp from September 1968 to January 1969, in which individuals put out a considerably larger work effort than would have been required if they had split up and dispersed into smaller groups of, say, 20 to 30. At other times the !Kung *were* observed to divide into smaller living groups and in those cases the work effort was observed to be modest.

These data indicate that the principle of least effort alone is not sufficient to explain the observed living groups of the !Kung and other hunters. It is at this point that ecological analysis must expand to include a wider range of social variables. The clue to the possible answer is found in Mauss's classic paper on the seasonal life of the Eskimo (1904–5). As noted in Chapter 12, the Eskimo division of the year into a large group (public life) phase and a small group (private life) phase is a pattern of life also observed among the !Kung and most of the world's hunter-gatherers.

Among the !Kung several groups aggregated during the winter dry season for a more intense period of social life. Visiting, feasting, trance dancing, hxaro trading, and marriage brokering were some of the activities carried out at these larger camps. But this intense social life also had its disadvantages: The large size of the group required people to work harder to bring in food, and fights were much more likely to break out in large camps than in smaller camps. Of 18 homicides among the !Kung, 15 occurred in camps of 40 to 150 people and only 3 in camps of less than 40 people (see Chapter 13).

In short, living in large groups was a mixed blessing. It offered the people a more intense social life, but it also meant harder work and a higher frequency of conflict. But, like many other hunter-gatherers, the !Kung sought both kinds of social existence – the intensity and excitement of a larger grouping and its attendant risks, and the domestic tranquility and leisure of smaller groupings. The small group was easier to support, but the larger group was possible to maintain if people were strongly motivated to stay together. Work effort was the sliding scale between group size and resources.

We now see the utility of the dialectical model of the foraging adaptation compared with a mechanical one. The principle of least effort is an example of a mechanical model in which the people act in a single direction – to minimize their work effort and maximize their leisure. But this mechanical model does not account for their behavior because the !Kung sought *social as well as ecological* rewards. Instead of contenting themselves with the smallest viable groupings, they periodically came together in much larger groupings in which the social advantages outweighed the ecological disadvantages and in which for a brief period they flaunted the thermodynamic constraints imposed by their environment. This important human aggregation has little in common with the herding or massing behavior observed in mammals and birds during the breeding season. It was and is a product of conscious purpose. The large group (public life) phase demanded increased work and increased cooperation of group members at a level that could be maintained only by a conscious effort of individual and collective will. People had to know what they were doing in order to stay together because staying together was not the path of least resistance. More, these collective gatherings were stabilized by a distinctly cultural method: the use of the sacred.

Large gatherings of hunter-gatherers were so often invested with a sense of the sacred perhaps precisely because they represent the group's distinctly cultural identity maintained in defiance of natural forces, a point emphasized by Durkheim (1912). Also the sacred may have been important as a means of maintaining order (sanctity) among large groups of people under difficult circumstances (Rappaport 1971a, b). At the same time the rise in conflict or threat of conflict served as a safety valve, forcing groups to separate to allow conflicts to cool and people to get back to quiet surroundings in preparation for the next round of public life.

This dynamic of movement in space–of coalescing and splitting, of rearranging groups, and of cycles of social intensity and tranquility– probably characterized the life of humankind for thousands of years before the cycle of movement was permanently altered by sedentarization accompanying the invention of agriculture. In thinking about the human past the dynamic of movement should hold a central place, as a mediating variable that unites the public and private life, work and leisure, in-group and out-group, and nature and culture.

MALE-FEMALE RELATIONS

Up to now we have been dealing with aspects of !Kung life that can be precisely quantified. Food, work, and spatial organization are all part of the economic base and are apt subjects for the uniformitarian approach. The dynamic of movement made the jump from base to superstructure because it showed how the necessity for mobility, a foraging universal, becomes structured in a uniquely human way into public life and private life phases of the annual round. The nature of male-female relations appears to be even more in the realm of superstructure. Starting with the basic biology of sex differences, foraging societies have evolved a variety

Plate 15.3. The spiritual power of women illustrated in the healing dance.

of modes of male-female relations, a multiplicity that is not easily predicted by the uniformitarian approach. Therefore, we must examine the mode of production for clues to account for the roles of women and men among the !Kung and other foraging societies.

Among the !Kung, women play an important role in production, providing a greater proportion of the subsistence than do the men (Marshall 1960; Lee 1968a). The same predominance of female over male work productivity has been observed among many other hunter-gatherers in tropical and warm temperate climates (McCarthy and McArthur 1960; Woodburn 1968a; Lee and DeVore 1968). The economic importance of women has led many observers to question the male-dominated patrilocal model of hunting and gathering society and to revise and upgrade woman's role in human prehistory (Leacock 1972; Morgan 1972; Hiatt 1974; Friedl 1975; Reed 1975; Rohrlich-Leavitt 1975; Slocum 1975; Tanner and Zihlman 1976). The counterposing of "woman the gatherer" to "man the hunter" has been part of a welcome and long overdue reexamination of the implicit and explicit male biases in anthropological theory (Golde 1970; Gough 1970, 1971; Rosaldo and Lamphere 1974; Reiter 1975; Voorhies and Martin 1975; Lamphere 1977; Reiter 1977).

The result of this rethinking has been a shift away from the simplistic formula that characterized hunter-gatherers as based on male domination and aggression in contrast to the female-dominated societies of the Neolithic horticulturalists based on fertility and vessels. For example:

> Paleolithic tools and weapons mainly were addressed to movements and muscular efforts: instruments of chipping, hacking, digging, burrowing, cleaving, dissecting, exerting force swiftly at a distance; in short every manner of aggressive activity. The bones and muscles of the male dominate his technical contributions . . . Under woman's dominance the neolithic period is pre-eminently one of containers: it is an age of stone and pottery utensils, of vases, jars, vats, cisterns, bins, barns, granaries, houses, not least the great collective containers like irrigation ditches and villages. [Mumford 1961:25]

Schemes like these echo nineteenth- and early twentieth-century sequences that equated hunters with patriarchy and horticulturalists with matriarchy (e.g., Bachofen 1861; Morgan 1877; Freud 1919). However, this long history of controversy should make us wary of formulas that simply invert the previous sequences and grant all political power to women in early society or postulate perfect equality between males and females in the preagricultural past. Rather than give a global assessment of male-female relations in !Kung society, I prefer to deal with the problem in a more cautious way by discussing in turn the various spheres in which men and women interact to show that dominance of one sex in one sphere does not necessarily lead to dominance in another.

Hunting versus gathering

!Kung men hunt and !Kung women gather; and gathering provides about
two-thirds of the diet and hunting one-third. Behind this simple statement
lie some not-so-simple qualifications. For example, there are at least three
ways of calculating the relative contributions of hunting and gathering to
the foraging diet: (1) by the weight or caloric content of food from each
source, (2) by the amount of work effort and the productivity per person-
hour, and (3) by the cultural evaluation the people themselves place on the
two kinds of subsistence. On the first count it is clear that gathered foods
provide about twice the food value of hunted foods. In July 1964 vegetable
products yielded 69 percent by weight and 71 percent of the calories of the
Dobe camp. At other seasons of the year, such as the late summer and fall
when the !Kung camp in mongongo groves or tsin fields, the proportion of
vegetable foods may rise as high as 80 percent. Is there ever a time when
hunting dominates over gathering? In some late spring and early summer
hunting camps the proportion of meat may sharply rise. In December 1964
the four hunters of a small camp of 12 at N/on/oni≠toa killed 29 animals in
17 days for a per capita consumption of almost 2 kg of meat per day. These
bursts of meat eating tend to be of short duration, however, and overall I
estimate that meat constitutes between 30 and 40 percent of the diet and
vegetables between 60 and 70 percent. Of course, not all the plant gathering is done by women. Men gather as well, and their work provides almost
a fifth of all the gathered food. Therefore, when we sum the overall contribution of each sex, the disparity is reduced. Men produce about 44 percent
and women 56 percent of the weight and calories of the food brought into
the camp.

Considering work effort and productivity adds a further dimension to
the differences between the sexes. Men put in a longer subsistence work
week than do women – about 2.7 days of work for men compared with 2.1
for women – but the productivity of women's work overall and per person-
hour is higher than the productivity of men's. A man brings back one
game animal for every 4 days of hunting, for a success rate of 25 percent;
a woman's rate of success in finding food during a day of gathering is 100
percent. It is true that a single game animal may provide a very large
input of food, as many calories as 50 days of gathering in the case of a
large kudu. But such kills are few and far between, and for the most part
men have to content themselves with smaller kills. For example, in July
1964, the four largest kills yielded only 55,000 Cal apiece, and the other
14 averaged less than 10,000 Cal each. Overall, each man-day of hunting
brought in about 7230 Cal compared with 12,000 Cal for each person-day
of gathering (Chapter 9). These differences in productivity account for
the fact that women provide a larger share of the food even though they
do less of the subsistence work.

In light of the greater importance of gathered food in the diet, it is curious that all !Kung, both men and women, value meat more highly than plant food. When meat is scarce in the camp, all people express a craving for it, even when vegetable foods are abundant. And the occasions when large animals are killed are usually marked by feasting, dancing, and the giving of gifts of meat. As game animals are scarce and unpredictable compared with plant foods, it is perhaps not so surprising that hunting is invested with more symbolic significance than gathering; and one should not lose sight of the fact that hunting provides essential nutrients, such as high quality protein, which are not as readily available from plant foods alone.

Women, men, and child care

The question of child care and how it should be divided between mother, father, and other caretakers is a key issue in contemporary Western society. The assignment of the majority of child care responsibilities to the woman of the modern household has come to be regarded as a key symbol of woman's oppression in the capitalist system. In arguing for a more equitable distribution of household labor, feminist anthropologists have turned to data on non-Western societies for evidence of a more just set of child care arrangements. At first glance, the !Kung data offer little support for this point of view: Over 90 percent of the work involved in caring for young children is borne by the mother aided by the other women. This is not to say that !Kung fathers ignore their children; they are attentive and loving and spend part of their leisure hours playing with and holding the young infants. But the !Kung father rarely takes sole responsibility for the child while the mother is absent, whereas the opposite occurs every day (Draper 1975; West and Konner 1978).

For their part, the women do not consider themselves oppressed by this state of affairs. They keenly desire children, are excellent mothers, and often complain that they do not have as many children as they would like.

In interpreting these attitudes one should avoid projecting the negative features we associate with child care on an entirely different cultural situation. The !Kung women consider childbirth and child care as their sphere of responsibility, and they guard their prerogatives in this area. For example, the fact that women go to the bush to give birth and insist on excluding men from the childbirth site is justified by them in terms of pollution and taboos; but the underlying explanation may be that it simplifies matters if a decision in favor of infanticide is made. Because the woman will commit a considerable amount of her energy to raising each child, she examines the newborn carefully for evidence of defects; if she finds any, the child is not allowed to live and is buried with the afterbirth. By excluding men from the childbed women can report back to the camp that the child was born dead without fear of contradiction. But if the child is healthy and wanted by the woman, she accepts the major responsibility for raising it. In this way the women exercise control over their own reproduction.

Another important reason why the !Kung woman's share of child care is not oppressive is that she is not isolated from the community in the same way a modern urban mother is. She is helped by all the other women in the camp, and there is no need to divide her productive work from her child care work. Gathering and food processing are carried out with the child on her hip – not left at home with a baby-sitter. In addition, men participate in the non-child-care aspects of housework. As noted in Chapter 9, men do between 20 and 40 percent of the housework of a four-person household. For these reasons, it is inaccurate to say that !Kung women are oppressed by the burden of child care responsibilities.

Marriage, divorce, and group structure

Their contribution to the food supply and their control over reproduction and child care give !Kung women influence in other areas, such as marriage and divorce. For a variety of reasons, there is an imposed scarcity among the !Kung of women of marriageable age. Parents of a girl can afford to be selective about a prospective son-in-law. As a result men usually have to prove themselves worthy by demonstrating their competence in hunting and ritual activities (see Chapter 8). This task takes many years, and men are often 7 to 15 years older than their wives at marriage. For example, the typical ages at marriage for the Nyae Nyae !Kung during the 1950s were 14 to 15 for women and 22 to 25 for men (Marshall 1959); in the Dobe area a decade later the ages were 16 to 17 for women and 23 to 30 for men. At marriage, the girl's people insist that the young couple live with them. The reasons given are of three kinds: (1) it must be seen that the man treats the daughter well, (2) he must prove his hunting abilities by providing meat, and (3) the girl is too young to leave her mother. In the majority of cases, the husband leaves his own group and takes up residence with his wife's group – a stay that may last 3, 5, or 10 years, or even a lifetime. Bride service is found among many of the world's hunter-gatherers and occurs even in northern Australia, an area usually regarded as the heartland of the patrilocal band (Shapiro 1971).

Thus there is a central paradox in the idea of Lévi-Strauss (1969:62–5) that in simple societies women are "scarce goods" and that they may have functioned as the original medium of exchange between men in early society. Their very scarcity makes women more desirable and allows them considerable scope to dictate their own terms of marriage. As a result, though most first marriages among the !Kung are arranged, many break up soon after, and the breakup is usually initiated by the wife, not the husband. Furthermore, there is a feedback relationship between the demography of marriage and its ideology. The fewer the women available for marriage, the greater the pressure to marry off girls at a younger age. However, the younger the girl, the longer the period of bride service necessary for the husband. By the time his bride service is completed, the husband's own parents may be dead, and such a man often decides to continue to stay with his wife's group.

The husband during the period of bride service is not exploited or treated as a menial by his wife's family (as was the daughter-in-law in the prerevolutionary Chinese family). Precisely the opposite is the case. The atmosphere is made as congenial as possible to encourage the son-in-law to stay on after the period of bride service. Usually the son-in-law forms strong ties with other men in the group, especially brothers-in-law. Recruiting sons-in-law adds hunting strength to the group and means more meat for the members, a point discussed further below.

Bride service and age differences at marriage are two of the factors that explain why women constitute the cores of !Kung living groups as frequently as do men. Statistically, mother-daughter bonds predominate, followed by sister-sister and brother-sister, but father-son and brother-brother bonds are also found. Thus it would be an overstatement to say that the !Kung group structure is a simple inversion of the patrilocal band model, with a female replacing the male at the group's core. Instead, the genealogical core consists of males *and* females, and no single rule of uxorilocal or virilocal postmarital residence accounts for the arrangements actually observed.

Women and political power

Does women's predominant role in production, their leverage in marriage, and their sharing of core group membership with men lead to power in the political arena as well? The answer in a broad sense is yes: !Kung women's participation in group discussions and decision making is probably greater than that of women in most tribal, peasant, and industrial societies (Chapter 12). But the level of their participation is not equal to that of men. The latter appear to do about two-thirds of the talking in discussions involving both sexes, and men act as group spokespersons far more frequently than do women (see Chapter 12).

This disparity between men and women comes into sharper relief when discussions and arguments turn to violence. In 34 cases of fights occurring in the period 1963–9 a man attacked a woman 14 times, whereas a woman attacked a man only once (Chapter 13, Table 13.1). As 11 of these 15 cases involved husband and wife, it is clear that in domestic scraps the wife is the victim in the great majority of cases. Similarly, in cases of homicide there were 25 male and no female killers (though it is worth noting that 19 of the 22 victims were males as well).

Remarkably, one major form of violence against women, rape, is rare among the !Kung. This kind of sexual violence, so common in other societies (Brownmiller 1975; Webster 1976), has been reported for the !Kung in only a handful of cases.

In summarizing the evidence concerning male-female relations, we see that women predominate in some spheres of behavior and men in others; the overall sense of the relations between the sexes is one of give and take. Both sexes work equally hard, with men working longer hours in subsistence and tool making and women working longer hours in housework and child care. Women's subsistence work is more efficient and productive than men's, so they provide more of the food despite their shorter work week. In marriage arrangements women exercise some control, and they initiate divorce far more frequently than men. On the other hand, the fact that the men are so much older than their wives at marriage may tip the balance of influence within the marriage in favor of the males. (It should be noted that in about one out of five !Kung marriages the woman is older than the man–up to 20 years older–and in these unions the woman's influence usually predominates.)

In the political sphere men do more of the talking than women, and it is my impression that their overall influence in "public" matters is greater, though I cannot present any data to confirm this point. Men exhibit more violent behavior than women, though women are rarely the victims in serious conflict; and rape, a primary form of violence against women in many societies, is not common among the !Kung.

On balance, the evidence shows a relatively equal role in society for the two sexes, and the !Kung data certainly do not support a view of women in "the state of nature" as oppressed or dominated by men or as subject to sexual exploitation at the hands of males. However, the comparative evidence suggests that the status of !Kung women is higher than that enjoyed by women in some other foraging societies, such as the Eskimo (Friedl 1975) and the Australian aborigines (Gale 1974).

THE SOCIAL RELATIONS OF PRODUCTION

The study of !Kung ecology has shown that the foraging way of life is not as rigorous and demanding as it is often made out to be. To understand these societies, we have to go beyond the overly simple argument that hunters are poor because the harsh environment and crude technology do not allow anything better. We must try and understand them on their own terms, as followers of a way of life that is adapted to their environment, that meets their needs, and that makes eminent good sense to them.

If the foraging way of life is viewed as a mode of production in its own right and not as a set of contrasts with which to highlight the advantages (or evils) of our own system, our understanding will be enhanced. In the spirit of Marx's research strategy (outlined above), I will set out the major features of the social relations of production that characterize the foraging mode of production and then sketch some of the main themes of the ideological superstructure that corresponds to it.

Several features appear to set the !Kung and other hunter-gatherers apart from tribal and centralized societies. An important one is their radically different conception of the relation between people and their environment. The wealth of agricultural and pastoral peoples is that which they have been able to develop out of the natural order by careful husbandry and improvement of land, livestock, homesteads, and durable goods. The !Kung, by contrast, make no sharp dichotomy between the resources of the natural environment and the social wealth. The unimproved land itself is the means of production, and because it is owned by no one exclusively, it is available to everyone who can use it. The !Kung do not amass a surplus because they conceive of the environment itself as their storehouse. The necessities of the hunter's life are in the bush no less surely than those of the agriculturalist are in the cultivated ground. The !Kung know a great deal about what their environment has to offer. This knowledge is, in effect, a form of control over nature: It has been developed over many generations in response to every conceivable variation in climatic conditions.

Because they know what to expect from the environment, they see little point in bringing the food and raw materials to camp before they are actually needed. The food collected by the members of a camp is distributed and consumed without delay within the boundaries of the camp or by the camp's immediate neighbors. No portion of the production is set aside for consumption at a later date or for distribution to more distant points. This lack of surplus requires that a constant level of work be maintained throughout the year. This uniformity of effort stands in sharp contrast to the management of subsistence in agricultural societies, in which intense periods of work (planting and harvesting) are followed by periods of relative inactivity. The actual amount of time devoted by the San to the food quest is modest, amounting to about 17 hours of subsistence effort per adult per week, or about 900 hours a year, a lower level of work than has been observed in many agricultural and most industrial societies (Chapter 9; Harris 1975:229–55).

Another outcome of this relation to the environment is the relatively small investment the !Kung make in what may be called the capital sector of their economy. Every household manufactures and maintains a basic set of utensils considered essential to the tasks of daily life. The list comprises less than 100 items. With the exception of iron, beads, and pots obtained from the Bantu, all the items of material culture, necessities and luxuries alike, are easily manufactured from locally available materials (Marshall 1961:246–8). Building a house for a rainy season camp is two day's work; shelters for the dry season camp are thrown up in a morning. The all-important digging stick can be whittled in an hour and lasts the user for several months. A complete set of bow, arrows, and quiver takes somewhat longer to make: A man assembles the materials over a period of weeks in the course of normal activities and then spends 5 or 6 days manufacturing the kit itself. These weapons then have a useful lifetime of several years (Chapter 9, Table 9.10).

Because of the ease with which articles can be made during the abundant leisure time, there is no lack of duplicate items. These are put into circulation through the hxaro gift-giving network. If an individual receives a valued good, such as an ostrich eggshell bead necklace, a thumb piano, or a finely carved pipe, he keeps it for several months and then passes it on to a trading partner. Months or even years later, his trading partner reciprocates with a similar item. The net effect is to maintain a constant circulation of goods and an equal distribution of wealth among the members of the society. Particularly active participants in the hxaro network are not richer than others in the sense of possessing a greater share of the world's goods. Rather, they are the people who have a greater than average number of trading partners and thus a more rapid turnover of goods. Nobody keeps hxaro goods very long.

This lack of wealth accumulation, even though the means for it – free time and raw materials – are at hand, arises from the requirements of the nomadic life. For people who move around a lot and did not keep pack animals until very recently, it would be sheer folly to amass more goods than can be carried along when the group moves. Portability is the major design feature of the items themselves. The total weight of an individual's personal property is less than 12 kg and can easily be carried from place to place. When a family is packing, it is remarkable to see all its worldly possessions – weapons, cooking utensils, water containers, medicines, cosmetics, pipes, musical instruments, children's toys, and beads – disappear into a pair of leather sacks the size of overnight bags.

The immediacy of food consumption, the modest investment in capital goods, and the lack of wealth disparities all contribute to the distinctive style of San social relations. With personal property so easily portable, frequent moving is not difficult. There is a similar lack of investment in fixed facilities such as village sites, storage places, and fenced enclosures. When groups come into conflict, parting company is a simpler solution than remaining together and resolving differences through adjudication or fighting.

A dynamic of movement informs the daily life of individuals and groups. Landownership is vested, not in a single individual, but in a collective of k"ausi, both males and females, who form the core of the resident camp and who must be approached for permission to use the resources of the area. Right of reciprocal access to food resources is a fundamental principle of land use. If group A visits group B in one season, it is expected that group B will repay the visit in the next. These visiting patterns tend to keep people in circulation from area to area, providing a change of scene and change of company. An individual's primary kin and close affines are always distributed at several different water holes, and through the far-reaching ties of the name relation he may establish close ties at a number of others. The outcome of these multiple options is that an individual may utilize the food resources of several water holes as long as he observes the elementary good manners of sharing fully with the members of the local camp. Whether an individual chooses to join a given camp depends on the history of his relations with the long-term residents. Many men and women who have a reputation for good humor, industry, or curing skills have standing invitations at many different camps. Even less popular individuals have strong primary kinship ties that make them welcome in at least two or three camps and tolerated in others.

This dynamic of movement coupled with the fact that both males and females form the core of groups leads to an emphasis in social relations on recruitment rather than exclusion. The older model of male-centered territorial bands (Service 1962; Fox 1967; Tiger 1969) assumed that the primary requirement of the foraging living group was the maintenance of exclusive rights to land, a task best shouldered by a core of male sibling defenders. In contrast, it is clear that the maintenance of *flexibility* to adapt to changing ecological circumstances is far more important in hunter-gatherer group structure than is the maintenance of exclusive rights to land. Flexibility favors a social policy of *bringing in* more personnel rather than keeping them out, hence the emphasis on the social principle of *recruitment* rather than *exclusion*. Because of the nature of production in hunter-gatherer society, the principal way to increase output is to add personnel; therefore, a primary social strategy of many hunter-gatherers is to recruit sons-in-law to augment the group's meat-getting capacity and at the same time to try to retain the sons. The net effect of this strategy is that many of the males in any group are outsiders and unrelated.

On the political level ,these characteristics of foraging life lead to a strong emphasis on egalitarian social relations. Egalitarianism is not simply the *absence* of a headman and other authority figures, but a positive insistence on the essential equality of all people and a refusal to bow to the authority of others, a sentiment expressed in the statement: "Of course we have headmen . . . each one of us is headman over himself." Leaders do exist, but their influence is subtle and indirect. They never order or make demands of others, and their accumulation of material goods is never more, and is often much less, than the average accumulation of the other households in their camp.

Two remarkable cultural practices at the level of consciousness accompany this egalitarian political ideal. They occur among the !Kung and among many other hunter-gatherers. The most serious accusations one !Kung can level against another are the charge of stinginess and the charge of arrogance. To be stingy, or far-hearted, is to hoard one's goods jealously and secretively, guarding them "like a hyena." The corrective for this, in the !Kung view, is to make the hoarder give "till it hurts," that is, to make him give generously and without stint until everyone can see that he is truly cleaned out. In order to ensure compliance with this cardinal rule, the !Kung browbeat each other constantly to be more generous and not to hoard. The importance of sharing and giving has been ably documented by Lorna Marshall (1961, 1976:287–312).

But deplorable as they regard the fault of stinginess, the !Kung's most scathing criticisms are reserved for an even more serious shortcoming: the crime of arrogance ($\neq twi$). A stingy person is antisocial and irksome, but an arrogant person is actually dangerous because, according to the !Kung, "his pride will make him kill someone." A boasting hunter who comes into camp announcing "I have killed a big animal in the bush" is being arrogant. A woman who gives a gift and announces to all her great generosity is being arrogant. Even an anthropologist who claims to have chosen the biggest ox of the year to slaughter for Christmas is being arrogant. The !Kung perceive this behavior as a danger sign, and they have evolved elaborate devices for puncturing the bubble of conceit and enforcing humility. These leveling devices are in constant daily use – minimizing the size of others' kills, downplaying the value of others' gifts, and treating one's own efforts in a self-deprecating way. *Please* and *thank you* are hardly ever found in their vocabulary; in their stead is a vocabulary of rough humor, back-handed compliments, put-downs, and damning with faint praise. In fact, the one area in which the !Kung are openly competitive is in recounting suffering. They try to outdo each other in tales of misfortune: cold, pain, thirst, hunger, hunting failure, and other hardships represent conversational gold, the obverse of the coin of arrogance, which they so strongly discourage.

To outsiders, these cultural preoccupations are disconcerting. We admire the !Kung from afar, but when we are brought into closer contact with their daily concerns, we are alternately moved to pity by their tales of hardship and repelled by their nagging demands for gifts, demands that grow more insistent the more we give.

These contradictions – generosity-stinginess, arrogance-humility, equality-hierarchy, sociability-withdrawal – are central themes in !Kung culture, and they afford us a glimpse into the internal workings of a social existence very different from our own. The essence of this way of life is

Plate 15.4. Composing sad songs on the thumb piano.

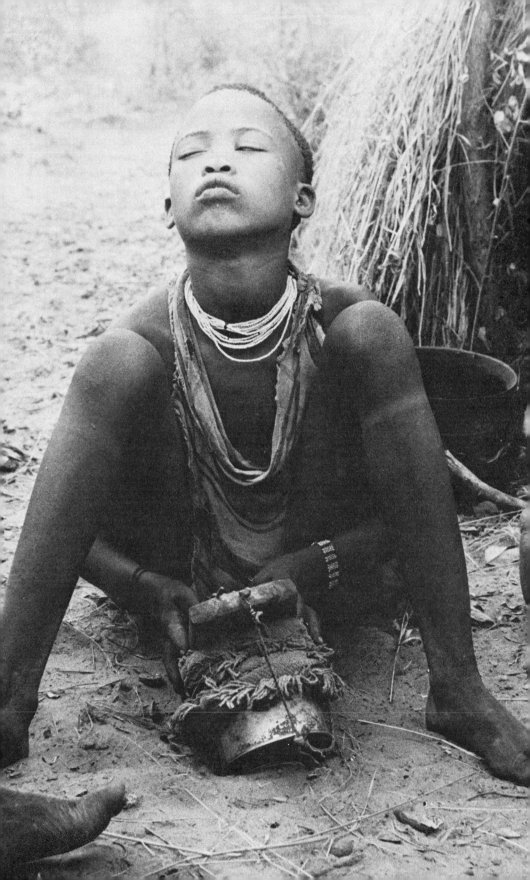

sharing, a practice that is extended more widely in the foraging mode of production than in any other. People share within the family and between families, and the unit of sharing extends to the boundaries of the face-to-face community and beyond. Visualize the kind of sharing that occurs around the dinner table in a Western household, but expanded in scale to include a group of 15 to 30 people, and you have some idea of the nature of sharing in a !Kung camp.

The principle of generalized reciprocity within the camp, the giving of something without an expectation of equivalent return, is almost universal among foraging peoples (Sahlins 1965, 1972). In the case of the !Kung, food is shared in a generalized familistic way; durable goods are exchanged according to the principle of balanced reciprocity (i.e., the transactions are expected to balance out in the long run). The fact that communal sharing of food resources has been directly observed in recent years among the !Kung and dozens of other foraging groups is a finding that should not be glossed over lightly. Its universality among foragers lends strong support to the theory of Marx and Engels that a stage of primitive communism prevailed before the rise of the state and the breakup of society into classes (Engels 1884). One should add the proviso, however, that this communism does not extend, as far as we know, to include sexual rights, as Marx and Engels, following Morgan (1877), originally believed.

Having declared that the foraging mode of production is a form of primitive communism, it would be a mistake to idealize the foraging peoples as noble savages who have solved all the basic problems of living. Like individuals in any society, the foragers have to struggle with their own internal contradictions, and living up to the demands of this strongly collective existence presents some particularly challenging problems. Sharing, for example, is not automatic; it has to be learned and reinforced by culture. Every human infant is born equipped with both the capacity to share and the capacity to be selfish. This observation is confirmed by studies of early childhood (Garvey 1977:51–3). Learning to receive an offered toy, to hand it back, and to extend the hand to receive it again is one of the earliest complex behaviors exhibited by young infants in Western society (Waterhouse and Waterhouse 1973). Western children between the ages of 5 and 8 years have been observed to share food in a natural and unselfconscious way (Dyson-Hudson and Van Dusen 1972:319–24). At the same time we all know that the word *mine* is one of the first few words learned by most Western infants (Garvey 1977:52). During the course of socialization, each society channels these impulses into socially acceptable forms, and every society expects some sort of balance between sharing and selfish behavior–between the needs of self and the needs of others. Among the foragers, society demands a high level of sharing and tolerates a low level of personal accumulation compared with Western capitalist norms. And living up to these demands, while it has its rewards, also takes its toll. I doubt whether any !Kung ever completely gives up the selfish impulse, and the tension to conform continues through life. Elderly !Kung in particular give voice to the contradictions between sharing and keeping. On one occasion ≠Toma//gwe asked me for a blanket and said, "All my life I've been giving, giving; today I am old and want something for myself." Similar sentiments have been expressed by other oldsters. Perhaps because they are old, their departures from the cultural norm are tolerated more than would those of younger adults.

Sharing food is accompanied by sharing space, and a second area of communal life that causes stress is the lack of privacy. Daily life goes on in full view of the camp. People rarely spend time alone, and to seek solitude is regarded as a bizarre form of behavior. Even marital sex is carried on discreetly under a light blanket shared with the younger children around the family fire. It is considered bad manners for others to look. Sullen, withdrawn behavior is regarded with concern and not allowed to continue. The person showing it is pestered and goaded until he or she loses his/her temper; the anger that follows helps clear the air and reintegrate the outsider. When people are depressed or their feelings are hurt, they express it by waking at night to compose sad songs, which they play for themselves on the thumb piano. These poignant refrains form a counterpoint to the night sounds of the crackling sleeping fires and the calls of the nightjars, and no one tells the players to pipe down or shut up.

It is clear that the demands of the collective existence are not achieved effortlessly; they require a continuing struggle with one's own selfish, arrogant, and antisocial impulses. The fact that the !Kung and other foragers succeed as well as they do in communal living in spite of (or because of?) their material simplicity offers us an important insight. A truly communal life is often dismissed as a utopian ideal, to be endorsed in theory but unattainable in practice. But the evidence for foraging peoples tells us otherwise. A sharing way of life is not only possible but has actually existed in many parts of the world and over long periods of time.

Appendix A. Unraveling the Dobe population figures for 1964

A review of the published data on the Dobe area !Kung shows more than one version of the census breakdown for November 1964. These discrepancies arise from two sources: (1) different ways of defining who is or is not in the population produced different results; and (2) my recensus of the !Kung in 1967 revealed a number of people I had missed in 1964. A few words of explanation are in order for those who wish to reconcile the conflicting figures given. The corrected data have been in the literature since 1972. Here is a brief account of how they were arrived at.

433 !KUNG IN THE DOBE AREA

In my doctoral thesis, written a few months after my first field trip, I wrote that "there were 433 Bushmen residents, all but one of them members of the !Kung tribe" (Lee 1965:39). A few pages later a table showed the breakdown of population by water hole and gave the total as 401. A footnote informed the reader that "the total of 433 is arrived at by the addition of 32 !Kung who were outside the Dobe area at the time of the census" (Lee 1965:43). There was no distinction made between residents and "alternators."

425 !KUNG IN THE DOBE AREA

In a paper published in 1969 but written in early 1967, I gave the number of *resident* !Kung as 336; and with the addition of 55 "alternators" and 34 "emigrants," the total number of !Kung came to 425 (Lee 1969a: 76–7). I had excluded the 8 people who had died during the period October 1963 to November 1964; hence the drop from 433 to 425. Perhaps more confusing to the reader was the subdivision of the residents into those in camps (248) and those associated with the Bantu (88), leaving four categories floating: residents in camps, residents with Bantu, alternators, and emigrants.

Returning to the Dobe area in August 1967, I resolved to try to clear up these census problems early in the new research. I undertook a complete recensus, using my November 1964 enumeration as a starting point. It soon became apparent that I had missed a number of people in 1964 and had double-counted a few others. Completing the recensus on November 10, 1967, I made the following entry in my field notes at that time:

> Master numbers 1–433 represent all those enumerated in November 1964. They include some 8 persons who died between October 1963 and November 1964. They also include 6 duplicates (No. 128 = No. 188; 129 = 189; 130 = 190; 131 = 191; 133 = 160; 199 = 215). (The 8 numbers of deceased were retired; the 6 duplicate numbers were reassigned.)

> Master numbers 434–560 plus the 6 duplicate numbers (133 numbers in all) were assigned to individuals first enumerated from August 28 to November 10, 1967. These new entries include four kinds of people:

> 1. New births during the period January 1, 1965, to November 10, 1967, still alive on latter date
> 2. New births from the same period who died before November 10, 1967
> 3. New immigrants and alternators
> 4. Residents who were present in 1964 but missed by me because of error or because they were away visiting

> The revised total 1964 population (x) consists of:

> (p) numbers 1–433 *less*
> (q) duplicates $(n = 6)$ *less*
> (r) those who died in 1963–4 $(n = 8)$ *plus*
> (d) residents and others missed in 1964 $(n = 47)$
> Therefore, $x = 433 - (6 + 8) + 47 = 466$

466 !KUNG IN THE DOBE AREA

These calculations provided the revised figure (466), which was included in subsequent papers. For example, in my paper "The !Kung Bushmen of Botswana" (published in 1972 but actually written in 1968), the following corrected breakdown was given for the population of the Dobe area for November 1964 (Lee 1972a:333):

> Residents = 379 (compared with 336 in Lee 1969a)
> Alternators = 87 (compared with 55 in Lee 1969a)
> Emigrants = 0 (compared with 34 in Lee 1969a)

The figures 248 and 88 (Lee 1969a:76–7) still have some limited usefulness as an enumeration of persons I counted at each water hole in November 1964, but they do not include the whole population present in 1964 or even present in November 1964. A majority of those people I missed the first time around had been living in small groups on the black cattle posts, particularly at /Xai/xai, which I had visited only briefly in 1963–4.

Two other changes have been made. The label "emigrants" turned out to refer to a noncategory. Most of the people I had recorded as "leaving" in 1964 had *moved back* or were still visiting in 1967. Therefore, I have combined them with other "alternators." The other change I have made is to relabel "alternators" as "marginals," a more accurate term to describe a category of persons ranging from those who regularly alternate in and out of the Dobe area to those who may visit the area only once in 5 years.

Appendix B. Plants of the Dobe area

T
ABLE B.1 lists all the plants known to the !Kung and for which we have botanical identifications. Plants are grouped alphabetically by families, and within families by genus and species. Specimens with a voucher number beginning with S were identified between June 1964 and February 1965 by Mr. W. R. Drummond at the National Herbarium, Salisbury, Rhodesia. Specimens with a P voucher number were identified in 1968–9 by Mrs. A. E. Van Hoepen of the State Herbarium, Pretoria, South Africa. Specimens with an L voucher number were identified in the field by the author without a herbarium specimen. The entire list was checked and revised in August 1978 by the staff of the National Herbarium, Ministry of Agriculture, Gaborone, Botswana. The voucher numbers listed are those of the Kalahari Research Group, not those of the cooperating herbariums.

In addition, Table B.2 lists by !Kung name 11 plants known to the !Kung but not botanically identified.

The last three digits in the voucher number contain a code that classifies plants according to type and use. An asterisk preceding the number indicates that plants in these categories are discussed in Chapter 6 and Appendix D.

*101–150	Trees with edible fruit (Table 6.1)
*151–200	Trees with edible gum (Table 6.3)
201–250	Trees, not edible, used otherwise
251–300	Trees not eaten or used
*301–350	Shrubs with edible berries (Table 6.2)
*351–400	Shrubs and other plants with edible melon or bean (Table 6.5)
401–450	Shrubs, not edible, used otherwise
451–500	Shrubs not eaten or used
*501–550	Plants with edible roots and bulbs (Table 6.4)
*551–600	Plants with edible leaves, cucurbits, or seeds (Table 6.5)
601–650	Medicinal plants
651–700	Plants with other uses
701–800	Other plants not eaten or used

The final column in Tables B.1 and B.2 lists further information on use. For edible species the code refers to a letter-number system introduced in Chapter 6: F =fruit, B = berry, G = gum, R = root or bulb, and O = other edible plant.

The total number of !Kung plants about which we have information comprises the 189 species in Table B.1, the 11 species in Table B.2, and 20 additional local species identified botanically but for which a !Kung name was not recorded: total =220 species.

Table B.1. *Plants known and named by the !Kung and found in the Dobe area*

Family Genus, Species	Voucher Number	!Kung Name	Use
Acanthaceae			
Asystasia sp.	SD64/36-666	//Hown	Dye
Amaranthaceae			
Achyranthes aspera L.	SD64/37-703	N≠achi≠xama	
Amaranthus sp.	SG18/64-556	!Kwe!Kwe	O1
Amaryllidaceae			
Ammocharis tinneana (Kotschy & Peyr.) Milne-Redh. and Schweickerdt	P669	Gon/ana	Glue
Crinum sp.	P685	//Ko	Tanning
Walleria muricata N.E. Br.	SDA39-507	Nchun	R34
Anacardiaceae			
Lannea edulis (Sond.) Engl.	P319	Kakatadebi	B13
Ozoroa paniculosa (Sond.) R & A Fernandes	P4988-605	Betata	V.D. medicine
Rhus tenuinervis Engl.	SD64/7-454	/Horube	
Rhus sp.	L455	//Hau	
Sclerocarya caffra (Sond.)	P102	Gai	F8
Annonaceae			
Annona stenophylla Engl. & Diels subsp. *nana* (Exell) N. Robson	P108	Twih	F2
Apocynaceae			
Diplorhynchus condylocarpon (Muell. Arg.) Pichon	SD64/55-254	//Gara	
Fockea capensis Engl.	P720	N/uä	
Asclepiadaceae			
Asclepias burchellii Schltr.	P764	//Kuie	
Brachystelma sp.	P502	!Gwitsau	R1
cf. *Ceropegia multiflora* Bak.	P524	!Gama	R2
Ceropegia sp.	SDA2-707	N!uie	?Water root
Dregea macrantha Klotzsch	SDG4/35-729	!Thama	
Ectadiopsis oblongifolia (Meisn.) Schlechter	SD64/54-667	Kau!Kuchara	Soap
Fockea sp. poss. *monroi*	P512	!Xwa	R16
Pentarrhinum insipidum (E. Mey)	P561	//Gwa	O13
Raphionacme burkei N.E. Br.	P518	!Gi!gi	R23
Raphionacme hirsuta (E. Mey) R.A. Dyer ex E.P. Phill	P534	N/won/washe	R24
Raphionacme sp.	P508	/Tama	R25
Asclepiadaceae	P537	!Xo!kama	R35
Possibly *Rhyssolobium* sp.	P543	!Gamn!n!gow	R26
Sarcostemma viminale (L.) R. Br.	P739	!Gubu!gubu	

Table B.1. (*cont.*)

Family Genus, Species	Voucher Number	!Kung Name	Use
Sarcostemma sp.	P503	N//ama	R27
Stapelia kwebensis N.E. Br.	P565	Tataba	O14
Asclepiadaceae	P542	!Ganibe	R37
Asclepiadaceae	P539	≠Dwan/i!kosi	R36
Bignoniaceae			
Catophractes alexandri D. Don	P708-449	!kai!kadi	Fire drill
Bombacaceae			
Adansonia digitata L.	P105	≠M	F1
Burseraceae			
Commiphora africana (A. Rich)	P206	N/ho!go	Soap
Commiphora angolensis Engl.	P207	N/hodi	Soap
Commiphora pyracanthoides Engl.	P206A	N/ho!go	Soap
Capparidaceae			
Boscia albitrunca (Burch.) Gilg. & Benedict	P107	Zan	F3
Celastraceae			
Maytenus senegalensis (Lam.) Excell	P451	!Go≠tobe	
Cassine transvaalensis (Burtt Davy) Codd	SDA12-209	Kwaye	Tanning
Salacia luebbertii Loes.	L313	!Goroshe	B14
Combretaceae			
Combretum apiculatum Sond.	P166	≠Doni	G9
Combretum hereroense Schinz	P251	!Xabi	G10
Combretum imberbe Wawra	P161	≠Do	G11
Combretum psidioides Welw.	SDA61-165	/Dwa	G12
Combretum zeyheri Sond.	P354	N//abe	G13
Combretum sp. cf. *collinum* Fresen.	P163	≠Dwah	G14
Combretum sp.	L355	//Gaiya	G15
Terminalia prunioides Laws	SE14-159	!Hu	G17
Terminalia sericea DC.	P160	Ziow	G18
Compositae			
Dicoma schinzii O. Hoffm.	SDA30-604	!Kabo!kabo	Medicine
Dicoma sp.	P4751-611	Tsaman/um	Medicine
Vernonia poskeana Vatke & Hildebr.	SDA28-705	!Gan!gani	
Convolvulaceae			
Ipomoea bolusiana Schinz	SD64/11-721	!Garube	
Ipomoea verbascoidea Choisy	P520	Nh!oru	R19
Merremia palmata Hall f.	SDA23-658	N≠arube	Twine
Crassulaceae			
Kalanchoe paniculata Harv.	SDA1-706	//Ku//kuha	
Cucurbitaceae			
Citrullus lanatus (Thunb.) Mansf.	SDA6-551	Dama	O5

467

Table B.1. (*cont.*)

Family Genus, Species	Voucher Number	!Kung Name	Use
Citrullus naudinianus (Sond.) Hook. f.	P552	Dcha	O6
Coccinia rehmannii Cogn.	P515	/Tan	R3
Coccinia sessilifolia (Sond.) Cogn.	P557	Kitwan	O7
Coccinia sp.	P514	N≠wara	R4
Coccinia sp.	P519	Nh/wi	R5
Corallocarpus bainessi (Hook f.) A. Meeuse	P522	!Gwara!kai	R6
Corallocarpus bainessi (Hook. f.) A. Meeuse	P564	/Horu	O8
Cucumis sp. cf. *C. kalahariensis* A. Meeuse	P506	Uhru	R7
Momordica balsamina L.	SD64/9-728	Wan	
Mukia maderaspatana (L.) M.J. Roem	SD64/93-555	Karu	O11
Trochomeria macrocarpa (Sond.) Hook. f.	P533	N≠wara!ko!ko	R31
Cyperaceae			
Cyperus fulgens C. B. Cl	P511	!Gau	R8
Cyperus rotundus L.	P509	!Hwi/wa	R9
Dichapetalaceae			
Dichapetalum cymosum (Hook.) Engl.	P316	Mai	B3
Ebenaceae			
Diospyros chamaethamnus Dinter ex. Mildbr.	SD64/65-314	Chaha	B4
Diospyros lycioides Desf. subsp. *sericea* (Bernh. ex. Krauss) de Winter	SD64/83-659	//Gwi//koroha	Toothbrush
Euphorbiaceae			
Cephalocroton puschelii Pax.	P309	≠Tedikuzū	B1
Croton gratissimus Burch.	P401	N≠wanaha	Tobacco substitute
Croton menyhartii Pax	SD64/39-402	N≠wana- han//ae	Tobacco substitute
Euphorbia monteiri Hook. f. subsp. *monteiri*	P768	!Hwa!ka!go	
Ricinodendron rautanenii Schinz	P101	//"xa	F7
Spirostachys africana Sond.	L210	K"xauie	Dye
Tragia okanyua Pax.	SDA18-704	Denekuchacha	
Gramineae			
Aristida sp.	P554	//Kai	O2
Elyonurus sp.	P653	≠Tomakəri	Aromatic
Panicum sp.	L554	//Kai	O12

Table B.1. (*cont.*)

Family Genus, Species	Voucher Number	!Kung Name	Use
Phragmites australis (cav.) Stend.	P651	!Kwa!kwa	Arrow shaft
Schmidtia pappophoroïdes Stend. ex J.A. Schmidt	SD64/45-730	/Twe//kai	
Themeda triandra Forsk.	P652	Kamakama	Thatch
Hydnoraceae			
Hydnora sp.	P516	//Hokxam	R18
Iridaceae			
Ferraria glutinosa (Bak.) Rendle	SD64/72-601	!Kaishe	Hallucinogen
Lapeyrousia coerulea Schinz	SD64/59-525	//Haru	R20
Lapeyrousia sp.	P528	≠Tədi	R21
Labiatae			
Hemizygia bracteosa Brig. syn. *Ocium bracteosum* Benth.	SDA72-660	N!ntsu	Aromatic
Leguminosae (Mimosoideae)			
Acacia fleckii Schinz	P157	N≠n̠	G2
Acacia erioloba E. Meyer	P154	/Tana	G3
Acacia hebeclada DC	SD64/52-453	!Go	
Acacia sp. cf. *hebeclada* DC.	SD64/86-153	!Gun	G4
Acacia (?) *karroo* Hayne	L156	//Koie	G5
Acacia mellifera (Vahl) Benth. subsp. *detinens* (Burch.) Brenan	P151	!Gan	G6
Acacia tortilis (Forsk.) Hayne subsp. *heteracantha* (Burch.) Brenan	P155	/Tadi	G7
Acacia (?) *erubescens* [Welw. ex] Oliv.	SD64/84-152	N!ha	G1
Albizia anthelmintica A. Brongn.	SDA25-204	Kəydi	Medicine
Dichrostachys cinerea (L.) Wight & Arn.	P158	/Twi	G16
Dichrostachys cinerea (L.) subsp. *Africana* var. *africana*, sens. lat.	P164	!Xhai	G16
Elephantorrhiza elephantina (Burch.) Skeels	P665	≠Twa≠tedi	Tanning
Leguminosae (Caesalpinioideae)			
Baikiaea plurijuga Harms	L252	!Gwa	
Bauhinia esculenta	P353	Tsin	O3
Bauhinia petersiana Bolle subsp. *serpae* (Ficalho & Hiern) Brummitt & J. H. Ross	P352	≠N≠dwa	O4
Burkea africana Hook	P162	!Xu	G8

Table B.1. (*cont.*)

Family Genus, Species	Voucher Number	!Kung Name	Use
Cassia sp.	SD64/27-608	Daman/um	Medicine
Guibourtia coleosperma (Benth.) J. Leonard	SE3-114	/Twi	F4
Peltophorum africanum Sonder	P205	!Gaietsau	Hut Building
Leguminosae (Papilionoideae)			
Abrus precatorius L.	SDA76-656	!Kube	Beads
Baphia massaiensis Taub. subsp. *obovata* (Schninz) Brummitt	SF15-661	/Gwi/goroha	
Indigofera flavicans Bak.	SD64/32-602	N≠aiego	Medicine
Indigofera trita L.f.	SD64/38-731	!Gow	
Lonchocarpus nelsii (Schinz) Heering & Grimme	P203a	//Hau	Hut Building
Mundulea sericea (Willd.) Chev.	P256	!Gai	Digging stick
Neorautanenia sp.	SDA53-715	!Gown!go	
Pterocarpus angolensis DC	L202	N≠hn	Kaross dye
Rhynchosia sp. ?*clivorum* S. Moore	P762	!Karube	
cf. *Rhynchosia* sp.	P563-775	N!odi	
Vigna sp. cf. *Vigna decipiens* Harv.	P517	Gani	R32
Vigna dinteri Harms cf. *Neorautanenia* sp.	P505	Sha	R33
Leguminosae			
Otoptera burchellii DC	SDA31-603	N!adi	Medicine
Hoffmannseggia burchellii (DC) Benth. ex. Oliv.	P541	N/omshan	R17
Liliaceae			
Aloe sp.	P716	N//ohru	
Asparagus sp.	SDA4-668	N≠həm≠dəm	Beads
Asparagus exuvialis Burch.	P655	!Gu!ko	Soap
Dipcadi glaucum Bak.	P559	!Gwaashe	O9
Dipcadi longifolium (Lindl.) Bak.	SD64/1-527	!Goro!go	R10
Dipcadi longifolium (Lindl.) Bak. or *Dipcadi marlothii* Engl.	P501	N!əmshe	R11
Dipcadi rigidifolium Bak.	P521	!Goro	R12
Dipcadi viride (L.) Moench	P538	N/ara	R13
Drimiopsis burkei Bak.	P717	//Go	
Eriospermum sp.	SDA38-719	!Kwi/wa kudenideni	
Gloriosa simplex L.	SD64/51-731	≠Tebenchn	Ornament
Ornithogalum seineri (Engl. & Krause) Oberm.	SD64/2-726	Damagoba	
Sansevieria scabrifolia Dinter	SDA8-654	!Khwi	Twine

Table B.1. (*cont.*)

Family Genus, Species	Voucher Number	!Kung Name	Use
Sansevieria sp.	P663	!Guma	Twine
Scilla sp.	P535	Tun	R28
Scilla sp.	P536	N!am	R29
Urginea sanguinea Schinz	SDA13-710	//Ka//ka	
Loganiaceae			
Strychnos cocculoides Baker	P109	N!o	F9
Strychnos pungens Solereder	SD64/82-110	Tha	F10
Loranthaceae			
Loranthus oleaefolius Cham. & Schhltd.	P4488-614	Chichi	Medicine
Malvaceae			
Abutilon angulatum (Guill. and Perr.) Mast.	SDA58-738	!Gu/wi	
Gossypium herbaceum L.	P664	//Gunago	Wild cotton
Menispermaceae			
Cissampelos mucronata A. Rich	P4829-618	N≠aiego!kan	Medicine
Cocculus hirsutus (L.) Diels	SB12-662	Duruwe	Twine
Nymphaeaceae			
Nymphaea sp.	L510	/Twe	R22
Ochnaceae			
Ochna pulchra Hook subsp. *pulchra*	P117	!Gi	F6
Olacaceae			
Ximenia americana L.	P104	!Xo!xoni	F12
Ximenia caffra Sond.	P103	//Gwe	F13
Orchidaceae			
Eulophia hereroensis Schltr.	P504	≠Do	R14
Eulophia sp.	P523	≠Dau	R15
Palmaceae			
Hyphaene sp.	P351	//Gən	O10
Hyphaene benguellensis Welw. var. *ventricosa* (Kirk) Furtado	P116	!Hani	F5
Pedaliaceae			
Dicerocaryum zanguebarium (Lour.) Merrill	P4478-617	//Gemi//gemi	Medicine
Harpagophytum procumbens D.C.	SD64/33-722	//Hxəmchi//koshe	
Sesamum schenckii Aschers.	SD64/10-606	Dama!xo!xo	Medicine
Phytolaccaceae			
Gisekia pharnaceoides L.	SD64/14-736	!Gwan!n	
Limeum fenestratum Heimerl. syn. *Semonvillaea fenestrata* Fenzl.	P750		
Plumbaginaceae			
Plumbago zeylanica L.	SF18-607	Khaba	Medicine

Table B.1. (*cont.*)

Family Genus, Species	Voucher Number	!Kung Name	Use
Polygalaceae			
Securidaca longipedunculata Fresen	P208	Chwechweha	Medicine
Oxygonum alatum Burch.	SD64/17-740	!Gwan!n	
Portulacaceae			
Portulaca kermesina N.E. Br.	SD64/41-741		
Talinum crispatulatum Dinter	P553	//Guea	O15
Talinum sp.	SD64/77-733	≠Ga≠garu	
Rhamnaceae			
Helinus spartioides (Engl.) Schinz ex Engl.	SDA26-701	Gwidoro	
Helinus integrifolius (Lam.) Kuntze	SB7,8-701a	Gwidoro	
Ziziphus mucronata Willd.	P106	N≠a̱	F14
Rubiaceae			
Vangueria sp.	P115	/Duru	F11
Solanaceae			
Solanum panduriforme E. Mey.	SDA3-713	N!hi!gan!un!twana	
Solanum renschii Vatke	SD3,4-714	!Gun!goma	
Solanum sp. nr. *coccineum* Jacq.	SD64/3-727	!Gən!go	
Sterculiaceae			
Hermannia angolensis K. Schum	P4831-615	/Gam	Medicine
Tiliaceae			
Grewia avellana Hiern	SD64/56-308	Zoma	B5
Grewia bicolor Juss.	P304	Kamako	B6
Grewia falcistipula K. Schum	SDA43-306	!Khwe	B7
Grewia flava DC	P301	N/n	B8
Grewia sp. ?*flavescens* Juss.	P302	/Tore	B10
Grewia retinervis Burret	P303	!Gwa	B9
Grewia sp.	L318	!Kama!koro	B12
Grewia sp.	P305	Da/m	B11
Verbenaceae			
Clerodendron lanceolatum Gurke	SD64/6-711	≠Tu≠tu	
Clerodendron sp.	P315	Dare	B2
Vitaceae			
Cyphostemma sp. cf. *congestum* (Bak.) Descoings	P718	≠Twoidama	
Zygophyllaceae			
Tribulus terrestris L.	SD64/12-709	≠Dnwa	
Terfezia sp. (truffles, a fungus)	L544	Chocho	R30

Table B.2. *Plants known to the !Kung but not botanically identified*

!Kung name	Voucher number	Use
Kona	P610	Fungus (medicinal)
N/wa	L210	Dye
N!ana	L317	B15
Tedi	L513	R39
!Gan!uhm	L735	Mushroom (poisonous)
!Guchigegebi	L723	
!Gwi	L526	R40
!Gxuku!hia	L734	
!Hu!gam!gae!gae	L724	
//"Aizheri	L529	R41
//Kore	L540	R38

Appendix C. Mammals of the Dobe area

T ABLES C.1, C.2, and C.3 list the 58 mammals of the Dobe area in three
groups: (1) those regularly hunted and eaten, (2) those occasionally hunted
and eaten, and (3) those rarely or never hunted and eaten. Identifications
are drawn from Smithers (1968). Within each group, the animals are listed alphabetically by families and within families by genus.

Table C.1. *Mammals regularly hunted and eaten*

Common name	Scientific name	!Kung name	Comment
Bovidae			
Impala	*Aepyceros melampus*	Kxara	Very rare
Cape hartebeest	*Alcelaphus buselaphus*	Ntso̲	Uncommon
Blue wildebeest	*Connochaetes taurinus*	!Ghi‿	Common
Roan antelope	*Hippotragus equinus*	N/ho‿	Uncommon
Gemsbok	*Oryx gazella*	!Gwe	Common
Steenbok	*Raphicerus campestris*	/Ton	Very common
Gray duiker	*Sylvicapra grimmia*	/Tau⁻	Very common
Cape eland	*Taurotragus oryx*	N!n	Uncommon
Greater kudu	*Tragelaphus strepsiceros*	N!hwa‿	Common
Giraffidae			
Giraffe	*Giraffa camelopardalis*	≠Dwa	Uncommon
Hystricidae			
Porcupine	*Hystrix africaeaustralis*	!Kum	Common
Leoporidae			
Scrub hare	*Lepus saxatilis*	!Hai⁻	Very common
Manidae			
Pangolin (scaly anteater)	*Manis temmincki*	N≠hwoi'	Common
Orycteropodidae			
Ant bear	*Orycteropus afer*	N/a‿	Common
Pedetidae			
Springhare	*Pedetes capensis*	N/hum‿	Very common
Suidae			
Warthog	*Phacochoerus aethiopicus*	/Wa	Very common

Table C.2. *Mammals occasionally hunted and eaten*

Common name	Scientific name	!Kung name	Comment
Bovidae			
African buffalo	*Syncerus caffer*	/Hau	Rare
Canidae			
Bat-eared fox	*Otocyon megalotis*	!Ku	Common
Equidae			
Burchell's zebra	*Equus burchelli*	/Twe	Rare
Felidae			
Cheetah	*Acinonyx jubatus*	!Gau	Common
Caracal	*Felis caracal*	≠Twi	Uncommon
African wild cat	*Felis lybica*	N/wa	Common
Mustelidae			
Honey badger	*Mellivora capensis*	//Hau	Common
Protelidae			
Aardwolf	*Proteles cristatus*	/Hi	Common
Viverridae			
Yellow mongoose	*Cynictus penicillata*	/Gaidoroha	Common
Small-spotted genet	*Genetta genetta*	Tswa	Common
Slender mongoose	*Herpestes sanguineus*	Tswanitsa	Common
Banded mongoose	*Mungos mungo*	/Gaidoroha	Common

Table C.3. *Mammals rarely or never hunted or eaten*

Common name	Scientific name	!Kung name	Comment
Order Carnivora			
Canidae			
Black-backed jackal	*Canis mesomelas*	/Tedi	Common
Wild dog	*Lycaon pictus*	/Du	Common
Felidae			
Serval	*Felis serval*	/Wi!kaun	Very rare
Lion	*Panthera leo*	N!haie	Common
Leopard	*Panthera pardus*	!Kum	Uncommon
Hyaenidae			
Spotted hyena	*Crocuta crocuta*	/Dwi	Very common
Brown hyena	*Hyaena brunnea*	!Hau	Very rare
Mustelidae			
Zorilla (striped polecat)	*Ictonyx striatus*	Da	Common
Order Chiroptera			
Hipposideridae			
Leaf-nosed bat	*Hipposideros commersoni*	//Gwa//gwama	Common
Nycteridae			
Egyptian slit-faced bat	*Nycteris thebaica*	//Gwa//gwama	Common
Rhinolophidae			
Dent's horse shoe bat	*Rhinolophus denti*	//Gwa//gwama	Common
Order Insectivora			
Soricidae			
Lesser red musk-shrew	*Crocidura hirta*	N/hwi	Common
Order Primates			
Cercopithecidae			
Vervet monkey	*Cercopithecus aethiops*	//Gai	Rare
Chacma baboon	*Papio ursinus*	/Dwara	Very rare
Lorsidae			
Night ape	*Galago senegalensis*	//Gore	Common

Table C.3. (*cont.*)

Common name	Scientific name	!Kung name	Comment
Order Proboscoidea			
Elephantidae			
African elephant	*Loxodonta africana*	!'Xo	Rare
Order Rodentia			
Muridae			
Red veld rat	*Aethomys chrysophilus*	N/hwi	Common ?
Namaqua rock rat	*Aethomys namaquensis*	N/hwi	Common ?
Gray pygmy climbing mouse	*Dendromus melanotus*	N/hwi	Common ?
Lesser gerbil	*Gerbillus paeba*	N/hwi	Common ?
Multi mammate mouse	*Mastomys natalensis*	N/hwi	Common ?
Pygmy mouse	*Mus minutoides*	N/hwi	Common ?
Pouched mouse	*Saccostomus campestris*	N/hwi	Common ?
Small fat mouse	*Steatomys minutus*	N/hwi	Common ?
Brant's gerbil	*Tatera brantsi*	N/hwi	Common ?
Peter's gerbil	*Tatera leucogaster*	N/hwi	Common ?
Woosnam's desert rat	*Zelotomys woosnami*	N/hwi	Common?
Muscardinidae			
Dormouse	*Graphiurus murinus*	N/hwi	Common ?
Sciuridae			
Bush squirrel	*Paraxerus cepapi*	!Wasa	Uncommon
Ground squirrel	*Xerus inauris*	N!au	Common

Appendix D. Major foods and nutritional assays

THOUGH the !Kung recognize 105 plant species as edible, only 14 species account for up to 75 percent of the vegetable diet by weight. The mongongo fruit and nut are discussed in Chapter 7. This appendix is devoted to the other major species: their botany, their ecology, their nutritional value, and how the !Kung use them. Table D.1 gives details of the nutritional composition of the major foods.

In the discussion that follows, each text heading gives the plant's code number, its common name, its !Kung and Setswana names, and its botanical name.

F1. BAOBAB (≠M, MUANA; *ADANSONIA DIGITATA*)

At the western water holes (Dobe, !Kubi, !Xabi, Mahopa) the baobab is second only to the mongongo as an important food plant. Groves of the giant trees are found on the molapo soils north of the Ahas and south of the upper !Kangwa River (Plate 6.1). The fruit and nuts are enclosed in a gray green oblong pod with a velvety exterior. The large pod, 10 to 15 cm long, weighs 80 to 200 g; specimens up to 400 g have been seen. Inside is a very dry white pulp enclosing 20 to 30 small, soft-shelled seeds. The proportions, by weight, in each pod are roughly: pulp 22 percent, seeds 31 percent, waste 47 percent.

Baobab is a winter food, with a season from May to September. The pods fall to the ground when ripe and are collected daily by men and women. Occasionally people throw sticks to knock down hanging pods or climb the giant limbs to reach accessible pods. Pegs are sometimes driven into a tree's trunk to facilitate climbing. In the camp the pods are easily cracked open and their contents emptied into a basin. The seeds are often difficult to separate from the pulp; in young pods both can be eaten together right from the pod. If the pod is mature, the pulp is pounded gently to separate it from the seeds; then with the seed removed the pulp is pounded to a fine flour. Water is added, and the fruit is usually eaten as a porridge or as a refreshing drink. The fruit's taste is pleasant and highly acidic. The seeds, when roasted, have a rich nutty flavor.

As a food the baobab is highly nutritious and is a good source of protein, calcium, phosphorus, potassium, and thiamine. The acidic taste of the pulp is attrib-

Table D.1. *Seasonal availability and nutritional composition of major San foods*[a]

	Mongongo nut	Mongongo fruit	Baobab fruit, nut	Vegetable ivory fruit	Marula nut	Wild orange fruit
Season of use	Year-round	Apr.–Nov.	May–Oct.	June–Oct.	Mar.–Oct.	Sept.–Dec.
Composition (g/100 g as eaten)						
Moisture	4.2	13.4	5.2	6.6	4.0	69.3
Ash	4.0	5.7	7.3	9.0	4.2	1.0
Protein	28.3	6.6	14.3	4.9	30.9	4.1
Fat	58.4	0.6	13.9	0.4	57.0	0.1
Fiber	1.5	3.5	10.7	9.6	2.4	1.4
Carbohydrate	3.7	70.2	51.4	69.6	—	24.0
Kilocalories supplied (per 100 g)	654	312	388	302	642	114
Composition (mg/100 g eaten)						
Calcium	249	89.6	272	103	106	22.3
Magnesium	500	195	630	196.5	467	23.2
Iron	2.07	0.74	9.51	2.04	0.42	0.33
Copper	1.90	0.45	2.47	0.47	1.99	0.10
Sodium	2.0	1.01	76.3	544.9	338	2.6
Potassium	686.6	1760	4173	2560	677	354
Phosphorus	704	46.0	1166	155.8	836	52.2
Zinc	4.09	1.39	6.96	0.56	—	0.11
B-Carotene	—	0	—	0.06	—	0
Thiamine	0.13	—	—	—	0.04	—
Riboflavin	0.14	0.11	—	0.10	0.12	0.11
Nicotinic acid	—	0.12	—	4.62	0.71	0.85
Vitamin C	0.57	8.51	—	19.7	—	18.1
Sample no.	1025/67	1029/67	682/67	1033/67	(Wehmeyer 1966:1103)	1037/67

[a]Analyzed by A.S. Wehmeyer, National Nutrition Research Institute, CSIR South Africa; unless noted otherwise sample numbers refer to samples submitted by M. G. Whiting and R. B. Lee, October–December 1967 and June 1968.
Dash (−) = no information.

utable in large part to the remarkably high levels of vitamin C, 213 mg per 100 g according to Wehmeyer (1966:1103). During the winter season the !Kung, simply by eating two or three baobab pods a day, can provide themselves with an almost therapeutic dose of vitamin C. In addition to its use as a food, a large baobab pod when carefully emptied of its content makes a serviceable water container with a volume of about 1 liter.

F5. VEGETABLE IVORY PALM (!HANI, MOKULANI; *HYPHAENE BENGNELLENSIS*)

This tall, handsome palm tree is relatively common west of Dobe and !Kubi, but absent at /Xai/xai and /Du/da. It grows on dark compacted soils on the edge of pans in association with anthills. The seed is round, about 5 cm in diameter, and consists of a thin, red, dry, inedible skin; a thin (3 to 6 mm) layer of edible pulp; and an inedible nutshell. The nut itself, inside the nutshell, is a 15-mm round ball of an extremely hard substance (hence the name "vegetable ivory"). The seeds weigh about 73 g, with a range from 48 to 97 g (n = 31). In ripe specimens early in the

Sour plum	Maphate berry	Mokomphata berry	/Tan root	!Xwa root	Sha root	Tsin bean	Tsama melon
Dec.–Feb.	Feb.–May	Mar.–June	Year-round	Year-round	Year-round	Feb.–July	Jan.–Sept.
67.2	17.6	10.6	82.0	90.0	78.4	5.2	91.3
1.4	3.2	3.7	4.1	1.5	1.0	2.9	1.9
3.1	7.5	5.4	2.2	0.6	3.0	31.6	0.4
1.3	0.6	0.2	0.1	0.7	0.1	36.1	0.1
0.7	23.3	12.6	2.2	1.6	0.9	1.0	1.7
26.3	47.9	67.5	9.4	5.6	16.6	23.2	4.7
—	227	293	47	31	79	544	21
5.9	375	157	201.9	—	15.2	136	62.3
2.0	195	172	944	—	58.0	258	30.6
0.20	4.11	4.7	0.45	—	0.90	3.3	0.20
0.10	0.43	0.4	0.16	—	0.20	1.0	0.14
4.60	7.4	31.0	11.1	—	16.1	89.0	3.7
737	816	655	262	—	319	849	135
14.5	89.9	—	19.2	—	16.4	484	3.8
—	0.60	1.6	1.01	—	0.40	3.8	0.10
—	0	—	0	—	0.03	0.22	0.68
0.04	0.08	—	0.06	0.05	0.09	0.94	1.76
0.04	0.15	—	—	0.02	0.05	0.82	0.03
0.81	2.35	—	1.00	—	0.86	1.86	0.98
22.5	14.7	—	3.35	5.84	9.82	2.19	7.53
(Wehmeyer 1966:1103)	1039/67B	527/68	668/67	1000/67	922/67	1036/67	1042/67

season about 33 percent of the total weight is edible pulp. As the seeds dry out, this proportion is reduced to 25 percent. Therefore, the edible yield per seed is 18 to 24 g. !Hani is a major food at Dobe during the winter and early spring (June to October), when men and women bring bags of the seeds into camp each week. The seeds, called *shumsi* ("testicles") by the !Kung, are collected from the ground around the base of trees or are knocked to the ground by thrown sticks. Back in the camp, !hani fruit is simply prepared: The dry skin is peeled off and the fruit is lightly pounded to loosen it from the shell; the pulp may be eaten directly off the shell, or peeled off with the fingers, or pounded in the mortar to a coarse meal. !Hani fruit is never cooked or salted or mixed with water. It may be mixed half-and-half with baobab fruit into a white and yellow flour, which is then eaten. The pulp of !hani has a golden crumbly texture with a pleasing datelike flavor. It is a good source of sodium, potassium, and nicotinic acid.

A dwarf form of *Hyphaene* palm, which may be a different species, is called //gɔn by the !Kung and yields an edible heart of palm (O10). This large, orange, fleshy organ is hacked out of the center of the shrub and can weigh up to 10 kg. It is roasted in a cooking pit in the same way that an animal is prepared. Marshall (1976:119) describes a case at /Gausha where a large heart of palm was shared like meat in a campwide distribution.

One September day during a week when meat was scarce at Dobe, three men shouldered weapons and headed west, only to return in the afternoon without meat but with an enormous quantity of !hani seeds, 715 in all. These the three men distributed to the 40 residents in the two camps at Dobe. It was the largest single collection of !hani fruit that we saw. The edible yield of the 715 seeds was about 12.9 kg of pulp (38,600 Cal), and this provided each of the 40 residents with a meal of 965 Cal, about what they would get if a small antelope were brought into camp.

F8. MARULA NUT (GAI, MARULA; *SCLEROCARYA CAFFRA*)

The marula is widespread in the Dobe area, growing on gray and rocky soils at all water holes. The seed ripens in March, and the season extends to October, when the rainy season tends to spoil the previous year's crop. The fresh seed is an oval about 2.5 cm long, consisting of a pale yellow skin, a juicy satiny pulp, and a hard shell containing a small nutmeat. A shell with a nut but without pulp or skin weighs about 5 g.

Despite its delightful flavor, the outer pulp is not as important a food as is the kernel. At /Xai/xai the people ignored the marula until the fall (April or May) when the fruit pulp has dried off the shell. They said the fresh pulp made the shell slippery and hard to crack. At the other water holes the pulp was eaten and the shells were sun-dried before being cracked. Marulas are easily collected on the ground where they have fallen, and they are brought back to camp in bags or karosses in lots of 3 to 8 kg. The shell, when cracked with nut-cracking stones, opens to reveal two fragile lobes of nutmeat. These have a superb taste, superior to that of the mongongo; but the marula is much smaller. Because of their fragility, the nutmeats must be picked out of the shell using a long thorn. This work requires patience, and women appeared to eat marula more frequently than men. The nuts are usually eaten straight, but they may be mixed with other foods in the same kinds of recipes as mongongo. Marula nuts are a good source of protein, magnesium, sodium, potassium, and phosphorus.

F9. WILD ORANGE (N!O, MAHOROHWANI; *STRYCHNOS COCCULOIDES*)

This is one of the top delicacies in the Dobe area and the one with the most unusual method of collection: N!o, and the related form da (*Strychnos pungens*), are common trees, 4 to 6 meters in height, growing on deep white sandy soils with *Burkea* and *Pterocarpus* (Plate 6.4). The fruit looks superficially like a large Sunkist orange about 10 cm in diameter. But the rich orange-colored rind is hard and woody, and the pulp inside is quite unlike an orange, consisting of about 30 lozenge-shaped pips surrounded by a sticky brown pulp. The fruits weigh from 250 to 580 g, with an average weight of 438 g (just under 1 lb).

The season of ripeness is from September to December, but the gathering process starts earlier. N!o is one of the very few !Kung foods that has an element of private property. The trees are not owned, and anyone may pick the fruit of a tree within his n!ore. The unusual element is that people come to the n!o groves in the late winter when the fruits are unripe, collect the fruits by knocking them down with thrown sticks or hooking them with the long springhare probe, and then *bury them* 0.5 meter deep to ripen in the ground. The burying hastens ripening and ensures that the fruit will not be spoiled by surface-dwelling insects. Once buried, the fruits belong to the person who buried them, and it is bad form for anyone else to dig them up without permission. During their time in the ground, the owner may turn the fruits once, and after a month they are ready for eating. Once back in camp the fruits are shared by the owner in the same way as other tasty vegetable foods.

The hard rind is easily opened with a knife and the pulp removed with a spoon or the hand. The taste is aromatic and pleasantly sweet. The seeds are thoroughly sucked to remove the pulp and then discarded. N!o oranges have been prized by the !Kung for generations. A camp with a good supply of n!o in its n!ore is a popular camp to visit in the early spring. Historically, /Xai/xai was an important spring meeting place not only for the strength of its water hole but also because of the abundant n!o in the vicinity. The blacks also love the n!o, and it is an item of trade between the !Kung and their neighbors.

The lesser form, da, is not buried in the ground. If it is found unripe, it is roasted in the shell to make it edible. Later in the season, when it is found ripe on the tree, it may be eaten raw. The !Kung older people caution the children never to eat either species unripe, saying that doing so will make them vomit.

F13. SOUR PLUM (//GWE, MORUTONOGA; *XIMENIA CAFFRA*)

This tart orange fruit and its related form, !xo!xoni (*Ximenia americana*), are found on brown sandy flats in association with *Grewia* species. It is an early summer fruit, with a season from December to February. The oval fruit, about 2 cm long, consists of a soft juicy skin with a stringent taste, a layer of tart orange pulp, and an inedible seed. The fruits are easily collected in season from the stalks of the tall bushes, but fruits that have fallen to the ground are not collected. Loads of 1 or 2 kg of the fruit are brought back into camp, where the plums are eaten raw with or without the peel or pounded to a pulp in the mortar. In spite of its tart flavor, sour plum is not mixed with other sweeter food, but is eaten straight. The sour plum is a good dietary source of potassium and vitamin C. The inedible seeds are roasted and widely used by the !Kung as medicine and cosmetic. The seed can be used as an antiseptic on sores and cuts; the ash of the charred seed is mixed with fat and rubbed into cuts to produce tattoos; at /Du/da the oil from crushed seeds is rubbed into the hair to lengthen the ringlets in the women's traditional coiffure.

B8. MORETHLWA BERRIES (N/N MORETHLWA; *GREWIA FLAVA*)
B9. MOKOMPHATA BERRIES (!GWA, MOKOMPHATA; *GREWIA RETINERVIS*)

These two are the most important of the eight *Grewia* species in the Dobe area. N/n is the main *Grewia* north of the Ahas, and !gwa is the main one south of the

Ahas and at Du/da. Both are medium-sized bushes, 2 meters in height, that form extensive groves numbering hundreds of bushes. N/n is found on the dark compacted soils of the molapo association; !gwa is found on sandier white and brown soils of the upper flats. These and the other *Grewia* species produce an edible pea-sized berry that consists of a thin, digestible skin; a fibrous, orange, edible pulp; and a tiny, hard, indigestible seed. In season people collect large volumes of these berries. A 1-liter pitcher of !gwa weighed 311 g. From 5 to 10 liters of the berry are typically gathered by a single person in a few hours. About half of the total weight is edible. Therefore, a 10-liter collection weighs 3.1 kg and yields about 1550 g of edible pulp. The berries are easily collected and prepared. The gatherers, usually women, go out to the groves and pick the ripe berries from the stalks (never from the ground). Back in the camp, basins full of berries may be passed from fire to fire. If ripe and juicy, the berries are eaten straight. Later in the season, when they have become dry, water is added and they are pounded in the mortar to loosen the stringy flesh from the seeds, or a long branched twig may be put into the mixture and twirled rapidly between the hands like a fire drill to agitate the seeds and separate the pulp. The mixture is then eaten as a tasty fruit porridge, or more water is added and the mixture is drunk as a refreshing beverage. The grewias are never cooked or roasted or mixed with other foods. The taste is pleasantly sweet, and the berries are a good source of sugar, calcium, iron, nicotinic acid, and vitamin C. The fiber content is exceptionally high.

The !Kung consume large quantities of the berries, including the pits. The latter are passed intact through the digestive system and expelled in massive wads in the feces. One of the hazards of eating *Grewia* in large quantities is the danger of fecal impaction. According to the !Kung, people have died from this condition though we never observed such a case in our studies.

These two main berries, along with other *Grewia* species, follow a ripening sequence that extends the *Grewia* season from December to July and beyond. In 1967–9 the ripening sequence for the five major species was as follows:

Zoma (*G. avellana*) in November
N/n (*G. flava*) in December
/Tore (*G. flavescens*) in February
!Gwa (*G. retinervis*) in March or April
Kamako (*G. bicolor*) in April or May

If autumn is dry, *Grewia* berries can remain edible into the winter and following spring. A rainy autumn, however, can cause the berries to rot on the bushes and thus end the season prematurely. In addition to their importance as food, *Grewia* plants are widely used for tools, digging sticks, house building, and fire making. And the *Grewia* berries are the main flavoring ingredient in the alcoholic home brew that the !Kangwa San have been making since 1967.

B14. WILD MANGO (!GOROSHE; *SALACIA LUEBBERTII*)

This is one of the tastiest of the major foods, and the one we know least about. !Goroshe was rarely seen in 1963–4, but by 1968 it appeared as one of the dominant foods at two water holes: /Twihaba and /Du/da. We have no nutritional data on it, and the botanical identification is drawn from Maguire (ca. 1954) and confirmed by Wilmsen (personal communication). Not in doubt, however, is its importance to the !Kung as food: We saw thousands of fresh !goroshe rinds littering the /Du/da camp in January 1969.

!Goroshe grows on a low shrub on the white and red sands of the dune association. The fruit is the size of a large cherry, about 3 cm in diameter. It has a rich, red, inedible rind; a bright orange stringy pulp the color, texture, and taste of a mango; and a hard seed the size of an apricot pit. During the season (January to March) the fruits are collected in large numbers and eaten as is. The peel is discarded, the delicious pulp is thoroughly sucked from the seed, and the latter is tossed away. Like most other berries, !goroshe is not mixed with other foods. Its flavor is superior to that of the sour plum and the *Grewia* berries and comparable to that of the wild orange.

R3. /TAN ROOT (/TAN, NAGHWA; *COCCINIA REHMANNII*)

One of the best roots for flavor, size, year-round availability, and widespread distribution, /tan is a member of the cucurbit family. It grows in all kinds of soil conditions, including molapos, flats, and dunes. The above-ground part is an inconspicuous climber that winds in the branches of shrubs and bushes. Below ground is an elongated yam-shaped root with a thick, coarse, knobby skin enclosing a fibrous, white, edible flesh. The root may weigh up to 10 kg, but the more typical sizes are 1 to 2 kg, and smaller specimens weigh as little as 30 g. /Tan is eaten year-round, but especially in winter and spring, when the storage organs tend to be fattest.

When the gatherer spots the /tan tendril above ground, she examines it closely to see if it is worth digging. /Tan, like most other root foods, is a perennial plant: The underground storage organ grows larger and larger with each succeeding year, though the top may die away after each season. The gatherer looks for signs of older dead tendrils, which if present in quantity may indicate a large edible root below ground. She then clears away old branches and grass that obstruct her work area and, using her digging stick, begins to excavate the root. /Tan is one of the deepest roots, lying 25 to 60 cm (10 to 24 in.) below ground. A large root could require 20 minutes or more of hard work to dig out. A very large root (over 8 kg) may have to be removed chunk by chunk, or part of it may have to be left in the ground.

Back in the camp, the /tan is always roasted before it is eaten. Eaten alone, its taste and texture are excellent. It also mixes well with other roots, with crumbled animal hide, with mongongo nuts, or with leafy greens. The !Kung caution that it can cause diarrhea or stomachache if eaten raw or underdone. It is a good source of calcium and magnesium.

R16. !XWA WATER ROOT (!XWA, LERUSSA; *FOCKEA* SP., POSSIBLY *MONROI*)

!Xwa root serves double duty: as a food and, more important, as a source of water. In the dry season people are able to live independently of the permanent water holes by digging and eating !xwa roots to satisfy their moisture requirements. The plant is a climber, found widely distributed on molapo soils in association with the common tree *Acacia mellifera*. The root is the size and shape (and color) of a football. The thin brown skin covers a soft white flesh that exudes a milky astringent juice. The roots can be dug year-round; they tend to be fatter and fuller during the summer and fall, and they grow thinner and more desiccated in the winter and spring. Even so, a specimen collected in November at the end of the dry season had a 90 percent moisture content. The roots can vary from 1 to 10 kg in weight (Plate 6.3).

When a group moves into waterless country, the members fill their canteens at the water hole to see them through the first day and night; then they spend part of each subsequent day digging !xwa roots. I accompanied one such group in November 1964 to !Kwi/wama, 19 km west of Dobe. The men I went hunting with on the second day spent about half their working hours digging !xwa roots in a molapo about 8 km from the base camp. !Xwa is buried 25 to 60 cm deep in the compacted gray soil of the molapo association and, therefore, is particularly difficult to dig out. After a root is dug out, it is cut into chunks and eaten, or the chunks may be squeezed by hand over a container to release the liquid, which is then drunk. Both techniques have advantages. Eating the pulp is an efficient way of processing the moisture, but it also requires eating a large amount of fibrous bulk. Squeezing the liquid out of the pulp solves the bulk problem, but it is an inefficient technique: In experiments only 63 percent of the water content could be recovered by the !Kung through squeezing. In a spring dry camp the per capita daily water requirement is about 4 liters. This amount can be provided by digging five to seven 1-kg !xwa roots or a smaller number of larger roots.

The taste and texture of !xwa are sweet and pleasant. !Xwa is a good starchy food that mixes well with mongongo nuts. If water is scarce, meat can be boiled in its juice. At some camps in the South, !xwa is dug and eaten as a food even when standing water is available. Curiously, the !Kung state that one must not wash in !xwa juice. One informant claimed that washing in it will make one weak in the knees. I found the sticky white juice unpleasant on the skin.

The taste of !xwa is much superior to that of the other emergency water sources, such as !gi!gi (*Raphionacme burkei*), n/won/washe (*Raphionacme hirsuta*), and n!oru (*Ipomoea verbascoidea*).

R33. SHA ROOT (SHA, CHADA; *VIGNA DINTERI*)

Sha is a popular, abundant, and easily excavated small root that grows in white sands of the flats association with *Burkea africana* and *Terminalia sericea*. The above-ground part is a creeper and is easier to identify than the tops of many other roots. The root itself is buried only 8 to 20 cm below ground and is relatively easy to dig out of the soft sand. The edible part consists of a string of golf-ball-sized little "potatoes" arranged in a series on a single long root. The edible parts range in weight from 10 to 75 g, with an average weight of 44 g. Sha roots are eaten at all times of year. They may be eaten raw, but are usually roasted. Both the thin reddish skin and the white crunchy inner flesh are edible. The taste is excellent eaten alone; sha is also commonly mixed with other roots and with leafy greens. Sha is the most popular representative of a group of about 20 other species of smaller edible bulbs and roots that are dug and prepared in the same way as sha and that are mixed with the same range of other foods. This group includes ≠do (R14), ≠dau (R15), nchun (R34), and tedi (R39) in the minor class, and R1, R2, R10, R12, R20, R25, and R35 in the supplementary class (see Chapter 6, Table 6.6).

O3. TSIN BEAN (TS'HI, MORAMA; *BAUHINIA ESCULENTA*)

The tsin bean is the second most important food of the !Kung in the southern parts of the Dobe area and in Nyae Nyae. It is rare north of the Ahas and east of the Namibian border. In its areas tsin is a superabundant ground runner that grows in the white sands of the upper flats association. The slender vines can grow to a length of 6 meters, and each vine can produce a dozen seedpods. In the Dobe area large tsin groves are found in the Ahas, southwest of !Kubi at Tsutsunana, west of /Xai/xai at !Garaha, and particularly at Hxore, 15 km southwest of /Xai/xai (see Chapter 12). The large (5 cm across), flat seedpod encloses a bean with a hard, inedible outer shell and an edible, two-lobed seed inside. The mature bean is an oval about the size of a thumbnail; each pod contains two to six beans, weighing about 3 g each. The tuber of tsin, called *n//n*, is also edible and may weigh up to 12 kg. A very large tuber may send out three or more runners, so that in a major tsin grove the long runners form a dense geometry of overlapping networks.

The beans begin to grow within the pods during the main rains of January. They ripen within the pods until April or May, when the pods explode, spilling the ripe beans inside their brown shells onto the ground. The beans remain edible on the ground for several months into the winter until they are attacked by ants and spoiled. The collecting season may start as early as January, when the immature beans are collected. Taken straight from the pod, the bean shells are soft and white; the beans must be carefully peeled and roasted before they are eaten. After April the bean shells are hard and brown; the beans may then be eaten raw or processed. Collecting is a simple matter: The gatherers fan out through the tsin fields and watch for the geometric patterns of bright green leaves and dark brown pods. Early in the season (January to March) the whole pod is collected, and the bean is pried out back at camp. In midseason (April and May) the bean alone is collected, making much less waste to carry home. Later in the season (June to August) collecting is more difficult. The leaves of the tsin plants have dried to a dark brown and are difficult to distinguish from the pods. Also the ants have made steady inroads on the crop. They build colonies around each fallen bean, so when the collector spots anthills around a tsin plant she passes it by. People sometimes set fires in the tsin fields at this time of year to burn off the old vegetation and increase visibility. Many hectares can be razed in a single fire.

A typical day's backload of 5 kg of tsin beans without pods has an edible/waste ratio of 70:30 and provides 3500 g of edible beans. Back in the camp, tsin beans are processed in several ways. Unripe beans may be sun-dried before further processing. A batch of 50 or so beans is roasted in the shell for a few minutes in the hot ashes and sand of the cooking fire. Slight bursts of steam from the roasting beans indicate they are ready for eating. Occasionally a bean explodes, but without much damage. The beans are removed from the ashes, placed on an anvil stone, and opened with a single light tap of a rock or stick. Each bean comes apart easily into halves. Eaten whole, the beans have a rich, strong nutty flavor. Alternately, the shelled beans may be pounded in the mortar and then mixed with hot water and eaten as a soup or porridge. The tsin bean is an excellent source of protein (31.6 percent), calories, potassium, phosphorus, thiamine, riboflavin, and nicotinic acid.

In addition to its use as food, the tsin bean has important ritual functions. The oil expressed from the bean is used to wash and anoint young men and women during initiation ceremonies and rituals connected with marriage. Whole beans may be drilled and strung to make attractive bead necklaces.

O5. TSAMA MELON (DAMA, MOKATE; *CITRULLUS LANATUS*)

The tsama melon is one of the most characteristic and abundant species growing in the central Kalahari Desert to the south. Countless thousands of tsamas litter the ground of the Central Kalahari Game Reserve after each rainy season. The more northerly Dobe area is far from the center of distribution, and the melons are not nearly as abundant there as further south; nevertheless, they still rank as a major food and as an important source of water. The tsama thrives on the brown sands of the lower flats with *Acacia* species. The plant is a runner that grows from an inedible storage organ and may extend for 3 meters along the ground. The melons begin to appear in January, are fully ripe by March, and may be collected and eaten through the winter into the following spring. The melons are round, pale green or yellow in color, and may weigh up to 2 kg; most are smaller, around 500 to 1500 g and 10 to 15 centimeters in diameter. Tsamas are conspicuous and easily collected. The whole melon is brought back to camp and may be cut into slices for distribution. The melon itself may be halved and used as a cup, while the pulp is pulverized with the blunt end of a digging stick. The seeds may be roasted and eaten as well. The flesh is white and hard in texture. Compared with the domesticated watermelon, the pulp is more bitter than sweet. Only a large tsama may have a slight sweetness at the center.

The tsama melon is a member of an extremely variegated species that includes domestic, wild, and feral varieties. Tsamas found growing near abandoned Herero villages are probably descendants of the cultivated forms. The complexities of cross-pollination of this species remain to be worked out. One tsama may be quite bitter and the one next to it quite sweet, apparently depending on the source of its pollination.

Distantly related to the tsama melon is the "bitter" melon, dcha (*Citrullus naudinianus*). This is a much more consistent form, with a characteristic yellow color, spiky appearance, and slightly bitter taste. Dcha is always cooked before eating to render it more palatable. In the Dobe area, dcha is ranked as a minor food, though at /Du/da, it is a major food exceeding the tsama in importance.

Appendix E. The hand-to-mouth existence: a note on the origin of human economy

Note: This hitherto unpublished paper about the importance of the carrying device in human evolution was written in 1968 and presented at a Wenner-Gren–sponsored conference on subsistence and social organization in primate societies in August of that year. Though the proceedings of the conference were never published, the various papers circulated through scientific networks, and occasional references to the argument of this paper began to appear in print (e.g., *Scientific American* 1970; Washburn 1976; Isaac 1978; Lancaster 1978).

Because the relations among carrying devices, infant carrying, and human origins have proved a fruitful topic for exploration (Sussman 1972; Denham 1974a, b; Slocum 1975), it seems worthwhile to publish this early contribution to the subject. Only minor editorial changes have been made, and the paper appears here in essentially the same form as it was originally written.

Among the changes are the incorporation of some footnotes into the body of the text, the omission of others, and the change of such phrases as "early man" to "early humans" to correct the sexist terminology prevalent in the 1960s.

On one substantive issue time has proved me wrong. I argued that "exchange of food . . . is absent from the societies of nonhuman primates." Van-Lawick Goodall and others, however, have shown that this is not the case. Chimpanzees in the wild and some baboons have been observed to share meat and other foods in a rudimentary way, often along lines of "kinship." Although this does not amount to *exchange* in the human sense, it does appear to be a rudimentary form of something that could be called *protoexchange*. This new evidence does not, I think, affect the basic argument.

The original paper owed much to S.L. Washburn's and Irven DeVore's writings on the home base (e.g., Washburn and DeVore 1961) and to extensive discussions with DeVore on primate subsistence and with Glynn Isaac on the implications of concentrations of exotic stone implements in East African sites.

IF evolution is a fact, human social and economic evolution can be no less so. It is commonplace in anthropology to assert that no contemporary human society even remotely resembles the societies of early man. Such an attitude, however exemplary, does not bring us any closer to an understanding of what early society may have looked like. As evolutionists, we must admit that early hominids lived in some organized manner and that this society had some economic basis. It is in the field of economics that the study of contemporary hunter-gatherers may give us important clues to the past. Arguments from kinship, incest taboos, language, and symbol using tend to accentuate the gap between animals and men. An economic approach – specifically the study of subsistence base – may help us reduce the gap.

What is the basic difference in economic organization between humans and their nearest relatives? The answer is summed up in the word *exchange*. Whereas each nonhuman primate organism (in common with most of the vertebrates) is a self-sufficient subsistence unit, no human eats or works alone. Much of a human individual's energy expenditure goes to feeding others, and much of what an individual consumes is food produced by others.

To take a specific example, the baboon troop leaves the sleeping trees each morning and forages en bloc across its range. Each individual, however, is a self-sufficient subsistence unit. Whatever its role in the social structure of the troop, it must "work" every day of its adult life if it is to survive. Chimpanzee organization in the forest is more flexible: Individuals and subgroups split up and recombine. They may go in different directions and eat different things, but the end result is the same: Each individual is a self-sufficient subsistence unit. Translated into input-output terms, there is an immediate relation in space and time between the production and consumption of food. Food is eaten on the spot within seconds of being picked. This is truly a hand-to-mouth existence.

The same epithet has been applied to the living hunting and gathering peoples, who, in contrast to our industrialized system of production and distribution, are characterized as existing from hand to mouth. But is it really so? The members of a !Kung Bushman camp, for example, move out each day, like the baboons, to forage for food, and, like the chimps, they may split up and go in several directions. But, unlike the beasts, the consumption of food is delayed. Gatherers and hunters may eat in the field, but they also bring a substantial portion of their "production" back to the camp. These resources are then pooled and distributed so that every member of the camp receives an equitable share. This kind of exchange, still persisting in some contemporary societies, represents an elementary form of economic life and is the essential basis for all subsequent economic developments. For by *exchange* humanity breaks down individual animal self-sufficiency. Agriculture, markets, money, craft specialization, and industrial organization, in this perspective, represent elaborations on and an unfolding of the possibilities inherent in the basic human pattern.

Exchange of food is basic to all human societies, even the most nomadic, yet is absent from the societies of nonhuman primates [*sic*]. The consequences of this pattern of food use for early human society were revolutionary. First, the expectation of exchange of foodstuffs led protohumans to develop the home base, an improved site where members of a group could rendezvous on successive days and pool resources. Second, exchange allowed the development of varied subsistence activities; individuals could forage in different parts of the range and concentrate on different foods; yet at the end of the day, each could receive a share of the whole group's production. Third, differentiation of tasks allowed a most important step in human affairs–*risk taking*–whereby an individual could attempt a difficult subsistence task such as hunting, which has a potentially great return but a rather small chance of success. With exchange, a hunter could come home empty-handed and still be fed at the end of the day. Finally, exchange and the home base permitted a breaking of the lockstep of primate subsistence; not everyone had to forage every day in order to survive. Among primates, the young, the old, the sick and disabled, and nursing mothers, all must keep up with the group or die. The human home base allowed rest and recovery without requiring the weak members to forfeit their lives or even a day's food.

The universality of this cluster of economic features in humans makes it likely that its origin is early and probably bound up with the very origin of human society itself. At least it is hard to imagine a hominid life way that lacked these features.

A further question can now be posed. Given its importance in human affairs, how did this cluster of features come into being? By what steps did early protohumans come to develop a way of life based on exchange and the home base? To answer this question we have to examine more closely the internal workings of this system–the relation between economic ends and means–to determine which elements are prerequisite and which are derived.

The existence of a home base as not only a sleeping site but also a locality where individuals meet to exchange goods implies that food is transported from one place to be consumed in another. But how was this transportation accomplished? Nonhuman primate means of transportation are limited in the extreme. Food can be eaten, of course, and "carried" in the stomach, but apart from that there are only the hands and, in some species, the cheek pouches, both with sharply limited capacities. This, as far as I am aware, exhausts the possibilities.

For the human system based on exchange to function, there must be some technical means of bringing things home. It is therefore necessary to postulate the existence of a carrying device as the essential prerequisite, the sine qua non, of human economy. This carrying device may have taken the form of a softened animal hide, a bark tray, a broad leaf, or a crude net. Given the perishable nature of the materials, it is not surprising that no carrying devices have turned up at archeological investigations. This absence, however, in no way lessens the extreme *functional* importance of the carrying device in human economic origins.

The functions of a carrying device are several: first and foremost, it greatly increases the weight of food an individual can carry, especially if the foodstuff is in small or unwieldy packages; second, it is the only means of transporting foods, such as nuts and berries, whose small size makes them impossible to carry more than a few feet without dropping; and third, it allows a user to carry goods while keeping one or both hands free.

In other words, the carrying device vastly improves the efficiency of labor. Having eaten its fill, a nonhuman primate stops foraging. A human, on the other hand, armed with a bag or net can easily collect in a few hours, three, five, or ten times the weight of food that can be consumed by oneself in the course of the day.

The invention of the carrying device made possible a human way of life, but with the increased efficiency of labor came the twin problems that have plagued humans ever since: the problem of surplus and the problem of leisure. The food in excess of daily needs can be put to two uses: It can be held over for consumption by the producer on the following day or it can be shared with others. In either case, the existence of a surplus frees a person for a brief space from the immediate task of feeding himself or herself. But whether protohumans used this potential for leisure or for pursuing other tasks not directly concerned with subsistence is a question we must now consider.

So far the argument has been couched in formal terms of the core features of human economy and the technical prerequisities of this economy. But the argument is not merely a construction of hypothetical events unanchored in space or time. I submit that empirical proof of this interpretation is already at hand. In fact, the way of life that includes the carrying device, home base, and exchange is intimately tied up with the tool-making revolution. It is the natural concomitant of the development of the new technology.

When hominids began systematically to fashion stone tools during the Lower Pleistocene in Africa, they faced a set of special problems. First was the separation in space between the source of the raw materials and the areas where the tools could be put to use. Further, neither of these areas was necessarily the ideal spot at which to fashion the tools. A second problem was time. The collecting of the raw materials and the manufacturing of tools took time, and the makers at least temporarily had to leave off foraging in order to pursue these tasks. Although the tools might ultimately be of use in getting food, the task of making them removed the maker from the food quest.

Assuming for the moment that early people used some of these first tools in hunting mammals, let us consider how each of these problems might have been met in practice. In the first hunts a person may have knocked down prey using any rock that was ready to hand. But this proved an unreliable means of production. With one rock in each hand, or at the most three or four cradled in the crook of the elbow, a hunter's arsenal would be soon exhausted. Further, an early empiricist would quickly note that the best stones were not always found near the highest concentrations of game. The inevitable solution, if hunting was ever to become more than a plant-gatherer's pastime, was a carrying device as the only means of transporting sufficient missiles of the correct size to the place where game was to be hunted.

If the tools themselves show systematic manufacture, we must assume that the procurement of the raw materials and the uses to which the finished products were put were systematic as well. A day spent in the vicinity of rock outcrops carefully selecting stones of suitable weight and shape and trimming others to conform to a preferred pattern would be time well spent for the early hunter who could fill the carrying device with a full load and return to the home base, ready for an early start the next morning to hunt.

Having killed the game, the hunter could then reach into the same carrying device for a tool with a sharp edge and butcher the prey on the spot. Game meat in itself does not require a carrying device. If the animal is small, it can be carried home intact; if large, it can be butchered down to convenient parcels for carrying home. It is in steps leading up to carrying the meat home – hunting, killing, and butchering – that the carrying device is necessary.

But even with the problem of transportation solved, there is yet another problem involved in the hunting of game. When you kill a large mammal, it yields far more meat than can be consumed by one individual in a day; but when you fail to kill one, the yield is nothing. Game hunting is in short a risky proposition. The contemporary Bushmen, for example, average only one kill for every 4 or 5 man-days of hunting. This problem is solved by the carnivores in a simple way: They kill or they starve. But the hominids were not carnivores; they were group-living, social primates evolving from a largely vegetarian baseline. It is therefore likely that plant foods remained important in the hominid diet throughout the early Pleistocene.

The same carrying device that may have begun originally as an aid in the more efficient use of tools in hunting could be put to equally good use in improving the exploitation of the basic primate subsistence source. Plant foods – nuts, berries, roots, and their insect analogs, grubs and caterpillars – come in small packages. A day's portion may consist of several hundred food items each weighing only a few grams. The collection of such a mass of minutiae is time-consuming, and if early people had to rely on the hand-to-mouth existence there would be little time left over for hunting mammals or for making the necessary preparations to hunt. With a carrying device, some members of the group could gather a surplus of plant foods and share this with others who had spent the day hunting when they rendez-voused at the end of the day. The same surplus of plant foods could be shared with others who had spent the day fashioning tools.

The outcome of this primitive exchange is to distribute the risk of a new and chancy activity – hunting – by combining it in a single economic system with a low-risk, tried-and-true productive activity – gathering. The corollary, of course, is that when the high-risk activity is successful and produces meat in excess of what can be eaten by the hunters themselves, the surplus is allocated to those who supported the hunters with food on the days the hunt failed.

The system of shared risk – combining the chanciness of hunting with the reli-ability of gathering – does not in itself imply a division of labor along sexual lines. Those who gather and those who hunt could exchange roles on alternate days, for the same carrying device that can bring tools to the hunting ground can bring plant foods back to the rendezvous. However, given the sexual dimorphism of both proto- and modern humans and the universal primate role of females as bearers of young, such role reversals probably rapidly gave way to the arrangement still found among hunting peoples today: women as gatherers of plant foods and men as hunters who may also gather.

In this view, the carrying device and the exchange of foodstuffs provided the logistic support that allowed the new subsistence source with its fledgling technol-ogy to thrive. No one doubts that hunting and tool making are closely bound up with the origins of the human economy. My point here is to show that food exchange is *essential* to these developments, not merely an adjunct or a consequence.

The evidence from early living floors of tool-making man indicates that by Lower Pleistocene times, the life style predicated on carrying device, home base, and exchange was already well established. The proof is in the concentrations of exotic stones found at Bed I Olduvai in association with the remains of early man. Some of these stones were transported from sites 15 km or more away from the deposits in which they are found, indicating that people had already solved the problem of the spatial separation of rock sources, living sites, and hunting grounds. That the carrying device played an essential role in the formation of these living floors cannot be doubted, unless we are willing to propose that every pair of stones in the deposit represents one 30-km round trip by a tool maker with one stone in each hand on the return leg. And, on the matter of exchange, think for a moment of the tremendous input of time and effort represented by the accumulation of these thousands of tools. It is likely that someone must have been feeding the makers while they engaged in their labors.

Unresolved is the question whether the carrying device was invented as an aid in hunting and was later adapted to gathering or whether it started as a gathering aid and was later adapted to hunting. There is a third possibility. The origin of the carrying device may be intimately tied up with the evolving biology of the species. The increasing helplessness of the newborn and the loss of body hair of adults conspired to make the carrying device the essential "tool" of the mother-infant complex. When the infant lost the ability to grasp, it must have been carried slung in a pouch suspended from the mother's shoulders. A mother's work would have been difficult indeed if she had had to use one arm to carry the baby on her hip and had had to set the baby down on the ground whenever there was work to be done. I may be wrong, but I do not think the demanding hominid infant would have allowed such treatment.

Whatever the actual sequence of events, the important point is that the *carrying device* plays a crucial role in each scenario. Without the carrying device, neither the tool making nor the home base nor the food-exchange adaptations would have been possible. Yet, *with* the carrying device, all these new modes of technology and organization not only become possible, but in a real sense become inevitable, as, over the course of generations, the possibilities inherent in this new technology began to unfold.

We have tended to think of tool making, hunting, exchange, division of labor, and infant helplessness as crucial developments in human evolution, but the structural relations among these features have remained unclear. The introduction of the carrying device into the discussion acts as a catalyst that may help to draw together in a more integrated way previously ambiguously related strands in the evolutionary argument.

Bibliography

Acocks, J.P.H. 1953. *Veld Types of South Africa.* Memoir of the Union Botanical Survey, No. 28. Pretoria: Government Printer.

Almeida, A. de. 1965. *Bushmen and Other Non-Bantu Peoples of Angola: Three Lectures.* Johannesburg: Witwatersrand University Press.

Bachofen, J. 1861. *Das Mutterrecht.* Basel: Schwabe.

Baines, T. 1864. *Explorations in Southwest Africa.* London: Longmans.

Balickci, A. 1964. *Development of Basic Socio-Economic Units in Two Eskimo Communities.* National Museum of Canada Bulletin, No. 202. Ottawa: National Museum of Canada.

Balikci, A. 1968. The Netsilik Eskimos: Adaptive processes. In R.B. Lee and I. DeVore (eds.). *Man the Hunter,* pp. 78–82. Chicago: Aldine.

Barnard, A. 1976a. Khoisan classification. *Bull. Int. Afr. Inst.* 46(4):12.

Barnard, A. 1976b. Kinship systems of the Khoi-speaking peoples. Doctoral dissertation, University of London.

Barnard, A. 1978. Kalahari Bushman settlement patterns. Paper presented at Association of Social Anthropologists conference, Cambridge, England, March 1978.

Basarwa Development Office. 1977. Report of a trip to Maun, March 1977. Ministry of Local Government and Lands, Gaborone. Mimeographed.

Beaucage, P. 1977. Enfer ou paradis perdu: les sociétés chasseurs-cueilleurs. *Can. Rev. Sociol. Anthropol.* 13(4):397–412.

Berman, M.L., K. Hanson, and I.L. Hellman. 1972. Effect of breast-feeding on postpartum menstruation, ovulation, and pregnancy in Alaskan Eskimos. *Am. J. Obstet. Gynecol.* 114:524–34.

Berndt, R.M. 1970. Comment on Birdsell (1970). *Curr. Anthropol.* 11:132–3.

Bernier, B. 1977. The penetration of capitalism in Quebec agriculture. *Can. Rev. Sociol. Anthropol.* 13(4):422–34.

Biesele, M. In press. *!Kung Folklore.* Cambridge, Mass.: Harvard University Press.

Billewicz, W., H. Fellowes, and C.A. Hytten. 1976. Comments on the critical metabolic mass and the age at menarche. *Ann. Hum. Biol.* 3:51–9.

Binford, L. 1968a. Methodological considerations of the archeological use of ethnographic data. In R.B. Lee and I. DeVore (eds.). *Man the Hunter.* pp. 268–73. Chicago: Aldine.

Binford, L. 1968b. Post-Pleistocene adaptations. In S.R. Binford and L.R. Binford (eds.). *New Perspectives in Archeology*, pp. 313–41. Chicago: Aldine.

Birdsell, J.B. 1968. Some predictions for the Pleistocene based on equilibrium systems among recent hunter-gatherers. In R.B. Lee and I. DeVore (eds.). *Man the Hunter*, pp. 229–49. Chicago: Aldine.

Birdsell, J.B. 1970. Local group composition among the Australian aborigines: A critique of the evidence from fieldwork conducted since 1930. *Curr. Anthropol.* 11(a):115–42.

Bishop, C. 1974. *The Northern Ojibwa and the Fur Trade: An Historical and Ecological Study.* Toronto: Holt, Rinehart and Winston.

Bjerre, J. 1958. *Kalahari.* Copenhagen: Carit Andersons.

Bleek, D.F. 1928a. *The Naron: A Bushman Tribe of the Central Kalahari.* London: Cambridge University Press.

Bleek, D.F. 1928b. Bushmen of central Angola. *Bantu Stud.* 3:105–25.

Bleek, D.F. 1929. *Comparative Vocabularies of Bushman Languages.* London: Cambridge University Press.

Bley, H. 1971. *South-West Africa Under German Rule: 1894–1914.* London: Heinemann.

Boas, F. 1888. The Central Eskimo. *Bur. Am. Ethnol. Annu. Rep.* 6:399–699. Washington, D.C.: Smithsonian Institution.

Boas, F. 1911. *The Mind of Primitive Man.* New York: Macmillan.

Böeseken, A. 1972. The meaning, origin and use of the terms Khoikhoi, San, and Khoisan. *Cabo* 1(1):5–10.

Böeseken, A. 1974. Dr. A.J. Böeseken replies to Professor R.H. Elphick. *Cabo* 2(2):8–10.

Böeseken, A. 1975. On changing terminology in history. *Cabo* 2(3):16–18.

Bohannan, P. 1960. Homicide among the Tiv of central Nigeria. In P. Bohannan (ed.). *African Homicide and Suicide*, pp. 30–64. New York: Atheneum.

Bongaarts, J., and H. Delgado. 1977. Effects of nutritional status on fertility in rural Guatemala. Paper presented at the Seminar on Natural Fertility, Institut National d'Etudes Démographiques, Paris, March 1977.

Bonte, M., and H. van Balen. 1969. Prolonged lactation and family spacing in Rwanda. *J. Biosoc. Sci.* 1:97–100.

Braverman, H. 1974. *Labor and Monopoly Capital.* New York: Monthly Review Press.

Bronte-Stewart, B., O.E. Budtz-Olsen, J.M. Hickley, and J.F. Brock. 1960. The health and nutritional status of the !Kung Bushmen of South West Africa. *S. Afr. J. Lab. Clin. Med.* 6(4):187–216.

Brooks, A., and J. Yellen. 1977. Archaeological excavations at ≠gi: A preliminary report of the first two field seasons. *Botswana Notes Rec.* 9:21–30.

Brown, R.C. 1974. Climate and climatic trends in the Ghanzi district. *Botswana Notes Rec.* 6:133–46.

Brownmiller, S. 1975. *Against Our Will: Men, Women and Rape.* New York: Simon & Schuster.

Brues, A. 1959. The spearman and the archer: An essay on selection in body build. *Am. Anthropol.* 61:457–69.

Carr-Saunders, A. 1922. *The Population Problem: A Study in Human Evolution.* Oxford: Clarendon Press.

Carstens, W.P. 1966. *The Social Structure of a Cape Coloured Reserve*. Cape Town: Oxford University Press.

Cashdan, E. 1977. Subsistence, mobility, and territorial organization among the //Ganakwe of the Northeastern Central Kalahari Game Reserve, Botswana. Department of Anthropology, University of New Mexico. Mimeographed.

Chapman, J. 1868. *Travels in the Interior of South Africa*. London: Bell & Daldy.

Clapham, W.B. 1973. *Natural Ecosystems*. New York: Macmillan.

Clark, J.D. 1951. Bushmen hunters of the Barotse forests. *N. Rhodesia J.* 1:56–65.

Clark, J.D. 1970. *The Prehistory of Africa*. London: Thames & Hudson.

Coale, A.J., and P. Demeny. 1966. *Regional Model Life Tables and Stable Populations*. Princeton: Princeton University Press.

Cohen, M.N. 1977. *The Food Crisis in Prehistory: Overpopulation and the Origins of Agriculture*. New Haven: Yale University Press.

Colson, E. 1960. *The Plateau Tonga: Social and Religious Studies*. Manchester: Manchester University Press.

Colson, E. 1973. *Tradition and Contract: The Problem of Order*. Chicago: Aldine.

Cooke, H.B.S. 1964. The Pleistocene environment of Southern Africa. In D.H.S. Davis (ed.). *Ecological Studies in Southern Africa*, pp. 1–23. The Hague: Junk.

Cooke, H.J., and T. Baillieul. 1974. The caves of Ngamiland: An interim report on exploration and fieldwork, 1972–74. *Botswana Notes Rec.* 6:147–56.

Cowley, C. 1968. *Fabled Tribe*. New York: Atheneum.

Damas, D. (ed.). 1969a. *Band Societies*. National Museum of Canada Bulletin, No. 228. Ottawa: National Museum of Canada.

Damas, D. (ed.). 1969b. *Ecological Essays*. National Museum of Canada Bulletin, No. 230. Ottawa: National Museum of Canada.

Damas, D. 1969c. Characteristics of central Eskimo band structure. In D. Damas (ed.). *Band Societies*, pp. 116–38, National Museum of Canada Bulletin, No. 228. Ottawa: National Museum of Canada.

Damon, A., H. Stondt, and R.A. McFarland. 1966. *The Human Body in Equipment Design*. Cambridge, Mass.: Harvard University Press.

Dawson, J.L.M. 1973. Attitude change and conflict. In G.E. Kearney, P.R. de Lacey, and G.R. Davidson (eds.). *The Psychology of Aboriginal Australians*. New York: Wiley.

Denham, W.W. 1974a. Infant transport among the Alywara tribe, central Australia. *Oceania* 44(4):253–77.

Denham, W.W. 1974b. Population structure, infant transport, and infanticide among Pleistocene and modern hunter-gatherers. *J. Anthropol. Res.* 30(3):191–8.

Dice, L.R. 1952. *Natural Communities*. Ann Arbor: University of Michigan Press.

Draper, P. 1975. !Kung women: Contrasts in sexual egalitarianism in the foraging and sedentary contexts. In R. Reiter (ed.). *Toward an Anthropology of Women*, pp. 77–109. New York: Monthly Review Press.

Draper, P. 1976. Social and economic constraints on child life among the !Kung. In R.B. Lee and I. DeVore (eds.). *Kalahari Hunter-Gatherers*, pp. 199–217. Cambridge, Mass.: Harvard University Press.

Draper, P. 1978. The learning environment for aggression and antisocial behavior among the !Kung. In A. Montagu (ed.). *Teaching Non-Aggression*, pp. 31–53. New York: Oxford University Press.

Drucker, P. 1955. *Indians of the Northwest Coast.* Garden City, N.Y.: Natural History Press.

Durkheim, E. 1912 (1961). *The Elementary Forms of Religious Life.* Tr. by J.W. Swain. New York: Collier Books.

Durnin, J., and R. Passmore. 1967. *Energy, Work and Leisure.* London: Heinemann.

Dyson-Hudson, R., and R. Van Dusen. 1972. Food-sharing among young children. *Ecol. Food Nutr. 1*:319–24.

Edholm, O. 1967. *The Biology of Work.* New York: McGraw-Hill.

Edmond, W., and S. Fleming. 1975. *All Work and No Pay: Women, Housework and the Wages Due.* London: Power of Women Collective and Falling Wall Press.

Eibl-Eibesfeldt, I. 1972. *Die !Ko-Buschmanngesellschaft: Gruppenbindung und Aggressions-Kontrolle.* Munich: Piper.

El-Minawi, M., and M. Foda. 1971. Postpartum lactation amenorrhea. *Am. J. Obstet. Gynecol. 111*:17.

Elphick, R. 1974. Professor R.H. Elphick replies to Dr. A.J. Böeseken. *Cabo* 2(2):3–7.

Elphick, R. 1975. Professor Elphick's final rebuttal of Dr. Böeseken's argument. *Cabo* 2(3):12–15.

Elphick, R. 1977. *Kraal and Castle: Khoikhoi and the Founding of White South Africa.* New Haven: Yale University Press.

Engels, F. 1884 (1972). *The Origin of the Family, Private Property and the State.* Edited, with an introduction by E. Leacock. New York: International Publishers.

Esche, H. 1976. Hunter-gatherer influence on ecology with reference to plant resources. Department of Anthropology, University of Toronto. Mimeographed.

Esche, H., and R.B. Lee. 1975. Is maximal optimal? Reflections on overnutrition, underdevelopment, and the size of human beings. Paper presented at 74th Annual Meeting of the American Anthropological Association, San Francisco.

Esterman, R.P. 1946–9. Quelques observations sur les Bochimans !Kung de l'Angola meridionale. *Anthropos 41–4*:711–22.

Forde, D. 1934. *Habitat, Economy and Society: A Geographical Introduction to Ethnology.* London: Methuen.

Forde, D. 1954. Foraging, hunting, and fishing. In C. Singer and A. Holmyard (eds.). *A History of Technology*, pp. 154–86. Oxford: Clarendon Press.

Fourie, L.M. 1928. The Bushmen of South West Africa. In C. Hahn, H. Vedder, and L. Fourie (eds.). *The Native Tribes of South West Africa*, pp. 79–106. New York: Barnes & Noble.

Fox, R. 1953. A study of energy expenditure of Africans engaged in various rural activities. Ph.D. thesis, London University.

Fox, R. 1967. *Kinship and Marriage.* Baltimore: Penguin Books.

Freeman, L.G. 1968. A theoretical framework for interpreting archeological materials. In R.B. Lee and I. DeVore (eds.). *Man the Hunter*, pp. 262–7. Chicago: Aldine.

Freeman, M.R. 1971. The significance of demographic changes occurring in the Canadian East Arctic. *Anthropologica 13*:215–36.

Frere, H.B. 1882-3. On systems of land tenure among aboriginal tribes in South Africa. *J. Anthropol. Inst. 12*:258-60.

Freud, S. 1919. *Totem and Taboo*. London: Routledge & Kegan Paul.

Fried, M.H. 1967. *The Evolution of Political Society*. New York: Random House.

Friedl, E. 1975. *Women and Men: An Anthropologist's View*. New York: Holt, Rinehart and Winston.

Friedman, J. 1975. Tribes, states and transformations. In M. Bloch (ed.). *Marxist Analyses and Social Anthropology*, pp. 161-202. ASA Monographs, No. 3. London: Malaby Press.

Frisancho, A.R., D. Pallardel, and J. Sanchez. 1972. Differential offspring survival related to maternal body size in an impoverished Highland population. Center for Human Growth and Development, University of Michigan. Unpublished.

Frisancho, A.R., J. Sanchez, and D. Pallardel. 1973. Adaptive significance of small body size under poor socio-economic conditions in Southern Peru. *Am. J. Phys. Anthropol. 39*:255-62.

Frisch, R.E. 1974. Critical weight at menarche: Initiation of the adolescent growth spurt and control of puberty. In M.M. Grumbach, G.D. Growe, and F.E. Mayer (eds.). *Control of Onset of Puberty*, pp. 403-23. New York: Wiley.

Frisch, R.E. 1975. Demographic implication of the biological determinants of female fecundity. *Soc. Biol. 22*:17-22.

Frisch, R.E., and J. McArthur. 1974. Menstrual cycles: Fatness as a determinant of minimum weight for their maintenance or onset. *Science 185*:949-51.

Frisch, R., and R. Revelle. 1970. Height and weight at menarche and a hypothesis of critical body weights and adolescent events. *Science 169*:397-8.

Gale, F. (ed.). 1974. *Woman's Role in Aboriginal Society*. Australian Aboriginal Studies, No. 36. Canberra: Australian National University Press.

Garvey, C. 1977. *Play*. Cambridge, Mass.: Harvard University Press.

Gioiosa, R. 1955. Incidence of pregnancy during lactation in 500 cases. *Am. J. Obstet. Gynecol. 70*:162.

Godelier, M. 1972. Structure and contradiction in Capital. In R. Blackburn (ed.). *Ideology in Social Science: Readings in Critical Social Theory*, pp. 334-68. London: Fontana.

Godelier, M. 1973. *Horizon, trajets marxistes en anthropologie*. Paris: Maspero.

Godelier, M. 1974a. Anthropology and biology: Towards a new form of cooperation. *Int. Soc. Sci. J. 26*(4):611-35.

Godelier, M. 1974b. Considerations théoriques et critiques sur le problème des rapports entre homme et son environnement. *Inform. Sci. Soc. 13*(6):31-60.

Godelier, M. 1975. Modes of production, kinship, and demographic structures. In M. Bloch (ed.). *Marxist Analyses and Social Anthropology*, pp. 3-28. ASA Monographs, No. 3. London: Malaby Press.

Golde, P. (ed.). 1970. *Women in the Field: Anthropological Experiences*. Chicago: Aldine.

Gordon, T., and W.B. Kannel. 1973. The effect of overweight on cardiovascular diseases. *Geriatrics 27*:80.

Gorges, E. 1918. *Report on the Natives of South-West Africa and Their Treatment by Germany*. Union of South Africa Report. London: HMSO.

Gough, K. 1970. *Women in Evolution*. Boston: New England Free Press. Pamphlet.

Gough, K. 1971. The origin of the family. *J. Marriage Fam.* 33:760–71.

Grey, D.R.C., and H.J. Cooke. 1977. Some problems in the Quaternary evolution of the landforms of northern Botswana. *Catena* 4:123–33.

Grove, A.T. 1969. Landforms and climatic change in the Kalahari and Ngamiland. *Geog. J.* 135(2):191–212.

Guemple, L. 1972. Eskimo band organization and the "D P Camp" hypothesis. *Arctic Anthropol.* 9(2):80–112.

Guenther, M.G. 1976. From hunters to squatters: Social and cultural change among the farm San of Ghanzi, Botswana. In R.B. Lee and I. DeVore (eds.). *Kalahari Hunter-Gatherers*, pp. 120–33. Cambridge, Mass.: Harvard University Press.

Guenther, M.G. 1977. More on Khoisan classification. *Bull. Int. Afr. Inst.* 47(1):3.

Guttmacher, A.F. 1952. Fertility of man. *Fertil. Steril.* 3:281–9.

Hahn, T. 1881. *Tsuni- //Goam, the Supreme Being of the Khoi-Khoi.* London: Trubner.

Harpending, H. 1976. Regional variation in !Kung populations. In R.B. Lee and I. DeVore (eds.). *Kalahari Hunter-Gatherers*, pp. 152–65. Cambridge, Mass.: Harvard University Press.

Harris, M. 1968. *The Rise of Anthropological Theory.* New York: Crowell.

Harris, M. 1975. *Culture, People, Nature: An Introduction to General Anthropology.* New York: Crowell.

Harrison, G., J. Weiner, J. Tanner, and N. Barnicot. 1964. *Human Biology.* London: Oxford University Press.

Heinz, H.J. 1966. Social organization of the !Ko Bushmen. Masters thesis, Department of Anthropology, University of South Africa, Pretoria.

Heinz, H.J. 1969. Search for Bushmen tribes of the Okavango. *Geog. Mag.* 41:742–50.

Heinz, H.J. 1972. Territoriality among the Bushmen in general and the !Ko in particular. *Anthropos* 67:405–16.

Heinz, H.J. 1975. Acculturative problems arising in a Bushman development scheme. *S. Afr. J. Sci.* 71:78–85.

Helm, J. 1965. Bilaterality in the socio-territorial organization of the Arctic drainage Dene. *Ethnology* 4:361–85.

Hentig, H. 1948. *The Criminal and His Victim: Studies in the Sociobiology of Crime.* New Haven: Yale University Press.

Hermans, J. 1977. Official policy toward the Bushmen of Botswana: A review. Part 1. *Botswana Notes Rec.* 9:55–68.

Hiatt, B. 1974. Woman the gatherer. In F. Gale (ed.). *Woman's Role in Aboriginal Society*, pp. 4–15. Australian Aboriginal Studies, No. 36; Canberra: Australian National University Press.

Hiatt, L.R. 1962. Local organization among the Australian aborigines. *Oceania* 32:276–86.

Hiatt, L.R. 1965. *Kinship and Conflict: A Study of an Aboriginal Community in Northern Arnhem Land.* Canberra: Australian National University Press.

Hindess B., and P. Hirst. 1975. *Precapitalist Modes of Production.* London: Routledge & Kegan Paul.

Hitchcock, R., J. Ebert, and M. Ebert. 1976. Regional studies in eastern Botswana. *S. Afr. Assoc. Archaeol. Newsletter* 8:3–4.

Hobbes, T. 1651 (1969). *Leviathan*. London: Routledge & Kegan Paul.

Hobsbawm, E. (ed.). 1965. *Marx's Precapitalist Economic Formations*. New York: International Publishers.

Holmberg, A. 1950. *Nomads of the Long Bow: The Siriono of Eastern Bolivia*. Publications of the Institute of Social Anthropology, No. 10. Washington, D.C.: Smithsonian Institution.

Howell, F.C., et al. 1965. *Early Man*. New York: Time-Life Books.

Howell, F.C. 1968. Comment. In R.B. Lee and I. DeVore (eds.). *Man the Hunter*, pp. 287–8. Chicago: Aldine.

Howell, N. 1973. The feasibility of demographic studies in "anthropological" populations. In M. Crawford and P. Workman (eds.). *Method and Theory in Anthropological Genetics*. Albuquerque: University of New Mexico Press.

Howell, N. 1976a. Toward a uniformitarian theory of human paleodemography. *J. Hum. Evol.* 5:25–40.

Howell, N. 1976b. The population of the Dobe area !Kung. In R.B. Lee and I. DeVore (eds.). *Kalahari Hunter-Gatherers*, pp. 137–51. Cambridge, Mass.: Harvard University Press.

Howell, N. 1979. *Demography of the Dobe Area !Kung*. New York: Academic Press.

Hunter, J.M. 1967. Seasonal hunger in a part of the West African savanna: A survey of body weights in Nangodi, north-east Ghana. *Trans. Inst. Br. Geog.* 41:167–85.

Hurlich, S., and R. Lee. 1978. Colonialism, apartheid and liberation: A Namibian example. In G. Smith and D. Turner (eds.). *Challenging Anthropology*, pp. 353–71. Toronto: McGraw-Hill–Ryerson.

Isaac, G. 1978. The food-sharing behavior of protohuman hominids. *Sci. Am.* 238(4):90–108.

Jain, A., T. Hsu, R. Freedman, and M. Chang. 1970. Demographic aspects of lactation and postpartum amenorrhea. *Demography* 7:255–71.

Jelliffe, D.B. 1966. *The Assessment of the Nutritional Status of the Community*. WHO Monograph Series, No. 53. Geneva: World Health Organization.

Jelliffe, D.B., and P. Jelliffe. 1974. Letter: Universal growth standards for preschool children. *Lancet* 2:47.

Jenkins, T., and G. Nurse. 1977. *Health and the Hunter-Gatherers*. Johannesburg: Witwatersrand University Press.

Jenkins, T., and P.V. Tobias. 1977. Nomenclature and population groups in southern Africa. *Afr. Stud.* 36(1):49–55.

Johnson, A. 1975. Time allocation in a Machiguenga community. *Ethnology* 14(3):301–10.

Johnston, F., R. Malina, and M. Galbraith. 1971. Height, weight and age at menarche and the "critical weight" hypothesis. *Science* 174:1148.

Johnston, F., A. Roche, L. Schell, and H. Wettenhall. 1975. Critical weight at menarche: Critique of a hypothesis. *Am. J. Dis. Child.* 129:19–23.

Jones, R. 1969. Fire stick farming. *Aust. Nat. Hist.* 16:224–8.

Jordaan, K. 1975. The Bushmen of southern Africa: Anthropology and historical materialism. *Race and Class* 17(2):141–60.

Katz, R. 1976. Education for transcendence: !Kia-Healing with the Kalahari !Kung. In R. Lee and I. DeVore (eds.). *Kalahari Hunter-Gatherers*, pp. 281–301. Cambridge, Mass.: Harvard University Press.

Keay, R.W.J. (ed.). 1959. *Vegetation Map of Africa South of the Tropic of Cancer.* London: Oxford University Press.

Keettel, W., and J. Bradbury. 1961. Endocrine studies of lactation amenorrhea. *Am. J. Obstet. Gynecol.* 82:995.

Kippley, S. (ed.). 1975. *Breast-Feeding and Natural Child Spacing.* Baltimore: Penguin Books.

Kippley, S., and J. Kippley. 1975. The relation between breast-feeding and amenorrhea: Report of a survey. In S. Kippley (ed.). *Breast-Feeding and Natural Child Spacing*, pp. 163–78. Baltimore: Penguin Books.

Knodel, J. 1977a. The influence of child mortality on fertility in European populations in the past: Results from individual data. University of Michigan. Mimeographed.

Knodel, J. 1977b. Breast feeding and population growth. *Science* 198:1111–15.

Koch, C. 1958. *Preliminary Notes on the Coleopterological Aspect of the Arrow Poison of the Bushmen.* South African Biological Society Pamphlet, No. 20. Cape Town.

Kolata, G. 1974. !Kung hunter-gatherers: Feminism, diet, and birth control. *Science* 185:932–4.

Komarek, E.V. 1966. The meteorological basis for fire ecology. *Tall Timbers Fire Ecol. Conf. Proc.* 5:85.

Komarek, E.V. 1967. Fire and the ecology of man. *Tall Timbers Fire Ecol. Conf. Proc.* 6:143.

Konner, M. 1976. Maternal care, infant behaviour and development among the !Kung. In R.B. Lee and I. DeVore (eds.). *Kalahari Hunter-Gatherers*, pp. 218–45. Cambridge, Mass.: Harvard University Press.

Lamphere, L. 1977. Review essay: Anthropology. *Signs* 2(3):612–27.

Lancaster, J.B. 1978. Carrying and sharing in human evolution. *Hum. Nature* 1(2):82–9.

Lancaster-Jones, F. 1963. *A Demographic Survey of the Aboriginal Population of the Northern Territory with Special Reference to Bathurst Island Mission.* Canberra: Australian Institute of Aboriginal Studies.

Lancaster-Jones, F. 1970. *The Structure of Australia's Aboriginal Population.* Canberra: Australian National University Press.

Lanham, L., and D. Hallowes. 1956. An outline of the structure of Eastern Bushman. *Afr. Stud.* 15(3):97–118.

Laughlin, W. 1968. Hunting: An integrating biobehavior system and its evolutionary importance. In R.B. Lee and I. DeVore (eds.). *Man the Hunter*, pp. 304–20. Chicago: Aldine.

Leach, E. 1954. *Political Systems of Highland Burma.* Boston: Beacon Press.

Leacock, E. 1954. *The Montagnais "Hunting Territory" and the Fur Trade.* American Anthropologist, Memoir No. 78. Washington, D.C.: American Anthropology Association.

Leacock, E. 1955. Matrilocality in a simple hunting economy (Montagnais-Naskapi). *Southwest. J. Anthropol.* 11:31–47.

Leacock, E. 1969. The Montagnais-Naskapi band. In D. Damas (ed.). *Band Societies*, pp. 1–17. National Museum of Canada Bulletin, No. 228. Ottawa: National Museum of Canada.

Leacock, E. (ed.). 1972. *Engels' "The Origin of the Family, Private Property and the State."* New York: International Publishers.

Leacock, E. 1978. Women's status in egalitarian society: Implications for social evolution. *Curr. Anthropol.* 19(2):247–75.

Leacock, E., and N. Lurie (eds.). 1972. *North American Indians in Historical Perspective.* New York: Harper & Row.

Lee, R.B. 1965. Subsistence ecology of !Kung Bushmen. Ph.D. dissertation, University of California, Berkeley.

Lee, R.B. 1968a. What hunters do for a living, or, how to make out on scarce resources. In R.B. Lee and I. DeVore (eds.). *Man the Hunter,* pp. 30–48. Chicago: Aldine.

Lee, R.B. 1968b. The sociology of !Kung Bushman trance performances. In R. Prince (ed.). *Trance and Possession States,* pp. 35–54. Montreal: Bucke Memorial Society.

Lee, R.B. 1968c. Comment. In S. Binford and L. Binford (eds.). *New Perspectives in Archeology,* pp. 343–6. Chicago: Aldine.

Lee, R.B. 1969a. !Kung Bushmen subsistence: An input-output analysis. In A.P. Vayda (ed.). *Environment and Cultural Behavior,* pp. 47–79. New York: Natural History Press.

Lee, R.B. 1969b. Eating Christmas in the Kalahari. *Nat. Hist.* (December), pp. 14–22, 60–3.

Lee, R.B. 1969c. !Kung Bushmen. *S. Afr. Med. J.* 43:48.

Lee, R.B. 1972a. The !Kung Bushmen of Botswana. In M. Bicchieri (ed.). *Hunters and Gatherers Today,* pp. 327–68. New York: Holt, Rinehart and Winston.

Lee, R.B. 1972b. !Kung spatial organization: An ecological and historical perspective. *Hum. Ecol.* 1(2):125–47.

Lee, R.B. 1972c. Work effort, group structure and land use in contemporary hunter-gatherers. In P.J. Ucko et al. (eds.). *Man, Settlement, and Urbanism,* pp. 177–85. London: Duckworth.

Lee, R.B. 1972d. Population growth and the beginnings of sedentary life among the !Kung Bushmen. In B. Spooner (ed.). *Population Growth: Anthropological Implications,* pp. 329–42. Cambridge, Mass.: MIT Press.

Lee, R.B. 1972e. The intensification of social life among the !Kung Bushmen. In B. Spooner (ed.). *Population Growth: Anthropological Implications,* pp. 343–50. Cambridge, Mass.: MIT Press.

Lee, R.B. 1973a. The evolution of technical civilizations. In C. Sagan (ed.). *Communication with Extra-Terrestrial Intelligence,* pp. 85–94. Cambridge, Mass.: MIT Press.

Lee, R.B. 1973b. Mongongo: The ethnography of a major wild food resource. *Ecol. Food Nutr.* 2:307–21.

Lee, R.B. 1974. Male and female residence arrangements and political power in human hunter-gatherers. *Arch. Sex. Behav.* 3(2):167–73.

Lee, R.B. 1975. The !Kungs' new culture. In *Science Year 1976,* pp. 180–95. Chicago: World Book Encyclopedia.

Lee, R.B., and I. DeVore (eds.). 1968. *Man the Hunter.* Chicago: Aldine.

Lee, R.B., and I. DeVore (eds.). 1976. *Kalahari Hunter-Gatherers: Studies of the !Kung San and Their Neighbours.* Cambridge, Mass.: Harvard University Press.

Lee, R.B., H. Harpending, and N. Howell. 1977. Letter to the editor. *Science* 197:1234.

Legros, D. 1977. Chance, necessity and mode of production: A Marxist critique of cultural evolutionism. *Am. Anthropol.* 79(1):26–41.

Le Roy Ladurie, E. 1960. *Le Climat depuis l'an mil.* Paris: Presses Universitaires de France.

Le Roy Ladurie, E. 1976. *The Peasants of Languedoc.* Urbana: University of Illinois Press.

Levins, R. 1966. The strategy of model building in population biology. *Am. Sci.* 54:421–31.

Levins, R. 1968. *Evolution in Changing Environments.* Princeton: Princeton University Press.

Lévi-Strauss, C. 1949. *Les Structures élémentaires de la parenté.* Paris: Presses Universitaires de France.

Lévi-Strauss, C. 1969. *The Elementary Structures of Kinship.* Boston: Beacon Press.

Lewis, H.T. 1971. The role of fire in the domestication of plants and animals in Southwest Asia: A hypothesis. *Man* 7:195–222.

Lyell, C. 1830. *Principles of Geology.* London: Murray.

McCarthy, F., and M. McArthur. 1960. The food quest and the time factor in aboriginal economic life. In C.P. Mountford (ed.). *Records of the American-Australian Scientific Expedition to Arnhem Land,* pp. 145–94. Melbourne: Melbourne University Press.

McKeown, T., and J. Gibson. 1954. A note on menstruation and conception during lactation. *J. Obstet. Gynecol. Br. Emp.* 61:824.

Maguire, B. ca. 1954. A report on the food plants ("veldkos") of the !Kung Bushmen of the Gautsha pan and Cigarette areas of northeastern South West Africa, based on collections and observations from mid-December 1952 until February 1953 in collaboration with the Harvard-Peabody Anthropological Expedition to South West Africa. Peabody Museum, Cambridge, Mass. Manuscript.

Malthus, T. 1798 (1966). *First Essays on Population.* London: J. Johnson.

Marais, J.S. 1939. *The Cape Coloured People: 1652–1937.* London: Longmans Green.

Margalef, R. 1964. *Perspectives on Ecological Theory.* Chicago: University of Chicago Press.

Marks, S. 1972. Khoisan resistance to the Dutch in the seventeenth and eighteenth centuries. *J. Afr. Hist.* 13:55–80.

Marks, S.A. 1976. *Large Mammals and a Brave People: Subsistence Hunters in Zambia.* Seattle: University of Washington Press.

Marshall, J. 1956. *The Hunters* (film). Somerville, Mass.: Center for Documentary Anthropology.

Marshall, J. 1957. Ecology of the !Kung Bushmen of the Kalahari. Senior honors thesis in anthropology, Harvard University, Cambridge, Mass.

Marshall, J. 1973. *An Argument about a Marriage* (film). Somerville, Mass.: Center for Documentary Anthropology.

Marshall, L. 1957. The kin terminology system of the !Kung Bushmen. *Africa* 27:1–25.

Marshall, L. 1959. Marriage among !Kung Bushmen. *Africa* 29:335–65.

Marshall, L. 1960. !Kung Bushmen bands. *Africa 30*:325–55.

Marshall, L. 1961. Sharing, talking and giving: Relief of social tensions among !Kung Bushmen. *Africa 31*:231–49.

Marshall, L. 1965. The !Kung Bushmen of the Kalahari Desert. In J. Gibbs (ed.). *Peoples of Africa*. New York: Holt, Rinehart and Winston.

Marshall, L. 1968. Comment. In R.B. Lee and I. DeVore (eds.). *Man the Hunter*, p. 94. Chicago: Aldine.

Marshall, L. 1969. The medicine dance of the !Kung Bushmen. *Africa 39*:347–81.

Marshall, L. 1976. *The !Kung of Nyae Nyae*. Cambridge, Mass.: Harvard University Press.

Marx, K. 1859 (1972). Preface to "A Contribution to the Critique of Political Economy." In *Marx, Engels and Lenin on Historical Materialism*, pp. 136–40. Moscow: Progress Publishers.

Marx, K. 1867. *Das Kapital: Kritik der politischen Oekonomie*. Hamburg: Meissner.

Marx, K., and F. Engels. 1965. The German ideology. In E. Hobsbawm (ed.). *Precapitalist Economic Formations: Karl Marx*, pp. 121–39. Tr. by J. Cohen. New York: International Publishers.

Mauss, M. 1904–5. Essai sur les variations saisonières des sociétés eskimos: Etude de morphologie sociale. *Ann. Soc. 9*:39–132.

Meek, R. 1973. *Studies in the Labor Theory of Value*, 2nd ed. New York: Monthly Review Press.

Meggitt, M. 1962. *Desert People: A Study of the Walbiri Aborigines of Central Australia*. Sydney: Angus & Robertson.

Meillassoux, C. 1972. From reproduction to production. *Econ. Soc. 1*:93–105.

Meillassoux, C. 1973. On the mode of production of the hunting band. In P. Alexandre (ed.). *French Perspectives in African Studies*, pp. 187–203. London: Oxford University Press.

Meillassoux, C. 1975. *Femmes, grenier et capitaux*. Paris: Maspero.

Meissner, M., E.W. Humphreys, S.M. Meis, and W.J. Scheu. 1975. No exit for wives: Sexual division of labour and the cumulation of household demands. *Can. Rev. Sociol. Anthropol. 12*(4):424–39.

Metz, J., D. Hart, and H.C. Harpending. 1971. Iron, folate and vitamin B_{12} nutrition in a hunter-gatherer people: A study of the !Kung Bushmen. *Am. J. Clin. Nutr. 24*:229–42.

Michel, P. 1967. Les Grandes étapes de la morphogénèse dans les bassins de fleuves Sénégal et Gambie pendant le Quaternaire. Paper for 6th Pan African Congress of Prehistory, Dakar, Senegal. Mimeographed.

Miller, O.B. 1952. *The Woody Plants of the Bechuanaland Protectorate*. Cape Town: South African Herbarium.

Minaguchi, H., and J. Meites. 1967. Effects of suckling on hypothalamic LH-releasing factor and prolactin inhibiting factor, and on pituitary LH and prolactin. *Endocrinology 80*:603.

Minge-Kalman, W. 1977. On the theory and measurement of domestic labor intensity. *Am. Ethnol. 4*:273–84.

Monod, T. 1958. *Majabat al Koubra: Contribution à l'étude de l'Empty Quarter ouest-Saharien*. Institut Français d'Afrique Noire, No. 52. Dakar.

Moodie, D. 1840–2 (1960). *The Record or a Series of Official Papers Relative to the Condition and Treatment of the Native Tribes of South Africa.* Amsterdam: Balkema.

Moorehead, A. 1966. *The Fatal Impact: An Account of the Invasion of the South Pacific.* London: Hamilton.

Morgan, E. 1972. *The Descent of Woman.* Briarcliff Manor, N.Y.: Stein & Day.

Morgan, L.H. 1877. *Ancient Society.* New York: World.

Mosley, W.H. 1977. The effects of nutrition on natural fertility. Paper presented at Seminar on Natural Fertility, Institut National d'Edudes Démographiques, Paris, March 1977.

Mosley, W.H. (ed.). 1978. *Nutrition and Human Reproduction.* New York: Plenum Press.

Mumford, L. 1961. *The City in History: Its Origins, Its Transformations, and Its Prospects.* London: Secker & Warburg.

Museum of Modern Art. 1955. *The Family of Man.* New York: Maco Magazine.

National Academy of Sciences. 1977. *Study of Plants and Agricultural Potential of Selected Species of the Leguminosae Family.* Washington, D.C.: National Research Council, Commission on International Relations.

Needham, R. 1954. Siriono and Penan: A test of some hypotheses. *Southwest. J. Anthropol. 10*:228–32.

Netting, R. 1972. Sacred power and centralization: Aspects of political adaptation in Africa. In B. Spooner (ed.). *Population Growth: Anthropological Implications,* pp. 219–44. Cambridge, Mass.: MIT Press.

Oswalt, W. 1973. *Habitat and Technology.* New York: Holt, Rinehart and Winston.

Passarge, S. 1907. *Die Buschmänner der Kalahari.* Berlin: Reimer & Vohsen.

Peters, H., S. Israel, and S. Purshottam. 1958. Lactation period in Indian Women: Duration of amenorrhea and vaginal and cervical cytology. *Fertil. Steril. 9*:134.

Peterson, N. (ed.). 1976. *Tribes and Boundaries in Australia.* Canberra: Australian Institute of Aboriginal Studies.

Peterson, N. 1978. Rights, residence and the relevance of flux in Australia. Paper presented at Conférence Internationale sur les Sociétés Chasseurs-Collecteurs, Paris, June 1978.

Pfeiffer, J. 1969. *The Emergence of Man.* New York: Harper & Row.

Potgieter, E., and D. Ziervogel. 1955. *The Disappearing Bushmen of Lake Chrissie: a Preliminary Account.* Pretoria.

Potter, R.G., M. New, J. Wyon, and J.E. Gordon. 1965. Application of field studies to research on the physiology of human reproduction. *J. Chronic Dis. 18*:1125–40.

Radcliffe-Brown, A.R. 1930. The social organization of Australian tribes. Part 1. *Oceania 1*:34–63.

Rappaport, R.A. 1967. Ritual regulation of environmental relations among a New Guinea people. *Ethnology 6*(1):17–30.

Rappaport, R.A. 1968. *Pigs for the Ancestors.* New Haven: Yale University Press.

Rappaport, R.A. 1971a. Ritual, sanctity, and cybernetics. *Am. Anthropol. 73*(1):59–76.

Rappaport, R.A. 1971b. The sacred in human evolution. *Annu. Rev. Ecol. Systematics 2*:23–44.

Rasmussen, K. 1931. *The Netsilik Eskimos: Social Life and Spiritual Culture.* Report of the Fifth Thule Expedition, 1921–4, Vol. 8, Nos. 1, 2. Copenhagen: Gyldendalske Boghandel.

Redstockings Collective. 1971. The politics of housework. In D. Babcox and M. Belkin (eds.). *Liberation Now: Writings from the Women's Liberation Movement*, pp. 110–15. New York: Dell.

Reed, E. 1975. *Woman's Evolution from Matriarchal Clan to Patriarchal Family*. New York: Pathfinder Press.

Reeves, C.V. 1972. Earthquakes in Ngamiland. *Botswana Notes Rec.* 4:257–61.

Reiter, R. (ed.). 1975. *Toward an Anthropology of Women*. New York: Monthly Review Press.

Reiter, R. 1977. The search for origins: Unraveling the threads of gender hierarchy. *Crit. Anthropol.* (women's issue) 3(9–10):5–24.

Republic of Botswana. 1975. *Tribal Grazing Lands Policy (Amendment) Act*. Gaborone: Government Printer.

Rogers, E.S., and M.B. Black. 1976. Subsistence strategy in the Fish and Hare Period, Northern Ontario: The Weagamow Ojibwa, 1880–1920. *J. Anthropol. Res.* 32(1):1–43.

Rohrlich-Leavitt, R. (ed.). 1975. *Women Cross-Culturally: Change and Challenge*. The Hague: Mouton.

Rosaldo, M., and L. Lamphere. 1974. *Women, Culture and Society*. Stanford: Stanford University Press.

Rose, F.G.G. 1960. *Classification of Kin, Age Structure and Marriage Amongst the Groote Eylandt Aborigines: A Study in Method and a Theory of Australian Kinship*. Berlin: Akademie-Verlag. (London: Pergamon Press.)

Sahlins, M. 1958. *Social Stratification in Polynesia*. Seattle: University of Washington Press.

Sahlins, M. 1965. The sociology of primitive exchange. In M. Banton (ed.). *The Relevance of Models in Social Anthropology*, pp. 139–236. ASA Monographs, No. 1. London: Tavistock.

Sahlins, M. 1968. *Tribesmen*. Englewood Cliffs, N.J.: Prentice-Hall.

Sahlins, M. 1972. *Stone Age Economics*. Chicago: Aldine.

Sbrzesny, H. 1976. *Die Spiele der !Ko-Buschleute*. Munich: Piper.

Schaefer, O. 1970. Pre- and post-natal growth acceleration and increased sugar consumption in Canadian Eskimos. *Can. Med. Assoc. J.* 103:1059.

Schaefer, O. 1971. When the Eskimo comes to town. *Nutr. Today* 6(6).

Schapera, I. 1930. *The Khoisan Peoples of South Africa: Bushmen and Hottentots*. London: Routledge & Kegan Paul.

Schinz, H. 1898. Beitrage zur Kenntnis de Afrikanischen Flora. *Bull. Herb. Boissier* 6:729–51.

Scholz, C.H. 1976. Rifting in the Okavango Delta. *Nat. Hist.* (April), pp. 34–43.

Schrire, C. 1972. The ethno-archaeology of subsistence behaviour in Arnhem Land. In D.L. Clarke (ed.). *Models of Archaeology*, pp. 653–70. London: Methuen.

Scientific American. 1970. Man's bag. In Science and the Citizen. *Sci. Am.* 140:40.

Scudder, T. 1962. *Before Kariba: The Ecology of the Gwembe Tonga*. Manchester: Manchester University Press.

Scudder, T. 1971. *Gathering among African Woodland Savannah Cultivators; A Case Study: The Gwembe Tonga*. Zambian Papers No. 5. University of Zambia, Institute of African Studies.

Secombe, W. 1973. Housework under Capitalism. *New Left Rev.* 83:3–24.

Seiner, F. 1910. Die Buschmanner des Okavango and Sambesigebietes der Nord-Kalahari. *Globus* 97(22).

Service, E.R. 1962. *Primitive Social Organization: An Evolutionary Perspective.* New York: Random House.

Service, E.R. 1966. *The Hunters.* Engelwood Cliffs, N.J.: Prentice-Hall.

Service, E.R. 1971. *Primitive Social Organization: An Evolutionary Perspective,* 2nd ed. New York: Random House.

Shapiro, W. 1971. Wawilak: Ontogeny, phylogeny and sexuality in Miwyt ("Murn-gin") thought. Paper presented at 70th Annual Meeting, American Anthropological Association, New York.

Shaw, E.M. 1963. Bushman arrow poisons. *Cimbebasia: J. South West Afr. Sci. Soc.* 1(1):1–35.

Sheps, M., and J. Menken. 1973. *Mathematical Models of Conception and Birth.* Chicago: University of Chicago Press.

Shostak, M. 1976. A !Kung Woman's memories of childhood. In R. Lee and I. DeVore (eds.). *Kalahari Hunter-Gatherers,* pp. 246–77. Cambridge, Mass.: Harvard University Press.

Silberbauer, G.B. 1965. *Bushman Survey Report.* Gaborone: Bechuanaland Government.

Silberbauer, G.B. 1972. The G/wi Bushmen. In M.G. Bicchieri (ed.). *Hunters and Gatherers Today,* pp. 271–325. New York: Holt, Rinehart and Winston.

Silberbauer, G.B. 1978. Political processes in G/wi bands. Paper presented at Conférence Internationale sur les Sociétés de Chasseurs Collecteurs, Paris, June 1978.

Silberbauer, G.B., and A. Kuper. 1966. Kgalagari masters and Bushman serfs: Some observations. *Afr. Stud.* 25(4):171–9.

Sillery, A. 1952. *The Bechuanaland Protectorate.* Cape Town: Oxford University Press.

Sillery, A. 1965. *Founding a Protectorate: History of Bechuanaland, 1885–1895.* The Hague: Mouton.

Slocum, S. 1975. Woman the gatherer. In R. Reiter (ed.). *Toward an Anthropology of Women,* pp. 36–50. New York: Monthly Review Press.

Smithers, R.H.N. 1968. *A Checklist and Atlas of the Mammals of Botswana.* Salisbury: National Museums of Rhodesia.

Snyman, J.W. 1970. *An Introduction to the !Xũ Language.* Cape Town: Balkema.

Snyman, J.W. 1975. *Zuǀʾhõasi Fonologie en Woordeboek.* Cape Town: Balkema.

Solway, J.S. 1977. Foragers, pastoralists, and serfs: Socio-economic development among the Basarwa of Botswana. Department of Anthropology, University of Toronto. Mimeographed.

Southall, A. 1960. Homicide and suicide among the Alur. In P. Bohannan (ed.). *African Homicide and Suicide,* pp. 214–29. Princeton: Princeton University Press.

Spencer, B., and Gillen, F. 1899. *The Native Tribes of Central Australia.* London: Macmillan.

Spencer, R. 1959. The north Alaskan Eskimo: A study in ecology and society. *Bur. Am. Ethnol. Bull. 171.*

Speth, J., and D. Davis. 1976. Seasonal variability in early hominid predation. *Science* 192:441–5.

Steward, J.H. 1936. The economic and social basis of primitive bands. In R.H. Lowie (ed.). *Essays in Anthropology Presented to A.L. Kroeber*, pp. 331–50. Berkeley: University of California Press.

Steward, J.H. 1938. Basin-plateau aboriginal sociopolitical groups. *Bur. Am. Ethnol. Bull. 120.*

Steward, J.H. 1949. Cultural causality and law: A trial formulation of the development of early civilizations. *Am. Anthropol.* 51(1):1–27.

Steward, J.H. 1955a. *Theory of Culture Change: The Methodology of Multilinear Evolution.* Urbana: University of Illinois Press.

Steward, J.H. 1955b. The concept and method of cultural ecology. In J.H. Steward (ed.). *Theory of Culture Change: The Methodology of Multilinear Evolution*, pp. 30–42. Urbana: University of Illinois Press.

Steward, J.H. (ed.). 1956. *The Peoples of Puerto Rico.* Urbana: University of Illinois Press.

Steward, J.H. (ed.). 1967. *Contemporary Change in Traditional Societies.* Urbana: University of Illinois Press. 2 vols.

Steward, J.H. 1968. Causal factors and processes in the evolution of pre-farming societies. In R.B. Lee and I. DeVore (eds.). *Man the Hunter*, pp. 321–34. Chicago: Aldine.

Steyn, H.P. 1971. Aspects of the economic life of some nomadic Nharo Bushman groups. *Ann. S. Afr. Mus.* 56(6):275–322.

Story, R. 1958. *Some Plants Used by the Bushmen in Obtaining Food and Water.* Botanical Survey of South Africa, Memoir No. 30. Pretoria: Government Printers.

Story, R. 1964. Plant lore of the Bushmen. In D.H.S. Davis (ed.). *Ecological Studies in Southern Africa.* The Hague: Junk.

Stott, D.H. 1969. Cultural and natural checks on population growth. In A.P. Vayda (ed.). *Environment and Cultural Behavior*, pp. 90–120. Garden City, N.Y.: Natural History Press.

Strehlow, T.G.H. 1947. *Aranda Traditions.* Melbourne: Melbourne University Press.

Sussman, R.M. 1972. Child transport, family size and increase in human population during the Neolithic. *Curr. Anthropol.* 13:258–69.

Tanaka, J. 1969. The ecology and social structure of Central Kalahari Bushmen. In T. Umesao (ed.). *African Studies*, Vol. 3. Kyoto: Kyoto University.

Tanaka, J. 1976. Subsistence ecology of Central Kalahari San. In R.B. Lee and I. DeVore (eds.). *Kalahari Hunter-Gatherers*, pp. 98–119. Cambridge, Mass.: Harvard University Press.

Tanner, N., and A. Zihlman. 1976. Women in evolution. I. Innovation and selection in human origins. *Signs* 1:585–608.

Taylor, C., and O. Pye. 1966. *The Foundations of Nutrition*, 6th ed. New York: Macmillan.

Terray, E. 1972. *Marxism and "Primitive" Societies.* New York: Monthly Review Press.

Thomas, D.H. 1974. An archeological perspective on Shoshonean bands. *Am. Anthropol.* 76(1):11–23.

Thomas, E.M. 1959. *The Harmless People.* New York: Knopf.

Thomas, H. 1971. Population dynamics of primitive societies. In S.F. Singer (ed.). *Is There an Optimum Population?* New York: McGraw-Hill.

Thomson, D. 1939. The seasonal factor in human culture. *Proc. Prehist. Soc.* (n.s.) 5:209–21.

Tietze, C. 1961. The effect of breastfeeding on the rate of conception. Paper presented at the International Population Conference, New York.

Tiger, L. 1969. *Men in Groups.* New York: Random House.

Tinley, K.L. 1966. *An Ecological Reconnaissance of the Moremi Wildlife Reserve, Botswana.* Johannesburg: Okavango Wildlife Society.

Tobias, P.V. 1961. Physique of a desert folk: Genes, not habitat, shaped the Bushmen. *Nat. Hist.* 170(2):16–24.

Tobias, P.V. 1964. Bushman hunter-gatherers: A study in human ecology. In D.H.S. Davis (ed.). *Ecological Studies in Southern Africa,* pp. 69–86. The Hague: Junk.

Tobias, P.V. 1975. Stature and secular trend among South African Negroes and San (Bushmen). *S. Afr. J. Med. Sci.* 40(4):145–64.

Topkins, P. 1958. Letter to the editor. *J.A.M.A.* 167:144.

Topkins, P. 1959. The histologic appearance of the endometrium during lactation and its relationship to ovarian function. *Am. J. Obstet. Gynecol.* 77:921.

Traill, A. 1974. *The Compleat Guide to the Koon.* African Studies Institute Communication, No. 1, pp. 1–50. Johannesburg: University of the Witwatersrand.

Traill, A. (ed.). 1975. *Bushman and Hottentot Linguistic Studies.* African Studies Institute Communication No. 2, pp. 1–102. Johannesburg: University of the Witwatersrand.

Traill, A. 1976. *Research on the Non-Bantu African Languages.* Johannesburg: Department of Linguistics, University of the Witwatersrand.

Trigger, B. 1973. The future of archeology is the past. In C.L. Redman (ed.). *Research and Theory in Current Archeology,* pp. 95–111. New York: Wiley.

Truswell, A.S. 1977. Diet and nutrition of hunter-gatherers. In Ciba Foundation (ed.). *Health and Disease in Tribal Societies,* pp. 213–26. Amsterdam: Elsevier.

Truswell, A.S., and J.D.L. Hansen. 1968. Medical and nutritional studies of !Kung Bushmen in northwest Botswana: A preliminary report. *S. Afr. Med. J.* 42:1338–9.

Truswell, A.S., and J.D.L. Hansen. 1976. Medical research among the !Kung. In R.B. Lee and I. DeVore (eds.). *Kalahari Hunter-Gatherers,* pp. 166–94. Cambridge, Mass.: Harvard University Press.

Truswell, A.S., B.M. Kennelly, J.D.L. Hansen, and R.B. Lee. 1972. Blood pressures of !Kung Bushmen in northern Botswana. *Am. Heart J.* 84:5–12.

Turnbull, C. 1965. *Wayward Servants: The Two Worlds of the African Pygmies.* Garden City, N.Y.: Natural History Press.

Turnbull, C. 1968. The importance of flux in two hunting societies. In R.B. Lee and I. DeVore (eds.). *Man the Hunter,* pp. 132–7. Chicago: Aldine.

Tyson, J.E., and A. Perez. 1978. The maintenance of infecundity in postpartum women. In W.H. Mosley (ed.). *Nutrition and Human Reproduction,* pp. 11–27. New York: Plenum Press.

Udesky, I. 1950. Ovulation in lactating women. *Am. J. Obstet. Gynecol.* 59:843.

United Nations. 1970. *Demographic Yearbook.* New York: Statistical Office and Department of Social Affairs, United Nations.

U.S. Bureau of the Census. 1974. *Statistical Abstracts of the United States, 1973.* Washington, D.C.: GPO.

Vanek, J. 1974. Time spent in housework. *Sci. Am.* (November), pp. 116–20.

Van Ginneken, J.K. 1974. Prolonged breastfeeding as a birth spacing method. *Stud. Fam. Plan.* 5:201–6.

Vayda, A.P., A. Leeds, and D.P. Smith. 1961. The place of pigs in Melanesian subsistence. In V.E. Garfield (ed.). *Proceedings of the 1961 Annual Spring Meeting of the American Ethnological Society.* Seattle: University of Washington Press.

Vedder, H. 1910–11. Grundriss einer Grammatik der Buschmannsprache vom Stamm de !kŭ-Buschmänner. *Z. Kolonialsprachen* 1:5–25, 106–17.

Vierich, H. 1977. Report to the remote area dwellers office of a survey in the Kweneng District. Ministry of Local Government and Lands, Republic of Botswana. Mimeographed.

Voorhies, B., and K. Martin. 1975. *Female of the Species.* New York: Columbia University Press.

Wallerstein, I. 1974. *The Modern World System: Capitalist Agriculture and the Origins of European World–Economy in the Sixteenth Century.* New York: Academic Press.

Washburn, S.L. 1976. Foreword. In R. Lee and I. DeVore (eds.). *Kalahari Hunter-Gatherers.* Cambridge, Mass.: Harvard University Press.

Washburn, S.L., and I. DeVore. 1961. The Social behavior of baboons and early man. In S.L. Washburn (ed.). *Social Life of Early Man.* Chicago: Aldine.

Waterhouse, M., and H. Waterhouse. 1973. Primate ethology and human social behavior. In R. Michael and J. Crook (eds.). *Comparative Ecology and Behavior of Primates.* New York: Academic Press.

Weare, P., and A. Yalala. 1971. Provisional vegetation map of Botswana. *Botswana Notes Rec.* 3:131–47.

Webster, P. 1976. The politics of rape in primitive society. Paper presented at 75th Annual Meeting, American Anthropological Association, Washington, D.C.

Wehmeyer, A.S. 1966. The nutrient composition of some edible wild fruits found in the Transvaal. *S. Afr. Med. J.* 40:1102.

Weiner, J.S., and J.S. Lourie. 1969. *Human Biology: A Guide to Field Methods.* Philadelphia: Davis.

Wellington, J.H. 1955. *Southern Africa: A Geographical Study,* Vol. 1. London: Cambridge University Press.

Wellington, J.H. 1964. *South West Africa and Its Human Issues.* London: Oxford University Press.

West, M., and M. Konner. 1978. The role of the father: An anthropological perspective. In M. Lamb (ed.). *The Role of the Father in Child Development.* New York: Wiley.

Westphal, E.O.J. 1963. The linguistic prehistory of Southern Africa: Bush, Kwadi, Hottentot and Bantu linguistic relationships. *Africa* 33:237–65.

Westphal, E.O.J. 1971. The click languages of southern and eastern Africa. In J. Berry and J.H. Greenberg (eds.). *Linguistics in Sub-Saharan Africa,* pp. 367–420. The Hague: Mouton.

White, C., and N. Peterson. 1969. Ethnographic interpretations of the prehistory of western Arnhem Land. *Southwest. J. Anthropol.* 25:45–67.

White, F. 1962. *Forest Flora of Northern Rhodesia.* London: Oxford University Press.

White, L.A. 1949. *The Science of Culture*. New York: Farrar, Straus & Giroux.

White, L.A. 1959. *The Evolution of Culture*. New York: McGraw-Hill.

Wiessner, P. 1977. Hxaro: A regional system of reciprocity for reducing risk among the !Kung San. Ph.D. dissertation, University of Michigan, Ann Arbor.

Williams, B.J. 1968. The Bihor of India and some comments on band organization. In R.B. Lee and I. DeVore (eds.). *Man the Hunter*, pp. 126–31. Chicago: Aldine.

Williams, B.J. 1977. Investigations of a little-known way of life: Review of Kalahari Hunter-Gatherers. R.B. Lee and I. DeVore, eds. *Science 196*:761–3.

Wilmsen, E. 1974. *Lindenmeier: A Pleistocene Hunting Society*. New York: Harper & Row.

Wilmsen, E. 1976. Summary report of research on Basarwa in western Ngamiland. Report to the Government of Botswana. Museum of Anthropology, University of Michigan.

Wilmsen, E. 1977. Seasonal effects of dietary intake on Kalahari San. Paper presented to Federation of American Societies for Experimental Biology, Chicago. (To be published in *Federation Proceedings*, vol. 37.)

Wilmsen, E. 1979a. *Prehistoric and Historic Antecedants of a Contemporary Nopmiland Community*, Boston University, African Studies Center. Working Papers, no. 12.

Wilmsen, E. 1979b. *Diet and Fertility among Kalahari Bushmen*. Boston University, African Studies Center. Working Papers, no. 14.

Wilson, F. 1972. *Migrant Labour in South Africa*. Cape Town: Oxford University Press.

Wilson, M., and L. Thompson. 1969. *The Oxford History of South Africa*. London: Oxford University Press.

Windhoek Advertiser. Bushman military bases in the Caprivi. September 23, 1977.

Wolf, E.R. 1959. *Sons of the Shaking Earth*. Chicago: University of Chicago Press.

Wolf, E.R., and J. Jorgenson. 1970. Anthropology on the warpath in Thailand. *N. Y. Rev. Books 15*(9):26–35.

Wolfgang, M.E. 1958. *Patterns in Criminal Homicide*. Philadelphia: University of Pennsylvania Press.

Woodburn, J. 1968a. An introduction to Hadza ecology. In R.B. Lee and I. DeVore (eds.). *Man the Hunter*, pp. 49–55. Chicago: Aldine.

Woodburn, J. 1968b. Stability and flexibility in Hadza residential groupings. In R.B. Lee and I. DeVore (eds.). *Man the Hunter*, pp. 103–10. Chicago: Aldine.

Wyndham, C.H., J.F. Morrison, J.S. Ward, G.A.G. Bredell, M.J.E. von Rahden, L.D. Holdsworth, H.G. Wenzel, and A. Munro. 1964. Physiological reactions to cold of Bushmen, Bantu, and Caucasian males. *J. Appl. Physiol. 19*:868.

Yellen, J.E. 1971. Archeological excavations in western Ngamiland. *Botswana Notes Rec. 3*:276.

Yellen, J.E. 1972. *Aerial View of the Dobe Area*. Map. Cambridge, Mass.: Educational Development Corporation.

Yellen, J.E. 1977. *Archaeological Approaches to the Present: Models for Reconstructing the Past*. New York: Academic Press.

Yellen, J.E., and H. Harpending. 1972. Hunter-gatherer populations and archaeological inference. *World Archaeol. 4*(2):244–53.

Yellen, J.E., and R.B. Lee. 1976. The Dobe-/Du/da environment: Background to a hunting and gathering way of life. In R.B. Lee and I. DeVore (eds.). *Kalahari Hunter-Gatherers*, pp. 27–46. Cambridge, Mass.: Harvard University Press.

Index

513